The U.S. Military Intervention in Panama
★ ★ ★
Origins, Planning, and Crisis Management
June 1987–December 1989

CONTINGENCY OPERATIONS SERIES

THE U.S. MILITARY INTERVENTION IN PANAMA
ORIGINS, PLANNING, AND CRISIS MANAGEMENT
JUNE 1987–DECEMBER 1989

by

Lawrence A. Yates

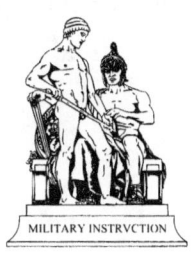

CENTER OF MILITARY HISTORY
UNITED STATES ARMY
WASHINGTON, D.C., 2008

Library of Congress Cataloging-in-Publication Data

Yates, Lawrence A., 1945–
 The U.S. military intervention in Panama : origins, planning, and crisis management, June 1987–December 1989 / by Lawrence A. Yates.
    p. cm. — (Contingency operations series)
  Includes bibliographical references and index.
  1. Panama—History—American Invasion, 1989—Causes. 2. Military planning—United States. 3. Panama—Military relations—United States. 4. United States—Military relations—Panama. I. Title.
  F1567.4.Y38 2008
  972.8705'3—dc22

2008026930

First Printing

CMH Pub 55–1–1

For sale by the Superintendent of Documents, U.S. Government Printing Office
Internet: bookstore.gpo.gov Phone: toll free (866) 512-1800; DC area (202) 512-1800
Fax: (202) 512-2104 Mail: Stop IDCC, Washington, DC 20402-0001

ISBN: 978-1-78039-284-4

Contingency Operations Series

Richard W. Stewart, General Editor

Advisory Committee
(As of October 2007)

Theodore A. Wilson
University of Kansas

William T. Allison
Weber State University

Joyce E. Morrow
Administrative Assistant to the
Secretary of the Army

James J. Carafano
Heritage Foundation

Brig. Gen. Mark E. O'Neill
U.S. Army Command and
General Staff College

Brig. Gen. Patrick Finnegan
U.S. Military Academy

Mark P. Parillo
Kansas State University

John F. Guilmartin
Ohio State University

Reina Pennington
Norwich University

Brian M. Linn
Texas A&M University

Ronald H. Spector
George Washington University

Howard Lowell
National Archives and Records
Administration

Col. Thomas Torrance
U.S. Army War College

Lt. Gen. Thomas Metz
U.S. Army Training and
Doctrine Command

Stephen F. Vogel
Washington Post

U.S. Army Center of Military History
Jeffrey J. Clarke, Chief of Military History

Chief Historian	Richard W. Stewart
Chief, Histories Division	Joel D. Meyerson
Chief, Publishing Division	Keith R. Tidman

Contents

☆ ☆ ☆

	Page
Foreword	xi
The Author	xii
Preface	xiii

Chapter

1. The Making of a Crisis, June 1987–February 1988 1
    - The United States and Panama 2
    - Noriega 9
    - Crisis in Panama 14
    - The Southern Command and the Crisis 21

2. Operation Orders and Security Enhancement, February–April 1988 33
    - Contingency Planning: ELABORATE MAZE 35
    - Sanctions 40
    - Phase V, Joint Special Operations Task Force, and U.S. Army, South 43
    - Security Enhancement 50
    - Showdown in Washington 57
    - Joint Task Force-Panama 59

3. Violence, "Fissures," and a PRAYER BOOK, April–May 1988 63
    - Noriega Perseveres 63
    - First Blood 66
    - Déjà Vu 77
    - The PRAYER BOOK 89
    - Fissures 97

4. Settling In, May 1988–January 1989 103
    - Woerner's Critique and Policy Proposals 104
    - Joint Training 109
    - The "Stage" 113
    - Rules of Engagement 118
    - The Redeployment Question 127
    - Enter the XVIII Airborne Corps 129

5. Toward a Tougher Posture, February–April 1989 135
    - Woerner's Woes 137
    - "Terror" in Panama 139
    - A Tougher Posture 150

Chapter	Page

6. Operation NIMROD DANCER, May 1989 157
    The Muse Affair 158
    Preelection Preparations 161
    The Election 165
    Deployments 170
    Adjusting and Adapting 178
    Harbinger: The "Invasion" of Fort Espinar 188

7. Asserting U.S. Treaty Rights, May–June 1989 191
    Triad and Fissures II 192
    Reasserting Treaty Rights: Convoys 196
    "Sliding into Something" 207

8. Ratcheting Up, June–September 1989 217
    BLADE JEWEL *and the* PRAYER BOOK 217
    Woerner's "Retirement" 223
    Ratcheting Up 224
    ALICE, BEATRICE, *and the Others* 231

9. From Black Tuesday to BLUE SPOON, October–December 1989 ... 241
    General Max Thurman 241
    "Black Tuesday": The 3 October Coup Attempt 248
    Ramifications 258
    Operation Order 1–90 and Operation Plan 90–2 263
    The Road to JUST CAUSE 270

10. Conclusions 277
    The Twilight Zone 279
    Joint Operations 282
    Personalities 284

Bibliography 287
Abbreviations and Acronyms 291
Index 295

TABLE

Buildup of U.S. Forces in Panama, 1988–1989 278

CHARTS

No.

1. Command Relationships: U.S. Southern Command 16
2. U.S. Southern Command Joint Staff Organization 17
3. Command Relationships: Joint Task Force-Panama (as of May 1988) .. 83

No.	Page
4. Initial BLUE SPOON Command Arrangements	90
5. Joint Task Force-Panama Organization for NIMROD DANCER	193
6. BLUE SPOON on the Eve of Operation JUST CAUSE: Operation Plan 90–2 Command and Control	267

MAPS

Central and South America, 1989	*Frontispiece*
1. Panama, 1989	4
2. Panama Canal Area, 1987–1989	26
3. Canal Area, Pacific Ocean Side, 1987–1989	86

ILLUSTRATIONS

President Theodore Roosevelt in Panama During the Construction of the Canal, 1906	2
Locks of the Panama Canal Under Construction	6
General Omar Torrijos	7
President Jimmy Carter and General Torrijos Sign the Panama Canal Treaty	8
General Manuel Antonio Noriega Moreno	10
General Frederick F. Woerner Jr. in Conversation	15
The Panama Canal	34
Maj. Gen. Bernard Loeffke Briefing the Troops	37
Admiral William Crowe	40
President Ronald W. Reagan Talking with Caspar Weinberger, Secretary of Defense During the First Months of the Panama Crisis	43
A Panama Defense Forces Antiriot Unit Using Water Cannon to Put Down a Demonstration Against the Regime	54
A Marine Patrol on the Arraiján Tank Farm	69
The Guard House at the Entrance to Quarry Heights, the Location of the U.S. Southern Command Headquarters	79
Paramilitary Dignity Battalion Members in Red T-shirts in the Streets Ready to Fight	106
Fort Clayton	110
Rodman Naval Station	116
President George H. W. Bush Speaks at an Armed Forces Review and Awards Ceremony	136
Demonstrators Bang Pots in Protest Against the Noriega Regime	158
Opposition Candidates Guillermo Endara and Ricardo Arias Calderón and Marchers Face the Panama Defense Forces	169
A Dignity Battalion Member Attacking Guillermo "Billy" Ford	169
U.S. Army Troops Arriving for Operation NIMROD DANCER	174
Albrook Air Station	176
Howard Air Force Base	208
AC–130 Spectre Gunship	216

	Page
Maj. Gen. Marc A. Cisneros and General Maxwell R. Thurman at the Former's Promotion Ceremony	225
Marines in Their Light Armored Vehicles	234
General Woerner Talks at the Change of Command Ceremony	242
General Thurman	243
Lt. Gen. Carl W. Stiner	246
Noriega Waves His Fist to Supporters After the Failed October 1989 Coup	259
Soldiers in an M113 Armored Personnel Carrier Guard an Entrance to Gorgas Army Hospital	273

Illustrations courtesy of the following sources: p. 2, Theodore Roosevelt Collection, Harvard College Library; p. 6, Office of History, U.S. Army Corps of Engineers; p. 7, http://www.country-data.com; pp. 10, 54, 106, 158, 169 (top/bottom), 259, Corbis; p. 40, Department of the Army; p. 69, http://www2.bc.edu; p. 79, http://william_h_ormsbee.tripod.com; p. 110, http://www.globalsecurity.org; p. 136, http://www.pubdef.net; p. 216, U.S. Air Force; and p. 246, XVIII Airborne Corps Historian. Cover and all other illustrations from Department of Defense files.

Foreword

Prior to Operation JUST CAUSE, the December 1989 U.S. intervention in Panama, American leaders had struggled for over two years with the increasingly difficult regime of General Manuel Antonio Noriega. At the time, the Panama Canal was still under U.S. administration, with the U.S. Southern Command based at Quarry Heights charged with its security. Led by General Frederick F. Woerner Jr. and supported by Maj. Gen. Bernard Loeffke, the command's Army component commander, American military leaders weathered a series of low-grade crises during 1988–1989, slowly culminating in a growing military confrontation with Noriega's military, paramilitary, and police forces. Detailed in Larry Yates' study are the contingency plans, rules of engagement, a host of varied operations—security patrols, guard duty, training exercises, shows of force, and police actions—and even the occasional firefight, all of which characterized this trying period.

But this history is much more than a precursor to JUST CAUSE. The book's true value lies in a careful examination of the complex relationships between a U.S. combatant command, one of the four American global military headquarters, and its Washington, D.C., superiors, to include Joint Chiefs Chairman Admiral William Crowe, Army Chief of Staff General Carl Vuono, Defense Secretary Richard Cheney, and Presidents Ronald W. Reagan and George H. W. Bush. Indeed, the able Woerner and his staff often found themselves walking a tightrope between a variety of ill-defined administration policies whose long-range goals were difficult to fathom and the exigencies of a steadily worsening local situation. The conflicting demands ultimately led to Woerner's untimely replacement by General Maxwell R. Thurman, an officer more comfortable with the Bush administration's approach to the crisis. Highlighted also are the roles played by the local joint and special operations headquarters, those U.S.-based commands charged with providing military reinforcements to the region, and those government officials responsible for regional diplomatic, intelligence, and economic affairs. The result is a rich mix of timeless experiences and insights especially attuned to the contingency fare so common in the post–Cold War era and an excellent primer for officers assuming duties in the joint defense commands and staffs that play a key role in today's defense establishment. The volume also marks another significant addition to the Center's expanding Contingency Operations Series.

Washington, D.C.
25 July 2008

JEFFREY J. CLARKE
Chief of Military History

The Author

Lawrence A. Yates is a native of Kansas City, Missouri. He received his Ph.D. in history from the University of Kansas in 1981, after which he joined the Combat Studies Institute at Fort Leavenworth, Kansas. During his twenty-four years with the institute, he taught and wrote about U.S. military interventions, contingency and stability operations, and unconventional warfare. In 1989, he was in Panama during Operation JUST CAUSE, the U.S. invasion of that country. Among his publications, he is the author of Leavenworth Paper 15, *Power Pack: U.S. Intervention in the Dominican Republic, 1965–1966*, and *The US Military's Experience in Stability Operations, 1789–2005*; coauthor of *My Clan Against the World: U.S. and Coalition Forces in Somalia, 1992–1994*; and coeditor of—and a contributor to—*Block by Block: The Challenges of Urban Operations*. In September 2005, Yates retired from government service. He is currently working on an official history of Operation JUST CAUSE, the companion piece to this volume.

PREFACE

On 20 December 1989, the United States invaded the Republic of Panama to overthrow the dictatorship of General Manuel Antonio Noriega. By capturing the general, defeating the military forces he commanded, and installing a democratic government in the country, Operation JUST CAUSE, the code name for the U.S. invasion, brought to an end in a matter of days a crisis in American-Panamanian relations that had defied resolution for over two years.

The swiftness and completeness of the U.S. victory immediately certified JUST CAUSE as an exemplary case study to be analyzed in military service schools and assimilated by doctrine writers, trainers, staff officers, commanders, organizational experts, strategists, and tacticians. The invasion offered lessons in joint and urban operations; unity of command; the rapid, decisive, yet restrained use of overwhelming force; the integration of conventional and special operations forces; and the applicability of the principles of war across the spectrum of conflict. For nearly a year after its conclusion, it also served as a force-projection model for what U.S. military operations in the post–Cold War world might resemble. Then, almost as quickly as it had attained this preeminent status, the Panama operation receded from view as an object of institutional study and emulation, a consequence of the American military's sudden shift of attention and resources to the Persian Gulf in response to Iraq's occupation of Kuwait. By early 1991, JUST CAUSE had been eclipsed by Operations DESERT SHIELD and DESERT STORM. So, too, had the broader context in which the invasion of Panama had taken place.

Today, nearly twenty years after the fact, the vast majority of U.S. officers can readily link JUST CAUSE with Panama and Noriega, but that association generally reflects the limits of what they remember about their own profession's involvement in the crisis. In the forefront of the military's collective memory, little has been retained regarding the role U.S. forces played in the stability and nation-building operations that began during the invasion and continued well after its official conclusion—this despite the continued availability of relevant studies by John T. Fishel and Richard Shultz Jr. Worse, on the subject of U.S. military activities in Panama during the 2½ years of tension leading up to the invasion, there is something approaching institutional amnesia. Of the several books about Operation JUST CAUSE (*see* Bibliography), most cover the pre-invasion crisis in an introductory chapter or two, with discussion confined to a handful of military milestones that, selected with the advantage of hindsight, suggest an inexorable movement to open hostilities.

My goal in this volume is to examine the Panama crisis from June 1987 to December 1989 not simply as a prelude to Operation JUST CAUSE but as a case study in its own right—as an extended series of interrelated actions and issues that U.S. military personnel had to confront on a daily basis in a process that imparted no sense of inevitability as to the outcome. If I am successful, the reader should easily realize that this example of crisis management offers numerous insights for today's officers, especially those operating under conditions in which conventional warfare is either a subsidiary endeavor or absent all together. In the

Panama crisis, this limbo between peace and war was labeled the Twilight Zone by some, a doctrinal wasteland in which officers, noncommissioned officers, and enlisted men who were trained almost exclusively in the straightforward art of traditional warfare had to adapt, in the furtherance of their country's policies, to an unfamiliar, complex, unorthodox, and highly ambiguous environment. This type of conflict placed a heavy emphasis on restraint in the face of provocation, and actions from the strategic level down through the tactical were driven more by political considerations and signals than by military necessity. In the process, warriors often found themselves acting as cops, peacemakers, and diplomats, and occasionally as victims.

The study is based largely on primary sources, many of which I collected during several trips to Panama while the crisis was still in progress. On these visits, I enjoyed access to file cabinets full of documents generated by Joint Task Force (JTF)-Panama, the U.S. Southern Command (SOUTHCOM), the Pentagon, and the XVIII Airborne Corps. I also conducted over two hundred interviews with civilians and military officers who were involved in the crisis. Equally important, I observed these people—commanders, staff officers, civilian employees, and troops in the field—as they worked long hours responding to dozens of simultaneous, often competing challenges affecting their wide range of regional responsibilities, of which the Noriega problem was only one. Of necessity, I have had to condense the detail and complexity of their experience into what I hope is a coherent narrative that provides some analytical insights while minimizing as much as possible the imposition of an artificial sense of order on a process that too often seemed disjointed and chaotic to those caught up in it.

Having stated in general terms what I have tried to accomplish, it is important to indicate what this study does not attempt to do. To begin with, this is not a history of the crisis from the perspective afforded the highest levels of government in Washington. The text will make only occasional excursions into the White House, State Department, Pentagon, and Central Intelligence Agency. Rather, attention is centered on the U.S. military as it dealt with the crisis at the strategic (SOUTHCOM) and operational (JTF-Panama) levels, with an incursion now and then into the tactical level that was largely the province of JTF-Panama's service components. Nor does this study make any pretense of being an in-depth look at the Panamanian side of the hill, either in terms of Noriega and the Panama Defense Forces, or in terms of the regime's political opposition. The focus, again, is on the role and activities of the U.S. military. Finally, this is an analytical narrative of a historical case study, not a political science model for crisis management, although I hope that those who deal in such schema will find useful data from the information contained herein.

Spanish-speaking readers of this book deserve a brief explanation on a convention I employed with respect to Spanish words in the text. Normally, when a Spanish word requiring an accent mark is used, the accent mark is included, thus informing the reader as to what syllable of the word should be emphasized. I have made an exception where a Spanish word is used frequently in English without an accent. For example, the word "río" (river) in Spanish is spelled "rio" in this text, as in Rio Hato.

I started researching this book in 1989, just two months before Panamanians voted in their presidential election in May. I finished writing the first draft of the manuscript on New Year's Day of 2001. During the years in between and since, I have become indebted to more people than I can possibly list here, and to all of them I extend my heartfelt thanks and appreciation. Certain individuals and institutions do require special mention, however, and if I do not include everyone that I should, I apologize in advance. To begin with, I am tremendously grateful to then-Maj. Gen. Bernard Loeffke and Col. John A. "Jay" Cope Jr. at U.S. Army, South (USARSO), for selecting me for the project, and to then-Maj. Gen. Marc A. Cisneros for continuing my involvement after Loeffke and Cope had left Panama for new assignments. The USARSO historians, especially Janet Len-Rios, offered invaluable assistance in expediting my trips to Panama, providing me office space, facilitating my access to documents, and handling a variety of administrative details. Once the Southern Command acquired an official historian, John Pitts, I was able to explore his file cabinets as well for pertinent documents.

Officers on the JTF-Panama and SOUTHCOM staffs were extremely generous with their time, as were numerous commanders in the field operating under one or both of these headquarters. Four such men were then-Col. Arnold T. "Arnie" Rossi, Col. Norman W. Higginbotham, Lt. Col. John T. Fishel, and Maj. Fred Polk. Back at Fort Leavenworth, of the student officers and faculty who rotated in and out of the Army's Command and General Staff College in the 1990s, dozens had participated in the Panama crisis and proved eager to relate their experiences to me. This included a number of my colleagues in the Combat Studies Institute, especially Lt. Col. John R. Finch and Maj. John Diviney. For one year of the project, Maj. Kelvin Crow was assigned as a research assistant who, besides visiting several archives in this country and abroad, also organized the mass of documents that became a discrete collection on the Panama crisis housed in the fort's Combined Arms Research Library (CARL). Over the years, the directors and staff at CARL have gone out of their way to ensure the integrity of that collection and to accommodate my work with it. Similar accolades can be directed at library personnel, archivists, and historians who assisted me at the Army War College, the U.S. Army Military History Institute, U.S. Forces Command, the Joint History Office, the U.S. Marine Corps History Division, and the U.S. Army Center of Military History (CMH). In the last organization, I am very grateful to the former chief of the Historical Resources Branch, Robert K. Wright Jr., who as an Army reservist conducted exhaustive research on Operation JUST CAUSE. Finally, the archives at the U.S. Special Operations Command (SOCOM) were opened to me, thanks to the efforts of John Partin, the SOCOM historian, and the assistance of Gaea Levy, the history office archivist.

U.S. Army, South, funded my research trips to Panama and elsewhere from 1989 through 1993. By the latter date, CMH was also involved in the project, funding additional research and reviewing completed drafts of each chapter. For authorizing this arrangement, I would like to thank Roger J. Spiller and Col. Richard Swain, both directors of the Combat Studies Institute, who, along with their successors, also sought to find me the time to complete the manuscript. At CMH, I would like to thank Jeffrey J. Clarke and Richard W. Stewart for their help and support throughout the project. I would also like to single out Brig. Gens. Harold W. Nelson and John S. Brown, both chiefs of military history at the Center, for their support.

In 2004, Jay Cope, John Fishel, Gabriel Marcella of the Strategic Studies Institute, Keith R. Tidman and Donald A. Carter of CMH, and Jeffrey Clarke participated in the Center's review panel of the manuscript. Their comments and criticisms were invaluable. So, too, has been the collaboration I have had with Diane Sedore Arms, a CMH editor, who has given me indispensable advice on improving the readability of this text. Like many authors, I preferred to think that in my draft manuscript "every word was carefully chosen, every sentence carefully crafted," to quote an acquaintance. Diane did a superb job of pointing out to me the fallacy of this thinking, and I am enormously indebted to her. S. L. Dowdy, the CMH cartographer, also did magnificent work on the maps for the book. Michael R. Gill collected the photographs and designed the handsome cover and layout as well as the charts. Contractor Anne Venzon created the detailed index for this volume. The author alone is responsible for all interpretations and conclusions, as well as for any factual errors that may have crept into the text.

Leavenworth, Kansas   LAWRENCE A. YATES
25 July 2008

The U.S. Military Intervention in Panama

Origins, Planning, and Crisis Management
June 1987–December 1989

1

THE MAKING OF A CRISIS

JUNE 1987–FEBRUARY 1988

When one nation uses force to resolve a conflict with another, questions generally arise as to whether hostilities were inevitable or could have been avoided. An answer requires, among other things, an analysis of the immediate, short-term, and long-term influences that broadened or narrowed the choices available to decision makers or, at least, the choices they perceived as being available to them.

The immediate reason for President George H. W. Bush's decision to execute Operation JUST CAUSE, the U.S. invasion of Panama in December 1989, seems clear enough. On Saturday night, 16 December, a car carrying four American servicemen ran a roadblock near the headquarters of the Panama Defense Forces (PDF) in Panama City. Guards manning the checkpoint opened fire on the car, wounding the driver and killing a passenger, a Marine lieutenant. Two witnesses to the shooting, a U.S. Navy lieutenant and his wife, were taken into police custody. Before being released, the lieutenant was severely beaten and his wife fondled and threatened with sexual abuse. News of these incidents, together with indications that other American citizens and U.S. service personnel in Panama were increasingly at risk, convinced Bush that the most appropriate and effective response available to him was to employ U.S. military force to topple the country's dictatorial regime, destroy its armed forces, and install a democratic government in its place.

The killing of an American citizen in a foreign country and the brutal mistreatment of two innocent American bystanders do not automatically constitute a *casus belli*. After monitoring the violent events of the sixteenth, several U.S. officers sitting in the operations center at Fort Clayton, Panama, expressed regret over the marine's death but, after referring to "an exceptionally bad Saturday night" in the capital city, voiced no desire for revenge.[1] President Bush, however, had to place the incident within the broader context of U.S.-Panamanian relations, which at the time were in a state of acute crisis. Since late 1987, both countries had been on a collision

---

[1] The author spent several hours in the U.S. Army, South, operations center at Fort Clayton late Saturday night and early Sunday morning, 16 and 17 December 1989, and noted the response to the shooting by several officers present. Subsequent conversations with other persons monitoring the Panama crisis confirmed the impressions of that night. The death of Marine Lt. Robert Paz was regarded as tragic but not necessarily a cause for going to war.

U.S. Military Intervention in Panama, June 1987–December 1989

President Theodore Roosevelt *(center)* in Panama during the construction of the canal, 1906

course, during which, on at least two occasions, Washington had augmented the number of troops normally based in Panama. Although neither side sought war, by late 1989 a combination of U.S. frustration and the increasingly shrill anti-American rhetoric and erratic behavior of Panama's strongman, General Manuel Antonio Noriega Moreno, had created the impression among key U.S. officials that events in the crisis were slipping out of control. The incident at the PDF checkpoint confirmed these fears, and Bush responded by ordering military intervention.

THE UNITED STATES AND PANAMA

If the shooting of the Marine lieutenant has to be considered in the context of an on-going crisis between the United States and Panama, understanding the nature of the crisis itself requires a look at the broader course of U.S.-Panamanian relations in the twentieth century.[2] The usual starting date for such a survey is 1903, at which time Panama was a part of greater Colombia, a status it had acquired in 1739, when Spain still controlled the area (called New Grenada), and which was reaffirmed after Spanish rule ended in 1821. Nearly a century later, the colonial legacy remained clearly visible across the Panamanian landscape. The population consisted of three principal groups: Spanish-speaking *mestizos* (mixed white and Indian blood), English-speaking Antillean blacks (descendants of African slaves brought to the New World beginning in 1517), and various Indian groups (descendants of the original inhabitants of the region). Roman Catholicism was the predominant religion, a further testimony to the Spanish era, as was a political system dominated by the light-skinned oligarchy and based primarily on *personalismo*, the loyalty to prominent individuals, rather than on ideological affinity or party affiliation.

In the decades following Spanish rule, various Panamanian leaders and groups intermittently sought to separate Panama from Colombia, but prospects for achieving independence had remained bleak until the new century, when the United States took an interest in Panama as the potential site of a transisthmian

---

[2] Unless otherwise noted, the brief survey that follows of U.S.-Panamanian relations up to the fall of 1983 is taken from Sandra W. Meditz and Dennis M. Hanratty, eds., *Panama: A Country Study* (Washington, D.C.: Headquarters, Department of the Army, 1989). See especially the chapter on the historical setting by Jan Knippers Black and Elmundo Flores.

canal. American business interests eager to cut costs and shipping time had been perennial advocates of a waterway linking the Atlantic and Pacific oceans. The U.S. military pursued the same goal for strategic reasons, especially after the Spanish-American War of 1898 demonstrated the need for America's growing navy to be able to sail from one ocean to the other without having to navigate Cape Horn. Supportive of both positions, the administration of President Theodore Roosevelt negotiated a treaty with Colombia giving the United States the right to build and control a canal through Panama. When, to Roosevelt's surprise, the Colombian senate refused to approve the agreement for ratification, an angry president threw his support to the cause of Panamanian independence. That support assumed a tangible form in November 1903, when advocates of independence engineered an uprising in Panama. To discourage any Colombian foray to put down the rebellion, Roosevelt ordered U.S. warships to take up positions off the Panamanian coast. A few Colombian troops did manage to land at Colón but could not suppress the nearly bloodless revolt. Within days, Roosevelt recognized a quickly organized junta as the government of an independent Panama *(Map 1)*.

The price for America's support of Panamanian independence was the Hay–Bunau-Varilla Treaty that gave the United States the right to build, use, and defend a canal across Panama. In addition, the newly independent country also granted the United States a strip of land ten miles wide along the length of the canal route (and three nautical miles into the sea on each end) that would serve as an operating area within which the U.S. government would exercise, in perpetuity, "all the rights, power, and authority . . . which the United States would possess and exercise if it were the sovereign of the territory."[3] In effect, the United States would occupy and control a large swath of territory—the Canal Zone—that bisected Panama. These concessions, together with provisions in the Panamanian constitution of 1904 that gave the United States the right to intervene in Panama to guarantee that country's sovereignty and, when deemed necessary, to restore order, formally relegated Panama to the status of a U.S. protectorate.

The Panama Canal, an engineering marvel even by today's standards, opened in 1914. Its operation and defense immediately became an integral part of America's strategic interests in the hemisphere. As for Panama, the waterway proved a mixed blessing. Many in the country benefited economically, as the canal's operations filled the pockets of the oligarchy and spurred the emergence of a Panamanian middle class of professionals and civil servants. The presence of the Canal Zone, however, together with the U.S. troops and thousands of American citizens living there exempt from Panamanian jurisdiction, aggravated nationalist sentiments and fueled resentment. The rise of the Arias family in Panamanian politics during the 1930s symbolized this discontent. Speaking for middle class *mestizos* and Panamanian nationalists, Harmodio Arias Madrid and his brother, Arnulfo, leveled verbal assaults at the country's white oligarchy and its acceptance of U.S. hegemony over Panamanian territory and the canal. Harmodio's election as president in 1932 paved the way for the 1936 Hull-Alfaro Treaty with the United States that, among its provisions, ended Panama's protectorate status. Brother Arnulfo's election

---

[3] Michael L. Conniff, *Panama and the United States: The Forced Alliance* (Athens, Ga.: University of Georgia Press, 1992), p. 69.

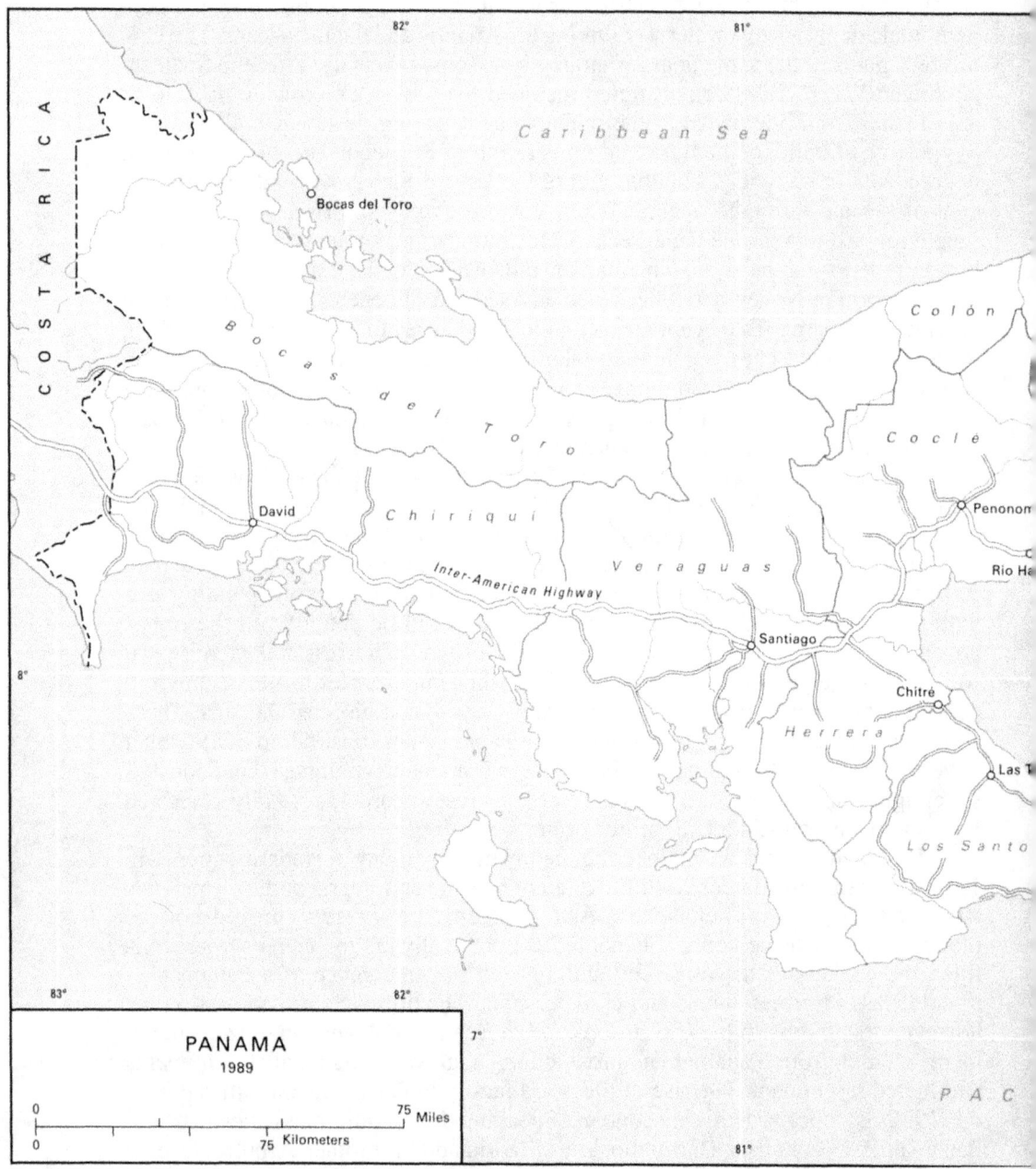

Map 1

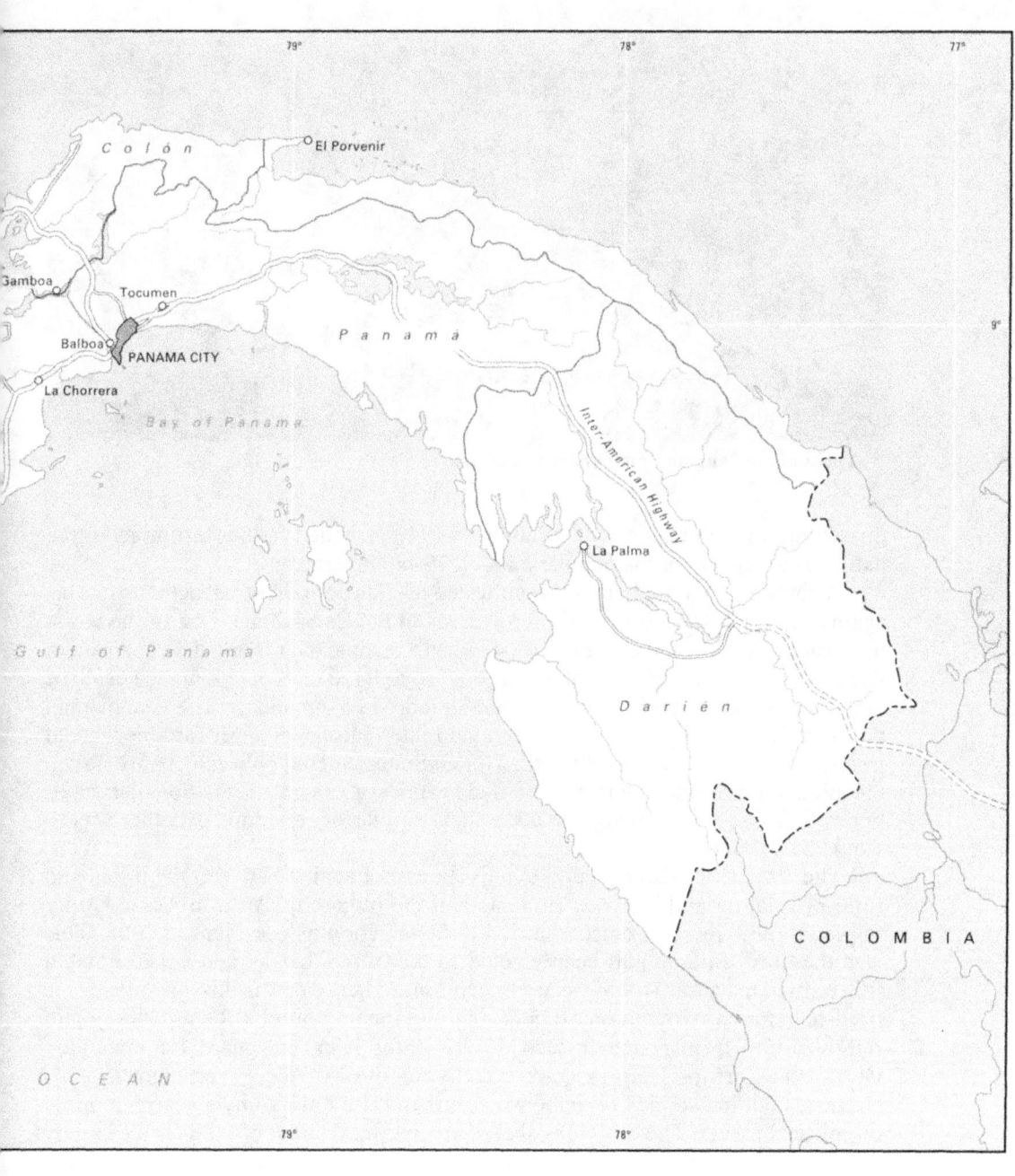

U.S. Military Intervention in Panama, June 1987–December 1989

Locks of the Panama Canal under construction

three times to the presidency beginning in 1940 provided further testimony to the nationalistic appeal of his popular *panameñismo* movement.

Panamanian nationalism also manifested itself in periodic street demonstrations against America's presence and prerogatives in the Canal Zone. One of the worst outbreaks of violence occurred in 1964, when a dispute over flying the Panamanian flag at an American high school in the zone led to three days of rioting, the death of two dozen people, and injuries to several hundred Panamanians. The Panamanian government skillfully used the riots to gain international support for a new canal treaty, the negotiations for which the United States entered only reluctantly. When the initial draft of a new agreement failed to appease Panamanian nationalists, their opposition was vocal enough to necessitate further negotiations. Another accord would be a decade in the making.

The 1964 riots also exacerbated divisions in Panama between the urban and rural population and between students and the oligarchy. Arnulfo Arias' ability to play on this internal discontent led to his election as president in 1968. This was the third time he had been elected to the office, but he had yet to finish a full term. This time would be no exception. When early in his presidency he tried to remove two senior officers of the Panama National Guard, the guard removed him from power instead. Five months later, the guard's commander, Col. Omar Torrijos Herrera, took effective control of the government and the country. In doing so, he broke the white, urban-based oligarchy's near monopoly of political power. The oligarchs shared an abiding distrust of the guard's largely *mestizo* membership, but once Torrijos emerged as the country's strongman, they had no recourse but to acquiesce in the military's ascendancy and, when possible, reach an accommodation with the new rulers. Over time, the imperfect democracy Panama had known to that point became little more than a façade for a military-dominated authoritarian regime.

In 1972, a constitutional assembly dutifully named Torrijos, now a brigadier general, chief of state—he also answered to the title "Maximum Leader of the Panamanian Revolution"—and adopted a new constitution that gave the dictator

THE MAKING OF A CRISIS

General Torrijos *(right)*

vast civil and military powers. To create a popular foundation for this political authority, the general forged a coalition that included such disparate groups as guardsmen and students, campesinos, urban workers, and the middle class, all of whom, for one reason or another, harbored grievances against the oligarchy. Critics denounced Torrijos as lazy and disorganized, a drunk and a charlatan, a Socialist if not a Communist, but their voices were drowned out by the accolades of his supporters. Even though he had no combat record of which to boast (his most significant use of force had been against his own people during the 1964 riots), the new military strongman in Panama quickly became a national hero by virtue of his charisma, his flamboyant demeanor, his populist program of social reform and civic action (which also served to increase the guard's political and economic influence throughout the country), and his vocal commitment to Panamanian nationalism.

Partly to validate his credentials as a populist and a nationalist, Torrijos made completion of a new canal treaty one of his top priorities. Progress toward this goal occurred in 1974, when Panamanian and U.S. diplomats reached agreement on the principles that would guide further negotiations. Three years later, the negotiators' hard work achieved the breakthrough they sought, and, on 7 September 1977, the general and President Jimmy Carter signed two documents that, if ratified, would restructure U.S.-Panamanian relations.

The first document, the Panama Canal Treaty, abrogated the Hay–Bunau-Varilla Treaty of 1903 and all other bilateral agreements pertaining to the canal. Under the terms of the new treaty, Panama would assume immediate jurisdiction over territory in the Canal Zone, which would cease to exist as a formal entity, but would allow the United States to operate, maintain, and manage the canal until noon, 31 December 1999, at which time the treaty would be terminated and Panama would assume full control of the waterway. The interim organization for running the canal would be the Panama Canal Commission (PCC), a U.S. government agency to be established under the terms of the treaty. Initially, the administrator of the commission would be an American; on 1 January 1990, a Panamanian would

President Carter and General Torrijos sign the Panama Canal Treaty.

move into the position. The treaty also mandated that both countries participate in the protection and defense of the canal. The vehicle for doing so, the Combined Board, would consist of an equal number of U.S. and Panamanian officers, an arrangement that further strengthened the political role of the military in Panama by making the national guard instead of the civilian government the direct link with the United States for specific foreign policy and national security issues concerning the canal. Finally, the treaty stated that the U.S. military presence in Panama would end on or before the termination date of the treaty.

The second treaty signed by Carter and Torrijos committed the United States and Panama to guarantee the neutrality of the canal. Unlike the first document, the neutrality treaty had no termination date. The two leaders also signed a series of executive agreements, including two that defined what areas in the former Canal Zone the United States alone would hold until 2000 in order to operate and defend the canal, what areas would be open for use by the armed forces of both countries until that date, what areas would be turned over to Panama upon ratification of the treaties, and what areas would be turned over before 2000.

Troubling questions surrounding the treaties, particularly queries concerning whether the United States could intervene unilaterally to maintain the operation and neutrality of the canal, generated emotional debate in both countries. A Panamanian plebiscite revealed only lukewarm acceptance of the treaties largely because they did not formally prohibit U.S. intervention in the future. In the United States, where the canal was a symbol of American power and technology, a vocal opposition excoriated the Carter administration for giving away U.S. territory and a militarily strategic asset. (In his quest for the Republican Party presidential nomination in 1976, Ronald W. Reagan had excited crowds by declaring of the canal, "We built it, we paid for it, it's ours and we are going to keep it.") The acrimony the canal treaties generated throughout much of the country was mirrored on Capitol Hill, where, after the longest debate in Senate history, the upper house approved the documents for ratification by only one vote. On 1 October 1979, the treaties entered into force. At that time, the Canal Zone was formally abolished, Panama took control of 64 percent of the territory that had been contained therein, while another 18 percent became the "canal operating area," controlled by the new canal commission. What was left remained under U.S. military control, with the process of turning it over gradually to Panama to be completed by the turn of the century.[4]

Many American opponents of ratification worried that the security of the canal could not be entrusted to a "tin-horn" dictator, meaning Torrijos. That the general actively supported Communist-led Sandinista guerrillas in Nicaragua was, in the critics' minds, just one proof of his capacity for willfully disregarding U.S. national security interests. Bedeviled by these allegations, Torrijos also found himself under pressure from the Carter administration to democratize his government, while at home he was plagued by growing disillusionment over the treaties and his regime's faltering economic and social programs. To ease the criticism, the general took steps to amend the constitution of 1972 and to make a small gesture toward more popular participation in Panamanian politics. In October 1978, he also stepped down as chief executive but continued to command the national guard, which still ran the country. The Panamanian legislative election in 1980, stacked in favor of Torrijos' own creation, the Democratic Revolutionary Party (Partido Revolucionario Democrático, or PRD), represented, according to one historian, "a small step toward restoring democratic political processes" in Panama. But it also "demonstrated that Panama's political party system was too fragmented to form a viable united front against the government."[5]

How far Torrijos would have taken the democratization process remains a matter of conjecture. On 31 July 1981, the "maximum leader" was killed in a plane crash in western Panama. In the political turmoil that followed, one condition remained constant: the national guard continued to dominate Panamanian politics. In August 1983, Manuel Noriega took over as the guard's new commander.

NORIEGA

The illegitimate son of a Panamanian civil servant and the family maid, Manuel Noriega emerged from childhood with a distrust of the ruling oligarchy and a resentment toward the privileged classes.[6] A self-conscious introvert whose pockmarked face garnered him the sobriquet "*La Piña*" ("the pineapple"), Noriega did not betray signs of assertive behavior until he entered high school in 1947. There, he encountered a half-brother, Luis Carlos Noriega Hurtado, he did not know he had. Under Luis Carlos' tutelage, Noriega became deeply involved in the

---

[4] For texts of the two treaties, see Meditz and Hanratty, eds., *Panama*, pp. 273–93. Reagan's quote is from *Washington Times*, 11 Jun 2004. Regarding the one-vote margin in the Senate, a handful of senators were reported to be preparing to shift their negative votes into the positive column if such action was needed to permit ratification.

[5] Meditz and Hanratty, eds., *Panama*, p. 59.

[6] The brief biographical sketch that traces Noriega's career up to the murder of Hugo Spadafora is taken primarily from Frederick Kempe, *Divorcing the Dictator: America's Bungled Affair with Noriega* (New York: G. P. Putnam's Sons, 1990), pp. 38–71. I have also incorporated observations made by Gabriel Marcella and General Frederick F. Woerner Jr., U.S. Army (Ret.), The Road to War: The U.S.-Panamanian Crisis, 1987–1989, draft article, 6 May 91.

General Noriega

nationalistic, anti-oligarchic politics in vogue at the school, with his participation in the leftist-oriented Panamanian Student Federation serving more as an outlet for his personal resentments and frustrations than as a basis for any formal ideological commitment.

After graduation, Noriega worked as a hospital laboratory assistant, after which, again as a result of his half-brother's influence, he entered the Chorrillos Military Academy in Lima, Peru. Wearing a uniform imparted to Noriega a sense of self-esteem, while the hardships of cadet life taught him lessons about the efficacy of brutality as a means of control. In 1962, a meeting with Torrijos, then a commander in the province of Colón, so impressed Noriega that he joined the Panama National Guard. Torrijos, for his part, took a liking to the young officer, often assigning him important, even sensitive, duties and covering for him when episodes of sexual brutality, rape, drunkenness, and other aberrant behavior threatened his military career.

As Noriega rose through the ranks, he acquired greater responsibilities, together with many of the more sinister talents that would later so disgust, infuriate, and confound his enemies. In the mid-1960s, when the U.S. military intelligence unit located in Panama helped the national guard put together an intelligence-gathering capability, Torrijos, by then commander in Chiriquí Province, put Noriega, chief of the province's traffic police, or *tránsitos*, in charge of the local effort. Noriega further honed his intelligence skills in courses taught by the U.S. military in the Canal Zone and at Fort Bragg, North Carolina. While attending these and other classes, he developed a fascination for psychological operations that later motivated him to write a manual on the subject. As time passed, he turned the modest military intelligence assets initially available to him into a sophisticated espionage network with agents planted inside numerous Panamanian organizations. The information he collected and his willingness to use it for blackmail and intimidation made him an increasingly dangerous man to cross. According to some sources, his files included one full of damaging information on Torrijos, which helped Noriega keep his patron tractable.

Together with Torrijos and other officers, Noriega participated in the 1968 coup against Arnulfo Arias. As a major in command of an infantry company, Noriega hunted, fought, and occasionally tortured guerrillas operating in Chiriquí Province in support of the ousted president. A year later Noriega's timely assistance saved Torrijos himself from a coup attempt plotted by rival officers in the guard. Torrijos rewarded Noriega by making him chief of military intelligence in Panama and promoting him to lieutenant colonel. From that vantage point, *La Piña* was able to expand his collection efforts and to establish contacts and share information with other intelligence services throughout the world.

After Torrijos' death, Noriega skillfully outmaneuvered his fellow officers within the guard's inner circle to emerge in August 1983 as Panama's new strongman. Soon thereafter, he secured passage of Law 20 that created the Panama Defense Forces. The national guard retained its identity but only as one among several organizations—to include ground, air, and naval forces and the police—constituting the PDF. While the president of Panama ostensibly exercised control over the armed forces, the law in fact rendered that role largely symbolic. According to one account, the new organization "enjoyed administrative autonomy that in effect allowed it to determine its own internal procedures in regard to personnel policies, disciplinary sanctions against [PDF] members, organizations created to further the social welfare of the members, and recommendations for the defense budget." As commander in chief of the new organization with the rank of *general de fuerzas*, Noriega expanded the PDF's roster, intensified its training, and purchased more equipment. In the process, the Panama Defense Forces became a much more militarized organization than its institutional predecessor. Moreover, as commander in chief, Noriega acquired under Law 20 the responsibility for implementing "measures needed to guarantee the security of inhabitants and their property and the preservation of public order and social peace," while keeping the country's president informed of national security developments.[7]

In the political arena, Noriega made little pretense of following through on Torrijos' tentative measures to reduce the military's role in Panamanian politics. To the contrary, the new commander quickly ousted another of Panama's civilian presidents and, less than a year later, helped engineer the fraudulent election that placed the PDF-backed candidate, Nicolás Ardito Barletta, in the presidential palace. (There is general agreement that the actual winner in the 1984 election was Arnulfo Arias, who was thereby denied, thanks to Noriega, the opportunity to begin—much less finish for the first time—yet another term as president.) As with Torrijos, Noriega used the Partido Revolucionario Democrático as the military's official political party. In coalition with the smaller Partido Laborista Agrario, in which Noriega's brother-in-law would serve as secretary general, the PRD controlled the legislative branch of government.

Noriega also deepened the military's role in the economic life of the country. Prudence had always dictated that Panamanian businessmen not ignore the military. An officer with a position on a firm's board of directors could offer valuable services in advancing the company's fortunes. Law 20 expanded the role of the military in the economy by placing elements of the Panama Defense Forces in control of Panama's ports, airports, immigration, and other revenue-generating enterprises. Many officers also moved up from their symbolic positions as board members to become owners of lucrative enterprises. Torrijos had challenged the political power of the oligarchy; now, the PDF under Noriega began to encroach—

---

[7] The quotes are from Meditz and Hanratty, eds., *Panama*, p. 225.

through formal and informal means and legal and illegal enterprises—upon the elite's economic livelihood.

Noriega's actions generated opposition, but his growing reputation as a ruthless, even sadistic, man silenced most critics. One notable exception was Dr. Hugo Spadafora, a physician, revolutionary, and former government official. In response to the 1968 coup against Arias, Spadafora had vowed to depose Torrijos, but, strangely enough, after the general had the doctor arrested, the two men ended up becoming good friends. During the period when Torrijos supported the Sandinistas' war against Nicaraguan President Anastasio Somoza Debayle, Spadafora was given a "brigade" of a few hundred Panamanian volunteers with which to join the fight. After the Sandinista victory, disillusionment with the new Marxist-Leninist government in Managua compelled Spadafora to support the CIA-sponsored Contra insurgency against his erstwhile comrades.

Spadafora's exploits as a guerrilla warrior, his good looks, his machismo, and his charisma stood in stark contrast to Noriega's appearance, experience, and demeanor. Even before Torrijos' death, Spadafora had privately charged Noriega with corruption, war profiteering, and drug trafficking. After Noriega took control of the country, the doctor continued his verbal assaults, which precipitated a highly publicized test of wills. Given Spadafora's popularity and the apparent validity of his charges, Noriega decided to make an example of his nemesis. On 13 September 1985, Spadafora crossed into Panama from Costa Rica, where he was living in exile. Three days later, the doctor's decapitated, mutilated body was found in a U.S. mail sack back across the Costa Rican border. Although Noriega was in Paris at the time, few doubted that the systematic torture and barbarous murder of such a prominent opposition figure could have been carried out without the general's authorization.[8]

The death of Spadafora spread fear and uncertainty among Noriega's detractors, further intimidating them into keeping their silence. Next to the murder itself, what was most disturbing was that, despite his reputation for brutality, Noriega generally had not been perceived as sanctioning political killings. The Spadafora episode changed that perception and shed a little more light on what was becoming Noriega's modus operandi for dealing with opposition to his power. There would be no "dirty war" in Panama, no death squads roaming the country, no lists of missing persons numbering in the thousands. Rather, opponents of the regime would be targeted selectively, individually, or in small groups; harassed and intimidated, incarcerated if need be, in many cases tortured and sexually abused; but killed only in the most extreme cases, such as that of Spadafora. Word of these activities would spread, invariably embellished by the hyperbole of rumor and gossip. The resulting terror was always more psychological than physical. The important thing was the effect: acquiescence. You did not have to kill your opponents, or even harm them physically, to silence them.

In the short-term, the grisly details of Spadafora's death had the desired effect. Allegations leveled against the general by the doctor's family fell on sympathetic ears, but, given the climate of fear, professions of indignation did

---

[8] Accounts of the Spadafora murder can be found in Kempe, *Divorcing the Dictator*, pp. 126–41; Kevin Buckley, *Panama: The Whole Story* (New York: Simon & Schuster, 1991), pp. 21–31.

not translate into any serious challenge to Noriega's power. President Barletta attempted to investigate the murder, only to find himself forced to resign in favor of Vice President Eric Arturo Delvalle. Barletta considered fighting his dismissal, but a threat to the safety of his family, delivered personally by a PDF officer, convinced him otherwise. If there were any lingering doubts as to who ran the government, Spadafora's murder and Barletta's resignation removed them.

Having silenced all but a handful of his domestic critics, Noriega felt secure in his position of power. The United States occasionally expressed its preference for a more democratic Panama, but the general believed that his ties to the Reagan administration were strong enough that Washington would overlook his indiscretions at home or, at worst, give him a perfunctory slap on the wrist. After all, had not U.S. Secretary of State George P. Shultz attended Barletta's inauguration in 1984, despite charges that the presidential election had been fraudulent.[9] Similarly, in the aftermath of the Spadafora episode and Barletta's removal, Noriega had attended two amicable meetings with U.S. officials ostensibly sent to reprimand him. His continuing relations with various American agencies and organizations, including the U.S. military command in Panama, bolstered his feeling of confidence. The general thus received an unpleasant surprise when, in the spring of 1986, he became the target of two investigations by the U.S. Senate. Surprise turned to shock when, during a visit to the United States in June, he was treated to a front-page story in the *New York Times* detailing his alleged involvement in drug trafficking, money laundering, arms shipments to Communist guerrillas, and the selling of restricted U.S. technology to Cuba. Written by investigative reporter Seymour M. Hersh, the exposé also linked Noriega directly to the Spadafora murder and claimed that the general provided intelligence information to both the United States and Cuba.[10]

Quoting anonymous U.S. government officials, past and present, and relying on classified documents leaked to him, Hersh revealed how several departments and agencies responsible for America's national security benefited from "the Panama connection." Noriega allowed the U.S. military command based in Panama "extensive leeway" in its activities, and, over the years, he had provided useful intelligence to the United States on Latin American insurgencies and on Cuban activities in the region. Also, according to Hersh's sources, the general permitted various U.S. organizations to maintain intelligence-gathering facilities in Panama. What the Hersh exposé did not say was that Noriega had been recruited by U.S. military intelligence as early as 1952, that he was currently supporting U.S. Drug Enforcement Administration efforts in Panama (some say by turning in his competitors or insignificant underlings), and that,

---

[9] Barletta had been a student of Shultz's at some point in the 1960s when Shultz had been head of the business school at the University of Chicago.

[10] *New York Times*, 12 Jun 86. On the Spadafora affair, Hersh cited sources who claimed that the United States had intelligence linking Noriega directly to the murder. The existence of this evidence was confirmed to me in an interview with a military intelligence officer who had served in Panama at the time of the murder. Interv, author with Col Paul F. Morgan, U.S. Army, 7 Jul 89, U.S. Special Operations Command, MacDill Air Force Base, Fla. Colonel Morgan was the deputy chief of staff for intelligence (DCSINT) at U.S. Army, South (USARSO), a U.S. Southern Command (USSOUTHCOM) component, from 1985 to 1989.

at the request of the Reagan administration, he was assisting the Contras in their war against the Sandinista regime in Nicaragua.

The Hersh article and subsequent revelations showed that many U.S. government officials had important ties to Noriega and believed that his value to America's strategic interests in the region warranted their downplaying his friendly relations with Cuba and his various illicit activities. As one source told Hersh regarding Noriega's selling of U.S. intelligence to Cuba, "The station chiefs loved him. . . . As far as they were concerned, the stuff that they were getting was more interesting than what the Cubans were getting from Noriega on us."[11] This forgiving assessment seemed to reflect a broader sentiment among State Department, Pentagon, Central Intelligence Agency (CIA), Drug Enforcement Administration, and National Security Council officials in mid-1986 that the devil you know is better than one you do not. Whatever Noriega's faults, the Reagan administration would continue to overlook them.

Hersh's exposé did not address what administration officials might do if the machinations of the Panamanian dictator turned into a serious threat to U.S. national security interests. Would an anti-Noriega consensus emerge to counter the danger, or would there be a breaking of ranks, with some U.S. officials arguing for cutting the general loose and others defending the current arrangements? Already, there had been some divergence from the status quo. The new U.S. ambassador to Panama, Arthur Davis, had on his arrival in the country called for the restoration of Panamanian democracy and an investigation into the Spadafora murder. There were also indications that Elliott Abrams, assistant secretary of state for inter-American affairs, harbored serious doubts about Noriega's continued usefulness to U.S. agencies. Still, when the administration held a policy review on Panama, Abrams supported the decision to shelve official concerns about Noriega until the conflict with the Sandinistas in Nicaragua was resolved.[12]

Crisis in Panama

Once Hersh's revelations ceased to stir public comment, the Reagan administration enjoyed a year's grace period during which no compelling reason arose for further reevaluating the relationship with Noriega. Then, on 1 June 1987, the general cashiered an ambitious rival within the Panama Defense Forces, Col. Roberto Díaz Herrera, the organization's chief of staff. Three days later, Noriega announced that he himself would remain the PDF commander for another five years. Díaz Herrera swiftly retaliated, publicly accusing the general of fraud, corruption, and drug trafficking. He also told reporters that Noriega was responsible for the murder of Spadafora and, even more damning, the plane crash that killed Torrijos. Coming from such a high-ranking member of the PDF leadership, the allegations rocked the country. Angry Panamanians in the capital gathered at Díaz Herrera's home in support of the colonel, and, when Noriega sent his special antiriot unit, the Dobermans, to disperse the assemblage, the troops had to employ bird shot and tear gas. In the days that followed, spontaneous demonstrations erupted throughout Panama City and in Colón at the northern end of the canal, with men and women waving white handkerchiefs and banging pots, two gestures of defiance that almost overnight became symbols of the

---

[11] *New York Times*, 12 Jun 86.
[12] Kempe, *Divorcing the Dictator*, pp. 169–80; Buckley, *Panama*, pp. 41–52.

opposition to Noriega. That opposition acquired an organizational framework when leading Panamanian businessmen—some motivated by principle, others resentful of PDF encroachments on their economic turf—formed the National Civic Crusade (NCC) on 10 June. Such diverse groups as students, teachers, workers, medical organizations, and religious leaders proclaimed their support. When the NCC began organizing mass demonstrations, a national strike, and car caravans through the capital as part of its protest, and as the regime responded with the Dobermans and counterdemonstrations, Panama suddenly found itself in a serious political crisis.

The firing of Díaz Herrera and the public protests that days later followed his allegations against Noriega bracketed a significant event for the U.S. military in Panama, a change in the top position at the U.S. Southern Command (SOUTHCOM). Located at Quarry Heights, the name given two man-made terraces near the summit of Ancon Hill overlooking Panama City, the headquarters had been established in the Canal Zone in 1963 as a successor to the U.S. Caribbean Command and as the latest affirmation of the American military presence in Panama. As a unified command, SOUTHCOM included components and staff officers from each service as well as Special Operations Forces (*Chart 1*). Its mission, in general terms, was to oversee U.S. military programs and activities in Central and South America, including the defense of the Panama Canal.

On 6 June, General Frederick F. Woerner Jr. became commander in chief of the Southern Command (CINCSO)(*Chart 2*). Woerner was a West Point graduate, a battalion commander in Vietnam, and a soldier-scholar, fluent in Spanish and the recipient of a master's degree in Latin American history. Of his several assignments in the region, his most recent had been as commander of the 193d Infantry Brigade, stationed in Panama, and, simultaneously, as commander of the U.S. Army Assistance Agency for Latin America. Given his experience in the theater, he took the reins at Quarry Heights with definite ideas on the course his new command should chart He was concerned that Washington's preoccupation with Central America since the early 1980s, specifically with the wars in Nicaragua and El Salvador, had slighted other countries in the region, especially the principal nations of South America. As CINCSO, he hoped to place more emphasis on theater-wide issues. He also sought to promote the spread of democracy in

General Woerner in conversation

CHART 1—COMMAND RELATIONSHIPS: U.S. SOUTHERN COMMAND

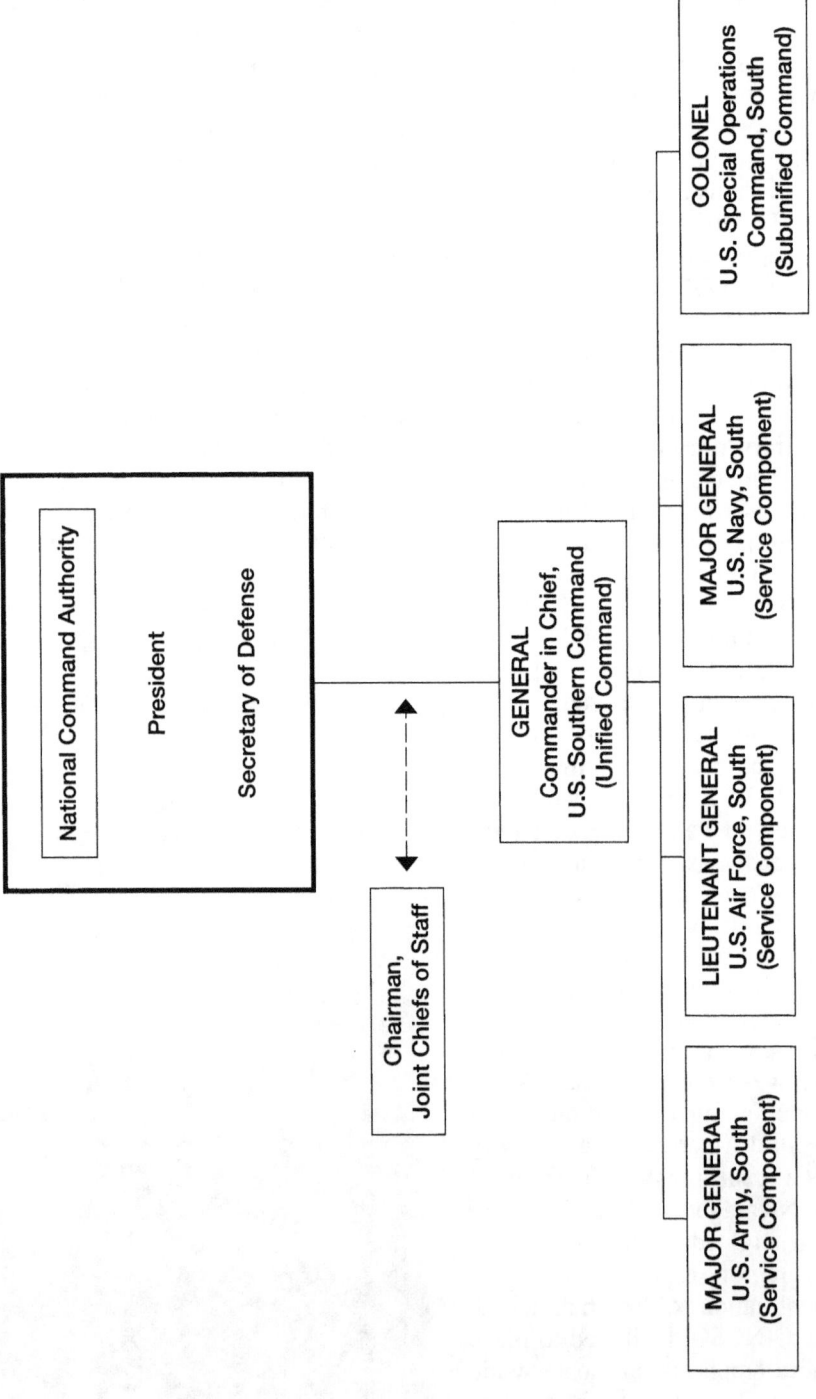

CHART 2—U.S. SOUTHERN COMMAND JOINT STAFF ORGANIZATION

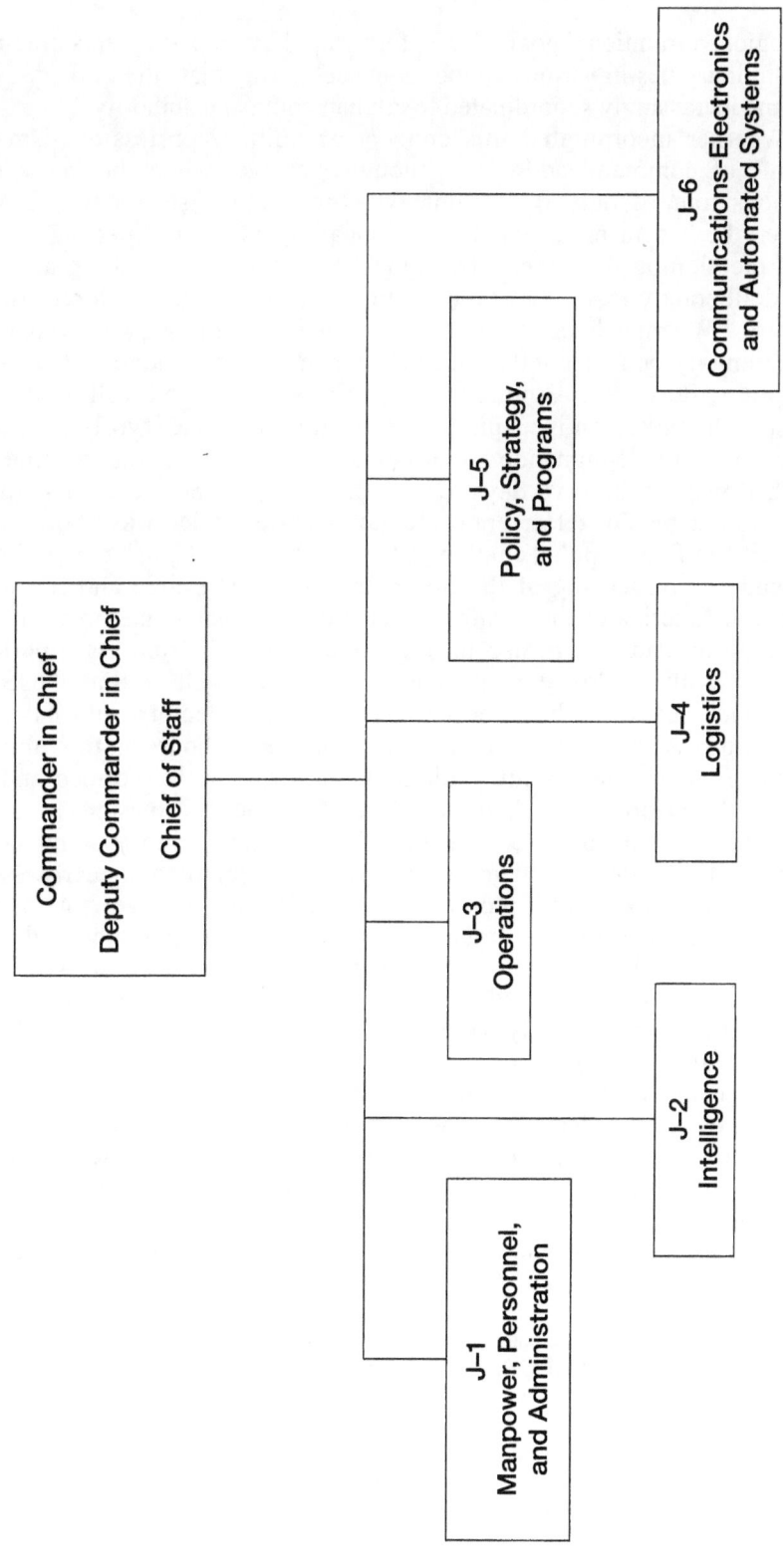

the region, a traditional goal of U.S. foreign policy, in part by encouraging closer civil-military ties in various countries in such a way that "the military . . . would become increasingly subordinated to civilian command authority."[13]

Woerner incorporated this concept of military professionalism into his change of command address. Although Noriega, whom he knew from his previous tour of duty in Panama, was one among several Latin American officers he had in mind when he personally drafted the speech, he refrained from mentioning the general by name. "I would not be making a speech that was deliberately insulting to the commander of the military forces of the host country," Woerner later insisted.[14] Nevertheless, Noriega, who was present at the ceremony, considered the speech a personal affront and refused to attend the reception afterwards. Although neither man had time to dwell on the episode, the speech marked an inauspicious renewal of a strained working relationship between the two commanders that would, within the months to come, become much worse. Within two days of the ceremony, the political crisis in Panama precipitated by Díaz Herrera's allegations was under way. For Noriega, it marked the first popular challenge to his position of power. For Woerner, it portended a refocusing of the Southern Command's time and resources, not on South America or the theater in general, as he had contemplated, but more narrowly on Panama. It also meant a telephone call from his superior, Navy Admiral William Crowe, chairman of the Joint Chiefs of Staff (JCS), asking with mock solemnity how the new commander in chief could have screwed things up so badly in Panama after only forty-eight hours on the job.[15]

On 10 June, the day the National Civic Crusade was formed and one day after PDF antiriot troops had used force to disperse protesters in the capital, President Delvalle declared a state of emergency.[16] The ensuing crackdown temporarily quelled the demonstrations, but, beginning in early July, NCC leaders again mobilized public opposition to the regime, this time for a more sustained effort. As organized protests spread throughout the country, Noriega adopted a hard-line policy in response. In subsequent confrontations between demonstrators and the Panama Defense Forces, only a handful of protesters were actually killed, the first fatality occurring on 26 July, but scores were wounded and hundreds arrested. A select few were tortured to serve as an object lesson to the others and to stoke rumors that beatings and same-sex rape by AIDS-infected PDF were just two of the abominations awaiting any of Noriega's critics who ended up behind bars. The government also exiled some opposition leaders and seized the property of others. The PDF, which owned three newspapers, a television station, and several radio stations, used these assets to discredit its detractors, while censoring or closing pro-opposition media.

---

[13] Woerner discusses his career, his views about the Southern Command in the 1980s, and his philosophy on the democratic potential of Latin American militaries in Interv, General Frederick F. Woerner Jr., U.S. Army (Ret.), U.S. Army Military History Institute (MHI), Carlisle Barracks, Pa.

[14] Ibid.

[15] Ibid.

[16] A chronology of the demonstrations that rocked Panama in the summer and fall of 1988, together with a chronology of U.S. government and U.S. Southern Command reactions, is included in USSOUTHCOM, Historical Report 1988. I have also incorporated observations from Marcella and Woerner, The Road to War, 6 May 91.

The Making of a Crisis

Against this impressive array of government power, Panamanians who took to the streets soon discovered that white handkerchiefs were no match for tear gas, truncheons, water cannon, and bird shot. The lesson was driven home on 22 October when Noriega unleashed not the Dobermans, but Battalion 2000, a full-fledged military unit with helicopters, to break up an antigovernment demonstration. The unit's antiriot tactics so disrupted the rally that the National Civic Crusade did not schedule another until 13 November. The opposition harbored few zealots or willing martyrs; thus, fighting back against well-armed troops and police was not a practical option. Yet, so long as critics of the regime continued to agitate in any way, Noriega felt compelled to respond. Each response, in turn, generated more adverse publicity at home and abroad. How the United States would react was of particular concern to the PDF commander, who orchestrated his campaign against the opposition with one eye on the internal crisis and the other on Washington.

What he saw in Washington was not reassuring, particularly when he looked to Capitol Hill. On 26 June, the U.S. Senate by a vote of 84-2 passed a resolution that called for the government of Panama to restore constitutional rights suspended under the state of emergency, ensure free elections, remove the Panama Defense Forces from nonmilitary activities and organizations, and investigate the Spadafora murder. Delvalle denounced the resolution, although he did declare an end to the state of emergency.

In the wake of the Senate's action, Noriega intensified the campaign to shore up his political support in Panama, combining populist appeals to Panamanian nationalism and *torrijismo* with a strong dose of anti-American rhetoric. This last tack was nothing new in Panamanian politics, and, during past occurrences, U.S. officials had generally accepted it for what it was, a calculated ploy designed primarily for domestic consumption. But this time Noriega overplayed his hand. Four days after the Senate passed its resolution, progovernment demonstrators gathered outside the U.S. Embassy in Panama City. As the PDF looked on, the mob threw rocks and paint-filled balloons at the building, broke windows, and damaged cars in the area. An outraged Ambassador Davis angrily denounced the attack, demanded compensation (which was later paid), and recommended the suspension of economic and military assistance to Panama.

Noriega presumably reckoned that his close ties with various U.S. agencies and departments within the executive branch would allow him to tweak the Senate and even insult the State Department without causing severe damage to the bureaucratic consensus that had tolerated his illicit activities in the past. He soon discovered, however, that the consensus was much shakier than he thought. The demonstrations, the anti-American rhetoric, the attack on the embassy, and, most of all, the drug trafficking in which he was allegedly involved had finally turned him into a public embarrassment for the Reagan administration. The State Department, prodded by Elliott Abrams, had been on the verge of disavowing him for over a year. Now, buoyed by the administration's putative successes in promoting democracy in the Philippines and Haiti (where the United States had facilitated the removal of Presidents Ferdinand Marcos and Jean-Claude Duvalier, respectively), the department called for a campaign of economic pressure aimed at ridding Panama of an unsavory dictator and the United States of a troublesome "friend."

The CIA and the Pentagon, while conceding Noriega's transgressions, were less eager to take action against the general (although the CIA agreed to remove him from its payroll in the wake of the embassy demonstration). The director of central intelligence, William Casey, and others for whom support of the Contra insurgency in Nicaragua had become a near obsession continued to value Noriega as a source of information and assistance in the administration's battle against the Sandinista government. At the Pentagon, Secretary of Defense Caspar Weinberger and Admiral Crowe did not regard Noriega as an indispensable asset but argued against any precipitate action that might undermine what still constituted a productive working relationship between the U.S. military and the Panamanian armed forces, despite the friction generated by the general's anti-American bombast.

Woerner agreed. In a message to Crowe in early September, the general made the case for a "prudent" and "balanced" strategy for dealing with the crisis. He stated that the Southern Command wanted to see democracy established in Panama, basic civil rights protected, and freedom of the press reestablished. The Panama Defense Forces, he argued, would be an important player in the attainment of these objectives. To think otherwise would be to ignore the country's traditions and culture. Even if Noriega were to step down, "the significant involvement of the PDF in Panamanian politics would continue. A completely apolitical PDF is a fantasy." Woerner reiterated his personal goal of helping Panama's military "support a genuine transition to democracy and evolve into a professional organization friendly to US interests and capable of defending the Canal." This objective, though, could not be pursued if Congress cut off security assistance to Panama. "Neither long-term nor short-term US interests in Panama are furthered by severing completely our professional military-to-military contacts with the PDF," however "strained and deteriorating" they might be at the moment. Crowe apparently agreed. A note on Woerner's copy of the message indicated it "won raves from the JCS."[17]

The message's contents would have received less enthusiastic reviews from Congress and the State Department, which for the remainder of the year advocated economic warfare against the Delvalle regime. President Reagan lent his support to this approach on 22 December when he signed a bill restricting U.S. assistance to Panama until that country's government could provide evidence of a meaningful transition to democracy. The sanctions hurt the Noriega dictatorship but also had an adverse effect both on the businessmen who formed the core of the opposition movement and on the Panamanian people as a whole.

Economic sanctions and appeals for Panamanian democracy fell short of a coherent, interagency approach by the Reagan administration to the situation in Panama. Critical questions remained unanswered. Was Noriega's removal from power a prerequisite for democracy? The State Department seemed to accept this condition, and Woerner and Crowe made no strong remonstrations. But various elements in the CIA and the Pentagon continued to balk at discarding a man whom they still considered an important asset. Another question, raised in Woerner's message to Crowe, was how the Southern Command should deal with the PDF and its commander on a day-to-day basis. As Reagan's national security team deliberated over these and related issues, no consensus materialized on what to do.

---

[17] Msg, USSOUTHCOM to Joint Chiefs of Staff (JCS), 031830Z Sep 87.

With other, more pressing matters demanding attention elsewhere in the region and the world, the administration procrastinated on devising a comprehensive approach for handling its predicament with Noriega. In late 1987, more assertive action probably would have been premature anyway. As Woerner often observed, the crisis in Panama was primarily an internal affair that should be resolved internally, if at all possible, by means of a Panamanian solution to a Panamanian problem. The situation, in his opinion, should not be allowed to degenerate into a full-scale U.S.-Panamanian confrontation, Noriega's rhetoric and Washington's economic sanctions notwithstanding.

THE SOUTHERN COMMAND AND THE CRISIS

During his first months as SOUTHCOM's commander, Woerner did what he could to prevent an open break between the Southern Command and the Panama Defense Forces, despite the increasing strains the crisis in Panama placed on the relationship. Personally, he felt nothing but contempt for Noriega, a man he regarded as a scoundrel, a thug, and an obstacle to the PDF becoming a more professional organization. Still, Noriega was the PDF's commander, so Woerner was occasionally compelled to meet with him. The SOUTHCOM commander insisted, though, that the meetings be conducted on an "unofficial" basis. This meant following a routine in which Woerner would agree to a request by Noriega for a face-to-face conversation, drive to Noriega's office at Fort Amador and enter through the back door, and talk with the general one-on-one, with no media coverage. These "discreet" meetings, to use Woerner's description, allowed both men to discuss issues and problems of mutual concern, without providing Noriega a "photo opportunity" to use in his propaganda war against the domestic opposition. Noriega accepted these conditions and, according to Woerner, never violated the confidentiality of the meetings.[18] On an official level, contacts with PDF officers continued through such mechanisms as the Combined Board and military-police liaisons. SOUTHCOM also continued to plan for routine exercises the headquarters had customarily conducted with the PDF and its national guard predecessor. In late 1987, however, President Delvalle had placed that kind of activity in limbo when, in response to additional economic sanctions passed against Panama by the U.S. Congress, he announced that the Panama Defense Forces would not participate in KINDLE LIBERTY, the annual combined exercise for the defense of the Panama Canal, scheduled for early 1988. In January 1988, the U.S. Congress raised the ante by passing a resolution prohibiting all military training and exercises with the Panamanian military. As Woerner looked on, the SOUTHCOM-PDF relationship he valued was increasingly becoming a casualty of the worsening crisis.

Salvaging a professional relationship that would allow U.S. forces to exert a salutary influence on the Panama Defense Forces was only one of Woerner's crisis-related concerns. He also had the responsibility to do what he could to insulate the people under his command from the violence in the streets. This was no simple task. Among the more than 50,000 U.S. citizens living on Panamanian territory, especially in and around the capital, there were several thousand U.S. service personnel and their dependents. From their homes and apartments—sometimes as the residences filled with smoke or tear gas—many could observe at close range

---

[18] For Woerner's account of his approach to meeting with Noriega, see Woerner MHI Interv.

the clashes between Panamanian forces and opposition demonstrators. In one case, an American dependent watching a demonstration from her balcony received superficial wounds from stray shotgun pellets. There was also the risk that military personnel driving to and from any of the several U.S. installations that remained in the former Canal Zone might inadvertently land in the middle of an angry mob or find themselves surrounded by overturned cars and burning tires. To minimize these risks, Woerner and his component commanders did the best they could to keep Americans in Panama informed about day-to-day developments in the crisis.

To monitor the turmoil, the Southern Command set up crisis action teams whenever the situation warranted. Generally, these teams operated out of "the Tunnel," SOUTHCOM's secure command post dug into the side of Ancon Hill, and included SOUTHCOM staff officers and liaison officers from the service components. Once activated, a team's primary function was to collect and collate information on the crisis, relying heavily on U.S. military intelligence assets in Panama to provide the data.

The process was not necessarily an easy one. Even before the crisis, SOUTHCOM's intelligence shop; the intelligence officers of the service components, especially U.S. Army, South's (USARSO) deputy chief of staff for intelligence; and the Army's Panama-based 470th Military Intelligence Brigade, the principal "collector" of military intelligence in Panama, all worked under significant handicaps while trying to fulfill the requirements placed on them for timely information. To begin with, the intelligence database for Panama was smaller than it could have been because, officially, the country was a friendly nation hosting American armed forces. Because of this status, legal and political considerations prevented Panama from becoming a target of extensive U.S. clandestine intelligence operations. Helping to compensate for these shortfalls, at least during the precrisis years, was the fact that a good deal of useful information could be obtained from open sources and overt methods: covering the Panamanian media, traveling through the country, and exploiting contacts American servicemen cultivated with Panamanian civilians and the Panama Defense Forces. U.S. intelligence officers, for example, enjoyed daily liaison with their Panamanian counterparts and had ready access to PDF bases and posts, as well as to the posted orders of the day. Panamanian forces also "tacitly cooperated" with American efforts to collect intelligence on other countries in the region, especially El Salvador, Nicaragua, and Cuba. In sum, despite legal and other barriers, U.S. intelligence activities aimed at and involving Panama prior to the crisis were accomplished without excessive constraints and risks.[19]

When the crisis began to erode the cooperative relationship between U.S. intelligence personnel and the Panama Defense Forces, open sources remained available and valuable but other avenues of collection began to close down. The Southern Command tried to adapt to the deteriorating situation, but, according to one midcrisis assessment, "the entire US intelligence complex was ill-prepared to

---

[19] This description of U.S. military intelligence assets in Panama during the early stages of the crisis is based on Intervs, author with Brig Gen John Stewart Jr., U.S. Army, 14 Jun 89, Quarry Heights, Panama; Col M. J. Flynn, U.S. Army, Mar 89, Corozal, Panama; Morgan, 7 Jul 89; Maj Gen Bernard Loeffke, U.S. Army, 31 May 89, Fort Clayton, Panama; Col John A. Cope, U.S. Army, 29 Mar 89, Fort Clayton, Panama; Lt Col Michael Mallory, U.S. Army, 29 Mar 89, Fort Clayton, Panama; and Ed McConnell, 19 Jun 89, Fort Clayton, Panama.

initiate intensive collection operations against Panama." Nor did doctrine provide any practicable guidelines for action since it did not cover what the 470th defined as "diplomatic/economic war" against a hostile host country "under conditions characterized as 'neither peace nor war, nor classic low intensity conflict.'" The process of adjustment thus took time and improvisation, at the beginning of which military intelligence units simply did not have enough people or resources to cover the numerous targets offered by the PDF and by anti- and pro-government activists. As one example of the recurring frustration experienced in obtaining timely information, intelligence officers often acquired and processed crisis-related material only to find they had been scooped by the news media, particularly CNN (Cable News Network).[20]

Together with the small number of clandestine operations that remained active, the overt sources and contacts that continued in play during the early months of the crisis provided the 470th and U.S. Army, South, with the information required to publish periodically a classified order of battle that depicted the PDF's organization, if not its tactical capabilities. USARSO's deputy chief of staff for intelligence also issued routine intelligence summaries that, for the most part, reported broad political and economic trends in the country. When available, information on the times and places of opposition demonstrations was disseminated to the American community via such media as SOUTHCOM's newspaper, the *Southern Command News*; the command's television station, SCN (Southern Command Network); U.S. Embassy announcements; and various other official channels. On a more personal level, Woerner and his component commanders met with military families in an attempt to elucidate events, calm fears, and solicit cooperation in what was becoming a trying experience for many dependents. The Southern Command also implemented a four-tiered system of personnel movement limitations (PMLs) designed to restrict off-base military travel during periods of heightened tension. When PML Alpha, the least restrictive of the four, was in effect, Americans in Panama were advised to "exercise caution" and to "avoid crowds, meetings and demonstrations." Should the situation necessitate enacting the highest PML, Delta, American citizens would be told not to travel unless it would be onto a U.S. defense site or a treaty-designated Military Area of Coordination.[21]

To reduce the possibility of an unwarranted or unintended provocation, SCN and the *Southern Command News* frequently reminded their audience that, under the terms of the canal treaties, Americans were prohibited from interfering in the internal affairs of Panama. To this end, the SOUTHCOM Public Affairs Office adopted measures to keep it from being perceived as a vehicle for anti-Noriega propaganda. For example, when it ran wire service stories on the crisis—stories often critical of the Panamanian regime—it did so with the disclaimer that the contents and opinions expressed in the stories were not those of the U.S. government. In another step to avoid the appearance of meddling in Panama's internal troubles, the Southern Command and the U.S. Embassy began monitoring training exercises and other routine U.S. military activities in the canal area much more closely. For at least one operations officer in USARSO's 193d Infantry Brigade, the more intense scrutiny meant frequently having to brief the U.S. ambassador or a SOUTHCOM

---

[20] The source for this assessment and the quotes is Msg, 470th Military Intelligence (MI) Bde to U.S. Army Intelligence and Security Command (INSCOM), 232235Z Feb 89.

[21] USSOUTHCOM, Personnel Movement Limitations (PML) Handout, n.d.

general to reassure the individual that some pending military undertaking would not provoke an adverse reaction from the Panamanian government or the Panama Defense Forces.[22]

The warnings, advisories, and other precautions did not prevent isolated episodes in which Americans inadvertently became embroiled in street protests and demonstrations, and thus subject to mistreatment by Panamanian forces. Initially, the *Southern Command News* indicated that these incidents could have been avoided had the Americans involved only heeded SOUTHCOM's PML levels.[23] As the crisis continued, however, the PDF appeared to launch a deliberate campaign of harassing U.S. military personnel. The evidence was not conclusive at first, since low-level harassment, such as soliciting bribes for alleged traffic violations, had gone on for years before the crisis began. But as incidents of U.S. servicemen being illegally detained and, in some cases, physically abused increased in the last quarter of 1987, Woerner faced a dilemma. To take too strong a stand could risk a SOUTHCOM-PDF confrontation, even hostilities, over PDF transgressions that were deplorable but hardly cause for a war that neither the SOUTHCOM commander nor the Reagan administration desired. But to limit SOUTHCOM's response to written protestations that contained no serious threats of punitive measures risked encouraging further harassment and a concomitant decline in the morale of U.S. forces stationed in Panama.

The dilemma for Woerner was real, as demonstrated in a telling episode in late 1987. Official letters protesting PDF infringements on the rights of U.S. forces in Panama emanated from SOUTHCOM's Center for Treaty Affairs. At one point, the treaty affairs office drafted a letter from Woerner to Noriega, in which the SOUTHCOM commander expressed his "deepening concern" over the incidents of harassment, the "growing polarization" between U.S. forces and the PDF, and the potentially "debilitating impact" future incidents would have on the combined mission to defend the canal. If Woerner signed the strongly worded missive, which had attached to it an annotated chronology of illegal PDF activity against U.S. service personnel, the process of engaging in formal protests would have been elevated to the commanders' level. After weighing the possible consequences of the recommended action, Woerner decided not to sign the letter, preferring instead that its contents be conveyed to the PDF by Brig. Gen. Marc Cisneros, the command's director of operations, in an informal meeting with Panamanian colonels. (The verbal remonstration, not surprisingly, had only a transitory impact.) Disinclined to employ force at this point and barred by Washington from even threatening its use as a counter or a deterrent to PDF improprieties, Woerner possessed little leverage with which to compel Noriega's regime to stop the harassment and treaty violations. The offenses, in fact, would continue, their intensity oscillating according to the dynamics of the crisis. As predicted, the morale of U.S. service personnel in Panama began to suffer, and in time, many started to question the degree of SOUTHCOM's concern for their safety and security. Given the broader issues at

---

[22] Various issues of the *Southern Command News* throughout the summer and fall of 1987. As for the monitoring of U.S. exercises in Panama, see Interv, author with Maj Billy Ray Fitzgerald, U.S. Army, 28 Apr 89, Fort Clayton, Panama.

[23] For example, the *Southern Command News*, 24 Jul 87, carried an article citing three incidents involving U.S. military personnel that took place during a major opposition rally on 10 July. Each of the incidents, the article flatly stated, could have been avoided by the Americans in question.

stake and the cautious guidance Woerner received from above, these doubts about the SOUTHCOM commander and his staff may have been misplaced, but they nevertheless stigmatized the command well into the crisis.[24]

Another issue troubling Woerner also involved the safety of U.S. service personnel. What would happen if a pro-Noriega mob attacked U.S. military facilities the way demonstrators had attacked the U.S. Embassy in June? In contemplating this scenario, U.S. Army, South, SOUTHCOM's largest service component, headquartered at Fort Clayton, about ten minutes from Ancon Hill, reviewed both its role as a reaction force and its capabilities for handling civil disturbances. On 9 January 1988, those capabilities were put to a test when about two hundred progovernment demonstrators gathered at the back entrance of Quarry Heights. The occasion was Martyrs' Day, the annual holiday commemorating the Panamanians who died during the 1964 anti-American riots. In a display of "political theater," the mob carried placards and spewed forth verbal abuse, actions that prompted Col. Gar E. Thiry, SOUTHCOM's vice director of operations, to request that military policemen standing by at Fort Clayton be dispatched to the scene. Neither USARSO's chief of staff, Col. Arnold T. Rossi, nor the military police (MP) commander on the scene, Maj. Al Mansfield, was convinced the situation warranted such a deployment, but Thiry insisted, and the MPs arrived at Quarry Heights about an hour after the first summons. The demonstrators eventually dispersed, having inflicted no damage on the SOUTHCOM headquarters.[25]

In the wake of the demonstration, an argument ensued as to whether the Southern Command had overreacted in ordering the military police to the scene. On one point, however, there was consensus: the Martyrs' Day protests marked a small turning point in the crisis in that, for the first time, Noriega had targeted a U.S. military installation. The vulnerability of other U.S. military facilities would have to be assessed, as the issue of USARSO's ability to handle civil disturbances acquired a new sense of urgency *(Map 2)*.

Following Martyrs' Day, the remainder of January seemed fairly calm. Neither side in Panama's internal crisis seemed eager to confront the other during the holiday season. On the nineteenth, the government even allowed the opposition press to reopen. The lull in the crisis encouraged the USARSO commander, Maj. Gen. Bernard Loeffke, to send a memorandum to Woerner suggesting ways to improve relations with the Panama Defense Forces. Although military-to-military relations had become increasingly strained over the last months of 1987, neither Woerner nor Loeffke considered the downward slide to be irreversible. Loeffke noted that, although U.S. Army, South, had minimized its contacts with the Panamanian military, the cooperation between American military police officers and the PDF major who met biweekly with the provost marshal was improving. Based on these encouraging signals and on indirect overtures he had received from Noriega, Loeffke recommended the inclusion of Panamanian forces in various USARSO activities "in a low visibility environment." SOUTHCOM agreed and

---

[24] Southern Command's Center for Treaty Affairs (SCTA) draft Ltr, Woerner to Noriega, n.d., and Encls.

[25] Material on the Martyrs' Day incident is contained in Telephone Interv, author with former USSOUTHCOM staff officer, 25 Oct 90; Memo, Lt Col Shaun Darragh for U.S. Army, South (USARSO), Deputy Chief of Staff for Operations (DCSOPS), 8 Jan 88; Memorandum for the Record (MFR), Col Gar Thiry, 11 Jan 88; Cope Interv, 29 Mar 89.

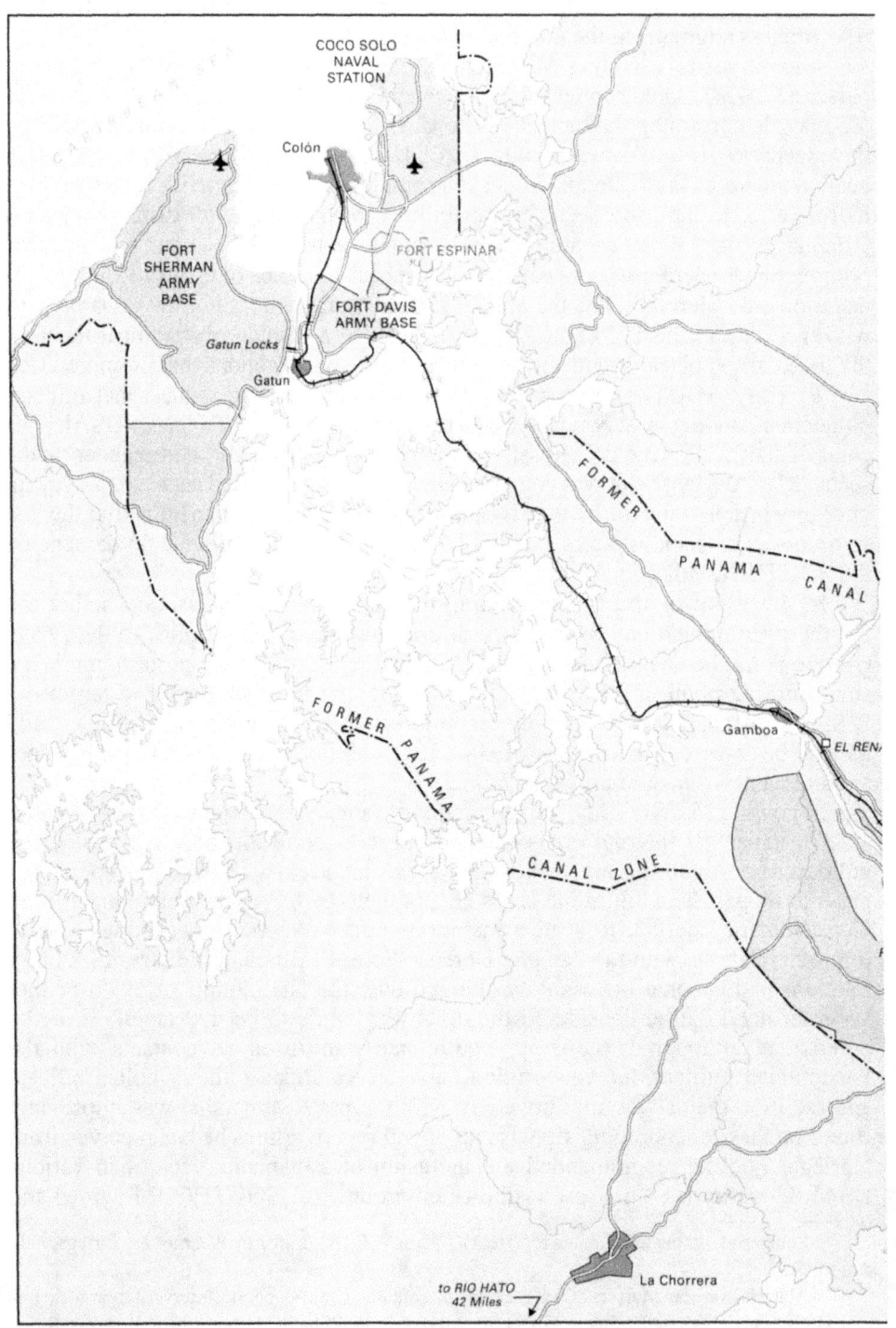

Map 2

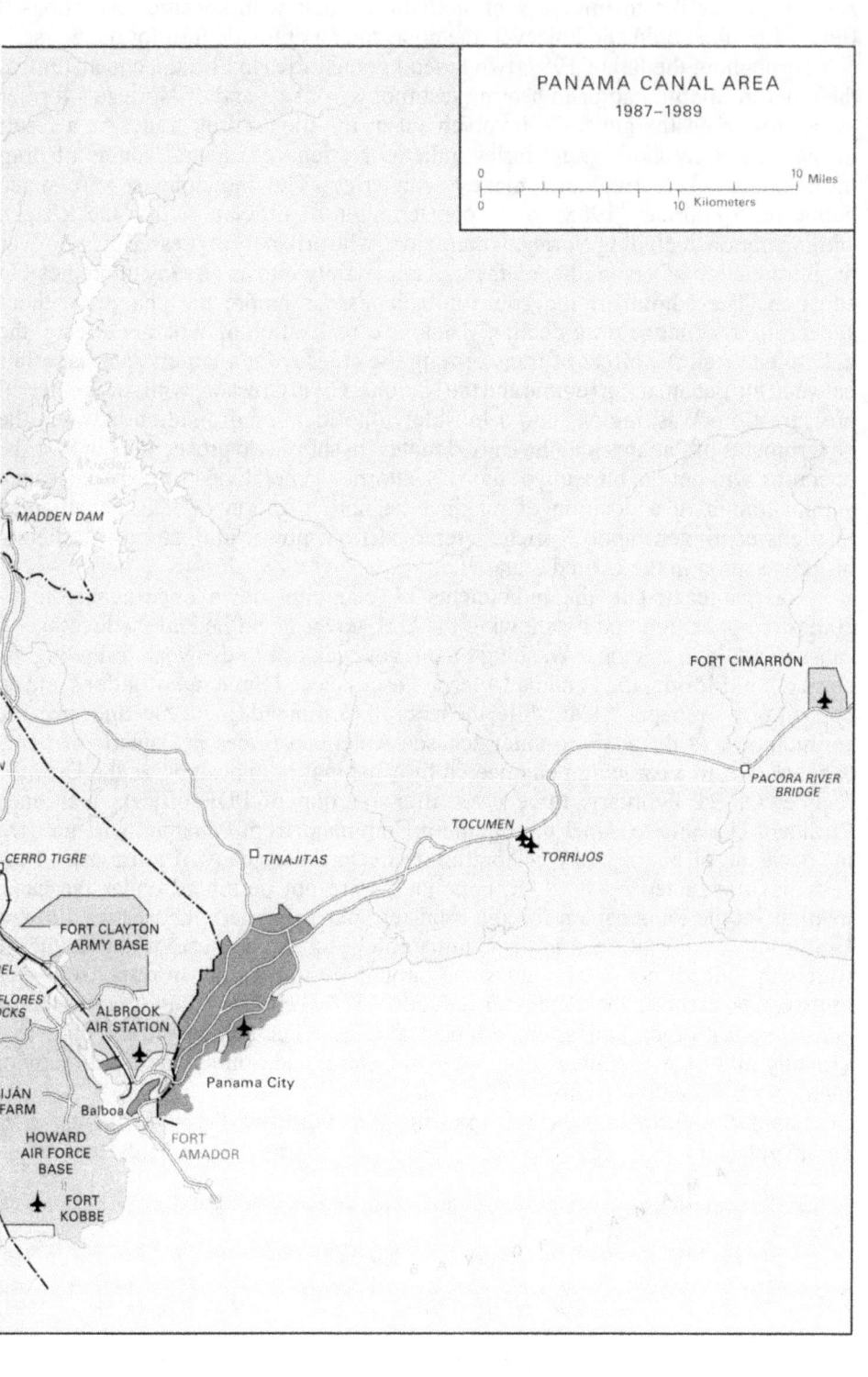

authorized Loeffke to initiate such activities, albeit with specific restrictions.[26] Before Loeffke could act, however, the crisis took a dramatic turn for the worse.

Throughout the fall of 1987, two federal grand juries in Florida, one in Tampa, the other in Miami, had been hearing testimony from several of Noriega's former associates about the general's involvement in the illegal drug trade. As a result of that testimony, both grand juries indicted Noriega on several counts of drug trafficking, racketeering, and money laundering. The indictments were made public on 5 February 1988, to the consternation of officials within the Reagan administration, including Noriega's detractors, who privately expressed dismay over the introduction of yet another element of uncertainty into an already unpredictable situation. The administration could not dismiss or ignore the charges without appearing to condone drug dealing. Thus, in a realization of Woerner's fears, the indictments had the effect of transforming the crisis from a largely internal affair between the Panamanian regime and the National Civic Crusade, with some external pressure from Washington, into a full-blown political confrontation between the governments of Panama and the United States. In short, two prosecutors in Florida, operating without the blessing of the U.S. attorney general, had placed the Reagan administration in a position of making the normalization of U.S.-Panamanian relations contingent upon Noriega's removal from power and, at least in theory, his prosecution in the United States.[27]

Noriega reacted to the indictments by clamping down once again on his domestic opposition and by showing the U.S. government he had the leverage to cause it untold problems if Washington did not back off. In the week following the news out of Florida, the Panama Defense Forces closed three radio stations and an opposition newspaper. Meanwhile, the tenor of Combined Board meetings became acrimonious, as the PDF co-chief accused American forces in Panama of being "aggressors" in a campaign engineered by Washington to destabilize the Delvalle regime. On 11 February, three days after a group of PDF officers petitioned President Delvalle to expel the Southern Command from Panama, Noriega used the occasion of his birthday celebration to declare that many, if not most, of the activities conducted by the U.S. command were not permitted under the canal treaties. As the Panamanian foreign minister later explained, the treaties allowed U.S. troops to be stationed in his country solely for the purpose of defending the waterway, not for conducting missions throughout the region. In response to this propaganda gambit, the Pentagon defended SOUTHCOM's missions as being consonant with the treaties, while a host of U.S. officers endorsed the logic that virtually all of the command's activities in Central and South America directly or indirectly affected the security of the canal.[28]

Amid the furor and verbal sparring that followed the indictments, U.S. commanders in Panama were careful to avoid alarmist statements that might

---

[26] Memos, Loeffke for Commander in Chief, U.S. Southern Command (CINCSO), 22 Jan 88, 25 Jan 88.

[27] The story behind the indictments against Noriega can be found in Buckley, *Panama*, pp. 114–25; Kempe, *Divorcing the Dictator*, pp. 236–57; John Dinges, *Our Man in Panama: How General Noriega Used the U.S.—and Made Millions in Drugs and Arms* (New York: Random House, 1990), pp. 275–98.

[28] Quote from *Tropic Times*, 12 Feb 87. USSOUTHCOM, Historical Report 1988, pp. 116–17; MFR, 470th MI Bde, 12 Feb 88; Loeffke Interv, 31 May 89.

exacerbate the crisis. Woerner informed the Joint Chiefs of Staff that Noriega would likely not seek a direct confrontation with the United States but would try to establish the "moral high ground" by reiterating nationalistic themes. At U.S. Army, South, Loeffke, in one of his periodic updates to General Carl Vuono, the chief of staff of the Army, echoed SOUTHCOM's public position that the "situation in Panama is not as bad as the newspapers might describe it," and that, while "minor isolated incidents" had occurred, the "overall situation is not directed to the American soldier." Yet, he conceded, Panama was tense, and U.S. troops were expressing concern about what course of action the Reagan administration intended to pursue in the days and weeks ahead.[29]

The thousands of American citizens living in and outside the former Canal Zone shared that concern. They could easily become the targeted victims of any regime-sponsored retaliatory measures against U.S. policy; they could even be potential hostages in the event of a U.S.-Panamanian military showdown. Among these citizens were the military dependents living on U.S. bases, often in direct contact with PDF units as the result of certain treaty provisions. For example, at Fort Amador, family housing for American military personnel was located directly across a recreation field from the PDF 5th Infantry Company barracks. (A similar arrangement existed on the Atlantic side of the canal at Fort Espinar.) Crimes against property on the bases continued to rise as the Panamanian economy worsened and the crisis intensified. And while harassment of Americans by the Panama Defense Forces could still be categorized as low-keyed, the mounting possibility of a more intense campaign of intimidation exacted a psychological toll upon the potential prey.

Responding to these concerns, the Southern Command sought to reassure U.S. servicemen, their dependents, and other civilians that the harsh rhetoric, increased tension, and general sense of instability in Panama following the indictments did not pose a greater threat to the American community. In mid-February, only a week after news of the indictments was made public, the *Tropic Times*, the successor of the *Southern Command News*, noted a decline in incidents of PDF harassment of U.S. personnel, praised the cooperative attitude of the PDF in helping to resolve a variety of problems, and declared SOUTHCOM's conviction that the government of Panama would continue to ensure the safety and security of American citizens. As Loeffke informed Vuono, Army officers were talking to as many soldiers as possible in an attempt to "appease their fears." But he also added that U.S. Army, South, was taking "precautions," to include a review of "our response packages and our evacuation plan," even though "we have not visibly practiced them for fear of aggravating the political situation."[30]

Loeffke's report to Vuono in mid-February illustrated the predicament of military commanders in Panama from Woerner on down. They still viewed the crisis as a political problem with adverse ramifications for the military. Yet, even though they regretted the increased tension between Americans and Panamanians, they could not ignore the possibility of a confrontation with Panamanian forces or anti-American demonstrators. Thus, while the *Tropic Times* and military

---

[29] Msgs, CINCSO to JCS, 112300Z Feb 88, and CDR, USARSO, to Chief of Staff, Army (CSA), 122140Z Feb 88.

[30] Msg, CINCSO to JCS, 112300Z Feb 88; *Tropic Times*, 12 Feb 88. Quotes from Msg, CDR, USARSO, to CSA, 122140Z Feb 88.

spokespersons were issuing statements to allay public concerns, the Southern Command and its components were prudently addressing various military contingencies that might arise. As Colonel Thiry emphasized in a message from the SOUTHCOM Operations Directorate, the headquarters could not be perceived as having failed to prepare for hostile actions by the PDF against U.S. targets. He cautioned against any provocative action by U.S. forces but called for an immediate planning effort to update the command's security posture.[31]

U.S. Army, South, concurred and once again assessed its capability for handling civil disturbances, this time requesting the Department of the Army's help in acquiring more antiriot gear, on-call combat service support, and armored vehicles. (The Army granted the first two requests but denied the armored vehicles.) As for the evacuation plans Loeffke mentioned, they had been under routine review since October. Geared exclusively to a "permissive or benign" environment, they contained no provision for a "noncombatant evacuation operation" in a "nonpermissive," or hostile, environment, including one in which combat operations might be under way. The plans, in short, would have to be updated.[32]

As the Southern Command and its components undertook a variety of precautionary measures, the crisis again showed signs of worsening. On 21 February, Noriega's daughter and son-in-law were stopped for speeding on Albrook Air Station, a facility divided into U.S. and Panamanian sectors. When the son-in-law became belligerent, he was handcuffed. PDF retaliation was swift. Over the next two days, Noriega's men detained thirty-three American soldiers, charging most of them with wearing their uniforms while riding motorcycles to their bases. The United States protested the detainments, which for most soldiers were not that long, while Loeffke confided to his diary the serious nature of the provocation. The incidents marked a significant escalation in the pattern of PDF harassment and, in his opinion, represented "the start of our problem with Noriega." Cisneros met with senior PDF officers on the matter and, after making a forceful protest, received assurances that Panamanian forces would not tolerate threats aimed at U.S. servicemen, dependents, or facilities.[33]

The Albrook episode and the regime's response were quickly eclipsed by another major development related to the U.S. indictments against Noriega. Throughout the crisis, President Delvalle had come under increasing pressure from friends and associates to salvage his personal honor by stripping the general of his power. Delvalle had made several trips to the United States beginning in 1987, ostensibly for medical reasons but also to meet secretly and discuss possible courses of action

---

[31] Msg, CINCSO to CDR, USARSO, et al., 11 Feb 88. While Thiry's message called for enhanced security, with U.S. forces being alerted for emergency situations, the colonel, in an attempt to reduce tension, also endorsed providing the Panama Defense Forces unclassified information concerning U.S. training in the country. U.S. Army, South, disagreed with both positions. Security alerts might be seen as provocative, while the sharing of information with the PDF might be interpreted as a sign of being "soft." Draft msg, n.d., in USARSO DCSOPS files.

[32] Msg, CDR, USARSO, to Department of the Army (DA), 191350Z Feb 88; Note, Chief of Staff, USARSO, to Commanding General (CG), USARSO, 26 Jan 88; Memos, William D. Clark for Maj Gen Bernard Loeffke, 11 Jan 88, and Clark for SecArmy, 11 Jan 88.

[33] Quote from Diary, Bernard Loeffke, 21 Feb 88. *Tropic Times*, 26 Feb 88; Fact Sheet, SCTA-J, 22 Apr 88; Ortiz chronology; Interv, author with Brig Gen Marc Cisneros, U.S. Army, 1 May 89, Quarry Heights, Panama.

with top U.S. foreign policy officials. On 25 February, the beleaguered president acted. In a pretaped address to the nation, he dismissed Noriega as commander of the Panama Defense Forces. The general's retaliation was immediate. That evening, the pro-Noriega National Assembly ousted Delvalle and his vice president and, at 0400 the next morning, swore in education minister Solis Palma as minister-in-charge of the presidency. When the Reagan administration declared it would continue to recognize Delvalle as the legitimate president of Panama, the die was cast. Neither Reagan nor Noriega would be able to retreat from the position he had staked out without losing face.[34]

As one consequence of President Reagan's decision, General Woerner received orders that he was to have no further contact with Noriega on the legal grounds that the dictator commanded the armed forces of a government the United States now considered illegitimate. From the onset of the crisis, Woerner had maintained that a professional working relationship between the Southern Command and the Panama Defense Forces would strengthen the security of U.S. interests in Panama. But the federal indictments brought against Noriega in early February 1988 and the Reagan administration's backing of Delvalle rendered a return to normal military-to-military relations untenable. According to one military intelligence summary of events, U.S. policy had transformed American forces and their dependents "from neutral observers in a CCN-PDF struggle to active participants in a US-PDF politico-military struggle."[35]

What the U.S. military role in that struggle would be was by no means clear in late February. Woerner was opposed to hostilities against the PDF, except as a last resort, and with Crowe's support, he would continue his efforts to avoid provocative actions on the part of his command. Even so, he could not dismiss the possibility of a war or any other military contingency. Staff officers at the Southern Command and its components thus began reviewing the existing plans for the defense of American interests in Panama. Not surprisingly, the scenarios they encountered, written well before the crisis, were found wanting. What was needed were new contingency plans that addressed the current troubles.

Informal planning began in early 1988. To ensure that the Southern Command had the resources and cooperation it needed from military headquarters outside its jurisdiction, Woerner requested that the Joint Chiefs of Staff authorize the initiative. On 28 February, he received orders from the Joint Chiefs directing SOUTHCOM to begin formal planning in a "crisis action mode" for possible military operations against the Panama Defense Forces. The message also notified several other commands and agencies of their requirement to support the effort.[36] A few days

---

[34] USSOUTHCOM, Historical Report 1988.

[35] Woerner MHI Interv; Msg, 470th MI Bde to INSCOM, 232235Z Feb 89. CCN is the Spanish acronym for the National Civic Crusade (NCC).

[36] Msg, JCS to CINCSO, 281944Z Feb 88. In "Planning for Post-Conflict Panama: What It Tells Us About Phase IV Operations," John Fishel recounts that, soon after Noriega was indicted by the two U.S. grand juries, General Woerner directed the appropriate SOUTHCOM staff to prepare contingency plans for the defense of the canal and U.S. bases. In these plans, the Panama Defense Forces would be considered a hostile force. "At the same time," according to Fishel, "he requested the chairman of the Joint Chiefs of Staff to direct him to develop plans for conflict with the PDF." Fishel's article can be found in *Turning Victory into Success: Military Operations After the Campaign*, Brian M. De Toy, ed. (Fort Leavenworth, Kans.: Combat Studies Institute Press, 2005), p. 169. (The book

later, on 4 March 1988, Woerner's director of operations produced the first draft of a new contingency plan geared particularly to the crisis. It was submitted for review just as the crisis was entering a new phase, one which would include a buildup, or "security enhancement," of U.S. forces in Panama.

---

contains papers and presentations made at the second annual military symposium sponsored by the U.S. Army Training and Doctrine Command and hosted by the Combat Studies Institute at Fort Leavenworth.)

2

OPERATION ORDERS AND SECURITY ENHANCEMENT

FEBRUARY–APRIL 1988

Since the end of World War II, American presidents had confronted a succession of local crises around the world within the larger framework of the Cold War, the ideological and geopolitical conflict that pitted the United States and its allies, clients, and friends against the Soviet Union, the People's Republic of China (after 1949), and their respective allies, clients, and friends. Over the course of four decades, as the struggle went through several distinct phases, the U.S. response to such scattered and diverse conflicts as the Greek Civil War, the Huk insurrection in the Philippines, the travails of a divided Korea, political turmoil in Lebanon and the Dominican Republic, and hostilities in Vietnam often stemmed more from the perceived need to contain the spread of communism than from any inherent or vital American interest in the afflicted countries themselves.

The Noriega problem, erupting as it did in what turned out to be the Cold War's final years, in many respects fit this pattern. To be sure, the strategic importance of the Panama Canal and the need to minimize foreign influence in the Caribbean area had been long-held tenets of U.S. foreign policy. But without the Cold War dynamic, the American posture vis-à-vis Noriega in 1987–1988 might have assumed a very different form. At that time, however, few observers imagined the impending collapse of the Soviet Union. The Reagan administration therefore viewed the dictator's growing ties to Soviet-supported governments in Cuba and Nicaragua, his procurement of Communist-bloc arms, and the presence of Cuban military advisers and trainers in his country as worrisome developments that had to be countered in the name of anticommunism and in the interest of U.S. security in both the region and, by extrapolation, the world.

The Cold War also influenced the way the Pentagon addressed the crisis in Panama. Beginning in the 1970s, developments within the U.S. armed forces moved along lines that in the 1980s would parallel the Reagan administration's fixation on the central Cold War theme of Soviet-American confrontation. In the aftermath of the Vietnam War, the Army in particular had been revamping its doctrine, force structure, weapon systems, training, and education in an effort to refocus its attention away from the myriad of local and regional hot spots around the world and onto the perceived Soviet military threat in central

U.S. MILITARY INTERVENTION IN PANAMA, JUNE 1987–DECEMBER 1989

The Panama Canal

Europe. As an institution, the Army benefited from this overhaul, but the ramifications were not necessarily helpful for military officers still trying to cope with local crises. In the case of Panama, for example, SOUTHCOM staff officers preparing to write the contingency plan called for in the Joint Chiefs' message of 28 February found themselves working in what was virtually a doctrinal wasteland.[1]

The Army constituted the largest service component under the U.S. Southern Command, and the centerpiece of Army doctrine in the 1980s was AirLand Battle, the authorized concept for how U.S. soldiers would fight an all-out war against Warsaw Pact troops in Germany's Fulda Gap. The tenets of AirLand Battle postulated large conventional units engaged in a mobile, highly technological, large-scale multinational fight for survival, a scenario that had little to do with the situation in Panama. Nor did the Panama crisis fit neatly into any of the categories that U.S. military doctrine provided for operations below the level of total war. Some Army officers spoke of *low intensity conflict* (LIC) in Panama, but others argued that the current LIC field manual, FM 100–20, did not cover any scenario similar to that into which the Southern Command was being drawn. Although the manual was in the process of being revised, an Army lieutenant colonel involved in the update, when asked if the situation in Panama qualified as low intensity conflict,

---

[1] My assessment of the perceived relationship of the Panama crisis to military doctrine in this section is based on several conversations with military personnel in Panama and the United States. Both General Woerner and Colonel Rossi used the terms attributed to them in conversations with me, and I was present at the briefing during which the lieutenant colonel expressed his opinion that the crisis in Panama could not be described as a low intensity conflict.

OPERATION ORDERS AND SECURITY ENHANCEMENT

thought for a minute and responded that it did not. Conditions there simply did not fit any of the four subcategories of LIC—counterinsurgency, counterterrorism, peacetime contingency operations, and peacekeeping—slated for incorporation into the revised edition. General Woerner personally described the crisis as "low-probability conflict," while Col. Arnie Rossi, the USARSO chief of staff, employed a more familiar reference, "The Twilight Zone." Rossi's term, while evocative of Trotsky's well-known dictum, "neither war nor peace," more readily conjured up memories of a once-popular science fiction television program known for its ambiguous and sometimes surrealistic plot lines. What the term lacked, of course, was doctrinal status or prescriptive advice.

In the months to come, the Panama crisis would continue to evolve in a doctrinal void. With the corpus of U.S. military doctrine and international law geared to war or peace, there was little to cover the limbo in between. Since the United States was not at war in Panama, it had to be at peace, technically speaking. As a result, military personnel caught up in the crisis would continue to plan and operate according to peacetime codes and rules, "making it up" when those guidelines proved inappropriate or irrelevant to the pressing issues at hand. If, in the meantime, there was a need for additional ground troops to bolster security or to play some other role, the units most likely to be committed were U.S. marines and elements from Army "light" infantry divisions. The problem here was that, although touted as being LIC-oriented, these units, too, had been immersed in AirLand Battle doctrine. Consequently, they were trained primarily for small-scale conventional combat operations. Conversely, they rarely learned how to perform the political, economic, police, humanitarian, and various other functions inherent in the kinds of military operations that require daily interaction with large numbers of civilians and nonmilitary officials while pursuing objectives that generally range well beyond strictly military concerns.

CONTINGENCY PLANNING: ELABORATE MAZE

In contrast to the dearth of U.S. military doctrine applicable to the Panama crisis, standardized procedures did exist to assist a joint, or multiservice, headquarters in the task of contingency planning. In early 1988, staff officers at the Southern Command; U.S. Army, South; and elsewhere referred to these guidelines as they drafted the new set of crisis-related operation orders (OPORDs) authorized by the Joint Chiefs.

When the crisis began in June 1987, the principal on-the-shelf operation plan (OPLAN) pertaining to Panama was CINCSO OPLAN 6000–86 for the defense of the canal. Few officers on the SOUTHCOM and component staffs knew the contents of the plan, but those who did recognized that its execution was predicated on two scenarios, both of which were considered improbable. The first pictured a war between the Soviet Union and the United States in which Moscow's surrogates would carry out acts of terrorism and sabotage against canal facilities. The second scenario envisaged a threat from leftist groups in Panama. In 1987, the prospects for war with the Soviets seemed remote, while left-wing organizations in Panama were kept under strict control by the Panama Defense Forces.[2]

---

[2] Intervs, author with Maj Dan Augustine, U.S. Army, 13 Jun 89, Fort Clayton, Panama; Col John A. Cope Jr., U.S. Army, 29 Mar 89, Fort Clayton, Panama; and Lt Col Robert Pantier, U.S. Army, 21 May 91, Fort Leavenworth, Kans.

Under the Deliberate Planning Process dictated by the Joint Operations Planning System, CINCSO OPLAN 6000–86 was due for a biennial review. The process began in late 1987, when relations between American and Panamanian troops had deteriorated to a point where U.S. staff officers tasked with conducting a mission analysis of the plan could not ignore the possibility, however remote it seemed at that early stage of the crisis, of hostilities between the two forces. OPLAN 6000–86 provided for no such confrontation. It assumed, instead, that the defense of the canal would be conducted either in partnership with the Panamanian military or, in the worst case, against hostile Panamanians encouraged by an officially "neutral" PDF. Although General Woerner and his staff discussed ways to overcome the plan's irrelevance with respect to the existing crisis, until they received a directive from the Joint Chiefs of Staff to write a new plan, OPLAN 6000–86's scenarios and assumptions remained unchanged, at least on paper.[3]

There was one provision of OPLAN 6000–86 to which U.S. Army, South, paid particular attention during the review process. In the event the plan had to be executed, the SOUTHCOM commander was to activate a joint task force (JTF) to conduct military operations. The commanding general, USARSO, would become the commander, Joint Task Force-Panama, with most of that multiservice organization's key staff positions being filled by USARSO personnel. As for the more than two hundred remaining staff slots, those would be filled from SOUTHCOM's components, according to a manning document attached to the operation plan. To acquire some sense of how this arrangement might actually function, a command post exercise took place in February 1988. Code-named BLACK TOUCAN, the exercise encountered several problems, especially in getting the service components to "think purple," meaning in joint terms. BLACK TOUCAN also reaffirmed the preference of Maj. Gen. Bernard Loeffke, the prospective JTF-Panama commander, for a smaller, more manageable organization pared to just over eighty staff positions. A more questionable conclusion concerned the Panama Defense Forces. Although BLACK TOUCAN was conducted in the wake of the U.S. indictments against Noriega, the after action review maintained that, should the execution of OPLAN 6000–86 prove necessary, "close cooperation with PDF to coordinate convoy movements within AO's [areas of operations]" would be required.[4] Yet, even as this observation was being disseminated, doubts were multiplying as to its practicability.

Soon after BLACK TOUCAN, SOUTHCOM staff officers prepared a "talking paper" listing a number of issues General Woerner would have to address should the Panamanian military deliberately commit a belligerent act. To the key questions, "At what threshold or point should the PDF be designated as hostile?" and "When should USCINCSO recommend armed intervention?" the paper avoided a direct answer but provided instead a refresher course on peacetime rules of engagement

---

[3] Intervs, author with Augustine, 13 Jun 89; Cope, 29 May 89, Fort Clayton, Panama; and Capt Carlos Puentes, U.S. Army, 28 Mar 89, Fort Clayton, Panama.

[4] Intervs, author with Augustine, 7 Jun 89, Fort Clayton, Panama, and Cope, 29 May 89; Telephone Interv, author with John A. Cope, 7 Nov 91; Memo, Col John A. Cope Jr., USARSO DCSOPS, for CDR, Special Operations Command, South (COMSOCSO or COMSOCSOUTH), et al., 14 Feb 88; Milestone chart, JTF OPLAN 6000, n.d. Quote from Briefing slides, JTF-Panama, CPX BLACK TOUCAN.

OPERATION ORDERS AND SECURITY ENHANCEMENT

General Loeffke briefing the troops

(ROE).[5] Even so, the questions themselves reflected what many staff officers by this point had accepted as inevitable: a new operation plan geared to the crisis at hand would have to be written. The Joint Chiefs' February message, issued at Woerner's request, formally cleared a path for the SOUTHCOM commander to do just that.

In light of the volatile situation in Panama, drafting the new CINCSO contingency plans followed the procedures for crisis action planning set forth in the Pentagon's Joint Operations Planning System. This meant that chief responsibility for the initiative rested with Woerner's director of operations, General Cisneros, and that the published product would be an operation order, as opposed to an operation plan. In providing Cisneros guidance for writing the order, Woerner incorporated elements of 6000–86, his own strategic thinking, comments from the chairman of the Joint Chiefs, and a concern for the safety of the more than 50,000 Americans living in Panama. The new OPORD was to contain a "phased" plan that covered such contingencies as a gradual buildup of U.S. forces, defensive and offensive operations, and a noncombatant evacuation operation. Woerner also wanted the plan written so that the SOUTHCOM commander could execute any one phase at any given time, independently of the other phases, or, if need be, simultaneously or in sequence with any or all of them.

Operations security prevented Woerner from disseminating the strategic thinking behind his guidance. Simply put, he hoped that, should the National Command Authority order him to take military action, the prerequisite buildup of U.S. troops in Panama would in and of itself be the "catalytic event" that would compel the Panama Defense Forces to remove Noriega, thus providing the "Panamanian solution to a Panamanian problem" that he advocated. As Woerner confided to his innermost circle of advisers, once a buildup of U.S. troops began, he intended to contact top-ranking PDF officers privately, beginning with the PDF

---
[5] Draft Talking Paper, SCJ–5-DPJ, 18 Feb 88; Msg, JCS to CINCSO, 281944Z Feb 88.

chief of staff, Col. Marco Justines. Woerner would explain to Justines that the troop buildup was real, that U.S. forces would soon take action to remove Noriega, and that, if Justines did not engineer Noriega's ouster before these troops were forced to act, the chief of staff would find himself sharing his boss' fate. Woerner would not be bluffing. If Justines rejected the SOUTHCOM commander's advice, his name would, in fact, be added to the list of PDF officers to be deposed. Woerner would then move down to the next officer in the PDF chain of command and convey the same message to him. At some point, Woerner judged, an officer inclined to save himself and Panama's military institutions would orchestrate an effort to overthrow the dictator.[6]

Most of the officers in the small group drafting the new contingency plan were ignorant of this strategic vision as they began to develop a concept of operations and to select appropriate courses of action. Working under the immediate direction of Lt. Col. John McCutchon, chief of the Plans Division, Operations Directorate, members of the group had only a few days, not weeks or months, to generate an acceptable product. Furthermore, despite having Woerner's input, they had to achieve their goal without the advantage of clear and coordinated political guidance from Washington with respect to essential missions and objectives. From OPLAN 6000–86, the group salvaged part of the U.S. order of battle, the list of critical facilities to be defended, and certain command and control relationships. The officers refined each of these elements, aware that much of what they were writing could already be considered compromised because many of the details appeared in a U.S.-PDF version of the existing plan for defending the canal.[7]

Despite these and other obstacles, CINCSO OPORD 2–88, code-named ELABORATE MAZE, was ready by 4 March for transmission to the Joint Chiefs.[8] As appropriate for a CINCSO-level plan, the document discussed in only general terms the nature of the threat and possible U.S. responses. A Panamanian order of battle updated by military intelligence estimated the current strength of the Panama Defense Forces, which was defined in the plan as a hostile force, at 14,000. Of that total, 4,000 were combat forces constituting seven infantry companies and six platoons, a small air force, and a coast guard. The majority of PDF combat and police personnel belonged to units headquartered near or in Panama City and Colón, the country's two largest cities located, respectively, at the southern and northern ends of the canal. The infantry units, furnished mainly with small arms and a limited number of heavier weapons, were judged "a well-trained and disciplined force at the small unit tactical level," but a force that suffered from a reliance on overly centralized command and control arrangements, a paucity of professional leadership, and a lack of standardized weapons, communications, and equipment.

---

[6] Interv, author with General Frederick F. Woerner Jr., U.S. Army (Ret.), 30 Apr 91, Fort Leavenworth, Kans.

[7] Intervs, author with Cope, 29 Mar 89, and Puentes, 28 Mar 89.

[8] The discussion of CINCSO OPORD 2–88 that follows, including all quoted material, is based on the text contained in Msg, CINCSO to JCS, 042255Z Mar 88. The plan, as noted in the text, was labeled an operation order (OPORD) instead of an operation plan because it was written in the crisis action planning mode. The content of the message, however, is characteristic of an OPLAN, not an OPORD.

According to the operation order, the Panama Defense Forces had become increasingly estranged from the Panamanian people and was attempting to retain control of the country through intimidation, press censorship, political manipulation, and, in league with pro-Noriega political parties, a highly nationalistic, anti-American propaganda campaign. The harassment of Americans in Panama had to date been more reactive than calculated, the planners suggested, but, should the crisis intensify and should Noriega and the PDF believe that their survival was in jeopardy, the intimidation of U.S. personnel and the threats to American interests could increase dramatically. Although the Panamanian military would not likely seek an all-out armed confrontation with the United States, Noriega had other options available to him, ranging from the disruption of normal activity on U.S. bases, to the use of limited military operations to seize vulnerable U.S. facilities. These options could be implemented over a period of weeks and months, or they might occur during a sudden escalation of the crisis. In either case, once hostile actions by the regime warranted a U.S. military response, the SOUTHCOM commander under ELABORATE MAZE had the mission to conduct "joint operations to protect U.S. lives, property and interests in Panama and to assure the full exercise of rights accorded by international law and the U.S.-Panama treaties." He also had to be prepared to conduct a noncombatant evacuation operation in a permissive or nonpermissive environment.

Prior to execution of the plan, in what became known as Phase 0, certain preliminary measures were required, including the activation of JTF-Panama and a joint special operations task force (JSOTF). Then, military operations could proceed selectively in accordance with ELABORATE MAZE's menu of four operational phases, any of which could be conducted independently, in sequence, or concurrently with any of the others, as Woerner had directed. The first three phases defined the circumstances under which the United States would augment its forces in Panama for the purpose—depending on the threat—of defending critical facilities, executing an evacuation of civilians, and ensuring the continued operation of the canal. Phase IV involved offensive operations against the Panamanian military. In this eventuality, the commander, JTF-Panama, would neutralize the Panama Defense Forces within his area of operations and conduct on-order operations to secure other critical areas. Simultaneously or soon thereafter, the commander, joint special operations task force, would launch surgical strikes against "key PDF leadership, command and control facilities, military and civilian airfields, and other critical nodes within the Republic of Panama." The operation order listed the troops that would be available to each joint task force commander, discussed in general terms the rules of engagement that would be sufficient to protect U.S. forces while limiting "the scope and intensity of the conflict," and instructed that "offensive operations will be conducted in a manner to reduce collateral damage and loss of life."

ELABORATE MAZE briefly addressed civil affairs and civil-military operations (CMO), but principally as follow-on measures to the combat operations covered in the operation order's fourth phase. At one point, the planners noted that U.S. "objectives following Phase IV operations must be defined for continued CMO planning." This requirement appeared later in the text as a "Command Concern" asserting that "clear national policy objectives must be available delineating what [U.S. government] goals are for the period following hostilities with the PDF. Such objectives and goals are essential for making operational decisions when planning and executing military actions."

SANCTIONS

While the SOUTHCOM staff was writing ELABORATE MAZE, Woerner was becoming increasingly curious about the Reagan administration's future policy initiatives toward Panama. He generally regarded Washington's recently imposed economic sanctions against the country as ineffective and counterproductive, yet he feared that worse could follow. On 8 March, during a meeting with staff and component representatives, he informed those present about a telephone conversation he had just had with Admiral Crowe, the chairman of the Joint Chiefs of Staff. According to Crowe, the State Department, prompted by Assistant Secretary of State for Inter-American Affairs Elliott Abrams, "smells blood" and wanted to pile additional economic sanctions on Panama in hopes of forcing Noriega's immediate removal from power. Crowe and Secretary of Defense Frank Carlucci opposed this course of action, arguing that Abrams' recommendations were rash and based on a short-term and short-sighted assessment of U.S. interests in Latin America. Better, they counseled, to move incrementally, gradually building up the pressure on the Noriega regime. In Crowe's opinion, as relayed by Woerner to his subordinates, discussions in Washington lacked any appreciation for Panamanian realities.[9]

Admiral Crowe

As reflected in the general's telephone conversation with the admiral, Abrams' campaign for additional U.S. economic sanctions against Panama had been picking up momentum since the dismissal of Panamanian President Eric Delvalle in late February. From Washington's perspective, Woerner later observed, "Panama seemed particularly vulnerable to economic pressure: a small service-oriented economy, where the United States had unusual leverage. There was a large presence of American citizens and businesses, and the currency was the dollar." The Reagan administration's position that Delvalle was still the legitimate president of Panama permitted the ousted leader, together with Panamanian opposition figures in the United States, their legal and political advisers, and the State Department, to obtain a court decision to freeze over $35 million in Panamanian assets in four American

---

[9] MFR, Col John A. Cope, 9 Mar 88.

banks. On 29 February, Delvalle issued a proclamation from his hiding place in Panama to the effect that money owed his government should be paid into an escrow account in the United States. The impact of these measures was immediate and, combined with an opposition strike, "provoked a profound economic crisis within Panama," according to Woerner, in which the "entire Panamanian economy has reverted to a cash-only basis." Banks closed, pensioners demonstrated, and the Noriega-controlled Solis Palma regime pondered how to meet upcoming government payrolls.[10]

With some in the Reagan administration looking for more economic screws to turn, Crowe prepared for another round of bureaucratic infighting by consulting his allies in the confrontation, including Woerner. Responding in a personal message to the chairman, the SOUTHCOM commander conceded that further "economic sanctions are the next logical step." Yet, the general considered "of the utmost importance" an administration approach that avoided "a broad, unfocused, economic embargo. Such a measure would be premature and would almost certainly impact overwhelmingly on both U.S. interests and on those Panamanians whom we are seeking to help." Woerner declared his support for "surgical economic measures designed to impact the [government of Panama] at minimal cost to the private sector and the poor." In this vein, he addressed his comments to two of five sanctions that an interagency Panama Review Group, formed in Washington soon after the crisis began, was putting forward for consideration. (The group's other three proposals, he indicated, were "throwaways" that did not affect U.S. military interests.) The first of the two sanctions, one that called for placing into escrow the revenue owed from an oil pipeline passing into Panama, Woerner endorsed as a measured response that would "live up to our commitment to the Panamanian people and . . . preempt the U.S. Congress from once again taking the foreign policy lead and imposing a scale of sanctions contrary to our interests." He opposed, however, a similar proposal to put the Panama Canal Commission's annuity and tonnage payments in escrow. That move, he argued, would politicize the administration and operation of the canal, thus setting a "dangerous precedent."[11]

Crowe took Woerner's advice to heart. In the telephone conversation of 8 May, he told the SOUTHCOM commander that he would oppose both the pipeline and canal sanctions and work instead for a policy that was less extreme and more in line with long-term U.S. interests. He also asked Woerner to advise him on how Noriega might respond to the enactment of sanctions. Woerner, in tasking his staff to prepare a response, directed that they "*not* consider" as a possibility the extreme case of the Panama Defense Forces invading the canal area.[12]

Woerner's message to Crowe late that night suggested that "long-term damage between our two militaries may be the . . . result of additional pressure against Panama." In reiterating this theme, the general recalled that, in the past, the

---

[10] First quote from Gabriel Marcella and General Frederick F. Woerner Jr., U.S. Army (Ret.), The Road to War: The U.S.-Panamanian Crisis, 1987–1989, draft article, 6 May 91, p. 33. Second quote from Msg, CINCSO to JCS, 090327Z Mar 88, sub: Possible Responses to USG [U.S. government] Sanctions. John Dinges, *Our Man in Panama: The Shrewd Rise and Brutal Fall of Manuel Noriega*, rev. ed. (New York: Times Books, 1991), pp. 297–98.

[11] Msg, CINCSO to JCS, 070730Z Mar 88, sub: USCINCSO Views on Panama Sanctions.

[12] MFR, Cope, 9 Mar 88.

Panamanian military had reacted to U.S. pressure with measures that included bureaucratic foot-dragging in dealing with American citizens, the arrest and physical assault of U.S. service personnel, and a "systematic internal indoctrination campaign" against the United States. A "hostile, aggressive PDF," he elaborated, would have an adverse impact on Southern Command's regional missions, as "even Canal defense would be a job of significant proportions." Furthermore,

regional intelligence gathering missions could be exposed and air space control bureaucratically constrained; deliberate actions by the PDF could severely limit USSOUTHCOM's ability to continue support to U.S. embassies and security assistance organizations throughout both Central and South America. Support for anti-drug operations out of Panama could be hindered. Direct communications access to MILGRPs [military groups] and embassies could be hampered. Training of foreign nationals in Panama could be denied or severely curtailed. Refusal to allow refueling of U.S. helicopters at PDF bases would preclude or restrict flights to Honduras, Costa Rica, and other countries in the region.

Local SOUTHCOM missions, the "quality of life" on U.S. bases, and the "anxiety levels" of service personnel would also be affected adversely by continued PDF harassment and by any regime initiative to disrupt electricity, water and sewage service, unsecured communications, garbage collection, logistical support, and the Panamanian work force.[13]

In short, as Woerner perceived the situation, "possible retaliatory measures are virtually limitless," although some could be discounted as lacking credibility. He doubted, for example, whether the Panama Defense Forces would take "direct actions against USSOUTHCOM assets or the Canal." Rather, Noriega would probably pursue a "restrained approach," with demonstrations at the U.S. Embassy and verbal attacks on embassy officials. He would also continue his propaganda campaign, playing on the theme of Panama as a small and hapless victim of U.S. aggression, while denouncing as a prelude to invasion the TOTAL WARRIOR exercises then in progress between U.S. Army, South, and two successive Army National Guard units rotating in from the United States. (Almost as an aside, Woerner indicated that "a healthy respect by Noriega for our military capability to reinforce USSOUTHCOM provided by these exercises is beneficial to the [U.S.] government position.") The PDF was also likely to increase the sporadic harassment of American citizens and to irritate U.S. officials with administrative slowdowns.[14]

In subsequent messages, Woerner continued to advise Crowe on the military implications of economic sanctions that had been proposed or enacted for their political impact. At one point, the general warned about the "questionable legal ground" the United States might be on in responding to a démarche from Delvalle that, under Panama's constitution, required legislative approval.[15] In offering this kind of wide-ranging counsel, Woerner, like his predecessors and contemporaries, demonstrated why many considered taking the helm of a unified command to be as much a diplomatic as a military assignment.

On 11 March, President Reagan announced that Panama Canal Commission monies legally owed to the government of Panama would be placed in an escrow account. He also called upon U.S. government agencies to identify additional sources

---

[13] The discussion and all quotes are from Msg, CINCSO to JCS, 090327Z Mar 88, sub: Possible Responses to USG [U.S. government] Sanctions.
[14] Ibid.
[15] Msg, CINCSO to JCS, 070730Z Mar 88, sub: USCINCSO Views on Panama Sanctions.

Operation Orders and Security Enhancement

President Reagan talking with Caspar Weinberger, secretary of defense during the first months of the Panama crisis

of funds due or payable to the government of Panama. In response to the presidential statement, Woerner activated a crisis action team to monitor Noriega's reactions and again advised Crowe about the negative impact of stringent economic sanctions.[16] By that point, however, the admiral was fully engaged in staving off another State Department initiative: the call for decisive U.S. military action in Panama.

Phase V, Joint Special Operations Task Force, and U.S. Army, South

While administration officials debated the efficacy of economic penalties against the Noriega regime, officers working for Lt. Gen. Thomas Kelly, the director of operations for the Joint Staff in the Pentagon, studied the CINCSO version of Elaborate Maze and provided detailed feedback to the planners at Quarry Heights. On 11 March, the Joint Chiefs weighed in, formally approving continued planning on the four-phase operation order. One of the changes they directed added the mission "to stabilize the situation and restore law and order

---

[16] Msgs, CINCSO to JCS, 121830Z Mar 88, sub: SCJ3 Sitrep No. 3, and CINCSO to Secy of Defense/JCS, 212155Z Mar 88, sub: Payments to Government of Panama. In a draft article dated 6 May 1991, General Woerner and Gabriel Marcella, SOUTHCOM's international affairs adviser when Woerner was SOUTHCOM commander, reassess the impact of economic sanctions on Panama during the crisis. Citing several studies, together with their own observations, they conclude that the sanctions were a failure for a variety of reasons. They quote one analyst as saying, "Sanctions alone were no more likely to remove Noriega from power than sanctions against Chicago would have removed Al Capone." Woerner and Marcella, themselves, state that the "sanctions caused great inconvenience and hurt more the lower and middle classes, but did not achieve decisive political results." The reasons they offer for the failure include conflicting U.S. policy goals, a policy of incrementalism that allowed the regime time to adjust to any one initiative, a reluctance to impose sanctions that really hurt the government, the tenacity of Noriega, and the inability of Washington policymakers, most lacking expertise in Latin American affairs, to devise a coordinated and multifaceted strategy for confronting Noriega. Marcella and Woerner, The Road to War, 6 May 91, pp. 33–39.

until a legally constituted government is installed." This requirement authorized the Southern Command to develop "a Phase V to impose U.S. military control over those areas with significant concentrations of U.S. citizens and those facilities critical to the functioning of government." With respect to the American citizens, the Joint Chiefs perused the ELABORATE MAZE annex devoted to the evacuation of noncombatants and concluded that the arrangements might best be written as a separate operation order, given the magnitude of the planning effort required. Finally, the SOUTHCOM commander was also directed to work out arrangements for the operational control of the U.S. Navy aircraft carrier battle group called for in Phase IV of the plan.[17]

The Joint Chiefs directive to add a fifth phase to ELABORATE MAZE was, like the February message to Woerner, the Pentagon's go-ahead for an initiative already under way at Quarry Heights. Right after Cisneros' staff finished the first draft of the operation order, two civil affairs officers at SOUTHCOM reviewed the plan and were surprised to find that it contained no phase for civil-military operations. The deputy director of the command's Policy, Strategy, and Programs Directorate (SCJ-5) told the two to prepare a briefing for General Woerner delineating a plan "for the restoration of Panama in the wake of U.S. combat operations against the PDF." Such a plan, the three decided, "should follow the post–World War II formula for military government." At the briefing later that day, Woerner approved the overall approach and provided additional guidance. According to one account, he directed the planners to assume that the "CINC would be in charge of the government of Panama for a period not in excess of 30 days. Military government would be transitional and would last only as long as necessary. If it were not necessary to institute military government, then some other alternative would be exercised. General Woerner assumed that he would be in charge after a military operation." As incorporated into ELABORATE MAZE, Phase V made no direct reference to the thirty-day assumption but stated that once circumstances permitted, "USCINCSO direction and control of selected governmental functions will be transferred to the US Country Team and/or the [government of Panama]." With this and other revisions, Woerner resubmitted ELABORATE MAZE to the Pentagon.[18]

In their 11 March message, the Joint Chiefs had also authorized the writing of supporting plans to the CINCSO operation order. At the echelon immediately below SOUTHCOM, this translated into two operation orders, one for a joint special operations task force, the other for JTF-Panama. The JTF-Panama supporting plan

---

[17] Msg, JCS to U.S. Commander in Chief, Europe (USCINCEUR), et al., 120056Z Mar 88, sub: OPORD—ELABORATE MAZE.

[18] First quote from John T. Fishel, *The Fog of Peace: Planning and Executing the Restoration of Panama* (Carlisle Barracks, Pa.: Strategic Studies Institute, 1992), pp. 7–8, and see also pp. 9–15. Second quote from Msg, CINCSO to JCS, 181945Z Mar 88, sub: USCINCSO/001/ELABORATE MAZE/OPORD 2–88. The full CINCSO version of KRYSTAL BALL/BLIND LOGIC was drafted in SOUTHCOM's Policy, Strategy, and Programs Directorate by teams from the 361st Civil Affairs Brigade, SOUTHCOM's CAPSTONE reserve unit, coming to Panama on 31-day temporary tours of active duty. (CAPSTONE refers to the formal relationship between an Army Reserve unit and its active component headquarters.) Besides drafting the CINCSO OPORD, the teams also worked on the civil-military operations task force supporting plan. Full versions of both operation orders, complete with a series of functional annexes, were ready by August 1988. One factor that would come into play later: the KRYSTAL BALL/BLIND LOGIC planners in Policy, Strategy, and Programs Directorate did not have contact with BLUE SPOON planners in the Operations Directorate.

would cover conventional operations in all five phases of ELABORATE MAZE; the JSOTF supporting plan would confine itself to combat operations in Phase IV, the phase that called for offensive action against the Panama Defense Forces.

Initially, nearly all involved in the planning process assumed that the Special Operations Command, South (SOCSOUTH), a subunified command under SOUTHCOM with its headquarters at Albrook Air Station in Panama, would form the nucleus of the joint special operations task force. Indeed, following the Joint Chiefs' 28 February message, Col. Chuck Fry, the SOCSOUTH commander, had sent a few of his officers to Quarry Heights to assist in planning the special operations segments of ELABORATE MAZE. But Fry's headquarters was overextended, with many of his people in other Latin American countries working on theater missions. When the time neared to write the JSOTF supporting plan for the CINCSO operation order, he did not have the resources to do it. He had previously discussed this problem with Woerner and with General James J. Lindsay, the commander in chief, U.S. Special Operations Command (SOCOM), headquartered at MacDill Air Force Base, Florida. Woerner, in turn, had informed the Joint Chiefs that SOUTHCOM could not put together a joint special operations task force. When the Joint Chiefs' message of 11 March arrived, it recommended that the U.S. Special Operations Command provide assistance to the Special Operations Command, South, for planning purposes.[19]

Fortuitously, the Army's 1st Special Operations Command, headquartered at Fort Bragg, North Carolina, was at Hurlburt Air Force Base, Florida, conducting an exercise, CASINO GAMBIT, as part of the Army Training and Evaluation Program for a battalion of the 7th Special Forces Group. Since other Special Operations Forces were stationed at the base, a joint special operations task force had been activated for the exercise under 1st SOCOM's deputy commander, Col. Joseph S. Stringham. Aware of the work on ELABORATE MAZE then under way in Panama, Stringham had assembled a small group that met nightly to discuss planning for the worsening crisis. Once SOUTHCOM received its tasking to proceed with writing the JSOTF supporting plan to ELABORATE MAZE, the colonel volunteered his group's services, received General Lindsay's approval, reported to MacDill to obtain Lindsay's specific guidance, took charge of a nine-man planning team composed mostly of majors, and set off for Panama, arriving the evening of 13 March.[20]

Fry briefed the team upon its arrival at his headquarters at Albrook. After the briefing, Stringham asked to meet personally with Woerner the next morning. The colonel had three questions he wanted to ask the general, the first of which concerned Noriega. Stringham had been told that, in the event the United States executed Phase IV operations against the Panama Defense Forces, Noriega was to be "taken out." At the meeting, the colonel asked Woerner if that meant killing or abducting the dictator, "because if you want to either kill him or snatch him," Stringham later recalled saying, "that is beyond my authority and I will have to connect you

---

[19] Interv, author with Col Chuck Fry, U.S. Army, 1 May 89, Albrook Air Station, Panama; Msgs, COMSOCSOUTH to CINCSO, 302342Z Mar 88, sub: Commander's Sitrep No. 001, and JCS to USCINCEUR et al., 120056Z Mar 88.

[20] Intervs, author with Maj Dan Priban, 14 May 92, Fort Leavenworth, Kans., and John Partin with Brig Gen Joseph S. Stringham, 29 Aug 89, Fort Bragg, N.C.; Msg, COMSOCSOUTH to CINCSO, 302342Z Mar 88, sub: Commander's Sitrep No. 001.

with the people who do that." Woerner responded that he had no instructions to approve either course of action against Noriega and that he would have to receive permission from Crowe if the need surfaced to target the dictator personally. The second issue Stringham raised had to do with the degree of damage Woerner wanted the joint special operations task force to inflict on Panama's telephone exchanges and television and radio stations. The SOUTHCOM commander indicated that, should U.S. forces execute Phase IV, he only wanted such facilities temporarily disabled, so that they would be available when needed to assist in the task of restoring local order. Finally, Stringham wanted Woerner's guidance on what to do about "taking down" the Comandancia, the PDF headquarters compound in southeast Panama City, down the hill from Quarry Heights. Woerner expressed his fear that all-out combat at the compound might start fires that would spread throughout the city. He therefore told Stringham to try to "isolate" the position and persuade the Panamanian military to surrender. In fact, Woerner added, that should be the approach taken at any of the Special Operations Forces' targets. If U.S. troops could separate the PDF rank-and-file from their leadership, he went on to say, the former would likely surrender. What Woerner wanted, in Stringham's assessment of the meeting, was "neutralization of the [command and control] of the PDF. That was all he was after us to do."[21]

Over the next three days, Stringham's planning team at Albrook worked to translate Woerner's guidance into a supporting plan for Phase IV special operations.[22] Stringham directed the group, working closely with General Cisneros' staff at Quarry Heights and keeping USARSO's General Loeffke updated daily. In the colonel's opinion, the concept of operations developed by the Southern Command was "very loose," and the selection of targets had been "chaotic" and not "economical." There were, he related later, "some 30 targets all over the country, and they didn't know how they were going to focus the effort."

In trying to provide that focus, Stringham relied in part on a "template plan" he had written before the crisis. The document contained an overview of military activities special operators could conduct in most countries in the Caribbean area. It also included a list of the Special Operations Forces available for such operations, the airlift needed to get them to their objectives, and the capabilities they possessed to perform their missions. Combining this information with the guidance he received from Woerner and the CINCSO version of ELABORATE MAZE, the colonel steered his team toward two objectives: the capture of Noriega, if authorized, and the neutralization of the Panama Defense Forces. With a map before them, the planners identified airfields that would have to be secured to keep Noriega from flying out of Panama. They then looked at PDF garrisons that could reinforce the airfields. Finally, they targeted PDF command and control centers, the most important being the Comandancia. In the process, they reduced the number of targets from thirty to twenty-four.

Even this lower figure left one major problem unresolved. The forces available for special operations in Panama included the 75th Ranger Regiment(-), the 7th Special Forces Group, the Army's 160th Special Operations Aviation Regiment, the Air Force's 1st Special Operations Wing, and one or two Navy Sea-Air-Land

---
[21] Stringham Interv, 29 Aug 89.
[22] The account of the planning process at Albrook is based on ibid., and on the author's interview with one of the planning team headed by Colonel Stringham.

(SEAL) platoons. In the process of assigning targets to these units, the planners soon realized they did not have enough troops and equipment to ensure the timely success of the mission. They consequently cast a wider net to include other forces on hand, such as the Navy's Special Boat Unit 26, which belonged to SOUTHCOM's Navy component; whatever battalion-size unit was currently in Panama for a rotation through the Jungle Operations Training Center (JOTC) on the Atlantic side of the canal area; and a Marine expeditionary unit then in transit through the Panama Canal aboard the USS *Okinawa*.

By 17 March, Stringham's team had a draft COMJSOTF (commander, joint special operations task force), OPORD 2–88, ELABORATE MAZE, to brief to Woerner and Cisneros. The plan's concept of operations, which Woerner approved, called for the isolation, immobilization, and neutralization of designated enemy targets.[23] To accomplish this, three special operations task forces would conduct surprise surgical strikes against the objectives. Task Force Red, consisting primarily of two battalions of the 75th Ranger Regiment, would deploy from the United States and, in simultaneous air assaults, seize and secure both the Torrijos-Tocumen military and international airport complex outside Panama City and the PDF garrison at Fort Amador across the Bay of Panama from Quarry Heights. The Rangers would also isolate the Comandancia and PDF facilities nearby and, from a base of operations in Panama City, fan out to Tinajitas and Fort Cimarrón to compel the surrender of hostile units at each location. Task Force Black, consisting mainly of the 7th Special Forces Group, would seize various communications sites, neutralize the Panama Defense Forces at Fort Espinar on the Atlantic side of the canal, and maintain surveillance on PDF facilities and activities at Panama Viejo, Rio Hato, the Pacora River bridge, Cerro Gordo, and the airfield and PDF garrison in David near the Costa Rican border. The third task force, Task Force White, consisted mainly of Navy special operations assets. Its assignment was to isolate the PDF's own special operations unit, known by its Spanish acronym UESAT, on Flamenco Island and to deny enemy personnel the use of Paitilla airfield in Panama City. In carrying out their missions, the three task forces could each count on fire support from U.S. Air Force AC–130 Spectre gunships.

Once the special operations task forces had achieved their objectives, Stringham's plan called for an immediate handoff to conventional forces under JTF-Panama. Most of the special operations units would be redeployed within twenty-four to forty-eight hours. Those that remained would be placed under the commander, Special Operations Command, South, for use in Phase V stability operations as directed by the SOUTHCOM commander. Stringham's operation order made no mention of Noriega. The planning to prevent his escape from Panama in the event of hostilities was "compartmentalized" (meaning that it was developed separately and in secrecy from other aspects of the plan) and would remain so until September 1989.

---

[23] Quotes from Stringham Interv, 29 Aug 89. The account of the joint special operations task force concept of operations and missions is based on COMJSOTF OPORD 2–88, ELABORATE MAZE, 17 Mar 88. A preamble to the table of contents stated that the operation order "was produced within 48 hours from receipt of CINCSOUTH guidance and therefore does not necessarily follow JOPS [Joint Operation Planning System] format and will need further refinement by force listed unit planners."

After Woerner blessed the operation order, Stringham's team returned to the United States, where the planners briefed General Lindsay at the U.S. Special Operations Command. Stringham then returned to Hurlburt, where CASINO GAMBIT was winding down. The imminent end of the exercise raised an important issue with respect to ELABORATE MAZE command and control arrangements. On 24 March, as a part of Phase 0 of ELABORATE MAZE, Woerner had activated Stringham's joint special operations task force, originally set up in support of CASINO GAMBIT, as the headquarters responsible for conducting Phase IV special operations should the just-completed operation order for Panama be executed. Stringham discussed this decision with Lindsay, who suggested that the proposed JSOTF mission under ELABORATE MAZE might be more efficiently handled by a special operations organization that controlled greater assets than Stringham's makeshift headquarters. On 31 March, as a result of this conversation, 1st Special Operations Command handed over its Panama mission to the Joint Special Operations Command at Fort Bragg, North Carolina.

The COMJSOTF operation order that went with the mission contained several references to JTF-Panama. In the event of hostilities, that conventional headquarters would be tasked with providing essential support to the special operators before, during, and after their combat missions. There was just one problem. Whereas Woerner had activated the joint special operations task force called for in Phase IV of ELABORATE MAZE, JTF-Panama existed only on paper during the first month or so of contingency planning in early 1988. This meant that at U.S. Army, South, General Loeffke, the officer slated to become the joint task force commander once JTF-Panama was activated, did not have a joint staff to participate in the planning effort. He had to rely instead on a small ad hoc planning cell, or "study group," set up in USARSO headquarters at Fort Clayton, to write both the supporting JTF-Panama and the component Army Forces plans to CINCSO OPORD 2–88. U.S. Army, South, seemed barely up to the task. Authorized only 239 personnel slots, its threefold role as a major Army command, a theater Army, and a SOUTHCOM component stretched to the limit a staff composed of several captains, a few majors, "pitifully few" lieutenant colonels, and a handful of colonels. The degree to which Loeffke's staff was overtaxed became apparent after contingency planning got under way at Quarry Heights. USARSO's representative at the initial sessions in the Tunnel was a junior officer, Capt. Carlos Puentes.[24]

Puentes' early involvement in the SOUTHCOM planning process enabled him to play a leading role in the USARSO study group, in which he initially served as the conceptual consultant to one other captain, Mike Dearborn. Then, in early March, Col. John A. "Jay" Cope Jr., the USARSO deputy chief of staff, operations, put Maj. Dan Augustine in charge of the cell. Augustine took responsibility for structuring the overall planning process, leaving Puentes to operate the complicated and complex computer program for the phased deployment of any U.S. forces that would have to be brought into Panama in the event of hostilities. Majs. Chuck Herrick and Bruce Sneddon also joined the group in March, Herrick to write a new evacuation plan premised on a nonpermissive

---

[24] The account of USARSO planning efforts is based on Intervs, author with Cope, 29 Mar 89 (source of quote) and 29 May 91; Augustine, 7 Jun 89, 13 Jun 89, and 11 May 90, Fort Leavenworth, Kans.; Maj Chuck Herrick, 1989, Fort Clayton, Panama; and Puentes, 28 Mar 89.

environment, Sneddon to deal with compartmentalized planning. The irony was that these three majors and two captains were all U.S. Army officers; yet they found themselves writing the initial drafts of contingency plans for joint U.S. conventional operations in Panama.

The group received its guidance from several sources. Although the press of USARSO's numerous missions kept Cope and Rossi from giving their undivided attention to contingency planning, both colonels met nightly with Augustine and the others to provide advice, direction, and feedback. In keeping with the concept of operations passed down from SOUTHCOM's director of operations, Cope instructed his planners to concentrate on key PDF nodes in and around Panama City and on "isolating the battlefield," which meant blocking any hostile forces that could reach the capital. As additional U.S. forces arrived in Panama, JTF-Panama would extend its operations from critical PDF nodes to the entire city.

Although Cope usually served as the conduit for conveying SOUTHCOM guidance to the USARSO study group, there were occasions when the contingency planners at both headquarters communicated directly. In general, coordination between Cisneros' staff and Augustine's group never reached the level of effectiveness desired by the latter. Conversely, Washington's urgent requests for information often obliged the USARSO cell to disregard its chain of command and communicate directly with the Joint Chiefs and the Department of the Army, to the consternation of staff officers at Quarry Heights. Augustine and his group also dealt directly with SOUTHCOM's components and several U.S.-based headquarters responsible for providing the units included on the evolving troop list. In the midst of all this frenetic activity, Loeffke requested that small groups of U.S. officers be sent to Panama on ninety-day rotations to augment USARSO's planning effort. Toward the end of March, the first such group consisting of five majors arrived at Fort Clayton.

The work of the USARSO study group bore fruit on 21 March, when it forwarded its supporting plan, COMJTF-Panama OPORD 1–88, ELABORATE MAZE, to SOUTHCOM.[25] The mission statement and five-phase concept of operations were taken almost word for word from the CINCSO version of the plan. Should a buildup of U.S. forces in Panama take place during one of the pre-hostility phases of the plan, JTF-Panama would conduct an evacuation of noncombatants to remove American civilians from harm's way. Should hostilities occur, Phase IV of the plan called for JTF-Panama to conduct operations against command and control facilities, civilian communications sites, and selected airfields; to support JSOTF operations; and to be prepared to seize and secure PDF facilities at Rio Hato. The emphasis was on isolating and disarming PDF and paramilitary units in Panama City and Colón although the plan did not rule out operations throughout the country. To protect noncombatants and Panamanian property in the process, the rules of engagement in effect during Phase IV sought to limit the application of U.S. firepower to no more than was deemed necessary to accomplish the mission. In Phase V, JTF-Panama would provide military policemen, civil affairs and medical personnel, and other assets to help a U.S. military government and the State Department restore law and order and stability in the country. Among the forces available to JTF-Panama for

---

[25] The following account of the plan developed at U.S. Army, South, is based on Msg, CDR, Joint Task Force-Panama (COMJTFPM or COMJTF-Panama), to CINCSO, 220030Z Mar 88, sub: OPREP–1/COMJTFPM/001/ELABORATE MAZE/OPORD 1–88.

the operations described in the plan were in-country units, such as the 193d Infantry Brigade and 1st Battalion, 228th Aviation, and augmentation units from outside Panama, to include the 7th Infantry Division (Light), a mechanized battalion, a military police brigade, a psychological operations battalion, a Marine expeditionary brigade, and an aircraft carrier battle group.

Most of the staff officers who drafted the JTF-Panama and JSOTF supporting plans assumed that Phase IV offensive operations—tantamount to a U.S. invasion of Panama—would be executed in the near future, probably in March or early April. The two generals for whom they labored, however, took pains to disabuse them of that notion. At one briefing, Loeffke told the USARSO contingency planners, "You know this is a pipe dream." To his diary he confided that "Many Americans believe the military can do magic. Most are civilians who have never tasted war. They give more capabilities to the military than the military has." In assessing the short-term and long-term ramifications of open hostilities with the Panamanian military, Loeffke wrote, "Strongly oppose military action in Panama City. The animosity created would be too large."[26]

Woerner also judged military intervention in Panama as improbable, a point he emphasized during an impromptu visit to Stringham's team of special operations planners at Albrook. He also continued to recommend against the military option in his communications with Crowe, who was just as adamantly opposed to intervention as he. Crowe, too, had powerful allies. In Loeffke's diary, a flag officer note dated 2 April read, "We will prevail in this situation but hopefully we will do it in a way that is peaceful and without unnecessary suffering by the Panamanian people." The note was signed by Colin Powell, the national security adviser to President Reagan.[27]

SECURITY ENHANCEMENT

While the initial JSOTF and JTF-Panama operation orders were still being drafted, the Southern Command was determining how it might increase the protection it could afford American citizens, property, and interests in Panama. Two separate approaches to this end emerged: one sought to bring U.S. security forces in Panama up to full strength, while the other looked to bring in additional units, particularly some of those already listed on the ELABORATE MAZE troop list.[28]

In recommending a buildup of U.S. forces for security reasons, Woerner was concerned about the continued violence in the streets of Panama City. He also worried that, once the sanctions announced by President Reagan on 11 March began to be felt, Panama's economy could deteriorate to the point where Noriega might retaliate against some vulnerable American facility in an attempt to embarrass the United States. There was another reason for the SOUTHCOM commander to be uneasy as well. As PDF harassment continued and the level of burglaries and other economic crimes rose dramatically in housing areas on U.S. bases, morale among service personnel and their dependents declined. The degree of the dip was problematic, but as one countermeasure, Woerner and his immediate subordinates continued to hold meetings with the families affected by the turbulent events in

---

[26] Diary, Bernard Loeffke, n.d.
[27] Intervs, Woerner, 30 Apr 91; Priban, 14 May 92; Diary, Loeffke, Powell note.
[28] Augustine Interv, 11 May 90; Msg, CINCSO to JCS, 121930Z Mar 88, sub: Panama Security Enhancement.

Panama. At these "town hall" sessions, the commanders imparted information about developments in the crisis and received questions and comments from their audiences. In a report to General Vuono, Loeffke indicated that few of the families he talked to felt threatened or wanted to leave. A few days later, however, a specialist fourth class living in Panama City told the USARSO commander that "Enlisted men won't always tell you everything. They know you'll tell the chain of command. The chain in turn will chew them out."[29] In the context of this sentiment, a buildup of U.S. security forces in Panama could possibly reinforce other command initiatives to reassure apprehensive Americans.

Woerner asked for the additional troops as a "prudent" but not demonstrative measure. The augmentation was not to be a show of force but conducted in such a way as to cause as little alarm as possible within the Panamanian military. The general suggested that one way to avoid undue publicity was for the units designated for security enhancement to be sent to Panama in conjunction with the Florida National Guardsmen then en route for the annual training event, TOTAL WARRIOR. The deployment would thus have some semblance of being routine, although the security enhancement units would play no part in the exercise.[30]

Secretary of Defense Carlucci approved the buildup and Woerner's "low-key" approach to it. On 12 March, he authorized the Joint Chiefs to direct the commander in chief of the U.S. Atlantic Command to deploy a Marine Fleet Anti-Terrorist Security Team (FAST); the commander in chief, U.S. Forces Command, to deploy an Army military police battalion from Fort Bragg, an Army Arrival/Departure Airfield Control Group, and an Army Movement Control Team; the chief of staff of the Air Force to deploy an Airbase Ground Defense Flight and an Air Force Dog Flight; General Vuono to deploy a counterintelligence detachment (Spanish language qualified); and General Lindsay to deploy an Army signal battalion(-). The Military Airlift Command would provide the necessary transportation, and the Strategic Air Command would refuel those aircraft en route.[31]

The Joint Chiefs' order stated explicitly that the immediate threat to Americans was "one of rhetoric and minor harassment. Although there is currently no direct threat to US citizens, the situation could rapidly deteriorate and US lives and property could be at risk." The troop movement was to be conducted in such a way as to "give the impression of relatively normal operations at Howard AFB so as not to alarm the PDF." To drive home the point, the message stated emphatically that the deployment "does not constitute authority to execute ELABORATE MAZE." On the subject of command and control arrangements, the order indicated that, upon their arrival in the SOUTHCOM area of responsibility, the deploying forces would come under the SOUTHCOM commander's operational command.

Other issues addressed in the Joint Chiefs' message included psychological operations and the themes that needed to be reinforced, avoided, or counteracted when explaining the troop movements. For example, one point to be emphasized was that, despite allegations leveled by the Noriega regime, the newly arrived

---

[29] Woerner Interv, 30 Apr 91; Msg, CDR, USARSO, to CSA, 092300Z Mar 88. The specialist's observation is from Diary, Loeffke, 12 Mar 88.

[30] Msg, CINCSO to JCS, 121930Z Mar 88, sub: Panama Security Enhancement.

[31] Msgs, Commander in Chief, U.S. Forces Command (CINCFOR), to CDR, XVIII Abn Corps, 121755Z Mar 88, sub: Warning Order, and JCS to U.S. Commander in Chief, U.S. Atlantic Command (USCINCLANT), et al., 122000Z Mar 88, sub: Deployment Order for Security Forces to Panama.

American units were there only to augment "existing US military security forces," not "to invade Panama and set up a puppet government." Serving as a reminder to the units themselves on that score, the message directed that they would operate under peacetime rules of engagement, which allowed U.S. troops to respond to threats only with actions that "are appropriate to the provocation, are designed to limit the scope and intensity of the conflict, will discourage escalation, and will achieve political and military objectives."[32]

Of the first units to deploy, both the Marine FAST platoon and the Air Force Airbase Ground Defense Flight arrived in Panama the afternoon of 14 March without incident. The SOUTHCOM Public Affairs Office experienced some frantic moments, however, when ABC News broadcast word of the deployment, thereby compelling the command to issue a press release on the security enhancement buildup sooner than it had anticipated. The statement stressed that the dispatch of the troops under President Reagan's orders was not in response to any specific incident but merely a prudent measure in light of the unrest and tension in Panama. Inadvertently, the regime itself helped reinforce this characterization by not doing more to challenge it. As the National Guard unit for TOTAL WARRIOR and the remaining security enhancement troops began flowing into the country, the anti-American demonstrations the Southern Command had anticipated failed to materialize. One U.S. assessment of this missed opportunity suggested that, while the PDF hierarchy was aware of the force deployments, the buildup was small and dispersed enough to prevent Noriega and his inner circle from appreciating its full impact.[33]

Soon after the Pentagon issued the security enhancement order, the Southern Command began making a series of adjustments to the scheduled deployments. As a result, all Army units affected by the order remained in the United States for the time being. Meanwhile, Woerner reported to the Joint Chiefs on 15 March that the augmentation forces that had deployed were beginning to perform their security missions. Twenty-six members of the Fleet Anti-Terrorist Security Team, for example, were already patrolling the Arraiján Tank Farm, an aboveground Navy fuel depot just north of Howard Air Force Base. The facility's vulnerability had caused Loeffke and others to voice their concerns. In the same message, Woerner described the situation in Panama as volatile, a sentiment shared by Loeffke. In an update to Vuono, the USARSO commander warned of possible trouble over the next three to four days because of the worsening economic conditions. "Our basic concern," he emphasized, "is that the situation can quickly escalate."[34]

---

[32] Msg, JCS to USCINCLANT et al., 122000Z Mar 88, sub: Deployment Order for Security Forces to Panama. As a part of Noriega's propaganda war against TOTAL WARRIOR, the Panamanian Foreign Ministry delivered a note to the U.S. Embassy, charging in "hysterical" tones that a U.S. invasion of Panama was imminent. The note was returned to the ministry "unopened." Msg, AmEmb, Panama, to SecState, 252155Z Mar 88, sub: Panama Protests U.S. Military Activities.

[33] USSOUTHCOM, Historical Report 1988, p. 134; *Tropic Times*, 16 Mar 88; Fact Sheet, USARSO DCSOPS, 24 Mar 88.

[34] Msgs, CINCSO to JCS, 130500Z Mar 88, sub: SCJ3 Sitrep 035; CINCFOR to CDR, III Corps, 130630Z Mar 88, sub: Deployment Order (Corrected Copy); CINCSO to JCS, 131506Z Mar 88, sub: SCJ3 Sitrep 036; JCS to USCINCLANT et al., 131858Z Mar 88, sub: Change One—Deployment Order for Security Forces to Panama; CINCFOR to CDR, III Corps, 132215Z Mar 88, sub: Change One—Deployment Order for Security Forces to Panama; and CINCSO to JCS, 160650Z Mar 88,

Operation Orders and Security Enhancement

On 16 March, two days after Loeffke's warning, Col. Leonidas Macías, chief of Panama's police forces, and Maj. Fernando Quezada led a small group of mid-level PDF officers in an attempt to topple Noriega. The motives of the conspirators were mixed: all had been passed over for promotion; some feared a U.S. invasion and the destruction of the Panama Defense Forces as an institution if Noriega remained in command; some were uneasy over Noriega's growing ties with Cuba, Nicaragua, and Libya; some had recently returned from studying at military colleges in the United States; and some merely wanted to preempt higher-ranking officers from launching their own coup. What direction the crisis would have taken had the plotters succeeded is a matter of speculation. But the coup attempt, which Noriega possibly knew about beforehand, failed miserably, and its participants were arrested and, in some cases, imprisoned and tortured.[35]

Pro-Noriega spokespersons accused the United States of fomenting the revolt and of waging an "undeclared war" against Panama. The Reagan administration denied the allegations, although it certainly had not discouraged any such effort to oust Noriega. To the contrary, Secretary of State Shultz had made what one observer has called "a thinly disguised appeal to the officers of the Panama Defense Forces to rise up against Noriega, calling the PDF 'a strong and honorable force that has a significant and proper role to play' in a post-Noriega Panama." According to the same author, the secretary of state "secretly ordered U.S. embassies in several Latin American countries to 'inform Panamanian military attachés of U.S. desire to work with PDF, but inability to do so while Noriega remains. Message includes support for PDF's important role in Panama as a professional military subordinate to civilian authority and expresses desire to resume close cooperation once PDF puts its house in order.'"[36]

Noriega appeared in public immediately after the coup attempt, passing off the few shots fired that morning as nothing but "kisses." In the ensuing days, he used the incident as a rationale for purging the Panama Defense Forces and the government of several individuals whose loyalty he questioned and for tightening his "Mafia-like" network of "informal control" over the PDF by creating the Strategic Military Council composed of trusted subordinates. In Panama City, his opponents again took to the streets with the support of the National Civic Crusade, and workers already on strike cut off electrical power to the capital, prompting

---

sub: SCJ3 Sitrep 041. Quote from Msg, CDR, USARSO, to CSA, 142330Z Mar 88. Diary, Loeffke, 15 Mar 88.

[35] Kempe, *Divorcing the Dictator*, pp. 273–79. The coup attempt occurred while Colonel Stringham's team was working on the JSOTF supporting plan in Panama. Consequently, Stringham saw firsthand how the Panama Defense Forces dealt with the opposition. He was not impressed, dismissing the Panamanian military as a group of "thugs." He also observed the behavior of the civilian population, which just sought "to get out of the way." That convinced him that, should there be fighting between U.S. and Panamanian forces in Panama City, the civilian population would not interfere or get in the way. Stringham Interv, 29 Aug 89.

[36] Dinges, *Our Man in Panama*, rev. ed., pp. 298–99. A SOUTHCOM message covering events the day before the coup attempt referred to "recent actions taken by the U.S. government to encourage the separation of . . . Noriega from the . . . [Panama Defense Forces]." Msg, CINCSO to JCS, 160650Z Mar 88, sub: SCJ3 Sitrep 041. In light of subsequent recommendations, Woerner appears not to have objected to the concept of driving a wedge between Noriega and the PDF, but rather to the sanguine hopes voiced by the State Department as to the professional role the Panamanian military would assume as soon as its leader was gone.

A Panama Defense Forces (PDF) antiriot unit using a water cannon to put down a demonstration against the regime.

the Panamanian military to retaliate by seizing the power plants and other public utilities. On 18 March, the government declared a state of emergency, during which it again suspended various constitutional rights. In defiance, the opposition called a general strike for the twenty-first. At the same time, Civic Crusade leaders made known their feelings that getting rid of Noriega was now the responsibility of the United States. As this latest round of threats and violence intensified, it seemed to herald the kind of significant escalation in the crisis that Woerner, Loeffke, and others feared.

Behind the scenes, there existed a brief hope that the coup attempt might have actually shaken Noriega, perhaps to the point where, if offered the proper incentives, he would voluntarily step down from his dictatorial position. Publicly, the Panamanian strongman proclaimed that his "virility was proved" by his ability to hold onto power. Privately, he seemed to be looking for a deal through which he could leave the PDF but still retain much of that power. As one Panamanian observed, "The general is willing to go, but he's not going to be dragged out like a dog." When Noriega requested a meeting with State Department officials right after the coup attempt, Deputy Assistant Secretary of State William Walker and legal adviser Michael Kozak arrived with a proposal in which the United States would agree not to extradite Noriega for prosecution on drug trafficking charges if the general agreed to asylum in a third country. Walker and Kozak met with Noriega and a few of his close associates twice on 18 March. As if from a scene in the *Godfather*, there was much talk of "friendship" and "respect," but in the end, Noriega rejected the U.S. proposal.[37]

When news of the negotiations was made public, Panamanian opposition leaders strongly objected to not being informed in advance. Loeffke, too, expressed reservations, confiding to his diary that the State Department was the wrong agency

---

[37] On the Walker-Kozak mission, see Margaret E. Scranton, *The Noriega Years: U.S.-Panamanian Relations, 1981–1990* (Boulder, Colo.: Lynne Rienner Publishers, 1991), pp. 147–48.

Operation Orders and Security Enhancement

to be dealing with Noriega, since the PDF commander did not respond well to ultimatums. "We as soldiers could do a better job in negotiating with him," Loeffke concluded.[38] Back in the United States, Secretary Shultz and General Powell appeared on Sunday interview programs to indicate that time was running out for Noriega to go into voluntary exile. What the United States planned to do if the general ignored the warning remained unclear, especially after President Reagan, to the chagrin of several of his advisers, declared in the wake of the coup attempt that the United States would not use military force to remove the dictator.

Woerner's reaction to the failed coup was to recommend the continued deployment of security enhancement forces to Panama. Events, he informed the Joint Chiefs, had become "fluid, volatile, and unpredictable." He further warned that "clearly the situation is tending towards violence." Under those circumstances, he thought deploying more of the troops SOUTHCOM had requested, including the Army units that had initially been held back, was "prudent." The Joint Chiefs approved the recommendation.[39]

Among the units to deploy was the 503d Military Police Battalion with three MP companies from Fort Bragg. The battalion's arrival was well received by most staff officers at U.S. Army, South, which had been lobbying for more military policemen. The Military Police Command in Panama consisted of a headquarters company and two combat support companies. These units were responsible, among their other missions, for the security of about twenty U.S. installations and several U.S.-PDF military areas of coordination. As the crisis escalated in early 1988 and as evidence of hostile intrusions and criminal activities on U.S. facilities began to mount, security requirements exceeded the Military Police Command's ability to respond effectively. As an interim measure, USARSO directed infantry units from the 193d Infantry Brigade to join military policemen on patrols and overwatch programs, an approach that proved productive but at the expense of the 193d's primary missions. The newly arrived military policemen, together with the radio-equipped high mobility multipurpose wheeled vehicles (HMMWVs) they brought with them, increased manpower and mobility, thus allowing USARSO to provide police protection to a much broader area. At the same time, infantry units released from MP duties were free to launch patrols aimed at detecting PDF surveillance on U.S. facilities.[40]

Some staff officers at Fort Clayton questioned the decision to send an MP battalion to Panama at this point in the crisis. Better, they argued, had combat forces listed in the Elaborate Maze operation orders been flown in as a show of determination. This, however, was exactly the signal Carlucci, the Joint Chiefs, Woerner, Loeffke, Rossi, and Cope wanted to avoid. To them, the deployment of military police into a confrontational environment in which neither side wanted war was the appropriate gesture to make. The MPs were, after all, cops trained to "power

---

[38] Diary, Loeffke, 20 Mar 88.

[39] Quotes from Msg, CINCSO to JCS, 161815Z Mar 88, sub: Panama Security Enhancement. Msg, JCS to USCINCLANT et al., 170038Z Mar 88, sub: Deployment Order for Security Forces to Panama.

[40] Intervs, author with Lt Col Mike Michaelis, U.S. Army, 7 Jun 89, Fort Clayton, Panama; Capt Gary Holt, U.S. Army, 26 Sep 90, Fort Leavenworth, Kans.; Maj Gen Bernard Loeffke, U.S. Army, 27 Mar 88, 31 May 89, Fort Clayton, Panama; Cope, 29 Mar 89; and Col Arnie Rossi, U.S. Army, 24 May 89, Fort Clayton, Panama.

down" dangerous situations and restore order. They could take abuse without losing their discipline. They were perceived as being less likely than infantry to respond to violence with violence. As U.S. Army, South, tried to walk the fine line between protecting American lives and property without demonstrating a belligerent intent, the MPs were a "politically acceptable" symbol of law enforcement and restraint. Even the PDF could recognize that they were not there to start a war. As events in Panama evolved, the military police became a critical presence, the "major combat working unit" in the crisis. They were the "guys on the streets."[41]

So crucial was the role of the military police in the crisis that Loeffke asked Woerner for a second MP battalion from the United States. Cope worked up a fact sheet recommending the deployment of the 519th Military Police Battalion with two companies, together with a Headquarters and Headquarters Company from the 16th Military Police Brigade. In Cope's assessment, the second MP battalion would give U.S. Army, South, greater flexibility in several areas as the "threat to U.S. installations slowly grows and becomes more apparent." More military police would increase the available number of quick reaction forces (units on alert to respond to a dangerous situation within fifteen to thirty minutes), provide additional area security, protect unsecured facilities such as the USARSO headquarters building at Fort Clayton, assume all or part of the daily installation interior guard, and enhance the military's capability to react to any sudden outbreak of hostilities, dubbed by contingency planners as Bolt Out of the Blue (a play on words invoking the name of the 193d Infantry Brigade's commander, Col. William J. Bolt). Citing the political as well as the military logic contained in the earlier request for the 503d, Cope noted that "This type unit does not stigmatize the Reagan admin as wanting to take offensive action." In a similar vein, a second MP battalion coming into Panama was in keeping with Loeffke's comment, "Our biggest challenge is to be firm but not provocative."[42]

As additional military policemen arrived in Panama, some problems arose. Many of the MPs had little idea of why they were there. Having not been briefed by Forces Command prior to their departure, they anticipated entering a warlike environment for the purpose of conducting an evacuation of noncombatants. Some MPs were visibly distressed when they were met upon their arrival at Howard Air Force Base and told to doff their red berets so as not to appear in a "combat mode." Once in Panama, they regarded the information imparted to them as inadequate. Nor were they pleased with many of their security enhancement assignments. While some took part in mobile patrols, others received less satisfactory static missions of guarding gates and installations. Another source of displeasure was the negative reaction they received from the very people they had come to protect. Indeed, to some U.S. service personnel stationed in Panama, the newly arrived MPs seemed to have little to do besides issue parking tickets, check IDs, and make getting into the post exchange an inconvenience. Still, by 24 March, Loeffke could speak of

---

[41] Intervs, author with Augustine, 7 Jun 89, 13 Jun 89, and Rossi, 24 May 89. First quote from Interv, author with Michaelis, 7 Jun 89. Intervs, author with Holt, 26 Sep 90, and Loeffke, 31 May 89. Third and fourth quotes from Interv, author with Cope, 29 Mar 89. Second quote from Telephone Interv, author with Capt Anthony Schilling, U.S. Army, 30 Nov 90.

[42] First quote from Fact Sheet, USARSO DCSOPS, 24 Mar 88. Second quote from Msg, CDR, USARSO, to HQDA, 24 Mar 88, sub: USARSO Sitrep No. 10. Last quote from Msg, CDR, USARSO, to HQDA, 312200Z Mar 88, sub: USARSO Sitrep No. 17.

the "atmosphere of tranquility" created by the MP buildup and increased patrols in housing areas. By the end of the month, he was boasting of statistics that showed a decline in the break-ins on U.S. bases after the arrival of the military police.[43]

SHOWDOWN IN WASHINGTON

On the evening of 28 March, Lt. Col. Robert Pantier was running the Panama crisis action team in the Tunnel at Quarry Heights when Rear Adm. Richard C. Ustick, the SOUTHCOM chief of staff, telephoned to inquire about what was going on at the Marriott Hotel in Panama City. Pantier had received no information on any unusual activity at the hotel, but Ustick said CNN was reporting that, following an anti-Noriega march, the Panama Defense Forces had entered the premises and had apprehended opposition members and media personnel. The network was also running live footage of the PDF herding people into waiting vans. About fifteen minutes after the call from Ustick, Pantier began to receive reports of the incident.[44] The next day, the "storming" of the Marriott was the lead story on most morning news programs in the United States. Among the journalists arrested and roughed up by the PDF there had been five Americans. Plainclothes officers had also ransacked the offices of NBC, CBS, and ABC News located in the hotel.

In the furor created by the Marriott incident, the Joint Chiefs summoned Woerner to Washington to discuss the situation. En route, the SOUTHCOM commander and his staff examined the options policymakers were likely to consider. Despite President Reagan's public disavowal of any intention to use U.S. military force as a solution to the crisis, Secretary of State Shultz was still arguing for a "snatch" operation to apprehend Noriega. To this, Elliott Abrams added an even grander scheme. It called for sending 6,000 additional U.S. troops to Panama. Then, under the protection of these forces, Eric Delvalle, the ousted but U.S.-recognized president of Panama, and Col. Eduardo Herrera Hassán, Panama's ambassador to Israel, would restate the former's claim to being the country's legitimate president. In support of the claim, the opposition would take to the streets. These actions, combined with the abduction of Noriega, would end the crisis.

Crowe and Woerner considered the plan brash and impractical. In discussions among their staffs, it was referred to as "loony tunes" and "the Rambo option," the product of an imaginative civilian mind uninformed by personal military experience. The scheme presented other problems as well. Opposition leaders in Panama, remembering Delvalle's acts of repression under Noriega, had only reluctantly endorsed his claim to the presidency. Their support for Abrams' plan could therefore not be assumed. There was also the more pressing matter of Americans living in Panama. A rapid buildup of U.S. forces (as opposed to the

---

[43] Intervs, Augustine, 13 Jun 89; Michaelis, 7 Jun 89; Holt, 26 Sep 90; Telephone Interv with Capt Schilling, 30 Nov 90. Quotes from Msg, CDR, USARSO, to HQDA, 24 Mar 88, sub: USARSO Sitrep No. 10. Msg, CDR, USARSO, to HQDA, 312200Z Mar 88, sub: USARSO Sitrep No. 17.

[44] Pantier Interv, 21 May 91. There were several times during the crisis that officers manning operations centers at Quarry Heights and Fort Clayton would rely on CNN for up-to-the-minute news of an incident taking place. During normal days, for example, the emergency operations center at Fort Clayton would be lightly manned, with the television often turned to soap operas. Once an incident occurred, the channel would be changed immediately, and CNN monitored thereafter. In other offices in Panama (and in Washington), televisions were tuned to the news network during the course of a business day.

gradual buildup covered under ELABORATE MAZE) might trigger hostage-taking by the Panamanian military. Or the Americans could get caught in the crossfire if the PDF decided to fight the U.S. forces or the demonstrators. Woerner had initiated a reduction of off-post personnel earlier in March, but the process of bringing military dependents onto U.S. bases was slow and did not even affect the many thousands of private American citizens living in and around Panama City and Colón. Abrams could protest that presidential prestige was on the line, since Reagan had publicly demanded Noriega's resignation, but his argument carried little weight with U.S. officers who blamed the State Department, and Abrams in particular, for manufacturing much of the U.S.-Panama crisis in the first place and for dragging the president into it. There was also the vivid memory of the State Department's role in sending U.S. marines into Lebanon in the early 1980s and the tragic consequences of that commitment. Presidential prestige or no, the Joint Chiefs and most of the Pentagon were simply not amenable to having U.S. troops die in Panama for anything less than vital U.S. interests, none of which seemed immediately threatened. Finally, as Crowe explained personally to Reagan, "Why should good ol' boys from Peoria, Illinois, go down and die for people in Panama driving in Mercedeses?"[45]

A full review of U.S. options in the Panama crisis took place at the White House on 29 March. In terms of bureaucratic warfare, it was a bloody session in which the clash of issues and personalities that had been festering since the onset of the crisis came to a head. PDF provocations, the efficacy of current U.S. economic sanctions, Noriega's recent creation of paramilitary organizations known as Dignity Battalions, the prospect of hostage-taking and guerrilla warfare, and the influx into Panama of Cuban, Nicaraguan, Colombian, and Libyan weapons and advisers all received careful, if at times contentious, consideration. Crowe attacked the Abrams plan as too risky. Not only would Americans in Panama be placed in jeopardy, but military action there would cause other, strategically located countries in which the United States had base rights to reconsider whether a tangible U.S. military presence was a blessing or a potential threat. The admiral also estimated that the military force needed to execute Abram's scheme—a carrier battle group, commando units, and an amphibious assault team—was more than the Pentagon had available to send. Shultz angrily contested Crowe's force estimates as deliberate exaggerations. The secretary of state again proposed a snatch operation and again encountered Crowe's objections. The group considered other courses of action but reached no consensus. The president finally ruled out a military operation and decided instead to announce further economic sanctions and to send 1,300 additional troops to Panama for the purpose of security enhancement.[46]

The day after the White House meeting, Woerner met with the Joint Chiefs of Staff, who directed him to "plan for the deployment and employment of sufficient forces to protect US citizens, the Canal, and US installations." He indicated that he did not need more troops but understood the political rationale for sending them. After further discussion, the Joint Chiefs decided that the additional forces needed

---

[45] Crowe's quote from Kempe, *Divorcing the Dictator*, p. 297. On the military options advanced by Shultz and Abrams and the response by Crowe and other military officers, see ibid., pp. 289–97; Kevin Buckley, *Panama*, pp. 137–39; Interv, author with Maj Fred Polk, U.S. Army, 29 Mar 89, Fort Clayton, Panama; *New York Times*, 2 Apr 88, 3 Apr 88.

[46] Kempe, *Divorcing the Dictator*, pp. 302–04; *New York Times*, 2 Apr 88.

to satisfy the continuing security enhancement mission could be found among those units listed under Phases I, II, and III of ELABORATE MAZE. On a related matter, they also instructed Woerner to continue planning for a nonpermissive evacuation of noncombatants and to refine ELABORATE MAZE planning.[47]

JOINT TASK FORCE-PANAMA

If Woerner did not readily embrace the second round of security enhancement augmentation, Loeffke did. The PDF's repressive raid at the Marriott, according to the USARSO commander, "appears to be one more sign that Noriega is determined to take any action he deems necessary to demonstrate his hold on Panama." Because "our intelligence is still unable to provide us with General Noriega's military intentions," constant vigilance would be essential. The troops currently in Panama, in Loeffke's estimate, were adequate to respond to contingencies for two more weeks, although they could only defend U.S. bases and not "go on offensive operations or defend Canal installations." On the principle that "more is better," he wanted the second MP battalion that he had requested from Woerner, as well as a UH–60 and an assault helicopter company. "If the situation is aggravated," he wrote in a message to Vuono, "then we believe it will be necessary to start phasing in other combat forces."[48]

On 1 April, the Defense Department announced the second troop augmentation. The units that deployed to Panama over the course of the following week included the 519th Military Police Battalion that Loeffke and Cope had requested, the 16th Military Police Brigade Headquarters and Headquarters Company, an Army reconnaissance troop, three Air Force ground defense units, two Air Force canine squads, a Marine infantry company, and a combat aviation company from the 7th Infantry Division (Light), consisting of four OH–58 Kiowas, fifteen UH–60 Black Hawks, and seven AH–1 Cobras.

The 1,300 military personnel that were deployed, when added to the first augmentation round of 670, raised the number of U.S. forces in Panama to 12,000. The Pentagon again tried to quiet speculation that an invasion was imminent by insisting the relatively small buildup was in response to the "instability of the current situation in Panama, the heavy-handed tactics of Noriega in dealing with the situation and the potential for increased threats to U.S. citizens and interests in Panama." In classified message traffic, the Joint Chiefs again emphasized that, although the units listed in the 1 April announcement were also on the ELABORATE MAZE troop list, the deployment was not an authorization to execute the operation order. The State Department took a more belligerent line, though, with the suggestion that the augmentation was a warning to Noriega and his supporters that "it would not be advisable for them to take any actions against Americans." Pentagon officials conceded that some of the units being deployed, such as the Marine rifle company, were combat units but offered assurances that these units would not serve in a combat capacity. They would only bolster security forces already present.[49]

---

[47] Quote from Msg, JCS to USCINCLANT et al., 082317Z Apr 88. Woerner Interv, 30 Apr 91.

[48] First, second, and third quotes from Memo, Loeffke for CINCSO, 29 Mar 88. Fourth quote from Msg, CDR, USARSO, to HQDA, 29 Mar 88, sub: Sitrep No. 15.

[49] Quotes from *New York Times*, 2 Apr 88. *Tropic Times*, 4 Apr 88, 8 Apr 88.

Most of the units entering Panama were placed under the operational control of their SOUTHCOM service component (for example, the Air Force units went under the command's Air Force component). This meant that a unified command was essentially running tactical operations as it engaged in crisis management on a day-to-day basis. The task was nearly impossible, given the Southern Command's long list of other missions, commitments, and activities in the theater. This predicament had become especially acute during the last half of March, when, during the first wave of security enhancement deployments to Panama, the United States also mounted Operation GOLDEN PHEASANT in Honduras, sending light infantry units into that country to deter a possible invasion by the Sandinista government in Nicaragua. Since Honduras fell within the Southern Command's area of responsibility, staff officers at Quarry Heights suddenly found themselves stretched to the limit trying to monitor two simultaneous crises. Meanwhile, the USARSO cell Colonel Cope had set up under Major Augustine, while performing several joint task force planning functions, lacked formal authorization and the assets required of a joint organization. In short, the time had come, many thought, to establish JTF-Panama for the purpose of providing centralized control over the U.S. forces involved in security enhancement missions in Panama. The headquarters would also manage the tactical aspects of the crisis on a daily basis.

The activation of JTF-Panama was supposed to take place in Phase 0 of ELABORATE MAZE, before any troop deployments to Panama. Although that operation order had not been formally executed, many of the troops listed in it were arriving daily. Woerner had previously indicated he would place these forces under the operational control of JTF-Panama, yet, in late March and early April, he seemed hesitant to activate the joint task force. His reluctance stemmed from two considerations. The small size of his Army component and the fact that it had theater-wide missions caused some staff officers at Quarry Heights to question USARSO's ability to function effectively as the core of JTF-Panama. In lengthy discussions on this point, some senior officers at SOUTHCOM even expressed doubts about whether their counterparts at U.S. Army, South, were personally up to the challenge. There was also the more sensitive issue of the PDF's reaction. Having had access to plans for the combined defense of the canal, the Panama Defense Forces knew that activation of JTF-Panama could indicate imminent hostilities. There were some U.S. officers in Panama who argued that sending Noriega this signal would not hurt, but Woerner was not among them.[50]

Loeffke and Rossi supported Woerner's cautious approach to the crisis, but still needed the SOUTHCOM commander to activate the joint task force. Without the authority to call on the other services for assistance and support, U.S. Army, South, could not hope to respond effectively to the joint responsibilities that were already being thrust upon it by contingency planning and the security enhancement buildup. Fortunately for USARSO, it had two high-ranking friends in court at Quarry Heights, SOUTHCOM's deputy commander and chief of staff.

---

[50] Msg, CINCSO to CINCFOR, 0220017Z Apr 88; Intervs, author with Polk, 29 Mar 89; Col Gar Thiry, U.S. Army, and Col Tom Braaten, U.S. Marine Corps (USMC), 12 Dec 89, Maxwell Air Force Base (AFB), Ala. During his visit in March for the purpose of planning special operations, Colonel Stringham had made the point to SOUTHCOM officials that he did not believe U.S. Army, South, had sufficient combat assets to serve as the core around which JTF-Panama could be constructed. Stringham Interv, 29 Aug 89.

Both officers began to press the issue with Woerner, while U.S. Army, South, launched its own campaign. On 4 April, Loeffke informed his superior that a secure JTF-Panama communications net had been established. In another message to Woerner, he restated his position that he did not require a full JTF staff, but one of just over eighty billets, 85 percent of which would be filled by personnel from U.S. Army, South. The next day, Cope directed the writing of an operation order for conventional Phase 0 preparations under ELABORATE MAZE. USARSO also activated a separate operational staff for JTF-Panama planning. Colonel Rossi even went so far as to draft the order activating JTF-Panama, his "ultimatum," as he called it. In just a few days, these efforts bore fruit. On 6 April, a kidney stone compelled Woerner to enter the hospital, where, while convalescing, he agreed to the entreaties of his deputy and chief of staff. On 8 April, the Southern Command issued the order for the activation of JTF-Panama at noon the next day.[51]

The order called for a joint task force staffed at "a modified manning level using in-theater assets for the purpose of enhancing the readiness and command and control of on site security enhancement forces." As stated in the SOUTHCOM contingency plans, the commanding general, USARSO, was designated commander, JTF-Panama, and would receive operational control of Navy Forces (NAVFOR), Marine Forces (MARFOR), Air Force Forces (AFFOR), and Army Forces (ARFOR). "The activation of JTF-PM is a most sensitive issue," Loeffke was reminded, "and is to be handled in a low key and prudent manner. Take reasonable precaution in achieving the needed posture of readiness so as not to precipitate a confrontation."[52]

On the day before he formally became the JTF commander, Loeffke sent a personal message to Vuono updating the Army chief on the situation in Panama. Loeffke noted that a nervous PDF was taking measures, on the one hand, to reassure Americans that their lives and property were safe and, on the other, to prepare for possible hostilities with the United States. In terms of how the Reagan administration should respond to the crisis, Loeffke stood with Crowe and Woerner in preferring a "phased force build up" over military intervention or a snatch operation. "If we nab Noriega and his supporters nab several American hostages," Loeffke commented, "what do we do next?" As for the "attack now" option, he expressed concerns over the high costs of an invasion in lives, property, and chaos. "The collateral damage to the civilian population (both Panamanian and ours) will not be small. . . . The situation may turn into widespread looting. If we strike and destroy the effectiveness of the PDF there will be almost no Panamanian security forces. Without Panamanian police and [with] the presence of the 1000 or so bad elements who are eager to fight the U.S. the situation may become difficult to control in the city. At the present our families are hostages." Should the United States intervene, he cautioned, "we will need to be prepared to re-establish law

---

[51] Msg, CDR, USARSO, to CINCSO, 042330Z Apr 88; Memos, Loeffke for CINCSO, 4 Apr 88, and USARSO DCSOPS to Crisis Action Team (CAT) Team Chief, 5 Apr 88; Msg, CDR, USARSO, to CINCSO, 052330Z Apr 88. Quote from Interv, author with Rossi, 24 May 89. Intervs, author with Cope, 29 Mar 89, 29 May 89; Draft Activation Order, CINCSO to CDR, USARSO, n.d.; Msg, CINCSO to CDR, USARSO, 082210Z Apr 88.

[52] Msg, CINCSO to CDR, USARSO, 082210Z Apr 88.

and order in Panama. Establishing services to a large city and reconstituting the Panamanian Defense Forces will be major endeavors."[53]

Opinions continued to differ as to when or if President Reagan would order an invasion of Panama. Some Americans and Panamanians predicted U.S. military action at some point in the future, despite the president's decision on 29 March not to resort to armed intervention. Others shared Woerner's belief that military force would not have to be used to resolve the crisis. In prescient words, Loeffke wrote on 9 April, the day JTF-Panama was activated, "It has become apparent that this crisis will not be quickly resolved."[54]

---

[53] Msg, CDR, USARSO, to Department of the Army, 082126Z Apr 88. An earlier draft of the message, "sent by mistake," included a paragraph that read, "History. The future will evaluate us as whether or not we were men of judgment. At the present time common sense dictates we increase the force presence, and give the diplomats and others an opportunity to offer options to Noriega." Msg, CDR, USARSO, to DA, 081609Z Apr 88.

[54] Sitrep 26, USARSO, 9 Apr 88.

3

Violence, "Fissures," and a Prayer Book

April–May 1988

President Reagan's rejection of military intervention to oust Noriega and the failure of William Walker and Michael Kozak to negotiate a settlement did not preclude the use of force or diplomacy to resolve the crisis in Panama at some future date. Meanwhile, contingency planning under SOUTHCOM's auspices continued, as did the flow of U.S. security enhancement forces into the country. As Woerner watched the troop buildup, he warned close advisers of a self-fulfilling prophecy in which the deployment itself could increase the chances for a military showdown. His prediction seemed to gain credence when, on 12 April, the marines sent to Panama for "political" reasons engaged in a two-hour firefight against armed intruders on a U.S. fuel facility. Yet the incident, which could have provoked wider hostilities, instead marked the high point of tension in early 1988. Despite subsequent intrusions and shootings, all of a lesser magnitude, Woerner's fears of events racing out of control were not realized. Indeed, the Reagan administration maintained some hope that Noriega might still be persuaded to resign and leave the country. To that end, direct talks between Kozak and Noriega resumed just days after the firefight. One month later, the United States found itself well removed from the brink of war, although no closer to its policy goal of deposing Noriega.

Noriega Perseveres

As part of the campaign to pressure the general into retirement, the Reagan administration on 8 April announced new economic sanctions. Invoking the International Emergency Economic Powers Act of 1977, the president signed an executive order prohibiting American citizens and companies operating in Panama from paying any taxes or fees owed the Panamanian government. The initiative, portrayed to the news media as a tough measure, only antagonized those American businessmen who, in dealing with Panama, were more concerned about profits and a friendly working environment than the administration's problems with Noriega. Also the Treasury Department, convinced that Noriega would survive the sanctions but that an already depressed Panamanian economy might not, demonstrated its opposition to the move by erecting bureaucratic obstacles to the order's implementation. As one U.S. official observed, "We have ruined a healthy economy, weakened the pro-American middle class, and created conditions for growing Communist influence. You've got to give yourself credit: That's a hell of an achievement for diplomacy!"[1]

Many of Panama's opposition leaders, particularly middle- and upper-class professionals and businessmen who were often the unintended victims of the sanctions, voiced a similar sentiment as they surveyed the economic desolation around them. Panama's banks, which had closed in early March, would not begin reopening until mid-April, and then only for limited services. In the meantime, the unemployment rate moved toward 40 percent as numerous industries folded. Pensioners continued to be hard hit by the cash shortage, as were government workers, who quickly found themselves resorting to the expedient of using their paychecks as currency. The National Civic Crusade continued its efforts to turn economic hardship into organized dissent, but the Panama Defense Forces became increasingly adept at disrupting antigovernment rallies and marches. One opposition leader conceded that widespread fear prevented large turnouts at the NCC's well-publicized demonstrations. But, he noted, somewhat unconvincingly, just the news of a scheduled protest forced the PDF into the streets on a daily basis. The opposition's new strategy: "We plan to wear them out."[2]

The flaw in the strategy was that Noriega and the Panama Defense Forces showed no signs of weakening. To the contrary, the general had recovered quickly from the 16 March coup attempt and had strengthened his control over Panama's armed forces and the government. As for the economic crisis, porous U.S. sanctions, outside assistance, competent advice, and inventive measures kept the economy afloat just enough to avoid political chaos. By the end of March, soon after Assistant Secretary of State for Inter-American Affairs Elliott Abrams assured the world that Noriega was "hanging on by his fingernails," the general, in fact, appeared to have a firm grip on the reins of power.[3]

The PDF's brutal actions at the Marriott Hotel on 28 March served to drive home this point. So did the fact that Noriega was still capable of staging progovernment rallies in which thousands of Panamanians loyal or indebted to him, or threatened with the consequences of nonattendance, filled the streets of the capital, chanting nationalistic slogans and hoisting placards warning that Panama would become another Vietnam for U.S. troops. Noriega himself often referred or alluded to the Vietnam analogy, as, for example, when he somberly told a visiting journalist that, should the United States intervene in Panama, "American mothers are going to see their sons fighting in a nation without necessity." Anti-U.S. propaganda permeated the cities. Regularly, the Ministry of Health reported that U.S. troops entering the country were drug fiends infected with Acquired Immune Deficiency Syndrome (AIDS). The PDF-controlled media also gave an anti-American twist to longstanding social and political divisions within Panama. One broadcast, for example, had black Panamanians of West Indian descent denouncing the United States for trying to reestablish a racist, class-oriented regime in the country. Noriega also suggested that, if necessary, he would go public with information that would cause the Reagan administration great embarrassment. The thinly veiled threat encouraged a flurry

---

[1] Quote from Buckley, *Panama*, p. 136, and see also pp. 133, 135.

[2] Ibid., pp. 128, 134; *Tropic Times*, 20 Apr 88; Msgs, CDR, JTF-Panama, to AIG 9029, 122230Z Apr 88, sub: Panama INTSUM [Intelligence Summary] 56–88, and 132230Z Apr 88, sub: Panama INTSUM 57–88.

[3] Buckley, *Panama*, pp. 133–35.

of speculative editorials and cocktail party gossip in Washington, not to mention unrecorded moments of introspection by top government officials who, at some point in their careers, had crossed paths with "our man in Panama."[4]

On a daily basis, the anti-American propaganda, which served as a political barometer in the crisis, was not nearly so troublesome as the regime's continued harassment of U.S. service personnel and their dependents. The torments inflicted by Panamanian bureaucrats, police, and armed forces acting in concert ranged from the petty annoyances of identity card checks, interrupted travel, traffic bribes, confiscated equipment, night court, and detainment or questioning, to the indignities of sexual insinuations and verbal abuse, physical intimidation and humiliation, intense and threatening interrogations, the occasional strip search, and arrests at gunpoint. Noriega, American military intelligence reported, had personally ordered an intensification of the harassment campaign. The Panama Defense Forces, according to one source, was supposed to detain U.S. servicemen "wandering around the downtown area" and, if need be, "work them over." Noriega reportedly had also created a contingency planning group and directed it to prepare for guerrilla warfare against U.S. forces in Panama. The most publicized and threatening move of the regime's anti-American campaign came in early April, when the general formed the Dignity Battalions, fourteen paramilitary units composed of "patriotic" Panamanians who, according to one intelligence source, were supposed to carry out provocative acts against the forces of "American imperialism" in the country. The so-called battalions, portrayed as a popular militia, had an estimated 2,000 members recruited largely from hoodlum elements, the poor, the Panama Defense Forces, Noriega loyalists, and workers who owed their jobs to the government. How well armed and trained they were was not immediately clear to American military intelligence officers.[5]

More easily detectible were the Soviet-made weapons, mainly AK47s and RPG7s, that began appearing in PDF hands, the result of an arms deal between Noriega and Cuba's Fidel Castro in early March, according to the revelations of a PDF officer who had defected after the failed 16 March coup. There was also sufficient evidence to indicate that the weapons had not arrived unaccompanied. Intelligence sources agreed that the number of Cuban functionaries in Panama had taken a sudden jump, although no one seemed to know for certain just why they

---

[4] The Vietnam-related quote is from ibid., p. 141, and see also p. 132. Msgs, 242330Z Mar 88; Foreign Broadcast Information Service (FBIS) Chiva Chiva to AIG 4677, 051437Z Apr 88; CDR, JTF-Panama, to AIG 9029, 122230Z Apr 88, sub: Panama INTSUM 56–88.

[5] A fact sheet written by SOUTHCOM's Center for Treaty Affairs, dated 22 April 1988, listed eighty-three cases in which the Panama Defense Forces harassed U.S. service personnel and their dependents between 21 February and 19 April 1988. The list included everything from minor inconveniences to a firefight at the Arraiján Tank Farm on 12 April (see this chapter, pp. 69–71). A typical entry told of a military policeman who "was detained, threatened with being shot and humiliated (i.e., he was directed to drop his pants, jump in the air and shake his underwear)." See also Msgs, Air Force Office of Special Investigations (AFOSI), Howard Air Force Base Base, to HQ, AFOSI, 242030Z Mar 88; Naval Investigative Service Agency (NAVINVSERVRA) to JCS, 042147Z Apr 88, sub: IIR; ibid., 052240Z Apr 88, sub: IIR; ibid., 081900Z Apr 88; CDR, 470th MI Bde, to U.S. Defense Attaché Office (USDAO), 102355Z Apr 88, sub: Current Attitudes and Future Actions and Intentions of the FDP; ibid., 152316Z Apr 88, sub: SOCSOUTH Sitrep #18; CDR, SOCSOUTH, 061820Z Apr 88, sub: Sitrep No. 6; and CDR, 470th MI Bde, to USDAO, 102350Z Apr 88, sub: Panamanian Military Adopts New Measures in the Face of the Continuing Crisis.

were there. Maj. Gen. Bernard Loeffke recorded in his diary that the Cubans had come to assist in the propaganda war against the United States. Other, unconfirmed reports placed them with PDF units. One source indicated that at least thirteen Cuban "academic instructors" were living on the military base at Rio Hato, allegedly teaching the natural sciences to PDF personnel stationed there.[6]

In late March, three Cubans were apprehended while videotaping the main flight line at Howard Air Force Base. The episode linked the men directly to another concern of U.S. officials in Panama: the increased level of PDF surveillance of American housing areas, bases, and facilities. The surveillance served as an unambiguous reminder of the acute vulnerability of the American community in Panama. Although the Southern Command postulated that the Panamanian military might only be trying to obtain advance warning of any impending evacuation of American civilians, a sure signal of imminent hostilities, that explanation, even if accurate in some cases, did not explain why the PDF was continuing its surveillance of uninhabited facilities such as the Arraiján Tank Farm north of Howard.[7]

There was another unanswered question regarding the surveillance: was it linked to the increased number of Panamanian intrusions onto U.S. bases and facilities? Many of those installations were surrounded by thick, double-canopied jungle and had always been regarded by burglars, hunters, and poachers as violable territory. As the country's economy declined, more and more of these people risked capture or worse in order to eke out a living. But some intruders that were sighted and occasionally apprehended by U.S. patrols wore camouflage suits and paint, thus raising concerns about surveillance and possible sabotage. The Southern Command and its components had identified many "soft" targets where a small hostile force could inflict enough physical damage to have a significant political impact. Part of the mission of the incoming security enhancement forces would be to prevent this from happening.

First Blood

Military police arriving in Panama generally assumed responsibility for the security of U.S. Army facilities, while augmented Air Force security police patrolled Howard Air Force Base. But guarding U.S. Navy facilities, such as the Rodman Naval Station, the Farfan antenna site, and the Arraiján Tank Farm, required more manpower than the Marine security force company billeted in barracks on Rodman had to spare, even after it had been augmented by the Marine Fleet Anti-Terrorist

---

[6] Msg, CDR, 470th MI Bde, to USDAO, 102355Z Apr 88, sub: Current Attitudes and Future Actions and Intentions of the FDP; Buckley, *Panama*, p. 130; *Tropic Times*, 23 Mar 88; Diary, Bernard Loeffke, 13 Apr 88; Msgs, NAVINVSERVRA to JCS, 052240Z Apr 88, sub: IIR, and CDR, JTF-Panama, to AIG 9029, 122230Z Apr 88, sub: INTSUM 56–88; Interv, author with Lt Col Michael Mallory, U.S. Army, 29 Mar 89, Fort Clayton, Panama. Col. Paul Morgan, the USARSO deputy chief of staff for intelligence at the time, noted later that, while the Cubans and Nicaraguans gave Noriega some advice and assistance, neither country wanted to become too close to the general for fear of tarnishing their image throughout the rest of Latin America, where Noriega was generally despised or ridiculed. Interv, author with Col Paul Morgan, U.S. Army, 7 Jul 89, U.S. Special Operations Command, MacDill AFB, Fla.

[7] Msgs, 221710Z Mar 88; NAVINVSERVRA to JCS, 042147Z Apr 88, sub: FDP Continues Surveillance of US Military Installations; CDR, 470th MI Bde, to USDAO, 102350Z Apr 88, sub: IIR; ibid., 081900Z Apr 88; CINCSO to JCS, 120600Z Apr 88, sub: SCJ3 Sitrep 012 April; and CDR, JTF-Panama, to AIG 9029, 132230Z Apr 88, sub: INTSUM 57–88.

Violence, "Fissures," and a Prayer Book

Security Team platoon. Once the Joint Chiefs informed Woerner that a reinforced Marine rifle company would be sent to Panama in the wake of the Marriott incident, the decision was made to have small detachments from the unit bolster security at Rodman and the Farfan site, next to Howard. These dispositions would leave the bulk of the company to move onto the Arraiján Tank Farm.

Before Company I, 3d Battalion, 4th Marines, left the United States, its commander, Capt. Joseph P. Valore, received photographs of the three Navy sites and learned of his assignment to guard them. Even so, the marines were not entirely clear as to the extent of their mission in Panama. Would they engage strictly in security enhancement, or would they also be the advance element for a brigade-size combat force? The question arose because ELABORATE MAZE listed a Marine expeditionary brigade on its time-phased force deployment list, and all indications were that such a unit would be deployed within ten days. Consequently, on 1 April, a three-man advance element from the 6th Marine Expeditionary Brigade stationed at Camp Lejeune, North Carolina, arrived in Panama to discuss prospective troop movements with officers from U.S. Army, South, and U.S. Navy, South (NAVSO), SOUTHCOM's naval component. The group was followed on 6 April by Col. William J. Conley, the brigade's chief of staff, who flew into Howard on the same day as Company I. Conley believed that his primary mission was to prepare the way for the deployment of up to two of the brigade's infantry battalions together with Marine aviation assets. For this reason, he initially regarded Valore's rifle company not just as a security enhancement element, but as the core around which a much larger combat force would soon be built. As the senior marine present, Conley assumed command of the Marine reinforcements arriving in Panama. His Marine Forces headquarters, in turn, was placed under NAVSO's operational control.[8]

On 7 April, Valore toured the Arraiján Tank Farm, then returned to Rodman Naval Station, where Company I had "planted its flag," to meet with members of the Marine FAST platoon. Since its arrival in March, the platoon had been conducting mobile patrols on the tank farm in response to an increasing number of unauthorized intrusions, about which Valore was briefed in detail. The next day, the captain deployed his men in accordance with guidance received from Conley. A squad(+) moved to the Farfan antenna site, while a platoon(-) remained at Rodman to bolster perimeter security. The rest of Company I moved into the fuel depot. The facility, according to the Marine Corps' official history of the Panama crisis, "covered approximately two square kilometers of rolling grassland, apparently designed to resemble a golf course from the air, but was surrounded by dense jungle, which provided excellent avenues of approach both to the [37] storage tanks and to Howard Air Force Base to the south. In the jungle, visibility was limited to a few feet, even by day, and movement was slow and exhausting. . . . But for the most part the tank farm was not fenced as it bordered the Pan-American, or Thatcher, Highway, the best high-speed avenue of approach in the country." Valore's Marine element on the depot included two infantry platoons, an 81-mm. mortar section (two mortars), a DRAGON and a TOW (antitank weapons)

---

[8] Intervs, Benis Frank with Maj Joseph P. Valore, USMC, 29 Mar 90, Camp Lejeune, N.C.; Col Donald F. Anderson, USMC, 30 Mar 90, Camp Lejeune, N.C.; and Janet Len-Rios with Col William J. Conley, USMC, 2 Sep 88, Rodman Naval Station, Panama. U.S. Marine Corps, USMC Command Chronology and Supporting Documents, 6 April 1988–31 May 1990, History and Museums Division, Headquarters, U.S. Marine Corps, Washington, D.C.

section, an artillery forward observer team, a heavy machine gun squad, and a detachment of engineers. The previous year, the unit had received jungle training on Okinawa.[9]

Valore divided the grounds of the tank farm into two zones, each of which became a tactical area of responsibility (TAOR) for an infantry platoon. The captain's original intention was to use a system of shifting patrol bases as a means of securing the facility, but he soon decided to conduct patrols out of "one set of good positions" instead. One reason for the change in tactics was his realization that the frequent relocation of bases would "waste time and effort moving command posts and communications equipment." Another reason was the constant surveillance his marines were coming under. Once on the tank farm, the Leathernecks noticed an increasing number of disabled Panamanian vehicles near the northern perimeter and the main entrance. A report noted that the "drivers appeared to be taking an inordinate amount of time to repair their cars."[10]

Valore established his operations center and ordered his men to set up observation and listening posts and to begin aggressive patrolling. Additional sensors were also positioned around the perimeter of the tank farm and along the jungle-covered trails into the facility. These measures produced quick results, as the sensors indicated significant movement in the vicinity. On 9 April, Company I had its first glimpse of intruders when a Marine patrol sighted two men dressed in camouflage suits and paint.[11]

On their fourth night on the tank farm, the marines spotted a group of about nine intruders. When a patrol began to pursue them, the unidentified men split up into two or three smaller groups. Whenever the marines came close to capturing one group, the other intruders would maneuver to envelop the patrol. The patrol itself finally split into two teams in an effort to outmaneuver the targets. Suddenly, a trip flare went off, followed by bursts of gunfire. When the shooting stopped, Marine Cpl. Ricardo M. Villahermosa lay wounded. He was evacuated to Gorgas Army Hospital on Ancon Hill, where he died an hour after midnight, the first American military fatality connected with the Panama crisis. It was suspected and quickly confirmed that the mortal wound had been inflicted by friendly fire.[12]

The death of Villahermosa "got everyone upset," according to Valore. Maj. Eddie Keith, the commanding officer of the security company at the Marine barracks at Rodman, told the captain that his men should not have been on patrol with rounds in the chambers of their weapons. To go out "locked and loaded," Keith elaborated, violated standing procedures for security duty on the tank farm. In response, Valore explained that Colonel Conley, an officer who remembered well how a restrictive weapons policy had contributed to the deaths of 241 marines in the 1983 Beirut bombing, had authorized placing magazines in the M16 rifles and rounds in the chambers. Furthermore, Valore made clear with Conley's backing,

---

[9] Valore Interv, 29 Mar 90; USMC Command Chronology and Supporting Documents, 6 April 1988–31 May 1990. The description of the Arraiján Tank Farm is from Lt. Col. Nicholas E. Reynolds, *Just Cause: Marine Operations in Panama, 1988–1990* (Washington, D.C.: History and Museums Division, Headquarters, U.S. Marine Corps, 1996), pp. 3–4.

[10] Valore Interv, 29 Mar 90. First and second quotes from Reynolds, *Just Cause*, p. 6. Third quote from USMC Command Chronology and Supporting Documents, 6 April 1988–31 May 1990.

[11] USMC Command Chronology and Supporting Documents, 6 April 1988–31 May 1990.

[12] Ibid.; Valore Interv, 29 Mar 90; Reynolds, *Just Cause*, p. 7.

he intended to continue this less restrictive policy.[13] The next day the marines dealt with the death of their comrade as they went about their routine activities and prepared for another night of guard duty and patrolling. They had no way of knowing that, on the heels of the previous night's tragedy, they were about to participate in the most violent and the most controversial incident of the two-year crisis in Panama preceding Operation JUST CAUSE.[14]

The first indication of what was to come occurred at dusk on 12 April, when the platoon responsible for the west side of the tank farm reported probing activity by up to ten armed people. An hour or so later, reports began coming into Company I's operations center concerning another, larger body of intruders, possibly forty to fifty, moving about Arraiján. At that time, Valore had a surveillance and target acquisition (STA) team of thirteen marines and a corpsman in the western extreme of the tank farm, about 700 meters from friendly lines. In addition, an element from the 3d Platoon was out on patrol, while another from the 1st Platoon was about to begin patrolling. The reports prompted Valore to move with his first sergeant to a better vantage point where they could confirm the sightings firsthand and assess the situation. Once at their new location, the two men observed at least a dozen intruders between the tanks and the Inter-American Highway.

A Marine patrol on the Arraiján Tank Farm, *with jungle in the background*

As the Marine company's 1st Platoon consolidated near Valore's location, shots were

---

[13] Valore Interv, 29 Mar 90; Reynolds, *Just Cause*, pp. 6–8.

[14] The following account of the 12 April 1988 tank farm incident is based on the following sources: Intervs, author with Maj Tom King, U.S. Army, and Maj Clyde Vaughn, U.S. Army, 18 May 89, Fort Leavenworth, Kans.; Maj Billy Ray Fitzgerald, U.S. Army, 28 Apr 89, Fort Clayton, Panama; Maj William Graves, U.S. Army, 20 Aug 91, Fort Leavenworth, Kans.; and Maj John Mulholland, U.S. Army, 30 May 91, Fort Leavenworth, Kans.; Frank with Valore, 29 Mar 90; and Len-Rios with Conley, 2 Sep 88. Log, JTF-Panama Duty Officer, 12 Apr 88; Note, Anderson to SOUTHCOM Dir of Opns (SCJ–3), 130600R Apr 88. Msgs, CDR, JTF-Panama, to AIG 9029, 131600Z Apr 88, sub: INTSUM 1–88; CDR, Marine Forces-Panama (COMMARFORPM) to CDR, JTF-Panama, 131700Z Apr 88, sub: Arraiján Tank Farm Incident Report #1; CDR, USARSO, to CDR, JTF-Panama, and CINCSO, 132000Z Apr 88, sub: USARSO Sitrep No. 30; SecDef to CINCSO, 132027Z Apr 88, sub: Public Affairs Guidance-Arraiján Tank Farm Incident; CDR, JTF-Panama, to CINCSO, 132200Z Apr 88, sub: COMJTF-PM Sitrep No. 2; CDR, JTF-Panama, to CINCSO, 140022Z Apr 88, sub: Special Sitrep-Firing at the Arraiján Tank Farm; CINCSO to JCS, 141830Z Apr 88, sub: Arraiján Tank Farm Incident No. 2; and USSOUTHCOM to Chairman, Joint Chiefs of Staff (CJCS), 142025Z Apr 88, sub: Arraiján: CINCSO Assessment. Memo, Loeffke for CINCSO, 14 Apr 88, sub: Update #54; Reynolds, *Just Cause*, pp. 8–10.

fired from a ravine located to the front, between the captain's position and the highway. As the marines returned fire, Valore received an urgent report from the STA team, which moments earlier had reported probing in its area. Trip flares were going off, he was told, and ten to fifteen armed intruders were maneuvering against the small group. The platoon sergeant with the STA team requested illumination rounds from the company's 81-mm. mortars, but Valore initially denied the request. He relented after receiving reports that convinced him the intruders were moving with hostile intent against another platoon in the southwest sector of the tank farm. As the volume of small arms and illumination fire increased, the STA team reported intruders still moving to encircle it and implored Valore to authorize the use of high explosive rounds. "Sir, I need some f——g mortars," the captain heard the team sergeant whisper urgently over the radio. Although the surveillance team had yet to come under direct fire, Valore approved the request on the grounds that other units were taking fire and firing back. He was not going to risk letting the intruders maneuver to within grenade range of the STA team.

Within minutes, "all hell broke loose" in the vicinity of the surveillance team. Then the 1st Platoon took more fire from the front. "At that time," Valore recalls, "all bets were off, and we opened up with the machine gun and the Mark19 that was available."[15] The first sergeant directed the fire into a ravine in front of the platoon. The effect of the Mark19 chain gun, which could fire over three hundred 40-mm. antipersonnel rounds per minute, was "devastating," causing marines who moments before had perceived themselves in immediate jeopardy to cheer loudly.

Word of the firefight spread rapidly. Valore maintained continuous communications with Conley and the Marine barracks. These reports were relayed up the chain of command to the JTF-Panama operations center at Fort Clayton and to Colonel Rossi, the joint task force's chief of staff. From his office and, later, from the operations center, Rossi, joined by Cols. Jay Cope and Paul F. Morgan, JTF-Panama's ranking operations and intelligence officers, respectively, began the process of crisis management at the tactical level. One of his first actions was to place the 193d Infantry Brigade, the 16th Military Police Brigade, and the 1st Battalion, 228th Aviation, on full alert. The 193d's mortar platoon began setting up its weapons on the athletic field at Fort Kobbe, preparing to fire them over Howard Air Force Base into the Arraiján Tank Farm. An infantry platoon at Kobbe was ordered to move to Howard's flight line, adjacent to the fort, for possible employment. Meanwhile, at the air base, security forces closed off the installation and shut down the main access road curving through it. A total of ten helicopters were placed on strip alert: 3 UH–60 Black Hawks, 3 UH–1 Hueys, 2 AH–1 Cobras, and 2 OH–58 Kiowas. Of these, only an OH–58 actually deployed over the tank farm, providing aerial lighting for the marines. An AC–130 Spectre gunship on hand at Howard was also launched to track the intruders with its infrared camera. At one point in the evening, the Marine command post at Rodman informed the operations center at Fort Clayton that PDF buses were speeding with their headlights turned off from the vicinity of the Bridge of the Americas toward the tank farm, perhaps to reinforce the intruders. The marines at Rodman asked

---

[15] Valore Interv, 29 Mar 90.

permission to block the road. Rossi and Cope discussed the request, then ordered the Inter-American Highway blocked as a prudent defensive measure.

While Rossi, Cope, and Morgan issued orders on behalf of JTF-Panama, the SOUTHCOM Center for Treaty Affairs was contacting key PDF leaders, including the director of operations, Col. Elías Castillo. Castillo denied PDF involvement in the firefight but agreed to send a senior officer to the tank farm in an attempt to arrange a cease-fire and disengage the forces. Another Panamanian officer, Capt. Moisés Cortizo, commander of the 5th Infantry Company at Fort Amador, agreed to provide PDF elements to assist in controlling the massive traffic snarl on the blocked Inter-American Highway. Cortizo himself went to the Arraiján Tank Farm, where he met with Conley.

Around 2200, General Loeffke arrived. The general had decided to go personally to the tank farm after he learned that Valore was requesting fire support from Cobra attack helicopters. The problem was that Cobras could not be launched except by order of the JTF-Panama commander, and Loeffke wanted to have a firsthand look at the situation before making any such decision. When he arrived at the Marine operations center dressed in civilian clothes, the company's exasperated executive officer asked him who the hell he was. The answer sufficed to have Loeffke promptly escorted to the front of the tank farm, where he received an account of the night's activities directly from Valore.

By that time the shooting, which had gone on intermittently for over two hours, had tapered off. Loeffke ordered a cease-fire and, accompanied by Cortizo and others, rode with lights on and horns blaring into the area separating the marines and the intruders. With the end of the firefight, Valore recalled the surveillance and target acquisition team and his men still on patrol. The marines, once assembled, reported no casualties. The captain then asked permission to police the battlefield to determine the extent of any damage inflicted on the intruders. Loeffke, to Valore's surprise, denied the request. The general also refused to let a Special Forces (SF) team do an immediate patrol outside the tank farm. A sweep of the area, Loeffke had decided, would not take place until dawn, several hours away. In the meantime, Valore was told to report with a good portion of his company to the Marine barracks for a debriefing.

Rossi and Conley presided over the "hot wash" with the marines that commenced around 0100. During the session, Valore and his men answered questions, and JTF-Panama component commanders discussed the lessons to be derived from the just-concluded incident. While the hot wash was in progress, marines remaining on the tank farm watched through night-vision devices "as a number of the intruders apparently received first aid" and as others "either wounded or dead" were dragged away and evacuated. From various other sources came reports of blacked-out ambulances and PDF buses speeding from the Arraiján Tank Farm toward Panama City.[16] There was thus every reason to believe that the intruders had suffered serious casualties. At issue was whether there would be any remaining evidence to substantiate this assumption by the time the sweep scheduled for 0700 commenced.

Conley was in charge of the sweep. Rossi, at SOUTHCOM's direction, was present "to ensure that a USARSO team is on hand to observe the sweep and make sure it is well done," a hint of doubt concerning the marines' ability to do the job.

---

[16] Reynolds, *Just Cause*, p. 8.

Rossi later reported to Cisneros that, as of noon on 13 April, no evidence had been found to suggest the marines had been fired on or had inflicted casualties. That afternoon, in accordance with a decision Loeffke had made during the incident, a battalion from the 193d relieved Company I on the tank farm. Valore's men were being "stood down" for forty-eight hours of "rest and recreation." In the meantime, officers at the Southern Command and JTF-Panama tried to reconstruct what exactly had happened to the marines the night of 12 April.[17]

The initial findings passed up the chain of command tried to superimpose order over a chaotic event. Predictably, the reports contained inaccurate, even some contradictory information, but by and large they supported, with a few qualifications, the marines' version of the firefight. USARSO military intelligence assets available to JTF-Panama reported that at least five sensors had been activated on the tank farm, "indicating the likelihood of an intrusion of a relatively large group." For his part, Loeffke informed Woerner, "I am convinced that hostile activity led to both firefights [11 and 12 April]." Cisneros, with Woerner's authorization, reported to the Joint Chiefs that, although no evidence of the opposing force or its whereabouts had been found, movement sensors at the Arraiján Tank Farm had detected at least ten to twelve intruders. Other intelligence sources spoke of ambulances arriving at the site and estimated up to twenty-three casualties among the intruders. On 14 April, Woerner made his own assessment in a message to Crowe. The SOUTHCOM commander admitted to the limited evidence available, but cited sensor activations and Marine sightings as indication that perhaps ten to fifteen intruders had entered the tank farm. The physical evidence of a firefight was less conclusive, he added, but, in his judgment, a PDF element had gone onto the tank farm, fired a few rounds, and initiated other hostile actions as part of Noriega's efforts to disparage and to sow confusion among the newly arrived security forces.[18]

In the days that followed, the regime's psychological warfare, which according to JTF-Panama demonstrated "a high degree of sophistication in propaganda and disinformation," made the most of Villahermosa's death and the firefight a night later. A communiqué from the Panamanian Ministry of Government and Justice expressed sympathy over the death of the marine, denied PDF involvement in the incident, and taunted that "not even the most naive could believe that a foreign patrol could infiltrate the largest US military air base . . . in Latin America without having a single one of its members captured, injured or killed by the most powerful army in the world." As for the 12 April incident, Cortizo was quoted as calling it a

---

[17] Quotes from ibid. See also Note, Anderson to SCJ–3, 130600R Apr 88. Using the analogy that getting right back on a horse after a fall was the best remedy, the commander, 1st Battalion, 508th Infantry, urged that the Marine company be allowed to stay on the tank farm but was told by Colonel Conley and the Navy officer commanding at Rodman that the decision to pull the marines out was final. That Captain Valore had approved mortar fire on his own authority was a cause of great concern, even with the battalion commander. Interv, author with Lt Col Robert Barefield, U.S. Army, 7 Nov 90, Fort Leavenworth, Kans.

[18] Interv, Benis Frank with Col Thomas W. Roberts, USMC, 30 Mar 90, Camp Lejeune, N.C. Quotes from Msg, CDR, JTF-Panama, to CINCSO, 132200Z Apr 88. Msgs, CINCSO to JCS, 141830Z Apr 88; and USSOUTHCOM to CJCS, 142025Z Apr 88. One potential source of evidence as to the number of intruders was the videotapes from the AC–130 that had flown over the tank farm. The tapes showed thirty to forty people, but the poor quality of the images made determining if the individuals were marines or intruders impossible. Msg, CDR, JTF-Panama, to AIG 9029, 182200Z Apr 88, sub: INTREP No. 5–88.

"provocation, an illegal action in Panamanian territory." "If there was shooting," the PDF captain added, "it was among the US soldiers who are killing themselves." In what would become a recurrent theme, regime-controlled media depicted the marines as hysterical, doped-up hotheads firing their weapons at themselves and at jungle foliage. The whole incident showed that "they are even afraid of palm trees," Noriega quipped.[19]

The "Night of the Swaying Palm Trees" became a contentious issue, but not, as one might have expected, between the marines and the Panamanian military. Company I's 1st Sgt. Alexander Nevgloski dismissed Noriega's gibes by saying, "We don't shoot at palm trees unless they're shooting at us." What puzzled and then embittered the marines were insinuations emanating from JTF-Panama and the Southern Command that the PDF propaganda might be true. The problem began with the debriefing at the Marine barracks, which in one form or another was repeated over the course of several days. While Valore recalled several of the colonels present saying positive things to him, others privy to the interrogation likened it to the Spanish Inquisition. The questioning seemed excessively critical at times and intended to cast doubt on the veracity of Company I's account of the incident. This was also the impression being passed to the commander of the 1st Battalion, 508th Infantry (Airborne), elements of which were about to relieve the marines at the tank farm: in some way, not specified, the Leathernecks were said to have "screwed up." The matter came to a head at a press conference held by SOUTHCOM's Public Affairs Office. Sergeant Nevgloski had no more finished depicting the intruders as "highly professional," when "an informed U.S. source" told reporters that "anomalies" existed in the marines' account of events of 11–12 April, that there was a lack of evidence to indicate an intrusion took place on the twelfth, and that the marines were inexperienced, did not know the terrain, and were nervous about being "put into what they felt was a combat situation early after their arrival in Panama." The company(-) had been taken off the tank farm after the shootings, the spokesperson added, presumably to compose itself. In the meantime, they had been replaced by "more seasoned troops of the 193rd Light Infantry Brigade." When pressed for further information, including whether the marines had been "shooting at shadows," a SOUTHCOM information officer replied, "At this point in time, we don't categorically rule anything out."[20]

Confronted with an apparent lack of official support, Valore, with Conley's support, refused to alter his account of the firefight. Loeffke, for his part, did not question Valore's insistence that hostile forces had fired on the marines. But a rumor began circulating that the general, together with key members of his staff and their counterparts at the Southern Command, regarded the marines' conduct on the twelfth as overreactive—"undisciplined" and "trigger happy." The marines, with their professionalism and competency being called into question, began to

---

[19] All quotes except Noriega's from Msg, CDR, JTF-Panama, to AIG 9029, 132230Z Apr 88. Translation of *La Crítica* editorial, "Marines Make Fools of Themselves," 14 Apr 88. Noriega quote from Buckley, *Panama*, p. 140.

[20] All quotes except the second, eighth, and last from *Tropic Times*, 18 Apr 88. Interv, author with Roberts, 30 Mar 90. Second quote from Interv, author with Graves, 20 Aug 91. *Washington Post*, 16 Apr 88. Eighth quote from *New York Times*, 14 Apr 88. Last quote from Buckley, *Panama*, p. 140. Valore Interv, 29 Mar 90; Maj Robert B. Neller, USMC, Marines in Panama: 1988–1990 (Paper, USMC Staff College, Quantico, Va., 1991); Reynolds, *Just Cause*, p. 9.

speak out critically on what they considered the "garrison attitude" of the U.S. forces stationed in Panama. Company I had been sent to Panama on an "operational mission," only to find "a business as usual as much as possible mentality" on the part of the in-country forces. "We were down there to take care of a mission," one Marine officer declared. "We weren't going home at night." Several marines voiced their opinion that Woerner would feel more comfortable in a pinstriped suit. At the root of the charges and countercharges was a difference of perception, in which the viewpoints of high-ranking officers based in Panama, for whom the crisis was a politico-military minefield and who had been told not to exacerbate the situation or start a war, clashed with those of the newly arrived marines, who had been given an assignment that placed them squarely in the line of hostile fire. This perceptual gap would widen as the crisis continued. At the outset, however, what seemed painfully obvious to the marines was that they could not count on the support of JTF-Panama and the Southern Command in any incident that carried with it the danger of drawing the United States into a military confrontation with the Panama Defense Forces.[21]

Behind the scenes, in a two-track response to the events of 12 April, the Southern Command took steps to prevent a further escalation of the crisis, while making the gravity of the situation clear to the Panamanian military. To begin with, the command approved Loeffke's request to postpone a company-size airmobile exercise at Madden Dam that JTF-Panama had planned as a joint training event and show of force. Citing increased tension in the crisis, Cisneros went even further in declaring that SOUTHCOM's Operations Directorate would require at least seventy-two hours' notice to consider all future exercises. At the same time, he conveyed a message to the Panama Defense Forces that was anything but conciliatory. Woerner, in keeping with orders he had received from Washington following Delvalle's ouster, had discontinued his meetings with Noriega. Cisneros, however, continued to consult with PDF colonels on treaty matters. After the firefight, he met with Colonel Castillo and delivered a virtual ultimatum. Not only would the Panamanian military be held responsible for armed intrusions on U.S. facilities, but the death of any U.S. serviceman by hostile fire would assuredly produce a military response. When the colonel swore that Panama's armed forces were not involved in any provocations, Cisneros countered that Noriega was using the intrusions in hopes of creating a Panamanian martyr. The PDF colonel charged that Cisneros was calling him a liar. Cisneros replied that the colonel was, in fact, either a liar or a dupe. The confrontation ended on this note of mutual recrimination, casting doubts over how productive any future meetings might be.[22]

---

[21] The quotes concerning the marines' perception of the in-country forces come from Intervs, author with Valore, 29 Mar 90; Conley, 2 Sep 88; and Anderson, 30 Mar 90. The first two quotes expressing the joint task force's perceptions of the marines come from several informal conversations between the author and JTF-Panama officers and enlisted men. The Marine Corps later awarded Valore and Sergeant Nevgloski the Bronze Star for their actions on the tank farm.

[22] Msg, CINCSO to CDR, JTF-Panama, 150006Z Apr 88, sub: SCJ3 Guidance Message No. 4; Interv, author with Brig Gen Marc Cisneros, U.S. Army, 1 May 89, Quarry Heights, Panama. Msg, CINCSO to CDR, JTF-Panama, 092154Z Apr 88, sub: SCJ3 Guidance Message No. 1, had directed JTF-Panama to develop a major training event to be used as a show of force.

Violence, "Fissures," and a Prayer Book

From the perspective of Fort Clayton, the "initiation by fire" on 11–12 April validated the need for JTF-Panama as an operational headquarters in the crisis, but highlighted several deficiencies in the organization just three days after its activation. As Loeffke informed Vuono, the firefight was "in a way beneficial: it forced our JTF to operate and get our procedures smoothed out." Within a few days of the tank farm incident, the JTF-Panama operations center, which had been the near-exclusive preserve of Army "green suiters," tended more to a "purple" hue, as the other service components began sending representatives, some on a daily basis, others at least during periods of rising tension. The command also moved to improve joint communications links. The hot wash conducted by Rossi after the firefight had revealed communication problems between military police at Fort Amador and Navy security police at the Rodman Naval Station, and between U.S. ground elements and the AC–130 conducting aerial reconnaissance of the Arraiján Tank Farm that night. To improve joint tactical communications, U.S. Army, South, on behalf of JTF-Panama, provided secure FM radios to the Air Force and Navy.[23]

The firefight also raised command and control issues that demanded immediate attention. After 9 April, Loeffke had assumed that, as the JTF-Panama commander, he exercised operational control over Company I through Colonel Conley, whom he understood to be his Marine Forces-Panama, or MARFOR, component commander. Yet, when Loeffke arrived at the tank farm in the last stages of the firefight, he found the Navy officer in command at Rodman wanting "to run the battle" on the conviction that Company I still fell under the Navy's control. "We stayed out of it until the marines started shooting HE mortar rounds and asking for Army air," Loeffke reported later to Vuono. "We then took over and asked [the] Navy captain to monitor only."[24]

The confusion surrounding who was in charge the night of the firefight apparently stemmed from the ambiguity surrounding command and control arrangements discussed shortly after Valore's rifle company and Colonel Conley had arrived in Panama. In talks between the colonel and the NAVSO commander, Rear Adm. Jerry G. Gneckow, the admiral informed Conley that Company I came under NAVSO's operational control and would provide direct support to the Marine security force company at Rodman for the purpose of securing naval installations in Panama. In the event that the SOUTHCOM commander activated JTF-Panama, Gneckow went on to say, then that joint headquarters, not NAVSO, would exercise operational control of the marines in Panama, with Conley assuming the role of the joint task force's MARFOR component commander. On 9 April, immediately after Woerner did activate JTF-Panama, Conley sent an officer to Fort Clayton to provide liaison with the new headquarters. At Rodman, he also continued to work on his original mission of planning for a follow-on flow of forces from the 6th Marine Expeditionary Brigade.

All of this seemed straight forward enough, except for the fact that the chain of command of the Navy captain at Rodman did not run directly through

---

[23] Intervs, author with Fitzgerald, 28 Apr 89; Majs Clyde Vaughan and Angel Rivera, U.S. Army, 16 Mar 89, Fort Leavenworth, Kans.; and Maj Gen Bernard Loeffke, U.S. Army, 27 Mar 89, Fort Clayton, Panama. Quote from Msg, CDR, USARSO, to DA, 152330Z Apr 88, sub: Update No. 9. Msg, CDR, JTF-Panama, to CINCSO, 140022Z Apr 88.

[24] Msg, CDR, USARSO, to DA, 152330Z Apr 88, sub: Update No. 9.

SOUTHCOM's Navy component, but rather back through a different chain to the U.S. Atlantic Command (LANTCOM), a unified headquarters in Norfolk, Virginia, commanded by a full admiral. From the Navy captain's perspective, therefore, Valore's company was not a SOUTHCOM or a NAVSO asset but a unit assigned by headquarters under LANTCOM in support of the Marine security force company at Rodman. To complicate matters further, the tank farm was a facility that fell under the naval station's direct responsibility. Thus, when the firefight erupted, the Navy captain arrived on the scene to direct the marines he believed to be under his control. His encounter with Loeffke, who also claimed control over the marines, revealed an urgent need to reach an understanding on command and control arrangements now that JTF-Panama was a functioning headquarters.[25]

The matter took almost two weeks to sort out. The Navy, according to Cisneros, balked at placing the marines under the operational control of an Army general. But the Southern Command asserted its right to determine the assignment of combat forces in the theater, and on 25 April Conley formally became the commander of all Marine forces in Panama, to include Company I, the Marine security force company at Rodman, and the Fleet Anti-Terrorist Security Team platoon. Under JTF-Panama, these marines remained responsible for the security of the naval station, the tank farm, Galeta Island, and the Farfan antenna site. In summarizing the causes of the command and control snarl, Loeffke stated simply, "We didn't know one another." Rossi, after trying to explain the problem, remarked, "Now you know why we're all confused most of the time."[26]

As the issue of who controlled Company I was being worked out, Conley and the Air Force component commander for JTF-Panama requested more troops to perform the separate set of security enhancement missions assigned to each of them. The Air Force cited the vulnerability of Howard Air Force Base as the principal reason for wanting more security police. As for the marines, the 12 April firefight had only confirmed their predeployment belief that a company(-) was too small a unit to secure the tank farm properly. At minimum, a battalion was needed since it contained the personnel and the support assets that would enable the marines to perform their security enhancement mission more efficiently, while having the capability to sustain themselves from within their own organization. In that the Joint Chiefs had originally thought about sending a Marine brigade to Panama, Conley believed his request for a battalion reasonable and completely justified. (Valore noted later that, when JTF-Panama decided to pull his marines off the tank farm for 48 hours, elements from an Army battalion had taken their place.)[27]

Loeffke recommended to Woerner that the Southern Command approve the Air Force's request for a hundred additional security police for Howard, but he took a different tack on Conley's appeal. Instead of bringing in more marines, he suggested that MARFOR troop levels be increased by rotating USARSO units,

---

[25] Intervs, Frank with Valore, 29 Mar 90; author with Anderson, 30 Mar 90; and Conley, 2 Sep 88. USMC Command Chronology and Supporting Documents, 6 April 1988–31 May 1990; Reynolds, *Just Cause*, pp. 5–6.

[26] Msg, CDR, U.S. Navy, South (COMUSNAVSO), to CINCSO, 291846Z Apr 88; Neller, Marines in Panama; Intervs, author with Anderson, 30 Mar 90; Loeffke, 27 Mar 89; and Rossi, 24 May 89. The quotes are from the Loeffke and Rossi interviews, respectively.

[27] Memo, Loeffke for CINCSO, 19 Apr 88, sub: Update #55; Anderson Interv, 30 Mar 90.

namely military police and elements from the 193d, under Conley's operational control. The proposal stemmed in part from doubts Loeffke and his staff still harbored about the suitability of what they perceived as the marines' "warrior mentality" for security enhancement duties. There was also the issue of sending too warlike a signal to Noriega and the Panamanian military should more U.S. combat power be brought in from outside Panama. The deployment of Conley's headquarters and Company I to Panama had served the purpose of "priming the pump." Should a Marine expeditionary unit or a Marine expeditionary brigade be needed, the foundations had been set for its deployment. But there was no reason at the moment, Loeffke believed, to increase the Marine presence in Panama. Woerner agreed and approved Loeffke's recommendation to use USARSO forces to bolster the marines. The initial Army units to come under Marine Forces-Panama on a temporary basis included elements of the 519th Military Police Battalion and Company B, 1st Battalion, 508th Infantry.[28]

DÉJÀ VU

Valore and his men returned to their security mission on the tank farm a few days after the firefight. In the weeks that followed, they received additional equipment and manpower—beacons, loudspeakers, video equipment, additional sensors, Air Force and Navy dog teams, and the USARSO elements Loeffke had promised—to help them deal with trespassers on the facility. In related operations, other U.S. units were trying to get a handle on the exact composition and intentions of armed intruders in the Rodman Ammunition Supply Point north of the tank farm, and in the jungle west of Howard Air Force Base. As sightings and sensors indicated an increase in intruder activity, the issue quickly became a Priority Intelligence Requirement that would preoccupy the Southern Command and JTF-Panama commanders and staff for a better part of the year to come.

Woerner expressed his concern over the matter four days after the 12 April firefight when he directed Col. Chuck Fry, the SOCSOUTH commander, to conduct reconnaissance and surveillance missions to "find, fix, and capture intruders." Fry responded by setting up Task Force Gray, composed of three-man Special Forces teams; a twelve-man reaction force from the 3d Battalion, 7th Special Forces Group; and aviation assets from the 617th Special Operations Aviation Detachment. An AH–1 Cobra attack helicopter and an AC–130 Spectre gunship were on-call, as was an immediate reaction platoon from the 1st Battalion, 508th Infantry, the conventional Army unit barracked at Fort Kobbe, adjacent to Howard Air Force Base. Fry's three-man teams would conduct daytime patrols "followed by infiltration of observation posts to points along likely enemy infiltration routes." In the days following Woerner's directive, Task Force Gray set up three observation posts in the jungle west of Howard.[29]

Shortly thereafter, Lt. Col. Robert Barefield, commanding officer of the 1st Battalion, 508th Infantry, received word from the 193d Brigade headquarters that

---

[28] Quote on "priming the pump" from Memo, Loeffke for CINCSO, 19 Apr 88, sub: Update #55. Reynolds, *Just Cause*, p. 10. A Marine colonel ruminating on Woerner's decision later observed, "We tried our damnedest to get an infantry battalion on the ground," but "they did not want a lot of marines down there." Anderson Interv, 30 Mar 90.

[29] Interv, Frank with Valore, 29 Mar 90. Quote from Interv, author with Col Chuck Fry, U.S. Army, 1 May 89, Albrook Air Station, Panama.

Fry's teams would be operating in the vicinity of the air base. Because the 1st Battalion of the 508th was responsible for conventional patrols in the area and because the battalion's Company C had the "hot" platoon that would respond to any emergency involving the Special Forces, Barefield immediately called the 193d's liaison officer at Special Operations Command, South, and asked what the teams would be doing and where exactly they would be located. The reply he received surprised, then angered, him: the special operators did not believe he needed to know that information. When he persisted, asking for at least a radio frequency and a link-up point that the Special Forces team and his battalion might use in case of a problem, he was told not to worry. Frustrated, he informed SOCSOUTH headquarters that, given the risks inherent in uncoordinated operations, the Special Forces team should not call him should it require assistance in the event of an emergency.[30]

About 1445 on 20 April, a Task Force Gray team from the 7th Special Forces Group moved into the jungle, 150 meters west of the Howard flight line, close to what had been designated as Observation Post 2.[31] The location for the outpost had been selected for its proximity to the intersection of several trails running through the dense foliage. Reconnaissance had revealed a widening of the trails, together with a handful of "cave-like" areas, possibly rally points, that someone had cut into the jungle. At dusk, the team moved from its jungle cover to Observation Post 2 on the edge of a north-south trail. The men positioned themselves for a 360-degree line of sight and set three Claymore antipersonnel mines on the periphery of the outpost. An hour later, it was dark enough for one of the team to don his night vision goggles. He immediately saw about two dozen uniformed persons, each carrying a rifle, advancing toward his position. Equally alarming, every fourth person wore night vision goggles.

Two of the unidentified men were approaching an area covered by one of the Claymores. The two showed no sign of having seen the mine, but the Special Forces team leader could not take the chance that they would find it and reposition it to go off in the direction of the observation post. He therefore ordered the mine detonated. Following the explosion, about half of the unidentified intruders retreated eastward across a small rise. The others dropped to the ground and began crawling toward Observation Post 2 on its right and left flanks. Fearful of being encircled, the team opened fire with two M16 rifles and a squad automatic weapon (SAW). The men expended several hundred rounds, mainly from the SAW, and one team member observed what appeared to be the night vision goggles of one of the intruders shatter as the man fell backwards. When the Special Forces stopped firing, the team leader detonated a second Claymore to clear an escape route. The three men then retreated to a position about 200 meters southeast of Observation Post 2 and took cover.[32]

---

[30] Barefield Interv, 7 Nov 90.

[31] Unless otherwise noted, the account of the events that followed on the night of 20 April is based on Msgs, CINCSO to JCS, 210230Z Apr 88; SCJ–3 to JCS J–3, 221945Z Apr 88; AFOSI 721st Det to HQ, AFOSI, 212145Z Apr 88; CDR, 470th MI Bde, to USDAO, 240025Z Apr 88; and CDR, 470th MI Bde, to JCS, 070115Z May 88, sub: IIR. Intervs, author with Loeffke, 31 May 89; Cisneros, 1 May 89; Maj J. C. Hiett, U.S. Army, 27 Apr 90, Fort Leavenworth, Kans.; Barefield, 7 Nov 90; Graves, 18 May 91, Fort Leavenworth, Kans.; and King and Vaughn, 18 May 89.

[32] An Army officer standing on the porch of the mess hall at Fort Kobbe distinctly remembers hearing the two Claymores go off before the small arms fire began. Graves Interv, 18 May 91.

Violence, "Fissures," and a Prayer Book

During the confrontation, the Special Forces team had radioed for help. As the word passed from headquarters to headquarters, Cisneros made his way to the Tunnel at Quarry Heights, Colonel Rossi moved into the operations center at Fort Clayton, while Loeffke hastened to join Fry at the Task Force Gray operations room in a hangar at Howard. Fry, for his part, dispatched his twelve-man reaction force to link up with the Special Forces team at its new position. While this rescue force was en route, the colonel received approval from Quarry Heights to launch an AC–130 with infrared cameras to fly over the area. SOUTHCOM also directed Rossi to have JTF-Panama send elements of the Navy's Special Boat Unit 26 to check out reports of two small boats operating off the coast where the shooting had taken place. The Navy commander who took the call sent the boats but not before chiding Loeffke's chief of staff for trying to tell the Navy how to do its job.

The guard house at the entrance to Quarry Heights, the location of the U.S. Southern Command headquarters

When Loeffke arrived at Howard, Fry asked him to summon the on-call reaction platoon at Fort Kobbe. Loeffke called the 193d and directed that the platoon report to Howard and that the rest of Company C be placed on alert. Accordingly, Barefield assembled the company and prepared the reaction platoon to deploy. But he delayed sending anyone to Howard until he could ascertain the chain of command for the Special Forces involved. He went to the airfield himself, where, joining Loeffke, he received the briefing he had sought earlier in the day. The information confirmed his fears that there was no coordinated plan to extract the Special Forces team.

In due course, Company C's 3d Platoon arrived at Howard, accompanied by the company commander, Capt. William Graves. The captain, who had previously served in the 7th Special Forces Group, asked some of his former colleagues in the operations room about the situation. To his consternation, he received the answer Barefield had been given that morning: the information was too sensitive to disseminate. Graves thought this a strange reply under the circumstances: elements of his company were about to assist in extricating a Special Forces team in trouble. Irritated, the captain proceeded to an office in the hangar where Loeffke was briefing the reaction platoon on its mission. In essence, the platoon, accompanied by a Special Forces escort, would enter the Air Force ammunition depot at Howard, cut three passageways through the chain-link fence surrounding it, and wait for Fry's three-man team and the larger rescue force to come through the openings. Once the Special Forces soldiers were safely inside the depot, Loeffke said, the 3d Platoon from Fort Kobbe should shoot to kill anything that moved. After the briefing, the general accompanied the platoon to its dismount point. The men entered the depot area and were preparing to cut the fence when they received word to wait.

The reason for the delay was that Fry was talking with the stranded Green Berets over the radio, trying to coax them in. But they were reporting continuous movement in their vicinity and thus were refusing to budge from their fallback position. When the AC–130 over the area detected a group of twenty to twenty-five persons moving toward the ammunition depot, the SF team was advised of the group's presence, while the rescue force Fry had deployed was told to hold its position. Meanwhile, Loeffke talked to Cisneros about whether the gunship or the 3d Platoon should open fire on the unidentified group. Because of the mixture of friendly and hostile forces in the area and the uncertainty surrounding the whereabouts of either, neither general could say for certain that the group discovered by the AC–130's infrared camera was hostile. Given the circumstances, the judicious decision was to withhold fire.[33]

Once Fry realized that he could not extricate his men that night, he decided to pull them out after dawn. For this, he was given operational control of Company C from Fort Kobbe. Graves was uneasy with the mission. His company would be the third friendly element in the area, and he did not know where the other two were. There was also the possibility that the intruders might still be around, although the two groups that had been tracked by the AC–130—one near Observation Post 2, the other near the ammunition depot—had apparently withdrawn well before dawn. Despite Graves' misgivings, his soldiers entered the jungle from Howard at first light. Fry, his 9-mm. pistol drawn, led the way, walking point with a fire team from the company. The colonel's small group used a main trail, while Graves, two infantry platoons, and a scout platoon(-) shadowed them from the jungle. Fry found his three-man team on the trail in the middle of a perimeter set up by the original twelve-man rescue force. The colonel entered the perimeter several minutes ahead of Graves. By the time the captain arrived, Fry was visibly upset. The colonel had just learned that there had been no exchange of shots with intruders, but that the Special Forces team had done all the firing.[34]

As the colonel prepared to pull his men out of the jungle, Graves asked if Company C could stay and comb the area for evidence of what had occurred. After Fry consented, Graves sent out patrols that in due course found the site from which the Special Forces team had opened fire. Fragments from the two Claymores had penetrated the jungle foliage at a height of about three meters, a level unlikely to produce casualties. In fact, as with the tank farm firefight, no evidence of hostile casualties could be found, although an intelligence report later indicated that an ambulance, with the PDF clearing its way, had left the area the night of the

---

[33] Loeffke Interv, 31 May 89. Staff officers on duty in the U.S. Army, South, and JTF-Panama and the SOUTHCOM operations centers confirmed that, on the night of 20–21 April, they had no idea who the AC–130 was tracking. Subsequent evaluation of the AC–130 videotape and other evidence confirmed that the group was, in fact, intruders. Intervs, author with Hiett, 27 Apr 90; and King and Vaughn, 18 May 89. Msg, CINCSO to JCS, 221945Z Apr 88.

[34] In retrospect, both Fry and Loeffke commended the Special Forces team for its candor. The team members could easily have said that they had been fired upon, thereby avoiding the displeasure of their superiors. Their honesty, in Fry's opinion, established their credibility regarding the events of that night. Intervs, author with Fry, 1 May 89; Loeffke, 31 May 89; and Graves, 18 May 91.

shooting and crossed the Bridge of the Americas, thus lending some support to the account of the Special Forces team member who reported having seen one of the intruders fall.

As with the 12 April firefight at the tank farm, the shooting incident west of Howard on 20 April was shrouded in ambiguity and raised several questions for U.S. military headquarters in Panama involved in crisis management. Two issues of critical importance dealt with the relationship between Special Operations Forces under the Special Operations Command, South, and conventional forces under JTF-Panama. Each group adhered to vastly different doctrinal and operational procedures. The special operators went into the field in small teams, preferred to work alone, and, because of their vulnerability, insisted on operations security, which generally meant dispensing with such formalities as situation reports and communications checks. Above all, it meant shrouding their missions in secrecy, not just from the opponent, but from friendly forces as well. Conventional forces, although used to procedures that placed a premium on coordination and the sharing of information with friendly units, were generally content to let the Special Operations Forces units go their own way. An exception was when they had to work together and in proximity to one another. At that point, the commanders of the conventional troops sought coordination with the special operators and information as to their mission, composition, and location. To be denied such cooperation could result in the conventional units acting blindly in an emergency, possibly at risk from both hostile and friendly fire. Acquiescence in these demands for coordination and information, of course, was exactly what the special operators believed could compromise their mission, their procedures, and, given the small size of the teams involved, their lives.

After the 20 April incident, the issue of interaction between conventional and unconventional forces came to a head, resulting in several compromises. Fry provided JTF-Panama with a liaison officer, at least for the time being. The special operators also became more forthcoming in providing information to the commanders and staff of conventional units when the two forces worked in proximity to one another. Despite receiving these concessions, the conventional commanders still complained on occasion of being left uninformed about special operations that had the potential for placing conventional units in danger.[35]

---

[35] Intervs, author with Fitzgerald, 28 Apr 89; Col John A. Cope, U.S. Army, 29 Mar 89, Fort Clayton, Panama; Barefield, 7 Nov 90; and Hiett, 27 Apr 90. One example of continuing strains between Special Operations Forces and conventional forces at the tactical level is contained in the Loeffke Diary in an entry for 10 October 1988. Loeffke canceled an operation between the marines and the Special Forces when an Army platoon leader from Company C, 5th Battalion, 87th Infantry, told the general of coordination problems with the Special Forces. Loeffke requested the report be put in a disposition form (DF), the text of which follows. "During my company's commitment [5–11 September 1988] at the Arraiján Tank Farm we had a problem with coordination with a Special Forces unit. . . . On two occasions, for example, Special Forces teams came across our positions. In both cases we had no radio contact, no prior planned visual link-up, nor any kind of warning they were approaching our position. In the case I was personally involved in, a two-man team walked across our sector during the early morning (approximately 0530 hrs). Due to limited visibility, it was with great difficulty that we were able to identify them as friendly forces. . . . Due to this same lack of coordination, I was sending patrols into areas not knowing exactly where the Special Forces units might have been or they knowing where we were."

The problem of special operations and conventional forces working together at the tactical level raised another key issue, that of command and control. As commander of a subordinate unified command charged with the planning and execution of special operations, Fry worked directly for the SOUTHCOM commander. The night of 20–21 April, he was the officer who directed the efforts to extract the beleaguered Special Forces team, reporting to Woerner via Cisneros. Loeffke, after he arrived at Howard, did not challenge this arrangement. In his opinion, however, the special operations units, because they were engaged in a mission involving the Panama crisis and requiring JTF-Panama assistance, should have been under his operational control. With this in mind, he established his own "running dialogue" with Cisneros, a move that frustrated Fry, who later charged that Loeffke had undercut his handling of the situation. Fry was especially upset when, after the AC–130 had detected unidentified persons moving toward the ammunition depot at Howard, he had assembled forces to be flown into the area to set up an ambush, only to have those forces recalled while they were airborne. The recall came after Loeffke had informed Cisneros of the initiative, and the two generals had decided against it.[36]

Once the 20–21 April incident was over, Loeffke pushed for an immediate change in command and control relationships, as they pertained to JTF-Panama, between special operations and conventional forces (*Chart 3*). Cisneros agreed, and the next day, in a staff update briefing at Quarry Heights, Woerner told Fry that, on operations related directly to the crisis in Panama, the colonel worked for the JTF-Panama commander. Fry did not protest the SOUTHCOM commander's directive but sought clarification after the meeting, arguing that "there appears to be a serious misunderstanding of USCINCSO's intent." By this he meant that JTF-Panama would surely regard Woerner's decision as placing Special Operations Forces under Loeffke's operational control for "all phases of the crisis," not just the operations scheduled by Task Force Gray west of Howard. In Fry's opinion, JTF-Panama could establish missions, assign terrain, and provide administrative and logistical support to Special Operations Command, South, but Fry himself should direct the execution of any operation, with his men reporting straight to him, and he, in turn, to Loeffke. As the SOCSOUTH commander, he pointed out, he was obligated to exercise this control. Moreover, he had little confidence that conventional commanders and staff would employ his forces properly, ignorant as he believed most traditional officers were of special operations doctrine, procedures, and tactics. Loeffke, as Fry knew, had actually had eight years' experience with the Special Forces, but, counteracting that, in Fry's opinion, was the general's opposition in the past to formal efforts to "divorce" Special Operations Forces from conventional forces because the separation, in Loeffke's mind, would create an unacceptable "anomaly" within the Department of Defense.[37]

Loeffke, as Fry feared, clearly saw Woerner's decision as giving JTF-Panama operational control over Special Operations Forces employed in crisis-related

---

[36] Interv, author with Fry, 1 May 89. Quote from Interv, author with Loeffke, 31 May 89. Interv, author with Hiett, 27 Apr 90.

[37] The third and fourth quoted words from Interv, author with Loeffke, 31 May 89. Intervs, author with Cisneros, 1 May 89; Fry, 1 May 89; and Hiett, 27 Apr 90. Msg, CINCSO to CDR, JTF-Panama, 211813Z Apr 88. First and second quotes from Msg, CDR, SOCSOUTH, to CINCSO, 231701Z Apr 88, sub: SOF Command and Control.

Chart 3—Command Relationships: Joint Task Force-Panama (as of May 1988)

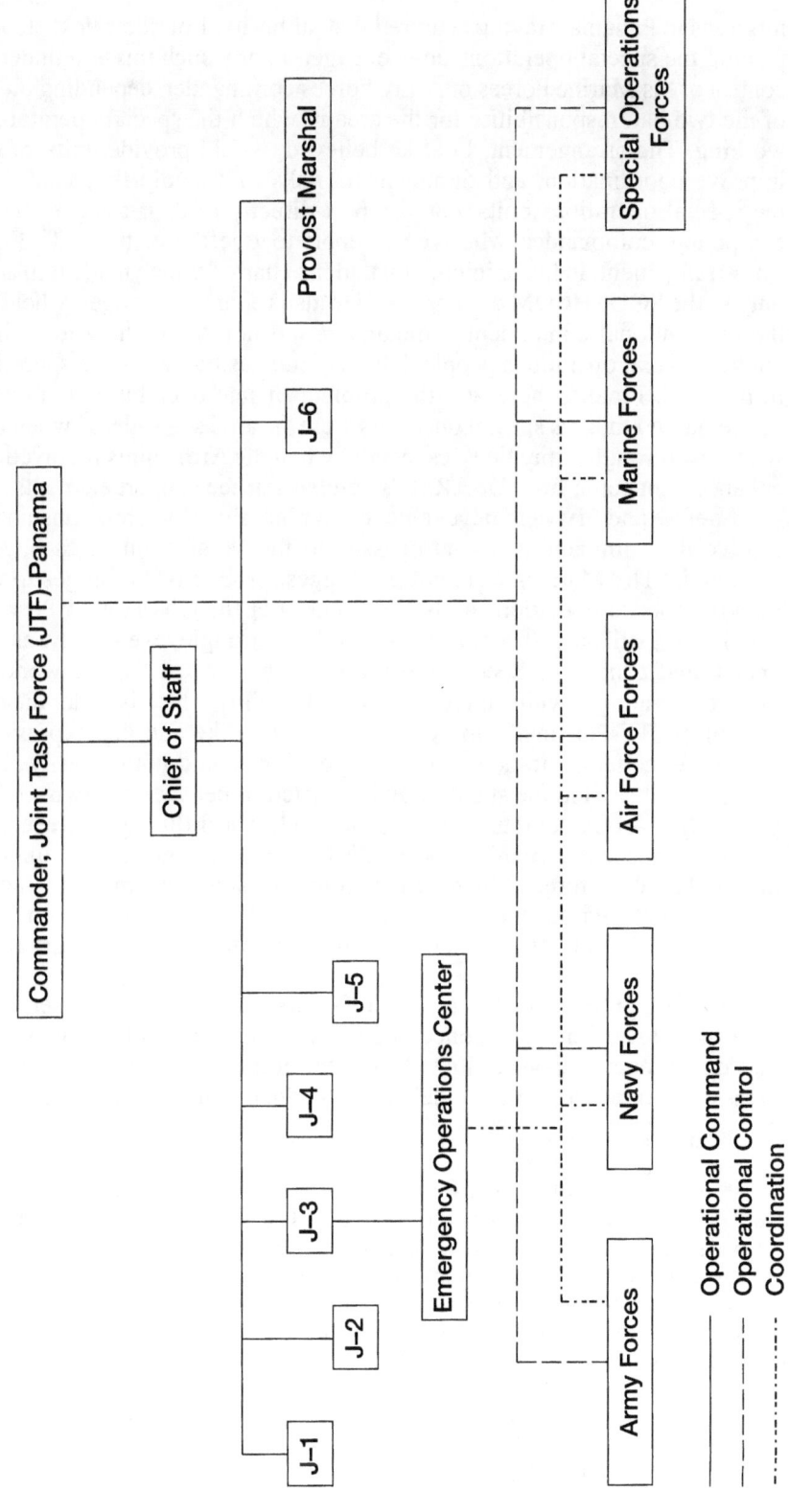

missions in Panama. Having acquired that authority, Loeffke's next step was to try placing the special operations units engaged in any such mission under the direct control of his Marine Forces or Army Forces commander, depending on which one of the two had responsibility for the area in which the special operators would be working. The arrangement, Loeffke believed, would provide unity of command, improve coordination, and diminish the risks of friendly fire. Under the setup, the special operations units would report directly to their assigned JTF-Panama component commander, who would report to Loeffke or his staff. Fry resisted. The arrangement, in his opinion, violated his charter, which made him accountable only to the SOUTHCOM commander. He also reiterated his deeply held belief that the conventional component commanders did not "know how to command and control special operations people," thereby increasing the risk to special operators in the field. Finally, there was the problem of interoperability. On one occasion Fry remarked that his special operators were "scared s——tless" when they had to withdraw through Army lines, especially when the Army units involved in security enhancement came from USARSO's combat service support elements.[38]

Loeffke and Fry were never able to establish a working relationship that would resolve the command and control issue to the satisfaction of each. As Loeffke lamented, "The Marines were not our biggest problem. Our biggest problem was with the special operations units."[39] A year after the Observation Post 2 incident, Rossi could still say, "There continues to be a struggle, even today, as to who has operational control of Special Operations Forces when they're working—when they're operating—within an Area of Responsibility which is under the operational control of JTF-Panama." On occasion, both Loeffke and Fry expressed a desire to resolve matters, but their respective positions could not be easily reconciled.[40] Observers attributed the standoff and the friction between the two to the forceful personality—some said stubbornness—of each. The difficulty, however, ran deeper, being in essence a systemic concern for how best to organize and direct two very different kinds of forces with divergent roles, missions, and modi operandi. For this reason alone, the issue would remain a source of contention between JTF-Panama and Special Operations Command, South, well after Loeffke and Fry had departed the scene.

Another problem with which Loeffke and Rossi found themselves grappling after the 20 April incident concerned the areas in Panama for which JTF-Panama had operational responsibilities. When the joint task force was activated, these areas conformed to the near indefensible hodgepodge of U.S. bases, facilities, and

---

[38] Interv, author with Loeffke, 31 May 89. Quotes from Interv, author with Fry, 1 May 89.

[39] Loeffke Interv, 31 May 89.

[40] Rossi Interv, 24 May 89. On 13 June 1988, Loeffke sent Fry a note emphasizing "integration" of conventional forces and Special Operations Forces as one of the three challenges Admiral Crowe had issued to the U.S. Special Operations Command. Fry responded in a letter in which he acknowledged that a "wall" had been erected between the two kinds of forces and cited the command and control system as "the root cause of our current problems." In closing, he wrote, "I pledge my efforts and solicit your assistance in making the system work." He signed the letter, "Chuck." Loeffke replied with a note scribbled at the bottom of Fry's letter. "My Friend," it began, "We *can* work together. However there has to be *one* man responsible for the overall fight." As to who that man should be with respect to Special Operations Forces, neither officer, despite good intentions, could reach agreement with the other. Fry interpreted Loeffke's note as a rebuff of his overture. Ltr, Fry to Loeffke, 17 Jun 88; Fry Interv, 1 May 89.

housing in Panama. On the east bank of the canal on the Pacific Ocean side of the country, Fort Clayton, Curundu, Quarry Heights, and several housing areas were Army responsibilities; Albrook Air Station belonged to the Air Force; and the Navy had responsibility for Fort Amador. On the west bank, the Air Force guarded Howard Air Force Base; the Navy had responsibility for Rodman Naval Station, the Arraiján Tank Farm, and the ammunition depot north of it; and the Army looked after Fort Kobbe (*Map 3*). As one staff officer described the arrangement of service responsibilities, there were "islands within islands." The 20 April shooting incident revealed many of the problems inherent in this setup. With a minimum of coordination and centralized direction, Army units, special operations teams and aviation, Air Force security police, and an AC–130 had all been involved in the action west of Howard. Fry was ostensibly in charge, but, in fact, "everybody was talking to everybody."[41]

"Goose eggs" were the solution JTF-Panama devised to unsnarl the tangle. Rossi simply drew three large circles on a map of the canal area and assigned the responsibility for security enhancement and coordination within each goose egg to a different commander answerable to JTF-Panama. The entire Atlantic side of the canal area went to an Army military police commander, while on the Pacific side, the Marine Forces commander, Colonel Conley, was given the west bank of the canal, and Colonel Bolt, the 193d Brigade commander, the east side. At this point, Conley, as promised by Loeffke, received operational control of an Army infantry company and two military police companies. The spectrum of these overhauled responsibilities was formally defined in JTF-Panama Operation Order 10–88, published on 25 April.

The key function that the goose eggs facilitated was coordination, which was now centralized, and not control, which varied from one area of responsibility to another. For example, on the west bank of the canal, Conley still did not have control over internal security at Howard Air Force Base. The Air Force was adamant that the security police would retain responsibility for that function, per Air Force—and joint Army–Air Force—doctrine. Nor could Conley order security police to carry out Marine Forces missions under JTF-Panama. As Cope bemoaned, "They will not twitch off the vicinity of that airbase." A similar situation existed at Albrook Air Station, where, again, the security police operated independently of the JTF-Panama component commander in charge of the area of responsibility, in this case Colonel Bolt. At Fort Kobbe, within the Marine Forces area of responsibility, the Army continued to provide security. Despite these anomalies, Loeffke could report to the Army chief of staff that JTF-Panama was becoming "a mature fighting force" that was "integrating daily the Navy, Marine, Army, and Air Force assets into one coordinated effort." Loeffke specifically noted that the Marine Corps area of responsibility included Howard Air Force Base, thus compelling the Air Force and the marines to talk to each other for "the first time" on air base ground defense, for which no joint doctrine existed between the aviators and the Leathernecks.[42]

---

[41] First quote from Interv, author with Vaughn and Rivera, 16 Mar 89. Second quote from Interv, author with King and Vaughn, 18 May 89.

[42] Intervs, author with King and Vaughn, 18 May 89; and Vaughn and Rivera, 16 Mar 89. First quote from Interv, author with Cope, 29 Mar 89. Interv, author with Augustine, 7 Jun 89. Msg, CDR, JTF-Panama, to COMNAVFORPM et al., 251600Z Apr 88, sub: JTF-PM OPORD 10–88. Remaining quotes from Msg, CDR, USARSO, to CSA, 271425Z Apr 88, sub: Update No. 10.

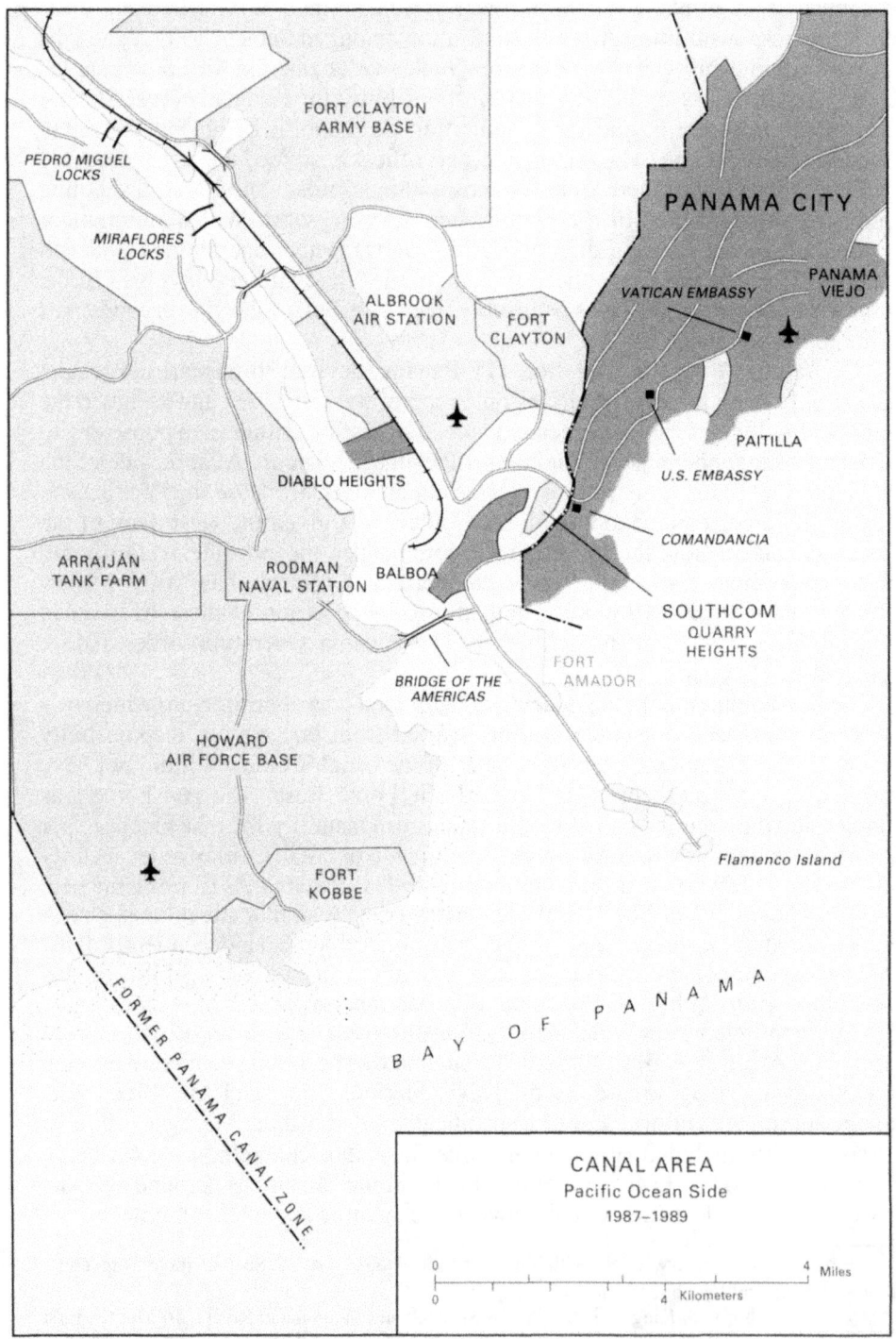

Map 3

Violence, "Fissures," and a Prayer Book

As JTF-Panama moved in the wake of the 12 April firefight and the 20 April incident to straighten out chain of command arrangements, geographical responsibilities, and operational procedures, the new headquarters also engaged the Southern Command in a dialogue over operational reporting. The issue had first been addressed on 9 April, the day JTF-Panama was activated, in the SOUTHCOM J–3 Guidance Message 1. In the message, Cisneros informed JTF-Panama and its components that they needed to monitor the timeliness and accuracy of their reports so that the Southern Command could make sound decisions and provide prompt answers to queries from the president, the secretary of defense, and the Joint Chiefs of Staff. In a series of follow-on messages, Cisneros prohibited JTF-Panama and its components from sending information copies of their situation reports to commanders outside the theater. Information copies sent directly to other headquarters without SOUTHCOM's review and input, Cisneros argued, could be misleading in that they would lack the broader assessment of events that only the unified command could provide, given its access to various intelligence sources off-limits to subordinate commanders and staff. Cisneros did insist, however, that information copies of component situation reports to JTF-Panama be submitted directly to the Southern Command. This procedure, he asserted, would further ensure that Washington and out-of-theater commanders received timely reports, thus saving Woerner from the avalanche of outside requests for clarification that inevitably followed the issuance of incomplete or erroneous accounts.[43]

Staff officers at JTF-Panama readily acknowledged the need for better reporting. During the 12 April firefight, for example, much of the information received in the operations center at Fort Clayton had been inaccurate, vague, and conflicting. "Rumor rather than fact often clouded the issue," Rossi informed Cisneros after the incident. Rossi and Cope also agreed with Cisneros' directive that prohibited JTF-Panama's components from reporting to their service headquarters and outside commands. Both men had experienced the frustration of being informed by a Navy admiral or Marine commander from a headquarters outside Panama of an event that should have been reported first through the JTF-Panama chain of command. But Loeffke's staff objected to Cisneros' decree that JTF-Panama's components had to send information copies of their situation reports to the Southern Command. Inexact component reports arriving at SOUTHCOM could result in Cisneros and his staff themselves setting off the dreaded "avalanche" of inquiries from higher authorities. Accurate reporting could be better served, Rossi and Cope proposed, by having the components send their reports solely to JTF-Panama, which would consolidate and verify the information before passing them to the Southern Command in the form of a single report. Cisneros considered the proposal but rejected it on the grounds that a single situation report would take too long to reach SOUTHCOM, thereby impeding Woerner from responding promptly to the Joint Chiefs or National Command Authority.[44]

From the perspective of JTF-Panama, the conditions Cisneros set for both timely and accurate reports seemed mutually exclusive. If SOUTHCOM wanted

---

[43] Msgs, CINCSO to CDR, JTF-Panama, 092154Z Apr 88, sub: SCJ3 Guidance Message No. 1; 121939Z Apr 88, sub: SCJ3 Guidance Message No. 3; 150006Z Apr 88, sub: SCJ3 Guidance Message No. 4; and 160300Z Apr 88, sub: SCJ3 Guidance Message No. 5.

[44] Quote from Msg, CDR, JTF-Panama [Rossi], to CINCSO [Cisneros], 140022Z Apr 88, sub: Special Sitrep—Firing at the Arraiján Tank Farm. SCJ–3 Guidance Message No. 3.

critical information within minutes, even while an incident or event was in progress, accuracy was bound to suffer. That "the first report is always wrong" was taken as axiomatic within the joint task force staff, as reports from the field during the tank farm firefight and the special operations fracas west of Howard had clearly demonstrated. Indeed, as the result of precipitous reporting during the 20 April incident, Woerner's first message to the Joint Chiefs, written before the Special Forces team had been recovered, stated that the intruders had fired first, when, in fact, they had not fired at all. Right after the event, Cisneros sent a personal communication to Loeffke stating the obvious: "significant improvements" still needed to be made in operational reporting.[45]

Concerning the dissemination of information, Loeffke often referred to the Southern Command as the buffer that kept him from having to engage in public relations with the news media or deal directly with the Joint Chiefs' inquisitiveness. Yet, as Cope observed, the buffer could at times become a "conduit" for passing downward unreasonable demands from the highest authorities for information that, in the midst of an incident, JTF-Panama could not provide if it hoped to render an accurate report. Cope cited one recurring sequence in which the Joint Staff would receive word (often through CNN) about something happening in Panama; Lt. Gen. Thomas Kelly, the director of operations in the Pentagon, would call and "beat up" on Cisneros for information; and Cisneros, in turn, would call JTF-Panama, wanting the information "yesterday." As Woerner explained in later years, Washington too often preferred fast, even inaccurate, information to no information at all. From the outset, then, the contradictions inherent in the desire for accuracy and the demand for timeliness became a source of friction between the Southern Command and JTF-Panama. Staff officers at Fort Clayton complained about undue interference and micromanagement on the part of the unified command, whereas their counterparts at Quarry Heights believed that the issues at stake in the crisis necessitated a close monitoring of JTF-Panama's tactical communications network.[46]

The SOUTHCOM staff also began questioning whether JTF-Panama had the resources to exercise crisis management on a day-to-day basis. Of immediate concern to both headquarters was the number of troops available to the joint task force to carry out its security enhancement mission following the violent events of mid-April. Loeffke was especially worried about such vulnerable facilities as Howard Air Force Base and the Rodman Ammunition Supply Point. In an update to Woerner, he now recommended approving not only the Air Force request for more security police, but also Conley's request for an additional Marine company, one that would deploy with amphibious light armored vehicles (LAVs), ideally suited to the terrain in Panama. Loeffke further noted that the Army might have to

---

[45] Msg, CINCSO to JCS, 210230Z Apr 88. Cisneros quote from Msg, CINCSO [Cisneros] to CDR, JTF-Panama [Loeffke], 211847Z Apr 88. Of the inaccurate "first reports" that flooded the JTF-Panama operations center during the crisis, one that took on a special urgency was the information phoned in that the Panama Defense Forces were drowning opposition members in a river. Persons sent to verify the report discovered a mass baptism in progress. Intervs, author with Vaughn and Rivera, 16 Mar 89.

[46] Interv, author with Loeffke, 31 May 89. Quoted words from Interv, author with Cope, 29 Mar 89. Intervs, author with General Frederick F. Woerner Jr., U.S. Army (Ret.), 30 Apr 91, Fort Leavenworth, Kans., and Col Arnie Rossi, U.S. Army, 27 Mar 89, Fort Clayton, Panama.

send a mechanized unit to serve as an evacuation and quick reaction force. "The type of aggressiveness that the enemy has exhibited warrants this precaution," he explained. In an update to Vuono a few days later, he reiterated that the threat to American interests in Panama had increased, thus forcing JTF-Panama to consider asking for additional forces, the formal request for which would be made through Woerner to the Joint Chiefs.[47]

THE PRAYER BOOK

The units that Loeffke indicated might be needed in Panama were, as in the case of the earlier security enhancement forces, listed in contingency plans for the crisis. Those plans had been evolving at a steady pace since the completion of SOUTHCOM's draft of ELABORATE MAZE in mid-March. In early April, during a trip to Washington following the Marriott incident, Woerner met with the Joint Chiefs and received further planning guidance. To begin with, U.S. units identified in the first three phases of ELABORATE MAZE, which covered defensive operations and the buildup of forces in Panama, were to be consolidated into one force "module" in an operation order code-named ELDER STATESMAN. Troop deployments envisaged under ELDER STATESMAN were to be reviewed and revised so that "combat forces are front loaded on the flow list to the maximum degree possible." Woerner was also to submit separate operation orders for a nonpermissive evacuation of U.S. civilians, code-named KLONDIKE KEY; offensive operations—Phase IV of ELABORATE MAZE—now code-named BLUE SPOON; and Phase V stability operations, code-named KRYSTAL BALL.[48] In effect, ELABORATE MAZE, with its five interactive phases, had been divided into three separate operation orders, purportedly to rationalize and simplify the planning process. At the same time, the plan for an evacuation of noncombatants had been elevated in status from an ELABORATE MAZE annex to an operation order in its own right. When taken together, the set of four operation orders that replaced ELABORATE MAZE—and were derived from it—acquired the code name PRAYER BOOK.

In the SOUTHCOM Operations Directorate, staff officers working for Lt. Col. John McCutchon and monitored by Cisneros wrote the new operation orders within a week, and late on 13 April Woerner began sending them to the Joint Chiefs. One of the first to be transmitted was KLONDIKE KEY, which described in general terms a coordinated program of military escorts, psychological operations, and public affairs announcements that would go into effect should the National Command Authority through the Joint Chiefs order an evacuation of U.S. citizens from Panama. JTF-Panama would take charge of the operation, with the commander of a Navy carrier battle group supporting the effort. Woerner's intent was to conduct the evacuation swiftly, protect American lives and property in the process, and accomplish the mission using the minimum force necessary. In this last point, the key word was "necessary," in that U.S. troops participating in the operation were to demonstrate their resolve and take whatever actions the situation required to safeguard the evacuees. The Southern Command did not anticipate Panama's

---

[47] Memos, Loeffke for CINCSO, 21 Apr 88, sub: Update #58, and 26 Apr 88, sub: Update #60; Msg, CDR, USARSO, to CSA, 271425Z Apr 88, sub: Update No. 10.

[48] Msg, JCS to USCINCLANT et al., 082317Z Apr 88, sub: Panama Situation Planning Update. The "K" in KRYSTAL BALL is not a typographical error or an unintentional misspelling on the part of the author.

U.S. Military Intervention in Panama, June 1987–December 1989

Chart 4—Initial Blue Spoon Command Arrangements

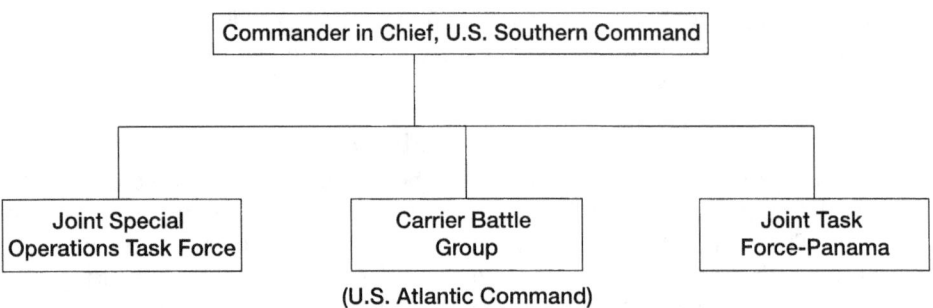

police or military using force to interfere with an evacuation, but the command could not rule out "plausibly deniable" hostile actions by regime-backed "goon squads."[49]

Within a minute after the Southern Command forwarded Klondike Key to Washington, CINCSO OPORD 5–88, Blue Spoon, for offensive military operations in Panama, followed.[50] Reiterating the concept of operations contained in Elaborate Maze, the plan called for U.S. forces to seize PDF command, control, and communications sites together with key airfields. The Panamanian military and any other groups employing armed resistance would be "neutralized." Anticipating a breakdown of law and order during the fighting, the plan called for Woerner to assume full "political-military" authority over all U.S. interests in Panama. Civil-military operations initiated under Blue Spoon would be expanded during the postcombat phase, covered by Krystal Ball.

In Blue Spoon, as in Elaborate Maze, surgical strikes by U.S. Special Operations Forces, the majority of which would deploy from the United States under the control of a joint special operations task force, remained the central feature of open hostilities in Panama (*Chart 4*). The list of targets was also virtually the same, to include the Comandancia, the Torrijos-Tucumen airport complex, the Paitilla and Curundu airfields, Fort Cimarrón, David, Rio Hato, Tinajitas, and Panama Viejo. Depending on the enemy units involved and their locations, the plan called for a variety of operations, ranging from isolating and neutralizing the Panama Defense Forces (Comandancia) and seizing key facilities (Torrijos-Tucumen), to reconnaissance and surveillance activities (Tinajitas). JSOTF elements would also perform civil-military operations as required and conduct hostage rescue missions. Throughout Blue Spoon operations, the joint special operations task force would receive support from JTF-Panama.

Besides supporting JSOTF missions, JTF-Panama under Blue Spoon was to conduct follow-on operations to neutralize the Panama Defense Forces and other combatants; to relieve special operations strike forces once they had achieved their objectives; and to stand ready to conduct offensive operations against Fort Espinar, Fort Amador, Fort Cimarrón, and Tinajitas. The conventional joint task force

---
[49] Msg, CINCSO to JCS, 140326Z Apr 88, sub: Klondike Key OPORD 4–88.
[50] Msg, CINCSO to JCS, 140327Z Apr 88, sub: Blue Spoon OPORD 5–88.

would also be given operational control of an amphibious task force, composed of a battalion-size Marine expeditionary unit, for employment at David, Rio Hato, and in the Panama City area. The plan carried the proviso that should offensive operations be necessary before special operations units could deploy, JTF-Panama would execute the JSOTF missions as required.

BLUE SPOON also called for the SOUTHCOM commander to receive operational command of a Navy aircraft carrier battle group from the U.S. Atlantic Command. Once deployed, the battle group could be used to block any reinforcements and weapons dispatched from Cuba, to provide close air support for JTF-Panama, to conduct air strikes against specified targets, and to augment SOUTHCOM's reconnaissance efforts and intelligence collection. The BLUE SPOON operation order concluded with a statement of Woerner's intent to bring the offensive operations to a "swift and decided end."

Of the three major subordinate organizations answerable directly to the SOUTHCOM commander under BLUE SPOON, two—the joint special operations task force and JTF-Panama—were up and running as of late April, but the status of the carrier battle group was problematic, even for planning purposes. From the Navy's perspective, relinquishing command and control of a carrier group, the crown jewel of the fleet, to an Army general was anathema. A non-naval officer was certain to misuse this prized asset. For Woerner, however, the principle of unity of command dictated that the carrier battle group be under him. Cisneros and his Navy counterpart at the Atlantic Command tried to work out an agreement that would satisfy both headquarters, but, after several heated telephone conversations, the effort collapsed. Woerner then took his case to the chairman of the Joint Chiefs of Staff, Admiral Crowe. "USCINCSOUTH," Woerner wrote, "must be able to command air/land/sea forces toward a single focal point to accomplish identified objectives." Any command and control arrangement that interfered with this necessity would violate the clear intent of JCS Publication 2 and the Goldwater-Nichols Department of Defense Reorganization Act of 1986: namely, that the "supported CINC" be provided authority commensurate with his assigned responsibility and mission.[51] Crowe, in responding, sided with Woerner and against his own service. In the event BLUE SPOON was executed, the admiral decreed, the SOUTHCOM commander would exercise operational command over a carrier battle group. As events would demonstrate, issuing such a directive was easier than enforcing it.

KRYSTAL BALL OPORD 6–88 for civil-military operations in Panama was the last of the separate plans derived from SOUTHCOM's ELABORATE MAZE, and it reached the Joint Chiefs late on 14 April.[52] Like Phase V of its parent plan, the operation order assumed that, as a result of U.S. combat operations against armed elements in Panama, the country would experience varying degrees of damage, a security vacuum, and a disruption of basic services, especially in the two largest urban areas, Panama City and Colón. Hostile acts by isolated pockets of military and paramilitary groups, criminal elements, and, possibly, international terrorists could complicate progress toward the restoration of law and order and the installation of a government recognized by the United States. Based on these

---

[51] Msg, CINCSO to JCS, 142045Z Apr 88, sub: ELABORATE MAZE Planning.

[52] All quotes contained in the discussion of KRYSTAL BALL are from Msg, CINCSO to JCS, 150125Z Apr 88, sub: CINCSO OPORD ELABORATE MAZE: KRYSTAL BALL, OPORD 6–88.

assumptions, Woerner's civil affairs planners conceived of KRYSTAL BALL being executed in three stages, to be concentrated first in Panama City and Colón, then expanded to other areas as required. In the first, or immediate, stage, U.S. stability operations would concentrate on public safety, health problems, and population control to eliminate life-threatening conditions. The second, "sustained," stage would concentrate on restoring essential services and transferring responsibility for the rebuilding of Panama from the U.S. military to the U.S. Embassy's country team and to Panamanian institutions. In stage three, the United States would work through Panamanian institutions to ensure a stable, democratic Panama.

During KRYSTAL BALL, a civil-military operations task force (CMOTF) would answer to the SOUTHCOM commander and have operational control over civil affairs assets, SOUTHCOM's treaty affairs center, and a variety of units and personnel specializing in security and stability operations. Given this arrangement, the operation order raised "command concerns" over whether the president would authorize the call up of the necessary reservists under the Presidential Selected Reserve Call-up, a critical question given that most of the military's civil affairs capability was in the reserves. The issue was also raised as to whether adequate cash would be available to jump-start Panamanian bank operations. As for the CMOTF's specified missions, one included responsibility for the "reconstitution, reformation, and retraining of the PDF as a responsible Panamanian institution." This task was predicated on the Panama Defense Forces remaining intact after BLUE SPOON but as an apolitical organization that would support and facilitate democratic government in Panama.

Because SOUTHCOM's commander would be in charge of an interim U.S. military government in Panama during and following hostilities and because of the sensitive nature of the plan and Woerner's concerns about it leaking to the media or to the Panamanian government, KRYSTAL BALL was kept under tight wraps at Quarry Heights. In the ensuing weeks and months, SOUTHCOM's Civil Affairs Branch of the Policy, Strategy, and Programs Directorate, supported by reservists on 31-day temporary tours of active duty, refined the CINCSO and the supporting Commander, CMOTF, versions of the plan.[53] The other PRAYER BOOK operation orders were farmed out, as ELABORATE MAZE had been, to subordinate commanders for their supporting plans. The joint special operations task force, working out of Fort Bragg, concentrated on its portion of BLUE SPOON, while JTF-Panama developed supporting operation orders for ELDER STATESMAN, BLUE SPOON, and KLONDIKE KEY. In formulating the new supporting plans, both the joint special operations task force and JTF-Panama relied almost entirely on what they had written for ELABORATE MAZE.

Indeed, the same U.S. Army, South, planning cell that had cobbled together the JTF-Panama version of ELABORATE MAZE now took on the task of writing the supporting operation orders for the PRAYER BOOK. For Maj. Dan Augustine, the leader of the small team that still worked under the watchful eyes of Colonel Cope and Colonel Rossi, that meant tackling ELDER STATESMAN. The process, over a hectic ten days, contained its share of twists and aggravations. To begin with, Augustine and Cope were skeptical of the guidance they received from higher headquarters

---

[53] Woerner Interv, 30 Apr 91; Fishel, *The Fog of Peace*, pp. 7–12. As Fishel relates, "SCJ5 requested a team of CA officers principally from the SOUTHCOM CAPSTONE reserve unit, the 361st CA Brigade, to draft the full plan."

requiring that the plan schedule combat units, or "shooters," to arrive in Panama at the beginning of any troop buildup. The U.S. military in Panama simply did not have the logistical base to support several thousand combat troops deploying with only their basic loads. There was also the Friday afternoon, both men recalled, when they received word that the Joint Staff in the Pentagon wanted the list of forces required for an ELDER STATESMAN troop buildup in Panama. Augustine was still working on a mission statement, a prerequisite for determining the necessary forces, but the Joint Staff persisted in demanding the list of troops, even if the units did not have missions assigned to them. Augustine and Capt. Carlos Puentes, another member of the original USARSO planning cell, referred back to ELABORATE MAZE and put together a troop list that they briefed to Cope on Saturday. Sunday they briefed the deputy director of operations at Quarry Heights, even though their list was already on its way to the Joint Chiefs. "That's dumb, but that is the crisis action system," was Cope's verdict. Not everything concerning the process, however, received such a negative assessment. Augustine, for example, did not have to draft both the JTF-Panama and the Army Forces versions of ELDER STATESMAN, as the USARSO cell had done for ELABORATE MAZE, because a group from the 7th Infantry Division (Light) arrived in Panama to write the ARFOR plan. Also during this time, Lt. Col. Robert Pantier moved from the Southern Command to U.S. Army, South—which also meant to JTF-Panama—on 13 April to fill the position of director of plans. Later that month, enough augmentees arrived at U.S. Army, South, on temporary duty to help ease the planning burdens of the command.[54]

By the time the JTF-Panama ELDER STATESMAN OPORD 6–88 was transmitted to the SOUTHCOM commander on 18 April, the code name had been changed to POST TIME. In general, the document described PDF actions, capabilities, and intentions since the 16 March attempted coup and listed defensive operations JTF-Panama would execute on its own or in conjunction with a troop buildup. These operations included protecting and defending U.S. defense sites, housing areas, the U.S. Embassy, and treaty-designated areas of military coordination. Addressing the logistical issue, POST TIME noted USARSO's concern that the support base for forces already in country was severely strained and would likely not improve. Since additional combat service support units were not scheduled to arrive until the fifth day of the projected buildup, Southern Command and JTF-Panama support groups would, through a consolidation and centralization of their efforts, try to sustain initial operations.[55]

---

[54] Interv, author with Augustine, 7 Jun 89. Quote from Interv, author with Cope, 29 Mar 89.

[55] Msg, CDR, JTF-Panama, to CINCSO, 181730Z Apr 88, sub: COMJTFPM POST TIME OPORD 6–88. The Army Forces-Panama (ARFORPM), POST TIME Operation Plan, written by a group of planners from the 7th Infantry Division (Light), was submitted to JTF-Panama on 3 May 1988. It assumed that, at the beginning of any buildup of U.S. forces, the United States would not be involved in open conflict with the Panama Defense Forces but that relations would be strained and hostilities could begin at any time. The plan also assumed that a noncombatant evacuation operation would not be conducted prior to the arrival of POST TIME forces. A noncombatant evacuation operation, the plan argued, would detract from the Army's defensive mission during the buildup and would interfere with the buildup itself. The concept of operations consisted of five phases, based on what units were already deployed to Panama and the extent of the area they had to defend. Msg, CDR, ARFOR/CDR, 7th Inf Div (Light), to CDR, JTF-Panama/CDR, USARSO, 031900Z May 88, sub: ARFORPM OPLAN 1–88, "POST TIME."

If at any point in the crisis the National Command Authority ordered an evacuation of U.S. civilians from Panama, JTF-Panama, by direction of the Southern Command, would be in charge of the operation. Thus, as Augustine was working on the ELDER STATESMAN (POST TIME) operation order, Maj. Chuck Herrick was grappling with JTF-Panama's evacuation plan, KLONDIKE KEY. The magnitude of the problem had not changed since March when he had worked on the ELABORATE MAZE evacuation annex. There were still around 50,000 American noncombatants living in Panama, most in or around Panama City and Colón in housing areas that were often isolated or adjacent to PDF facilities. To bring these people together and to facilitate their evacuation, Herrick identified assembly and holding areas, rally points, ground and sea routes, helicopter landing zones, and the procedures for extricating Americans from what could easily be a chaotic state of affairs. "The extraction force commander," JTF-Panama assured the Southern Command, "must be sensitive to the need first to avoid a confrontation with PDF elements. At the same time he must provide for the defense of his element and the evacuees under his charge." If force had to be used in any instance, it needed to be "limited in intensity, duration, and magnitude to that reasonably required to counter successfully the hostile act or hostile intent."[56] Each of these statements was in keeping with emphasis on minimum force Woerner had approved in the SOUTHCOM version of KLONDIKE KEY.

Herrick briefed the evacuation plan to Loeffke and Rossi. He also briefed it twice to officers at Quarry Heights. During one of the SOUTHCOM briefings, he turned what had been a relatively sedate meeting into pandemonium when he announced that each family being evacuated could take only one pet dog or cat with them. During the ensuing uproar, one colonel was heard to claim—presumably with some exaggeration—that he would rather leave his family than his dogs behind. For days, Herrick "caught hell" over this "incredibly emotional" issue.[57]

Meanwhile, Captain Dearborn was working on the JTF-Panama operation order for BLUE SPOON, which was submitted to the Southern Command on 18 April, a few hours after the POST TIME message. On D-day, according to the plan, JTF-Panama forces, in support of JSOTF strike forces, would continue to defend key facilities in Panama. But there would also be offensive missions to execute. JTF-Panama would secure Fort Amador and Fort Espinar, neutralize the Panama Defense Forces at both installations, control and demilitarize the area between Fort Amador and Albrook Air Station, isolate Panama City and prevent Panamanian armed forces from reinforcing the Comandancia, secure selected communications facilities and utilities, and take control of Colón. On D plus 1, JTF-Panama could expect to relieve JSOTF elements and begin law and order and stability missions that would continue as long as necessary.[58]

While JTF-Panama was drafting its four supporting plans for the PRAYER BOOK, special operations planners at Fort Bragg concentrated on BLUE SPOON. Their JSOTF supporting plan, submitted to the Southern Command on 21 April,

---

[56] Conversation, author with Maj Chuck Herrick, 1989, Fort Clayton, Panama. Quotes from Msg, CDR, JTF-Panama/CDR, USARSO, to CINCSO, 130100Z Apr 88, sub: OPREP–1, ELABORATE MAZE OPORD 4–88.

[57] Herrick Conversation, 1989.

[58] Msg, CDR, JTF-Panama, to CINCSO, 182200Z Apr 88, sub: BLUE SPOON, COMJTFPM OPORD 7–88.

posited a concept of operations consisting of four phases, the first two of which dealt with the predeployment of some special operations equipment and strike forces to Panama several days in advance of executing offensive operations. Phase III would begin at H-hour with a Ranger battalion under Task Force Red deploying from the United States and seizing the Torrijos-Tocumen airport complex. A second Ranger battalion, constituting the remainder of Task Force Red, would deploy to Howard Air Force Base, board waiting helicopters, and move to isolate and, on order, neutralize the Panama Defense Forces at the Comandancia. Other JSOTF task forces, namely White, Black, Blue, and Green, would simultaneously carry out other offensive operations called for in SOUTHCOM's version of BLUE SPOON. AC–130 gunships and AH–6 Little Bird helicopters would act in direct support of the special operations strike forces against those targets that planners anticipated would offer the greatest resistance. During these operations, the JSOTF operations center would be "the central node for maneuver, airspace, and fire support decision making." The fourth, and final, phase of the operation would begin when targets secured by Special Operations Forces were turned over to JTF-Panama.[59]

The complexity of the BLUE SPOON plans alone required careful and frequent coordination among the Southern Command, the joint special operations task force, JTF-Panama, and Special Operations Command, South. Certain portions of the plans had to be clarified. The JSOTF commander, for example, wanted to know exactly what was meant by the term *neutralization* that appeared frequently in the operation orders in reference to the Panama Defense Forces. There were also more sensitive issues that had to be sorted out. Panama City and the area surrounding it would be the primary battlefield during offensive operations, and both joint task forces would have troops operating in close proximity to one another. The special operations planners believed that, once the hostilities began, JSOTF should control the major combat assets employed, with the exception of those used by JTF-Panama for defensive missions. As Col. Joe Stringham, who helped draft the original JSOTF Phase IV operation order, asserted, the job of conventional forces on D-day was to hold what they had and "stay out of the way." The problem was that JTF-Panama also had offensive BLUE SPOON missions, albeit only a few, to conduct at H-hour. Early in April, Colonel Fry had questioned whether JTF-Panama could "simultaneously defend all vital installations and defend/assault at Ft Espinar and Ft Amador?" JTF-Panama believed that it could, and the operation orders remained unchanged. Between 14 and 17 April, the special operations planners from Fort Bragg visited Panama to "deconflict facilities and terrain with all JTFPM customers." Some issues were resolved, others were not. Among the latter was the allocation of air support. In JTF-Panama's copy of the JSOTF operation order of 21 April, next to a sentence reading, "All JTF-PM helicopters will return to their departure location and not be used during the rest of BLUE SPOON," someone had written in bold letters, "NO!"[60]

---

[59] Msg, CDR, JSOTF, to CINCSO, 212332Z Apr 88, sub: COMJSOTF OPORD 8–88, BLUE SPOON.

[60] Ibid. Stringham quote from Interv, John Partin with Brig Gen Joseph S. Stringham, U.S. Army, 29 Aug 89, Fort Bragg, N.C. Fry quote from Msg, CDR, SOCSOUTH, to CINCSO, 080120Z Apr 88, sub: Commander's Sitrep No. 010. Last quote from Msg, CDR, JSOTF, to CINCSO, 212332Z Apr 88, sub: COMJSOTF OPORD 8–88, BLUE SPOON.

On 23 April, Lt. Gen. Gary Luck, the special operations commander at Fort Bragg, sent a message to Woerner, stating that the mid-April coordination meetings had helped to refine and integrate the supporting plans for BLUE SPOON. To sustain the momentum of the process, he advocated a "continuous dialogue" between conventional and special operations planners and called for another coordination visit at JTF-Panama's earliest convenience. The list of major issues that needed to be discussed included intelligence collection and dissemination; gray, white, and black lists of enemy or unfriendly personnel; operations security and command and control; vulnerability analyses of Howard Air Force Base, Rodman Naval Station, and Albrook Air Station; JSOTF–JTF-Panama hand-off procedures; coordination of psychological operations and fire support; JTF-Panama AC–130 requirements; the availability of tactical air support; logistical issues; deception plans; rules of engagement; and communications.[61]

The second coordination visit took place 27–29 April. After evaluating its results, Luck sent Woerner a list of what had been resolved and what had not. Among the former, Luck listed over a dozen issues. They included procedures for JSOTF hand-offs to JTF-Panama; assignments of areas of responsibility; the insertion of JTF-Panama forces into Tinajitas; airspace management (the joint special operations task force would control all air activities from H minus 2 to H plus 10); the validation of JSOTF requirements for certain communications channels; the jamming of PDF air traffic control radar and communications; and support for psychological operations. The list of unresolved issues was just as long and included airspace management in connection with a JTF-Panama assault on Fort Amador; the daily operation of the Torrijos-Tocumen airport complex once the Rangers had departed; command and control arrangements for the 3d Battalion, 7th Special Forces Group, during BLUE SPOON; "reinitiating" reconnaissance operations by Special Operations Command, South; the allocation of AC–130 assets; the control of Volant Solo (a C–130 transport plane converted into a PSYOP platform); the vulnerability studies of specific U.S. installations in Panama; command and control of close air support; logistical information; and tactical deception "integral to JSOTF planning." To help reach consensus on these and other issues, the special operations delegation from Fort Bragg left Panama agreeing to attend bimonthly targeting meetings with JTF-Panama for the purpose of further BLUE SPOON planning.[62]

Although many issues raised in the contingency plans for U.S. military operations in Panama remained open for discussion, the procedures for coordinating and refining the plans had been established by early May. The writing and revising of the CINCSO and CMOTF KRYSTAL BALL operation orders were confined to a few planners in SOUTHCOM's Policy, Strategy, and Programs Directorate, assisted by reservists coming in on 31-day temporary tours. On matters pertaining to POST TIME and KLONDIKE KEY, the Southern Command and JTF-Panama would work closely together. On BLUE SPOON, coordination efforts involved the SOUTHCOM Operations Directorate and two of the three headquarters directly answerable to

---

[61] Msg, CDR, JSOTF, to CINCSO, 230700Z Apr 88, sub: JSOTF BLUE SPOON Coordination Visit.

[62] Quotes from Msg, CDR [JSOTF] to CINCSO, 041700Z May 88, sub: JSOTF BLUE SPOON Coordination Visit. Msg, CDR, SOCSOUTH, to [JSOTF], 300135Z Apr 88, sub: Commander's Sitrep No. 032.

Violence, "Fissures," and a Prayer Book

Woerner under the plan—JTF-Panama and the joint special operations task force—with the Atlantic Command remaining recalcitrant on making a carrier battle group available, even after Crowe's ruling that it should. On 9 May, the Joint Chiefs of Staff approved the series of updated PRAYER BOOK operation orders for further "execution planning."[63] One contingency not mentioned in the message concerned what to do about Noriega should the United States take military action against his regime. Plans for possible actions along those lines continued to remain highly sensitive and compartmentalized.

Fissures

Whether the PRAYER BOOK plans, particularly BLUE SPOON, should be executed became a subject of debate. There were Americans in and out of uniform who claimed that national honor and the growing threat to U.S. citizens in Panama demanded military action. To this small chorus was added the voices of several Panamanian opposition leaders. On 13 April, a JTF-Panama intelligence summary noted that the National Civic Crusade's failure to remove Noriega through protests, demonstrations, and strikes had demoralized the opposition, causing many Panamanians, in their private conversations with U.S. officials, to express "hope for a U.S. military solution." Against this significant, but never excessive pressure, President Reagan held fast to his 29 March decision against the use of armed force. Consequently, SOUTHCOM's guidance to JTF-Panama was to continue security enhancement measures but to avoid actions that could be construed by the Panamanian armed forces as overly aggressive.[64] This approach suited Woerner, Loeffke, and key members of their staffs, who did not waiver in their belief that U.S. intervention in Panama would be a disaster for American interests and policy in Latin America.

The real danger, in their view, was war by accident. The Panama Defense Forces, intelligence reports confirmed, would not deliberately provoke the United States to the point of open hostilities. But there was always the possibility that an unforeseen incident could escalate into a confrontation neither side desired. The continuous intrusions by armed persons on U.S. installations and the incidents of 12 and 20 April had demonstrated the risks involved in crisis management. In early May, the U.S. intelligence community in Panama submitted its first detailed assessments of the composition and intentions of the intruders. According to these reports, soldiers from the PDF jungle operations school and the 7th Infantry Company (also known as the *macho de monte*, or "Wild Boars") had conducted reconnaissance missions against U.S. facilities in mid-March. Noriega had subsequently created a special operational element made up of select PDF members from several units and possibly trained by Cuban advisers at Rio Hato. Captain Cortizo, who had made an appearance at the tank farm the night of the firefight, had apparently been picked by Noriega to exercise overall control of this special element's activities. After training for ten days, the unit had returned to staging areas near La Chorrera and Arraiján and had begun its intrusions into the fuel depot, the Rodman Ammunition Supply Point, and the area west of Howard

---

[63] Msg, JCS to USCINCLANT et al., 091709Z May 88, sub: Approval USCINCSO OPORDs.

[64] Buckley, *Panama*, pp. 136–37. Quote from Msg, CDR, JTF-Panama, to AIG 9029, 132230Z Apr 88, sub: Panama INTSUM 57–88. Msg, CINCSO to CDR, JTF-Panama, 092154Z Apr 88, sub: SCJ3 Guidance Message No. 1.

Air Force Base. The reasons for the intrusions were not readily apparent, although sabotage, intelligence gathering, training, and psychological warfare were offered in the reports as possibilities. One point, however, was clear. The intruders had stopped short of "engaging in a decisive conflict which would provoke a major US response."[65] The marines could take some comfort in this assessment, which seemed to vindicate their argument that there had indeed been intruders on the tank farm the night of 12 April. (The episode remained controversial, however, as did the related issue of whether the marines had overreacted to any intrusion that had taken place.)

By the time these reports were issued, the danger of accidental war was receding, as were the tensions that had led Loeffke in late April to consider asking Woerner for more combat units. During the first week in May, in fact, the intrusions had dropped off sharply, although the reason seemingly owed to special circumstances: Noriega was at a crucial stage in his renewed negotiations with the United States.[66]

A second round of talks with the dictator had begun with Michael Kozak's return trip to Panama in mid-April. There would be another, extended visit from late-April through mid-May and another covering 22–25 May. The purpose of these talks mirrored that of the first round in mid-March: to reach an agreement that would allow Noriega to relinquish his power in Panama peacefully. The Southern Command was kept out of the secret negotiations, but, during Kozak's mid-April visit, the headquarters did convene discussion groups to consider the kind of interagency campaign plan that would be necessary to achieve U.S. policy goals, should the negotiations fail. Those goals, in what came as close to specific policy guidance as the Southern Command would receive, had recently been disseminated in classified form by White House chief of staff Howard Baker. They included the protection of U.S. citizens, the defense of the canal and U.S. facilities, the "placement of the [U.S. government] in the best possible position to maneuver in a post-Noriega regime," and the "removal of General Noriega (preferably without resorting to a military option)."[67] Among the U.S. government agencies represented in the weekend discussions at Quarry Heights were the Southern Command, the State Department, the U.S. Embassy, and the CIA. At times the attendees broke

---

[65] Msgs, CINCSO to JCS/Defense Intelligence Agency (DIA), 091350Z May 88, sub: Panama Intelligence Weekly, PDF "Special Operational Element," and CDR, JTF-Panama, to AIG 9029, 111900Z May 88, sub: INTREP 16–88 May. One question not addressed in these reports was whether or not Cubans took part in the 12 April intrusion at the Arraiján Tank Farm. Several high-ranking U.S. officers have indicated to the author that they had reason to believe the Cubans were involved and suffered casualties. In *Divorcing the Dictator*, pp. 283–84, Kempe cites a source "with access to U.S. military intelligence reports" telling him that the intruders on the tank farm were made up primarily of Cuban commandos and that three were wounded, one of whom died later. At the time, New York Senator Alfonse D'Amato accused the Pentagon of withholding information regarding Cuban involvement so as not to heighten tensions between the United States and Panama. On post-JUST CAUSE information relating to the 12 April 1988 firefight, see Reynolds, *Just Cause*, pp. 9–10. During a trip to Panama in 1990, the author also saw interrogation reports that support what Reynolds writes in his official history.

[66] Msgs, CDR, USARSO, to CSA, 132330Z May 88, sub: Update No. 11, and CINCSO to JCS/DIA, 091350Z May 88, sub: Panama Intelligence Weekly, PDF "Special Operational Element."

[67] Baker's goals are listed in Memo for CINCSO, 13 May 88, sub: Panama Campaign Plan, signed by Brig Gen James J. LeCleir, U.S. Air Force (USAF), SCJ–5.

into small groups to brainstorm political, economic, military, and psychological initiatives that, if integrated into a comprehensive program, might secure the goals set forth by Baker.

The proposed interagency campaign plan that emerged from the sessions underwent revisions and rewrites, but its fundamental approach remained constant: a coordinated effort to create and exploit what Woerner referred to as "fissures" within the Panama Defense Forces. One of SOUTHCOM's key roles in this stratagem would be to deliver a series of messages in face-to-face meetings with Panamanian officers who were close to Noriega or who favored a long-term PDF-U.S. relationship. The messages would be designed to convince the selected officers that Noriega was placing the PDF's existence as an institution in jeopardy by courting a military confrontation with the United States. The U.S. government, as SOUTHCOM officers would emphasize, supported the preservation of the Panama Defense Forces as an organization and was committed to the fulfillment of U.S. treaty obligations. The implicit message was that the Panamanian military had to take charge of its own destiny, place loyalty to its institutions (and concern for one's career) above loyalty to Noriega, and remove the general from power before the United States was forced to do the job, in which case the PDF would fall with the general. The proposed guidance for delivering these messages cautioned against conveying the impression that U.S. officers were imposing a *gringo* solution to a Panamanian problem or that they were making promises regarding future aid or favors. Woerner also emphasized that the SOUTHCOM initiative would not work in a vacuum but had to be bolstered by a reduction of off-post personnel, military shows of force, increased activity by the Panamanian opposition, and a fully developed set of interagency political, economic, and psychological measures for increasing the pressure on Noriega and the Panama Defense Forces.[68]

The scope and magnitude of the interagency campaign plan was formidable. A revised version, submitted by the SOUTHCOM Policy, Strategy, and Programs Directorate to Woerner on 13 May, postulated a sequence of actions calculated to generate popular support for the opposition and to motivate and strengthen the opposition movement, to convince the Panamanian military to act on its own to preserve itself as an institution, to position the U.S. government for future actions in Panama, and to convince Noriega that he would be forced to leave Panama, "one way or another." The démarche consisted of three phases, or "packages." Package A, the "soft" approach, contained thirty initiatives, each assigned to the appropriate U.S. "execution authority"—SOUTHCOM's commander, the U.S. Embassy, the Joint Chiefs, the State Department, the Panama Canal Commission, or the Interagency Policy Review Group in Washington. If Package A failed to achieve results after about sixty days, Package B would be executed. Intentionally designed "to be hard-line and more provocative," the eight or so actions included bringing additional combat units into Panama, commencing "show of force military exercises," and enacting a selective economic embargo. If Noriega still clung to power, Package C would begin a flow of "full combat assets" and an evacuation of U.S. citizens, enact a total economic quarantine, and set the stage for Woerner to deliver an ultimatum to Noriega to step aside or suffer the consequences. An interagency campaign staff, composed of the U.S. ambassador to Panama, the

---

[68] Woerner Interv, 30 Apr 91; Paper, Creating and Exploiting Fissures in the PDF, 29 Apr 88, Woerner Papers, MHI.

SOUTHCOM commander, the Panama Canal Commission administrator, and a CIA representative would supervise execution of the plan and ensure the initiatives were properly coordinated.[69]

To be effective, the proposed campaign plan needed to be executed as an integrated whole. An uncoordinated, piecemeal implementation of the plan would likely ensure its failure, a point Woerner tried to get across to his superiors in Washington. As Woerner recalls telling the Pentagon, "What you can't do is tell me to execute one, two, three, four, or five elements of this plan and think that you have a strategy. . . . And I got back: 'Implement paragraph 3A, 4C.' But that is exactly what I said would not work." At one point in late May, the interagency group in Washington did approve most aspects of one version of the plan but withheld authority for certain other critical initiatives.[70] This came at a time when the behind-the-scenes negotiations between Noriega and Kozak had become public knowledge, and the Reagan administration was engaged in controlling the damage caused by rumors, true to be sure, that the president was prepared to drop the indictments against the general if Noriega agreed to step down from power.

Despite a Senate nonbinding resolution and the urgings of Vice President George H. W. Bush not to drop the indictments in a deal with Noriega, President Reagan authorized one last round in the talks in late May. Kozak returned to Panama, where after two days of intense negotiations, he believed he had reached an agreement with the general. A last-minute snag developed, however, when Noriega balked at issuing a public statement. Frustrated, Secretary of State Shultz ordered Kozak to break off the talks. On 25 May, Shultz announced that the United States had taken all offers off the table and contemplated no further negotiations.[71]

With a diplomatic solution to the crisis beyond reach for the foreseeable future, Woerner again raised the fissures campaign plan with the Joint Chiefs but without success. Thus, with the interagency approach moribund and with the president continuing to resist the use of U.S. military force in the crisis, the question of policy guidance arose once again. What did the administration want the Southern Command to do? The answer came that summer. With the presidential election campaign impending and with Vice President Bush, the probable Republican nominee, vulnerable on the Panama issue because of his previous dealings as CIA director with Noriega, Woerner was told face-to-face and by way of telephone to put the crisis on the back burner and to keep the situation under control lest an intensification of the crisis hurt Bush's chances for the Republican nomination and the presidency.[72] Several officers at the Southern Command who knew of the

---

[69] Memo for CINCSO, 13 May 88, sub: Panama Campaign Plan.

[70] Woerner is quoted in Thomas Donnelly, Margaret Roth, and Caleb Baker, *Operation Just Cause: The Storming of Panama* (New York: Lexington Books, 1991), pp. 33–34. See also Woerner Interv, 30 Apr 91; Msg, SecDef to AmEmb, Panama/CINCSO, 272036Z May 88, sub: Implementation of PDF Fissures Plan.

[71] Just how close Kozak was to an agreement with Noriega became a controversial issue. The account of the negotiations in Kempe, *Divorcing the Dictator*, pp. 309–31, suggests that Shultz's impatience scuttled an accord. Buckley, in *Panama*, pp. 140–45, argues that Noriega was just stringing the United States along, buying time to consolidate further his position in Panama and to make the Reagan administration look foolish in the process. See also *Tropic Times*, 27 May 88.

[72] Msg, CINCSO to JCS, 272331Z May 88, sub: USCINCSO PSYOP Campaign Plan; Kempe, *Divorcing the Dictator*, p. 333; Donnelly et al., *Operation Just Cause*, pp. 35–36; author's informal conversations with a SOUTHCOM officer who worked directly for Woerner. According to Kempe's

new guidance believed that the White House had improperly involved the military in partisan politics. But orders were orders. Noriega was not going away, efforts by the United States to effect his ouster had been put on hold, and the Southern Command was left to contemplate an indefinite stay in the Twilight Zone.

---

account, National Security Adviser Colin Powell delivered this message to Woerner personally, while Admiral Crowe, the chairman of the Joint Chiefs, and Secretary of Defense Frank Carlucci conveyed it over the telephone.

4

SETTLING IN

MAY 1988–JANUARY 1989

After the recall of the Kozak mission in late May 1988, the crisis in U.S.-Panamanian relations, with all its attendant risks, settled into something of a routine. On the diplomatic front, President Reagan maintained economic sanctions against the Solis Palma regime, continued U.S. recognition of Eric Devalle as the legitimate president of Panama, and, in general, continued to seek Noriega's removal from power. Still, beyond monitoring these and a series of less publicized initiatives, the administration's interest in Panama seemed to wane as, for the remainder of the year, Reagan turned his attention to more pressing foreign policy matters, beginning on 29 May with a summit meeting with Soviet leader Mikhail Gorbachev in Moscow.

A similar shift in priorities occurred as well within the American news media. Once reporters, analysts, and columnists had conducted their postmortems on the Noriega-Kozak negotiations, the crisis in Panama nearly vanished from newsprint and the airwaves. Other events now vied for media coverage, chief among them the U.S. presidential election. As 1988 unfolded, Republicans and Democrats held state primaries followed by national conventions; they then took aim at each other in the campaign proper. The election and Panama were linked, of course, but not in any way clearly visible to the American voter. And that was how the administration intended to keep it, as evidenced by its directive to Woerner not to let matters in Panama deteriorate to the point where the inevitable publicity might raise as a campaign issue the Republican presidential candidate's former ties with Noriega. The SOUTHCOM commander and his staff agreed, albeit for reasons far removed from partisan politics, that everything possible should be done to prevent the crisis from spinning out of control.[1] A serious escalation, they feared, might culminate in a U.S.-PDF military confrontation. Such a showdown would likely damage not only long-term interests of the United States in Panama but America's standing and policies throughout Latin America as well.

---

[1] On the intrusion of partisan politics into the crisis, see Chapter 3. Woerner's instructions to keep the lid on are cited in Donnelly, Roth, and Baker, *Operation Just Cause*, p. 36. The author's talks with key staff officers who were at the Southern Command in mid-1988 confirm the receipt of the directive and the resentment expressed among the officers privy to it.

Noriega, needless to say, was not visited by an injunction similar to that imposed on Woerner. The dictator, though, had a knack for sensing just how far he could go in taunting the United States without provoking a military response that he could not hope to survive politically. Since at this point in the crisis, he had no intention of crossing the line marking the limits of American tolerance, he became a silent partner in advancing the Reagan administration's goal of containing the crisis. But if he was an unsolicited accomplice in this effort, he was also an unpredictable one, in that he remained a despot willing to do what he regarded as necessary to retain control over his country. With the diplomatic impasse and Washington's subsequent preoccupation with the election and other issues, he detected a low-risk opportunity to bolster his position at home by intensifying his anti-American rhetoric and authorizing further PDF intrusions onto U.S. military facilities. With his blessing, the Panama Defense Forces and the regime it propped up also continued to violate the canal treaties when circumstances permitted and to engage in the physical, psychological, and bureaucratic harassment of U.S. forces and citizens in Panama. Statistics compiled on the harassment, intrusions, and treaty infractions fluctuated from week to week and month to month, with each upsurge conveying the message that Noriega, should he choose, could make life extremely difficult, even dangerous, for many of the Americans living or stationed in Panama. Thus, despite the desire of key leaders in both countries to prevent the situation from escalating toward armed conflict, so long as the crisis persisted, with its low-grade intimidation and provocations, there was always the chance that, in the words of one U.S. general, "Sooner or later, somebody's going to get killed out there."[2]

WOERNER'S CRITIQUE AND POLICY PROPOSALS

In the absence of such a dramatic event, the staff at SOUTHCOM and JTF-Panama believed that, for the foreseeable future, the situation in Panama would continue to be handled as a "crisis on the cheap," with decision makers in Washington allocating few resources for managing the problem and little guidance for resolving it.[3] Some high-placed officers in the Pentagon appeared to question whether or not the situation in Panama even constituted a serious threat. The country's cities were not in flames, blood was not flowing through the streets, and the only fatality U.S. forces had suffered to date had been the result of friendly fire. Lt. Gen. Thomas Kelly, the director of operations on the Joint Staff, conveyed this message during a visit to the Southern Command in 1988. In a conference room

---

[2] The officer's quote is from Interv, author with Brig Gen Marc Cisneros, U.S. Army, 1 May 89, Quarry Heights, Panama.

[3] The discussion that follows of SOUTHCOM's perception of the policy-making process regarding the Panama crisis is based on Intervs, author with Maj Dan Augustine, U.S. Army, 13 Jun 89, Fort Clayton, Panama; Cisneros, 1 May 89; Col John A. Cope Jr., U.S. Army, 25 May 89, Fort Clayton, Panama; Brig Gen John F. Stewart Jr., U.S. Army, 14 Jun 89, Quarry Heights, Panama; General Frederick F. Woerner Jr., U.S. Army (Ret.), 30 Apr 91, Fort Leavenworth, Kans.; Col Paul F. Morgan, U.S. Army, 7 Jul 89, MacDill Air Force Base, Fla.; Briefing, Brig Gen Cisneros, 14 Apr 89, Fort Leavenworth, Kans.; Presentation, General Woerner, 30 Apr 91, Fort Leavenworth, Kans.; Conversations, author with Maj Fred Polk, U.S. Army, 1989; Msg, CINCSO to CJCS [personal, General Woerner for Admiral Crowe], 042115Z May 89, sub: Policy Initiatives Post Elections. The phrase "crisis on the cheap" was used by Colonel Cope in a conversation with the author in early 1989.

full of officers, he explained that, from his vantage point in the Pentagon, the so-called crisis was something akin to a "pimple on an elephant's ass."[4]

A "pimple" it may have been, but it was causing enough irritation, in Woerner's opinion, to detract from SOUTHCOM's ability to treat even uglier blemishes in the region, such as narco-trafficking. Even so, the crisis was not so festering as to goad the Reagan administration into applying an effective remedy in the form of a comprehensive policy designed to compel Noriega and his cronies to step aside. Instead of policy, the Southern Command was the recipient of what Woerner referred to derisively as tactical guidance and naïve counsel. There had also been the stream of ill-conceived, even counterproductive, measures emanating from Washington, against which he had objected, to little avail. The administration's selective economic sanctions, for example, were indeed beginning to have an adverse effect on the Noriega-backed regime, but the penalties continued to exact an even higher toll on businessmen and professionals opposed to the dictator, and on the Panamanian people in general. A continuation of that trend, Woerner feared, could "nudge" the opposition into an accommodation with the dictator.

The SOUTHCOM commander also was not pleased with the instructions he had received to sever almost all contacts with the Panama Defense Forces. In a message to Elliott Abrams, the assistant secretary of state for inter-American affairs, Woerner argued that the tactic "could be playing into Noriega's hands" by increasing the apprehensions of Panamanian officers that the United States was out to destroy the organization itself, not just to remove its tainted leadership. If the policy stood, the general warned, the likely consequences included the loss of a valuable source of information, an intensified feeling on the part of even the more professional and moderate PDF officers that their future was linked to Noriega's political survival, and, concomitantly, a decreased likelihood that Panama's military would act against its leader in a way that would constitute the kind of Panamanian solution to a Panamanian problem that Woerner had advocated from the outset of the crisis. "We may well be unifying the PDF, rather than creating the critical wedges—which should be our objective," he concluded.[5]

Another impediment to an effective U.S. policy for Panama, Woerner insisted with increasing frustration, was the continued inability to achieve interagency consensus in Washington. Differences that had divided the State Department, the Defense Department, the White House, the CIA, the Joint Chiefs, the Southern Command, the U.S. Drug Enforcement Administration, and other bureaucratic organizations from the beginning of the crisis did not lend themselves easily to compromise or resolution. The result, in Woerner's words, was a policy of "incrementalism by committee," in which policy makers sought the "lowest common denominator"—that is, the minimal response to the crisis that they could make without any one agency sacrificing critical points on its closely held agenda. So long as these turf battles persisted, any all-inclusive policy put forward for interagency consideration was likely to be only partially implemented or, worse,

---

[4] Kelly's use of the phrase, "pimple on an elephant's ass," was related to the author by a former SOUTHCOM officer present at the general's briefing.

[5] Quotes from Msg, USSOUTHCOM to State/RCI [personal, Woerner to Abrams], 271530Z Oct 88, sub: Clarification of Panama Policy–Business as Usual. Trip Rpt, 23 Nov 88, sub: Trip Report—CINC Washington Visit 21–22 November 1988; Stewart Interv, 14 Jun 89; Presentation, Woerner, 30 Apr 91.

U.S. Military Intervention in Panama, June 1987–December 1989

Paramilitary Dignity Battalion members in red T-shirts in the streets ready to fight

confined to bureaucratic limbo. The fate of Woerner's "fissures" plan in April–May 1988 had demonstrated to the SOUTHCOM commander the difficulty of trying to forge a comprehensive approach to resolving the crisis.[6]

Throughout the remainder of 1988, Woerner found few reasons to alter his critical opinion of Washington's handling of the affair. While the Joint Chiefs accepted or approved several of his proposals pertaining solely to military aspects of the crisis, his more comprehensive economic, political, and psychological recommendations requiring an integrated interagency program continued to be tabled or only partially implemented. In early October a SOUTHCOM report held out little hope that "bold new initiatives" would be approved by Washington for at least another six months. In the message, Woerner's Policy, Strategy, and Programs Directorate predicted that, even after the presidential election, the winner, whether Michael Dukakis or George H. W. Bush, would probably take a cautious "wait-and-see" approach until he entered the White House in January and had a chance to review U.S. policy toward Central America and Panama.[7]

Woerner saw little profit in procrastination. Much of the information and intelligence available to the Southern Command indicated that Noriega was strengthening his hold on power and that, given Washington's preoccupation with other issues and the National Civic Crusade's relative quiescence, he was under no real pressure to abandon his criminal and dictatorial ways. The Kozak mission, besides allowing Noriega time to regroup after the 16 March coup attempt, had demonstrated the futility of reaching a political accommodation with the general, at least in the near future. That realization notwithstanding, President Reagan showed no inclination to reverse his decision against U.S. military intervention,

---

[6] Quotes from Presentation, Woerner, 30 Apr 91. The "fissures" plan is discussed in Chapter 3.
[7] Information Paper, USSOUTHCOM J–5, 5 Oct 88, sub: Support for U.S. Policy in Panama.

a decision with which Woerner still concurred. The SOUTHCOM commander, though, strongly believed that, between the extremes of negotiation and war, there was much room for effective action and that difficult decisions about the crisis should be made sooner rather than later. With this in mind, he persisted in seeking a comprehensive interagency strategy based on a series of continuously updated proposals he submitted to Washington through the chairman of the Joint Chiefs of Staff.

One set of proposals went to Admiral Crowe in a message dated 7 October. Woerner began by advising the chairman that the time had come for "the U.S. to apply additional pressure to the Noriega regime." The paragraphs that followed outlined an interagency plan for covert U.S. psychological operations that would improve the flow of information from "non-regime sources" in Panama to the Panamanian people. Because of "legal limitations on covert activities by DOD [Department of Defense] and our need not to be seen as being directly tied to the opposition," Woerner recommended that the military serve in "a supporting and advisory role to whichever agency is given the lead." The plan included the use of electronic and written media, such as a radio station offshore or in an adjacent country, a mobile van, an airborne platform, tapes, an illustrated comic book, and issues of the *Tropic Times*; advice and assistance to the opposition in targeting its desired audience, developing a campaign plan, learning information dissemination techniques, and gaining access to polls and surveys conducted by agencies outside Panama; and activities that would exploit the PDF's sensitivity to its image in Central America. In addition, a "leak of a professionally written psychological profile on Noriega showing serious personality defects of a kind not compatible with Latino culture," Woerner suggested, "might serve to strain relationships between Noriega and his key supporters in the PDF."[8]

Woerner followed this message nine days later with another, setting forth a campaign that would, through overt means, convey positive information about the goals of the United States in the region. In the pages of the *Tropic Times* and the broadcasts of the Southern Command Network's television channel and radio station, SOUTHCOM had already increased its own news coverage of the crisis. Additional measures, however, were still required. A survey had revealed that, among U.S. service personnel in Panama, 60 percent did not understand America's policy in the crisis, and more than 90 percent wanted U.S. officials to explain what the policy was. SCN radio and television could address this need, Woerner wrote, without becoming "politicized or used in a psyop role." He also proposed that the U.S. Treaty Implementation Plan, a classified document that established milestones for the withdrawal of U.S. forces from Panama by the end of the century, be declassified in an effort to counter Noriega's allegations that the United States had no intention of honoring the canal treaties. Additional recommendations included running a series of *Tropic Times* articles and television and radio programs on U.S. treaty rights; having senior American officials address issues such as regional democracy, economics, and security assistance; and publicizing U.S. military activities in Panama so

---

[8] Msg, CINCSO to CJCS [personal for Lt Gen Riscassi, JCS; Asst SecDef Armitage; Chargé d'Affaires Maisto, AmEmb; and Col Rankin, USCINCSO, Liaison Officer (LNO)], 071845Z Oct 88, sub: Panama–Covert Psyops Proposal.

as to demonstrate America's determination to defend the canal and protect its citizens. The implementation of these proposals, Woerner maintained, would keep U.S. forces and Panamanian citizens better informed and, thus, lessen their vulnerability to "hostile disinformation."[9]

Soon after Bush was elected president, Woerner threw a third cluster of proposals into the interagency arena. In a visit to Washington in late November, the general met with officials in the Pentagon and the State Department and laid out his "Panama scenario." The assessment he presented was bleak, and he followed it with an appeal for the United States to become more "proactive" by promoting an "aggressive but subtle" initiative in which the Panamanian opposition to Noriega would take the lead in publicizing human rights violations in the country. The goal of such action would be to increase international and domestic pressures on the Solis Palma regime and Noriega (but not on the PDF, lest its officers "circle the wagons") and to "ensure the most propitious electoral conditions possible" for Panama's presidential balloting, scheduled for May 1989. As in Woerner's covert psychological operations plan, the United States government, with the State Department playing the leading role, would not become outwardly involved in the human rights campaign but would restrict itself to behind-the-scenes advice and support for Panama's opposition groups and other interested parties such as the Catholic church, human rights organizations, and private citizens.[10]

From experience, Woerner knew that his recommendations might never emerge from the bureaucratic labyrinth of interagency politics. He had another concern as well. Two of his three sets of comprehensive proposals were predicated on the Panamanian opposition taking the initiative, and he was not at all confident that the National Civic Crusade was up to the task. This perception of the Civic Crusade was widely shared within the U.S. military community in Panama. Opposition leaders had at times shown remarkable bravery, but on the whole, the movement seemed to have run out of steam, despite its periodic demonstrations. The NCC itself conceded as much. In mid-June 1988, after a year of challenging Noriega and the government, one opposition leader remarked, "The time of white handkerchiefs, pot banging and marches is over. We need to find something new." Little of substance followed. In Woerner's view, the Civic Crusade lacked strong, charismatic leadership, was prone to fragmentation, and might even be inclined to seek an accommodation with Noriega. Some companies owned by opposition members continued to do business with the Panama Defense Forces, even as the owners called for U.S. intervention. In short, Woerner concluded that Noriega's well-to-do critics wanted a solution to the crisis that would not entail undue risk or sacrifice on their part.[11]

Brig. Gen. John F. Stewart Jr., SOUTHCOM's director of intelligence, agreed that the opposition was "sitting on its hands," when it should have been taking to the streets in an effort to garner labor and student support and to confront the regime

---

[9] Msg, CINCSO to CJCS et al., 160030Z Oct 88, sub: USCINCSO Public Information Plan.

[10] Quoted words from Trip Rpt, 23 Nov 88, sub: Trip Report—CINC Washington Visit 21–22 November 1988. Paper, n.d., "Human Rights Initiative."

[11] The opposition leader is quoted in *Tropic Times*, 13 Jun 88. Woerner's critique of the opposition can be found in Trip Rpt, 23 Nov 88, sub: Trip Report—CINC Washington Visit 21–22 November 1988; Msg [draft?], CINCSO to Crowe, Nov 88, sub: Outlook for the Next Six Months in Panama; Woerner Interv, 30 Apr 91.

with continuous turmoil. "Freedom is not free," Stewart declared. Yet few in the opposition seemed willing to pay the necessary price, whatever that might be. There was also the problem of relations between the National Civic Crusade and the Panama Defense Forces. Woerner's strategy for toppling the Noriega dictatorship called for the civilian opposition, at some point, to join in common cause with sympathetic elements within the Panamanian military. But, as Stewart noted, the two groups were natural antagonists, despite their alleged business connections. The PDF regarded itself as representing labor and the lower classes, while the opposition's leaders came primarily from the white business and professional classes who resented the steady encroachment of the armed forces on the Panamanian economy. PDF members, therefore, had good reason to believe that the opposition, should it come to power, would not hesitate to dismantle their institution. Thus, even those officers who despised Noriega regarded the Civic Crusade as an unacceptable alternative. Until a reluctant and intimidated opposition built bridges to the Panama Defense Forces, the prospects for an internal solution to the crisis remained problematic.[12]

As 1988 drew to a close, Woerner and his principal advisers came to suspect that the development of a comprehensive U.S. policy for dealing with the crisis in Panama would have to await the inauguration of the new American president, the rejuvenation of the Panamanian opposition, and perhaps Panama's presidential election the coming May. In the meantime, Woerner would continue his efforts to keep the volatile situation under control. Left to "grope and cope," as one USARSO officer put it, SOUTHCOM's commander, his staff, and key action officers met regularly with their counterparts in the U.S. Embassy and other agencies to discuss and coordinate various routine undertakings that the crisis required. Also, as SOUTHCOM's Center for Treaty Affairs continued to deliver formal protests regarding PDF misconduct and treaty violations, Woerner, in an effort to reduce the risks to Americans, initiated on his own authority limited measures to reduce the number of service personnel and their dependents living in Panama proper and not on U.S. military bases. The measures included cutting back on dependent travel, granting liberal environmental and morale leave, and allowing for the early return of dependents to the United States. As a part of this effort, Woerner successfully sought to change the length of military tours in Panama from thirty-six to thirty months for service personnel accompanied by dependents and from twenty-four to fifteen months for unaccompanied personnel.[13] All the while, SOUTHCOM's commander waited for the appropriate time to mount another appeal to Washington for policy guidance.

Joint Training

Managing the tactical aspects of the crisis remained the responsibility of Joint Task Force–Panama. As the year progressed, the friction that had characterized aspects of the command relationship between that headquarters and the Southern Command persisted, with staff officers at Fort Clayton complaining that their counterparts at Quarry Heights had a habit of not coordinating or consulting

---

[12] Stewart Interv, 14 Jun 89.

[13] The "grope and cope" quote is from Morgan Interv, 7 Jul 89. On interagency meetings in Panama, see Intervs, author with Col Curt Ely, and Lt Col Mike Michaelis, both U.S. Army, 7 Jun 89, Fort Clayton, Panama. On the reduction of off-post personnel (ROPP), see Information Paper, USSOUTHCOM J–5, 5 Oct 88, sub: Support for U.S. Policy in Panama.

Fort Clayton

with the joint task force but rather issuing decrees from above that often ignored tactical realities. Also from the perspective of JTF-Panama, there were too many people in the higher headquarters who wanted to be operators, the result being micromanagement, facilitated in this case by the fact that Quarry Heights and Fort Clayton were just a ten-minute drive from one another. But unsolicited guidance on minor issues could come as well from as far away as Washington, as in the case of the Pentagon dictating the appropriate garb (helmets and flak jackets) for military policemen standing guard in Panama. For JTF-Panama, this kind of "interference" only complicated the command's task of orchestrating day-to-day operations.[14]

As commander of the joint task force, General Loeffke had the mission to ensure that the troops under his command were prepared to provide security and, if required, execute combat operations. This necessitated a good deal of training, and, from the outset, Loeffke insisted to his staff and component commanders that this function be truly joint. At JTF-Panama's daily briefings, the general would listen to each service component's training schedule, then suggest ways to combine the separate training events into a joint undertaking. Staff officers for the components, after experiencing some consternation over this seemingly haphazard and short-notice reordering of their training timetables, began to anticipate Loeffke's wishes. This led to a weekly meeting at which each service's operations officers would discuss the training needs of their units, devise a plan that would satisfy some of these needs through joint training, then present the plan to Colonel Cope, the JTF-Panama director of operations, and, once he approved it, to Loeffke.[15] Before long, the weekly coordination meetings for joint training

---

[14] Intervs, author with Morgan, 7 Jul 89; Cope, 25 May 89; and Col Arnie Rossi, U.S. Army, 27 Mar 89, Fort Clayton, Panama. Conversation, author with Maj Chuck Herrick, USARSO Secy of the General Staff (SGS), Summer 1989, Fort Clayton, Panama.

[15] Msg, CDR, USARSO, to CSA, 310200Z Jan 89, sub: Update No. 20; Interv, author with Maj Billy Ray Fitzgerald, U.S. Army, 28 Apr 89, Fort Clayton, Panama. The systematic planning of joint

became routine, to Loeffke's deep satisfaction. Areas covered by the joint training plans included administration, logistics, communications, intelligence, patrolling, land navigation, linkup procedures and passage of lines, rules of engagement, civil disturbances, interior guard duty, and the use of night-fighting equipment.

Loeffke mandated at least one battalion-size joint training event every other week, and he zealously scrutinized the results. Some of his component commanders showed less enthusiasm for the undertaking. Citing the purely defensive mission of the marines, Colonel Conley, the Marine Force commander, initially resisted joint training but soon relented. The Navy's participation in any scheduled joint training event, on the other hand, could never be taken for granted, and SOCSOUTH's Colonel Fry, whose special operations forces occasionally came under Loeffke's operational control, thought the general had gone too far in making joint training one of the JTF-Panama's primary missions. Fry was characteristically blunt: "This became thought of as a goddamn training experience and not real goddamn operations. . . . I don't play those games. I do not send people on real missions where they can get shot [just] to train them." This skepticism notwithstanding, joint training quickly became a hallmark of JTF-Panama. The sight of a target being attacked simultaneously by a 105-mm. cannon of an Air Force AC–130, the mortars of a Navy special boat unit, and Army gunships was not uncommon, Loeffke informed the chief of staff of the Army. Finally, Loeffke's decision to shuffle several USARSO units in and out of the Arraiján Tank Farm, where they came under the operational control of the Marine Force commander, allowed soldiers to learn the ways of marines and vice versa.[16]

One of the principal goals of joint training was to identify and resolve problems of interoperability. Of the several difficulties that came immediately to the fore, one of the most critical entailed jargon and communications. As Colonel Conley advised Colonel Cope, differences in service terminology and acronyms were leading to misunderstandings and confusion. Some JCS publications helped "high-level staffs" overcome this obstacle, but these were of no use to units at the tactical level. "The potential is present," Conley warned, "to cause a disaster if the wrong terms were to be used in a critical situation." Over time, the problem of terminology was mitigated by several methods, including interservice coordination on a regular basis, the exchange of liaison officers, and simply the ongoing daily routine of a functional joint task force.[17]

Communications were Loeffke's recurring nightmare. The FAX machines, STU III secure telephones, and multichannel hotlines set up in Panama early in the crisis facilitated communication between JTF-Panama, its components, and

---

training events did not completely resolve the problem of JTF-Panama making last-minute changes to the agreed-upon schedules, even though, for optimum effectiveness, these schedules needed to be approved weeks in advance. Interv, Lt Col Robert L. Barefield, 7 Nov 90, Fort Leavenworth, Kans.

[16] Msg, CDR, USARSO, to DA [Loeffke to Schwarzkopf], 100150Z Jun 88, sub: Update No. 13. Intervs, author with Maj Gen Bernard Loeffke, U.S. Army, 27 Mar 89, Fort Clayton, Panama; Barefield, 7 Nov 90; and Lt Col John R. Finch, U.S. Army, 17 Mar 89, Fort Leavenworth, Kans. Quote from Interv, author with Col Chuck Fry, 1 May 89, Albrook Air Station, Panama. Msg, CDR, USARSO, to CSA, 310200Z Jan 89, sub: Update No. 20.

[17] Conley's remarks are from Lessons Learned Rpt, CDR, MARFOR, JTF-Panama, n.d. (but in response to Colonel Cope's memo of 19 May 1988, calling for JTF-Panama components to submit lessons learned to DCSOPS, USARSO, every Monday morning). See also Intervs, author with Maj Tom King, U.S. Army, and Maj Clyde Vaughn, U.S. Army, 18 May 89, Fort Leavenworth, Kans.; and Col Thomas W. Roberts, USMC, 24 Mar 89, Rodman Naval Station, Panama.

higher headquarters, but the tactical-level networks between the components and their units did not always function properly. For this reason, Loeffke insisted on redundant communications and emphasized before every major joint training event that he wanted "the comms stressed to the max." Early problems included the different times at which each service changed its frequencies and variables, the lack of a joint key list for "crypto" variable compatibility, the inability to determine call signs for want of joint communications-electronics operating instructions, and the general incompatibility of one service's equipment with that of another's. Coming up with solutions to these problems on paper was not necessarily difficult, but implementation often took time. Moreover, despite the emphasis Loeffke placed on communications, every time he thought that the nets were operating efficiently, some new glitch would surface to induce yet another nightmare. In an incident in 1989, for example, a Panamanian citizen handling an unexploded artillery shell on the U.S. Army's Empire Range was killed when the shell exploded. Afterwards, Rossi drew a diagram of all the U.S. officers who had used the communications network in reacting to the incident. The network had been overwhelmed. By Rossi's calculations, of the twenty officers who had tied up communications, only five had a legitimate reason for doing so.[18]

As the JTF-Panama director of operations, Cope grappled with another problem highlighted by the joint training events: many of the U.S. troops rotating in and out of Panama for the security enhancement mission simply were not trained or qualified to operate in what he and others regarded as a low intensity conflict. The Cobra crews arriving as part of Task Force Hawk offered a case in point. Trained to destroy Soviet tanks on a European battlefield, they could not readily adjust to a mission that called for close air support for ground troops. Nor were they adept at hitting slow-moving targets in the Bay of Panama, a competition in which the Navy's special boat unit regularly bested them.[19]

The Cobra crews, in Cope's assessment, illustrated a larger problem plaguing the Army: the lack of realistic training for a low intensity conflict. The National Training Center and the Joint Readiness Training Center were essential, Cope conceded, for giving commanders and their troops a feel for combat. But at both locations, training was conducted in a "sterile" force-on-force environment. Innocent civilians and "people-related problems" found in many low intensity conflicts were absent from the training centers. So, too, were various constraints on the use of massive combat power. Rather, there was an emphasis on "kill and destroy," using any means available. Such training tended to reinforce traditional thinking about the role of the military as a conventional instrument, to be employed, after the "failure" of diplomacy, to resolve a problem through the use of force, free from political constraints. "Sterile" training, Cope believed, obscured the inextricable link between politics and military

---

[18] First quote from Interv, author with Loeffke, 29 Mar 89. Second quoted word in both Intervs, author with Loeffke, 31 May 89 and 27 Mar 89. Intervs, author with Rossi, 27 Mar 89; Cope, 29 Mar 89; and Fitzgerald, 28 Apr 89. Msg, item 001, CDR, MARFOR, sub: Communications Interoperability, USMC Command Chronology, 6 April 1988–31 May 1990: Lessons Learned, History and Museums Division, Headquarters, U.S. Marine Corps, Washington, D.C. At some point in mid-1989, Loeffke noted that just when he thought the importance of using the same communications variables during joint training events had been learned, a MEDEVAC exercise was held in which key elements were using different variables. Author's notes on Comments, Maj Gen Loeffke, mid-1989.

[19] Cope Interv, 29 Mar 89; Author's notes on Comments, Maj Gen Loeffke, mid-1989.

power inherent in a low intensity conflict. In his opinion (and that of others), the U.S. military needed to redirect a portion of its training programs to deal with the restraints, politically mandated constraints, and large numbers of civilians found on the nonlinear, unconventional, often urban "battlefield" characteristic of an unorthodox LIC environment.[20]

To facilitate the Army's understanding of low intensity conflict, Loeffke directed Cope to compile "lessons learned" files featuring the insights acquired from the joint training events and from the daily operations of JTF-Panama and its components. Cope consequently instructed staff officers in the field to submit weekly reports containing the required material. Some of the units complied readily; others did so only reluctantly, equating *lessons learned* with *mistakes*. Whichever the case, Cope's staff screened the incoming information, always pulling a few select items to brief at JTF-Panama update meetings. Lessons ranged from the problems encountered in using dogs in the jungle to broader operational issues. Critics of the program charged that the material presented was tilted more toward tactical minutiae than overriding issues dealing with joint interoperability, and Rossi, in reading summary sheets, came to believe that the lessons submitted had been "relearned" rather than learned. Yet, if there was a serious flaw in the program, it was to be found outside of Panama, where various agencies failed to take advantage of the information Cope provided them. At the Center for Army Lessons Learned at Fort Leavenworth, for example, officers expressed appreciation for the USARSO/JTF-Panama reports, but under the erroneous assumption that the center was receiving raw, not processed, material, confined the reports to rarely opened file drawers.[21]

Loeffke, for his part, never tired of disseminating the *lessons* of JTF-Panama, whether in hosting official visitors to U.S. Army, South, or in giving briefings back in the United States. The bottom line, in his view, was that his troops were in an ever-increasing state of readiness to conduct joint operations should the crisis suddenly turn "ugly." In this light, he regarded the joint training program as the "success story" of JTF-Panama, an organization, he told a variety of audiences, that had in many ways become the "joint training center for DOD."[22]

THE "STAGE"

There were concerns voiced early on at the Southern Command and JTF-Panama that an expanded program of joint training throughout the canal area carried with it the slight risk of provoking an unwanted confrontation with the Panama Defense Forces.[23] As scheduled training events proceeded, however, these fears receded, as

---

[20] Cope Interv, 29 Mar 89.

[21] Intervs, author with USARSO staff officer, early 1989; Fitzgerald, 28 Apr 89; Loeffke, 27 Mar 89; and Rossi, 27 Mar 89. Memo, Colonel Cope for CDR, MARFOR, et al., 19 May 88, sub: Input of Lessons Learned on JTF-Panama.

[22] Quotes from Loeffke Interv, 31 May 89. Msg, CDR, USARSO, to CSA, 310200Z Jan 89, sub: Update No. 20.

[23] A SOUTHCOM Disposition Form dated 8 July 1988 raised the possibility of a confrontation. In a note attached to the DF, Cope maintained that Noriega had probably drawn a line on a map. If JTF-Panama crossed that line, even for training purposes, the Panama Defense Forces might well respond with military force. Cope thought the best course was to find out where the line was, perhaps by using U.S. aviation assets, not so much for the purpose of avoiding it as challenging it. To leave the line unchallenged, he argued, might prompt Noriega to move it closer to the canal.

potentially explosive encounters between U.S. troops and Panamanian forces failed to materialize. The same could not be said of concerns raised by the situation on the Arraiján Tank Farm and the Rodman Ammunition Supply Point, where American forces continued their daily security enhancement duties. For a short period in May, during the Noriega-Kozak negotiations, intrusions onto these two U.S. facilities tapered off, prompting Loeffke to express his relief. "Ninety days on alert began to wear thin," he confided to General Vuono. But in June, after the negotiations had collapsed, the intrusions picked up again. From July through October, they escalated sharply, numbering well over a hundred a month.[24] Small arms fire was often exchanged, although, with one exception, the intensity of the shooting in no way approached that of the 12 April firefight. Still, the tank farm and the adjacent ammunition supply point had become the "stage," as Woerner called the area, on which the most dangerous aspects of the Panama crisis were being acted out.

Under Rossi's goose egg approach, the tank farm and the ammunition supply point were in the Marine Forces area of responsibility. Since the marines did not have sufficient personnel to secure both facilities as well as other terrain assigned to them (such as Sierra Miñon, a nearby hill overlooking Howard Air Force Base), Loeffke kept a company-size element from the 193d Infantry Brigade under the MARFOR's operational control. Military police also drew guard duty at the ammunition supply point, even though several MP commanders protested that this static defense mission did not properly employ their mobile assets.[25]

In Loeffke's opinion, the use of infantry and military policemen on the tank farm and ammunition supply point, while helpful in promoting jointness, tied down Army units needed for other duties. Their employment also prevented combat service and combat service support units in Panama from learning their rear area security missions. To remedy the situation, the general gave USARSO's 324th Support Group, band members, communications personnel, and other noncombat elements four weeks to prepare for guard duty on the two facilities. The preparations revealed that the designated units and personnel were not equipped to carry out the mission. They lacked armored vests, night-vision devices, sniper weapons, and adequate communications. Reviewing the statistics, Loeffke concluded that JTF-Panama had surfaced a major weakness in Army training. Efforts were made to correct the deficiencies, and by the end of the year he could boast that USARSO/JTF-Panama had the best-trained combat support and combat service support units in the theater, if not the Army. The units were physically fit, he argued, could fire as well as any U.S.-based infantry unit, and had been exposed to real-life dangers. To the infantry and MPs guarding the Arraiján Tank Farm and Rodman Ammunition Supply Point, the additional manpower came as welcome relief. The Special Forces

---

[24] Loeffke's relief was expressed in Msg, CDR, USARSO, to CSA, 232000Z May 88, sub: Update No. 12. For the situation on the tank farm and ammunition supply point for the last half of 1988, see Msg, CDR, MARFOR, to CG, 6th Marine Expeditionary Brigade (MEB), 18 Mar 89, USMC Command Chronology for 6 April–31 December 1988, History and Museums Division, Headquarters, U.S. Marine Corps, Washington, D.C.; Fact Sheet, SOUTHCOM J-3, 25 Oct 88, sub: Intrusion Incidents.

[25] Telephone Interv, author with Capt Anthony M. Schilling, U.S. Army, 20 Nov 90, Fort Sill, Okla. The military policemen had chafed at the static security mission they performed at the ammunition supply point as an inappropriate use of troops who operated best when they could employ their mobility and their ability to interact with people. Michaelis Interv, 7 Jun 89.

were less enthusiastic, worrying that inexperienced "kids" in combat support and combat service support units might compromise ongoing special operations west of Howard.[26]

While the primary mission of U.S. troops at the tank farm and ammunition supply point was to defend and protect the facilities, JTF-Panama was also supposed to gather evidence of the reported intrusions and, if possible, identify the intruders and determine their motives. Military intelligence personnel worked on the problem, but the findings were largely inconclusive. When field commanders complained that they needed more extensive and precise data, Col. Paul F. Morgan, the JTF-Panama director of intelligence, fired back, "No way! This is not the battlefield of Europe where you can see them coming." Tracking the whereabouts of a PDF unit going about its routine business was relatively easy for intelligence officers; tracing a handful of individuals using guerrilla tactics to infiltrate U.S. facilities was next to impossible. Also, as General Stewart noted, legal and peacetime constraints that ruled out most covert collection operations compounded the difficulty of acquiring accurate and timely intelligence "beyond the line of sight." Even when official dispensations were forthcoming, establishing a productive intelligence network based on human sources [HUMINT] took time, as did the procedures essential for the protection of sources and collectors alike.[27]

Tactical commanders worked under many of the same constraints as intelligence personnel. Troops on the tank farm under MARFOR control, for example, could have acquired information through deep patrols, surveillance, and ambushes, but the rules of engagement prohibited such activities. Routine U.S. patrols would at times pursue intruders and hope to surround them before they escaped the area, but, aside from the jungle terrain making this tactic almost impossible to realize, higher headquarters explicitly stated that intruders trying to get away should be permitted to do so. Avoiding an unwanted and perhaps deadly incident trumped the requirement for information. Highly sophisticated sensors, photographic equipment, and night-imagery devices were employed to provide tangible proof of the armed intrusions, but the results were generally less than satisfactory. Finally, one could police an area in which intruders had been sighted or in which there had been an exchange of shots, but as General Cisneros noted, you could run a herd of elephants through the thick jungle and an hour later find no evidence of their presence. Rossi put it more bluntly: "We have fired thousands of rounds to a distance of six meters away, and we haven't hit s———t."[28]

---

[26] Intervs, author with Loeffke, 27 Mar 89; Fitzgerald, 28 Apr 89; and Fry, 1 May 89. Comments, Maj Gen Loeffke, n.d. [Spring 1989]; Msg, CDR, USARSO, to DA, 292325Z Sep 88, sub: Update No. 17. On several occasions, Loeffke required his staff officers to visit the tank farm and ammunition supply point, even to the point of spending the night. Morgan Interv, 7 Jul 89.

[27] Intervs, author with Morgan, 7 Jul 89, and Stewart, 14 Jun 89.

[28] Intervs, author with Stewart, 14 Jun 89; Maj John Mulholland, U.S. Army, 30 May 91, Fort Leavenworth, Kans.; Maj William Graves, U.S. Army, 20, 27 Aug 91, 18 May 92, Fort Leavenworth, Kans.; Maj Dan Augustine, 13 Jun 89, Fort Clayton, Panama; Lt Col Robert Pantier, U.S. Army, 21 May 91, Fort Leavenworth, Kans.; Fry, 1 May 89; Cisneros, 1 May 89; and Rossi, 27 Mar 89. The efforts to obtain hard evidence of intruders did produce at least one videotape of armed personnel, but some officers who saw it argued that ascertaining for certain whether the individuals were on U.S. property or not was impossible. On the existence of the videotape, see Fact Sheet, SOUTHCOM SCJ–3, 25 Oct 88, sub: Intrusion Incidents, which reported that the "best hard evidence of intrusion was only recently obtained on 25 October with video footage of intruders being secured by Army/

U.S. MILITARY INTERVENTION IN PANAMA, JUNE 1987–DECEMBER 1989

Rodman Naval Station

Although conclusive evidence regarding the intruders may have been lacking, what information did exist supported what military intelligence, staff officers, and commanders had surmised since early May. Intrusions of armed personnel on the Arraiján Tank Farm and Rodman Ammunition Supply Point did take place, the violations of U.S. facilities was a campaign orchestrated by the PDF, and the units involved were probably the 7th Infantry Company or the special forces of the Special Security Antiterrorist Unit (known by the Spanish acronym UESAT)— or perhaps both—engaged in training exercises. The identity of the unit or units was really immaterial, according to one U.S. intelligence officer. More critical was the intention of the intruders. As of late October 1988, the list of probable motives included trying to make U.S. troops look incompetent and unprofessional, attempting to unnerve U.S. troops, testing the efficacy of PDF psychological operations, determining the limits of the rules of engagement and other operational constraints under which U.S. troops operated, and, in the event of a "failure" (being captured or killed by U.S. troops), "providing a 'martyr' around which to rally future campaigns against the US."[29] Missing from this list was any suggestion that the presumably well-armed intruders sought to inflict casualties on the Americans, an act that would have precipitated the military showdown with the United States that Noriega wanted to avoid.

While officers discussed the nature and purposes of the intrusions, guard duty on the tank farm and ammunition supply point settled into a nightly routine for the troops involved. At dusk, the assigned units would engage in a night-firing

---

Marine forces in the ATF." As to the quality and the handling of the tape and the release of apprehended intruders, the author's comments are based on conversations with a handful of officers in Panama, not on hard documentation.

[29] A concise presentation of what was known about the intrusions in the latter part of 1988 is provided in Fact Sheet, SOUTHCOM SCJ–3, 25 Oct 88, sub: Intrusion Incidents. That a large number of U.S. officers in Panama accepted these findings is attested to in messages and interviews too numerous to cite here.

exercise that consisted of each person firing twenty M16 rounds with the help of night-vision scopes. Ten hits on the target were required before one could advance to the next test, the identification of various objects through night-vision goggles. There followed "spot tests" on the rules of engagement then in effect and on "survival Spanish," a series of Spanish words and sentences (printed on a small card) that Loeffke deemed appropriate for security enhancement duties. Once the troops had "qualified," they took up their positions and began acclimating to the nighttime sounds of the jungle. (To facilitate the acclimatization process, JTF-Panama initiated the practice of sending newly arrived Marine units to the Jungle Operations Training Center on the Atlantic side of the isthmus. After a short tour there introduced the Leathernecks to the terrain and sounds unique to Panama's jungles, they would be sent to the tank farm and ammunition supply point to assume their duties.)

If, while on guard duty, a soldier or marine spotted an armed individual or group moving in his direction, the rules of engagement directed that he issue the verbal challenge, *alto* (Spanish for "stop"). If the person or group did not stop but continued to maneuver toward the guard's position, the guard was authorized to lock and load his weapon and fire a warning shot. If the intruders opened fire prior to a warning shot, the guard was authorized to return fire. Most "firefights" involved the exchange of only a few shots, after which the intruders would withdraw. Any sighting of armed men was reported to the JTF-Panama operations center at Fort Clayton. In those cases where shots had been fired, the operations center notified Colonel Rossi immediately, who in turn informed Loeffke. All shooting incidents required a debriefing afterwards. JTF-Panama would then analyze the incidents and draw what conclusions were possible, then forward the information in situation reports to the Southern Command. SOUTHCOM, if a particular incident was serious enough, would pass the information further up the chain to the Joint Chiefs.

Although most shooting engagements after the 12 April firefight were small affairs, there were exceptions. The most noteworthy occurred on 31 October, Halloween night. At 2015, eleven marines in separate listening posts on the Arraiján Tank Farm detected movement and heard voices around the southern edge of the facility. When they sighted armed intruders in the jungle nearby, the marines issued the required verbal challenge. The intruders thereupon opened fire with automatic weapons and other small arms. The marines fired back. Over the next two and a half hours, six more firefights broke out, four started by the intruders and two by marines responding to what they perceived as threatening movements. Once the small arms firing stopped, the marines, in what they considered a prudent measure, continued to fire illumination rounds from their grenade launchers and 81-mm. mortars throughout the night. The Leathernecks sustained no casualties during the fighting, and, after dawn, patrols relieved the men in the listening posts.

Panama's regime-controlled media played up the Halloween theme, claiming that the marines had been shooting at witches on broomsticks. The JTF-Panama/Southern Command assessment was more down to earth. The incident, an intelligence report claimed, was the most violent since the 12 April firefight. And for once, there was a good deal of physical evidence to indicate that multiple intrusions and hostile firing had taken place, although ascertaining whether or not the intruders had suffered casualties proved impossible. The implications of the night's events were particularly unsettling. The 31 October intrusions displayed a tactical sophistication not normally associated with the Panama Defense Forces, raising again the possibility of participation by more experienced, non-Panamanian personnel, possibly Cubans. More alarming was the apparent readiness of the intruders to fire on the marines without provocation. There was also evidence that the trespassers possessed a thorough knowledge of the U.S. rules of engagement.[30]

RULES OF ENGAGEMENT

This last point touched upon a contentious issue within the U.S. military community in Panama. When officers observed unidentified armed personnel on the tank farm and ammunition supply point, the intruders not only seemed to have a "total awareness" of U.S. rules of engagement, but even appeared to know when the rules had been modified, oftentimes before the changes had been implemented in the field. How the intruders acquired that information was certainly a source of concern. More troubling to the troops performing guard duty, however, were the rules themselves. Since the beginning of the security enhancement mission, the content and interpretation of the rules of engagement had been a source of confusion and frustration.

Rules of engagement set forth policies and procedures for engaging a hostile force. Because the United States and Panama were not at war, U.S. troops performing security enhancement duties in the area of the canal operated under peacetime rules of engagement contained in a SOUTHCOM letter of instruction dated 29 December 1987. The SOUTHCOM rules, in turn, were based on JCS guidelines and subject to modification by the Joint Chiefs or the SOUTHCOM commander.[31]

"The inherent right of self-defense is the basis for these Rules of Engagement," the SOUTHCOM document asserted, and the right to use force in self-defense depended on two elements: necessity and proportionality. *Necessity* constituted a response to the commission of a hostile act or the demonstration of hostile intent. *Proportionality* was the requirement that the use of force be "limited in intensity, duration, and magnitude to what is reasonably required to counter the hostile act or hostile intent and ensure the safety of US forces." A *hostile act* consisted of an attack or use of armed force against U.S. forces, American citizens, or their property. *Hostile intent* was defined as "the threat of the imminent use of armed force" against these and other targets. A justifiable use of deadly force required the presence of one of these threats, or the designation in advance by the SOUTHCOM commander that an opposing force was hostile, in which case U.S. troops could employ deadly force "without respect to the commission of a hostile act or the demonstration of hostile intent."[32]

---

[30] Accounts of the 31 October firefights are contained in Reynolds, *Just Cause*, pp. 11–12; CDR, MARFOR, to CG, 6th MEB, 18 Mar 89, USMC Command Chronology for 6 April–31 December 1988; USSOUTHCOM News Release, 3 Nov 88, sub: Armed Intruders Encountered at Arraiján Tank Farm Monday Night; Intelligence Rpt (INTREP) 10022–88, n.d., in Colonel Rossi's files, USARSO/JTF-Panama.

[31] USSOUTHCOM, 29 Dec 87, sub: Letter of Instruction (LOI), Peacetime Rules of Engagement (ROE).

[32] Quotes from Ibid. Excerpt, JCS Deployment Order, 122000Z Mar 88.

Elaborating and, in some cases, qualifying these general guidelines were supplemental rules of engagement, issued by the Southern Command and the Joint Chiefs, that specifically addressed the situation in Panama. For example, U.S. troops performing security enhancement missions at the tank farm and ammunition supply point were to "attempt to control" an incident without using force. "When time and conditions permit," SOUTHCOM's letter of instruction read, "the hostile forces should be warned and given the opportunity to withdraw or cease threatening actions." U.S. troops could employ force only as a "measure of last resort" and just to the degree needed to establish control over a situation. Pursuit of a hostile force was not allowed except when the disablement or destruction of that force was "required in self-defense."[33]

Accompanying the rules of engagement were rules of conduct that called upon U.S. troops to respect Panamanian property and to deal courteously with Panamanian citizens. Also closely associated with the rules of engagement were a series of orders that one Marine Forces commander characterized as "operational constraints." In the early part of the security enhancement mission, JTF-Panama decreed that only Army military policemen, Air Force security police, and Navy security personnel could carry loaded weapons, mainly side arms. Other troops, including those guarding and patrolling the Arraiján Tank Farm and Rodman Ammunition Supply Point, were not permitted to have magazines in their weapons, much less rounds in the chambers. Should a threat arise, a field commander could direct that magazines be taken out of ammunition pouches and inserted into the weapons, although the prohibition against chambering a round remained in effect unless the use of force was required.[34]

As soon as the rules of engagement and other operational constraints went into effect, problems surfaced. To begin with, the Joint Chiefs of Staff and the Southern Command wanted component and subordinate commanders to have copies of the SOUTHCOM letter of instruction. The commanders, in turn, were to brief all incoming troops on the rules of engagement. At JTF-Panama, Loeffke believed that one way to ensure the widest possible dissemination was to issue the troops a wallet-size card listing, in general terms, the appropriate rules. His proposal ran into bureaucratic obstacles, however, because several of the rules were classified Confidential. JTF-Panama appealed to the SOUTHCOM staff to intercede with the Joint Chiefs, who would have to approve declassification of the rules in question. On 11 May, the SOUTHCOM staff judge advocate talked with a legal officer assigned to the Joint Staff but failed to receive permission to declassify the rules in question. Loeffke bridled at a decision that in essence meant "as a technical matter . . . we should not brief those soldiers on these ROE." "That, of course, is absurd and unacceptable," he wrote Woerner, adding that, unless the

---

[33] Quotes from USSOUTHCOM, 29 Dec 87, sub: Letter of Instruction (LOI), Peacetime Rules of Engagement (ROE). Excerpts, JCS Deployment Order, 122000Z Mar 88.

[34] Memo, Lt Col Joseph Cornelison, Staff Judge Advocate, USARSO, for JTF-Panama J–3, 27 Apr 88, sub: Minimizing the Effect of U.S. Military Operations on Panamanian Civilians. Quote from Interv, Benis Frank with Col Thomas W. Roberts, USMC, 30 Mar 90, Camp Lejeune, N.C. Intervs, author with Graves, 20, 27 Aug 91, 18 May 92; and Fitzgerald, 28 Apr 89. Msg, CDR, JTF-Panama, to CDR, Army Forces-Panama (COMARFORPM), et al., 131330Z Apr 88, sub: Policy for Carrying Ammunition; Memo, Lt Col Joseph Cornelison for CDR, JTF-Panama, 15 Apr 88.

SOUTHCOM commander objected, JTF-Panama intended to publish the card, not as rules of engagement but as orders or guidelines from Loeffke.[35]

Woerner did not object. Nor did he let the matter drop with the Joint Chiefs. On 20 May, he sent a message to the Pentagon in which he strongly urged "expeditious action" in declassifying the rules of engagement and approving issuance of the card. Getting an answer took almost three weeks. At that point, the Joint Chiefs informed Woerner that they had no objection to certain classified rules being published in a "bullet format" (short, concise statements listed without elaboration) but that they also wanted some changes in the way certain rules were worded. In the end, the troops responsible for protecting U.S. facilities in Panama received a card listing, in sequence, the appropriate steps they should take when confronted by intruders and at what points the use of deadly force was deemed permissible.[36]

Although the cards provided U.S. forces with written guidelines, problems concerning the rules of engagement continued to mount. Both commanders and troops expressed frustration at what they regarded as the vague and inconsistent wording of the rules. The frequent changes made to specific rules and other operational procedures compounded their confusion. Inquiries from the field piled up. When specifically could you chamber a round? When specifically could you open fire? What specifically constituted a "threat"? Commanders briefing their troops had difficulty providing intelligible answers, largely because the officers themselves did not always fully comprehend the rules. Early in the security enhancement phase of the crisis, troops often expressed incredulity at what they were told. As they became accustomed to the briefings, a sense of resignation encouraged sarcasm and cynicism. As one company commander recalled his experience briefing the troops on rules of engagement, "It's kind of like a bad comedian in front of a crowd of hecklers." Yet, the same officer conceded that when higher headquarters attempted to add specificity—and thus clarity—to the rules, the length and complexity of the resulting guidance only made briefing the changes more difficult.[37]

Without a clear understanding of the rules of engagement, marines and soldiers on guard duty or patrol often had doubts about what they could do under certain circumstances. They also began to worry about the consequences of their actions should they employ deadly force, even in self-defense. Would they incur the wrath of higher headquarters, perhaps to the point of facing court-martial and incarceration? Several commanders whose units had exchanged fire with intruders on the tank farm and ammunition supply point complained that the debriefings

---

[35] Memo, Loeffke through Chief of Staff, SOUTHCOM, for CINCSO, 18 May 88.

[36] On the issue of providing the troops a wallet-size rules-of-engagement card, see Excerpt, JCS Deployment Order, 122000Z Mar 88; Msg, CINCSO to CDR, JTF-Panama, 212315Z Apr 88, sub: USCINCSO Directed Standing Order; Memo, Loeffke through Chief of Staff, SOUTHCOM, for CINCSO, 18 May 88. First quote from Msg, CINCSO to JCS, 200316Z May 88, sub: ROE Classification. Second quote from Msg, JCS to CINCSO, 072220Z Jun 88, sub: ROE Classification. Msg, CDR, USARSO, to Headquarters, DA (HQDA), 260105Z Mar 88, sub: Briefing for Soldiers Arriving in Panama.

[37] The company commander's observations come from Graves Interv, 27 Aug 91. See also Augustine Interv, 13 Jun 89; Msg, item 8, 193d Inf Bde (Light), Lessons Learned, n.d., sub: OPLAN 6000.

conducted by JTF-Panama and the Southern Command afterwards were generally contentious sessions akin to an interrogation, with the guards who had fired their weapons often believing that their behavior, not that of the intruders, was on trial. At one point, the marines even had to account for every round expended in the course of a shooting incident. As an Army officer observed, the troops' uncertainty surrounding the use of force, when combined with the perception that support from higher headquarters was lacking, left the "guy on the ground in the lurch." The result, according to another officer, was a "hesitant soldier," a soldier who might wait too long to load his weapon and defend himself. In the jungle, where distances were compressed and a patrol could encounter hostile elements unexpectedly, hesitation could prove fatal.[38]

In an attempt to clear up some of the doubts and confusion surrounding the subject, Colonel Rossi provided JTF-Panama components a memorandum on 12 August designed to serve as an authoritative, single-source document on the rules of engagement currently in effect for ground forces in Panama. In addition to the rules previously indicated, specific guidelines stated that unarmed intruders on U.S. facilities would be warned by voice or loudspeaker that they were in a restricted area and that they should stop. If the intruders obeyed the order to stop, they would be apprehended. If they attempted to flee, no warning shot would be fired. Armed intruders would receive a similar warning, together with one to lay down their weapons. If they failed to heed the command, U.S. troops could fire a warning shot. But, Rossi emphasized, the troops could fire at the intruders only if fired upon, if irrefutable evidence existed of hostile intent, or if clearly acting in self-defense. With this sort of directness, Rossi's memorandum did provide a comprehensive and comprehensible set of guidelines for the rules of engagement, but, as the colonel himself conceded, JTF-Panama continued to receive requests for clarification and changes.[39]

The combination of uncertainty, doubt, and hesitation produced by the rules of engagement was inextricably linked to the larger issue that pitted the right of individual and unit self-defense against the need for discipline and restraint in a complex and politically charged situation. The ensuing debate was intense and controversial. Published rules of engagement proclaimed in capital letters, "NOTHING IN THESE RULES NEGATES A COMMANDER'S OBLIGATION TO TAKE ALL NECESSARY AND APPROPRIATE ACTION FOR HIS UNIT'S SELF DEFENSE."[40] Yet, there were those in the field who questioned this claim. The rules were too restrictive, they argued, and were more concerned with preventing Panamanian casualties than with protecting American troops. The marine or soldier who gave a verbal warning, "*alto*," to an intruder or who waited for clear evidence of a hostile act or hostile intent before chambering a round in his weapon, or who fired a warning shot before employing deadly force against a hostile element, risked giving away his position and exposing himself to hostile fire. Col. Thomas W. Roberts, the MARFOR commander who

---

[38] Reynolds, *Just Cause*, p. 11. For the comments and quotes of the two officers, see, respectively, Intervs, author with Augustine, 13 Jun 89, and Graves, 27 Aug 91.

[39] Memo, Col A. T. Rossi for ARFOR [and other JTF-Panama components], 12 Aug 88, sub: Rules of Engagement; Rossi Interv, 27 Mar 89.

[40] USSOUTHCOM, 29 Dec 87, sub: Letter of Instruction (LOI), Peacetime Rules of Engagement (ROE).

succeeded Conley, insisted that young men engaged in the profession of arms on the tank farm and ammunition supply point had to be trusted to go on a mission with a loaded weapon. To proscribe this and other commonsense measures, he asserted, represented a training failure and placed young marines or soldiers in vulnerable positions. To both Roberts and his predecessor, the existing rules of engagement conceded the initiative to a hostile force and, in the event of a major confrontation, increased the likelihood that a U.S. soldier or marine would take the first bullet.[41]

To a number of officers on the SOUTHCOM and JTF-Panama staffs, the criticism emanating from the Marine Forces component reinforced the view held in both those higher headquarters since the 12 April firefight that the marines were "loose cannons," obsessed with the 1983 Beirut terrorist bombing in which 241 marines had been killed. That tragedy, according to some Army staff officers, had rendered the marines unable to function in a politically sensitive and nuanced environment in which the probability of hostilities was low and the need for discipline and restraint high. The chain of command from Crowe through Woerner to Loeffke had emphasized that the object of the security enhancement mission in Panama was strictly protective; it was not to kill Panamanians. The peacetime rules of engagement were carefully calculated to avoid unnecessary violence and casualties, even when encountering armed and unfriendly forces. In this sense, the Southern Command and JTF-Panama both affirmed, the rules had served U.S. military objectives well. No American installations had been destroyed, no U.S. troops had been killed by hostile fire, and American forces had not created martyrs by killing Panamanian citizens, armed or otherwise. The problem, Rossi explained, was to get this message across to a security force, composed largely but not exclusively of marines, that was well armed, preoccupied with force protection, proud of its warrior ethos, accustomed to thinking in traditional terms of wartime rules of engagement, and that believed the presence of any armed Panamanian in an unauthorized area constituted hostile intent.[42]

What made the issue so contentious was not that one side in the debate believed U.S. troops in Panama had a right to defend themselves and the other side did not. Rather, the friction derived from what each side perceived as the most appropriate way of ensuring the protection of those troops. The MARFOR commanders readily conceded their preoccupation with the Beirut tragedy but argued that, even if a marine had never set foot in Lebanon in the mid-1980s, they would have been concerned about the limitations they perceived higher headquarters had placed on the ability of their troops in Panama to act in self-defense. In a

---

[41] Intervs, Benis Frank with Col Donald F. Anderson, USMC, 30 Mar 90, Camp Lejeune, N.C., and Roberts, 30 Mar 90; author with Fitzgerald, 28 Apr 89; Loeffke, 27 Mar 89; and Roberts, 24 Mar 89, Rodman Naval Station, Panama. Reynolds, *Just Cause*, pp. 11–12.

[42] Intervs, author with Finch, 17 Mar 89; Rossi, 27 Mar 89; Morgan, 7 Jul 89; Loeffke, 27 Mar 89; Cisneros, 1 May 89; and Cope, 29 Mar 89. Diary, Bernard Loeffke 5 Nov 88; Comments, Maj Gen Loeffke, n.d. [Spring 1989]; Handwritten note, Col Michael Bigelow to SCJ–3, 21 Jun [88]. The "loose cannons" phrase was used by the JTF-Panama command group on several occasions. One Army company commander whose unit frequently came under the MARFOR's operational control on the tank farm noted that all he heard from the Marine commander and staff was "No more Beiruts." In his opinion, however, this concern made the marines overly cautious, not unduly aggressive. Graves Interv, 27 Aug 91.

Settling In

measure of interservice harmony, most Army commanders in the field also favored greater latitude in dealing with hostile forces than was allowed under the rules of engagement. From the perspective of the Southern Command and JTF-Panama headquarters, however, less restrictive rules could make the situation more, not less, dangerous. In a note to Woerner, the SOUTHCOM deputy director of operations argued that "US/PDF (intruders) appear to have entered into a situation where *both sides* are abiding by ROE designed to avoid armed conflict, or at least that has been the effect. . . . For the US forces to modify this situation, ie, more aggressive ROE, may invite an escalation in terms of military/terrorist activity which is not in our best interests at the present time."[43] Even the security enhancement forces conceded that, if the Panama Defense Forces really wanted to kill U.S. troops or destroy American facilities, they could easily do so virtually anytime, anywhere. Noriega, most observers acknowledged, did not want a shooting war; he sought only to enjoy the benefits of his psychological warfare campaign. As Woerner and Loeffke saw the situation, an overreaction by U.S. troops to armed threats on the Arraiján Tank Farm and Rodman Ammunition Supply Point would, at best, provide Noriega with the propaganda victories he sought. At worst, the crisis could escalate out of control. Thus, until intelligence or other sources revealed that the Panamanian military intended to inflict casualties on American troops, U.S. forces on guard duty and patrol were to continue to exercise discipline and a high level of restraint.[44]

While the Southern Command and JTF-Panama publicly insisted on compliance with the strict rules of engagement, expediency and a desire to minimize friction with units in the field occasionally resulted in both headquarters turning a blind eye when troop commanders chose to ignore or apply their own interpretation to a specific rule. In one example of this, Loeffke, whose views concerning the nature of the crisis and how best to handle it at no time detracted from his genuine concern for the safety and morale of the troops he controlled, more or less resigned himself to the fact—common knowledge at the time—that Marine and Army units under the MARFOR's operational control on the tank farm generally went on guard duty at night locked and loaded.[45]

On occasion, arguments generated by the rules of engagement carried over to related issues and procedures. One such concern had to do with the pursuit of hostile forces. Early in the security enhancement mission, an MP on guard duty at the ammunition supply point expressed her frustration directly to Loeffke. "General, why are we here?" she asked. "We hear them all around us and when we say '*alto*' they laugh and withdraw. Why can't we go after them? Why should we be on guard if we are not allowed to chase them?"[46] At Quarry Heights, Cisneros was asking the same questions. As the SOUTHCOM director of operations, he favored a more assertive policy toward the intruders, although not so assertive as

---

[43] Handwritten note, Bigelow to SCJ–3, 21 Jun [88].

[44] Ibid.; Comments, Maj Gen Loeffke, n.d. [Spring 1989]; Intervs, Frank with Anderson, 30 Mar 90; author with Loeffke, 27 Mar 89; Morgan, 7 Jul 89; Rossi, 27 Mar 89; and Lt Col Michael Mallory, U.S. Army, 29 Mar 89, Fort Clayton, Panama.

[45] My conversations with several officers who served on the Arraiján Tank Farm and with JTF-Panama staff officers who admitted knowing that the rule regarding ammunition was consciously being violated.

[46] MFR, Loeffke, n.d.

to provoke open hostilities. At one point, he suggested that Colonel Fry at Special Operations Command, South, develop a plan to ambush and capture an armed intruder on U.S. property. Fry submitted the plan to Loeffke, who forwarded it for approval to Woerner. In an accompanying memorandum, the skeptical joint task force commander explained that the proposed operation would violate JCS supplements to the SOUTHCOM rules of engagement in two ways. First, the ambushes might exacerbate the crisis, and, second, the Special Operations Forces would be employing force as an initial step, not as a last resort, and would make no attempt to warn a hostile force or give it a chance to withdraw. "This may be too aggressive for the situation at this time," Loeffke penned at the bottom of the memo. Despite this reservation and an opinion by another general officer on Woerner's staff that the plan was too risky and served little purpose, other SOUTHCOM staff directorates recommended that the commander approve the proposal.[47]

Loeffke quickly followed his dissenting memo on the ambush plan with another proposal related to the rules of engagement. Under pressure from his MARFOR component following a series of shooting incidents on the tank farm and ammunition supply point in July, he suggested that Woerner declare the intruders a "hostile force." Such a designation would allow U.S. troops to fire at armed intruders without first yelling a warning and firing a warning shot, both of which ran the risk of giving away U.S. positions. Messages were drafted for the SOUTHCOM commander's signature, but after a month of considering the proposal, Woerner decided to put it on hold, to be reconsidered only if the situation should further "heat up." (There was some speculation that, given Loeffke's concerns about intensifying the crisis, JTF-Panama might have raised the issue with Woerner knowing that he would not approve it. Meanwhile, Loeffke could tell the marines that he had argued their case with his immediate superior.)[48]

Despite this setback, the MARFOR commander continued his efforts to modify the rules of engagement. On 29 October, Colonel Roberts sent a memorandum to JTF-Panama indicating his intention to rewrite the wallet-size cards his troops carried. The new card would begin with the statement, "ROEs are based on the inherent right of self-defense," thus emphasizing and clarifying a point that he believed the original card obscured. The next rule would read, "Use the minimum force necessary to contain the threat" (instead of "to control the situation," the wording of the original). The rule following that one would read, "If fired on, return fire," thus omitting the phrase dictated by the Joint Chiefs, "if necessary for self-defense." Colonel Cope, then acting as the JTF-Panama chief of staff, replied

---

[47] On the ambush proposal, see Memo, Loeffke through Chief of Staff, SOUTHCOM, for CINCSO, 8 Jul 88, sub: Operation to Apprehend Intruder, which contains the quote. Staff Action Summary Sheet, 11 Jul 88, sub: ROE for Panama; Draft msg (unsigned), CINCSO to CDR, JTF-Panama, Jul 88, sub: Adjusted ROE for Special Operations. Handwritten notes, Col Gar Thiry to Brig Gen LeCleir, SCJ–5, and Col Berrean, SCJ–2, 11 Jul [88]; LeC [Brig Gen LeCleir, SCJ–5] to Vice SCJ–3, 12 Jul [88]; and Denny [?] to VJ–3 [Col Gar Thiry, USMC], 12 Jul [88]. Memo, Col G. E. Thiry, USMC, Vice Dir SCJ–3, through Dep CINC and Chief of Staff, for CINCSO, 14 Jul 88, sub: Proposed SOF Operation.

[48] Memo, Loeffke for CINCSO, 26 Jul 88, sub: Rules of Engagement; Draft msg (unsigned), CINCSO to CJCS, n.d. [drafted 28 Jul 88], sub: Rules of Engagement; Handwritten note, Woerner to J–3, 4 Sep [88], attached to Staff Action Summary Sheet, Brig Gen Cisneros through Chief of Staff and DCINC to CINCSO, 29 Jul 88, sub: Rules of Engagement.

to the memo two days later, informing Roberts that the proposal was being staffed. "You may not be aware," Cope added, "that the JCS only blessed the current ROE card after we incorporated their verbiage; so we must remain consistent. Your rules 2 and 3 deviate. Until we resolve inconsistencies, continue using the current JTF-P card."[49]

The rash of firefights on the tank farm the night of 31 October resulted in a general review of security enhancement policies and rules of engagement in effect on both the fuel depot and ammunition supply point. The review took place during a meeting in Woerner's office on 2 November. Loeffke opened with an assessment of the current situation, which, as a result of the 31 October incidents, he again described as increasingly dangerous. He was particularly worried about the intruders' willingness to answer U.S. verbal warnings with gunfire. Troops guarding the two sites, he went on to say, were beginning to feel like "sitting ducks." To ameliorate their predicament, he proposed three options for Woerner to consider. Loeffke himself did not endorse each of the options but believed he had the duty to raise them with the SOUTHCOM commander. The first deleted from the rules of engagement the requirement to issue a verbal warning to armed intruders before engaging them with deadly force. Instead, every thirty minutes, U.S. troops would broadcast warnings to intruders that they were in a restricted area and thus subject to being fired on. Option two applied only to the Arraiján Tank Farm and involved pulling all observation posts and listening posts out of jungle areas surrounding the facility. This option, Loeffke warned, would reduce the MARFOR's early warning capabilities and was not doctrinally sound. The third option called for Woerner to pull all guard personnel out of defensive positions and to have the Marine Force component use vehicular patrols to provide security for the area.[50]

Woerner asked for comments from those in the room, then proceeded to render his decision. He noted that the current rules of engagement had served their purpose and that he would not change them. Rather, he would order tactical changes on the tank farm and ammunition supply point. These changes amounted to accepting Loeffke's second option, one that the JTF-Panama commander did not personally support. Each day after dark, Woerner directed, observation and listening posts would be pulled inside the perimeter of the tank farm. Loudspeaker broadcasts would continue but so would the requirement to issue a verbal warning to intruders. To provide maximum protection for the guards, Woerner insisted that those issuing

---

[49] The quotes of Roberts and Cope are taken respectively from Memos, Col T. W. Roberts, CDR, MARFOR, for CDR, JTF-Panama, 29 Oct 88, sub: Rules of Engagement, and Col John A. Cope, Actg Chief of Staff, for Col Roberts, USMC, 31 Oct 88, sub: Guidance Based on Incidents over the Last 72 Hours. See also Roberts Interv, 24 Mar 89.

[50] Memo, Brig Gen Marc Cisneros for CDR, JTF-Panama, 18 Nov 88, sub: Tactical Changes to Support Current Rules of Engagement (ROE). Quote from MFR, Col Charles E. Bonney, 2 Nov 88, sub: Rules of Engagement (ROE) at Arraiján Tank Farm (ATF) and Ammo Supply Point (ASP). According to the MFR, besides Woerner and Loeffke, General Eugene H. Fischer (deputy CINCSO), Rear Adm. Richard Ustick (SOUTHCOM chief of staff), Rear Adm. Jerry G. Gneckow (NAVSO commander), General Cisneros, Col. Charles Carleton, Col. T. Hayden, and Col. Charles E. Bonney attended the meeting. The day before, Loeffke had provided Woerner a memorandum outlining the three options discussed at the meeting. See Memo, Loeffke for CINCSO, 1 Nov 88, sub: Update No. 121, Options.

any warning be located in well-covered positions. Daylight patrols were authorized so long as they did not go more than 300 meters beyond the perimeter; they also had to return by 1700.[51]

After the meeting, Cope informed Roberts of Woerner's decisions. The MARFOR commander was livid. In a tersely worded memorandum to Loeffke, Roberts charged that his forces were being placed at a tactical disadvantage and requested that the decisions be rescinded. Any immediate reconsideration of Woerner's ruling, however, was out of the question, and, over the course of several days, "a system of bunkers and trench lines" sprang up on the Arraiján Tank Farm and Rodman Ammunition Supply Point, as the marines sought to protect themselves by digging in. The marines' presence at the fuel farm was also reduced to one platoon(+), with a second platoon serving on the ammunition depot, and a third providing a reaction force in reserve. Roberts continued his protests, Loeffke sympathized, and by mid-month, the two achieved a partial reversal of policy. The troop reductions for each location remained in effect, but Roberts was able to order the bunkers and trenches "razed," as the marines returned to "light infantry tactics" in an effort to deter intruders on the two facilities.[52]

Although they advocated divergent courses of action, both Woerner and Roberts sought the same result: to reduce the number of incursions at the tank farm and ammunition supply point. By late 1988, if not sooner, several officers in the Southern Command and JTF-Panama had concluded that the increasing tempo of hostile activity at both sites could be attributed mainly to the large number of U.S. troops present there on guard duty. By serving as a lucrative target for PDF training exercises and psychological warfare, the troops who had been deployed to secure the facilities from intruders had ironically and unwittingly invited the very activities they were there to curtail. In becoming "obsessed" (Rossi's term) with the intrusions, JTF-Panama, the Southern Command, and the Joint Chiefs of Staff had managed to respond in ways that only played into Noriega's hands. Woerner and Roberts (and others) now attempted to reverse such counterproductive policies, Woerner by pulling most of the troops out of each facility, Roberts by employing aggressive tactics that would make further intrusions too risky for the Panama Defense Forces. In a message to Admiral Crowe, the SOUTHCOM commander described the tank farm and ammunition supply point as being "more theater and stage than battlefield." If he reduced the number of troops—the "audience"—at the two locations, the intruders, he thought, would quickly lose interest in performing before something well short of a "full house." Roberts, on the other hand, maintained that aggressive patrolling and the setting of ambushes would make the Panamanian military "think twice before entering the storage facilities."[53]

---

[51] Memo, Cisneros for CDR, JTF-Panama, 18 Nov 88, sub: Tactical Changes to Support Current Rules of Engagement (ROE); Diary, Loeffke, 5 Nov 88; MFR, Col Charles E. Bonney, 2 Nov 88, sub: Rules of Engagement (ROE) at Arraiján Tank Farm (ATF) and Ammo Supply Point (ASP).

[52] Memos, Col John A. Cope Jr. for Col Tim Roberts, USMC, 2 Nov 88, sub: Results of Meeting with CINC, and CDR, MARFOR, for CG, JTF-Panama, 6 Nov 88, sub: Rule [sic] of Engagement. Msg, CDR, MARFOR, to CG, 6th MEB, 18 Mar 89, USMC Command Chronology for 6 April–31 December 1988; Maj Robert B. Neller, USMC, Marines in Panama: 1988–1990 (Paper, USMC Staff College, Quantico, Va., 1991). Quotes from Reynolds, *Just Cause*, pp. 11–12.

[53] The Woerner quotes are from Msg, CINCSO to JCS [personal, Woerner to Crowe], 141831Z Dec 88, sub: Security Enhancement Forces. The quote summarizing Roberts' views is from Reynolds,

Subsequent events could be used to vindicate either Woerner's decision or Roberts' tactics. By the end of 1988, the number of incidents at the Arraiján Tank Farm and Rodman Ammunition Supply Point had dropped off sharply.[54] These statistics, while encouraging, needed to be read with caution. To apply Woerner's theater metaphor, Noriega's players might, in fact, be a traveling troupe that, when attendance fell off at one location, would simply move its stage production to another.

THE REDEPLOYMENT QUESTION

Having removed much of the "audience" from two key facilities, Woerner had to determine where to send it. The obvious answer was "home," which suggested inactivating the MARFOR headquarters and redeploying the Marine security enhancement rifle company. (There was also a growing feeling at Quarry Heights and even Fort Clayton that JTF-Panama had outlived its usefulness and should be inactivated, a measure that would be expedited by redeploying units under its control, such as the Marine company, that were based outside of Panama.) But, as Woerner knew from experience, bringing troops into a country was easier than sending them back home, even though many of the stateside headquarters that had been highly supportive in contributing to the security enhancement effort were now clamoring to have specific units returned to them. Policy makers in Washington would have to determine whether to pull the troops out, a decision the Reagan administration was not about to make before considering all the ramifications.

The issue of redeployment had first surfaced in late May 1988 when, after the collapse of the Noriega-Kozak negotiations in Panama, President Reagan indicated that he was not going to order an invasion of the country. At that time, Woerner had taken the position that there should be no reductions in security forces until a settlement with the Noriega regime had been concluded. Other headquarters, though, expressed concerns about this open-ended commitment. The 7th Infantry Division (Light), for example, had deployed Task Force Hawk, about a third of the division's aviation assets, to Panama, and, while the division expressed its willingness to support the detachment so long as the crisis warranted, it also

---

Just Cause, p. 12. In a message to the Pentagon, Admiral Ustick, the SOUTHCOM chief of staff, carried the "stage" metaphor into the 1989. A reduction in the security forces, he contended, would "take away [Noriega's] audience to where his applause meter would eventually reach zero." Msg, CINCSO to Joint Staff [personal, Rear Adm Ustick to Lt Gen Johnson], 162026Z Feb 89, sub: Panama—Update.

[54] On the decrease in incidents at the tank farm and ammunition supply point, see Msgs, CDR, USARSO, to CSA, 281829Z Dec 88, sub: Update No. 19; CDR, USARSO, to CSA, 042131Z Apr 89, sub: Update No. 22; and CINCSO to Joint Staff, 162026Z Feb 89. USMC Command Chronology for 6 April 1988–31 December 1988; Msg, Commanding Officer (CO), MARFOR, Panama, to CG, 6th MEB, 19 Jul 89, sub: Command Chronology [for 1 January 1989–30 June 1989], History and Museums Division, Headquarters, U.S. Marine Corps; Loeffke Interv, 27 Mar 89; Neller, Marines in Panama; Reynolds, *Just Cause*, p. 12. In early 1989, an American soldier, Special Forces S. Sgt. John C. Brite, was fatally wounded from a shotgun blast fired by a Panamanian, presumably a hunter. That incident took place on the Atlantic side, not at the tank farm or ammunition supply point, and an investigation convinced the U.S. command, as well as most of Brite's associates, that the shooting was a tragic accident. *Tropic Times*, 3 Feb 89; Diary, Loeffke, n.d. [entry on Brite shooting]; Notes, n.d., Loeffke Papers; Intervs, author with Rossi, 27 Mar 89; Fry, 1 May 89; and Mulholland, 30 May 91.

noted that "This tasking obviously degrades the readiness and deployability of this division as well as its ability to participate in JCS directed exercises. . . . Additionally, combined arms training within the division is severely restricted; we can airlift only platoon sized elements." Given these requirements and shortfalls, the 7th Division requested that Task Force Hawk be redeployed by 15 July.[55]

Military police commanders voiced similar concerns. By August, they could see no justification for keeping eight MP companies in Panama. The commander of the U.S. Forces Command (FORSCOM), the Army headquarters in Atlanta, Georgia, responsible for providing combat-ready regular and reserve forces for deployment overseas, also chimed in. FORSCOM had overseen the deployment of 1,550 soldiers for the security enhancement mission. On 7 July, in a message to the Joint Staff and the SOUTHCOM director of operations, the command expressed its continued support for SOUTHCOM's needs in the crisis but also addressed the adverse impact of the security enhancement deployments on scheduled unit training and exercises, reserve component support, National Training Center rotations, and various joint endeavors. "Our current challenge is to satisfy all competing demands and still retain a viable response force," the message stated. With that in mind, Forces Command suggested that the Joint Chiefs and the Southern Command "look for ways to subtly reduce the 1557 plus soldiers to the minimum essential," with an emphasis on redeploying aviation assets, military police, and various support units.[56]

Reaffirming U.S. security needs in Panama but recognizing "competing requirements in other environs," Woerner directed Loeffke to conduct a thorough review to determine what forces were essential to the security enhancement mission. When the review was completed, the Southern Command recommended that several elements be redeployed, including the MP brigade headquarters, an MP battalion headquarters, and three MP companies. On 28 July, the Joint Chiefs authorized redeployment of all the units the Southern Command named except the military police. Both the State Department and the National Security Council expressed concern that bringing those units home would signal a weakening of America's determination to see Noriega removed from power. Not until September were the MP units allowed to redeploy.[57] By then, a second review concerning the disposition of augmentation forces was under way at

---

[55] On Woerner's views in May 1988, see Msg, Loeffke through Chief of Staff, USSOUTHCOM, to CINCSO, 15 Jul 88, sub: JTF-Panama Force Requirements Review. On Task Force Hawk and for the quotes, see Msg, 100900Z Jun 88, sub: Task Force Hawk's Role in Panama Security Augmentation.

[56] Msg, CINCFOR to JCS [personal, Maj Gen Wiegand to Lt Gen Kelly and Brig Gen Cisneros], 072241Z Jul 88, sub: Panama Security Enhancement. See also Telephone Interv, author with Capt Anthony Schilling, U.S. Army, 30 Nov 90.

[57] Quote from Msg, CINCSO to CDR, JTF-Panama, 131620Z Jul 88, sub: Force Requirements Review. Memo, Loeffke through Chief of Staff, SOUTHCOM, for CINCSO, 15 Jul 88, sub: JTF-Panama Force Requirements Review; Congressional Background Paper, SOUTHCOM J–3-Operations (SCJ–3-O), 2 Aug 89, sub: Security Augmentation Forces—A Historical Perspective (Deployment/Redeployment). When the 16th Military Police Brigade had deployed from Fort Bragg, the brigade's commander, a full colonel, had insisted that the MP command in Panama fell under his operational control. The MP commander in Panama, also a full colonel, unsuccessfully resisted the move. The resulting friction, often erupting into "bloodletting" verbal confrontations between the two officers had a detrimental impact at brigade headquarters, where staff officers stationed in Panama were abruptly and unceremoniously removed from their offices. The tension did not subside

Quarry Heights and Fort Clayton. The consequent recommendations, made that December, called for substantial reductions in security enhancement forces, including redeployment of the Marine headquarters and rifle company. Again, the idea of reducing U.S. forces in Panama collided with concerns at higher levels about how Noriega would interpret such a move. The Southern Command submitted a revised redeployment schedule designed to allay those concerns, but by then the press of current and impending events made sending home anything other than small support units impossible. An upswing in treaty violations and harassment in Panama in the beginning of 1989, the desire in Washington to keep the pressure on Noriega, and the uncertainties surrounding the impending Panamanian presidential election all militated against a large-scale drawdown of U.S. security enhancement forces.[58]

ENTER THE XVIII AIRBORNE CORPS

These same considerations also affected planning efforts related to the crisis. Throughout 1988, Woerner held to the position that U.S. military intervention in Panama was to be avoided if possible. Yet, as he understood from the outset, unanticipated events could leave the White House with little choice but to commit American forces to combat operations in the country. Prudence therefore still demanded that planners at the Southern Command, JTF-Panama, the Joint Special Operations Command, and other headquarters continue to update and revise the PRAYER BOOK series of plans, with special attention to POST TIME, which included a buildup of U.S. forces in Panama, and BLUE SPOON, which called for offensive combat operations against the Panama Defense Forces and regime-sponsored paramilitary groups.

In the Operations Directorate at Quarry Heights, Cisneros oversaw the Southern Command's work on the CINCSO version of both of these operation orders. The general also provided guidance to JTF-Panama and the joint special operations task force as those two headquarters modified their supporting plans and tackled a lengthy list of difficult and unresolved issues. There was, for example, the question of how much time would be required to complete a buildup of U.S. forces in Panama. The original POST TIME operation order called for seventeen days, which seemed excessive, even if the purpose of a buildup under Woerner's strategy was more psychological than military. By expunging extraneous units from the troop list, Lt. Col. John McCutchon and Lt. Col. Robert Pantier, the SOUTHCOM and JTF-Panama chiefs of plans, respectively, were able to cut the time to twelve days. The two officers also discussed how to get a brigade of the 7th Infantry Division (Light) into Panama prior to the beginning of any offensive actions. If this could be accomplished, JTF-Panama would be

---

until the brigade headquarters was redeployed and the MP commander in Panama reassumed command authority. Conversation, author with Lt Col Mike Michaelis, Jun 89, Fort Clayton, Panama.

[58] Congressional Background Paper, SCJ-3-O, 2 Aug 89, sub: Security Augmentation Forces—A Historical Perspective (Deployment/Redeployment); Msgs, CINCSO to JCS [personal, Woerner for Crowe], 141831Z Dec 88, sub: Security Enhancement Forces, and JCS to CINCSO, 130045Z Jan 89, sub: Deployment Order—Panama Augmentation Forces. In February 1989, the marines were told that they would, in fact, redeploy, but subsequent events overrode this decision. Msg, CDR, MARFOR, Panama, to CDR, JTF-Panama, 9 Feb 89, sub: Operational Implications of the Redeployment of Company C, 1st Battalion, 6th Marine Rgt.

better prepared, should the Panamanian military launch preemptive strikes, to carry out defensive and offensive combat operations on its own until BLUE SPOON units based outside Panama could arrive in the country.[59]

If BLUE SPOON did have to be executed, better that operations be conducted on a timetable set by the U.S. military, beginning with H-hour. In order to ensure maximum tactical surprise and to prevent normal commercial air operations at Torrijos International Airport from interfering with U.S. attacks on targets (including the airport itself) in and around Panama City, the planners recommended that combat operations commence at 0100 on D-day. The initial fighting would thus take place after dark, an advantage to U.S. forces trained and equipped for night operations. On a related matter, planners decided that evacuating American citizens from Panama shortly before or during BLUE SPOON would not be feasible. An evacuation operation conducted prior to hostilities would give away the element of surprise deemed essential to a swift and economical victory, while one conducted simultaneously with BLUE SPOON would tie up airfields and aircraft, create mass confusion, and obstruct combat operations. Staff officers did not welcome the prospect of thousands of U.S. citizens being placed at risk, but there seemed to be no course of action, save the rapid defeat of the PDF, that would protect civilians without jeopardizing the mission itself. In a slightly different vein, the safety of the special operations personnel who would be flown in to execute BLUE SPOON posed another set of insuperable challenges. AC–130 gunships could counter surface-to-air missiles (SAMs), but C–141 troop transports could not. If the Panama Defense Forces managed to shoot down one or two aircraft carrying Ranger units to their D-day objectives, the triumph U.S. planners correctly saw as inevitable would quickly become a pyrrhic victory.[60]

These and other conundrums were discussed at meetings held in Panama and the United States throughout 1988 and into the new year. One session held at Fort Bragg between 6–10 February 1989 was of special significance. It witnessed a changeover from JTF-Panama to the XVIII Airborne Corps as the executive agency for planning conventional BLUE SPOON operations. The transition had its origins fairly early in the planning process when the question arose as to whether the U.S. Army's contingency corps should be brought into the crisis upon the execution of either POST TIME or BLUE SPOON. General Loeffke and the USARSO staff vehemently opposed the move on the grounds that full-scale involvement of the corps was unnecessary. A USARSO-dominated JTF-Panama, they believed, had the prerequisite expertise, the firsthand knowledge of Panama and the crisis, the equipment, the familiarity with the plans, and the capability to perform PRAYER BOOK missions, especially given the short span of control required and the limited geographical area involved. To call on the XVIII Airborne Corps instead would require a "steep learn-up curve" for a stateside headquarters that knew "virtually nothing about this part of the world." Furthermore, Loeffke and his staff contended, what was the point of the Southern Command and JTF-Panama having contingency plans if an "outside" organization had to be brought in to execute

---

[59] Intervs, author with Lt Col Robert Pantier, 13 Jun 90, Fort Clayton, Panama, and 21 May 91, Fort Leavenworth, Kans.; Memo, Col Wesley Taylor, 75th Ranger Rgt, for CDR [JSOTF], and CDR, 1st SOCOM, 23 Sep 88; Briefing, Lt Col Robert Pantier, 21 May 91, Fort Leavenworth, Kans.

[60] Memo, Taylor for JSOTF and 1st SOCOM, 23 Sep 88; Intervs, author with Maj John Diviney, U.S. Army, Mar 89, Fort Leavenworth, Kans., and Augustine, 13 Jun 89.

them. In USARSO's view, the XVIII Airborne Corps would be justified in directing combat operations in Panama only if the fighting escalated because of Cuban or Nicaraguan intervention.[61]

Initially, Woerner and Cisneros accepted this argument. By June 1988, however, they had begun to have doubts about USARSO's ability to serve as an operational headquarters should the new contingency plans be executed. U.S. Army, South, had only limited resources and had to apply them to a wide range of missions, given the headquarters' three distinct roles as a SOUTHCOM component, a major Army command, and the nucleus of JTF-Panama. There was also a question of command and control to consider. The USARSO commander was a two-star general. As a wartime commander executing BLUE SPOON, he would not have seniority over at least two other general officers whose forces would be deployed, in one case under JTF-Panama's operational control. Making the commander of the joint task force a three-star billet by bringing in the XVIII Airborne Corps headquarters would resolve that problem. Finally, Woerner recognized, as did General Kelly in the Pentagon, that "if it became necessary to bolster JTFPM forces with brigades from the United States, a corps headquarters would be needed to run the operation." With these considerations in mind, Cisneros invited Col. Thomas H. Needham, XVIII Airborne Corps' director of operations, and Lt. Col. Timothy L. McMahon, the corps' chief of plans, to Panama to discuss what role their headquarters might play in the crisis. At one point during the visit, Cisneros asked the two if the corps would be willing to take over as JTF-Panama should war break out. The proposal came as a surprise to both officers, but they responded that the XVIII Airborne Corps was capable of performing the mission.[62]

Maj. David Huntoon, who had arrived at Fort Bragg in July as a regional war planner for the corps, was given the Panama desk and the assignment of defining the precise role that the XVIII Airborne Corps might play with respect to the PRAYER BOOK. A series of messages passed between SOUTHCOM, JTF-Panama, and the corps headquarters, followed by a conference in Panama from 9–12 August 1988. Throughout, USARSO's position was that corps assets could certainly be used to augment the existing JTF-Panama, but the corps itself should not come in as the "war-fighting" headquarters unless the Army Forces component of the joint task force exceeded one division on the ground, a prospect Loeffke did not consider likely unless there was outside intervention by countries hostile to the United States, also an unlikely prospect. The threat in Panama was "puny," Loeffke always maintained, and JTF-Panama, acting in tandem with the joint special operations task force, possessed enough military power to meet any local challenge. Huntoon's response was that, in the event the contingency plans were

---

[61] Memo, Loeffke for CINCSO, 11 Mar 88, sub: #41, Plus and Minuses of 18th Airborne Corps. See also Intervs, author with Cope, 29 Mar 89; Augustine, 13 Jun 89; and Morgan, 7 Jul 89.

[62] Donnelly, Roth, and Baker, *Operation Just Cause*, p. 36. Intervs, author with Woerner, 30 Apr 91; Cope, 29 Mar 89; Augustine, 13 Jun 89; Cisneros, 1 May 89; Pantier, 13 Jun 90; and Maj J. C. Hiett, U.S. Army, 27 Apr 90, Fort Leavenworth, Kans. Conversation, author with Lt Tim McMahon, 20 Dec 89, Fort Clayton, Panama; Telephone conversation, author with Maj David Huntoon, 27 Jun 90; Comments, Maj Fred Polk, U.S. Army, to author, 1989. Quote from Ronald H. Cole, *Operation Just Cause: The Planning and Execution of Joint Operations in Panama, February 1988–January 1990* (Washington, D.C.: Joint History Office, Office of the Chairman of the Joint Chiefs of Staff, 1995), p. 10, and see also p. 9.

executed, the corps should be brought to Panama as early as possible to assume the role of the joint task force in charge of conventional operations. In doing so, the corps would not be interested in sharing command with the current JTF-Panama nor would it allow its resources to be used simply to augment that organization. The XVIII Airborne Corps "does not piecemeal out its assets," Huntoon declared. After intense and detailed discussion, the participants agreed on a compromise. Upon execution of POST TIME or BLUE SPOON, XVIII Airborne Corps would deploy a 31-man group to serve as an advance party for the corps headquarters, should SOUTHCOM's commander request its deployment. The anticipated "trigger" for that request would be the commitment to the fight of one or more brigades from the 82d Airborne Division.[63]

During the August conference, Cisneros approved a manning document Huntoon had drafted in coordination with McCutchon and Pantier for a corps-led JTF-Panama. After further staffing, Woerner sent the document and a message to the Joint Chiefs of Staff, asking the chairman to add a corps headquarters to the BLUE SPOON force list. On 19 October, Admiral Crowe approved the request, with the formal response coming in a message from General Kelly on 21 November. Kelly, whom USARSO staff officers correctly regarded as the XVIII Airborne Corps' "friend in court," had been lobbying since April to have the corps serve as the operational headquarters for BLUE SPOON. He thus agreed with most of Woerner's position but made one significant change to the August compromise: the corps would deploy to Panama and become JTF-Panama as soon as a troop buildup began under POST TIME.[64]

This message, which the Pentagon had not coordinated or staffed in advance with U.S. Army, South, came as a surprise to staff officers at Fort Clayton, who referred to the contents as Kelly's "diktat." A USARSO memorandum opposing the decision claimed there would be "no end to the confusion" created in a transition from a USARSO-led to an XVIII Airborne Corps joint task force. U.S. Army, South, understood the nuances of the situation in Panama and provided the expertise and continuity necessary to make the transition from peace to war. It also had responsibility for all Army personnel in the theater. Kelly's decision relegated the command "to a position of kibitzing from the sidelines." If allowed to stand, Rossi predicted, "We will necessarily be starting down a path in which CONUS based forces are seen as the only answer for Latin American issues." The USARSO chief of staff also candidly noted, "In my opinion, this condition will serve as a strong argument for the eventual deactivation [sic] of USARSO, if and when it

---

[63] First quote from Telephone conversation, author with Huntoon, 27 Jun 90. Interv, author with Pantier, 13 Jun 90. Second quote from Interv, author with Loeffke, 31 May 89. USARSO Memo 1–1, Staff Action Summary, 9 Sep 88, sub: XVIII Airborne Corps Deployment to JTF-PM. The role of the advance party between its deployment and any CINCSO request to deploy the corps headquarters seems to have been interpreted differently by the various parties involved. Huntoon indicated later that the small advance element would be augmented by JTF-Panama and U.S. Army, South. USARSO staff officers clearly believed that the thirty-one men would augment the existing JTF-Panama until the corps deployed.

[64] Telephone conversation, author with Huntoon, 27 Jun 90; Msg, CINCSO to JCS, 272115Z Oct 88; Msg, JCS to CINCSO, 212122Z Nov 88; Cole, *Operation Just Cause*, pp. 9–10.

is returned to [the United States], because if a stateside command can plan and prepare to execute the plan, why do you need another similar command?"[65]

Arguing that the SOUTHCOM commander had the authority to run his operation plan the way he desired, U.S. Army, South, recommended that Woerner challenge Kelly's position on the timing of the corps' deployment. Woerner, despite contrary advice from Cisneros, was inclined to do so. Since his message to the Joint Chiefs, his views on the subject had not changed, in that he still acknowledged the need for a larger command element under certain conditions but was no more eager than before to involve the XVIII Airborne Corps—a group of outsiders—until absolutely necessary. On this point, he and Loeffke were in complete accord. In overruling Kelly, Woerner simply held fast to his original intention: as the SOUTHCOM commander, he would determine when the flow of BLUE SPOON units reached a level requiring the deployment of all or part of the corps for command and control purposes. Put more directly, the corps in some configuration would not be brought to Panama until combat operations were well under way. Neither Kelly nor the new corps commander, Lt. Gen. Carl W. Stiner, was happy with the prospect of having the XVIII Airborne Corps deploying and assuming operational control from JTF-Panama in the midst of heavy fighting. Kelly consequently continued to argue for an earlier deployment, but Woerner held firm and Crowe supported the combatant commander on the scene.[66]

With the command and control issue temporarily settled (or, as Woerner's critics would argue, left hanging), the Southern Command and the XVIII Airborne Corps addressed a second aspect of Kelly's message: the corps was to conduct a detailed review of the PRAYER BOOK plans. When, in early December, Cisneros formally requested the review, the XVIII Airborne Corps responded with a request to be designated the executive agent for Panama planning. Pantier and Huntoon met in January to discuss the shift in responsibility, and the hand-off, as previously noted, took place in February at Fort Bragg.

Initially, XVIII Airborne Corps planners worked mainly with JTF-Panama and other organizations responsible for conventional operations. There was also coordination with Joint Special Operations Task Force-Panama, but that headquarters continued to work directly for the SOUTHCOM commander, despite appeals from the corps to integrate conventional and special operations planning. There was another issue that also troubled corps planners. The airborne command preferred operations in which U.S. forces struck rapidly with overwhelming power, defeated the enemy, and then withdrew, to be ready for the next contingency. The BLUE SPOON operation order called for such an attack, but, in Woerner's preferred scenario, only after a gradual buildup of U.S. forces in Panama under POST TIME had had a chance to intimidate PDF officers into taking steps to depose Noriega

---

[65] Most of this paragraph and the quotes therein are taken from MFR, Col A. T. Rossi, 19 Dec 88, sub: XVIII Airborne Corps Designation as COMJTF-PM. See also Cope Interv, 29 Mar 89; Fact Sheet, 9 Dec 88, sub: PRAYER BOOK Command and Control, Submitted by CPT Patrick Collins, USARSO DCSOPS Plans Division.

[66] Memo, Lt Col J. R. McCutchon, Chief of Plans Division, for SCJ–3, 23 Nov 88, sub: Corps Level JTF-PM; Handwritten note, Cisneros, attached to ibid.; MFR, Col Rossi, 19 Dec 88; Staff Action Sheet, Maj Kiser (through Chairman, PRAYER BOOK Planning Cell, and SCJ–3-DD), to SCJ–3, 1 Dec 88, sub: XVIII Airborne Corps Designation as COMJTFPM; Cole, *Operation Just Cause*, p. 10.

themselves. Since the buildup would take almost two weeks, this did not fit the corps' modus operandi. But Woerner saw no reason to change the concept, and in that he was the "supported" commander in chief, the corps had no choice but to "salute" and follow SOUTHCOM's guidance. Moreover, given XVIII Airborne Corps' worldwide commitments and the open question as to when it might be called upon to deploy to Panama, Stiner soon delegated planning responsibilities back to JTF-Panama, choosing merely to monitor that headquarters' efforts. As he said later, "We didn't pay too much attention to [BLUE SPOON] in the early stages, except to know that we had that responsibility, because we had a full plate of our own training activities."[67]

At this point in early 1989, the crisis in U.S.-Panamanian relations had settled into a regularized if not comfortable dynamic. Tensions continued between the two governments, intrusions onto U.S. installations accompanied by the occasional exchange of gunfire ebbed and flowed, planning for contingency operations proceeded apace, and incidents of harassment and treaty violations occurred with varying frequency and severity. Throughout all this, the Reagan administration took few policy initiatives after May 1988, as it awaited the outcome of the U.S. presidential election. Once George H. W. Bush became the president-elect, military and foreign policy specialists generally assumed that the situation in Panama would remain on the back burner until after his inauguration. What tack the new administration would then take vis-à-vis Noriega elicited much speculation on the part of all parties to the crisis. Presumably, the answers would be forthcoming.

---

[67] The quote about corps planners having to "salute' is from Telephone conversation, author with Huntoon, 27 Jun 90. Stiner quote from Interv, Dr Robert K. Wright Jr. with Lt Gen Carl W. Stiner, 2 Mar 90, Fort Bragg, N.C. Cole, *Operation Just Cause*, p. 10.

5

TOWARD A TOUGHER POSTURE
FEBRUARY–APRIL 1989

On 20 January 1989, George H. W. Bush took the presidential oath of office. To mark the occasion, General Noriega led 5,000 Panamanians in a demonstration that included burning outgoing President Ronald Reagan in effigy. Reagan offered no public comment on the spectacle. There was no need. He had already taken his parting shot at his antagonist to the south. In an interview given shortly before leaving the White House, Reagan suggested that the United States should reconsider adhering to the canal treaties if Noriega were still in power when the time came to turn the waterway over to Panama.[1]

Any attempt to abrogate the canal treaties a decade after their ratification would entail widespread ramifications, most of them negative. America's credibility would be undermined, public opinion in Panama and the rest of Latin America would be inflamed, and Noriega would be provided ammunition for his propaganda war. For these reasons and others, the new president showed no inclination to act on his predecessor's suggestion. What policy, then, would Bush adopt in the crisis? That remained an open question. In 1988, as vice president he had opposed any diplomatic solution that would drop the federal indictments against Noriega as the price for the dictator leaving Panama. Some attributed this position to political posturing, but the hard line did not change after the election. When Noriega, through his lawyers, put out feelers in early 1989 for better relations with the United States, the new president authorized the State Department, in behind-the-scenes contacts, to reiterate his uncompromising conditions for the dictator's departure. So long as Bush held to this position, the diplomatic impasse would continue.[2] That left the president to choose among three options: continuing Reagan's policies, downplaying the whole issue, or devising new initiatives of his own to end the crisis.

Bush initially followed the first course, letting word circulate that he would propose no new policies or change any existing ones until he had put together his own national security team, an undertaking that proved more difficult than anticipated. The president's first choice for secretary of defense, former Senator John Tower of Texas, failed to win confirmation after a heated debate in the Senate

---
[1] *New York Times*, 21 Jan 89, p. 9.
[2] For a brief, very general sketch of these contacts, see James D. Baker III, with Thomas M. Defrank, *The Politics of Diplomacy: Revolution, War and Peace* (New York: G. P. Putnam's Sons, 1995), p. 180.

President Bush speaks at an Armed Forces Review and Awards Ceremony. At the left is Richard Cheney and at the right is General Colin Powell.

along partisan lines. Bush immediately submitted a new candidate, Republican Congressman Richard Cheney of Wyoming. Cheney received quick and unanimous Senate approval, but by then almost two months had been lost trying to fill the position. Meanwhile, another key post in the national security bureaucracy remained vacant. Elliott Abrams had resigned as assistant secretary of state for inter-American affairs, conceding in late 1988 that Noriega's removal from power would not likely occur on Reagan's watch.[3] Press reports suggested that Secretary of State James D. Baker wanted Bernard Aronson, a Democrat, to fill the position, but a handful of Republicans in Congress and the administration, skeptical of Aronson's party affiliation, indicated that they might try to stall his confirmation.

In the midst of the political wrangling in Washington, the Southern Command picked up indications that significant new White House initiatives in the Panama crisis would be held in abeyance even longer than first thought, until after the Panamanian presidential election on 7 May. The lack of timely decisions caused Woerner to make some candid comments that, to his dismay, got him off on the wrong foot with the new administration, a misstep from which he never fully recovered. Soon thereafter, an incident involving U.S. schoolchildren in Panama outraged Americans there and in the United States and opened a highly publicized and emotional debate on the whole issue of PDF treaty violations and harassment. Meanwhile, out of the public limelight, planners in JTF-Panama (with the XVIII Airborne Corps looking on) and at the Joint Special Operations Command at Fort Bragg continued to update the PRAYER BOOK series of operation orders.

---

[3] What made Abrams' concession newsworthy was that, in the early phases of the crisis when he had encouraged military action against Noriega, he made statements to the effect that the dictator was barely holding onto power. By November 1988, however, he had become more cautious. In a private meeting with Woerner, he simply emphasized the need to solve the problem in the coming year lest it develop into a "holy mess" during the 1990s. Trip Rpt, 23 Nov 88, sub: Trip Report—CINC Washington Visit 21–22 November 1988.

Then, near the end of March, as Bush's national security team finally settled in, speculation surfaced that those advisers predisposed toward a tougher American stance with respect to Noriega would have the president's ear. Within the command groups at Quarry Heights and Fort Clayton, these rumors only added to the apprehension concerning future U.S. moves in the crisis.

WOERNER'S WOES

From the outset of the troubles in Panama, Woerner had regarded Admiral Crowe, the chairman of the Joint Chiefs of Staff, as an ally in Washington policy debates over the crisis. During the rancorous exchanges within Reagan's inner circle in 1988, Crowe had generally tried to restrain the hard-liners like Abrams and Secretary of State Shultz and had argued successfully against military intervention, a position Woerner keenly supported. The problem for Woerner was that, other than Crowe, he had no strong ally or base of support in the capital; nor, in Crowe's view, did the SOUTHCOM commander fully appreciate the byzantine nature of Washington politics. Woerner was virtually unknown to Congress, and he had never served a tour in the Pentagon. He also had vocal critics well placed within the military. In the Joint Staff, for instance, Lt. Gen. Tom Kelly continued to question the command and control arrangements for BLUE SPOON, while at Fort Bragg, commanders and operations officers in the joint special operations task force and the XVIII Airborne Corps saw little merit in Woerner's concept of a gradual buildup of U.S. forces in Panama should the White House find military escalation unavoidable. Crowe generally backed Woerner's positions in these arguments—at times, some said, against the admiral's own preferences.[4]

Woerner, for his part, grew increasingly frustrated at the inability of the national security establishment to fashion an interagency approach to the festering crisis. He truly appreciated President Reagan's decision not to use military force in the spring of 1988 but found himself disappointed time and again as SOUTHCOM's proposals for a comprehensive set of initiatives went unanswered or were diluted and rendered ineffective by bureaucratic politics. He had been told to keep the crisis under control during the U.S. presidential campaign, but the election was now several months in the past and Bush was in the White House. Would there finally be a concerted effort to resolve the crisis? Given the multitude of domestic and international problems facing the new president and the difficulties Bush was having getting key national security personnel on board, Woerner was skeptical. He had no problem with the administration gearing new U.S. policies to Panama's upcoming presidential election but feared that crucial decisions regarding those initiatives were being left to the last minute. "Of the few remaining non-violent options to force the ouster of Noriega," he informed Crowe in early January 1989, "the May elections present us with the best opportunity, but only if we can quickly plan for and execute a comprehensive action plan."[5]

The first public pronouncements by Secretary Baker on the subject reinforced Woerner's concerns. In an appearance before the House Foreign Affairs Committee

---

[4] On Woerner's status in Washington, see Donnelly, Roth, and Baker, *Operation Just Cause*, pp. 16, 26–27; Bob Woodward, *The Commanders* (New York: Simon & Schuster, 1991), p. 83; Cole, *Operation Just Cause,* p. 10.

[5] Msg, CINCSO to JCS [personal for Crowe, Armitage, Abrams, Amb Davis], 031320Z Jan 89, sub: May 89 Panamanian Elections—An Opportunity.

in mid-February, the secretary of state asserted that the Bush administration would not normalize relations with Panama so long as Noriega remained in power. He added that there would be a review of existing policy with the intention of making improvements, but what those improvements might be was left unsaid. Later, senior officials in the administration told reporters that, despite the objections Baker had raised to wide-ranging financial sanctions against Panama when he was treasury secretary under Reagan, President Bush had no intention of lifting the embargo.[6] In short, pending a policy review at some undetermined point in the future, the old and, in Woerner's view, ineffectual and piecemeal measures for dealing with the crisis would remain in place.

Shortly after Baker's testimony, the *New York Times* reported a luncheon speech given by Woerner to the Central American Chambers of Commerce in Panama City.[7] At this point, Bush had been president for just a month, the Tower affair was still in the headlines, and Aronson's nomination to the position vacated by Abrams was still rumor, not fact. When Woerner accepted the invitation to address the business group, he knew that he would be asked about any impending changes in U.S. policy toward Panama. To preempt a barrage of questions on the topic, he decided to field the first such question with a comprehensive statement on the crisis as he saw it.

As expected, the luncheon address afforded him such an opportunity. Citing an "absence" of U.S. policy toward Panama, he asserted the urgent need for debate and for decisions concerning "what our actions are to be on May 8 [the day after the Panamanian elections] given a variety of scenarios." Would such deliberations take place in the immediate future? Woerner doubted that they would. "We are frankly ill prepared to do that now because, as you well know, we have a vacuum in Washington in the absence of an appointment of an assistant secretary of state for Latin American affairs. . . . Until we get that position filled and the debate can commence, I offer you little hope of an articulated policy."[8]

"What I said, I said deliberately," Woerner later asserted. He had anticipated expressing his views on the policy process, and he had. He had also anticipated that his comments, while made off the record, would be reported by someone in the news media. They were. So that he would have an accurate account of what he said, he had asked his public affairs people to make a tape recording of the remarks. What he had not anticipated was the way his remarks would be interpreted in the media. The *New York Times* article, under the headline, "General Sees Lack of Policy," characterized Woerner's words as harsh and alleged that he was "[a]dding his voice to critics who say the Administration has moved slowly in formulating its foreign policy." As soon as the article appeared, Woerner recalled, "all hell hit the fan."[9] Numerous callers wanted to know exactly what he had said, and armed with a transcript of his remarks, he was able to tell them. He also sent the tapes and transcript to his superiors in Washington, emphasizing that his remarks, taken in context, clearly did not refer to a policy vacuum but to the vacancy at the State Department. In other words, nothing he said was intended as criticism of

---

[6] *New York Times*, 24 Feb 89, p. 3.
[7] The account of Woerner's speech and the furor that followed is based on ibid.; Interv, author with General Frederick F. Woerner, Jr., U.S. Army (Ret.), 30 Apr 91, Fort Leavenworth, Kans.
[8] *New York Times*, 24 Feb 89, p. 3.
[9] Quotes from ibid.; Woerner Interv, 30 Apr 91.

the president. Initially, he was led to believe that the White House accepted this explanation and that the tempest had blown over.

A few weeks later, while on an official visit to the capital, he found out otherwise. At the end of a meeting he had with Crowe and Brent Scowcroft, Bush's national security adviser, the latter asked Woerner to remain behind. "The president is infuriated," Scowcroft scolded the general. Surprised by the rebuke, Woerner asked if Scowcroft had read the transcript, and Scowcroft replied that he had. "What you said is true," he conceded, "but you shouldn't have said it." Woerner thereupon apologized for the remarks and assured Scowcroft that his aim had not been to embarrass the president. When Woerner rejoined Crowe, the admiral asked if Scowcroft had raised the speech issue. Woerner answered yes, at which point Crowe became visibly displeased. "He had no right to bring it up!" Woerner remembers the admiral saying in anger. Apparently, the White House had led Crowe to believe that the whole matter was a "dead issue."[10]

Two years after the episode, Woerner still defended his remarks and rejected the interpretation that he was being critical of the new administration. "If you get to four stars," he reflected, "you might not be very smart, but you've got enough sense not to criticize your commander in chief." But he also added, "If I had it to do all over again, I wouldn't do it. . . . I wouldn't make the speech."[11] But the damage was done. Woerner survived the furor over his luncheon remarks, but his standing in Washington had slipped even further. To his military critics at Fort Bragg and in the Pentagon were now added civilian antagonists within the president's inner circle, even, perhaps, the president himself. Within this group, the impression grew over the ensuing weeks and months that Woerner was not a "team player" and that his reading of the crisis was out of sync with that of the policy-making bureaucracy. To make matters worse, charges were beginning to circulate that he was a general who could not, or would not, protect the men and women serving in his command.

"Terror" in Panama

Since early in the crisis, there had been a "continuous ebb and flow" in the level of harassment and treaty violations directed against Americans and U.S. installations in Panama. By the end of 1988, service personnel, their dependents, and employees of other U.S. agencies had grown accustomed to a variety of aggravations. For one, PDF *tránsitos* continued to solicit bribes from American motorists they stopped, and, despite SOUTHCOM guidance not to pay, many of the victims, anxious to get on with their business, chose to hand over the widely accepted "fine" of $20. The likely outcome for those who refused to part with their cash, or who failed in some way to dissuade their tormentors, was night court, where any judgment against a U.S. serviceman usually had tacked onto it a gratuitous $300 fine for showing "disrepect to the PDF." Besides the bribes and night court, the Panama Defense Forces regularly detained American service personnel performing official duties, occasionally roughing them up in the process.

The SOUTHCOM Center for Treaty Affairs issued periodic fact sheets summarizing the incidents, which numbered in the hundreds by the end of 1988. Seven categories of infractions were covered: denial of freedom of movement, excessive force and endangerment, procedural guarantee violations, other violations

---
[10] Woerner Interv, 30 Apr 91.
[11] Ibid.

of treaty documents or arrangements, detentions without charges, confiscation or destruction of personal or U.S. government property, and violations of U.S. installations.[12] What these categories and the terse summary of individual incidents under each one failed to reveal were the feelings, ranging from annoyance to abject fear, experienced by the numerous service personnel and their dependents who were variously detained, handcuffed, interrogated, strip-searched, sexually intimidated, verbally abused, denied legal counsel, bullied, photographed for propaganda purposes, and subjected to many other indignities. SOUTHCOM treaty affairs officers who recorded these activities empathized with the plight of the victims and grew increasingly frustrated over the futility of official protests.

While the illegal activity and harassment directed against Americans could be nerve-racking, most of the intimidation consisted of low- to medium-grade inconveniences, aggravations, and provocations. On occasion, however, more serious incidents broke the pattern. One such case involved the violation of U.S. rights at the port of Las Minas on the Atlantic side of the canal area. In blatant defiance of the canal treaty, the Panama Defense Forces periodically interfered with the movement, unloading, and processing of U.S. cargo at the port. The Southern Command had protested the disruptions but to little avail. Then, on 29 September 1988, Panamanian authorities at Las Minas seized a 120-mm. gun tube that the Army had sent to Panama for testing. When SOUTHCOM officials arrived at the scene, they were denied access to the port, with one of the uniformed Panamanians present using his AK47 to push away an American MP liaison officer. The Southern Command demanded return of the gun tube while rejecting Panamanian charges that the tube was linked to U.S. "subversive activities." Woerner also decided that the provocation was so flagrant as to require action beyond a formal protest. Using open communication lines, SOUTHCOM officers initially played down the issue, deliberately misleading eavesdropping Panamanians as to the seriousness of the SOUTHCOM commander's intentions. Meanwhile, the 1st Battalion, 508th Infantry, at Fort Kobbe was placed on alert and units were moved to the Atlantic side of the canal area to be closer to the port. The show of force "surprised the devil" out of Noriega, according to one U.S. intelligence officer. The next day, the gun tube was returned, accompanied with an apology. What might have transpired had the Panama Defense Forces remained intransigent is a matter of speculation. But as Loeffke noted in his diary, "We were ready to go and fight the PDF to take back the weapon."[13]

The Las Minas affair involved a threat to U.S. property. Other incidents that exceeded routine petty harassment involved threats to, and in some cases actual abuse of, American citizens. On several occasions, the Southern Command had to protest the use of excessive physical force against U.S. servicemen in PDF hands. One such incident involved an allegedly drunken PDF officer using a night stick on a U.S. enlisted man and his pregnant wife. Another report charged four unidentified

---

[12] Fact Sheets, SCTA-J, 22 Apr 88, 22 Nov 88, sub: Recap of Recent PDF–US Forces Incidents. Quote from Interv, author with Maj William Graves, U.S. Army, 27 Aug 91, Fort Leavenworth, Kans.

[13] Third quote from Diary, Bernard Loeffke, 30 Sep 88. Second quote from Interv, author with Brig Gen John Stewart, U.S. Army, 14 Jun 89, Quarry Heights, Panama. First quote from Fact Sheet, SOUTHCOM J–3, 25 Oct 88, sub: Las Minas Events. Fact Sheet, SCTA-J–3, 22 Nov 88; *Tropic Times*, 30 Sep 88, 3 Oct 88.

PDF officers with pulling an American civilian from his rental car, accusing him of working for the CIA, and beating him unconscious. In a similar incident, a PDF officer repeatedly kicked a U.S. serviceman and placed a gun to his head. Besides physical force, the Panama Defense Forces also tried to employ intimidation, as when they arrested General Woerner and Secretary of the Army John O. Marsh Jr. while the two men were jogging on the Fort Amador causeway. In an even more brazen episode, Dr. Marcos Ostrander, an international lawyer employed by the U.S. Army, South, left his home one morning in September to find a decapitated and mutilated human body propped against his car. At the time, Ostrander was involved in preparing a report proving that American citizens did not receive fair trials in Panama. The body was assumed to be a warning against publishing his findings. A Panamanian officer Ostrander knew attributed the grisly act to radical elements within the Panamanian military and advised the lawyer to take the threat seriously.[14]

While the psychological impact of PDF harassment, intimidation, and abuse was felt throughout the American community in Panama, news of these incidents was rarely reported in the United States. When stories of PDF misconduct did surface, as in the *New York Times* in August and September 1988, they produced no discernible backlash. SOUTHCOM's Public Affairs Office took notice, however, and prepared a response to "set the record straight." "While basically factually accurate," a command spokesperson conceded, "this harassment pattern is not considered a campaign by the General Manuel Noriega regime, as the articles suggest, but rather a continuation of a trend which began in February [1988]" as a result of PDF officers taking advantage of the climate created by their commander's anti-U.S. posture and disinformation campaign. The majority of the incidents reported, the Southern Command assured the news media, were not serious, and the command's Center for Treaty Affairs diligently protested each infraction. That the Panama Defense Forces by and large ignored the protests was regrettable, but at least the official effort served to put the Southern Command "on record on the way business should be conducted." As a further response to the increased harassment, public affairs officers stressed, the command had moved about 1,400 of the 2,450 families of military personnel and Defense Department civilians to safer locations in Panama or back to the United States. But "short of other kinds of military actions," there was not much else U.S. officials could do to remedy the situation.[15]

If the American public was largely indifferent to the situation in Panama, many important officials in Washington were not. An officer in the Pentagon described the PDF's conduct as "appalling," while unidentified sources in the State Department criticized the Southern Command as being more interested in conducting "business as usual" with Noriega than with mounting a vigorous campaign against PDF

---

[14] *New York Times*, 29 Sep 88; Interv, author with Lt Col Robert Barefield, U.S. Army, 7 Nov 90, Fort Leavenworth, Kans.; Diary, Loeffke, 1 Nov 88, 10 Nov 88. According to one source, Loeffke was so angered by the threat to Ostrander that he had his provost marshal deliver a message to Noriega through a PDF officer that the dictator would pay a "devastating price" if the USARSO lawyer "so much as developed a hangnail." See Kurt Muse and John Gilstrap, *Six Minutes to Freedom* (New York: Citadel Press, 2006), p. 63.

[15] *New York Times*, 24 Aug 88, 27 Aug 88, 29 Sep 88. Quotes on SOUTHCOM's position on PDF harassment are from *Tropic Times*, 26 Aug 88.

harassment. Some U.S. officials even suggested that Woerner and his generals had issued a gag order prohibiting disgruntled colonels and majors from reporting incidents to the Defense Department. (The *New York Times* mitigated the effect of this accusation by reminding the paper's readers that the White House itself had placed restrictions on negative publicity about Panama for the duration of the presidential campaign.) Soon after the election, Woerner went to Washington to discuss possible U.S. initiatives in Panama during the coming year. Most of the conversations he held highlighted to one degree or another concern over the harassment problem. In one meeting, Admiral Crowe raised the issue but ordered no specific actions to resolve it. Most officials recognized that Woerner had few options available to him. Military force had been ruled out at the highest level, while any decision to impose curfews on U.S. service personnel and to declare certain areas off-limits would mean, in effect, abdicating several of America's treaty rights in Panama.[16]

When, in late January 1989, a *Washington Post* article made a passing reference to the harassment in Panama and characterized morale among U.S. troops as having hit "rock bottom," Loeffke dismissed the analysis as "pure malarkey." The Southern Command preferred the term "ill-informed" and denied allegations of a "cover up or downplaying" of the incidents. Yet, by coincidence, the piece appeared just as harassment in Panama was again on the upswing. In the weeks that followed, not only did the number of incidents increase, but the Noriega regime demonstrated the multiplicity of ways in which it could disrupt the lives of Americans in the country, especially in areas that previously had offered only a potential target or had received only negligible attention. The upward trend in "confrontational events," Rear Adm. Richard C. Ustick informed the Joint Staff, "seems to be approaching a new threshold to test our limits."[17]

Ustick singled out PDF interference with U.S. "freedom of movement" in Panama as a treaty violation that, left unchallenged, could hamper SOUTHCOM's ability to perform assigned missions. Throughout the crisis, Panamanian authorities had tried to control and restrict the movement of U.S. vehicles being used for official business, but, on 19 January 1989, the Panamanian cochairman of the Combined Board signaled an intensification of this effort when he informed his American counterpart that the Panama Defense Forces had "placed fixed sentry posts at the entry points of the canal area" to assist American personnel who got "lost" in Panama. In fact, the PDF used the checkpoints to stop, search, reroute, detain, and impound U.S. government and government-leased vehicles. One tactic involved taking advantage of the unwritten but mutually accepted definition of a U.S. military "convoy," which, by law, required a PDF escort. Over the years, both sides had agreed that four official vehicles traveling together

---

[16] First quoted word from *New York Times*, 29 Sep 88. Second quote from *Army Times*, 20 Mar 89 Trip Rpt, 23 Nov 88, sub: Trip Report—CINC Washington Visit 21–22 November 1988. In a handwritten note attached to a copy of the trip report, Col. Arnie Rossi at JTF-Panama indicated that he was "most interested" in the fact that the harassment and human rights issues had dominated the "dialogue" about Panama in Washington.

[17] *Washington Post*, 21 Jan 89, 7 Feb 89. For Loeffke's response, see Msg, CDR, USARSO, to CSA, 310200Z Jan 89, sub: Update No. 20. SOUTHCOM's position and Admiral Ustick's comments are from Msg, CINCSO to Joint Staff [personal, Rear Adm Ustick to Lt Gen Johnson], 162026Z Feb 89, sub: Panama-Update.

to a single destination constituted a convoy. With the upsurge in harassment, the PDF began stopping and detaining single vehicles traveling independently to different locations. Once four vehicles had been stopped, the Panamanian officers present designated them a convoy, which could then be turned back for not having coordinated its movements with the proper authorities and for not having the required escort.

In addition to the convoy ploy, the Panama Defense Forces sought to limit the freedom of movement of American officials and troops in Panama by refusing to recognize the decals that were used to identify U.S. government vehicles. This flagrant disregard of an important treaty provision raised concerns about how the PDF on any given day would deal with the legal status of those vehicles and the protection to which they were entitled. The Southern Command again protested vigorously, again to no avail.[18]

Another form of harassment inconvenienced American military personnel living in housing units that, under the treaty, had reverted from U.S. to Panamanian control. In 1984, the Southern Command had arranged to lease the units, most of which were located in the Balboa and Diablo Heights areas of Panama City, as a means of lessening the demand for limited on-base housing. With the crisis and the economic sanctions invoked by President Reagan in early 1988 under the International Emergency Economic Powers Act (IEEPA), the rent due on the units was diverted from the Solis Palma regime controlled by Noriega into an escrow account. In retaliation, the regime began hinting that Americans who had failed to pay their rent would be evicted. The threat hung in the air until February 1989, when the Panamanian housing ministry ordered electricity and water to seventy-eight of the residences shut off. The Southern Command responded by terminating the leases and moving over a hundred Americans affected by the cutoff to other quarters. Many of the families requested permission to pay the rent, but U.S. law imposed a steep fine for those who willingly violated the IEEPA sanctions. In his diary, Loeffke lamented the hardship caused by the "evictions." "This was a lousy way to get us out."[19]

The regime found other ways to turn its bureaucracy and the IEEPA issue against Americans in Panama. On 20 February 1989, it announced that all U.S. service personnel would have to obtain a *Paz y Salvo* ("Peace and Safety") certificate from the government before they could receive 1989 license plates for their cars and vans. Although American citizens were exempt from this procedure under the treaty, the Southern Command had no realistic option but to protest, an ineffectual response. With only one week before the new plates would be required, many U.S. military personnel stood in line up to eight hours to get the prerequisite certificate. Several thousand failed to meet the deadline and found themselves subject to fines for driving with expired plates.

---

[18] On the attempts to limit U.S. freedom of movement in Panama, see *Tropic Times*, 24 Feb 89; Msg, CINCSO to Joint Staff, 162026Z Feb 89, sub: Panama-Update; Author's notes on Treaty Affairs briefing, 23 Mar 89, Fort Clayton, Panama; Msg, CINCSO to VCJCS [personal, Gen Woerner to Gen Herres], 060115Z Mar 89, sub: Panama Assessment.

[19] Diary, Loeffke, 16 Aug 88, 3 Oct 88, 18 Feb 89, n.d. [Feb 89]. On the rent issue and evictions, see also *Tropic Times*, 22 Feb 89; Msgs, CINCSO to Joint Staff, 162026Z Feb 89, sub: Panama-Update, and CINCSO to VCJCS, 060115Z Mar 89, sub: Panama Assessment.

The inconvenience was enormous for the American military community but did not match the problems confronting Panamanian citizens employed by the U.S. government. For them, a *Paz y Salvo* certificate was proof of having paid their national taxes. But, under the IEEPA sanctions, money withheld from their paychecks for income and education taxes did not go to the regime but into the aforementioned escrow account. Panamanians employed by the United States were thus unable to obtain the certificate. Without it, not only were they unable to purchase license plates, but they could not engage in a variety of business activities and their personal property was subject to government seizure. Admiral Ustick did not understate the facts when he described the *Paz y Salvo* controversy as "another highly emotional issue involving all of our Panamanian employees and their families." The U.S. administrator of the Panama Canal also noted the disruption to the waterway's operations caused by the PDF's detaining Panamanian employees with expired license plates.[20]

In addition to the regime's psychological and bureaucratic warfare, the physical mistreatment of U.S. government employees and service personnel continued, with the Southern Command concerned over the increasing propensity of the Panama Defense Forces to resort to violence. Two incidents in February 1989 called attention to the problem. In the first, a civilian employee of the U.S. Navy received an official summons to appear at the local National Investigation Department (DENI) station to make a statement. When he arrived, the PDF lieutenant who met him outside the building began to hit him. An MP liaison at the scene reported that the Navy employee was pushed into the station while being hit in the face. When the military policeman tried to intervene, he was knocked aside. Inside the DENI station, the U.S. civilian was handcuffed and thrown into a cell. The PDF later beat him with a rubber hose and repeatedly kicked him in the head, telling him throughout the ordeal that he was going to die. Meanwhile, the MP liaison returned with another PDF lieutenant, and subsequent negotiations secured the release of the employee, who emerged with a broken eardrum and bruises on his back, buttocks, and hands. The Southern Command protested the incident, and the Panama Defense Forces, in essentially a meaningless concession, apologized.[21]

Two weeks later, in the second incident, a U.S. Navy lieutenant bird-watching in a marshy area near the old Tocumen airport was confronted by two PDF officers, who took him into custody. While in detention, he was accused of being a spy, denied contact with U.S. military liaison officers, strip-searched twice, hit in the head, back, and kidney area, threatened with sodomy and death, and photographed with his bird-watching equipment, which included binoculars and a camera. After nine hours of illegal confinement, the Panamanian military released him. The next day, while driving in Panama City, the lieutenant was stopped by a PDF *tránsito* for an alleged traffic violation. Fearing a repetition of

---

[20] Ustick's comments are contained in Msg, CINCSO to Joint Staff, 162026Z Feb 89, sub: Panama-Update. For additional information on the *Paz Y Salvo* issue, see Msgs, CINCSO to VCJCS, 060115Z Mar 89, sub: Panama Assessment, and CDR, USARSO, to CSA, 221840Z Mar 89; *Tropic Times*, 1 Mar 89, 3 Mar 89.

[21] *Tropic Times*, 10 Feb 89; Fact Sheet, SCTA-JC, 10 May 89, sub: Recap of Recent–US Forces Treaty Violations/Incidents from 01 Feb to 28 Feb 89; Msg, CINCSO to VCJCS, 060115Z Mar 89, sub: Panama Assessment.

the previous day's ordeal, the American fled the scene in his vehicle. As he raced back to Quarry Heights, he lost control of the car and ran into a retaining wall, incurring severe leg injuries. When an ambulance arrived, the driver was forced by a PDF officer to take the lieutenant to a Panamanian hospital instead of Gorgas Army Hospital. U.S. military liaison officers were finally able to intervene in the case, and sometime later the lieutenant was transferred to Gorgas, where he underwent surgery for his injuries.[22]

The harassment of Americans in Panama reached a new plateau on 3 March, in what would become one of the most emotional and publicized incidents of the crisis.[23] Shortly after 0700, several U.S. military headquarters began receiving reports that the Panama Defense Forces were stopping and holding American school buses at gunpoint. The buses were owned and driven by Panamanians, but the transportation they provided was a service contracted by the U.S. Navy. In keeping with SOUTHCOM's protests over the *Paz y Salvo* problem, the Navy had placed U.S. government license tags instead of Panamanian plates on the vehicles. PDF personnel were now detaining the buses for displaying improper licenses. What alarmed U.S. officials was that American schoolchildren, many of elementary school age, were still on the buses.

Of the twenty-one vehicles detained by the Panama Defense Forces, twelve were released after the drivers were issued tickets. Nine buses, however, were taken to the *dirección nacional de transporte terrestre* (DNTT). Maj. Alan Mansfield, a veteran of the crisis who ran the USARSO Provost Marshal Office at Fort Clayton, rushed to the scene, as did SOUTHCOM treaty affairs personnel, criminal investigation officers, and other U.S. representatives. When Mansfield and two other military policemen arrived, they closed off the area and collected the bus drivers' keys. Mansfield then confronted the ranking PDF officer on the scene in an unsuccessful effort to negotiate the removal of the children. When the Panama Defense Forces brought in a wrecker to tow away one of the buses with the children still on board, Mansfield ordered MP vehicles to block the route. At one point, a higher-ranking PDF officer arrived, as did more PDF troops and American MPs. As on many occasions during the crisis, Mansfield proved his skill in handling a highly charged situation. Every time a camera turned toward him, he coolly demanded to know why the Panamanians were abducting American schoolchildren. The PDF officer finally relented and released the children, many of whom had been detained on the buses well over an hour. American government vans called to the scene, as well as cars driven by distraught parents, were used to evacuate the children. In the meantime, the MP quick reaction force was placed on alert. The Panama Defense Forces detained the buses for another hour until the drivers, under extreme pressure, surrendered their licenses. The last bus was released at 0937.

The incident shocked and angered the American community in Panama, which viewed the "traumatization" of their schoolchildren as a major escalation

---

[22] Fact Sheet, SCTA-JC, 10 May 89, sub: Recap of Recent–US Forces Treaty Violations/Incidents from 01 Feb to 28 Feb 89; *Tropic Times*, 22 Feb 89.

[23] The following account is based on *Tropic Times*, 6 Mar 89; *Army Times*, 20 Mar 89; Log, SOUTHCOM Joint Operations Center, 3 Mar 89; Handwritten notes, n.d., titled J–3 Guidance; Telephone Interv, author with Capt Anthony M. Schilling, U.S. Army, 30 Nov 90; Interv, author with Lt Col Mike Michaelis, U.S. Army, 7 Jun 89, Fort Clayton, Panama.

in the crisis. "I can tell you that gets up close and personal, when they start screwing with your family like that," recalled a U.S. officer whose son was on one of the buses.[24] Many U.S. service personnel wanted the Southern Command to take strong action. When the command did little more than express outrage and issue a formal protest, the frustration that had been building throughout the crisis was vented, most of it at Woerner, Loeffke, the Joint Chiefs, and the Bush administration. A "unique opportunity" to take a "bold step" against the Panama Defense Forces had presented itself, one officer complained, "but nobody had the courage" to act. Sarcastic references to Woerner as "WIMPCOM" resurfaced. He was the "Philosopher King" whose policy of protecting his troops was "mind over matter—he didn't mind and we didn't matter." Anger and frustration also fueled the extracurricular activities of a few U.S. noncommissioned officers and enlisted men who, in groups of threes and fours, would go "hunting the PDF," that is, mugging or beating any PDF officer they could find and isolate. In a nonviolent but much more consequential move, someone at Quarry Heights sought retribution by leaking a copy of a classified document on PDF harassment to the Military Times Media group, which included the *Army Times*, a private newspaper circulated weekly to Army installations and personnel throughout the world.[25]

"Terror in Panama," was the banner front-page headline on that newspaper's 20 March 1989 issue. An article with that title reported that U.S. servicemen in Panama had been abducted, beaten, threatened, and submitted to psychological torture. The story also quoted Elliott Abrams on what the former assistant secretary of state asserted was a "shameful" and "pusillanimous" official response to the harassment in "a real effort to downplay it and not have that information circulated widely in Washington." Abrams went on to call Admiral Crowe's larger policy objectives "legitimate" but to voice his objection to carrying out the policy "over the bruised bodies of the men in Panama." An interview with a Navy petty officer, Mike Nieves, seemed to lend credence to Abrams' criticism. Nieves recounted his encounter with several PDF policemen who, after abducting him for parking an official van in a no-parking zone at Torrijos airport, took him out on a dirt road; robbed, beat, and kicked him; then put a gun near his head and pulled the trigger while he was forced to beg for his life. The article went on to report congressional concern over the harassment. One outraged Republican congressman, Robert Dornan of California, declared, "The next time an American is beaten we should hit them with a ton of bricks. And sometimes a ton of bricks is spelled: 82d Airborne."[26]

When General Loeffke walked into the JTF-Panama meeting on 23 March, he was clearly distressed about the *Army Times* article. His first question to the staff and commanders sitting around the U-shaped table in the Simón Bolívar

---

[24] *Army Times*, 20 Mar 89, p. 3. Quotes from Barefield Interv, 7 Nov 90.

[25] Intervs, author with Maj John Mulholland, U.S. Army, 30 May 91, Fort Leavenworth, Kans.; Maj William Graves, U.S. Army, 20, 27 Aug 91, 18 May 92; and JTF-Panama staff officer. Conversations, author with several officers and enlisted men in Panama who expressed their criticism of higher authorities on condition of anonymity; Kempe, *Divorcing the Dictator*, p. 363; Donnelly, Roth, and Baker, *Operation Just Cause*, pp. 32, 45; Lt Col Paul J. Woodrow, 'Ni Un Paso Atras'-The Crisis in Panama, 1987–1989, U.S. Army War College Personal Experience Monograph (Carlisle Barracks, Pa.: U.S. Army War College, 12 April 1992), pp. 14, 16.

[26] *Army Times*, 20 Mar 89, p. 3.

conference room at Fort Clayton was whether or not Americans in Panama were really being "terrorized" or if the incidents of which all present were aware could be better characterized as "harassment" and "intimidation." Most around the table preferred the latter terms: the incidents did not constitute "terrorism." As the discussion progressed, however, some expressed their concern that the Southern Command and JTF-Panama might be minimizing what in fact had become a serious problem. Loeffke responded that Noriega was certainly a "thug," but that Panamanian officials could justify some of their actions because of the refusal of the United States to make various payments to the regime.

At one point, the exchange migrated from the conference table to the larger audience of officers and civilians in attendance. A Center for Treaty Affairs official volunteered that many incidents that might constitute "terror" were going unreported because of a prevailing belief that neither top military commanders in Panama nor policy makers in Washington would take decisive action on behalf of the victims. That viewpoint generated further comments, until the discussion worked itself back to where it had begun, with seeming agreement that "terror" was too harsh a word to describe what Americans were enduring in Panama. The debate carried into the corridors afterwards, with several officers who had been in the audience arguing that "psychological terror" did exist when military personnel and their dependents were afraid to go about their daily business for fear of being detained and abused.[27]

The discussion at that meeting revealed the nuances and complexity of the harassment issue and the differences of opinion it generated within the American military community. To many service personnel who lived and worked in Panama, the incidents were clear-cut violations of the canal treaty and required a strong U.S. response if Noriega was to be discouraged from continuing or further escalating his tactics. Several officers and civilians in SOUTHCOM's Center for Treaty Affairs who had dealt with the victims of harassment on a daily basis tended to side with this group. For one treaty affairs official, the solution was simple: evacuate U.S. citizens, bring in the U.S. 82d Airborne Division, and "blow them away," meaning the Panama Defense Forces and its commander. Other Americans, including many military personnel and their families, disagreed. PDF and regime harassment was clearly a concern and an annoyance, but with the exception of a few atypical incidents in which Panamanian authorities had exercised excessive force or poor judgment, the threat to Americans was not undue cause for alarm and certainly not a cause for war. Besides, as the wife of one officer told an interviewer, "A lot of the harassment stories, unless they were officially documented, were rumors. Some were just plain stupid."[28]

---

[27] This account of the JTF-Panama meeting is based on Author's notes, JTF-Panama Update Meeting, 23 Mar 89, Fort Clayton, Panama.

[28] Woodrow, 'Ni Un Paso Atras.' First quote from Briefing, Center for Treaty Affairs official to author, 23 Mar 89. Conversations, author with numerous military personnel in Panama who expressed their criticism of higher authorities on condition of anonymity. Second quote from Donnelly, Roth, and Baker, *Operation Just Cause*, p. 44. Loeffke's files contain an example of how rumors of harassment could get started. In January 1989, while leaving Howard Air Force Base, the general stopped to talk with a PDF officer he knew. A security policeman saw the two men conversing and reported that the Panamanian military had stopped Loeffke and searched his vehicle. Two days later, Woerner heard at a party that Loeffke had been beaten up by the Panamanian

Woerner, Loeffke, Ustick, Cisneros, and other key commanders and staff officers, in weighing reason against emotion, tried to keep the harassment issue in perspective. The days when the United States would go to war to prevent its citizens abroad from being maligned or roughed up were long over. In early 1988, President Reagan had agreed to send security enhancement forces to Panama to protect American lives and property, but neither he nor his successor condoned the use of U.S. military force unless Noriega placed those lives in imminent danger. The incidents of petty harassment in Panama, for all the inconvenience, irritation, anger, and psychological distress they produced, did not pose such an acute threat. As Woerner later explained, "I did not feel that Americans were threatened life and limb." Neither did Crowe, and neither did the White House. With the military option excluded, there was little the Southern Command could do to end the harassment without escalating the crisis. As Woerner pointed out, he could cut off electricity to a PDF facility on a U.S. installation in response to some incident, but Noriega could retaliate by shutting down electricity to an entire American housing complex. Noriega and his cronies held "most of the trump cards," Woerner advised the Pentagon. Under the circumstances, the Southern Command had few options except using the formal mechanisms still available to it under the treaty to issue a stream of official protests, most of which elicited only a perfunctory reply from their recipients.[29]

As for the more serious and increasingly well-publicized incidents that went beyond petty harassment, few were as clear-cut as reported, several were surrounded by ambiguity or mitigating circumstances, and some simply never happened. In the case of the Navy bird watcher, for example, he was apprehended near a PDF facility, pursuing his hobby with binoculars and military maps in hand—behavior bound to raise an adversary's suspicions. Early in his detainment, when his Panamanian interrogators told him to write a statement confessing to espionage, the officer instead wrote a letter to his girlfriend. His reference in the letter to Panama as a "Banana Republic," and the sentence, "This is a bunch of bulls——t," were presumably what provoked his tormentors into more brutal action. The beating was inexcusable, but many U.S. service personnel who heard the whole story could only marvel at the officer's foolhardy behavior from start to finish. In another incident that received a good deal of publicity, a PDF officer allegedly accosted a U.S. Army private first class and his wife sitting in their car, forced the man into the trunk at gunpoint, and raped, or attempted to rape, the woman. That the Southern Command only protested the outrage angered many Americans in Panama. What never caught up with the initial reports, however, was the conclusion, reached after a thorough investigation, that the rape (or attempted rape) never took place. Finally, even the detention of the school buses could be viewed as within the rights of the regime, although stopping them while the children were on board had betrayed a serious lapse of judgment (one for which the officer in charge had reportedly been disciplined).[30] Americans demanding stronger action

---

military. In his notes on the "incident," the JTF-Panama commander bemoaned this "gross information." Notes, n.d., Loeffke Papers.

[29] Woerner's comments are taken from Msgs, CINCSO to VCJCS, 060115Z Mar 89, sub: Panama Assessment, and CINCSO to Joint Staff, 162026Z Feb 89, sub: Panama-Update. See also Donnelly, Roth, and Baker, *Operation Just Cause*, p. 43.

[30] Several officers at the Southern Command and JTF-Panama expressed doubts to me about the alleged rape. Having access to the official report, I continued to believe that a rape had occurred

by the Southern Command regarded these reservations, qualifications, and denials as desperate rationalizations by commanders who did not take kindly to bad news that might intensify the crisis. In some cases, this argument was not without merit, but, generally speaking, it overlooked the substantial difficulties U.S. commanders had in determining the facts of a given case and acting upon them.[31]

Most of the critics who chided Woerner for his handling of the "terror in Panama" were also unaware of one important consideration: the directive from Washington that forbade the SOUTHCOM commander from taking any action that would provoke a military confrontation with the Panama Defense Forces and the Noriega regime. Originally, the "statute of limitations" on this verbal directive ran through the U.S. presidential election. After George Bush became the president-elect, it was extended to his inauguration in January and, following that, to the Panamanian elections in May. The latter extension was to allow the president's new national security team ample opportunity to review the crisis and determine appropriate courses of action.

In the meantime, on 6 March 1989, three days after the school bus incident, Woerner offered his assessment of the increasing harassment to the vice chairman of the Joint Chiefs. Up to this point, SOUTHCOM's official position had been that the pressures brought against Americans in Panama were not part of an officially directed campaign, but the logical consequence of the regime's pervasive anti-American attitudes, the declining economic conditions in Panama, and, on several occasions, the fact that Americans had truly been in the wrong. Now Woerner explicitly labeled the harassment as being directed by the regime, probably by Noriega himself. Why had the PDF commander changed tactics? Woerner offered three possibilities: retaliation for perceived attacks on the Panamanian government in the U.S. media, including the *Tropic Times*; an attempt to shore up support within the regime's power base of public workers, labor unions, the poor, and the Panama Defense Forces by focusing attention on the U.S. troop presence and alleged U.S. violations of Panama's sovereignty; and an endeavor to build a case for postponing or canceling the elections scheduled for May.[32]

With a view to the future, Woerner predicted that the harassment would not "diminish over time," although he continued to believe that Noriega would not "intentionally take [the] harassment campaign to [the] point where US lives will

---

until I interviewed a female MP officer who had taken part in the investigation. She convinced me that the story was a fabrication to cover up other activities by the three individuals involved. As for the Navy bird watcher, a copy of his handwritten letter to his girlfriend, which contains the quotes, was placed in a JTF-Panama file. The position that the Panamanian regime was within its rights in stopping the school buses was expressed on various occasions by Woerner, Loeffke, and Cisneros, among others, all of whom condemned stopping the buses while the children were on board. A couple of months before the bus incident, Woerner had informed Crowe that "Some of the recent incidents have appeared to be of a . . . serious nature. However, further investigation revealed that some of these incidents were either not as serious as indicated, or that there was less PDF involvement than initially reported." Interv, author with Maj Nancy Nykamp, 11 May 99, Fort Leavenworth, Kans.; Msg, CINCSO to JCS [personal, Gen Woerner to Adm Crowe], 141831Z Dec 88, sub: Security Enhancement Forces.

[31] On the other hand, one of the MP officers involved in investigating reports of harassment complained to me that, in the incident involving the gun being discharged near the Navy petty officer's face, the Southern Command "deliberately got in the way" of the investigation.

[32] Msg, CINCSO to VCJCS, 060115Z Mar 89, sub: Panama Assessment.

be directly threatened." Instead, Woerner argued, the dictator would continue to abridge and violate U.S. treaty rights through new and more severe bureaucratic measures and media attacks. In short, the tactical initiative rested with Noriega. The challenge facing the Southern Command, Woerner declared, was to seize the initiative from Noriega in such a way that would strike at the general's vulnerabilities without "providing grist for his propaganda/harassment mill." In words that would have confounded his critics had they seen the message, Woerner concluded by saying, "Noriega will push us until we push back in a forceful and effective manner."[33] How such a push might be accomplished became the focus of a full-scale Washington-SOUTHCOM review in the months preceding the Panamanian elections.

A TOUGHER POSTURE

Even before the Bush national security team was completely in place, Secretary of State Baker asked the acting assistant secretary of state for inter-American affairs, Michael Kozak, a veteran of the crisis, to prepare a paper listing steps the United States could take to secure Noriega's removal from power. Baker, himself, favored "a policy of escalating political, economic, and covert pressures." But he also realized that military force might have to be used to end a crisis that had dragged on far too long. Kozak's memorandum supported increased pressure on Noriega and indicated the time had come to make fundamental policy choices.[34]

After Cheney was sworn in as secretary of defense on 12 March 1989, he met frequently with Baker and Scowcroft to discuss additional measures to take against the Panama regime. Arthur H. Davis, the U.S. ambassador to Panama, also participated in the dialogue, with Baker receiving a "strongly worded" cable from the embassy in April that recommended a more assertive policy in place of the one that had "stagnated." In a similar message later that month, the ambassador argued for "sterner measures" with "no punches pulled." The United States, he recommended, should remove all "nonessential" American citizens from Panama, secure the canal area, and, assuming that Noriega would steal the 7 May elections, prepare to assert U.S. treaty rights more forcefully. A proper mix of military and psychological pressure, he continued, would likely force the dictator from power or convince the Panama Defense Forces to remove him as a preemptive measure to ensure the institution's survival. As a last resort, the United States itself needed to be ready to employ military force to get the job done. "I firmly believe," Davis wrote, "that before we undertake this plan, we must commit ourselves to the ultimate use of U.S. military power to achieve our policy objectives should it become necessary. Not to make that decision from the outset puts the U.S. into an untenable paper tiger position." The ambassador did not believe that a tougher policy would lead to a military confrontation, but he added that "any credible option" had to run that risk.[35]

According to Baker, Davis' position prompted "an even more direct internal memorandum" from Kozak, dated 14 April. Again calling for stronger measures

---

[33] Ibid.

[34] Baker, *Politics of Diplomacy*, p. 178.

[35] First and second quoted words from ibid., p. 180 and p. 181, respectively. The remaining quotes are from Msg, AmEmb to SecState, 271729Z Apr 89, sub: A Post-Election Action Plan. Cole, *Operation Just Cause*, p. 11.

to oust Noriega, the acting assistant secretary asserted, "And while we don't think U.S. military force should be necessary, the President must be prepared to use force as a last resort. The credible threat represented by our willingness to use force opens other options and is the only wedge which will separate Noriega from the Panama Defense Forces." If pressure on the Panamanian military had not brought the desired results by 1 September, Kozak concluded, "the President should order Noriega's removal by a snatch or U.S. military action." Of these two recommendations, Baker regarded the "snatch" operation as politically unrealistic. Although he believed such action to be legal, he knew that President Bush, at this early point in his administration, was not interested in kidnapping the Panamanian strongman.[36]

From his headquarters at Quarry Heights and in visits to Washington, Woerner weighed in on the policy review he considered long overdue. In meetings and telephone conversations and through a stream of messages, the SOUTHCOM commander offered a variety of suggestions for dealing with the crisis in general and with the Panamanian elections and their aftermath in particular. His specific proposals were quite detailed, but, broadly speaking, Woerner reiterated the need for a more comprehensive and better-organized approach at the interagency level. A task force needed to be established with one agency placed in charge of orchestrating an agreed-upon plan—a plan designed to provide U.S. support for the political opposition in Panama, discredit the current regime, keep the Panama Defense Forces from closing ranks even more tightly behind their leader, and, in the event of a fraudulent election, apply more effective pressure on Noriega to step down.[37]

One recommendation the SOUTHCOM commander continued to put forward during the policy review was for a human rights initiative geared to the elections. His staff had submitted the plan to Washington back in November, and Woerner had revisited the issue with Crowe and others in January, urging that the interagency working group give the proposal serious consideration. A well-organized initiative, he maintained, would emphasize the human rights abuses of the Panamanian regime, focus international attention on the importance of the upcoming elections, and

---

[36] Baker, *Politics of Diplomacy*, pp. 181–82. According to one U.S. planner in Panama, Special Operations Forces had responsibility for devising an operation to "snatch" Noriega. While the project took place in utmost secrecy, the planners involved kept their counterparts in Panama informed of basic developments so that their mutual efforts would not conflict. All were aware that one argument against a snatch operation was that it would risk PDF or popular retaliation against U.S. citizens in Panama.

[37] The recommendations Woerner presented before and during the policy review on Panama are contained in the following messages: Msgs, CINCSO to JCS [personal, Crowe, Armitage, Abrams, and Ambassador Davis], 031320Z Jan 89, sub: May 89 Panamanian Elections—An Opportunity; CINCSO to CJCS [personal, Gen Woerner to Adm Crowe], 281627Z Mar 89, sub: Panama Action Plan—Leveling the Playing Field; USSOUTHCOM to Special Security Office (SSO)/DIA [eyes only, Woerner to Crowe], 15 Apr 89, sub: Panamanian Election Fraud; CINCSO to CJSC, 261820Z Apr 89, sub: USG Policy Statement Before Panamanian Elections; CINCSO to CJCS [personal, Gen Woerner to Adm Crowe], 281822Z Apr 89, sub: May 8th—Pass, Punt or Fumble; USSOUTHCOM to JCS [eyes only, Gen Woerner to Adm Crowe], 022219Z May 89, sub: A Panama Dark Horse Option; CINCSO to CJCS, 031505Z May 89, sub: Toughening Our Panama Posture; and CINCSO to CJCS [personal, Gen Woerner to Adm Crowe], 042115Z May 89, sub: Policy Initiatives Post Elections.

improve the prospects for the emerging anti-Noriega coalition to win a "reasonably honest" contest. Furthermore, he implied, such an initiative could help elevate U.S. policy above the "trivia" in which he believed it to be currently mired.[38]

Conceding that a human rights campaign by itself probably would not "carry the day," Woerner proposed other ways in which Washington could "positively influence events" by supporting Noriega's political opponents. His list of recommendations included promoting unity within the historically fractious opposition; assisting the opposition in acquiring accurate polling data and helping it develop an effective advertising campaign; devising means to "get out the vote," in part by counteracting the Panamanian voters' sense of futility; providing communications facilities for the opposition; simplifying the issues by turning the election into a plebiscite on Noriega; and assisting the opposition with its most pressing financial needs. These covert operations and other actions in support of Noriega's opponents, Woerner warned, had to be conducted with utmost discretion lest they become public knowledge and an embarrassment to the people Washington most wanted to help. (The revelation in March that President Bush had authorized the CIA to spend $10 million in support of the electoral opposition to Noriega gave the strongman an instant boost in the propaganda war: soon after the news broke, pro-regime candidates held their largest rally of the campaign.)[39]

Woerner also warned against any pronouncements or actions by the United States that would cause the Panamanian armed forces to "circle the wagons" around their leader. If "carefully crafted," he asserted, any U.S. policy statement with respect to the election could "also serve to reassure the PDF that our argument is only with Noriega, and that it is not our desire to destroy the Defense Forces as an institution."[40]

Woerner assumed, as did most analysts, that no amount of outside backing for the Panamanian opposition could prevent Noriega from employing fraud and intimidation in a well-orchestrated program to "steal" the election for his hand-picked candidates. The recommended U.S. support to the opposition, however, might help drive the dictator to such blatantly obvious excesses in his illegal machinations that the predictable—meaning fraudulent—outcome of the vote would be open to challenge. The critical question for the Bush administration, therefore, was what policy and strategy to adopt for the postelection period. Woerner envisaged three possibilities. Washington could acquiesce in the results of a fraudulent election and continue with its current policy of economic sanctions. The SOUTHCOM commander deemed this option "unacceptable" in light of the ineffectiveness of U.S. policies to date and the threat Noriega's regime posed to U.S. citizens and American interests in Panama. For the same reasons, Woerner labeled as "disastrous" a second option, U.S. disengagement from Panama. The third option, the one he endorsed, was in harmony with the firmer policy being

---

[38] Quoted words from Msg, CINCSO to JCS, 031320Z Jan 89, sub: May 89 Panamanian Elections—An Opportunity. Paper, n.d., Human Rights Initiative; Msg, CINCSO to CJCS, 281627Z Mar 89, sub: Panama Action Plan—Leveling the Playing Field.

[39] First quote from Msg, CINCSO to JCS, 031320Z Jan 89, sub: May 89 Panamanian Elections—An Opportunity. Second quote from Msg, CINCSO to CJCS, 281627Z Mar 89, sub: Panama Action Plan—Leveling the Playing Field. *New York Times*, 23 Apr 89, p. 14.

[40] First quote from Paper, Human Rights Initiative, n.d. Second quote from Msg, CINCSO to CJSC, 261820Z Apr 89, sub: USG Policy Statement Before Panamanian Elections.

discussed by Baker, Kozak, and Davis: the United States should increase its pressure on Noriega to relinquish power.[41]

In Woerner's estimation, the stage for a tougher policy could be set even before the election if the White House or the State Department were to issue a statement proclaiming both America's commitment to a democratic solution to Panama's internal crisis and the Bush administration's determination not to recognize another Noriega-imposed regime. The president could also dispatch an emissary to Panama to convey this strong message directly to Noriega and his entourage. Having done so, the administration could then respond to any electoral fraud on 7 May with a campaign aimed at exposing the regime's corruption and denying international legitimacy to a stolen election. This campaign would itself be part of a broader, "comprehensive time-phased, interagency-approved action plan which applies maximum pressure on Noriega—political, economic, and military." The goal of the plan would be "to force Noriega out at [the] low end of [the] violence spectrum and as early as possible."[42]

In keeping with his repeated calls for a comprehensive plan, Woerner provided Crowe a list of political, diplomatic, economic, and military initiatives for the administration to consider. The strictly military portion of the list included such measures as increasing psychological operations against the Noriega regime; jamming certain Panamanian television and radio programs; making Panama an unaccompanied tour for U.S. troops together with shortening the length of the tour; reducing the reliance of U.S. forces on Panamanian sources of support in such vulnerable areas as logistics, communications, and utilities; redeploying nonessential units; and limiting the number of military dependents allowed into the country, sending many in Panama back to the United States, and bringing dependents living on Panamanian territory onto U.S. bases.[43]

Woerner freely admitted that these and other actions might not be sufficient to dislodge Noriega. Worse, they might even provoke a violent confrontation between Panamanian and U.S. forces. This was a risk he was willing to take. Having witnessed the failure of efforts to "nickel and dime" the dictator, he called for raising the ante, aware that "we should undertake these wide ranging initiatives only with [the] full understanding that our hand almost certainly will be called." The stakes were high and "Noriega doesn't bluff." Should the game turn violent, the United States had to have the "capability and intent to use military force, and be prepared to accept political and human costs." This was tough talk from a general who remained opposed to a U.S. military solution to the crisis, although Woerner still believed that, if Washington could craft and execute an effective plan of action, "it is possible that Noriega will go before we commit U.S. forces." The use of the conditional was intentional, as he continued to have strong doubts as to whether

---

[41] Msg, USSOUTHCOM to SSO/DIA, 15 Apr 89, sub: Panamanian Election Fraud. Quoted words from Msg, CINCSO to CJCS, 281822Z Apr 89, sub: May 8th—Pass, Punt or Fumble.

[42] Msgs, USSOUTHCOM to SSO/DIA, 15 Apr 89, sub: Panamanian Election Fraud; CINCSO to CJSC, 261820Z Apr 89, sub: USG Policy Statement Before Panamanian Elections; and USSOUTHCOM to JCS, 022219Z May 89, sub: A Panama Dark Horse Option. Quotes from Msg, CINCSO to CJCS, 281822Z Apr 89, sub: May 8th—Pass, Punt or Fumble.

[43] Msgs, CINCSO to CJCS, 281627Z Mar 89, sub: Panama Action Plan—Leveling the Playing Field; CINCSO to CJCS, 031505Z May 89, sub: Toughening Our Panama Posture; and CINCSO to CJCS, 042115Z May 89, sub: Policy Initiatives Post Elections.

the national security bureaucracy could devise and implement a comprehensive plan. But even if it could, he had always believed that prudence required him to keep all options open, including military intervention, albeit only as a last resort. In one message that he signed personally, he raised in four different paragraphs the need to be prepared to use military force, indicating that "this level of sacrifice, including possible loss of life, is justified to achieve policy objectives."[44]

Woerner accompanied his tough talk about the possible use of military force with a call for a U.S. troop buildup in Panama after the election. If, following 7 May, the crisis escalated to the point of a military showdown, having additional forces on the scene would clearly work to SOUTHCOM's advantage. But Woerner did not issue his appeal with the idea that the incoming units would constitute an invasion force. Consonant with his long-held strategy of using a troop buildup as psychological leverage, he viewed the move as a means for increasing pressure on Noriega to bow out. How this pressure might be applied was the topic of several high-level discussions in April and May 1989. One option frequently raised was to use a postelection buildup to compel the Panama Defense Forces and the Panamanian regime to abide by the guarantees granted U.S. forces under the canal treaties. As Woerner saw the situation, Washington had to be prepared "to violate Panamanian pseudo-legal constraints on our treaty rights."[45]

In the opinion of the SOUTHCOM commander and his key advisers, "the clearest provocation by the PDF to date" with respect to U.S. treaty rights concerned the "freedom of movement" issue Woerner and Ustick had previously raised with the Pentagon. From early in the crisis, the Panama Defense Forces had blatantly violated treaty guarantees by interfering with the movement of U.S. military vehicles and equipment. The time had arrived, SOUTHCOM's chief of staff now asserted, for a command policy serving notice that any further interference "will result in prompt, appropriate U.S. reassertion of that right." Woerner was equally direct. "Our response should be an aggressive reassertion of our full treaty rights, both in letter and in spirit," he informed Crowe. "We must convince Noriega and the PDF leadership that we will no longer accept harassment and interference with our freedom of movement or other rights."[46]

In the weeks preceding the elections, the Southern Command and the Pentagon discussed more precisely just what this course of action would entail. Woerner contended that, at some point, all military convoys of four or more vehicles should

---

[44] Fourth and fifth quotes from Msg, CINCSO to CJCS, 281822Z Apr 89, sub: May 8th—Pass, Punt or Fumble. Sixth quote from Msg, USCINCSO to VCJCS, 060115Z Mar 89, sub: Panama Assessment. Remaining quotes from Msg, CINCSO to CJCS, 042115Z May 89, sub: Policy Initiatives Post Elections.

[45] Msg, CINCSO to CJCS, 031505Z May 89, sub: Toughening Our Panama Posture.

[46] Msgs, USSOUTHCOM to SSO/DIA, 050209Z May 89, sub: Procedures for US Assertion of Treaty Rights, and CINCSO to CJCS, 031505Z May 89, sub: Toughening Our Panama Posture. First quote from Memo, Rear Adm Richard C. Ustick, USN, Chief of Staff, USSOUTHCOM, for JTF-Panama et al., 12 Apr 89, sub: Policy on Freedom of Movement of U.S. Forces Vehicles in the Republic of Panama. Remaining quotes from Msg, USSOUTHCOM to SSO, 280133Z Apr 89, sub: Aggressive Reassertion of Our Treaty Rights. On the freedom of movement issue, Article XV, section 2(e), Agreement in Implementation of Article IV of the canal treaty read that "the vehicles and equipment of the United States Forces may, when in performance of official duties, move freely in the Republic of Panama, without obligation of payment of taxes, tolls or other charges to the Republic of Panama and without any other impediment."

have an armed escort.⁴⁷ This proposal came shortly after he had asked Crowe, citing the need "vigorously to reassert our rights," for authority the day after the Panamanian elections "to use the minimum force required to ensure strict compliance with these rights, regardless of Panamanian law and/or PDF unilateral interpretation of the Carter-Torrijos Treaty." In the Pentagon, staff officers gave the request a cool reception and questioned the circumstances under which the SOUTHCOM commander might assert such authority. "The [SOUTHCOM] message does not give details of which rights would be defended," according to one staff action. "It is inconceivable that SECDEF would grant USCINCSO the carte blanche authority he appears to be requesting." Consequently, the officers vetting the recommendation suggested that the request be turned aside unless Woerner provided specific examples of how he might employ force to compel the Panama Defense Forces to comply with the canal treaties.⁴⁸ Woerner's armed convoy plan was a response to this query.

Although Woerner wanted to use a postelection troop buildup primarily to reassert U.S. treaty rights, he and the others discussing ways to toughen U.S. policy recognized that the additional units might end up having to execute contingency plans for the crisis.⁴⁹ With that possibility in mind, planners at the Southern Command, JTF-Panama, and the Joint Special Operations Command worked to update the PRAYER BOOK operation orders. At Fort Clayton, Colonel Cope called Maj. Dan Augustine back into the USARSO Plans Division to work on a reception plan for additional troops, should President Bush accept the recommendation for a buildup. At Quarry Heights, operation orders were reviewed and revised. The principal changes appeared in POST TIME and BLUE SPOON, the plans for a U.S. troop buildup and offensive operations in Panama. A third brigade from the 7th Infantry Division (Light), originally slated to be on-call, would be added to the incoming troops required under the plans. Appendixes concerning electronic warfare operations, airspace management, and liaison officer requirements were also added to the BLUE SPOON operation order. Meanwhile, the impasse between SOUTHCOM and the Navy over the use of a carrier battle group—a deadlock that had plagued planning efforts in 1988—eased somewhat when the Atlantic Command agreed in principle to provide a naval blocking force in the Caribbean to prevent Cuban interference in any U.S. undertaking. Finally, the commander of the XVIII Airborne Corps was designated in BLUE SPOON as the commander of Joint Task Force-Charlie—a headquarters that would supersede JTF-Panama—upon execution of the operation order.⁵⁰ The exact point at which this would occur, however, remained unspecified.

---

⁴⁷ Msgs, USSOUTHCOM to SSO, 280133Z Apr 89, sub: Aggressive Reassertion of Our Treaty Rights, and USSOUTHCOM to SSO/DIA, 050209Z May 89, sub: Procedures for US Assertion of Treaty Rights.

⁴⁸ First and second quotes from Msg, USSOUTHCOM to SSO, 280133Z Apr 89, sub: Aggressive Reassertion of Our Treaty Rights. Remaining quotes from Memo and FAX Cover Sheet, 3 May 89, sub: Aggressive Reassertion of Our Treaty Rights, JCS Papers.

⁴⁹ This point was emphasized, for example, in a telephone conversation between Cisneros and Brig. Gen. Henry Shelton, the vice director, J–3, of the Joint Staff. See Msg, CINCSO to JCS/Joint Staff, 100216 May 89, sub: CONOPS for Security Enhancement Forces.

⁵⁰ Intervs, author with Maj Dan Augustine, U.S. Army, 11 May 90, Fort Leavenworth, Kans., and 7 Jun 89, Fort Clayton, Panama, and Lt Col Robert Pantier, U.S. Army, 13 Jun 90, Fort Clayton, Panama. Msg, CINCSO to Joint Staff, 241355Z Apr 89, sub: USCINCSO PRAYERBOOK OPORDS.

No major revisions were made to KLONDIKE KEY, the operation order for evacuating American civilians, or to BLIND LOGIC, the plan for a post-invasion Panama. With respect to the latter, however, the Southern Command did list specific unresolved issues, along with a forceful reminder that reserve civil affairs forces would need to be called up should the order be executed. Simply put, civil affairs resources in the active component of the Army were insufficient to accomplish the BLIND LOGIC missions.[51]

Besides the PRAYER BOOK operation orders, the Southern Command and JTF-Panama staff and components developed plans for handling any civil disturbances that might erupt during the election period. The officers also determined what security measures they needed to adopt for the horde of election observers heading for Panama, including those, like former President Jimmy Carter, who had been invited, and others, like some prominent U.S. congressmen, who were coming with President Bush's blessing but without visas for entering the country. As for American forces in Panama, as the election approached they began raising their state of readiness, making sure to maintain a low profile in the process.[52]

On the eve of the Panamanian elections, then, the Bush administration was on the verge of taking tougher measures toward Noriega and his regime. The policy review that Woerner had been calling for since the beginning of the year was under way, and he was a principal participant in it. To his familiar appeals for an interagency approach to the crisis and for a Panamanian solution to the problem, he added his voice to those calling for a tougher line. Following his publicized remarks in February (or, perhaps, in part because of them), Woerner repeatedly pushed for a more aggressive policy. His recommendations, in fact, seemed almost identical to those of Ambassador Davis, with whom he had a very rocky relationship. The similarity was no coincidence, in that the Southern Command and the embassy had coordinated their recommendations, almost to the word.[53] Both the SOUTHCOM commander and the ambassador argued that the status quo was no longer acceptable and called for stronger measures; both recommended a reduction of U.S. citizens in Panama; both urged the reassertion of U.S. treaty rights; and both accepted that a tougher policy might entail the use of military force. Ironically, Davis' tough line garnered him rave reviews within the inner circle of the new administration, while Woerner continued to be regarded as the odd man out—a general not really in sympathy with administration policy, a reluctant warrior. This perception would ultimately cost Woerner his command, but not until after Panamanian voters had had a chance to go to the polls.

---

[51] Msg, CINCSO to Joint Staff, 241355Z Apr 89, sub: USCINCSO PRAYERBOOK OPORDS.

[52] Intervs, author with Col John A. Cope, U.S. Army, 25 May 89, Fort Clayton, Panama; Brig Gen Marc Cisneros, U.S. Army, 1 May 89, Quarry Heights, Panama; Pantier, 13 Jun 90; and Augustine, 11 May 90, 7 Jun 89.

[53] On coordination between the Southern Command and the embassy, see Msg, U.S. Ambassador to SecDef, 27 Apr 89, sub: A Post-Election Action Plan.

6

Operation Nimrod Dancer
May 1989

For nearly two years, as U.S. policy in the Panama crisis drifted through a series of critical events, speculation arose as to when Washington might take more decisive action against Noriega. The inauguration of George H. W. Bush as president had been the most recent occurrence to elicit expectations of more resolute measures, but, after 20 January 1989, a policy reassessment moved forward only tentatively while the new president waited for his national security and foreign policy advisers to come on board. By the time the new team was in place, the next milestone, the presidential election in Panama scheduled for 7 May, was fast approaching. Behind the scenes, the U.S. government, as Woerner and others had recommended, did what it could to assist the slate of candidates in opposition to Noriega, but any new public initiatives would have to await the outcome of the election. At that point, some U.S. officers in Panama anticipated, the president would have to determine "what in the hell we're going to do on this darn thing."

In the meantime, American officials closely monitored the Panamanian political scene. The candidates slated to receive Washington's sub rosa assistance were leaders of opposition parties who had managed to put aside their personal and philosophical differences for the sake of presenting a united front. Topping the opposition ticket was Guillermo Endara, a portly 52-year-old lawyer who had been a confidant of Arnulfo Arias, one of Panama's most prominent political figures until his death the previous August. Endara's two vice presidential running mates were businessman Guillermo "Billy" Ford of the National Liberal Republican Movement, and Ricardo Arias Calderón, a philosophy professor and member of the Christian Democrat Party. Together they would go up against Noriega's handpicked slate of candidates, headed by Carlos Duque, a business crony of the general.

Preelection polls conducted by U.S. and Latin American organizations indicated that Endara would overwhelm Duque in a fair election. Reinforcing these findings were the large crowds that showed up at opposition rallies to cheer wildly when the three candidates promised to depose Noriega and end the corruption endemic in his regime. The downside to this optimistic prognosis was the assumption, taken for granted by opposition leaders and U.S. officials alike, that Noriega had the means and the intention to rig the election. Sources reported that the regime was doctoring lists of eligible voters and jailing many Endara supporters. In open contempt of the opposition, Noriega first restricted, then curtailed its access to the

Demonstrators bang pots in protest against the Noriega regime.

media. Adding to Endara's woes were financial and organizational problems within his own movement. President Bush expressed his concern over electoral fraud by publicly calling for free and open elections and proposing that a group of impartial observers monitor the vote. Privately, through a presidential "finding" approved in February, he had formally authorized covert financial assistance to the opposition, a reported $10 million. The Central Intelligence Agency took charge of distributing the money, which was to be used primarily for communications and psychological operations.[1]

In March, news of the presidential finding leaked to the press. Predictably, Noriega denounced U.S. interference in Panama's internal affairs, while the opposition candidates emphatically denied receiving money from the CIA. Woerner had warned of an "embarrassment" should covert U.S. efforts on behalf of the opposition become public, and the regime did reap some short-term benefit from the disclosure. According to the polls, though, the popularity of Endara, Ford, and Arias Calderón remained strong. The dictator would have to find even more damaging evidence to use against his opponents. He soon had it.

THE MUSE AFFAIR

On 5 April, Kurt Muse, a 38-year-old American citizen who had been raised in Panama and, as a businessman selling printing and graphic arts, continued to reside there with his family, returned to the country after a trip to the United States. As he stopped before the immigration window in Torrijos International Airport, he noticed to his horror a sign taped to the other side of the glass. "Kurt Muse," it read. "American citizen. Arrest him on sight." Within minutes, Muse found himself in the custody of the Panama Defense Forces.[2]

---

[1] Buckley, *Panama*, pp. 169–75.

[2] Muse's own account of his arrest, incarceration, and rescue can be found in Kurt Muse and John Gilstrap, *Six Minutes to Freedom* (New York: Citadel Press, 2006). Details of his arrest appear on pp. 7–13.

The arrest was more than just another case of routine harassment. In October 1987, Muse and a small group of like-minded colleagues had graduated from "fooling around with their radios, playing tricks on PDF soldiers, dispatching them on useless missions to dead-end streets" to broadcasting intermittently a series of short anti-regime, pro-opposition messages over The Voice of Liberty, the name they gave the clandestine radio operation they had set up that was capable of overriding Panamanian commercial transmissions with its own. At one point, the conspirators required additional, more expensive equipment and money to maintain the leases on apartments in which the illegal transmitters were located. They quickly discovered the Central Intelligence Agency was ready to foot the bill. In early 1989, as the Panamanian elections approached, The Voice of Liberty prepared to intensify its campaign aimed at encouraging Noriega's opponents to go to the polls in mass. Before the prerecorded messages could be broadcast, however, Muse was betrayed by someone close to the group. Immediately following his being taken into custody, his collaborators scattered to avoid a similar fate. U.S. officials in Panama learned of the arrest from Muse's family the night it occurred, but, initially, the regime deflected all inquiries as to his status and whereabouts. When U.S. pressure finally forced an admission that Muse was being held, the disclosure was accompanied by a public announcement that the prisoner was a U.S. agent engaged in subversive activities with the help of opposition leaders and the U.S. Embassy. A search of Muse's apartment and possessions had, in fact, uncovered pamphlets, firearms, photographic and film equipment, and recordings of clandestine radio and television transmissions, all of which were put on display at a press conference arranged for the international news media.[3]

Newspapers controlled by Noriega ran banner headlines and photographs of Muse and his "subversive" material, which the Panamanian military charged was given to him by U.S. psychological operations officers. At the quickly arranged press conference, Muse admitted to the reporters present that he had made covert radio broadcasts, although he denied working for the U.S. government. Panamanian officers at the conference claimed that Muse's clandestine communications network encompassed seven FM radio stations and three television transmitters capable of jamming local frequencies and that the network had been broadcasting for at least two months. They charged further that broadcast tapes had been recorded in advance for the purpose of spreading allegations of electoral fraud, should the opposition candidates lose on 7 May. Muse conceded only that the prepared broadcasts sought to encourage Panamanians to vote. Finally, the Panama Defense Forces confirmed that Muse would be charged with crimes against state security, one of the "big five" criminal charges that, under the treaties, did not obligate the Panamanian government to relinquish custody of an American prisoner to U.S. Forces.[4]

---

[3] This paragraph summarizes material in ibid., pp. 7–139, with the quote on p. 36. Msg, Foreign Broadcast Information Service, Chiva Chiva, Panama, SSN 8464, 070112Z Apr 89, Serial PA0704011289, Country: Panama, sub: U.S. Citizen Arrested, Charged with Antistate Activities.

[4] When capitalized, "U.S. Forces" refers to a formal entity named in the Panama Canal treaties of 1977. Msg, CINCSO, SSN 686, 080045Z Apr 89. Msgs, FBIS, Chiva Chiva, Panama, SSN 8483, 081?39Z Apr 89, sub: Clandestine Radio, TV Stations Dismantled; SSN, 081558Z Apr 89, sub: DENI Director, Attorney General on Muse; SSN 8520, 081609Z Apr 89; SSN 8521, 081611Z Apr 89; and SSN 8522, 081613Z Apr 89, sub: Officials on 'Clandestine' Operation.

Prior to the press conference, a three-man delegation led by Lt. Col. Robert Perry from SOUTHCOM's Center for Treaty Affairs had arrived at the DENI station at which Muse was being held. Woerner had authorized the visit, but only after hearing that Muse's wife was a teacher in the Department of Defense Dependent Schools (DoDDS), thus making the prisoner a military dependent covered by certain rights under the canal treaty. The whole affair irked the SOUTHCOM commander, who was not pleased to learn about "another case of the CIA conducting ops on his facilities without him being aware of it." Once the press conference ended, the ranking Panamanian officer on the scene granted Perry's demand to meet with Muse, but not until the delegation was first shown the confiscated material, including a large cardboard box with labels on it indicating it had received priority shipping on U.S. military aircraft flying into Howard Air Force Base. The delivery address on the labels was the Program Development Group, a widely known euphemism for the CIA located in nearby Corozal. After perusing the items, the group was allowed to see the prisoner. One of Perry's entourage, Lt. Col. James Ruffer, M.D., examined Muse, who, although solemn, appeared to be in relatively good physical condition. Muse said he had not been mistreated, except for the PDF's refusal to let him sleep during the first 24 hours following his arrest. Under the circumstances, he later related, he thought it best not to mention that, at one point during his initial interrogations, a PDF officer had put a pistol to his head, and, at another point, he had been forced to watch while an alleged Colombian drug peddler was savagely beaten and then killed by the interrogators. When advised by Perry of his rights under the canal treaty, Muse acknowledged that the Panama Defense Forces had honored them. Perry then assured him that he would receive periodic visits from U.S. Forces representatives and that he should contact them whenever the need arose. The PDF officer present asked that Muse's status be conveyed accurately to decision makers in Washington.[5]

Soon after meeting with Perry at the DENI station, Muse was placed in a small cell at the Carcel Modelo, the jail located across the street from the Comandancia. He received visits every other day from SOUTHCOM and USARSO representatives, who inquired as to his health and the conditions of his imprisonment and kept him abreast of progress on his legal case. One of the regular visitors, Dr. Marcos Ostrander, the USARSO lawyer who had himself been the target of PDF harassment, conveyed messages to and from Muse's family, whom U.S. Army, South, and the CIA had arranged to fly out of Panama and relocate in Florida soon after Muse was arrested. With Noriega exploiting the affair as a conspiracy between the Bush administration and the opposition candidates to sabotage Panamanian democracy, the general feeling was that Muse would not be released before the election, if he were to be released at all. The charges against him were serious, and he had admitted making the broadcasts. He had, without question, violated Panamanian law, and on one of his trips to Washington, a friend in the State Department had told him that, if the clandestine operation was discovered, Muse would be on his own. Still, if the U.S. government had assisted him in his secretive activities—as it had— did it not bear a moral obligation to secure his release? George H. W. Bush was

---

[5] MFR, SCTA, n.d., sub: Joint Committee Coordination in Reference to Mr. Muse; Muse and Gilstrap, *Six Minutes to Freedom*, pp. 133, 147–49, 153–58.

convinced that it did. In the ensuing months, the frustration of trying to secure Muse's freedom would weigh heavily on the president.

Preelection Preparations

While the Center for Treaty Affairs worked to get Muse out of the Carcel Modelo, other U.S. officers and officials were trying to determine what precautionary measures American citizens in Panama needed to take before, during, and after the elections. The Southern Command was deeply concerned about the potential for violence, whether initiated by Noriega in an attempt to steal the election or by the opposition as a reaction to electoral fraud. Under the circumstances, trying to anticipate the range of threats that would place American lives, property, and interests in jeopardy seemed a logical and judicious inquiry.

Preparing for the elections necessitated coordination among and within the principal U.S. civilian and military agencies in Panama. On the military side, the Southern Command and JTF-Panama worked closely together on the matter, although not entirely without friction. On 5 April, the SOUTHCOM public affairs director, U.S. Air Force Col. Ronald T. Sconyers, sent a memorandum to General Cisneros, the command's director of operations, stating that the time had come to begin "war-gaming" what the U.S. military in Panama was going to do before, during, and after the election. That same day, U.S. Marine Corps Col. Gar E. Thiry, Cisneros' vice director, sent his own memo to the SOUTHCOM chief of staff, expressing the need to hold an executive-level meeting at Quarry Heights to discuss what "prudent precautionary measures" U.S. forces might take in connection with the election. Both memos went to JTF-Panama, where Colonel Rossi noted in the margins his concern that the Southern Command was once again trying to play "*crisis operator & manager*," the role that Woerner had created the joint task force to perform. "Before we are 'postured' by [SOUTHCOM] discounting [JTF-Panama] input," Rossi noted, "JTFPM needs to take the initiative."[6]

In the weeks leading up to 7 May 1989, the impending election absorbed both headquarters, once again at the expense of time they needed to be devoting to their regional responsibilities. By late April, staff activity had reached a frenetic pace; by early May, briefings occurred daily to determine how U.S. forces in Panama should be "postured" during the elections. The general guidance was for military personnel to maintain a low profile and a high state of readiness. On 5 May, U.S. forces would begin a period of increased vigilance that would extend as long after the election as necessary, although, for planning purposes, 15 May was generally projected as the date the troops would resume their routine duties.

Besides U.S. military personnel in Panama, there were the tens of thousands of military dependents and American citizens who also needed to be advised and informed about issues concerning the election. At the Southern Command, the *Tropic Times* and SCN began running stories in March to provide the American community insight into the country's electoral system and to keep U.S. citizens abreast of their own government's position on the elections. The

---

[6] Memos, Col Ronald T. Sconyers, USAF, Dir, Public Affairs, for Brig Gen Cisneros, 5 Apr 89, sub: Election Day, Before and After, and Col G. E. Thiry, USMC, Actg Dir, J–3, for Chief of Staff, 5 Apr 89, sub: PM Election. Rossi's handwritten comments are on Staff Action Cover Sheet, Lt Col Mike Michaelis to Chief of Staff, 10 Apr 89.

Tropic Times for 28 March reported that U.S. State Department officials were predicting election fraud and pledging that there would be "no accommodation with a Noriega-dominated regime." Articles in subsequent issues ranged over the potential for election irregularities; the complexity of Panama's voting procedures; Ambassador Davis' statement that Panama was living through the "blackest days of its history"; the regime's denunciations of U.S. covert activities and Noriega's efforts to bar American journalists from the country; and Secretary of State Baker's warning to the Panama Defense Forces to allow fair elections or "face the consequences." The newspaper also covered President Bush's call for "free and fair" elections, his praise for international observers traveling to Panama to "shine the light of world opinion on the Panamanian elections," his declaration that "the day of the dictator is over," and his vow that the United States would not recognize "the results of a fraudulent election engineered simply to keep Noriega in power."[7]

Keeping Americans in Panama informed was one matter; ensuring their physical safety and the security of U.S. facilities was quite another. Forces assigned to JTF-Panama were tasked with providing the necessary protection. The joint task force's mission essential task list called for deterring intrusions, conducting reconnaissance and surveillance, securing fixed sites, establishing secure military zones on defense sites onto which U.S. citizens could be relocated, executing specific contingency operations if necessary, and, in the event of the latter, ensuring a smooth transition from a peacetime to a crisis environment. Addressing these tasks meant in some cases repeating activities conducted the previous year during the March-April invasion scare. Plans for evacuating U.S. citizens were dusted off, as were those for defending vulnerable areas such as Panama Canal Commission housing. Contingency plans, including the recently revised BLUE SPOON operation order, were reviewed, together with arrangements for coordinating and collecting intelligence. Communications nets were tested repeatedly. Arrangements for providing on-post "safe havens" and "sponsors" for military personnel living off U.S. installations were updated. Lengthy checklists were compiled and numerous decisions made. As election day approached, marines from JTF-Panama augmented the guard at the U.S. Embassy. Helicopters stood ready to conduct aerial observation, and military policemen and soldiers designated as JTF-Panama's reaction forces were put on a shorter "string," meaning the time required for them to move out in response to an incident. Large traffic barriers were delivered to U.S. facilities in case they were needed. Staff officers also devised plans to transport ammunition from fixed supply points to sites where soldiers and marines could draw it more readily. (Because each trip from a fixed ammunition supply point would require a PDF escort, the whole undertaking could serve as a warning to Noriega that U.S. forces were prepared to react to any violence directed against Americans.) The precautionary measures enumerated in advance of the election seemed endless, as did the hours put into planning and implementing each one of them.[8]

---

[7] *Tropic Times*, 17 Mar 89, 28 Mar 89, 7 Apr 89, 14 Apr 89, 24 Apr 89, 26 Apr 89. Davis' quote from *Tropic Times*, 3 May 89. Baker's quote can be found in *Washington Post*, 2 May 89. The president's quotes are in *Department of State Bulletin* 89 (June 1989): 2, and (July 1989): 66.

[8] Briefing slides, 27 Apr 89, sub: In-Progress Review Panama Strategy; Memo, Col A. T. Rossi, Chief of Staff, USARSO, for JTF-Panama J–3 et al., 13 Apr 89, sub: Joint Task Force-Panama

Having prepared for the possibility of election-related violence, General Loeffke and his subordinate commanders and staff had to determine specifically what JTF-Panama would do should a direct threat to American lives and facilities actually materialize. As there was no contingency plan geared specifically to the election crisis, Rossi instructed the staff to develop scenarios for three "highly probable" situations in which JTF-Panama would have to conduct operations for up to thirty-six hours without reinforcement. In the first situation Rossi envisaged, U.S. citizens would not be the target of Panamanian violence but would nonetheless feel the impact. The second situation involved "domestic violence" being "deflected" by one side or the other against the American community. The third entailed violent acts deliberately directed against U.S. citizens and property. For each scenario, Rossi wanted the staff to develop an appropriate response, while gathering information on relevant command and control, logistics, intelligence, public affairs, and legal issues. On 21 April, JTF-Panama reviewed the staff's findings, including the measures proposed and the forces required. Around this time, Colonel Cope informed the component commanders that, in addition to Rossi's three scenarios, they should also be prepared to react to other possible threats, including mortar rounds landing at Fort Clayton, probes of U.S. perimeters, a firefight, and an influx of refugees.[9]

A command post exercise was scheduled the following week to allow Southern Command, Panama Canal Commission, and U.S. Embassy personnel to rehearse a variety of possible election-related activities. The new MARFOR commander, Col. James J. Doyle Jr., had already expressed the view that such an exercise would provide an "excellent platform" for addressing the "concerns and questions" component commanders had about the May elections and the execution of contingency plans in general. Requiring further attention and guidance, in Doyle's opinion, were questions regarding what to do with refugees who showed up at U.S. installations, how to handle prisoners and detainees, when to expect publication of a JTF-Panama fire support plan, who had operational control over certain forces, what arrangements had been made for emergency resupply, and so forth. During the hectic two weeks leading up to the election, these and other concerns were discussed, some more thoroughly than others, so that by 3 May enough of the issues had been clarified to allow publication of a JTF-Panama fragmentary order to the POST TIME operation order. The fragmentary order presented a four-part concept covering the emergency employment of U.S. forces in Panama to secure bases of operation, protect Quarry Heights, increase the American presence in military areas of coordination, and, if necessary, execute contingency plans.[10]

Preparation; Msg, CINCSO to JCS, 292105Z Apr 89, sub: Preparations for Panama Elections; Memo, Col John A. Cope Jr. for CDR, AFFOR, et al., 28 Apr 89, sub: Joint Task Force-Panama Security Enhancement; Intervs, author with Maj Jonathan House, U.S. Army, 17 Oct 89, Washington, D.C., and Lt Col Robert Pantier, U.S. Army, 13 Jun 90, Fort Clayton, Panama.

[9] Briefing slides, JTF-Panama, n.d. [24 April is handwritten on a paper copy of the first slide]. Quoted words from Memo, Col A. T. Rossi, Chief of Staff, USARSO, for JTF-Panama J–3 et al., 13 Apr 89. Memos, Maj Gen Bernard Loeffke for CINCSO, 26 Apr 89, sub: Update No. 172, Joint Task Force-Panama Preparation for Election Period, and Col John A. Cope Jr. for JTF-Panama CDRs, 25 Apr 89, sub: JTF-PM Working Paper.

[10] Quoted words from Memo, CDR, MARFOR-Panama, for CDR, JTF-Panama (for J–3), 14 Apr 89, sub: MARFOR JTFPM CPX Inputs. Briefing, Fragmentary Order (FRAGO) JTF-Panama,

As planners and commanders were fine-tuning this set of possible responses, other staff officers at the Southern Command and JTF-Panama were ensuring that they would be able to monitor any significant developments during the election. Woerner intended to set up a 24-hour response cell early on election Sunday. The Friday before, a crisis action team would begin operating out of the Tunnel at Quarry Heights. At Fort Clayton, Colonel Cope decided to activate two such teams, one for JTF-Panama, the other for U.S. Army, South. He believed this arrangement necessary because, even with the heightened sense of urgency created by the election, he still lacked enough officers from other services to fill every position on the joint team. Manning the Army team, however, could be accomplished through personnel shifts internal to USARSO, thus posing fewer problems. Concerning the JTF-Panama crisis action team, Cope did achieve one significant concession. After he "went to the barricades," the Southern Command agreed to place liaison officers from each service at Fort Clayton instead of Quarry Heights. (To Cope, having these officers at SOUTHCOM made no sense in light of JTF-Panama's mission to execute contingency plans should the need arise.) As election day drew nearer, the colonel held a tutorial for officers unfamiliar with the functions of a crisis action team. He also cautioned his audience that, although they would be at the "center of the storm," they should remain calm and refrain from "shooting from the hip."[11]

Besides being ready to monitor the election and respond to a variety of contingencies, both the Southern Command and JTF-Panama had to be prepared for the possibility that President Bush would send additional forces to Panama. During the policy discussions in April and early May, Woerner had recommended a postelection troop buildup.[12] Before requesting specific units, however, he had consulted with Loeffke, who as commander of JTF-Panama would have operational control over the newly arrived units. Loeffke counseled that the number of U.S. ground troops in a buildup should be kept to a minimum. Deployment of a large force, he argued, far from creating a more stable situation, would only increase the possibility of unwanted incidents between U.S. troops and the Panama Defense Forces. Also to consider was the problem U.S. Army, South, would face in having to house (and supply) incoming units on military sites that were already congested. "Consequently," Loeffke advised Woerner (in terms that reiterated much of the position the joint task force commander had taken during the security enhancement buildup of 1988), "an additional brigade is not the way to go." Instead, he recommended deploying a mechanized infantry company or battalion and a Marine company with its light armored vehicles, a modest buildup that would send Noriega a "dramatic signal." If need be, these units would also enhance JTF-Panama's ability to put infantry into Panama City, "bust barricades," and extract Americans from Panamanian territory in the event of an evacuation.[13]

---

n.d.; Memo, Maj Gen Bernard Loeffke for CDR, AFFOR, et al., 16 Jun 89, sub: Mission Guidance.

[11] Memo, Col G. E. Thiry, USMC, Vice Dir J-3, for E plus CDR, JTF-Panama, 25 Apr 89, sub: Crisis Action Team (CAT) Preparation. First quote from Interv, author with Col John A. Cope Jr., U.S. Army, 25 May 89, Fort Clayton, Panama. Remaining quotes from Briefing notes, Colonel Cope to CAT Personnel, n.d.

[12] See Chapter 5.

[13] Loeffke advice to Woerner from Memo, Maj Gen Bernard Loeffke for CINCSO, 2 May 89, sub: Update No. 179, Additional Forces. Msg, CDR, USARSO, to Chief of Staff, Army, May 89,

The previous year, the Southern Command had rejected a similar request from JTF-Panama for Marine LAVs and a mechanized unit. Now, the move toward a tougher U.S. posture brought the two headquarters closer—but not completely—together. In a message to Crowe, Woerner recommended the deployment of the mechanized battalion(-) and Marine company that JTF-Panama wanted. Contrary to Loeffke's advice, however, the SOUTHCOM commander also suggested sending an infantry brigade headquarters(-) to the Atlantic side of the canal, where, if necessary, it could assume operational control of any additional troops the situation might require in that area. By sending these units to Panama, Woerner believed, the United States would "convey the desired political signal." The move would also give his command "additional operational capabilities."[14] The message made no direct reference to the year-old contingency plans for Panama, but the fact that the units Woerner requested were already on the troop list for POST TIME was no coincidence. The timely arrival of a brigade headquarters, a mechanized battalion, a Marine company from a light amphibious infantry (LAI) battalion, and possibly an infantry battalion for assignment to the Jungle Operations Training Center would certainly pave the way for an even larger deployment if the election led to a direct confrontation between U.S. forces and the Panamanian military.

THE ELECTION

As election Sunday drew near, the Southern Command enacted a "stay close to home" policy, advising U.S. service personnel, their dependents, and federal employees to avoid demonstrations and polling places over the weekend and to refrain from venturing outside U.S. facilities. To encourage compliance, the command placed restrictions on unnecessary travel and asked that various installations stage entertainment and other special events. Monday was declared a training holiday for military personnel, while civilian employees were encouraged to take leave and DoDDS teachers received an "in-service" day. All of these measures, the *Tropic Times* emphasized, were designed to "lessen off-base travel—not encourage three-day trips." As part of its information campaign, SOUTHCOM's Public Affairs Office activated a rumor-control hotline to keep U.S. citizens apprised of election developments. Finally, at 1800 Saturday night, Personnel Movement Limitation Bravo went into effect, one additional measure to keep Americans out of harm's way.[15]

While these precautions assisted Panama's American community in maintaining a low profile, other measures increased the ability of the U.S. military to deal with any contingency. As security forces under JTF-Panama prepared to go to an "advanced readiness status," the crisis action teams at Quarry Heights

---

sub: Update No. 24, Panama Elections [the day in May is not typed in, although Loeffke initialed the message]; Cope Interv, 25 May 89; Msg, CINCSO to CJCS, 031505Z May 89, sub: Toughening Our Panama Posture. According to one officer at USARSO, a mechanized company was all that was required to participate in an evacuation. A mechanized division, however, would balk at deploying just one company, and, if two companies were sent, they would be accompanied automatically by a maintenance "slice," which, in turn, would require a battalion headquarters. Interv, author with Maj Dan Augustine, U.S. Army, 11 May 90, Fort Leavenworth, Kans.

[14] Msg, CINCSO to CJCS, 031505Z May 89, sub: Toughening Our Panama Posture.

[15] Msg, CINCSO to JCS, 292105Z Apr 89, sub: Preparations for Panama Elections. First and second quotes from *Tropic Times*, 28 Apr 89, and 5 May 89, respectively, and see also 21 Apr 89.

and Fort Clayton began operations on Friday, 5 May. The location and status of PDF units were monitored as closely as possible, while a flood of last-minute reports and rumors were processed in an effort to anticipate events. Watch officers, however skeptical they might be over specific news items, could discount nothing, even though some of the information and speculation reaching them seemed far-fetched. According to one rumor, the Panama Defense Forces intended to pick up Americans and charge them with interfering in the election. Another held that Panamanian officials were going to dispense cocaine to American citizens, then charge them with drug possession. Most rumors proved groundless, although the PDF, as anticipated, did begin setting up checkpoints and roadblocks throughout Panama City, some located on routes leading into U.S. facilities.[16]

Reports of PDF activities were mixed with news concerning the arrival and movements of various groups of election observers. The Southern Command had assumed responsibility for receiving, transporting, and housing the observers—no mean logistical feat under the circumstances. The most prestigious group was an international team headed by former U.S. President Jimmy Carter, whose participation in the election had been approved by Noriega and blessed by President Bush. (Bush's advisers saw Carter's mission as a "no-win" situation for Noriega: the general could not refuse to receive the former president, still a hero in Panama because of the canal treaties; yet, Carter's unbiased team of observers would likely uncover and publicize election irregularities.) Other groups arrived and went to work without fanfare. One last-minute addition was the official U.S. observation team, also approved by Bush and led by Democratic Congressman John P. Murtha of Pennsylvania. Consisting of twenty-one U.S. senators, congressmen, officials, and aides, the delegation flew into Howard Air Force Base, despite statements by regime officials that the observers would not be welcome in Panama. Complicating matters further, Washington's policy of denying diplomatic recognition to Noriega's regime meant that the group arrived at the U.S. facility without having obtained the documents necessary for entering Panamanian territory.

Woerner and Ambassador Davis were waiting at Howard when the aircraft carrying this congressional delegation touched down. To those on the plane who could see the two men from their windows, the general and the ambassador seemed engaged in a heated argument. What the senators and congressmen did not yet know was that, sometime before their arrival, Woerner had personally been advised by the head of PDF intelligence that Noriega might have the uninvited observers arrested if they entered Panama illegally, that is, without proper documentation. Davis reportedly "scoffed" at Woerner's concern, reminding the general that, in the view of the United States, Panama had no legal government and, thus, had no authority to take such action. If the Panamanian immigration officer at Howard refused to issue visas for the group, Davis said, the congressional party would be escorted into Panama City anyway. In addressing the delegation on board the aircraft, the ambassador reiterated this position, which Woerner considered irresponsible. When Davis finished, Woerner stepped forward and, in contrast to the ambassador's reassuring remarks, advised the delegates not to resist if detained or arrested; the Southern Command would go through legal channels to secure their release. Republican Senator John McCain of Arizona bristled at the SOUTHCOM

---

[16] Author's notes, JTF-Panama Update Meeting, 2 May 89, Fort Clayton, Panama.

commander's words. In what Woerner described later as "an openly belligerent tone," the senator expressed his incredulity at hearing a U.S. Army general declare that he could not guarantee the security of U.S. officials on a mission approved by the president. That Woerner had no legal jurisdiction to prevent Panamanian authorities from arresting foreigners traveling on Panamanian soil without the necessary papers did not seem relevant to the senator.[17]

As the delegates at Howard boarded buses that would take them into Panama City, an embassy official arrived with their passports, all stamped. With that, the prospect of a confrontation with the Panama Defense Forces passed. Not so, however, the hard feelings the episode left in its wake—hard feelings exacerbated in a later meeting between Woerner and the delegation during which the possible evacuation of U.S. citizens became a topic of discussion. McCain was demonstrably unhappy with the estimates Woerner projected for the time needed—several months—to move Americans out of Panama with the least possible disruption to their lives. The meeting ended with McCain turning his back on Woerner and walking out. Not surprisingly, when the delegation returned to Washington after the election, the senator (and, reportedly, two of his fellow delegates, Republican Senator Connie Mack of Florida and Congressman Murtha) urged Bush to relieve Woerner. "That man is no damned good," McCain is reported to have said. Bush, for the moment, demurred. As for Woerner, in retrospect he conceded he should have been more diplomatic with the senators and congressmen, even though he had no sympathy with their position that seemed to place them above Panamanian law, even if they considered the regime administering it illegitimate.

On Sunday, 7 May 1989, several polling places opened late. If this was, as some speculated, a ploy by the regime to hold down the vote, it failed. Throughout the day, Panamanians turned out in large numbers to cast their ballots. That afternoon a Dutch priest, vocal in his charges of election fraud, was shot to death by a PDF officer in Chiriquí Province. This brutal incident notwithstanding, the voting generally seemed to go peacefully, albeit with irregularities. Official observers heard a catalog of complaints, including charges that members of the Panama Defense Forces were driving around to several polling stations, voting at each; or that the registration lists had been fixed to disfranchise known opposition sympathizers; or that opposition ballots had not been readily available when the polls opened. Aware of these allegations, some members of the U.S. congressional delegation voiced concern, but former President Carter indicated that, from what he had seen, the vote seemed to be "clean." Toward the end of the day, both sides claimed victory, although no returns had yet been posted.

Preelection polls had indicated the opposition would win by a two-to-one margin. On the basis of the large turnout on Sunday, coupled with comments made by Panamanians leaving the voting stations, this estimate seemed to have been borne out. Noriega was reported to be genuinely shocked at the magnitude of his candidates' impending defeat. In a last-ditch effort to salvage the situation, he had dispatched the Panama Defense Forces and paramilitary teams Sunday night to

---

[17] The story of the U.S. delegation and its interaction with General Woerner is from *Washington Post*, 6 May 89, p. A15. Donnelly, Roth, and Baker, *Operation Just Cause*, pp. 44–45, 47. Davis quote from Buckley, *Panama*, p. 177, and see also pp. 176, 178. Baker, *Politics of Diplomacy*, pp. 183–84; Intervs, General Frederick F. Woerner Jr., U.S. Army (Ret.), MHI, Carlisle Barracks, Pa., and author with Woerner, 30 Apr 91, Fort Leavenworth, Kans.

seize ballot boxes, trash polling stations, and, in some cases, burn ballots. But these highhanded moves only added to the mounting criticism. By Monday morning, opposition leaders and members of the U.S. congressional delegation were publicly proclaiming fraud. When opponents of the regime marched to protest the "stolen" election, they ran into the batons and birdshot of riot police and Dignity Battalions. On Monday afternoon, after members of his delegation had conferred with the Southern Command about security measures, Carter held a press conference to accuse the regime of "taking the election by fraud." Noriega's government, Carter charged, was "robbing the people of Panama of their legitimate rights. . . . I hope there will be a worldwide outcry of condemnation against the dictator who stole this election from his own people." Senator Mack went even further: if Noriega rejected the opposition's victory, he said, he would introduce legislation to abrogate the canal treaties.[18]

Mack's threat attracted little support. To abrogate the treaties, various senators and U.S. officials calmly pointed out, would play into Noriega's hands, unite the Panamanian people against the United States, alienate most of Latin America, and call into question the word and honor of the U.S. government. Still, the broader issue implicit in Mack's comments had to be addressed: how should the United States respond to fraudulent elections? Unaware of the administration's preelection planning, prominent senators and congressmen on both sides of the aisle agreed that President Bush should not rule out the option of using military force; indeed, by Tuesday reports circulated that the White House was, in fact, considering sending more troops to Panama. But Bush refused to be rushed. Noriega had not yet allowed the "official" results of the vote to be announced. Until the regime actually "stole" the election, any action taken by the president would be premature.[19]

Matters came to a head on Wednesday. A protest march led by the opposition candidates and joined by thousands of Panamanians was disrupted at several points along its route by riot police using tear gas, shotguns, batons, and water cannon. At one point, the uniformed officers stood aside while Dignity Battalion members dressed in red T-shirts and wielding clubs charged the crowd. In the ensuing melee, Endara fell to the ground unconscious, a large gash in his head from an iron pipe. Arias Calderón was hit several times before his bodyguard pushed him to safety. Billy Ford managed to get into a car, only to have his bodyguard slump against him, mortally wounded by a gunshot to the head. When Ford got out of the car, his shirt soaked in the bodyguard's blood, he, too, was beaten. What had begun as an orderly march turned into a scene of violence and disarray, as demonstrators sought safety and medical assistance. In the meantime, Panama City's jails began to fill with several hundred opposition members arrested by the Panama Defense Forces.[20]

---

[18] This brief account of the election in Panama is based on Buckley, *Panama*, pp. 178–80. The author has a videocassette tape of election coverage by U.S. television news media. President Carter's comments can be found in both sources.

[19] Author's videocassette tape of election coverage.

[20] Buckley, *Panama*, pp. 180–83; Panama chronology, n.d. The source of this chronology is not indicated on the cover sheet, but the document contains summaries of official U.S. message traffic relevant to the Panamanian election crisis between 14 and 16 May 1989.

Opposition candidates Guillermo Endara *(left)* and Ricardo Arias Calderón and marchers face the Panama Defense Forces during the post–May 1989 election protest.

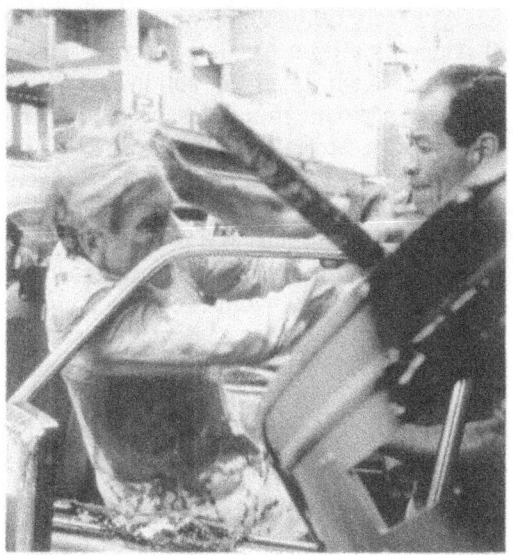

A Dignity Battalion member attacking Guillermo "Billy" Ford *(left)*

As the crisis action teams at Quarry Heights and Fort Clayton tried to construct a coherent picture of the confrontation and to determine the whereabouts of Endara, Arias Calderón, and Ford, U.S. troops reviewed their alert status. At 1640, the command put Personnel Movement Limitation Charlie into effect, further restricting the movement of U.S. citizens in Panama. DoDD Schools were closed (later followed by a decision to end the school year early). That afternoon, Ambassador Davis announced that embassy employees would be moved onto U.S. military bases Thursday. The first of some 150 fearful Panamanians were already making that trip, the beginning of what would become a "flood" of refugees into the canal area. About a dozen journalists covering the election learned that they had been declared personae non gratae and must leave the country. Reports that U.S. servicemen had been arrested at the time of the opposition march, when combined with rumors that the Panama Defense Forces were preparing to take American hostages in the event of an invasion, fueled media speculation that U.S. citizens in Panama would become the target of further regime-sanctioned violence. The movement of PDF military units into Panama City to reinforce the police in no way allayed these concerns. Finally, there were also reports of frenetic activity at the Carcel Modelo, where many of the arrested opposition members had been incarcerated. In short, as of Wednesday night, Panama once again seemed in chaos. In this charged atmosphere, the regime announced that the election had been annulled.[21]

In Washington that evening, Bush met with his national security advisers. The next afternoon, the president made a brief announcement to the press. He began by praising the commitment to "elected constitutional government" in most of Latin America but acknowledged that "in many parts of our hemisphere, the enemies of democracy lie in wait to overturn elected governments through force or to steal elections through fraud." Turning to events in Panama, he denounced the dictatorship for using "massive fraud and intimidation" and ultimately "violence and bloodshed" to steal the election. "The United States," he continued, "will not recognize nor accommodate a regime that holds power through force and violence at the expense of the Panamanian people's right to be free." The crisis in Panama, he said, was "between Noriega and the people of Panama." Pointedly, he expressed the hope that the Panama Defense Forces would stand with the people. In words that reflected Woerner's longstanding position, the president emphasized that a "professional Panamanian Defense Force can have an important role to play in Panama's democratic future."

After reiterating U.S. commitments to democracy in Panama, to the protection of Americans living in the country, and to the "integrity of the Panama Canal Treaties," Bush listed the actions he intended to take. The United States would support diplomatic initiatives by Latin American governments and the Organization of American States (OAS) to resolve the crisis. In the meantime, the American ambassador to Panama and much of the embassy staff were being recalled to the United States in protest. U.S. government employees and their dependents "living outside of U.S. military bases or Panama Canal Commission housing areas" would be relocated immediately "out of Panama" or onto "secure U.S. housing areas." Economic sanctions would "continue in force," and the United States would "carry out its obligations and . . . assert its treaty rights in Panama." There was only one strictly military measure in the list: a brigade-size force would be sent to Panama to augment U.S. forces already there. As the president neared the end of his statement, he warned that he did not "rule out further steps in the future."[22]

Deployments

The groundwork for the commitment of more troops to Panama, code-named NIMROD DANCER, had been laid several days before the president actually announced his decision. On 8 May, the day after the elections, the Joint Staff had requested a concept of operations for the additional security enhancement forces Woerner had listed in his 3 May message to Crowe. The Southern Command relayed the request to JTF-Panama, which found one aspect of the message troubling: included on the list of troops that might be sent to Panama was a light infantry battalion. Before

---

[21] Logs, SOUTHCOM CAT, 10, 11 May 89; Author's videocassette tape of election coverage; Msg, SOUTHCOM J-3 to NMC, 110710Z May 89, sub: Sitrep No. 10; Daily Operational Update, SOUTHCOM, 11 May 89.

[22] The full text of President Bush's statement can be found in *Department of State Bulletin* 89 (July 1989): 70–71.

the election, Loeffke had argued that the situation did not warrant sending the "light fighters" from the 7th Infantry Division (Light), and subsequent events had not changed his mind. The Pentagon, however, had decided otherwise. As Loeffke later noted, the unit "was force fed to us."[23]

The concept of operations drafted by planners at Fort Clayton stated in general terms what each of the headquarters and units designated for possible deployment could do to enhance the capability and flexibility of those U.S. forces already in Panama. Overall, the additional troops would add 1,716 soldiers and 165 marines to JTF-Panama, thus improving its ability to react to any situation and, if necessary, to execute PRAYER BOOK operations.[24]

On Wednesday, 10 May, soon after the assault on the opposition candidates and marchers, a meeting took place at Quarry Heights. Those present heard that, within thirty-six hours, President Bush would announce that he was sending more troops to Panama. Last-minute preparations had to be made, including a review of existing contingency plans, the drafting of reception plans for the soldiers and marines about to deploy, and the dissemination of the PDF order of battle. In Washington late that night, the Joint Chiefs alerted several headquarters to anticipate an execute order for Operation NIMROD DANCER. The next afternoon, as a result of the president's decision, both the State Department and the Pentagon activated special groups to monitor the crisis and coordinate actions on a 24-hour basis. The State Department also issued a travel advisory warning Americans of the unsettled conditions in Panama. Meanwhile, as another in a series of precautionary measures triggered by the crisis, Crowe ordered Woerner and SOCOM's General James J. Lindsay to "posture" special operations units called for in BLUE SPOON so that, if notified to do so, they could execute combat operations in Panama within seventy-two hours.[25]

Acting for the National Command Authority, the Joint Chiefs issued the order to execute NIMROD DANCER Thursday afternoon. As the message worked its way down the chain of command, the appropriate headquarters responded. The commander in chief, U.S. Pacific Command, prepared an amphibious task force for possible

---

[23] From the evidence available to the author, when the light infantry battalion was added to the troop list or who made the decision is unclear. Loeffke's observation that the unit had been "force fed" to the commanders in Panama was made in late May 1989. Two years after the fact, Woerner implied that he was not pleased with the size of the U.S. troop buildup in Panama after the elections. Journalist Bob Woodward also has written that Woerner tried to dissuade Crowe from sending too many troops. Quote from Interv, author with Maj Gen Bernard Loeffke, U.S. Army, 31 May 89, Fort Clayton, Panama. Interv, author with Woerner, 30 Apr 91. See also Bob Woodward, *The Commanders* (New York: Simon & Schuster, 1991), pp. 86–90.

[24] Msgs, CINCSO to JCS/Joint Staff [Cisneros to Brig Gen Shelton, Vice Dir, J–3, and Col Harbison, J–3, Joint Operations Division (JOD)], 100216Z May 89, sub: CONOPS for Security Enhancement Forces; CINCSO to CDR, JTF-Panama, 090400Z May 89, sub: CONOPS for Security Enhancement Forces; Intervs, author with Lt Col Robert Pantier, 13 Jun 90, and 21 May 91, Fort Leavenworth, Kans.; Msg, CINCSO to JCS, 120145Z May 89, sub: CONOPS for Additional Security Enhancement Forces; Panama chronology, n.d., entry for 13 May 89, 0200 Eastern Daylight Time (EDT).

[25] Augustine Interv, 11 May 90; Msg, CJCS to USCINCLANT et al., 110015Z May 89, sub: Operation NIMROD DANCER [alert order]; Chronology, n.d., entries for 10 May 89, 1315 EDT, and 12 May 89, 0010 EDT, 0306 EDT, 0308 EDT. Quoted words from Msg, CJSC to USCINCSO and USCINCSOC, 102346Z May 89, sub: BLUE SPOON. Msg, CDR [JSOTF] to USCINCSO et al., 110336Z May 89, sub: BLUE SPOON Alert Posture.

deployment to Panama on 72-hours' notice in case it was needed to ensure the safety of U.S. citizens. At Norfolk, Virginia, the commander in chief, Atlantic Command, received orders to ready a carrier battle group for possible deployment to the western Caribbean should there be an evacuation of Americans from Panama or, less likely, Cuban interference in the crisis. The Atlantic Command, as directed, also began the series of measures necessary for deploying a Marine company from a light amphibious infantry battalion. Similarly, the commander, U.S. Forces Command, located at Fort McPherson, Georgia, assumed responsibility for deploying the light infantry and mechanized Army units designated in the execute order. At Scott Air Force Base, Illinois, the Transportation Command (TRANSCOM) was the headquarters responsible for coordinating the physical movement of NIMROD DANCER units from the United States to Panama and for providing the necessary planes and ships, primarily from the Military Airlift Command (MAC) and from Department of Defense sealift assets. The Strategic Air Command, for its part, would refuel MAC aircraft en route to Howard Air Force Base.[26]

Before NIMROD DANCER units actually began their deployment, the Transportation Command and Military Airlift Command requested information on the PDF's capability to fire on planes flying into Howard or to attack the air base itself. Of special concern were any SA–7s, SA–14s, and mortars in the PDF inventory. The Southern Command and JTF-Panama responded that the Panama Defense Forces had received training in Nicaragua on the use of SA–7s but were not known to have any of these surface-to-air missiles in their arsenal. The number of SA–14s the Panamanian military might have was unknown, but not so the number of mortars, which were listed as sixty-four 60-mm., twelve 81-mm., and six 120-mm. The Panama Air Force had several trainer-fighters and helicopters, but, in the estimate of the JSOTF commander, no real air-to-air capability. If the need arose to suppress PDF air defenses, Woerner and Loeffke had Air Force security patrols at Howard, Marine patrols in the jungle outside the air base, quick reaction forces on alert, 60-mm. and 81-mm. mortars, Cobra helicopters, and an AC–130 gunship, with another on the way. What this reassuring inventory did not address was a chilling prospect that had haunted U.S. commanders and planners in Panama throughout the crisis: with all the U.S. equipment and firepower available, there was no way to guarantee that the Panama Defense Forces would not shoot down a transport or bombard Howard. The most that could be said in a positive vein was that, if the Panamanian military had this capability, they most likely lacked the desire or resolve to use it. The best estimate of PDF intentions at the time judged any interference with the airlift unlikely, although one analyst conceded that "anything is possible."[27]

As the commander who would receive operational control of the NIMROD DANCER conventional forces, Loeffke lobbied to get the mechanized battalion into Panama first. In the event the crisis took a marked turn for the worse, the unit's armored personnel carriers (APCs) would be sorely needed. Loeffke's priorities,

---

[26] Msg, CJCS to USCINCLANT et al., 111953 May 89, sub: Operation NIMROD DANCER [deployment order].

[27] Memo, Col Ben Anderson, CAT Dir, for Team Ch, CAT, 120835Z May 89, sub: Suppression of Enemy Air Defenses; Msgs, SOUTHCOM CAT to TRANSCOM CAT, 121542Z May 89, sub: Suppression of Enemy Air Defenses, and 61NAG Howard AFB to AIG 7110, 112100Z May 89, sub: Threat Assessment for MAC Aircraft.

however, ran afoul of the Joint Operations Planning System, the relative readiness of the deploying units, and the availability of MAC aircraft. There was also the limited facilities at Howard Air Force Base, a potential "chokepoint" in any attempt to sustain large-scale air operations into Panama.[28] These considerations would determine the order of deployment, which in this case meant that the Marine's Company A, 2d Light Amphibious Infantry Battalion, at Camp Lejeune, North Carolina, would probably arrive first, landing at Howard on Friday, one day after the president's announcement. The 165 marines brought with them the company's seventeen LAV–25s, fourteen of which boasted 25-mm. guns and could carry four infantry scouts. Of the remaining three, two served logistical purposes and one was configured for command and control. As Colonel Doyle, the MARFOR commander, observed, the light armored vehicles were ideal for operations in Panama, where a "water obstacle" ran the length of the MARFOR area of responsibility. Accompanying the newly arrived unit was an eight-man combat camera team, added to the deployment list at the last minute. After assembling at Howard, the marines crossed the Inter-American Highway into their billeting area at Rodman Naval Station. As with the security enhancement deployments in 1988, the small base was once again to experience the strains of accommodating an influx of additional forces whose home base was not in Panama.[29]

Friday afternoon, troops and equipment from the 7th Infantry Division (Light) began arriving at Howard.[30] The division, stationed at Fort Ord, California, had been on the POST TIME and BLUE SPOON troop lists for a year and thus was no stranger to the crisis in Panama. As the Panamanian election approached, planners at Fort Ord had begun preparing for a possible deployment. Although under the worst circumstances, the entire division might be involved, a two-man liaison team sent to Panama the week before the election learned that Woerner believed a much smaller commitment would be sufficient. Apprised of the SOUTHCOM commander's thinking, the G–3 shop at Fort Ord scurried to write an appropriate plan and, on 4 May, sent to Forces Command a one-page proposal for deploying variously sized task forces of up to three battalions. From Fort McPherson, the paper made its way to the Joint Staff in Washington. As was the case with USARSO planners a year before, 7th Infantry Division staff officers found themselves having to determine the force structure for deployment to Panama without having been told what the troop's precise mission might be.

---

[28] Memo, Col A. T. Rossi for Army Operations Center [MG Smith], 11 May 89, sub: Stationing of Augmentation Forces—Latest Package. Planes carrying NIMROD DANCER troops were originally scheduled to arrive at Howard at the rate of one every thirty minutes. Because of the airfield's limitations, the rate came closer to one every hour. Interv, Maj Larry Heystek with Maj Jeff Karhohs, U.S. Army, 26 May 89, Fort Sherman, Panama.

[29] Msg, USCINCTRANS/CAT to JCS, 120440Z May 89, sub: USTRANSCOM SITREP No. 1; Key Events, Operation NIMROD DANCER, WANG LC3 CAT1 459. Quoted words from Interv, author with Col J. J. Doyle, USMC, 14 Jun 89, Rodman Naval Station, Panama. Chronology, n.d., entry for 12 May 89, 1730 EDT.

[30] Unless otherwise noted, discussion of the 7th Infantry Division's deployment is based on Intervs, author with House, 17 Oct 89; Col David R. E. Hale, U.S. Army, 16 Jun 89, Fort Clayton, Panama; Maj Jeff Karhohs, 8 Mar 90, Fort Leavenworth, Kans.; Maj Robert Reese, U.S. Army, 19 Jun 89, Fort Clayton, Panama; Capt Richard Killblane, U.S. Army, 21 Jun 89, Fort Clayton, Panama; and Heystek with Karhohs, 26 May 89.

U.S. MILITARY INTERVENTION IN PANAMA, JUNE 1987–DECEMBER 1989

U.S. Army troops arriving for Operation NIMROD DANCER

When the order to deploy a battalion and brigade headquarters arrived at Fort Ord, the 1st Brigade—or, 9th Infantry regiment—was the division ready brigade, DRB1, capable of deploying within eighteen hours. The "Manchus," as the regiment was nicknamed, had just returned from an exercise at Fort Polk, Louisiana, with the 5th Infantry Division (Mechanized), which was also sending troops to Panama for NIMROD DANCER. Deploying with the 1st Brigade headquarters would be the 2d Battalion, 9th Infantry; an artillery battery from the 2d Battalion, 8th Field Artillery; and various supporting elements, for a total of 1,032 soldiers, 150 vehicles, and 6 105-mm. howitzers. On the night of 11 May, the Manchus took buses to Travis Air Force Base, California, where the plan called for them to board a fleet of C–141s for the flight to Panama. The discovery upon arriving at Travis that the Military Airlift Command had substituted thirteen C–5A Galaxy transports for some of the C–141s caused the division's movement officers to "really scramble" in reconfiguring the loading arrangements for troops and materiel to accommodate the larger transports. Despite these last-minute difficulties—not to mention the frustrations that virtually all the headquarters involved in NIMROD DANCER experienced from having to keep deployment arrangements Top Secret—the first transport carrying 7th Infantry Division troops took off from Travis Friday morning. Two days later, the last of the division's deploying units arrived at Howard. From there, the troops and equipment were moved via helicopters, trucks, and landing crafts, mechanized (LCMs), to Fort Sherman on the Atlantic side of the canal area.[31]

---

[31] According to the 9th Infantry's S–3, the movement of 7th Infantry Division's contribution to NIMROD DANCER from Howard Air Force Base to Fort Sherman was no simple accomplishment. First, the troops and equipment on the planes had to be unloaded and put into a ground convoy that moved to a holding area. From there, the force went to an embarkation point for LCMs, which took it up the canal, where it then unloaded and moved by a ground convoy into Sherman. Since the movement from Howard to Sherman began once the first units arrived, the "tail" was quite lengthy, running from Sherman back to Travis Air Force Base in California. Karhohs Interv, 26 May 89.

Operation Nimrod Dancer

Sandwiched between the marines and the light fighters was Company D, 1st Battalion(-), 5th Infantry Division (Mechanized), the one mechanized unit allowed to deploy immediately to Panama. The remainder of the battalion(-), composed of a second mechanized company, a battalion headquarters(-), and support elements, would not deploy until its equipment had made the three-hour overland trip from Fort Polk to the port of Beaumont, Louisiana, there to be loaded aboard the USNS *Bellatrix* for a sea voyage to Panama. Under these arrangements, the 5th Division's entire contribution of over seven hundred soldiers, nearly sixty armored personnel carriers, six mortar carriers, and over a hundred support vehicles did not finish deploying to Panama until 19 May. For command and control purposes, the mechanized forces were placed under USARSO's 193d Infantry Brigade, part of the Army Forces component under JTF-Panama.[32]

That the deploying mechanized force had the M113 armored personnel carrier in its inventory and not the newer Bradley infantry fighting vehicle was no accident. Compared to the Bradley, the M113 was narrower, carried more people (nine as opposed to six), and, in the event of an evacuation or the outbreak of hostilities, could maneuver more easily through the cramped streets of Panama's cities. At one point, the Joint Chiefs had raised with the Southern Command the possibility of sending a unit equipped with Bradleys, but JTF-Panama's chief planner responded to the inquiry with an emphatic protest up the chain of command. Not so easily resolved was the question of where the troops with their M113s would be lodged when they arrived. JTF-Panama wanted to use the mechanized force in support of possible operations in Panama City, but there was insufficient billeting space for the battalion on the east side of the canal. Consequently, only one company moved across the waterway from Howard to Albrook Air Station. The bulk of the force took up residence on the west side, at a facility known as Camp Rousseau. Should the armored personnel carriers at the camp be needed in Panama City, they would first have to cross either the Bridge of the Americas or a swing bridge in front of Fort Clayton.[33]

The Marine light amphibious infantry company and the Army light infantry and mechanized units constituted the core of the Nimrod Dancer deployments, and their arrival in Panama occasioned extensive media coverage. This tended to overshadow other movements of troops and equipment that were also critical to the operation. To begin with, some eighty-two officers and enlisted men from U.S. Army, South, were in Florida working with a National Guard brigade as part of its annual training. Prior to the election, Loeffke had decided to keep those USARSO personnel in the United States in line with the command's policy of making prudent preparations without overreacting. Now, with Nimrod Dancer under way, JTF-Panama requested the return of the soldiers, and Washington concurred. By 16 May, all were back in Panama. While this redeployment was taking place, the Joint Staff, in response to a mutual request from the Southern Command and U.S.

---

[32] Msgs, CINCFOR, Fort McPherson, to CDR, I Corps, Fort Lewis, and CDR, III Corps, Fort Hood, 110900Z May 89, sub: Oper/Nimrod Dancer, and Joint Staff to USCINCLANT et al., 112205Z May 89, sub: Change 1 to Nimrod Dancer Deployment Order; Interv, author with Maj Bill Epley, U.S. Army, 17 Oct 89, Washington, D.C. Chronology, n.d., entries for 12 May 89, 0120 EDT, 1115 EDT; 13 May 89, 1115 EDT; 15 May 89, 1755 EDT; and 16 May 89, 0830 EDT. Theresa L. Kraus, Working Chronology for Operation Just Cause, Working Paper, entries for 17, 19 May 89.

[33] Pantier Interv, 13 Jun 90.

Albrook Air Station

Army, South, directed the deployment of three intensive care nurses to augment the staff at Gorgas Army Hospital on Ancon Hill. Two UH–60 helicopters also arrived in Panama to fill out Task Force Hawk. Finally, amid all the publicized troop movements, certain special operations elements deployed secretly during NIMROD DANCER, occupying an office—dubbed the "no tell motel"—at Fort Clayton.[34]

With events moving swiftly and with international attention focused on Panama, Woerner looked to his Public Affairs Office to acquire and disseminate information about the crisis. The Army, Air Force, and Navy all deployed combat camera documentation teams to help out. Once they had arrived, Woerner activated a public affairs task force and a joint audio-visual detachment. The task force was to keep U.S. forces in Panama informed of the developing situation and to respond to queries from the media. Command policy was "maximum disclosure with minimum delay," although information would first be evaluated for accuracy and to determine if it would be of interest to the media. The mission of the joint audio-visual detachment was to provide video and photographic documentation of NIMROD DANCER operations, together with daily updates to Woerner and the Joint Chiefs. Woerner also asked the Pentagon to deploy the 28th Public Affairs Detachment from Fort Lewis, Washington, for thirty days. The commander of the detachment had worked on the operation orders for Panama and was thus familiar with the general situation. Finally, as a means of documenting events and capturing "lessons learned," Woerner encouraged his commanders to participate in taped interviews.[35]

---

[34] Augustine Interv, 13 Jun 89; Briefing slides, JTF-Panama, n.d., JTF-PM Posture, and JTF-Panama, n.d. [24 April 1989 written on first slide]; Chronology, n.d., entries for 13 May 89, 1630 EDT, and 14 May 89, 0156 EDT, 2240 EDT; Msgs, CINCSO to JCS, 252100Z Apr 89, sub: Medical Contingency Planning, and Col Rossi to Gen Pagonis, 14 May 89; Woodward, *The Commanders*, p. 90.

[35] Msgs, CINCSO to CDR, JTF-Panama, 150153[?] May 89, sub: Photo Documentation, NIMROD DANCER, and CINCSO to JTF-Panama, 150245Z May 89, sub: NIMROD DANCER Public Affairs. Quote

Operation Nimrod Dancer

While the Southern Command was moving to enhance and organize the public affairs assets available to it, efforts were under way to increase the security around Howard Air Force Base and other key installations in the event of hostilities. For the past year, Lt. Col. Bob Pantier, the chief planner for JTF-Panama, had been arguing that the introduction of countermortar radar (CMR) into Panama was urgently needed in light of the PDF's possession of 120-mm. mortars. In 1988, his appeals had been in vain, with Washington rejecting his requests presumably because deployment of the CMR sections, given their status as combat elements, might have run counter to White House efforts at the time to keep Panama off the front pages. The election crisis offered Pantier another opportunity. When JTF-Panama was directed to provide a concept of operations for Nimrod Dancer forces, he had been tapped to write the document. On his own authority, he inserted yet another request for two AN/TPQ–36 CMR sections. As he recalled his reasoning, "I figured it was better to ask forgiveness later on than permission." At the Southern Command, Cisneros deleted the request before sending the concept to the Joint Chiefs. Two days later, as Nimrod Dancer deployments into Howard again accentuated the air base's vulnerability, JTF-Panama prevailed on Cisneros to reconsider. He did. On 12 May, a follow-up message asked the Joint Chiefs for the two countermortar radar sections, one of which would be located at Howard Air Force Base at all times. The message also requested an AC–130 Spectre gunship, which would bring the number in Panama to two, thus allowing the command to have one or the other always ready to launch. Secretary of Defense Cheney authorized deployment of the CMR sections and the AC–130, with General Lindsay at MacDill Air Force Base providing the Spectre. (Soon after Cheney's decision was relayed to the appropriate headquarters, a teleconference among some of the key commanders revealed that the countermortar radar had been a part of the 7th Infantry Division's field artillery package for Nimrod Dancer all along.)[36]

There would be one other addition to the conventional forces deploying to Panama in the wake of the election violence. On 9 May, the Southern Command had raised the issue of having a "non-Panama based unit" replace the 193d's 1st Battalion, 508th Infantry (Airborne), in the Jungle Operations Training Center class scheduled to begin 21 May. Bringing in an additional combat unit for the expressed purpose of training would, without fanfare, bolster the number of troops on hand in the event of hostilities. Loeffke was not happy about removing the USARSO battalion from the JOTC rotation, but he did not object vehemently and

---

regarding command policy from Msg, SOUTHCOM PA to JTF-Panama, 150254Z May 89, sub: Nimrod Dancer Public Affairs. Msg, SOUTHCOM PA to JCS J–3, 150255Z May 89, sub: Request for Public Affairs Detachment; Chronology, n.d., entries for 15 May 89, 0337 EDT, 1145 EDT, 1235 EDT.

[36] Pantier's thinking on the countermortar radar issue is from Pantier Interv, 13 Jun 90. On the decision to deploy the countermortar radars and the AC–130, see Augustine Intervs, 13 Jun 89, 11 May 90; Presentation, Lt Col Robert Pantier, 21 May 91, Fort Leavenworth, Kans. Msgs, CINCSO to JCS/Joint Staff [Cisneros to Shelton and Harbison], 100216Z May 89, sub: CONOPS for Security Enhancement Forces; CINCSO to CDR, JTF-Panama, 090400Z May 89, sub: CONOPS for Security Enhancement Forces; CDR, JTF-Panama, to CINCSO, May 89, sub: CONOPS for Security Enhancement Forces; CINCSO to JCS, 120145Z May 89, sub: CONOPS for Additional Security Enhancement Forces; and CJCS to CINCFOR et al., 130218Z May 89, sub: Operation Nimrod Dancer Augmentation. Chronology, n.d., entries for 13 May 89, 0200 EDT, 0354 EDT, 1020 EDT, and 14 May 89, 1230 EDT.

his staff had no problem with JTF-Panama picking up operational control of 660 more soldiers. On 13 May, the 1st Battalion, 9th Infantry, from the 7th Infantry Division (Light) was designated the JOTC battalion.[37]

ADJUSTING AND ADAPTING

As NIMROD DANCER forces began arriving in Panama, JTF-Panama received a directive to provide the Southern Command detailed information on the disposition and employment of the new troops, the command and control arrangements under which they would operate, and how they would be integrated into contingency missions and Loeffke's joint training program. In complying with the directive, Loeffke's response would be based on PRAYER BOOK operation orders and the JTF-Panama fragmentary order for emergency action and would, as Colonel Doyle remarked, move U.S. forces in Panama "a notch closer to a contingency footing."[38]

In providing guidance to the JTF-Panama staff as it assembled the information SOUTHCOM wanted, Colonel Rossi once again drew "goose eggs" on a map. As was the case the previous year, there were three, each representing the creation of a new task force. Two were located on the Pacific side of the canal: Task Force Semper Fi on the west bank, Task Force Bayonet on the east, with the latter's area of responsibility extended north to the Tigris River. Across that divide and covering the other half of the canal area was the third oval, labeled Task Force Atlantic.[39]

As suggested by the name, Task Force Semper Fi was a Marine command; more precisely, it constituted a new designation for JTF-Panama's MARFOR component, which now added the newly arrived LAI company to the other Marine units falling under Colonel Doyle. For purposes of contingency planning, rehearsals, joint training, and the conduct of small-scale operations, Doyle would also exercise operational control over certain elements from U.S. Army, South, and, at times, over a company from the 7th Infantry Division brought down from the Atlantic side. As a result of these arrangements, Marine Forces-Panama experienced a net gain in assets and manpower, even though in the weeks following the May troop deployments, the number of units under Doyle's operational control would fluctuate continuously depending on the course of events in Panama and the theater. On several occasions, for example, crisis-related activities required that Task Force Semper Fi make its light armored vehicles available, on a short-term basis, to either Task Force Bayonet or Task Force Atlantic.[40]

Across from Task Force Semper Fi on the east side of the canal was Task Force Bayonet, commanded by Col. William J. Bolt and organized around USARSO's

---

[37] Quote from Msg, CINCSO to HQDA, 092302Z May 89, sub: Replacement Battalion for JOTC Training. Cope Interv, 25 May 89; Kraus, Working Chronology for Operation JUST CAUSE.

[38] Msg, CINCSO/SCJ-3 CAT to JTF-Panama/J-3, 142139Z May 89, sub: NIMROD DANCER Integration and Employment; Memo, Col John A. Cope Jr. for Department of the Army, CAT-Panama, 24 May 89, sub: Joint Task Force-Panama Organization. Quote from Doyle Interv, 14 Jun 89.

[39] Note, Col Arnie Rossi to DCSOPS, 16 May 89, sub: AORs.

[40] Doyle Interv, 14 Jun 89; Msg, CDR, JTF-Panama, to CDR, MARFOR; CDR, 9th Regimental Combat Team (RCT); CDR, 324th Support Gp, 231530Z May 89, sub: FRAGO (ASP Security); Memo, Cope for Department of the Army, CAT-Panama, 24 May 89, sub: Joint Task Force-Panama Organization.

193d Brigade, which he also commanded. In addition, he exercised operational control over the mechanized battalion(-) at Camp Rousseau on the west bank, the assumption being that, in a contingency operation, the employment of the battalion would be within Task Force Bayonet's area of responsibility. On a day-to-day basis, Bolt enjoyed the support of various military police, engineer, and naval assets, all of which remained under the control of their parent units.[41]

While modifying the organization and areas of responsibility of the two task forces on the Pacific side of the canal area entailed some significant adjustments, activating Task Force Atlantic on the northern side would require many more. In that Loeffke had never been fully convinced that light fighters from the 7th Infantry Division were needed at this stage in the crisis, JTF-Panama was at first reluctant to establish the task force, the core of which would be the division's 1st Brigade, commanded by Col. David R. E. Hale. Thus, when Hale set up his headquarters at Fort Sherman and began integrating his troops into activities on the Atlantic side, he discovered that he had no control over USARSO units and other elements already stationed in the area, most of which were commanded by lieutenant colonels. He immediately raised the issue with JTF-Panama and, after he "beat on the table," received the authority he sought. Soon thereafter, Task Force Atlantic was formally activated with Hale as its commander. Forces under his control included the light infantry and field artillery units from Fort Ord and, for activities connected with Operation NIMROD DANCER and the crisis in general, several USARSO assets, including two MP companies and an engineer battalion.[42]

The activation of Task Force Atlantic superseded the organizational and command and control arrangements JTF-Panama had created on the Atlantic side of the canal in 1988. The new configuration initially caused some confusion, largely because Loeffke and Hale, while personally agreeing on the setup, failed to notify all the affected parties. For example, the operations center at Fort Clayton received word of the changes only through an offhand remark Loeffke made when he showed up to conduct a tour for a visiting general. As for Lt. Col. Mike Michaelis, commander of the 549th Military Police Company and, under the old arrangement, the officer in charge on the Atlantic side, he never did receive written orders that put his company under Hale's operational control. To remove a potential source of friction, Michaelis asked Hale's provost marshal to use JTF-Panama as a conduit when giving the 549th an assignment. This procedure proved satisfactory to both parties, thus obviating any formal effort to "fix something [that] was not broken." Similarly, no one protested vigorously the arrangement under which JTF-Panama kept operational control over the Task Force Hawk aviation assets that Loeffke sent north in support of Task Force Atlantic, even though the aircraft involved had been in Panama for over a year courtesy of Hale's own 7th Infantry Division. As one officer summarized the situation, "everybody's working together."[43]

---

[41] Note, Rossi to DCSOPS, 16 May 89, sub: AORs; Memo, Cope for Department of the Army, CAT-Panama, 24 May 89, sub: Joint Task Force-Panama Organization.

[42] Quote from Augustine Interv, 7 Jun 89. Memo, Cope for Department of the Army, CAT-Panama, 24 May 89, sub: Joint Task Force-Panama Organization.

[43] Quote on relationship between Task Force Atlantic and the 549th Military Police Company from Interv, author with Lt Col Mike Michaelis, U.S. Army, 7 Jun 89, Fort Clayton, Panama. Intervs, author with Karhohs, 8 Mar 90, and Killblane, 21 Jun 89.

Occasionally, when a command and control issue did require formal clarification, Hale did not hesitate to refer it to JTF-Panama. One such instance involved the question of who had operational control over whatever battalion happened to be rotating through the Jungle Operations Training Center. Hale's concerns on this point were twofold. First, under the JOTC's hastily revised unit schedule, the 7th Infantry Division's own 1st Battalion, 9th Infantry, had deployed to the center for the expressed purpose of training. Hale did not want to "break faith" with the American people and the families at Fort Ord by using the unit for potentially dangerous operations. He did need its assistance, however, in such areas as contingency planning, communications, and force protection. If the unit were under his control during its rotation through the training center, he would be in a position to use—but not abuse—its assets in support of Task Force Atlantic. Hale's other concern stemmed from the fact that any battalion going through the jungle school had combat missions to perform should BLUE SPOON or the JTF-Panama fragmentary order be executed. In either contingency, one company from the JOTC battalion would be placed under Hale's operational control; the remainder of the unit would be assigned to Task Force Bayonet. Because preparing for those combat missions was one priority of the JOTC battalion and because Hale was the senior commander in the north responsible for contingency operations, he insisted that any battalion at the center come under his operational control for purposes of training. In mid-June, he raised the matter with Loeffke, who agreed.[44]

One command and control relationship required no clarification under a reorganized JTF-Panama: each of the three task force commanders answered to Loeffke on operational matters. As commander of USARSO's 193d Infantry Brigade, Bolt was accustomed to the arrangement, while Doyle had the experience of previous MARFOR commanders to draw upon. Hale adapted quickly, although he had to make some adjustments in the content of his staff's daily reports to Fort Ord. Designed to keep division headquarters abreast of the 9th Infantry's activities, the reports contained a wealth of information, including current intelligence estimates. As a courtesy, Hale provided JTF-Panama information copies of the messages, only to be told after a few days to omit the intelligence section in his reports to the division. This was in keeping with reporting procedures agreed upon by the Southern Command and JTF-Panama in 1988, which stipulated that all crisis-related intelligence had to be channeled through Fort Clayton and Quarry Heights. Hale complied, only to have 7th Infantry Division headquarters chide him for the omissions. Since he had to follow Loeffke's orders on the issue, Hale suggested that, to obtain intelligence reports, the division chief of staff talk directly to his JTF-Panama counterpart, Colonel Rossi.[45]

Some areas of potential friction between the JTF-Panama headquarters and the newly arrived commanders and staff officers were not so readily smoothed over, as was evidenced by the difficulties encountered in staff coordination. Soon after taking command of Task Force Atlantic, Hale observed that, initially, his greatest problem was simply learning to whom he had to talk and on what phone line. That was to be expected. What confounded some officers new to the theater, however,

---

[44] Quote from Hale Interv, 16 Jun 89. Memos, Col David R. E. Hale for CDR, JTF-Panama, 11 Jun 89, sub: Operating Procedures for JOTC Training Battalion, and Maj Gen Bernard Loeffke for CDR, MARFOR, et al., 16 Jun 89, sub: Mission Guidance.

[45] Hale Interv, 16 Jun 89.

were the obstacles they ran into even after they had learned what numbers to call. "So we talk to everybody that we think we can talk to and things don't work out," one Marine staff officer complained. The source of the problem, he indicated, was the joint task force itself. Despite the deeper shade of purple the presence of additional Navy and Marine liaison officers briefly lent to the emergency operations center at Fort Clayton during the early days of NIMROD DANCER, JTF-Panama was still predominantly an Army headquarters woefully understaffed for joint operations. And it would remain so unless PRAYER BOOK contingency plans were executed. In the meantime, USARSO's theater and administrative responsibilities as a SOUTHCOM component and a major Army command could not go unattended. Under these hectic conditions, coordination among the various staffs and components that constituted JTF-Panama was frequently the result of fortuitous circumstances rather than routine procedures.[46]

This was often the case in the area of training, which, as many of the forces entering Panama were surprised to learn, would be their top priority in the crisis. In the year since JTF-Panama had been activated, Loeffke's enthusiasm for joint training had only increased. The reasons soon became clear to the recent arrivals. Joint training acclimated them to the physical and operational environment in Panama. It also offered all involved the opportunity to work with their sister services and to become familiar with the array of resources that would be available for the conduct of combat operations. Most important, joint training enhanced the readiness of the troops to execute contingency plans; indeed, training events known as Purple Storms were still "rehearsals" in many respects, designed to approximate the movements and missions assigned to JTF-Panama units in the PRAYER BOOK and the emergency fragmentary order.

Coordinating training events, as well as other joint activities, sometimes proved frustrating for the newcomers. As in the past, Loeffke offered general suggestions at the daily JTF-Panama update meetings, and operations officers conferred in anticipation of his recommendations. But as his guidance worked its way down through the components and staff offices of his expanded command, different interpretations of his remarks sometimes surfaced. Reconciling these often entailed last-minute redrafting of the orders affected, which then had to be briefed to Lt. Col. Brett Francis, Cope's chief of operations, and, on occasion, to Cope himself. When the time came for execution, staff officers found that the operational details had not always been disseminated in a timely way. One possible solution, having the units involved coordinate laterally—for example, S–3 to S–3—risked leaving key personnel uninformed and sacrificing unity of command. Recurring problems of coordination sometimes led to confusion among the units scheduled to participate in a joint training event or operation. In one case, according to a Marine staff officer, "We not only caught the PDF by surprise; we caught the 193d as well." When asked about command and control arrangements, Francis conceded that "I think it's fair to say that [they are] confused," although he rightfully attributed some of the problems to commanders and staff officers who,

---

[46] Intervs, author with Hale, 16 Jun 89, and Doyle, 14 Jun 89. The quote from the Marine staff officer is from Interv, author with Maj Rick L. Horvath, USMC, 14 Jun 89, Rodman Naval Station, Panama.

for the sake of convenience, knowingly circumvented both the chain of command and JTF-Panama procedures.[47]

The demands NIMROD DANCER placed on JTF-Panama were enormous, not just in the area of operations but throughout the headquarters. Officers from the principal staff directorates at Fort Clayton worked long hours under considerable stress and with seemingly dwindling resources. Only two days after the election, the USARSO and JTF-Panama crisis action teams had been reduced in size, as component commanders and even some USARSO deputy chiefs of staff, under pressure themselves to meet a variety of requirements, recalled their liaison officers and representatives from Clayton's operations center. Other desperately needed personnel were being sent home under BLADE JEWEL, the code name for an operation—executed simultaneously with the NIMROD DANCER buildup of combat units—to reduce the number of U.S. military members and their dependents stationed in Panama. Requests submitted to beef up the joint task force headquarters with active duty augmentees made little headway, although several captains, a few majors, and at least one lieutenant colonel were sent from the reserve component to help out. Among the new arrivals, few were familiar with the crisis, or the organizations and people involved in it. Furthermore, in Francis' opinion, the captains and majors were being thrown into "an arena they cannot comprehend," mainly because "they don't have the lower-level experience . . . to truly grow into it."[48] In the meantime, higher headquarters and subordinate units alike still expected Loeffke's people to provide them a steady flow of timely and current information. Pressure also increased on JTF-Panama planners and operations officers to write, revise, and disseminate a succession of operation orders for contingencies, joint operations, and training events. Finally, combat units coming into Panama as part of the NIMROD DANCER buildup looked to JTF-Panama to provide them liaison officers and logistical assistance.

Logistics, as Col. Norman D. Higginbotham, JTF-Panama's J–4, commented with a sense of resignation, has been too often regarded by commanders and planners alike as a "peripheral" concern. Yet, without logistical support, "you're not going anywhere." This truism was embedded in the orders for NIMROD DANCER, which spelled out, at least in general terms, the supplies and support each deploying unit would need. But combat and support units do not always deploy together, in that the former usually enjoy a higher priority on the transport schedules than the latter. In these cases, the combat troops go in first with minimum support and arrange for the logisticians to follow. NIMROD DANCER offered no exception. Consequently, the mechanized and light infantry battalions setting up shop in Panama relied heavily at first on USARSO's logistical system.[49]

---

[47] Michaelis Interv, 7 Jun 89. First quote from Interv, author with Horvath, 14 Jun 89. Second quote from Interv, author with Lt Col Brett Francis, U.S. Army, 9 Jun 89, Fort Clayton, Panama.

[48] Francis Interv, 9 Jun 89. In one touch of irony, the BLADE JEWEL drawdown itself siphoned off staff officers, clerks, noncommissioned officers, and enlisted men needed to help run the Panama Relocation Center set up to process the departure of those Army personnel and dependents directed to leave Panama as part of the operation.

[49] Higginbotham's remarks from Interv, author with Col Norman D. Higginbotham, 30 May 89, Fort Clayton, Panama. On the issue of NIMROD DANCER logistics, see Msgs, CINCSO to USCINCLANT et al., 120445Z May 89, sub: USCINCSO OPORDER 1–89 (NIMROD DANCER), and CDR, USARSO, to Chief of Staff, Army, 142230Z May 89, sub: Update 25, Arrival of Forces.

By the end of May 1989, that system was stretched to the limit, with U.S. Army, South, providing logistical assistance to 4,000 service personnel in Panama over what it would normally support. Trucks were needed to transport troops and supplies. Rations had to be delivered. Laundry and mail facilities were essential to troop morale. Communications equipment was necessary to facilitate command and control and daily operations. "We have lost a good deal of flexibility with key USARSO resources—particularly ground transportation and communication equipment," a JTF-Panama staff officer observed in summarizing the situation. "We are now working in 3 arenas when we normally work in only one." Besides routine support to USARSO units, the command was also having to support the deploying forces, as well as the service personnel and dependents relocating from Panama City onto U.S. bases. In the face of these demands, Higginbotham predicted that, should the crisis worsen, U.S. Army, South, would have to bring in at least a transportation company, a service company, and a backup general supply base.[50]

There was yet another logistical issue with which U.S. Army, South, and JTF-Panama had to contend. For over a year, since the first contingency plans had postulated a buildup of U.S. forces in Panama, planners and logisticians had been pondering where the additional troops would be billeted, given the shortage of living facilities that already existed. Now, in May, the combined impact of the incoming NIMROD DANCER units and the surge of U.S. service personnel and families pouring onto U.S. bases brought those concerns to a head. U.S. Army, South, and JTF-Panama did what they could to accommodate the influx. On the Atlantic side, USARSO worked with Hale's brigade headquarters to obtain the necessary tenting for the troops and supplies. On the Pacific side, the command provided two air-conditioned "bubbles"—inflatable structures that could house up to two hundred soldiers each—for the mechanized elements at Camp Rousseau. To ease the housing and billeting crisis further, JTF-Panama, through the Southern Command, also requested that the Air Force send Harvest Eagle and Harvest Bare shelters to Panama. Harvest Eagle, which began arriving in mid-May, consisted of "tent cities" designed for temporary occupancy. Harvest Bare, on the other hand, consisted of more durable, accordion-like prefabricated units that, when unfolded and set up, could be used over a longer period as housing, dining, showering, and latrine facilities. Harvest Bare units began arriving in Panama in late May, after the Joint Chiefs authorized their use, and they were erected primarily at Howard Air Force Base to house the overflow of troops and civilians.[51]

The biggest adjustment NIMROD DANCER forces had to make was to the nature of the crisis itself. Prior to President Bush's announcement on 11 May, television news coverage of the election had graphically depicted the bloody breakdown of law and order in the streets of Panama City. The president's words themselves heightened the sense of danger and impending conflict, as did the fact that U.S. troops were actually being deployed. Taken together, these images and impressions led many soldiers and marines en route to Panama to assume that they would

---

[50] Quotes from Note, USARSO Staff Officer, n.d. Higginbotham Interv, 30 May 89.
[51] *Tropic Times*, 9 Jun 89, 31 May 89; Karhohs Interv, 8 Mar 90; Msg, SOUTHCOM J–3 to JCS J–3 CAT, 130355Z May 89, sub: Harvest Eagle/Prime Beef Augmentation; Log, SOUTHCOM CAT, 17 May 89; Daily Operational Update, SOUTHCOM, 17 May 89; Log, SOUTHCOM CAT, 18 May 89; Msg, SOUTHCOM J–3 to NMC, 210420Z May 89, sub: Sitrep 26.

soon be engaged in mortal combat with the Panama Defense Forces and Dignity Battalions. Others anticipated being immersed in utter chaos. Calmer assessments envisioned at best a tense situation.

The last prognosis proved the most accurate. By the time the marines, light fighters, and mechanized elements arrived in Panama, the capital was "tense but quiet." On 13 May, Bush publicly called on the Panamanian people and the Panama Defense Forces to "do everything they can" to oust Noriega, but neither group appeared eager to accommodate the president. In Panama City, incidents of petty harassment against Americans declined dramatically, while U.S. intelligence sources reported that the Panamanian armed forces seemed to be "operating under rules to avoid conflict with U.S. elements." Rumors spread throughout the capital that political prisoners in the Carcel Modelo were being tortured, but there was no mass demonstration in protest. The opposition did schedule a general strike for 17 May, but a disappointing response produced only a slowdown in business activity. The same day, the Organization of American States passed a resolution by a vote of 20 to 2, formally condemning Noriega's abuses but also warning against outside intervention in the internal affairs of a member state. In keeping with the resolution's call for "a transfer of power . . . with full respect to the sovereign will of the Panamanian people," the organization decided to send a diplomatic team to Panama to assist in the changeover. The Noriega regime denounced the resolution, while opposition leaders, which U.S. officials privately characterized as "cowed," called for rallies when the OAS delegation arrived on 23 May. Although few believed that the inter-American organization could engineer an agreement satisfactory to the principal parties, news of the mission afforded all sides a welcome breathing space. Thus, as NIMROD DANCER units began arriving in Panama, there was much news concerning the crisis but little disruptive activity. So calm did the situation appear from mid- to late May that newly arrived troops questioned whether they were really needed.[52]

As was the case with the security enhancement units rotating through Panama the previous year, the forces deploying for NIMROD DANCER had to adapt to a crisis in the Twilight Zone. Although American lives, property, and interests in Panama were at risk, there was no war or even the likelihood of one. The majority of Panamanians were friendly or indifferent, while the Panama Defense Forces and Dignity Battalions were keeping a low profile. In this tense but restrained environment, daily operations consisted largely (but not entirely) of guard duty, routine patrols, exercises, and a lot of police-type work, prompting Colonel Hale at one point to remark, not completely in jest, that he would gladly trade one of his rifle companies for a military police company. As during the first two years of the crisis, political considerations often determined military activities and virtually all operations were in some way politically sensitive. A company commander's

---

[52] *Tropic Times*, 15 May 89; Buckley, *Panama*, pp. 186–87; Chronology, n.d., entry for 13 May 89, 1345 EDT, and 15 May 89, 1351 EDT; Msgs, AmEmb to SecState, 12 May 89, sub: Torture, Business and Opposition Press Conference; SecState to Distribution, 18 May 89, sub: Situation Report; SOUTHCOM J–3 to Distribution, 20 May 89, sub: Situation Update; CDR [JSOTF] to JTF-Panama, 152235Z May 89, sub: COMJSOTF DISUM 005; CDR [JSOTF] to JTF-Panama, 172100Z May 89, sub: COMJSOTF DISUM 07; CDR [JSOTF] to JTF-Panama, 202100Z May 89, sub: COMJSOTF DISUM 10; CDR [JSOTF] to JTF-Panama, 232100Z May 89, sub: COMJSOTF DISUM 13.

operation orders, so the speculation went, sometimes had to be approved by the secretary of defense. There were restrictive rules of engagement and other operational constraints to assimilate, and the legal restrictions on the movement and activities of U.S. forces were complicated and numerous. There were also cultural differences with which one had to contend. The situation, in short, was complex, ambiguous, and fluid. Adapting to it would require maturity, flexibility, and discipline.

Of the incoming troops, the marines were perhaps the best informed about what to expect, able as they were to draw on the experience of the MARFOR units that had preceded them. This knowledge, however, did not make the rules of engagement and other constraints any less frustrating. The Army light fighters, for their part, were supposed to be ideally suited for low intensity conflict, but their experience at the Joint Readiness Training Center at Fort Polk, Louisiana, had been at the "combat end" of the spectrum, strictly force-on-force with no holds barred, as opposed to a politico-military simulation featuring a large civilian presence. The soldiers thus found themselves unprepared for "day-to-day existence in an environment where you're not going to see the enemy." As for the troops in the mechanized battalion, what they encountered in Panama bore little or no resemblance to any of the conventional operations for which they had trained. According to Colonel Hale, the process of adapting to the militarily unorthodox situation in Panama entailed, first, accepting the environment, then becoming increasingly proficient at operating in it.[53]

The program for integrating the new units into JTF-Panama and acclimating them to an unfamiliar and unorthodox environment was extensive if not always efficient, given the daily demands of crisis management. Senior commanders were briefed about the crisis upon their arrival.[54] After that, they could rely on their staffs and the daily JTF-Panama meeting to keep them abreast of current developments. As for the troops, the reception plan drawn up by JTF-Panama called for each incoming unit to be briefed. For the marines, Colonel Doyle set up an orientation program that included a "welcome aboard" briefing on the history of Panama, the background and nature of the crisis, the organization of MARFOR-Panama, the rules of engagement, the modus operandi of intruders on the Arraiján Tank Farm and Rodman Ammunition Supply Point, operations security, training programs, command policies, leave, and recreational opportunities and prohibitions. Likewise, Colonel Bolt met with the first elements of the mechanized battalion the day after they arrived to acquaint them with the crisis and assure them that they would receive the training they needed to perform their mission. Briefings to other units covered similar ground, some more thoroughly than others. The immediate scheduling of joint training events also accelerated the process of adjustment and acclimation, as did the efforts of Panama-based military policemen, staff officers,

---

[53] Intervs, author with Horvath, 14 Jun 89, and Hale, 16 Jun 89. Quote from Karhohs Interv, 8 Mar 90. Discussion notes, author with Col David R. E. Hale, 28 Sep 89, LICPRO Office, Fort Leavenworth, Kans.

[54] For Hale, his meeting with Loeffke was not soon enough. The minute he stepped onto the tarmac at Howard, he was asked to meet with the international press corps assembled there. After this awkward introduction to the crisis, he went off to meet with Loeffke. One of the 7th Infantry Division staff officers already in Panama maintained that JTF-Panama should have had someone present to brief Hale at the air base. Intervs, author with Hale, 16 Jun 89, and Killblane, 21 Jun 89.

and public affairs personnel to answer questions and disseminate information. In assessing the orientation program, Loeffke regretted that he could not make one change, the lowering of Personnel Movement Limitation Charlie back down to Alpha, a measure that would have allowed the new troops to go downtown where they could mingle with the Panamanian people and get to know them.[55]

Once NIMROD DANCER units received their orientation briefings and other pertinent information, they began the process of applying what they had learned. At Camp Rousseau, the mechanized battalion reworked its mission essential task list to incorporate nontraditional requirements necessitated by the crisis. At Fort Sherman, Hale told the press that, along with such routine concerns as operations security and perimeter defense, he was also emphasizing the troops' need to learn the rules of engagement.[56] Progress along these and other lines proved impressive, even though the reception programs and adaptation activities could not close the perceptual gap that, from the outset of the NIMROD DANCER buildup, separated the forces already stationed in Panama from the newcomers. To the former, the crisis had become a routine part of everyday life, a largely political confrontation in which Washington used the U.S. military to send signals to the other side, protect American interests, and keep the situation under control. A slide into open hostilities could not be discounted, but on a daily basis the more likely threat a U.S. soldier, airman, or sailor faced was harassment by a PDF *tránsito*. Under these conditions, to be ready for any contingency, to be able to respond to the surges in the crisis, but also to be able to back off during the periods of calm were the skills and flexibility required of American forces. Conversely, to go on a permanent war footing was neither cost effective nor psychologically wise, given the continuously changing and open-ended nature of the crisis. Such a posture might also inadvertently provoke the kind of military escalation that the Southern Command and JTF-Panama hoped to avoid.

Many Panama-based U.S. officers who embraced this assessment not surprisingly regarded some of the new troops as being too "warlike." The light fighters seemed the worst offenders. As part of their "persona," they donned "rag pots" (kevlar helmets with strips of cloth attached) and face paint, accouterments employed for camouflage but also intended to present a "fierce" image. When these painted "warriors" stepped off their transports at Howard, the JTF-Panama commander and staff had been appalled. Colonel Cope, concerned about the impression their appearance would have on the Panamanian people and the Panama Defense Forces, tried through channels to explain the "idiosyncrasies" of the 7th Infantry Division to the Panamanian military. But Cisneros, always more inclined than other top staff officers to put additional pressure on the Noriega regime, stopped the message. Subsequent efforts directed at Hale to have his soldiers don what JTF-Panama headquarters regarded as attire more appropriate to the situation met with strong resistance, from both the colonel and the division commander, Maj. Gen. Carmen Cavezza, who was adamant that combat troops should look like combat troops. The rag pot and face paint,

---

[55] Intervs, author with Doyle, 14 Jun 89, and Loeffke, 31 May 89; Telephone Interv, author with Capt Anthony M. Schilling, U.S. Army, 30 Nov 90; *Tropic Times*, 19 May 89. Also the author attended two orientation briefings, one given by Colonel Doyle, the other by Colonel Michaelis.

[56] *Tropic Times*, 19 May 89; Interv, author with Col Robert Barefield, 7 Nov 90, Fort Leavenworth, Kans.

which Cavezza associated with discipline and the warrior ethos, conveyed the troops' determination to meet any kind of challenge. On 22 May, the general flew to Panama to visit Hale's troops and to help "cement" relations between Task Force Atlantic and JTF-Panama. In a meeting between Cavezza and Loeffke, the issue of the rag pots and camouflage surfaced. Believing accommodation more conducive to harmony and efficiency than fiat, Loeffke acquiesced. At the next JTF-Panama update meeting, Hale arrived, as he had before, with his face painted black and green, his rag pot under his arm, and a 9-mm. pistol in a shoulder holster.[57]

When faced with criticism about the appearance and demeanor of their troops, commanders of the newly arrived marines and soldiers retorted that allegations concerning a "go-to-war" mind-set were grossly exaggerated. What the troops based in Panama had to realize, they argued, was that, in President Bush's assessment, the crisis had reached such dangerous proportions as to require the deployment of additional combat units. The troops in these units, therefore, needed to prepare for any operational contingency. What might appear excessive from the staff offices of Fort Clayton represented, from the perspective of the field, nothing more than essential precautions. If the barbed-wire defensive perimeters surrounding areas occupied by the new forces stood in stark contrast to the less visible security measures in place at most U.S. bases in Panama, then so be it. The same could be said of the mechanized infantry soldier who, clad in body armor and kevlar helmet and holding an M16, stood guard next to an M113 in full view of unarmed USARSO soldiers and civilian employees driving to work along Gaillard Highway. Incongruous as these and other sights might be, the reasoning behind them seemed sound to the new arrivals.

In a replay of yet another aspect of the security enhancement deployments of 1988, these differences in perception and perspective became a source of considerable friction at the tactical level between those troops based in Panama and those who were there as part of the NIMROD DANCER buildup. USARSO soldiers were restrained by the same travel restrictions as everyone else, but unlike the augmentation forces, they could go home at the end of the day, see the family or sweetheart, and have a beer. The newcomers quickly came to resent what they interpreted as a "laid back," "business as usual" approach to the crisis on the part of Panama-based troops. In fairness, USARSO units were no less prepared than the others under JTF-Panama to respond to any contingency. But to the guard in full combat gear at Albrook, to the light fighter in his rag pot and camouflage, and to the marines and soldiers denied access to even the simplest pleasures that Panama had to offer, leaning forward in the foxhole, as one soldier phrased it, proved difficult when you could see everyone around you going to the golf club.[58]

This resentment took its toll on morale among the augmentation forces. But so, too, did other problems, including boredom; adjusting to an unfamiliar, ambiguous, and unpredictable environment; being away from friends and families

---

[57] "Idiosyncrasies" quote from Interv, author with Cope, 25 May 89. Intervs, author with Maj Harry Tomlin, U.S. Army, 22 Mar 91, Fort Leavenworth, Kans., and Karhohs, 8 Mar 90. "Persona" quote from Interv, author with Hale, 16 Jun 89. Author's recollection of JTF-Panama update meeting during which Colonel Hale appeared as described.

[58] Intervs, author with Francis, 9 Jun 89, and Tomlin, 22 Mar 91. Quoted words from Karhohs Interv, 8 Mar 90. Killblane Interv, 21 Jun 89.

in the United States; personal problems having little to do with the crisis; and, initially at least, not knowing "When am I going home?" Marines had had a year to build and refine various programs to bolster morale, and, once headquarters elements from the mechanized battalion and 7th Infantry Division arrived in Panama, they, too, initiated activities that allowed the soldier to shed his uniform periodically and go swimming, watch movies, take part in athletic events, go on picnics or to the snack bar, or have a barbecue. Yet, beneficial as these efforts were, some soldiers experienced severe levels of stress and frustration. One Task Force Atlantic company commander had two of his men "explode in fits of anger," with one taking a rifle butt to furniture and other items, and the other, a sergeant, flinging his tray and food across the mess hall. When the captain asked a senior officer if these episodes were unique to his company, the reply was, "It's across the board." A noncommissioned officer with the mechanized troops offered a similar assessment: "Morale sucks." As Army officers newly arrived on the scene quickly realized, maintaining troop morale in an uncertain environment would tax their leadership techniques and skills to the utmost. Complicating the task was the fact that several officers, especially below field grade level, were themselves experiencing the psychological stress of operating on the unorthodox fringes of the Twilight Zone, in conditions that seemed to sap the self-esteem they acquired from being warriors.[59]

HARBINGER: THE "INVASION" OF FORT ESPINAR

Contributing to the stress experienced in the early days of NIMROD DANCER was a feeling that, no matter how calm the situation in Panama appeared and no matter how determined each side was to avoid open hostilities, every daily "milk run," in the words of one officer, contained a "potential flash point." The validity of that observation was brought home the night of 18 May 1989 in what became sardonically known as the "invasion" of Fort Espinar.

Soon after troops from the 7th Infantry Division arrived on the Atlantic side, a decision was made to move most of the 2d Battalion, 9th Infantry, onto Fort Davis, a U.S. base, with the battalion's Company B going instead to Fort Espinar, a military area of coordination in which the PDF's 8th Infantry Company was billeted right next to an American family housing area. The movement of Company B would involve about 140 combat troops, military policemen, logistics and communication personnel, and engineers. To minimize the possibility of an unwanted confrontation with the PDF company, Colonel Hale and his staff held a number of "skull sessions" trying to anticipate anything that might go wrong. Working in their favor and promising to help avoid trouble was the fact that, en route to Fort Espinar, the troops would traverse a highway that, under the canal treaty, was considered Panamanian territory. This meant that the Panama Defense Forces would be obliged to provide an escort for the column. On Tuesday, 16 May, U.S. officials notified the Combined Board about the convoy, stating that the move would take place the next day. The PDF members balked, arguing that they had not received the customary 24-hour notice. Although the canal treaty did not specify the time required for advance notification, the Americans decided not to press the point, in part out of concern for precipitating an incident while the Organization

---

[59] Discussion notes, author with Hale, 28 Sep 89; Killblane Interv, 21 Jun 89.

of American States was meeting in Washington to discuss the crisis. Company B's move was therefore postponed until Thursday.[60]

At 1700 Thursday, the company assembled for departure. The PDF escort arrived twenty minutes later, and the passage from Fort Davis to the Fort Espinar officers' club, Company B's new headquarters, took place without incident. Then, despite all the planning and prior coordination, the situation took a dramatic turn for the worse. The PDF 8th Infantry Company, described by Cope as "jittery to begin with," was not accustomed to having U.S. troops other than MPs inside Espinar. Furthermore, the 8th Company's commander apparently had been led to believe that the troops scheduled to enter the post would be a small group from the 29th Military Intelligence Battalion—a familiar unit on the Atlantic side—not over a hundred soldiers from the "2-9th Infantry." Faced with U.S. combat troops wearing face paint and rag pots, and the presence of HMMWVs with mounted machine guns, the 8th Infantry Company "went ballistic." Word quickly reached Company B that the PDF unit was setting up mortars. In response, Task Force Atlantic began training its artillery pieces on Fort Espinar. The tubes, located at Forts Davis and Sherman, had the capability of locating the source of rounds fired from enemy mortars. Attack helicopters from Task Force Hawk were also readied for action. As an additional measure, JTF-Panama called for an AC–130 gunship. The first confrontation to arise out of Operation NIMROD DANCER was under way.[61]

For several tense hours, U.S. officers monitoring the standoff could not tell whether their formidable show of force would compel the PDF to back down. In the operations center at Fort Clayton, Colonel Rossi personally got on the telephone with the watch officer at the Comandancia, Capt. Moisés Cortizo, commander of the PDF 5th Infantry Company. Cortizo, often quite vocal in his anti-American sentiments, ended up urging restraint. "We are not at war," he told Rossi, adding that both sides had to consider the welfare of the Panamanian people and avoid rash actions. After further discussion, reports reached JTF-Panama that the PDF company at Fort Espinar was beginning to stand down. By midnight the incident was over.[62]

The "invasion" of Fort Espinar raised serious concerns about an unanticipated flash point escalating into hostilities that neither side wanted. One reason for moving Company B into the fort had been to establish a military presence at a site targeted in JTF-Panama contingency plans. Another reason, the one made public, had been to demonstrate that the United States, under the canal treaty, had the right to station forces at Espinar. Throughout the crisis, the Panama Defense Forces had regularly violated provisions of the treaty. The Southern Command, as previously recounted, had submitted written protests over each violation but, under directives from Washington, had not sought to challenge the PDF militarily. That approach was now changing and, as the Fort Espinar incident revealed, so, too, were the risks involved.

---

[60] Quotes from Interv, author with Karhohs, 8 Mar 90. Intervs, Heystek with Karhohs, 26 May 89; author with Hale, 16 Jun 89; and Cope, 25 May 89.

[61] Intervs, Heystek with Karhohs, 26 May 89; author with Karhohs, 8 Mar 90; Loeffke, 31 May 89. Cope's quote from Interv, author with Cope, 25 May 89.

[62] Karhohs Interv, 26 May 89. Cortizo's entreaty was written on a blackboard in the Fort Clayton operations center.

7

ASSERTING U.S. TREATY RIGHTS
MAY–JUNE 1989

Two days after he announced the reinforcement of U.S. troops in Panama, President Bush met with reporters aboard Air Force One. In his comments, he touched on the prospects for resolving the two-year crisis, expressing his hope that the Panama Defense Forces would remove Noriega from power. Calling for the overthrow of a foreign dictator is not a routine presidential entreaty, but neither is it unique. The real news to come out of the session was what Bush left unsaid. He made no threat of military action against Panama's regime. The ouster of Noriega was for the Panamanians to arrange; it was not an objective of Operation NIMROD DANCER. Pentagon officials beginning with Admiral Crowe underscored this position in statements downplaying the chances for war. "The last thing we need to do is bomb and invade," one senior officer informed a *Washington Post* reporter.[1]

Until the veracity of the administration's temperate pronouncements could be tested, news agencies that had covered the 7 May 1989 election and its violent aftermath kept a spotlight on the crisis. For the troops deploying under NIMROD DANCER, this meant learning to cope with intrusive media coverage of their arrival and initial activities in Panama. Colonel Hale had to make the adjustment more quickly than most. As soon as he stepped off the plane at Howard Air Force Base, a waiting escort officer hustled him over to a nearby assemblage of the international press for an impromptu news conference. The unsuspecting colonel referred frequently to his mission statement, which emphasized U.S. rights and the protection of American citizens, to get through a barrage of questions, including the leadoff query, "Why are you invading Panama?" The marines, for their part, showed themselves old hands at dealing with the media. Soon after the company from Camp Lejeune arrived, Marine Forces-Panama staged an amphibious landing for the benefit of the cameras, prompting half-critical, half-admiring comments from Army officers on the Leathernecks' knack for "photo-ops."[2]

In the ensuing days, as NIMROD DANCER units took up their positions and began performing what appeared to be rather routine duties, most reporters

---

[1] *New York Times*, 14 May 89, p. 1. Quote from Donnelly, Roth, and Baker, *Operation Just Cause*, p. 48.

[2] Interv, author with Col David Hale, U.S. Army, 16 Jun 89, Fort Clayton, Panama; Conversations, author with Army officers who commented on the Marines' "photo-op."

concluded that war, in fact, was not in the offing and that the incoming troops had deployed, as indicated in the president's 11 May message, mainly to protect American lives and property (*Chart 5*). Several commentators lauded Bush for his cautious, yet sensible handling of the crisis, while the news media in general turned their attention to OAS mediation efforts, to certain well-publicized U.S. military exercises in Panama, and to stories breaking elsewhere in the world. By the third week in May, press coverage of the postelection crisis had dropped to the point where the confrontation at Fort Espinar on 18 May went virtually undetected, which is to say, unreported. To be sure, the evacuation of American dependents proceeded without letup; Ambassador Davis, an announcement stated, would not return to the U.S. Embassy in Panama City; and reports continued to circulate that several opposition members arrested during public protests against the regime were being tortured by their captors. Still, all this sobering news was overshadowed by other outward indications that the tension in Panama was abating and, together with it, the possibility of hostilities between U.S. and Panamanian forces.

Ironically, just as the news media were losing interest in NIMROD DANCER, U.S. forces in Panama were preparing to adopt a more assertive—some on the scene even used the term *provocative*—posture, a part of the tougher policy U.S. officials had agreed in advance to implement in the event Noriega stole the Panamanian elections. Beginning in late May, the range and intensity of U.S. military activities in Panama increased dramatically. Outside Panama, few Americans were aware of the change in course.

TRIAD AND FISSURES II

As the Bush administration prepared to increase the pressure on Noriega and his regime, General Woerner and his staff at the Southern Command once again recommended that a tougher military posture be but one part of a more comprehensive strategy for ending the crisis. In a message to Admiral Crowe drafted in mid-May, Woerner began by asserting that the United States faced its best opportunity thus far to dislodge the Panamanian dictator. "To accomplish our objectives," he continued, "all three legs of what I would like to term as the Panama Triad—enhanced U.S. force presence, international support/pressure, and opposition activities—must work in synchronization." In the remainder of the message, Woerner elaborated on the triad concept and the relationship of each leg to the other two.[3]

The first leg, the increased U.S. military presence in Panama, afforded the United States an opportunity to intimidate the Panamanian military. The tougher policy put into play by NIMROD DANCER called on U.S. troops to initiate a variety of activities to assert U.S. rights under the canal treaties. If properly conducted, these initiatives could "create fear and dissension in PDF ranks through the suggestion of the unknown." Noriega and the Panama Defense Forces, in other words, should always be concerned "with US military action directed at them." The United States, however, had to be careful. Military activities had to be orchestrated in such a way as to preclude Noriega's deflecting attention

---

[3] Unless otherwise noted, the presentation—including quotes—that follows Woerner's "triad" strategy is from Msg, CINCSO to CJCS, [15] May 89, sub: Panama Triad.

Chart 5—Joint Task Force-Panama Organization for Nimrod Dancer

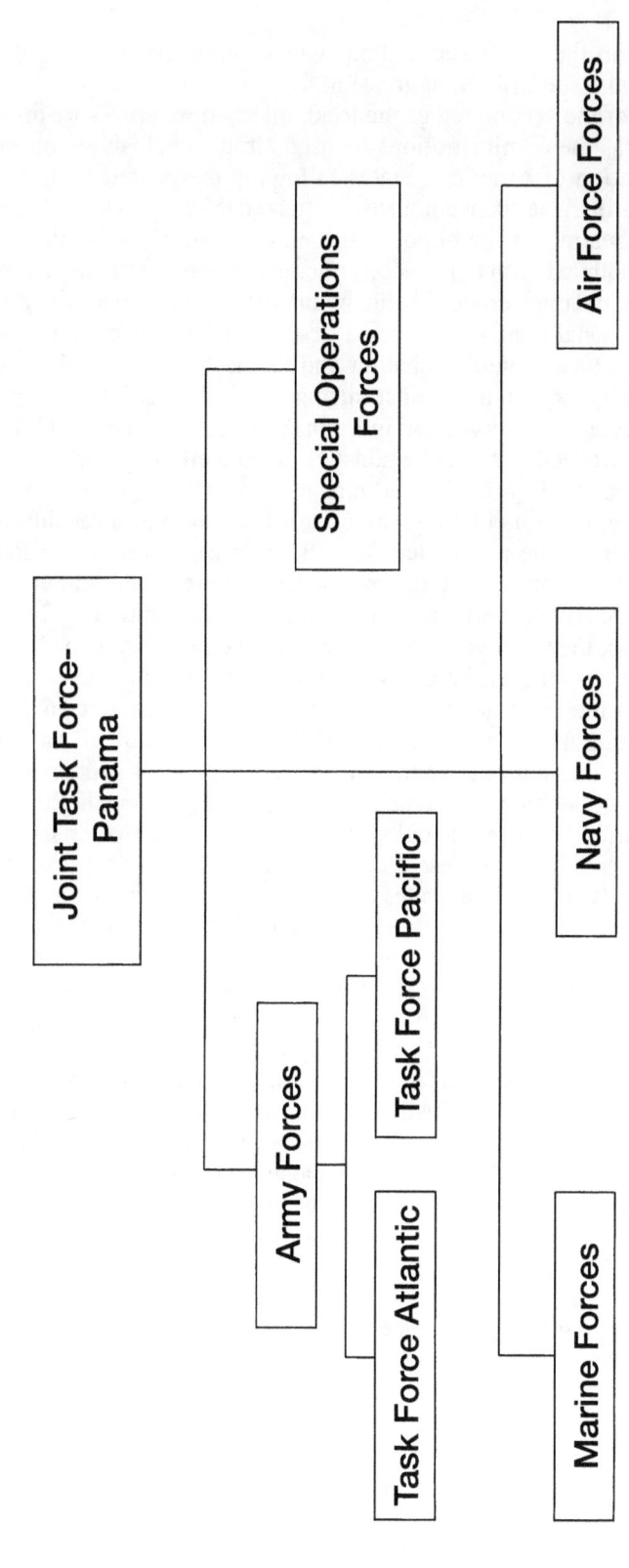

away from the real issue of Panamanian democracy to a bogus but potentially emotional issue of U.S. aggression.

As for the second leg of the triad, international pressure and support, Woerner (as well as the administration) focused almost exclusively on the activities of the Organization of American States following the postelection violence in Panama. Most Latin American countries criticized Noriega's annulment of the election and the beating of the opposition members, but these public denunciations were usually coupled with expressions of concern about outside (meaning U.S.) military activities and interference in Panamanian affairs.[4] Deliberations in the OAS reflected this traditional tension between a desire to take collective action in response to a member's unacceptable behavior and the need to uphold the principle of national sovereignty, especially against infringements by the United States, a country with a long record of intervention in Latin America. As a result, U.S. efforts to obtain a strongly worded statement against Noriega were only partially successful, despite pressure exerted by the Bush administration on the organization's delegates meeting in Washington. On 17 May, the organization passed a resolution that condemned Noriega by name and called for a transfer of power to the Panamanian people. Of the resolution, one commentator later wrote, "The language was so tame that even Jorge Ritter, Noriega's foreign minister, called it fair." To help implement the resolution, the OAS voted to send a commission to Panama.[5]

Woerner termed the OAS resolution "reassuring," even though he held little hope that the diplomatic démarche by itself could produce a solution to the crisis. In his opinion, the involvement of the Organization of American States served mainly to internationalize the situation, offer moral support to any U.S. effort to back the opposition in Panama, keep Noriega from casting the crisis in terms of a small nation beset by the colossus of the north (the real crisis being a beleaguered people beset by a ruthless dictator), and provide a "fig leaf" for U.S. actions in general.[6] If the United States hoped to capitalize fully on this regional support, Washington again had to be careful, avoiding any actions that could be construed as a unilateral attempt to impose a solution. Specifically, Congress should not move to reexamine the status of the canal treaties, and U.S. military forces in Panama should not engage in any provocative actions while protecting American lives and property and asserting U.S. treaty rights.

Concerning the third leg of the triad, the Panamanian opposition, the scheduled visit to Panama of an OAS delegation in late May would, in Woerner's words, provide a "security blanket" for the regime's critics to take to the streets. By moving "boldly and massively," opposition leaders could wear down Noriega and the Panama Defense Forces; if, however, the opposition failed to assert itself, it could negate the advantages generated by the other legs of the triad. Woerner was

---

[4] A list of messages from U.S. embassies throughout Latin America to the State Department, together with a summary of each message, is contained in a Chronology prepared during the election crisis. As the summaries in this Chronology reveal, most Latin American governments expressed mixed feelings about the situation in Panama, combining criticism of the regime with concerns about U.S. military intentions.

[5] On the response of the Organization of American States to the annulment of the Panamanian election, see Baker, *Politics of Diplomacy*, p. 183. Quote from Buckley, *Panama*, pp. 185–88.

[6] Interv, author with General Frederick F. Woerner Jr., U.S. Army (Ret.), 30 Apr 91, Fort Leavenworth, Kans.

not optimistic. At this "most critical juncture of the crisis," he stated, the opposition was not "doing its part." The general strike it had called was a failure, and it was not filling the streets with outraged citizens. The basic problem, as Woerner saw it, was that the United States had no formal procedures for synchronizing opposition activity with U.S. actions. "We must develop this mechanism now," he argued.

Having explained the triad concept, Woerner turned his attention to U.S. policy making at the interagency level, once again urging officials in Washington to devise and execute a plan to "drive a decisive permanent wedge between Noriega and the PDF." Woerner called such a plan Fissures II, a restatement of the idea and terminology he had enunciated during policy discussions over the past year. As was the case with the original Fissures proposal, the SOUTHCOM commander maintained that Fissures II could not be implemented piecemeal but required a series of integrated initiatives executed as part of a comprehensive strategy approved and managed at the interagency level.

Looking back from retirement on the crisis as a whole, Woerner later claimed that the United States never did come up with "a coherent and attainable strategic vision . . . or the institutional capacity within the structure of government—the decisive authority composed of political will, and consensus and resources—to carry it through." Because, in his opinion, "most agencies wished to avoid bearing the costs of solving the problem," Washington attempted to achieve the nonviolent removal of Noriega from power mainly through "wishful thinking," with "rhetoric outdistancing intentions."[7] Although the Pentagon supported a well-coordinated, interagency effort, the Bush administration, Woerner believed, had missed the opportunity afforded it by the Panamanian elections to jettison the limited and ineffectual approach of its predecessor in favor of a comprehensive, integrated blueprint that matched resources and means to objectives.[8]

Applying this very general critique to a postmortem of his specific recommendations of 1989, Woerner maintained that Fissures II suffered the same fate as Fissures I: the piecemeal implementation of disparate measures. As for his triad strategy, the synchronization of the three components essential to its implementation never occurred. The Panamanian opposition, after the beating it took (both literally and figuratively) in the postelection violence, shied from playing the active role Woerner deemed commensurate with its goals and responsibilities. As for efforts to internationalize the crisis, U.S. arrogance, he contended, prevented effective cooperation with the Organization of American States. The United States at the time was "on a roll," having applied pressure unilaterally to remove dictators such as Ferdinand Marcos in the Philippines and the young "Baby Doc" Duvalier in Haiti. In the hubris of the moment, Washington regarded OAS support for removing Noriega—always problematic given most members' suspicions of U.S. motives toward Latin America—as superfluous.[9]

---

[7] Gabriel Marcella and General Frederick F. Woerner Jr., U.S. Army (Ret.), The Road to War: The U.S.-Panamanian Crisis, 1987–1989, draft article, 6 May 91.

[8] On Pentagon preparations for a tougher policy, see Joint Staff Action Processing Form (and atchs.), through Director, Joint Staff (DJS), to Asst to CJCS, 13 May 89, sub: Strategy Position Paper on Panama; as well as the Atch., Position Paper, J–5 to DJS, 13 May 89, sub: US Strategy and Policy in Panama.

[9] Woerner Interv, 30 Apr 91. In his memoirs, James Baker, Bush's secretary of state, inadvertently supports this impression, implying that the administration's support for OAS initiatives was

Publicly, of course, the administration trumpeted its support for the Panamanian opposition and Organization of American States. It also stiffened some existing anti-Noriega measures, such as economic sanctions (which Woerner continued to view as misguided and misdirected). But most of all, Bush's tougher policy initiatives consisted of using the enhanced U.S. military presence in Panama to engage unilaterally in psychological warfare against Noriega and the Panamanian military. "We wanted Noriega to believe we were coming if he didn't leave first," Secretary of State Baker wrote in his memoirs. "More to the point, we also wanted to send the PDF a message: Noriega is the problem; either you remove him, or the U.S. military will."[10]

Throughout March and April, in the discussions leading to this tougher policy, Woerner had agreed that the time had come to step up the military pressure on Noriega and the Panama Defense Forces. In his triad message, he reiterated the specific measures U.S. forces could undertake to this end. These recommendations, in keeping with the Fissures concept of spreading disaffection within the Panamanian military and driving a wedge between it and the dictator, included refining and rehearsing relevant operation plans, maintaining an active training posture, mounting a SOUTHCOM public affairs campaign to emphasize U.S. military readiness and Noriega's isolation, continuing a "proactive" effort to collect intelligence, especially on Noriega, and vigorously defending U.S. treaty rights. Unlike the fate shared by many of Woerner's nonmilitary proposals, virtually all of these measures were implemented to one degree or another. The arrival in mid-May of a three-man team from Fort Bragg, led by Maj. Dave Huntoon from the XVIII Airborne Corps, signaled the more direct and active part the corps would play from that point on in reviewing and revising the existing PRAYER BOOK plans, specifically BLUE SPOON. Meanwhile, most restrictions imposed on U.S. intelligence gathering before and during the elections were lifted, thus enabling MI units to put their people back on the streets. Of even greater significance, however, were the more aggressive actions American forces began to take as a means of reasserting U.S. treaty rights in Panama.

REASSERTING TREATY RIGHTS: CONVOYS

In his communications with the Pentagon prior to the Panamanian election, Woerner had characterized repeated PDF interference with official U.S. vehicles and equipment in Panama as clear provocations and treaty violations. As one means of reasserting the freedom of movement guaranteed by the canal treaty, both he and Ambassador Davis proposed providing armed escorts for convoys of U.S. military vehicles. The Southern Command drew up the general procedures that an armed convoy would follow, and Woerner submitted them to the Pentagon.[11] The Joint Staff requested clarification on several points, as a rigorous assessment of the risks involved proceeded up the chain to the secretary of defense and the White House. Late on 11 May, the Southern Command sent the Joint Chiefs a message that added a sense of urgency to the deliberations. The

---

lukewarm at best. Washington, he wrote, had to give the Organization of American States a chance, "if for no other reason than to make it clear, should force become necessary, that the United States had exhausted every peaceful, diplomatic alternative." Baker, *Politics of Diplomacy*, p. 183.

[10] Baker, *Politics of Diplomacy*, p. 183.

[11] For the preelection discussion of freedom of movement and armed convoys, see Chapter 5.

potential for "state-sponsored violence" against Americans in Panama, Woerner claimed, had increased as a result of the country's internal disturbances. The situation was unpredictable, and the possibility existed that elements of the Panama Defense Forces would take further actions to restrict U.S. movement, including the construction of additional traffic barriers like those set up during the election.[12]

The following night, Woerner received a message stating that the National Command Authority had authorized him to defend American citizens in Panama and to conduct freedom of movement operations "under the conditions set forth herein." In protecting Americans, he was instructed to use the "minimum degree of force necessary" and, then, only if a U.S. citizen was in danger of "serious bodily harm." American property by itself would not be defended, nor could U.S. troops use force to protect Americans from minor harassment or from Panamanian units performing legitimate activities, such as arresting an American for a misdemeanor or serious crime. As for freedom of movement activities, the message authorized the use of force, as a last resort, to remove barricades or other obstructions blocking access to U.S. defense facilities; it also covered procedures the driver of an unescorted official vehicle should follow if stopped illegally by Panamanian authorities.[13]

Accompanying the general directives governing freedom of movement operations was specific guidance that also stemmed from the preelection exchange of messages between the Southern Command and the Joint Staff. The focus was on the armed convoys, which would quickly become the centerpiece of the initiative to reassert U.S. treaty rights in Panama. On 5 May, Woerner had outlined for Crowe the procedures convoys (four or more official vehicles) with armed escorts would follow. A convoy commander would operate under peacetime rules of engagement and, if stopped by Panamanian authorities, would produce a bilingual card containing in Spanish and English the treaty clause that guaranteed official U.S. vehicles unimpeded movement in Panama. If a recitation of the legal text failed to have the desired effect, the convoy commander would notify his headquarters by radio and, five minutes after that, inform the Panamanian officials on the scene that any use of force to detain the convoy further would be considered a hostile act and would be countered with armed force. Having made this point, the commander would order the convoy to proceed. If necessary, U.S. vehicles would push aside any obstacles to their advancement. U.S. troops could also employ deadly force if they thought they were in "imminent danger of death or serious bodily harm." This last prospect caused Woerner to propose forming a quick reaction force (QRF) capable of being inserted by helicopter to reinforce armed convoy escorts facing truly dangerous situations. Ideally, there would be no need to deploy this force, as the Panamanian military, according to U.S. analysts, would back away from any confrontation that threatened to escalate into a firefight. Whatever the PDF reaction, the main point conveyed in Woerner's recommendation was that the convoy would not be detained or turned

---

[12] Joint Staff Action Processing Form, through DJS to CJCS, n.d. [prepared 12 May 89], sub: Assertion of US Treaty Rights in Panama; Woerner Interv, 30 Apr 91. Quote from Msg, CINCSO to JCS/Joint Staff, 120250Z May 89, sub: Prudent Measures.

[13] Msg, CJCS to CINCSO, 122304Z May 89, sub: Procedures for US Assertion of Treaty Rights.

back; the United States would no longer tolerate PDF interference in the free movement of official U.S. vehicles.[14]

In notifying the Southern Command on 12 May of the NCA's authorization to conduct freedom of movement operations, Crowe's message reiterated the procedures Woerner had recommended for convoys, slightly modifying or emphasizing certain points. For example, while the general had mentioned the use of force in response to imminent threats, Crowe's reply made clear that this included not just "hostile actions" by the Panama Defense Forces, but "any demonstrations of hostile intent" as well. This amplification was balanced, however, by several cautionary notes. Only a convoy commander could declare "hostile intent" by the Panamanian military, and "only the minimum force necessary to counter any hostile act or hostile intent will be used." In a similar vein, a convoy commander faced with PDF resistance needed to determine "if the risks of proceeding are acceptable."[15]

In having Crowe convey these points to Woerner, the Bush administration was seeking to walk a difficult line between peace and war. The Pentagon was directing the Southern Command to assert U.S. treaty rights in an aggressive manner but not so aggressive as to start a war. The policy of toughness was calculated to put pressure on Noriega and the Panamanian armed forces, not to engage them in hostilities. This intent was driven home to Woerner in a secure phone conversation with Crowe in mid-May. As Woerner interpreted the exchange, he was to intimidate Noriega, show resolve in dealing with the Panama Defense Forces, and act tough. "But," Crowe told him emphatically, "understand that you are to do nothing provocative." To an outsider, such advice might have appeared ambiguous, even contradictory. Woerner was not an outsider but a veteran of the crisis. "The worst part about it," he later recalled, referring to the chairman's directive, "is I understood perfectly." The avoidance of armed conflict, he said, "was the operative guideline throughout my entire tenure."[16]

Upon receiving Washington's modifications of the convoy guidelines, Woerner passed them along to JTF-Panama and gave General Loeffke the mission to take responsibility for all convoy operations, to incorporate convoy procedures into a joint standard operating procedure (SOP), to establish secure communications for all aspects of the convoy movement, and to handle various other related details. With these taskings also came a set of CINCSO "implementing instructions." All convoys would be escorted by an armed security element, and the troops involved would "display a combat ready posture" and would not "place themselves at a tactical disadvantage." An air-ground reaction force would be on alert during convoy movements, with secure communications established between the convoy and the elements of that force. Convoy commanders who could not speak Spanish had to have an interpreter with them; they were also authorized to use force and, should they deem necessary, call in the reinforcements standing by. To ensure that the U.S.

---

[14] Msg, USSOUTHCOM to SSO DIA, 050209Z May 89, sub: Procedures for US Assertion of Treaty Rights.

[15] Msg, CJSC to CINCSO, 122304Z May 89, sub: Procedures for US Assertion of Treaty Rights.

[16] Crowe's quote is from Woodward, *The Commanders*, p. 92. The Woerner quotes are from Interv, General Frederick F. Woerner Jr., U.S. Army (Ret.), U.S. Army Military History Institute, Carlisle Barracks, Pa.

personnel involved understood the authorized procedures and had the opportunity to practice them, JTF-Panama was to conduct rehearsals involving all members of a convoy's security element and the reaction force supporting it. In accordance with treaty obligations, JTF-Panama, acting through the Combined Board, would also coordinate convoy movements with the Panama Defense Forces.[17]

There were several staff officers at JTF-Panama who reacted to the convoy directive with some perplexity. Not having been privy to the high-level policy discussions that preceded and followed the Panamanian elections, they questioned what the Bush administration hoped to achieve by the use of armed convoy escorts. Was the president trying to provoke a fight? To some, the obvious (albeit erroneous) answer was yes. Others, Colonel Cope among them, simply conceded that they did not know. All that was apparent was that Washington had deployed additional military assets to Panama. Was there a plan to use them? If there was a method to the madness, Cope confessed, it was not discernible to the staff at Fort Clayton. There were some officers, he indicated, presumably of a traditionalist bent, who had difficulty understanding Bush's apparent intention of using U.S. troops in Panama to convey strictly political signals to the Noriega regime. There were also some officers who, believing that the PDF's interference with official U.S. vehicles in the past had not been as extensive as the Southern Command was telling the Joint Staff, expressed the opinion that the more assertive convoy measures were provocative and unwarranted.[18]

Partly in response to Woerner's directive on the convoys and partly to rationalize and coordinate planning on a variety of issues that fell between daily operations and long-term projections, Cope set up the Operations Planning Group (OPG) within his office. To head up the effort, he once again tapped Maj. Dan Augustine, who after departing for the Command and General Staff College at Fort Leavenworth, was replaced by Lt. Col. Michael Menser, the U.S. Army Training and Doctrine Command's liaison officer to U.S. Army, South. Working with Menser on a variety of tasks, including procedures for freedom of movement operations, were Maj. Mark C. Collier and two national guardsmen.[19]

During intense planning sessions over the course of several days, Cope's people worked closely with the SOUTHCOM Operations Directorate in refining convoy preparations and procedures. As in the past, the interaction was not free from friction. There were still officers at Quarry Heights who did not have full confidence in USARSO's ability to handle major initiatives in the crisis. Consequently, Cisneros and his new vice director, Marine Col. Thomas A. Braaten, provided Cope's people with highly detailed guidance. This degree of oversight was not entirely appreciated at Fort Clayton, where Loeffke informed his staff and component commanders that JTF-Panama, not SOUTHCOM, had responsibility for tactical matters and that Cope could convey that message to Cisneros' people.

---

[17] Memo, General Fred F. Woerner for CDR, JTF-Panama, et al., 15 May 89, sub: Procedures for US Assertion of Treaty Rights.

[18] Intervs, author with Col John A. Cope Jr., U.S. Army, 25 May 89, Fort Clayton, Panama; Maj Dan Augustine, U.S. Army, 7 Jun 89, Fort Clayton, Panama, and 11 May 90, Fort Leavenworth, Kans.; Conversation, author with Maj Chuck Herrick, USARSO SGS, Summer 1989, Fort Clayton, Panama.

[19] Intervs, author with Augustine, 7 Jun 89; Maj Mark C. Collier, U.S. Army, 20 Jun 89, Fort Clayton, Panama, and 24 Jan 90, Fort Clayton, Panama.

In this spirit, members of the Operations Planning Group occasionally "blew off" what they considered to be inappropriate or unwarranted guidance from a unified command bent on micromanagement.[20]

Most of the guidance from Woerner's staff, of course, could not be readily dismissed. Loeffke, for example, had strong reservations about having armed U.S. troops escort convoys that, under the treaties, would have PDF escorts as well, but he could not ignore the SOUTHCOM directive calling for every convoy to have "at least one armed vehicle."[21] Menser and Collier thus hammered out a JTF-Panama operation order for the convoys that addressed such critical issues as the composition of the convoy and the weapons to be carried by the escorting troops, the rank of the officer who as commander of the armed security element would also be in charge of the convoy, the specific rules of engagement that would be in effect, the precise steps to take in the event of a confrontation, the communications setup, and the makeup of the quick reaction force. As planning proceeded, additional concerns surfaced. Cisneros, for example, wanted the operation order to address the treatment of wounded soldiers in the event of a firefight; there was also the question of what U.S. troops should do with any PDF personnel who had to be disarmed and detained. As the Operations Planning Group grappled with these issues, time became a precious commodity. Initial indications were that convoy operations would begin right after the OAS delegation left Panama, although Crowe informed Woerner that there would be no armed convoys before 18 May, itself a date that was approaching quickly.[22]

Initial guidance passed from the Joint Chiefs of Staff through the Southern Command called for a field grade officer to be in command of a convoy. That would have meant stripping staff personnel from the various headquarters involved, so JTF-Panama recommended, successfully, that a captain would suffice. Each convoy would contain MP vehicles, while a beefed-up infantry squad would serve as the armed security escort. The only visible weapons would be M60 machine guns on selected HMMWVs; ammunition belts for the M60s would be within reach of the gunners but not fed into the weapon. Any convoy commander delayed by the Panama Defense Forces would report the situation up the chain of command. Once given permission by higher headquarters to proceed—Woerner being the "decision authority" in "confrontational situations"—the convoy commander would notify the ranking Panamanian officer on the scene that the vehicles would proceed in five minutes.

Since Woerner's guidance called for a quick reaction force composed of an infantry platoon to be on "immediate response" alert in case a convoy needed assistance, JTF-Panama arranged for the required troops, together with the air and ground assets needed to transport and protect them. As part of that protection, a light helicopter gun team from USARSO's 1st Battalion, 228th Aviation, was made available to provide air cover for the quick reaction platoon, while Marine Forces-Panama was directed to station two light armored vehicles with the unit. The marines balked. From what they had heard, the evolving operation order would

---

[20] Quote from Augustine Interv, 7 Jun 89. Author's notes, JTF-Panama Update Meeting, 22 May 89, Fort Clayton, Panama.

[21] Interv, author with Maj Gen Bernard Loeffke, U.S. Army, 31 May 89, Fort Clayton, Panama. Quote from Msg, Woerner to CDR, JTF-Panama, 15 May 89.

[22] Theresa L. Kraus, Working Chronology for Operation JUST CAUSE.

end up requiring two convoys with armed escorts to be launched simultaneously, one from Fort Davis on the Atlantic side of the canal area, the other from Fort Clayton, on the Pacific side. Since each convoy would have a quick reaction platoon standing by, two of the amphibious vehicles would essentially be lost to Task Force Atlantic. Arguing that deploying these two assets across the isthmus without an LAI command and control element was ill advised, the MARFOR staff suggested that the vehicles in question be kept at Rodman, where, in the event of an emergency, they could be attached temporarily to other units for specific missions anywhere in Panama. JTF-Panama acquiesced. The LAVs would be available only to the quick reaction force on the Pacific side; the comparable force up north would have to use HMMWVs.[23]

If the marines seemed less than cooperative in supporting specific QRF requirements, the Air Force appeared eager to participate to the fullest in the freedom of movement exercises. Recognizing an opportunity to provide air crews some practical experience, Brig. Gen. Robin Tornow, JTF-Panama's newly promoted deputy and AFFOR commander, lobbied for a full "air cap" over the convoys. Loeffke evinced no enthusiasm for the proposal, but as a staunch advocate of joint cooperation, he made no concerted effort to oppose it. This created some difficult moments for planners in the Operations Planning Group. As they incorporated air support into the JTF-Panama operation order, AFFOR headquarters insisted on receiving 24-hours' advance notice as to which of its assets JTF-Panama would require for each daily convoy. When the planners informed the Air Force liaison officer to JTF-Panama that they could not guarantee the 24-hours' notification, the liaison's response was brusque: "Well, then we can't play." Tornow soon intervened to break the impasse, informing the officer in question that the 24-hour heads up was simply desirable, not essential. That issue aside, the arrangement with the Air Force called for each convoy to have four layers of air cover: from the bottom level up, the air armada consisted of OH–58 Kiowas, AH–1 Cobras, OA–37 Dragonflys, and A–10 Warthogs.[24]

While OPG planners worked on the convoy plan, Colonels Hale and Bolt prepared their troops to execute it. Hale's headquarters would be in charge of convoys leaving and arriving at Fort Sherman; Bolt's 193d Infantry Brigade would oversee those leaving and arriving at Fort Clayton. The transfer of responsibility from departing to arriving convoys would occur approximately at the midway point along the transisthmian highway connecting the Atlantic and Pacific sides of the country.

The troops assigned to accompany the convoys had to be well versed in the rules of engagement, a term not that familiar to many of the newly arrived platoon leaders and company commanders. From their perspective at the tactical level, the general ROE guidelines on the use of deadly force issued by the Joint Chiefs and the Southern Command raised countless questions as to how such guidance might be applied in a myriad of specific circumstances. What, for example, if PDF elements attempting to block a convoy had an "extended" (that is, ready to fire) Rocket-Propelled Grenade18 on the scene? Did the presence of that weapon alone

---

[23] Third set of quoted words from Msg, Woerner to CDR, JTF-Panama, 15 May 89. Memo, MARFOR, Panama, 17 May 89, sub: Employment of LAI; OPLAN XX–89; Notes accompanying briefing slides, n.d. First two sets of quoted words from FRAGO, 211800R May 89.

[24] Interv, author with Loeffke, 31 May 89. Quote from Interv, author with Collier, 20 Jun 89.

constitute hostile intent? Or did convoy security troops need to make allowances for the fact that the RPG18 was not collapsible (unlike its U.S. counterpart) and was thus always in a configuration from which it could be fired? Concerning this and other possible scenarios, there were no definitive answers, just an admonition to convoy leaders to be very careful and not to invoke deadly force without being sure it was necessary.[25]

Peacetime rules of engagement, as a JCS working paper dealing with the situation in Panama explained, did not require U.S. commanders faced with hostile intent "to take the first hit" before using force in self-defense. A commander's overriding responsibility had to be the safety of the troops, even if that entailed their being the first to open fire. Meant to be reassuring, this fundamental affirmation was greeted with skepticism by some officers in Panama. The United States was not at war, and there were limits to the precautions one could take in a politically sensitive crisis without appearing provocative, even when dealing with a clearly hostile adversary. Hale, for one, doubted that the rules of engagement would really allow U.S. troops, if threatened, to be in a position to fire the first shot, a point on which he conceded he was not always candid with his subordinates. As it turned out, he did not have to be. Several of his staff and company grade officers (as well as staff officers at Fort Clayton) had come to the same conclusion, expressing concerns that the rules of engagement for convoy operations were too general, too vague, and too difficult to apply in the "gray areas" of the Twilight Zone. In any confrontation, they feared, the Panamanian military might hold the initiative on the use of force, thus putting U.S. troops at a temporary, perhaps fatal, disadvantage. These misgivings, while discussed regularly by the officers involved, were not as a rule transmitted to the troops for fear of having a negative impact on morale.[26]

However worrisome their concerns surrounding convoy rules of engagement, ranking U.S. officers in Panama considered the PDF's use of deadly force at the outset of a confrontation highly unlikely. That being the case, the focus on ROE-related issues shifted to the initial actions convoy commanders would take in the event the Panamanian forces tried to obstruct a convoy's freedom of movement. The Joint Chiefs and the Southern Command had dictated the first step: the commander would dismount, approach the senior PDF officer on the scene, and read to him in English and Spanish the treaty clauses stating the U.S. military's right to conduct unimpeded convoy operations. Higher headquarters had also dictated the final step: the vehicles would proceed if the convoy commander deemed the risks of doing so acceptable. What steps the commander might take in between, short of deadly force, was largely a question for JTF-Panama to answer.

During planning sessions on each side of the canal area, officers considered possible options. Legal issues loomed large in the deliberations, as U.S. officials had emphasized that none of the actions contemplated should violate the canal treaties or other applicable laws. For this reason, Hale found himself (as did other commanders) relying as much or more on his staff judge advocate for advice as on his operations officer. After long days and late hours, JTF-Panama produced

---

[25] Interv, author with Maj Harry Tunnell, U.S. Army, 13 May 98, Fort Leavenworth, Kans.

[26] Atch. to Working Paper, JCS, n.d. [some pages of Working Paper stamped 11 May 89], sub: ROE for Panama, JCS Papers, CARL. Intervs, author with Augustine, 13 Jun 89, and 11 May 90, Fort Clayton, Panama; and Tunnell, 13 May 98. Discussion notes, author with Col David R. E. Hale, 28 Sep 89, Low-Intensity-Conflict Proponency Office, Fort Leavenworth, Kans.

a menu of measures from which a convoy commander could construct a course of action in the event of a confrontation. Some officers called these options "escalation standards"; Hale termed them *rules of confrontation* (ROC). Whatever the terminology, the goal was to attain such tactical superiority on the scene that any Panamanian force present would not wish to initiate hostilities. Repeatedly briefed and rehearsed, the rules of confrontation included such actions as dismounting the security platoon or squad from its vehicles; having the troops fix bayonets, lock and load, or "go to a knee" in a shooting position; firing illumination rounds from artillery in the rear; and giving concealed or open signals to the sniper or sniper team accompanying each convoy. (A sniper's assignment, in most cases, was to protect the convoy commander. This generally meant being prepared to target the senior PDF officer present. For the convoy commander, this meant learning the "first rule of confrontation": "Never block the sniper.")[27]

If those company grade officers who were about to serve as convoy commanders worried that the rules of engagement might rob them of the initiative in a confrontation, or that the rules of confrontation might escalate to the use of deadly force, they could take some small comfort in the aforementioned consensus surrounding PDF intentions. A JTF-Panama intelligence summary issued on the eve of the freedom of movement operations contended that the Panama Defense Forces might set up obstacles to block the convoys but, having interfered with a column's movement, would probably let the vehicles proceed, then formally protest the U.S. operation and try to exploit it for propaganda. The least likely scenario, according to the report, was any use of force by the adversary. Reports from the Southern Command echoed this assessment. Wary of American firepower and desirous of presenting a "low profile" during the imminent visit of the OAS delegation, the top PDF leadership, analysts indicated, had instructed subordinate commanders to avoid a confrontation with U.S. forces. The SOUTHCOM Intelligence (J–2) shop thus considered military conflict over the convoys unlikely, unless a PDF "hot head" ignored his instructions, or a PDF officer, lacking adequate direction in advance, made a "snap decision" or concluded that his orders required him to stop the convoy.[28] The report did not raise the possibility that, under certain circumstances, U.S. forces themselves might overreact or take some ill-conceived action that would precipitate a firefight.

By Thursday, 18 May, JTF-Panama stood poised to launch the convoy operations, only to be informed that Washington had put the undertaking on hold until the following Monday. The temporary delay afforded Loeffke the opportunity he needed to test the communications network that would facilitate command and control during the convoys. Given the sensitive nature of the freedom of movement mission and the potential, however slight, for conflict with uniformed Panamanians, the ability of the convoy commanders and higher headquarters to communicate

---

[27] Rules of confrontation quotes from Interv, author with Tunnell, 13 May 98. Interv, author with Hale, 16 Jun 89, Fort Clayton, Panama; Discussion notes, author with Hale, 28 Sep 89; Briefing, Col Hale to TRADOC Warfighter X Seminar, Sep 89, Fort Leavenworth, Kans.

[28] Msg, COMJTF-Panama to AIG 9029 et al., 212230Z May 89, sub: Panama Intsum 063-89U. Quoted words from Msg, CINCSO to AIG 7084, 230220Z May 89, sub: Freedom of Movement. Added to the concerns about an incident starting a firefight undesired by either side, Colonel Cope also raised the question of "how long the PDF are going to allow themselves to be provoked." Cope Interv, 25 May 89.

with one another at all times once the vehicles had made their scheduled departures was essential. Prior to the eighteenth, individual vehicles had reconnoitered the proposed route, setting up retransmission facilities and identifying communication "disconnects" and "blind spots." What Loeffke now authorized for Saturday, 20 May, was a major rehearsal, in which Bolt and Hale would each send out three vehicles containing a command and control element, an MP liaison, and a tactical air control party. This last element meant that the rehearsal would also include USARSO and AFFOR-Panama air assets.[29]

The rehearsal convoys moved out from Forts Clayton and Davis at 0800 Saturday. In the course of the round trip over the transisthmian highway, each ran into the Panama Defense Forces. In the case of the 193d vehicles from Fort Clayton, a PDF officer at one checkpoint attempted to break up the convoy over the objections of the convoy commander, who recited the applicable U.S. treaty rights. The legal niceties were lost on the Panamanian officer, but the impressive air armada of OA–37s and A–10s above the convoy was not. After a glance skyward, he allowed the vehicles to proceed.[30]

The rehearsal convoy from Fort Davis faced a potentially more dangerous situation. Before the vehicles departed, Task Force Atlantic insisted that a uniformed military policeman from the 7th Infantry Division ride in the lead vehicle, displacing to another vehicle a USARSO liaison MP dressed in civilian clothes. Once under way, the convoy stopped at a PDF checkpoint located at a fork in the road. There, the substitute military policeman, perhaps following directions from the Panamanians manning the checkpoint, made a wrong turn onto a route that led to a PDF encampment. The men in the camp were not expecting combat-clad soldiers with air cover; the 7th Division personnel, for their part, assumed that the PDF members were trying to stop the convoy. A tense situation quickly developed, defused only after the USARSO MP moved to the forefront and, in the course of some intense conversation, managed to calm down both sides. The incident failed to be included in the formal reports on the rehearsal, but all involved were aware of its occurrence and the dangers that it raised. One officer stated what others were thinking: this was the sort of inadvertent incident that could trigger a fight.[31] It had been another potential flash point, just two days after the one at Fort Espinar.

The results of the rehearsal were disappointing in other respects. At times, the dense rain forest on each side of the winding highway prohibited contact with the convoy via ground communications. The helicopters flying air cover were supposed to have radio contact with the vehicles, but one OH–58 launched by the 228th Aviation was equipped with a malfunctioning radio. The identification of the convoys as *yours*, *theirs*, and *ours* instead of using call signs added to the confusion, especially after command and control arrangements changed at the midway point. In another glitch, JTF-Panama personnel manning the operations center at Fort Clayton found they did not know how to call Task Force Atlantic. They also experienced difficulties with the equipment they were using, and when

---

[29] Orders for the communication rehearsal are from Draft FRAGO to OPLAN 2–89, 191200R May 89.

[30] Collier Interv, 20 Jun 89.

[31] Intervs, author with Maj Jeff Karhohs, U.S. Army, 8 Mar 90, Fort Leavenworth, Kans.; Collier, 20 Jun 89; and Loeffke, 31 May 89. Conversation, author with Lt Col Mike Menser, U.S. Army, 26 May 89, Fort Clayton, Panama.

they switched to tactical satellite (TACSAT) communications for backup, the system failed, at first because of bad batteries—"Changing batteries before an operation is usually a better idea than changing them during it," someone observed afterwards—and then again for reasons unknown. There were also numerous communication difficulties associated with aviation activities during the first leg of the rehearsal, although some of these problems were worked out before each convoy made its return trip. All told, the rehearsal had been a sobering experience. On the eve of the first major freedom of movement operation, the communications essential for effective command and control were deemed "poor to terrible."[32]

During much of the 20 May rehearsal, Cope and Menser were at Quarry Heights where, at the SOUTHCOM J–3's request, they were attempting to hammer out the final details of the convoy plan. While there, they received further indications that the first convoy operation would, in fact, leave that Monday, 22 May, one day before the OAS delegation was scheduled to arrive in Panama. After midnight, the two men returned to Fort Clayton and, Sunday morning, briefed the plan to Loeffke. The JTF-Panama commander, still unconvinced of the need to have an armed escort for the convoys, made a number of changes, then went to brief General Woerner. The plan Loeffke presented, JTF-Panama OPLAN 2–89, had taken over a week to write. It had undergone several revisions and had been coordinated with key personnel, including several military and civilian lawyers. The convoys were to be the showpiece of the effort to reassert U.S. treaty rights in Panama, and the proposed operations bore within them some potential for a violent confrontation with the Panama Defense Forces. Thus, when Woerner blessed the plan Sunday afternoon, Menser, who was present, likened the emotion of the moment to what a roomful of Allied officers in World War II must have experienced when they heard Eisenhower's famous "Go!" order for the 1944 D-Day invasion.[33]

The SOUTHCOM commander's approval of the operation plan may indeed have marked the emotional crescendo in the flurry of activity surrounding the proposed convoys. As events transpired, the initial execution of the freedom of movement operations proved, for the most part, anticlimactic. Two convoys assembled Monday morning, eleven vehicles at Fort Clayton, ten at Fort Davis. As called for in the canal treaties, the Panama Defense Forces received advance notification of the movement, twenty-four hours to be exact, as precedence, not law, dictated. When a PDF officer at Fort Clayton tried to delay departure of the convoy until the official escort (and television cameras) arrived, Loeffke waited an additional five minutes, then ordered Colonel Bolt to proceed. The Panamanian officer placed his hand on his holster but made no further threatening gestures. At 0905 the vehicles departed, leaving the tardy PDF escort to catch up. Neither convoy experienced any serious interference with its movement, and both arrived

---

[32] Draft memo, Lt Col Michael Menser for Col Cope, n.d., sub: Convoy COMMEX After Action Report. After convoy operations had been under way for several days, Cope conceded that there would always be communication problems. Partly in response to this issue, Loeffke would insist that many of the exercises run by JTF-Panama seek to "saturate the comms" in an effort to work out the glitches and to familiarize company grade officers with the equipment and procedures. Author's notes, JTF-Panama Update Meetings, 24 May, 6 and 9 Jun 89.

[33] Paper, Assertion of Treaty Rights Convoy 20 May, n.d.; Loeffke Interv, 31 May 89; Briefing slides [for convoy briefing on Sunday, 21 May 89], n.d. Author's notes written on the slides refer to weekend planning efforts and Menser's recalling Eisenhower's "Go!" order.

at their destinations pretty much on schedule. Throughout the operation, the Panamanian officers involved seemed confused although they did manage to film the convoys on videocassette. Late Monday JTF-Panama prepared two more convoys for departure the next day.[34]

The second day's operation also went without incident. Loeffke joined the convoy from Fort Clayton and experienced firsthand some of the communication problems that had yet to be resolved. Later that afternoon, he presided over the JTF-Panama daily meeting, where he informed the assembled staff officers and component commanders that General Woerner wanted to reduce the size of the convoys while increasing the number of daily runs. Cisneros had further indicated that the advance notification of convoy operations given the Panamanian military should be reduced from twenty-four hours to one hour. Loeffke then raised a third issue that was beginning to cause some uneasiness: the convoys were expensive to run, especially in terms of the fuel and maintenance required by the dedicated aviation assets. One way of lowering the costs, he suggested, might be to keep the Cobra helicopters on the ground at Howard, unless needed.[35]

At this point, Woerner joined the meeting. He confirmed the need for adjustments, declaring that he wanted to vary the pattern of convoy operations to put "pressure on the PDF so they can't keep up with *our* movements." The time had come, he said, "to harass *them*." In this context, he approved reducing the advance notification given through the Combined Board to one hour (later changed to two hours) and told Loeffke to decrease the number of vehicles per convoy. He declined to dictate the number of convoys JTF-Panama should run each day but reiterated that U.S. actions should not be predictable. Given this guidance, Loeffke directed the assembled officers to split each of the two large convoys scheduled for Wednesday into smaller groups. Staff officers in his operations shop were chagrined, in that the fragmentary order for Wednesday's convoys had already been disseminated. But with some frantic work and phone calls, the adjustments Woerner wanted went into effect the next day.[36]

---

[34] Loeffke Interv, 31 May 89; Msgs, CINCSO to Joint Staff, 22057Z May 89, sub: OPREP-3/ USCINCSO PM/038/May, and CINCSO to JCS, 230330Z May 89, sub: Panama Situation Update/ SCJ3/028/May; FRAGO, 231600R May 89 [for 23 May convoys].

[35] Author's notes, JTF-Panama Update Meeting, 23 May 89. On the issue of notifying the Panama Defense Forces about convoy movements, the canal treaties merely stipulated that the United States had to provide such notification. Informing the Panamanian military through the Combined Board 24 hours in advance was the result of precedent, not law. Reducing that time to one or two hours did not violate any legal aspects of the treaties. Also, withholding information on the purpose of the convoys and the contents of the vehicles, another ploy adopted during freedom of movement operations, was legal as well. Once convoy operations got under way, a movement control center took over the task of notifying the PDF two hours in advance. The procedure was cumbersome enough that word apparently did not always reach the other side until right before the convoys were set to move out. Author's notes, JTF-Panama CAT change of shift briefing, 31 May 89.

[36] Quotes from Author's notes, JTF-Panama Update Meeting, 23 May 89. The disgruntlement of the JTF-Panama staff officers affected by Woerner's directives was conveyed to the author in the days following the meeting. Some of the staff expressed the view that, at the update, Loeffke or someone else from JTF-Panama should have informed the SOUTHCOM commander that the fragmentary order for the next day's convoys was already in the field and that there would be less disruption if the adjustments were to go into effect Thursday instead of Wednesday. In another matter relating to changing the pattern of convoy operations, JTF-Panama reconsidered running simultaneous convoys from Fort Clayton and Fort Davis. At least one battalion commander taking part in the operations was

Over the weeks and months to come, convoy operations became routine, with Loeffke extolling the excellent training they provided lieutenants and captains.[37] In keeping with Woerner's directive, JTF-Panama varied the number of convoys from day to day. The composition of the air umbrella also changed frequently in response to ongoing concerns over aviation maintenance, fuel expenditure, and air space congestion. The Panamanian regime denounced the convoys as a prelude to an American invasion but made no credible threat of retaliation. Once U.S. officials were satisfied that, as their intelligence reports had predicted, the Panama Defense Forces would not confront or seriously interfere with the convoy operations, Woerner delegated to Loeffke the authority to approve the use of deadly force by the armed escorts, should it be needed, a responsibility Loeffke said he would exercise "gingerly."[38]

"SLIDING INTO SOMETHING"

The convoys with armed escorts were never meant to be the only military means by which the United States sought to reassert its rights under the canal treaties. At the same time the Southern Command and JTF-Panama were planning the convoy operations, Woerner was considering a number of "supporting efforts" that could "be implemented simultaneously with or prior to [freedom of movement] actions."[39] Just hours after Admiral Crowe gave him the green light for the convoys, the SOUTHCOM commander informed the Joint Chiefs that he and his staff were reviewing a variety of operations in keeping with the National Command Authority's guidance. The review turned into a continuous process, with Woerner evaluating recommendations, then informing JTF-Panama and the Joint Staff of those measures receiving his approval.[40]

The purpose of the supporting efforts, or "collateral operations," as Woerner called them, was not just the assertion of U.S. treaty rights. In keeping with the broader aims of the administration's tougher policy, Woerner also sought to heighten PDF concerns regarding U.S. military intentions, to strain PDF resources,

---

relieved, noting that, when simultaneous convoys heading toward one another reached the criss-cross point, the risk of friendly fire incidents increased dramatically. Interv, author with Lt Col William Huff III, U.S. Army, 29 Jan 90, Fort Clayton, Panama.

[37] Author's notes, JTF-Panama Update Meeting, 22 May 89.

[38] Author's notes, JTF-Panama Update Meeting, 26 May 89.

[39] Paper, SOUTHCOM J–3, Supporting Efforts for Freedom of Movement (FOM) Actions, 15 May 89. One of the "supporting efforts" implemented prior to the convoys was the insertion of Company B, 2d Battalion, 9th Infantry, 7th Infantry Division (Light), into Fort Espinar on 18 May. See Chapter 6. That move had been ordered, in part, to reassert "the right of the United States Government to house its force in areas of military coordination." See Memo for Occupants of Fort Espinar Government Quarters, 18 May 89, sub: American Troop Presence. The memorandum, signed by Colonel Hale and Lt. Col. Robert Henry, assured residents of Fort Espinar that the arrival of the 7th Infantry Division troops was not meant to be "provocative" or "confrontational."

[40] Paper, SOUTHCOM J–3, Supporting Efforts for Freedom of Movement (FOM) Actions, 15 May 89; Msgs, CJCS to CINCSO, 201833Z May 89, sub: Assertion of Treaty Rights, and CINCSO to JCS, 210420Z May 89, sub: Panama Situation Update/SCJ–3/026/May; Memo for CINCSO, 21 May 89, sub: Assertion of US Forces Treaty Rights; Msg, CINCSO to JCS, 230330Z May 89, sub: Panama Situation Update/SCJ–3/028/May; Memo, Brig Gen Marc A. Cisneros, Dir, SOUTHCOM J–3, for COMJTF-Panama; CDR, SOCSO, 24 May 89, sub: Measures to Support Freedom of Movement Operation; Msgs, CINCSO to JCS, 260415Z May 89, sub: Panama Situation Update/SCJ–3/031/May, and CINCSO to CJCS, 301426Z May 89, sub: Asserting Treaty Rights.

Howard Air Force Base, *with hangars and runway in the background*

and to increase the readiness of U.S. forces in Panama to execute contingency plans. By the end of May, these collateral measures constituted a wide range of activity and included, in general terms, conducting route reconnaissance and amphibious exercises using the Marines' light armored vehicles, executing high visibility Air Force maneuvers and air and amphibious assault operations, restricting PDF movement on U.S. defense sites, increasing MP patrols between these sites and military areas of coordination, openly rehearsing the extraction of key U.S. leaders from various locations, establishing artillery and mortar-firing positions on defense sites, and practicing artillery "raids." JTF-Panama and the Special Operations Command, South, also received a SOUTHCOM directive to develop deception plans that would accustom the Panama Defense Forces to seeing American forces operating in the vicinity of what U.S. planners knew to be BLUE SPOON targets and that would create in the mind of the PDF the perception that any attack on convoy movements or American citizens would "trigger immediate military intervention."[41]

Of the specific measures on Woerner's list of collateral operations for JTF-Panama to carry out, PROUD WARRIOR, an amphibious assault exercise around Howard Air Force Base, was one of the first. Executed on 23 May, it coincided with the second day of the convoy operations and involved 150 men, 4 LCM–8s, 2 patrol boats, 2 A–10s, and 5 UH–60s. Three days later, another "high visibility exercise," DEVIL I, put an MP quick reaction force into Fort Amador, then brought in another QRF by air to relieve the first. The same exercise also saw a company

---

[41] Msgs, CJCS to CINCSO, 201833Z May 89, sub: Assertion of Treaty Rights; CINCSO to JCS, 210420Z May 89, sub: Panama Situation Update/SCJ–3/026/May; CINCSO to JCS, 230330Z May 89, sub: Panama Situation Update/SCJ–3/028/May; and CINCSO to JCS, 260415Z May 89, sub: Panama Situation Update/SCJ–3/031/May. First quote from Msg, CINCSO to CJCS, 301426Z May 89, sub: Asserting Treaty Rights. Second quote from Msg, CINCSO to JTF-PM, 150753Z May 89, sub: ELOQUENT FURY Support to Ongoing Operations.

from the 1st Battalion, 508th Infantry, conduct an air assault to secure a Directorate of Engineering and Housing compound at Corozal. In early June, the 7th Infantry Division conducted PURPLE STRIKE, followed a week later by a major exercise, LIGHTNING THRUST I, involving the 193d Infantry Brigade and various units under its operational control or attached to it.[42]

Loeffke regarded these collateral activities as he did the convoys. On the one hand, they offered yet another opportunity to conduct joint training, exercises, and operations. Having U.S. service components working so closely together in Panama, he explained in a memo to Army Chief of Staff General Carl Vuono, enabled JTF-Panama to execute at least one joint operation a week and to review daily training schedules to see what could be accomplished jointly. On the other hand, Loeffke knew, collateral measures carried the same risks as the convoys of an unwanted incident. At minimum, an exercise or operation could backfire, providing the Panamanian regime a "propaganda showpiece." This, in fact, had actually happened during an exercise in which JTF-Panama deployed an MP quick reaction force to Fort Amador. Within hours of its arrival, Noriega himself had shown up with an entourage. Approaching one of the military policemen, he shook hands and theatrically offered himself up for arrest. "Here I am," he taunted. Panamanian cameramen captured the moment on film, leaving Loeffke to comment on the dictator's "magnificent" handling of U.S. pressure. The USARSO commander also vowed to avoid that kind of embarrassment in future exercises.[43]

Of greater concern was the risk acknowledged by all of an unanticipated "trigger event" igniting hostilities. By late May, the mounting number of exercises under NIMROD DANCER was bringing U.S. troops into almost daily confrontation with the Panama Defense Forces. The atmosphere was highly charged, and while the initial passive response of the PDF was encouraging, it did not preclude the chance of a fatal mishap. At some point, Loeffke feared, someone would point a weapon at someone else, the act would be interpreted as hostile intent, and a firefight would ensue. Wondering aloud if events might be close to spiraling out of control, he inquired of one observer, "Do you get the feeling that we're sliding into something?"[44]

The "invasion" of Fort Espinar and the inelegant convoy rehearsal had, within days of each other, demonstrated how miscommunication and misperception could result in an unplanned and unwanted confrontation. Both of those flash points had been defused, but others soon followed, despite the stringent rules of engagement and rules of confrontation and frequent injunctions to the troops to "follow the script closely" and avoid unnecessary conflict. At one JTF-Panama update, Loeffke spoke, without providing specifics, of three incidents in three days that had almost

---

[42] Memo, Cisneros for COMJTF-Panama, and CDR, SOCSO, 24 May 89, sub: Measures to Support Freedom of Movement Operation. For PROUD WARRIOR, see Msgs, CINCSO to JCS, 240415Z May 89, sub: Panama Situation Update/SCJ–3/029/May, and CDR, USARSO, to HQDA, 242300Z May 89, sub: Sitrep/COMJTF-PM/010/May; Author's notes, JTF-Panama Update Meeting, 23 May 89. For DEVIL I and quote, see Msg, CINCSO to JCS, 260415Z May 89, sub: Panama Situation Update/SCJ–3/031/May. For LIGHTNING THRUST I, see Author's notes, JTF-Panama Update Meeting, 6 Jun 89; Time Line for LIGHTNING THRUST I.

[43] First quote from Msg, CDR, USARSO, to CSA, Jun 89 [011245Z], sub: Update No. 27, Panama Update, Operations. Second and third quotes from Loeffke Interv, 31 May 89. Author's notes, JTF-Panama Update Meeting, 26 May 89.

[44] Comment, Loeffke to author, 24 May 89, Fort Clayton, Panama.

led to armed conflict. He attributed the near misses to misinformation, citing the lesson internalized in two years of crisis, "The first report is always wrong." In confidential comments and communications, he went even further, voicing a conviction shared by many USARSO officers: the "augmentees"—meaning the marines, the mechanized troops, and the light fighters—would be the ones most likely to get involved in an incident. U.S. forces organic to Panama, he stated, knew "the layout." The security enhancement and NIMROD DANCER combat forces, in his opinion, did not have such a clear perspective or understanding of the crisis.[45]

Loeffke's uneasiness over U.S. combat units from outside Panama was implied in a memorandum he sent Woerner on 31 May. The memo provided a brief account of two episodes, each of which, according to Loeffke, had contained the potential for an "armed confrontation by mistake." He began by advising the SOUTHCOM commander that there "are many soldiers and Marines who are very aggressive and need to be calmed down." The soldiers to which he referred in the first case were from the 7th Infantry Division (Light). On a visit to the Task Force Atlantic company billeted at Fort Espinar, he had inspected a defensive position on the roof of the officers' club. There, he found "machine guns in place aimed at a PDF guard." Loeffke ordered the machine guns removed, but the next day a SOUTHCOM general officer (Loeffke did not say who) visited the position and was reported to have told those present, "If anyone points a weapon at you, blow him away." Loeffke, while diplomatically suggesting that the general in question might not actually have made the remark, cited the confusion evinced by some of Colonel Hale's officers who, in his opinion, already had a tendency for "reading into hostile intent more than what it is meant to be."[46]

The second episode recounted in the memo raised the same issue but in the context of an even more dangerous situation. On 30 May, as part of a joint exercise run by JTF-Panama, the marines "swam" six LAVs from Rodman to Fort Amador. Although part of the effort to assert U.S. treaty rights and keep the Panamanian military off-balance, the undertaking was supposed to be uneventful. The initial reports indicated that it had been. The PDF had received advance notification, and JTF-Panama had selected a "nonprovocative" route for the amphibious vehicles to follow. At the joint task force update meeting late that afternoon, Loeffke seemed in good spirits. The Panama Defense Forces at Fort Amador had been having a "family day" (picnics instead of paychecks, according to U.S. intelligence), and Loeffke humorously noted, "We brought in LAVs to give them rides."[47] He obviously believed at that point that the exercise had been a success.

Toward the end of the meeting, however, Rear Adm. Gerald E. Gneckow, the JTF's NAVFOR commander (and SOUTHCOM's Navy component commander), requested that the principal participants stay after adjournment to discuss what he described vaguely as some concerns he had with the freedom of movement activities. What he was alluding to were reports concerning the guidance the marines had allegedly received regarding rules of engagement for the LAV exercise. As all

---

[45] Quote on frequent injunctions to the troops from Author's notes, JTF-Panama Update Meeting, 9 Jun 89. "The layout" quote from Loeffke Interv, 31 May 89.

[46] Memo for CINCSO, 31 May 89, sub: Update No. 184, Possible Confrontation. See also Author's notes, JTF-Panama Update Meeting, 25 May 89.

[47] Loeffke's remarks are from Author's notes, JTF-Panama Update Meeting, 30 May 89. See also Memo for CINCSO, 31 May 89, sub: Update No. 184, Possible Confrontation.

involved knew, the PDF 5th Infantry Company at Amador had several Cadillac-Gage V–300 armored reconnaissance vehicles, each with a 90-mm. assault gun. Just before the LAVs departed Rodman, the Marine platoon leader in charge had purportedly told his men that if one of the assault guns were aimed at them, they could fire on the offending vehicle. As the MARFOR commander, Col. J. J. Doyle defended the guidelines he had himself disseminated, arguing that his men could fire if fired upon or if they detected hostile intent. Having a weapon pointed at them, he declared, constituted hostile intent.[48]

Loeffke relayed this information to Woerner in the 31 May memorandum. "I believe this kind of attitude has been fueled by a feeling that we need to look aggressive," he indicated. "Some officers misinterpret exercising our rights with being aggressive, to the point that we will start an exchange of fire when not needed." Loeffke reiterated this point in his concluding recommendation that "we talk softer among ourselves and troops for fear of encouraging an aggressive action that we may not want to occur."[49]

The rules of engagement controversy raised by the LAV exercise led Woerner to convene a meeting at Quarry Heights on 2 June. What transpired was a debate that Colonel Braaten, one of the senior marines present, characterized as "reasonably heated." Doyle held to the position that PDF weapons pointed at his men constituted hostile intent and thus justified the use of deadly force. Woerner demurred. Having a weapon aimed at you, he maintained, did not necessarily reveal the intent of the person behind it. The Panama Defense Forces, he continued, knew that firing on an LAV would be suicidal, inasmuch as all the other LAVs would return fire. The PDF also knew that a firefight could lead to major hostilities that Panamanian forces had no hope of winning. Loeffke echoed this cautious line. As he later explained, a V–300 crew would always turn the turret in your direction simply as an act of bravado. U.S. military police at Amador had had it happen to them, yet they had shown the appropriate restraint and not opened fire. Confronted with a similar situation, Loeffke believed, the marines needed to adopt a "conservative" approach. Doyle disagreed and continued to argue the case for hostile intent, the result being that the meeting turned into a "marathon" session. Each time the issue seemed settled, someone would ask, "Is that clear, MARFOR?" and the answer would be that it was not, thus setting off another round of discussion. But the outcome was foreordained. Woerner refused to budge. According to Braaten, "everyone was not particularly happy, but understood what the CINC was saying."[50]

---

[48] Author's notes, JTF-Panama Update Meeting, 30 May 89; Loeffke Interv, 31 May 89; Msg, CDR, MARFOR, to COMJTF-PM [personal, Doyle for Loeffke], 121502Z Jun 89, sub: Rules of Engagement (ROE) Concerning Operation at Fort Amador. One Marine officer later indicated that Loeffke had tried to get Doyle personally to brief the Amador exercise to the unit involved but that Doyle had stuck by the "Marine way" of doing things, which meant giving his commanders guidance, then entrusting them to adhere to it in carrying out an operation. Interv, author with Maj Rick L. Horvath, USMC, 14 Jun 89, Rodman Naval Station, Panama.

[49] Memo for CINCSO, 31 May 89, sub: Update No. 184, Possible Confrontation.

[50] All quotes except Loeffke's from Interv, author with Col Gar Thiry, USMC, and Col Tom Braaten, USMC, 12 Dec 89, Maxwell AFB, Ala. Loeffke quote from Interv, author with Loeffke, 31 May 89. Author's notes, JTF-Panama Update Meeting, 2 Jun 89; Conversation, author with Col John Cope Jr., 3 Jun 89, Fort Clayton, Panama; Msg, CDR, MARFOR, to COMJTF-PM, 121502Z Jun 89, sub: Rules of Engagement (ROE) Concerning Operation at Fort Amador.

One ramification emanating from the LAV episode was to highlight, once again, the near impossibility of reaching a consensus on rules of engagement that would protect troops in the field while minimizing chances that they might employ deadly force unnecessarily. ROE-related issues that had been discussed throughout the crisis, most recently during the convoy planning, now demanded further clarification in the aftermath of the Amador exercise. The process would be divisive, difficult, and generally unsuccessful. "The tendency is to reduce [the rules of engagement] to black and white instructions: 'Do this if the PDF does that,'" the USARSO staff judge advocate (SJA) reported to Cope. "This simplification," he warned, "can make the use of armed force the result of reflexible [sic] reaction, rather than the result of the exercise of judgment after having considered the overall circumstances surrounding the PDF's actions." Context was critical, the judge advocate's report elucidated. "What might be deemed a hostile act or a demonstration of hostile intent in one setting, might not necessarily be so in another. For example, a drawn weapon could be merely an act of bravado [the term Loeffke had employed] or the preparatory act to firing." In such a situation, how was a soldier or marine to gauge the other side's intent? How was he to comprehend the "overall circumstances surrounding the PDF's actions"? He would, in effect, have to rely on available intelligence on PDF intentions, the past performance of the Panama Defense Forces, comments made at the scene, and the size of the opposing forces present to determine the context for assessing the threat.[51]

The SJA's report, the meeting at the Southern Command, and other messages and discussions served to elucidate each side's views in the contentious ROE debate, but the basic issues in question remained unresolved. As had been the case throughout the crisis, questions of context would remain at the heart of the ongoing controversy, as key U.S. commanders and staff officers never reached complete accord on what circumstances constituted hostile intent. Ten days after Woerner's conclave, Colonel Doyle continued to argue that the guidance he had given his marines for the Fort Amador exercise was consonant with the rules of engagement disseminated by JTF-Panama, the SOUTHCOM commander, and the Joint Chiefs. He had urged that his men show restraint, but he had also let them know that they could defend themselves with force appropriate to the threat should a weapon be pointed at them with what they perceived as hostile intent.[52] This last point, of course, could rarely be ascertained with certainty and would, thus, remain a matter of contention, with one side insistent that an overt act should suffice as proof of one's intent, the other side equally adamant that assessing context and the motive behind the act was essential.

The clash of views over the rules of engagement in general and the Fort Amador exercise in particular further served to aggravate relations between the JTF-Panama headquarters and its Marine Forces component. While a productive working arrangement between the two elements had been fashioned during the course of a year, the friction and suspicions that had followed the Arraiján Tank Farm firefight in April 1988 never completely dissipated. Throughout the crisis, Loeffke and his staff continuously questioned the Marines' fire discipline and "warrior"

---

[51] Memo, Col Joseph W. Cornelison, U.S. Army, USARSO Staff Judge Advocate, for J–3, JTF-Panama, 1 Jun 89, sub: Rules of Engagement.

[52] Msg, CDR, MARFOR, to COMJTF-PM, 121502Z Jun 89, sub: Rules of Engagement (ROE) Concerning Operation at Fort Amador.

mind-set. Furthermore, just days prior to inserting the light armored vehicles into Fort Amador, there had been a heated exchange at a JTF-Panama meeting in which the Army staff accused the marines of safety violations in their handling of ammunition at the tank farm. The MARFOR representative vigorously denied the allegations and testily rejected an offer to have an Army "safety team" advise the marines on proper procedures.[53] This clash, followed by the LAV episode, simply reinforced the strong reservations Loeffke's staff harbored regarding the suitability of the marines, with their "Beirut mentality," for employment in a crisis that required restraint, judgment, and restrictive rules of engagement. The MARFOR commander, with equal conviction, defended the performance and professionalism of his marines, asserting emphatically, "We are not 'cowboys.'"[54]

While tempers flared over ROE guidance during the Fort Amador exercise, the fact remained that, despite what a platoon leader might have told his troops concerning hostile intent, the marines had not fired on the V–300 training its assault gun on them. Still, in the eyes of the Southern Command and JTF-Panama, this had been a close call, warranting further discussion and renewed efforts to keep future confrontations from spiraling out of control. The problem, recognized by all parties, was that, even if there had been consensus over what constituted appropriate rules of engagement, there was only so much that detailed planning, reliable intelligence, good judgment, and reasonable restraint could contribute in reducing the possibility of an armed clash. In a complex environment, the element of chance could always intrude on events, often with unwanted and undesirable consequences.

In mid-June, that irrepressible element asserted itself forcefully during the course of a freedom of movement convoy. As a way of documenting the convoys, some of the helicopters flying over the vehicles carried Defense Department cameramen. On the afternoon of 15 June, an OH–58 involved in filming a Task Force Atlantic convoy on its return trip from Albrook Air Station hit a wire and crashed near the Madden Dam power plant. The wreckage spilled out onto the transisthmian highway.

The first U.S. forces on the scene were in the convoy the helicopter had been tracking.[55] When they arrived, the crash was already beginning to attract a crowd of Panamanian civilians, most wanting to help. Leaving one squad behind to provide security for the vehicles, the convoy commander, Capt. Daniel Tarter, had the rifle platoon leader and the remaining squad accompany him to the crash site, where they found the bodies of the pilot, copilot, and defense cameraman. The squad then set up a perimeter to maintain the integrity of the site until the bodies could be removed. In the meantime, the crowd began to grow, weather conditions worsened, attempts to call in a helicopter to evacuate the bodies were hampered by poor communications,

---

[53] The exchange over whether safety violations were taking place occurred at the JTF-Panama meeting on 25 May 1989. Author's notes, JTF-Panama Update Meeting, 25 May 89.

[54] Msg, CDR, MARFOR, to COMJTF-PM, 121502Z Jun 89, sub: Rules of Engagement (ROE) Concerning Operation at Fort Amador.

[55] This account of events on the afternoon of the helicopter crash are based on Intervs, author with Karhohs, 8 Mar 90; Maj Reginald Sikes, U.S. Army, 7 May 99, Fort Leavenworth, Kans.; Col Robert Barefield, U.S. Army, 7 Nov 90, Fort Leavenworth, Kans.; and Reginald Sikes, Operation NIMROD DANCER: A Personal View of Lessons Learned (Paper, A645, U.S. Army Command and General Staff [CGSC], Fort Leavenworth, Kans., 15 Feb 98).

and the Panamanian news media and an armed PDF platoon arrived on the scene. The situation had the ingredients for one of the "worst-case scenarios" envisaged during the convoy planning: the intermingling of Panamanian civilians, U.S. troops, the media, and the Panamanian military under unanticipated circumstances.

The PDF officer leading the platoon stated that the wreckage was in Panamanian territory, thus giving the Panama Defense Forces jurisdiction over the site. Captain Tarter, acting on orders to secure the scene until the cause of the crash could be investigated, refused the PDF demand to take charge. A heated argument followed, with the PDF officer, at one point, ordering his men into the nearby jungle. As the armed Panamanians disappeared into the foliage, U.S. riflemen could hear the sound of AK47s being locked and loaded. In response, the convoy's security platoon leader had an M60 gunner lock and load his weapon and aim it at the jungle line. After a few minutes, the PDF soldiers reemerged and returned to the highway, their weapons slung over their shoulders. In the meantime, a U.S. helicopter arrived but experienced difficulties in removing the bodies, thus prolonging the standoff.

Once the bodies were flown out and a platoon(-) from Bravo Company, 5th Battalion, 87th Infantry, arrived to relieve the convoy's armed escort and to provide site security, the tension eased somewhat, but the episode was far from over. Until an investigation team from Fort Rucker, Alabama, could be brought in to examine the wreckage, U.S. troops had orders to keep any Panamanians at bay. Meanwhile, the regime-controlled media charged that the downed helicopter had flown dangerously low over a populated area. PDF officers also objected to the continued monitoring of the scene by U.S. military personnel, although just how far they would go to challenge the Americans' presence was unclear. When Loeffke inspected the wreckage the day after the crash, a PDF major he encountered appeared cooperative. The officer did request that the number of troops guarding the site be reduced so as not to give the impression of an "invasion." When Loeffke sardonically remarked, "Isn't that what you've been waiting for?" the PDF major replied, "That's for novels." A tone of accommodation, not confrontation, characterized the exchange. Loeffke, while not reducing the U.S. force, did order the men to wear soft caps instead of helmets, to remove magazines from their weapons, and to carry their rifles pointed downward.[56]

That night, the situation took a dramatic turn for the worse.[57] Around 2100, three PDF officers visited the site and insisted on taking over security duties. A U.S. guard refused. Shortly after midnight, a PDF contingent of thirty to forty-five armed men showed up, approximately twice the number of American soldiers present. The Panamanian troops brought wreckers with them and said they were going to cart the remains of the helicopter to Howard Air Force Base. Bravo Company's executive officer, a lieutenant, was the ranking U.S. officer at the

---

[56] Msgs, CINCSO to JCS, Jun 89, sub: Panama Situation Report No. 43, and CINCSO to JCS, 171900Z Jun 89, sub: No. 44; Author's notes, JTF- Panama and USARSO CAT change of shift briefing, 18 Jun 89. Quotes from Author's notes, JTF-Panama Update Meeting, 16 Jun 89. Interv, author with Lt Col William Huff III, U.S. Army, 29 Jan 90.

[57] This account of the confrontation at the crash site is based on Author's notes, JTF-Panama and USARSO CAT change of shift briefing, 17 Jun 89; MFR, Maj Gen Bernard Loeffke, 17 Jun 89, sub: Crisis at Helo Crash Site; Conversation, author with Loeffke, n.d. [17 Jun 89], Fort Clayton, Panama; Msg, CINCSO to JCS, 181830Z Jun 89, sub: Panama Situation Report No. 45; Daily Operational Update, SOUTHCOM, 18 Jun 89; Huff Interv, 29 Jan 90.

scene, and he rejected the demand, telling the PDF officers that an investigation team would be there at dawn and that the wreckage would be cleaned up after that. The Panamanians refused to be placated and began "mingling" with the U.S. troops, who, hearing movement in the jungle around them as well, got into the best defensive positions they could. Tensions mounted with each passing minute. To one U.S. guard, his comrades seemed almost as if they were moving in slow motion, putting on their helmets and flak jackets, picking up their weapons, locking and loading, and maneuvering for position. Meanwhile, the Panamanian soldiers were unslinging their rifles and locking and loading.

Loeffke received word of the standoff around 0100. He immediately called Colonel Bolt and ordered him to move elements of the NIMROD DANCER mechanized battalion to Fort Amador as a show of force. He also directed two officers—Lt. Col. William Huff III, the battalion commander of the U.S. guards at the crash, and Maj. Alan Mansfield, the provost marshal at Fort Clayton—to go to the site. Additional military police were sent there as well, and an AC–130 was dispatched (although difficulties in launching it delayed its arrival over the scene of the confrontation). Loeffke himself headed for the Comandancia, where he encountered two PDF officers, one a lieutenant colonel. In blunt terms, he told both men that if the Panama Defense Forces fired on U.S. soldiers at the site, he was prepared to "react accordingly." Using his hand-held radio so that the PDF officers could hear him, he again talked to Bolt, issuing directives concerning the quick reaction force, the mechanized battalion, and other units on alert.

While at the Comandancia, Loeffke also talked over a radio with Col. Guillermo Wong, Noriega's intelligence chief and the senior PDF officer at the crash site.[58] Wong informed Loeffke that armed Dignity Battalion members were scheduled to demonstrate at the site around 0530 and demanded that the American guards leave before then. The Panamanian military, he said, would help the U.S. troops depart. Loeffke rejected the demand, indicated that his soldiers would leave around noon after the investigation had been completed, and notified Wong that any attack on the unit guarding the wreckage would be considered a hostile action by the Panama Defense Forces against U.S. forces. Wong took exception to the rhetoric but did not respond with threats of his own. He fared no better in advancing his cause after Huff and Mansfield arrived. Huff refused to talk to the colonel directly but had Mansfield convey a blunt message: if the PDF touched the wreckage, Wong would die. At one point, Wong received a call, presumably from Noriega, after which he appeared to Mansfield "a chastened man." By dawn, both sides had "deescalated," in Huff's words. The confrontation was over. Soon thereafter, the investigation team arrived, and, once its members had completed their work, the wreckage was removed. Later that day, Loeffke assessed the incident in what were for him fairly grave terms: "It was the toughest I've been and the closest I thought we were going to get into something."[59]

By the time of the helicopter crash, the exercises and operations conducted by JTF-Panama to assert U.S. treaty rights had, according to intelligence reports, caused some stress and disruption within the Panama Defense Forces, but not to the extent that would compel the institution as a whole or any group or officer in

---

[58] In *The Commanders*, pp. 89, 92, Bob Woodward identifies Wong as a "secret source" providing information to the Southern Command.

[59] Quotes from Huff Interv, 29 Jan 90. Conversation, author with Loeffke, n.d. [17 Jun 89].

AC–130 Spectre gunship

it to move against Noriega. Meanwhile, although the Panamanian military had not used force to resist the tougher U.S. actions, they had on about a half-dozen occasions been involved in confrontations that could have escalated into firefights. President Bush did not want a war but to remove that risk completely would have entailed reverting to pre–NIMROD DANCER policies, thereby raising the prospect of the crisis continuing indefinitely. That option was unacceptable. The alternative was to continue applying pressure in hopes both of rupturing the bond between the PDF and its commander and of compelling PDF officers to put the good of the institution over loyalty to its leader. While that strategy thus far had produced marginal results, there were still additional, more assertive measures that might yet yield the desired outcome. Of course, resorting to such measures meant entertaining additional, not fewer, risks.

Thus, at the very time Loeffke was talking tough over the face-off at the helicopter crash site, an initiative involving the Southern Command, the Joint Chiefs, and the National Command Authority was already well under way to "ratchet up" U.S. military activities in Panama. In July, President Bush would sign a national security directive authorizing the intensification of military pressure through a series of new actions. In doing so, his objective remained the same: to remove Noriega and bring the crisis to a satisfactory conclusion without having to execute an all-out U.S. invasion of Panama.

8

RATCHETING UP
JUNE–SEPTEMBER 1989

One month into Operation NIMROD DANCER, the results of the troop buildup and the Bush administration's tougher policy had been mixed. Measures to reassert U.S. treaty rights and to create fissures within the Panama Defense Forces had boosted morale within the American community and allowed JTF-Panama to hone its operational skills, but, as of mid-June, there was no end to the crisis in sight. Meanwhile, the Southern Command and its components had to deal with a host of other crisis-related issues, such as relocating military dependents, updating plans, and briefing visiting VIPs. These competed for time and personnel with other pressing requirements in the theater, including U.S.-sponsored construction and humanitarian projects in several Latin American countries, counterinsurgency efforts against Salvadoran and Peruvian guerrillas, the impending elections in Sandinista-controlled Nicaragua, and the drug war in general. To complicate matters further, this was also the time of the year when many U.S. military personnel would be retiring or transferring to new assignments.

BLADE JEWEL AND THE PRAYER BOOK

For USARSO officers also serving as JTF-Panama component commanders and staff, one of the most disruptive and frustrating issues to intrude on the conduct of daily business and the freedom of movement operations was Operation BLADE JEWEL. The purpose of this undertaking was to effectuate what President Bush had called for in three sentences of his 11 May statement: "U.S. Government employees and their dependents living outside of U.S. military bases or Panama Canal Commission housing areas will be relocated out of Panama or to secure U.S. housing areas within Panama. This action will begin immediately. It will be completed as quickly and in as orderly a manner as possible."[1]

As with the troop buildup and assertion of treaty rights, American officials had begun discussing a reduction in U.S. government employees and dependents in Panama weeks before that country's 7 May elections. In fact, well before May, there was already in effect a Reduction of Off-Post Personnel program to achieve those ends, and Woerner was content with the steady progress it was making, taking exception to those who would have him accelerate the process unduly.

---

[1] President Bush's statement can be found in *Department of State Bulletin* 89 (July 1989): 70–71.

Unless the Bush administration intended to invade Panama, which he assumed it did not, there was no need in his opinion to rush matters. Such a move would not intimidate Noriega but would result in "screwing around traumatically with the lives of our people for U.S. domestic reasons, not for strategic reasons." Woerner conveyed this sentiment in a conversation he had with Senator John McCain during the visit of the congressional election observers in May. The meeting served only to deepen the discord between the two men, as the senator came away incredulous over what he considered to be the SOUTHCOM commander's exaggerated claim that a drawdown of U.S. personnel would take several more months to implement. The State Department, the Central Intelligence Agency, and the National Security Council shared McCain's impatience, believing the required reductions could be made within thirty days. Consequently, Washington overrode Woerner's reservations and, once the president's policy went into effect, gave the general until the end of June to implement it. In a measure to help ensure that the Southern Command would meet that deadline, the Pentagon moved forward to June permanent change of station (PCS) transfers scheduled originally for July and August for military personnel.[2]

Since soldiers far outnumbered their sister service counterparts in Panama, the impact of BLADE JEWEL fell mainly on U.S. Army, South. On paper, the task sounded simple enough: bring command-sponsored families living off post onto a U.S. base or send them back to the United States. In practice, the process proved to be complicated, contentious, and disruptive. Over 1,000 families, meaning several thousand people, would have to be moved on short notice. Two to three thousand people would return to the United States; others would move into housing on Fort Clayton, Fort Amador, and other Army bases. Of those moving on post, some would move in with other families, creating no small amount of inconvenience. In other cases, occupants of on-post housing were told (in accordance with regulations) to vacate and return to the United States in order to make room for families, some of them civilian employees, moving in from off post. Families leaving Panama would have to find housing when they got to their destination. For service personnel scheduled to change assignments, this meant finding quarters at their new duty station, or, depending on the date that they were eligible to return from overseas (DEROS), sending their families ahead to do so without them. The problem was that, with tours in Panama being cut short by up to sixty days, housing at the new posts might not be available for families arriving early. Some would have to "stay with mother" while awaiting quarters, apparently without reimbursement in the form of temporary duty (TDY) funds and often without their sponsor.

Aggravating matters, many Army personnel coming to U.S. Army, South, as their new duty station would not arrive in time to fill the void created by those who were departing early. Moreover, after the 7 May elections, the status of official duty in Panama was changed to an unaccompanied tour, inflicting a last-minute hardship on many of the incoming replacements who, scheduled to arrive in July and August, had looked forward to their new assignment with the understanding that their families would be coming with them. The change in status also required

---

[2] For Woerner's quote, as well as Woerner's views on the personnel issue, see Interv, author with General Frederick F. Woerner Jr., U.S. Army (Ret.), 30 Apr 91, Fort Leavenworth, Kans. See also Baker, *Politics of Diplomacy*, pp. 183–84; Donnelly, Roth, and Baker, *Operation Just Cause*, p. 49.

U.S. Army, South, to convert many of its on-post family housing units into bachelor quarters, thus further exacerbating the plight of the families uprooted from their homes in Panama proper, including ones they owned, and brought onto a nearby base only to find the quarters that they were slated to occupy now designated for unaccompanied personnel. As the tensions generated by the election and the buildup of U.S. forces seemed to subside in late May, many of these families questioned the need for such radical measures. In short, the list of problems and inconveniences associated with BLADE JEWEL seemed endless to all involved. The reluctance of Washington to grant the operation the status of an evacuation, with the supportive measures that such an undertaking would have entailed, only increased the myriad of complaints and annoyances.

In Colonel Cope's opinion, BLADE JEWEL succeeded in bringing some people on post, sending others home, and "pissing off" just about everyone.[3] The drawdown of dependents was not all that confusing in principle, he contended, but the broad procedures applied to the process did not make allowance for the myriad of individual problems that arose. This was a defect criticized almost daily at JTF-Panama updates by Army component commanders looking out for the welfare of their troops. Loeffke sympathized but found himself repeatedly reminding all concerned that U.S. Army, South, "was writing the book" for this kind of activity. One chapter he himself contributed was the creation of a relocation center at Fort Clayton, where USARSO Deputy Chief of Staff for Resource Management Col. William Connolly and his staff worked long hours to rationalize the process and assist the uprooted families. To answer the variety of questions that surfaced daily, the command published the *Pangram,* a frequently updated newsletter focusing on BLADE JEWEL issues. Loeffke and other officers also addressed groups of families, keeping them abreast of developments and listening to their problems. Meanwhile, Rossi dealt with the Department of the Army (and the Pentagon in general), traveling back and forth to Washington to convey the extent of the upheaval created by BLADE JEWEL and to plead for financial and other assistance for the families involved. Among his accomplishments, he was able to get the Army to authorize TDY funds for families returning to the United States prematurely. To relieve the housing shortage, U.S. Army, South, also requested Harvest Eagle quartering packages from the Air Force.

At the peak of his frustration over BLADE JEWEL, Loeffke wrote the following to the chief of staff of the Army, a poignant reminder that the relocation process involved people, not statistics.

Anguish. This week was the first time in my Army career that I felt we were doing our families an injustice. When I farewelled the 225 families leaving yesterday, I went to shake hands with a wife. She was furious and proceeded to let me know it. She said to me: "Don't touch me general. I've waited ten months in the U.S. until my husband got quarters on post. My three children and I lived with friends in the U.S. It was miserable and crowded. I no sooner get settled in Panama, and you give me a week to move to Bragg. You won't let my husband go because it will hinder your readiness. I won't get priority for a house at Bragg. What do I do? I can't afford to live in a motel. I left a good job to join him here. I have lost that, so don't even talk to me."[4]

---

[3] Interv, author with Col John A. Cope Jr., U.S. Army, 29 May 91, Fort Leavenworth, Kans.

[4] Msg, CDR, USARSO, to CSA, 011245Z Jun 89, sub: Update No. 27, Panama Update, Operations.

Despite the magnitude of the relocation effort and the problems it entailed, BLADE JEWEL achieved the stated goal at the end of June. As Woerner informed Admiral Crowe, 6,300 service personnel and their dependents had been relocated; 1,625 sets of household goods had been moved within Panama, with another 1,600 sets shipped to the United States. All leases for off-post quarters had been terminated, although seventy families still remained in Panama proper for one reason or another, pending various actions by the Defense Department. At the Southern Command and U.S. Army, South, the end of BLADE JEWEL brought a sense of relief but little joy. If the purpose of the operation had been to put U.S. citizens in Panama out of harm's way or at least to convey the impression to Noriega and the Panama Defense Forces that Washington was clearing the decks for action, the impact was diluted by the fact that 30,000 U.S. citizens not employed by the U.S. government or under its control still lived on Panamanian territory. Nor did the families brought on post necessarily feel safer if they ended up on installations such as Fort Amador, where PDF combat units lived in barracks next to American housing areas. Looking back on BLADE JEWEL from the perspective of a few years, Woerner judged the whole operation a "shameful feint." Many who had suffered through the ordeal agreed. For U.S. Army, South, it had been, in Rossi's opinion, a crisis within a crisis.[5]

While BLADE JEWEL and the operations to assert U.S. treaty rights took place in public view, behind the scenes, military planners had to determine the impact of both enterprises on the PRAYER BOOK series of contingency plans. The noncombatant evacuation operation plan, KLONDIKE KEY, certainly needed to be reassessed in light of the BLADE JEWEL drawdown. A more pressing concern was how the NIMROD DANCER troop buildup would affect both POST TIME and BLUE SPOON planning and operations. In one change to BLUE SPOON made after the activation of Task Force Atlantic at Fort Sherman, units under Colonel Hale's control received the wartime mission of taking down the PDF 8th Infantry Company at Fort Espinar, an operation originally assigned to units from the 1st Battalion, 508th Infantry, 193d Infantry Brigade. The change freed the 193d units to hit targets closer to their headquarters on the Pacific side of the canal area. Similarly, the newly arrived mechanized battalion, which under the existing plans had combat missions on the Atlantic side of the country, was stationed under NIMROD DANCER on the Pacific side instead, where it picked up new BLUE SPOON missions in and around Panama City.[6]

Although the battalions sent to Panama from the 7th Infantry Division (Light) and the 5th Infantry Division (Mechanized) had been listed among those forces designated to deploy under POST TIME, the operation order itself, which called for a much larger buildup, had not been executed. The possibility that it might be, despite the Bush administration's calming words on the protective mission of NIMROD DANCER forces, was something Lt. Gen. Carl W. Stiner, commander of the XVIII Airborne Corps, had to consider. From the corps' perspective, the execution of POST TIME would likely be the prelude to a full-scale invasion under BLUE SPOON,

---

[5] Msg, CINCSO to CJCS, 011608Z Jul 89, sub: Status BLADE JEWEL Personnel Moves-Panama. The "shameless feint" quote is from Woerner Interv, 30 Apr 91.

[6] Intervs, author with Lt Col Robert Pantier, U.S. Army, 13 Jun 90, Fort Clayton, Panama, and Col Robert L. Barefield, U.S. Army, 7 Nov 90, Fort Leavenworth, Kans.; Joint After Action Report (AAR), USSOUTHCOM, Operation JUST CAUSE, 14 Feb 91, sec. A.

in which case Stiner and his staff would deploy at some undetermined point to run the war as a joint task force. Given this scenario, the general thought it essential that he receive timely information on developments in the crisis. With that in mind, he ordered a three-man advance party to Panama, the group arriving at Quarry Heights in mid-May.[7]

The team was led by Maj. David Huntoon, the corps' chief planner for Panama. Accompanying him were Capt. Mike Findlay from G–2 plans and Maj. Ed Lesnowicz, a marine. During the first week of their stay, the three worked out of the Tunnel at Quarry Heights. Once they concluded that additional POST TIME units were not going to deploy as part of NIMROD DANCER, they gravitated to Fort Clayton, where they joined JTF-Panama's Lt. Col. Bob Pantier and his staff in further refining the BLUE SPOON operation order for conventional forces. The reception they received at U.S. Army, South, was a bit chilly, with Loeffke, Rossi, and Cope still hoping to limit the corps' involvement in the planning process. Even so, all parties recognized that JTF-Panama needed the group's expertise in some areas, and Pantier stood ready to tap into it.[8]

One of JTF-Panama's most pressing requirements with respect to BLUE SPOON planning was to sort through a variety of fire support and battlefield coordination issues. One set of concerns had to do with special operations platforms, such as AC–130s, that would be used in any invasion. Other questions revolved around what artillery assets would have to be deployed under BLUE SPOON, and how indirect fire support would be coordinated. Neither the Southern Command nor JTF-Panama had a planner who could answer these questions, so Pantier relied heavily on Lesnowicz, the corps' deputy fire support officer. (Lesnowicz occupied what was traditionally a Marine billet on the staff of an Army headquarters.) Back in April, Pantier and Lesnowicz had started work on the structure for a fire support element (FSE) and a battlefield coordination element (BCE), and they continued this collaboration after the three-man team arrived in May. Doctrine served as their general guideline, but when necessary they made modifications to reflect conditions in Panama. The battlefield coordination element they set up, for example, did not require the doctrinally correct thirty-man staff.

While Lesnowicz concentrated on FSE and BCE issues, Findlay applied his expertise to a number of intelligence-related matters, including the need to ensure timely information from the field to the operations center in the event of a U.S. invasion. (In working these issues, Findlay found disconcerting the fact that the military intelligence people at the Southern Command and U.S. Army, South, were not always communicating with one another.) He also helped introduce into the BLUE SPOON plan the kind of tactical jargon that he believed subordinate headquarters and units would more readily understand.

---

[7] Telephone conversation, author with Maj David Huntoon, 27 Jun 90; Interv, author with Lt Col David Huntoon, U.S. Army, 7 Apr 92, Fort Bragg, N.C.

[8] For the activities of the three-man team, see Telephone conversation, author with Huntoon, 27 Jun 90; Intervs, author with Pantier, 13 Jun 90, and Maj Mike Findlay, U.S. Army, 8 Feb 90, Fort Leavenworth, Kans. While at Fort Clayton, Huntoon ran into Loeffke in a hallway. As they talked, Loeffke said something to the effect, "By the way, we don't think we're ever going to need you guys. We think we can do this ourselves, but we sure appreciate your coming down and doing this coordination." Huntoon Interv, 7 Apr 92.

By the time Huntoon and his party returned to Fort Bragg in mid-June—to be replaced by a team led by Lt. Col. Charles Bergdorf—they had contributed significantly to refining BLUE SPOON. They had also confirmed their belief that JTF-Panama was not "robust" enough to be given responsibility for executing the plan. The headquarters was adequate, they concluded, for managing such operations as freedom of movement convoys, but it could not hope to oversee a full-scale intervention. That assessment, in combination with the tougher U.S. policy that had gone into effect with NIMROD DANCER, compelled the XVIII Airborne Corps to become more actively engaged in the planning mission the Joint Chiefs had assigned it the previous year. From the corps' perspective, Stiner recounted later, Panama moved during this time "from the back burner to the front."[9]

The most significant revision to BLUE SPOON made in the wake of the Panamanian election and U.S. troop buildup originated with the SOUTHCOM commander and the joint special operations task force at Fort Bragg. At issue was the fate of the PDF commander in the event of a U.S. invasion. In compartmentalized sessions, planners had discussed a covert operation to snatch Noriega, but as of mid-1989, the approved D-day targets for BLUE SPOON conventional and special operations forces included PDF units and sites, not individuals. In the opinion of JSOTF planners, however, locating Noriega at any of the specified targets once hostilities commenced was unlikely. Unless Noriega himself was identified as an H-hour target, he would probably "go to ground" and become "virtually impossible to find." The critical question was, would having the Panamanian dictator on the loose once BLUE SPOON began matter?[10]

Woerner contended that it did. Following SOUTHCOM discussions with the Joint Staff in the Pentagon and after receiving a formal request from the joint special operations task force at Bragg to make Noriega a target, the SOUTHCOM commander concluded that U.S. policy objectives as stated in BLUE SPOON would not be satisfied fully if Panama's strongman remained at large. Should Noriega escape to a friendly country such as Cuba, he could mount a propaganda campaign in support of guerrilla warfare in Panama, thus complicating the transition to a democratic government during or following a U.S. invasion. To avoid a "long term problem," Woerner advised Crowe, "the capture of Noriega and disreputable elements of the present command and control structure of the PDF is not only a desirable objective for BLUE SPOON but a legitimate and necessary objective for successful mission accomplishment."[11]

On 1 June 1989, the capture or neutralization of the PDF commander became a formal BLUE SPOON mission to be executed by special operations personnel. Planning Noriega's removal from power remained compartmentalized at Fort Bragg, with Pantier and other key planners for conventional operations keeping abreast of the plan's details in order to avoid any potential conflict between the new SOF mission and the conventional ones contained in BLUE SPOON.[12]

---

[9] Interv, Robert K. Wright Jr., U.S. Army Center of Military History, with Lt Gen Carl W. Stiner, U.S. Army, 2 Mar 90, Fort Bragg, N.C., JUST CAUSE Interview Tapes (JCIT) 024.

[10] Msg, COM[JSOTF] to CINCSO, 181915Z May 89, sub: BLUE SPOON Tasking.

[11] Msg, CINCSO to CJCS, 231245Z May 89, sub: BLUE SPOON Planning.

[12] Joint AAR, USSOUTHCOM, Operation JUST CAUSE, 14 Feb 91, sec. A; Interv, author with Pantier, U.S. Army, 21 May 91, Fort Leavenworth, Kans. In *The Commanders*, p. 115, journalist Bob Woodward comments on the legal basis for targeting an individual. On 21 June 1989, the U.S. Justice

Ratcheting Up

Woerner's "Retirement"

Accelerated work on the Prayer Book operation orders continued throughout Nimrod Dancer, both in Panama and in the United States. In the meantime, those responsible for planning at the Southern Command and JTF-Panama had to deal with the disruptive effects of Blade Jewel and the flurry of military retirements and reassignments that occurs every year in June and July. Many planners would themselves be leaving Panama; so, too, would other key staff officers and commanders. At Albrook Air Station, SOCSOUTH's Col. Chuck Fry prepared for retirement, while Brig. Gen. John Stewart, the SOUTHCOM J–2 and one of Woerner's inner circle, packed his bags for a posting with the Army Staff. At U.S. Army, South, Col. William Bolt, who was also heading for the Army Staff, was ready to turn command of the 193d over to Col. Michael J. Snell; Colonel Cope anticipated his new assignment as Bernard Aronson's military assistant in the State Department; Colonel Rossi looked to retirement; and General Loeffke awaited a tour in Washington as chairman of the Inter-American Defense Board and commandant of the Inter-American Defense College. These officers and others, especially the host of generals and colonels leaving Panama, took with them their expertise and long-term familiarity with the crisis. Their replacements would need time to acquire a similar degree of expertise. The orientation process for the newcomers, which included highly detailed, four-hour briefings on the Prayer Book, could not hope to produce an immediate mastery of such a complex, nuanced, and dynamic issue.

Mitigating this turnover in military personnel was the continuity guaranteed by the presence of two key officers who were not leaving the country (while a third, Rossi, would be extended at U.S. Army, South, into the fall). Brig. Gen. Marc Cisneros, SOUTHCOM's operations director, had received orders to assume command at Fort Clayton, which meant he would receive a second star (in late October) and, like Loeffke, serve as commander, JTF-Panama. And Woerner, a calming influence in an increasingly turbulent period, had been asked to extend his tour as SOUTHCOM commander into 1991. For those who believed a U.S. invasion of Panama to be ill advised, the continued presence of these two officers seemed reassuring. Both would provide a steady hand at the helm of their respective headquarters as the host of new component commanders and staff officers acclimated themselves to the intricacies of the crisis.

That line of reasoning received a sudden setback in early July. On the sixth, Woerner received a telephone call from Chief of Staff of the Army General Carl Vuono, who said that he was coming to Panama to speak personally with the SOUTHCOM commander. Woerner received the call in his office. After he hung up, he told others in the room, "I am going to be relieved." Those present disagreed, but Vuono's arrival confirmed the CINC's premonition. "Fred," Vuono said once they were together, "the President has decided to make a change." In the discourse that followed, Vuono advised Woerner to resign rather than face removal, but the SOUTHCOM commander realized that, despite any graceful exit that could be arranged for him, he had been sacked. "In my terms," he would say later, "I'm

---

Department issued a 29-page legal opinion "stating that the President had legal authority to direct the FBI to abduct a fugitive residing in a foreign country for violations of U.S. law." According to Woodward, government officials believed that the opinion could be applied to Noriega.

being relieved—the first time in my career." When he asked Vuono the reasons for the decision, the Army chief pleaded ignorance: the secretary of the Army had offered no explanation. A few days later, Woerner was in Washington, where he met with Admiral Crowe at the Pentagon. The JCS chairman, too, said that he had not been consulted on the matter and suggested they go upstairs and talk to Secretary of Defense Cheney. In the course of that audience, Woerner tried every way he could to obtain a specific answer as to why he was being replaced, but Cheney only conceded that the decision was "purely political" and had nothing to do with Woerner's performance. Woerner, the secretary stated, had done exactly what the administration had asked of him in executing U.S. policy in the crisis.[13]

After thirty-four years' service, to be retired in this way hurt Woerner deeply and caused him to reflect on a higher principle. "I was disappointed and concerned professionally that the military officer, therefore the military institution, would be used for political gain." Crowe also believed the dismissal to be unjust. To the chairman, the White House had shown a lack of courage and the secretary of defense had seemed indifferent to the fate of a four-star general. There were others who deplored the decision, but, on the whole, there was little public backlash to a matter that received only passing attention in the news media.[14] Faced with an irrevocable decision, Woerner informed Cheney that he would like to remain at his position for ninety days. New officers coming to Quarry Heights in the "incredible turnover" that summer had to be brought up to speed on the crisis. Woerner also wanted to make a last visit to the Latin American countries in his area of responsibility. Cheney listened but agreed only to a sixty-day interval between the formal announcement of Woerner's retirement and the ceremony itself. That meant the latter would occur at the end of September.[15] General Maxwell R. Thurman, then scheduled to step down as commanding general, U.S. Army Training and Doctrine Command, would become the new SOUTHCOM commander.

RATCHETING UP

Two weeks before Woerner received word of his retirement, he had participated in a change-of-command ceremony at Fort Clayton, during which Cisneros took over as the commanding general, U.S. Army, South. Both men used the occasion to make strong statements about the crisis, with Cisneros calling Noriega a "dime store dictator," and Woerner warning that the United States would use whatever

---

[13] Second quote from Woodward, *The Commanders*, p. 96, and see also pp. 97–98. First and third quotes from Intervs, General Frederick F. Woerner Jr., U.S. Army (Ret.), U.S. Army Military History Institute, Carlisle Barracks, Pa. Last quoted words from Interv, author with Woerner, 30 Apr 91. The closest any ranking Bush administration official would come to a public but candid explanation of the specific reasons for Woerner being relieved appears in Secretary of State James Baker's memoirs. Baker claims that Woerner opposed the tougher policy advocated by the Bush administration and had developed a case of "clientitis" with Noriega. The "final straw" was what was perceived in the administration as Woerner's "leisurely timetable" for drawing down U.S. military dependents in Panama. (Baker does not address the issue that these perceptions of Woerner might not have been accurate.) According to Baker, he, Cheney, and Scowcroft strongly recommended to Bush that Woerner be replaced. Baker, *Politics of Diplomacy*, pp. 183–84.

[14] See, for example, newspaper columns on the subject by retired U.S. Army colonel, Harry Summers. Quote from Woerner MHI Interv.

[15] Woerner MHI Interv; Woodward, *The Commanders*, pp. 97–98; Woerner Interv, 30 Apr 91.

force necessary to protect American citizens and U.S. treaty rights in Panama.[16] What neither realized at the time, of course, was that in three months Woerner would be gone and Cisneros would become the principal repository of the military's "institutional memory" of the crisis among senior U.S. officers in Panama. As the SOUTHCOM operations director, Cisneros had always been candid about leaning toward the Woerner camp. Both he and his boss had been critical of Washington's failure to advance a coordinated policy to resolve the situation, both believed that the United States should execute BLUE SPOON only as a last resort, and both favored a comprehensive interagency program to put pressure on the Panama Defense Forces and the Noriega regime. Where the two differed somewhat was on the nature of the pressure to be applied, with Cisneros generally favoring a more aggressive, confrontational approach than Woerner found comfortable.[17]

In an incident that occurred shortly after the change of command at Fort Clayton, Cisneros offered a glimpse of just how aggressive he intended to be, given his new authority. The episode involved two PDF *tránsitos* pursuing a thief across the mud flats separating Panama City from Fort Amador. When one of the police officers opened fire at the suspect with an AK47, a stray round hit an inside wall of a U.S. colonel's family quarters on the fort. Upon receiving the report, Cisneros immediately moved a quick reaction force with its M113s and .50-caliber machine guns onto Amador. When the troops arrived, they investigated what had transpired and reported back. Cisneros then ordered them to return but over a route that would take them in front of the PDF 5th Infantry Company barracks. The QRF's guns were to be locked and loaded and pointed directly at the buildings. With this show of force, Cisneros established his credentials as the new USARSO and JTF-Panama commander, lived up to his reputation for wanting more confrontational action, and sent a clear message to both the Panamanian military and the American community in Panama: as commanding general at Fort Clayton, he would move decisively and with force against any perceived threat to U.S. military personnel and their dependents.[18]

In the days and weeks that followed, Cisneros made his mark in several other ways

General Cisneros (*left*) and General Thurman at the former's promotion ceremony

---

[16] The remarks are from Donnelly, Roth, and Baker, *Operation Just Cause*, p. 49.

[17] Ibid.; Conversation, author with Brig Gen Marc Cisneros, 13 Dec 89, Fort Clayton, Panama.

[18] John T. Fishel, The Panama Intervention of 1989: Operation Just Cause and Its Aftermath, copy in author's personal files.

related to the crisis. As Woerner's J–3, he had monitored the daily activities of JTF-Panama, and he was not always pleased with what he saw. In an observation with which Loeffke would have disagreed vigorously, Cisneros maintained that the organization was not sufficiently oriented to combat. He therefore implemented measures to increase the joint task force's operational preparedness while enabling it to exert greater pressure on the Panama Defense Forces. Contingency readiness exercises (CREs), which he had witnessed while stationed in Germany, constituted one such new measure. Supplementing the Purple Storms and joint training program Loeffke had promoted soon after the joint task force was activated, Cisneros specifically wanted the CREs to reduce to two hours the time needed for the bulk of U.S. forces under his command and control to muster and deploy for defensive or offensive operations. The exercises would also allow the troops additional opportunities to rehearse, without their knowledge, JTF-Panama's POST TIME and BLUE SPOON contingency plans, although operations security and deception plans dictated that units would not go to their actual battle locations. Soldiers from the 193d, for example, in conducting several air assault exercises into Fort Amador, would generally land in front of the PDF 5th Infantry Company barracks, whereas the BLUE SPOON plan called for a flanking attack.[19]

In addition to the contingency readiness exercises, Cisneros inaugurated a series of small-scale exercises that Rossi dubbed Sand Fleas. In common with the insect endemic to Panama, a Sand Flea exercise was designed to irritate the Panama Defense Forces, thereby aggravating the stress already generated by the regime's inability to pay and feed many of the organization's members. In practice, the line between Purple Storms, contingency readiness exercises, and Sand Fleas was often indistinct. But all three presented an opportunity to train U.S. forces, rehearse contingency plans, deceive the Panamanian military with false "signatures" and "footprints," force the PDF to react to each and every undertaking, and observe those reactions, which often included troop movements. Theoretically, the resulting strains on PDF resources, time, and patience would, in line with the new U.S. policy, increase friction and lower morale within the institution. But Cisneros also hoped the numerous U.S. exercises would gradually lull Noriega's men into a false sense of security, causing them ultimately to respond with an indifferent "Ah, the gringos aren't going to do anything. This is all just psychological warfare."[20]

To be sure, the exercises were, in some measure, psychological operations (PSYOP), an arena in which Cisneros was especially eager to become more confrontational toward the Panama Defense Forces. At one point right after he arrived at U.S. Army, South, this inclination nearly cost him his job. On 8 July, he gave a newspaper interview in which he asserted that he saw little chance of

---

[19] Donnelly, Roth, and Baker, *Operation Just Cause*, p. 49. Intervs, author with Maj Gen Marc Cisneros, U.S. Army, 30 Jan 90 and 29 Jun 90, Fort Clayton, Panama; and Col Michael J. Snell, U.S. Army, 16 Dec 89, Fort Clayton, Panama.

[20] Donnelly, Roth, and Baker, *Operation Just Cause*, p. 49. Quote from Interv, author with Maj Gen Marc Cisneros, 30 Jan 90, Fort Clayton, Panama. Intervs, author with Lt Col Robert Pantier, U.S. Army, 21 May 91, Fort Leavenworth, Kans., and 13 Jun 90; and Lt Col Brett Francis, U.S. Army, 14 Dec 89, Fort Clayton, Panama. Presentation, Lt Col Robert Pantier, 21 May 92, Fort Leavenworth, Kans.

either a diplomatic resolution to the crisis or the PDF overthrowing Noriega. He went on to say, "I've been thinking more and more that the United States should impose a military solution that would give this country an opportunity to have a government that isn't criminal." Most Americans would support such a move, he continued, most Latin American governments would privately applaud it, and most PDF personnel would not fight to save their commander. Cisneros stated that he was expressing a personal opinion. "Any U.S. military action is decided by the President."[21]

Word that the commander of U.S. Army troops in Panama was openly espousing military intervention created a sensation among people involved in the crisis. Spokespersons for Noriega's regime railed against Cisneros (as they had many times in the past), accusing him of sponsoring an invasion of their country. Reaction at the Pentagon, while expressed privately, was hardly more restrained. That Cisneros really was not an advocate of intervention and that the interview was part of a larger PSYOP stratagem aimed at rattling the Panamanian regime and its armed forces mattered little. Admiral Crowe was furious over what he considered a deliberate and unauthorized provocation. Woerner, who was in Washington after hearing about his own relief, called Cisneros and twice warned the new USARSO commander that "*his* head was on the block," and that he, too, might be relieved. In the end, Cisneros weathered the storm but not before taking to heart Woerner's admonition not to grant any more sensational interviews.[22]

In making the controversial statements, Cisneros never intended to appear to his superiors as an erratic, bellicose commander, a "loose cannon." With ample justification, he firmly believed his remarks, not to mention his handling of the shooting near Fort Amador or his introduction of the contingency readiness exercises, to be consonant with the Bush administration's tougher approach to Noriega and his regime.[23] Moreover, at the time of the interview, he knew that Washington was about to approve even stronger measures, the result of a month-old initiative that had begun on the eve of the first freedom of movement convoy in the last part of May and in which Cisneros himself had played a prominent role.

The initiative was partly prompted by a request from the Joint Staff on 19 May for the Southern Command to provide a list of additional actions U.S. forces in Panama might take to assert America's treaty rights and, in general, to advance the president's new policy. Woerner's J–3 shop, of which Cisneros was still the director at that time, had already enumerated several such "supporting efforts." After revising the proposals and adding some new options, Cisneros forwarded the list to the SOUTHCOM commander and the Pentagon on 21 May. Some of the proposed measures fell into the category of low-risk "collateral operations," which Woerner simply approved on his own authority while keeping Crowe informed. Other options entailed greater risks and required further analysis and discussion. By 30 May, the day Woerner formally submitted SOUTHCOM's recommendations to the Joint Chiefs, rumors were beginning to circulate around Quarry Heights and

---

[21] Quotes from both Press Releases, SOUTHCOM PAO, 10 Jul 89, and USARSO PAO, 10 Jul 89.
[22] Cisneros Interv, 30 Jan 90.
[23] Conversation, author with Cisneros, 13 Dec 89.

Fort Clayton that there might be an escalation in the U.S. military activities then under way to put pressure on Panama's regime and the Panama Defense Forces.[24]

In his message to Crowe, Woerner expressed the need for just such a course of action. While acknowledging the success of the convoys and the collateral operations he had authorized to that point, he also noted the low-key nature of the PDF's response, confined mainly to a disinformation PSYOP campaign against American imperialism. In order for the United States to "maintain the initiative," Woerner requested authority to execute new measures in early June, immediately following a scheduled OAS meeting on the crisis. The proposed actions included reoccupying various U.S. facilities currently being used by the Panama Defense Forces, asserting U.S. access to the Fort Amador causeway, and diverting public traffic around, instead of through, Howard Air Force Base. "Because some of these are confrontational," he warned, "they will require the same degree of resolve as the freedom of movement operations."[25]

About a week after sending the message, Woerner flew to Washington to talk with senior officials about the next steps in the crisis. A memorandum summarizing the nature of the discussions indicated that a major topic was "how to make both Noriega and the OAS think the US had military intervention on its mind" (presumably short of having the USARSO commander openly announce it to them, along with the rest of the world). Woerner indicated that there were numerous measures that could be employed to that end. Meanwhile, in Lt. Gen. Thomas Kelly's operations shop in the Pentagon, staffers drafted a paper in preparation for an interagency Policy Coordination Committee meeting on 14 June.[26] The paper recommended approval of the actions Woerner had discussed in his 30 May message and listed additional options for increasing pressure on Noriega and the Panama Defense Forces by "overstressing their centralized command structure system." The proposals included night training operations and highly visible joint training exercises, publicizing the completion of BLADE JEWEL, reconnaissance and surveillance operations in the vicinity of PDF command and control facilities and other sites, an evacuation exercise, deploying U.S. Air Force aircraft to Panama for training purposes, the visible placement of logistical supplies in Panama, simulating logistical and operational preparations for a large military operation, and placing operational forces on Fort Amador. The lieutenant colonel who wrote the paper acknowledged that there were risks attached to the proposed courses of action. Although increased pressure might "polarize the PDF-Noriega relationship," the measures might just as easily backfire, solidifying the PDF's loyalty to its

---

[24] Joint Staff Internal Staff Paper to DJS, 21 May 89, sub: Options for Exercising Panamanian Treaty Rights. First quoted words from Paper, SOUTHCOM J–3, Supporting Efforts for Freedom of Movement (FOM) Actions, 15 May 89. Second quoted words from Memo, Cisneros for CINCSO, 21 May 89, sub: Assertion of US Forces Treaty Rights. Memo, Cisneros for CDR, JTF Panama; CDR, SOCSO, 24 May 89, sub: Measures to Support Freedom of Movement Operation; Interv, author with Maj Gen Bernard Loeffke, U.S. Army, 31 May 89, Fort Clayton, Panama.

[25] Msg, CINCSO to CJCS, 301426Z May 89, sub: Asserting Treaty Rights.

[26] The Policy Coordinating Committee was made up of Bernard Aronson from the State Department, William Price from the National Security Council, Richard Brown from the Office of the Secretary of Defense, and Brig. Gen. David Meade from the Joint Staff. See Ronald H. Cole, *Operation Just Cause: The Planning and Execution of Joint Operations in Panama, February 1988–January 1990* (Washington, D.C.: Joint History Office, Office of the Chairman of the Joint Chiefs of Staff, 1995), pp. 11–12.

commander. Furthermore, the actions could increase the danger to U.S. citizens in Panama, while outside groups, including the Organization of American States, might view the moves as overly provocative, a reversion to "gunboat diplomacy." Still, despite the risks involved, an attachment to the staff paper called for the coordination and implementation of new policy initiatives.[27]

On 13 June, the day before the interagency meeting in Washington, staff officers at Quarry Heights reviewed the latest, updated Joint Staff paper concerning future military action in the crisis. Key SOUTHCOM directorates questioned some of the options, modified some, and added others. The next day, Woerner provided this feedback to the Pentagon. While the list of actions "to increase PDF perceptions that the U.S. is preparing for a military solution to the 'Crisis' in Panama" took up the bulk of the memorandum, what was of even greater importance were the general observations that preceded and followed the list. Woerner began with a very forceful statement: "While these options may be successful in intimidating Noriega and his thugs, there is a real possibility that he and the PDF may react (by accident or design) and test U.S. resolve. As a consequence, the signal that these options will send should not be sent, unless we are prepared to use military force."[28] As in the past, the SOUTHCOM commander was not advocating a military solution to the crisis; he was simply warning Washington that the process of convincing Noriega of Washington's seriousness concerning a military solution to the crisis might itself create a situation in which the United States would actually have to exercise that option.

Woerner also detailed the risks involved in adopting the new measures. Latin American allies might rally around the "banner of non-intervention," while Noriega would simply wait out any pressure he perceived as a bluff, which was likely if the United States in effect cried "wolf" again by employing "a series of piecemeal tactics which are not a part of a larger campaign plan." Here, the SOUTHCOM commander reiterated familiar themes. He raised again the triad concept as the best approach for exploiting Noriega's vulnerabilities and urged that the military options under consideration be incorporated into his latest proposal for an interagency campaign plan, BLACK GNAT, that he had just submitted to Admiral Crowe. In concluding, Woerner noted that "we are moving from one set of military missions (protect American lives & property/exert Treaty Rights) to a very different mission of threatening invasion. I therefore caution again that the aforementioned actions . . . must be accomplished as a part of a larger plan, and that the decision process for deception should include an agreement ahead of time that the signals we send may have to be executed."[29]

The next day, Woerner repeated these sentiments in a message to Air Force General Robert Herres, the vice chairman of the Joint Chiefs of Staff. But in addition to the long-standing plea for putting contemplated military actions within the context of an interagency campaign plan, the SOUTHCOM commander made a telling point. "I am also concerned," he wrote, "that by undertaking deception plan

---

[27] Memo for [SOUTHCOM] Chief of Staff, 13 Jun 89, sub: Deception Tactics. Quotes from Talking Paper [and atchs.], JCS J–3 Joint Operations Division, n.d., sub: Options to Increase PDF Uncertainty of US Intentions.

[28] Memo, General Fred F. Woerner for Maj Gen Graves, 14 Jun 89, sub: Options to Heighten PDF Concerns.

[29] Ibid.

which implies U.S. invasion, we may be going beyond President's publicly stated primary objectives of protecting U.S. lives and asserting U.S. treaty rights."[30] One can only speculate at this point on the impact these cautionary messages might have had on those key administration and military officials then planning the escalation of U.S. pressure in the crisis. Woerner was again implying that American policy makers had yet to accept responsibility and face up to the need for a truly integrated strategy. He was warning them that the additional military measures they were considering could result in the use of U.S. force, in effect the execution of BLUE SPOON. And he was questioning whether, in revising the military's mission in Panama, these policy makers were acting in accordance with President Bush's wishes. Conceivably, these sentiments reinforced the perception of the president's principal national security advisers that Woerner was not a "team player." If so, the messages he sent in mid-June 1989 could have influenced the president's decision to relieve him.

Whatever the impact of Woerner's advice, another month would pass before President Bush issued formal guidelines for implementing more assertive military measures in Panama. As the administration deliberated, staff officers at the tactical level, anticipating the tougher initiatives, engaged in a series of brainstorming sessions to fashion various ways in which JTF-Panama could turn up the heat on the Noriega regime. The goal, as the participants understood it, was to make U.S. troops more visible to more people in Panama and, by forcing the Panama Defense Forces to react to the new initiatives, to sow confusion and discontent within that institution. Headed by Colonel Menser and Major Collier from the Operations Planning Group, the meetings, informally dubbed Operation RATCHET, convened in mid-June at Fort Clayton, just a week before Cisneros took command at U.S. Army, South, and included representatives from all the services as well as from SOUTHCOM's Center for Treaty Affairs, the U.S. military intelligence community, and the Panama Canal Commission.

The atmosphere during these sessions was relaxed but thoughtful, with a premium placed on creative thinking. Few serious ideas were dismissed out of hand, and there was no shortage of suggestions. SOUTHCOM's Center for Treaty Affairs kept the attendees apprised of the legal latitude they had under the canal treaties, and, to the surprise of many, the room for maneuver turned out to be considerable. The revelation, for example, that military exercises did not have to be restricted to the canal area opened up all sorts of possibilities. Treaty affairs personnel also suggested that the best way to confuse the Panamanian military was not to keep quiet about imminent U.S. activities but to provide PDF members on the Combined Board just enough information to satisfy the law while leaving them wondering about what specifically was going to happen and what they might have to do in response. After much discussion, the U.S. officers participating in these sessions produced a wide range of options, which were then consolidated by Menser and Collier for presentation to the incoming USARSO and JTF-Panama commander.[31]

---

[30] Msg, CINCSO to JCS, 150003Z Jun 89, sub: Dangers in Crying Wolf.

[31] Intervs, author with Maj Mark C. Collier, U.S. Army, 20 Jun 89, and 24 Jan 90, Fort Clayton, Panama.

Alice, Beatrice, and the Others

Woerner's call for tougher measures, Cisneros' move from Quarry Heights to Fort Clayton, and Operation RATCHET all combined to increase the operational tempo of U.S. forces throughout July. Rare was the daily situation report that did not contain references to one or more Sand Fleas, contingency readiness exercises, or Purple Storms. Moreover, if any of these undertakings did result in a confrontation with Panamanian forces, the chances were that the whole affair would be documented on film, as each side increasingly made use of hand-held video cameras. An exercise recorded on videotape could, at the very least, serve as useful footage for evening newscasts. More important for the Southern Command, videotaping would capture any PDF provocations and presumably demonstrate PDF culpability in any escalation or resort to violence. (Whether the presence of cameras would actually encourage the kind of PDF posturing that might lead to violence remained an open question.) Film documentation, however, could be a two-edged sword. As U.S. troops came to suspect, the footage might also capture their own mistakes or lapses in judgment. Furthermore, knowing that one's actions were being filmed could conceivably prove a distraction in any confrontation; an officer might hesitate to act or might overreact in the presence of the cameras. These potential drawbacks notwithstanding, increasingly frequent references to "dueling cameras" and "the camcord war" indicated the degree to which videocassettes were becoming standard issue for planned operations and exercises. The use of recording devices also demonstrated that both sides saw in the increased military activity an opportunity to influence public opinion in Panama.[32]

JTF-Panama mounted more exercises and operations in July than in June or May, although most of the daily ventures were still fairly routine and did not entail inordinate risks for U.S. forces. One exception involved a Purple Storm executed to regain U.S. access to the Panama Canal Causeway between Fort Amador and Naos, Perico, and Flamenco islands. Under Article III of the implementing treaty, the United States had the "right to use any portion of the Canal operating areas for military training." The causeway and certain facilities on the islands fell under that clause. The problem was that the very specific language of the treaty to this effect had not been reflected in the color-coded treaty maps of the canal area, which showed the causeway and the islands as strictly Panamanian territory. According to Woerner, the time had come to rectify the mistake. On 18 July, he informed the Pentagon that, once the OAS delegation currently in Panama had concluded its business, the next series of U.S. exercises would include the causeway, which he referred to as "one of the prime areas" for the next step in asserting U.S. treaty rights.[33]

---

[32] Colonel Hale offered a two-hour course in "counterpropaganda" for his battalion commanders. The employment of videotaping was an integral part of that course. Discussion notes, author with Col David R. E. Hale, 28 Sep 89, LICPRO Office, Fort Leavenworth, Kans.

[33] Msg, CINCSO to CJCS, 301426Z May 89, sub: Asserting Treaty Rights; JCS Internal Staff Paper (and atchs.) to CJCS, 20 Jul 89, sub: Military Activities in Panama. Second quote from Msg, CINCSO to Joint Staff, 182215Z Jul 89, sub: Military Activities in Panama. A handwritten note, not dated, provided the following legal opinion on the causeway: "The Causeway issue (a COA [Canal Operating Area] under the Treaty but white on the MAP) *must* be resolved by State, for the Commission, before *we* the U.S. Forces can patrol it. *Technically* JOINT Patrols are for *green* areas & not *pink*. Only good relationship w[ith] the PDF could allow such a thing."

The magnitude of the exercise and the challenge it posed to accepted, though erroneous, legal interpretations of certain treaty clauses sounded alarms in the Joint Staff and the interagency arena, where Woerner's proposal was regarded, as he intended it to be, as "an escalatory step." The problem was not so much the increased risks involved, but the timing of the exercise. President Bush was "personally engaged" in supporting the OAS effort at the time and had deferred a decision on employing tougher military measures in the crisis. But barring an OAS breakthrough on Panama, which was considered highly unlikely, those around Bush assumed he would approve the new initiatives in a matter of days. Following that, the National Command Authority would require 24-hours' notification before troops in Panama executed the causeway plan.[34]

On 22 July, as expected, the president approved NSD-17, a national security directive setting new guidelines for U.S. military actions in Panama to assert treaty rights and to keep Noriega and his followers off guard. The directive divided operations into four categories, based on a matrix of risk and visibility. Low-risk, low-visibility activities fell under Category I. As examples, NSD-17 listed such measures as publicizing the evacuation of U.S. government dependents, expanding media and psychological campaigns against the regime, and placing PDF members under formal escort whenever they entered a U.S. base. Low-risk, high-visibility activities constituted Category II, which included increasing MP patrols between U.S. installations, training Apache helicopter crews and battalion-size units in Panama, and practicing amphibious and combat operations at night. Category III consisted of medium-risk, high-visibility measures, such as the increase of U.S. armed patrols and reconnaissance in the vicinity of key PDF installations. The most sensitive and dangerous category, Category IV, encompassed high-risk, high-visibility operations and exercises. Examples included reestablishing U.S. access to the causeway and reasserting U.S. control over certain facilities at Fort Amador, Fort Espinar, and Quarry Heights. Because of the elevated level of risk, all Category III and IV proposals had to be submitted to the Joint Chiefs for approval at the interagency level or higher.[35]

Following dissemination of the new guidance, Woerner resubmitted the causeway proposal up the chain of command, notifying the National Command Authority that he was scheduling this Category IV event for 10 August. He quickly received the necessary authorization. At JTF-Panama, staff officers code-named the operation ALICE, which, according to one source, caused Cisneros some consternation at first. Why pick a female name? he wanted to know. Why not something stronger, given the magnitude of the undertaking? Rossi provided the answers. To begin with, he pointed out, there were definite security advantages to the term ALICE, should Noriega's people overhear anyone discussing the operation. He also noted the negative impact ALICE would have on PDF machismo once the operation had been executed and the code word publicized. Cisneros accepted the explanation.[36]

Just as the Southern Command and JTF-Panama were ironing out the final details of the plan, an unforeseen event intruded. On 8 August, just two days before

---

[34] JCS Internal Staff Paper (and atchs.) to CJCS, 20 Jul 89, sub: Military Activities in Panama.
[35] Cole, *Operation Just Cause*, pp. 11–12.
[36] JCS Internal Staff Paper (and atchs.) to DJS, 8 Aug 89, sub: Notification of Cat IV Activity—Operation ALICE; Collier Interv, 24 Jan 90.

Alice, a routine Sand Flea exercise turned into a serious confrontation.[37] The exercise, code-named Westward Ho, had six light armored vehicles from Task Force Semper Fi conducting a motorized reconnaissance that, at times, took them into Panamanian territory. This was allowed under the treaty, but legal niceties did not prevent two PDF *tránsitos* from stopping one of the LAVs while it was in a White, or Panamanian, area on the color-coded treaty map. The purpose behind this interference became apparent, as a group of Panamanians began what American sources described as a "small demonstration" at the site. The "outrage" of the demonstrators was duly filmed for Panama's evening newscasts. Some tense moments ensued, during which a reaction force with five light armored vehicles arrived and extricated the LAV being detained.

The LAVs then proceeded to link up with the main body of the reconnaissance force, which, en route to its destination, noticed that it was being followed by six PDF vehicles. At one point, the pursuers, without realizing or without caring, trailed the light armored vehicles into a Green zone, or area of coordination. The canal treaties forbid the Panama Defense Forces to enter such an area without prior coordination with U.S. forces, so the MARFOR commander ordered all six cars stopped. Thirteen Panamanians—four in uniform, nine in plain clothes—were removed from the vehicles at gunpoint and disarmed. When the marines began the process of detaining each person, five of the plain-clothed individuals awaited their turn by videotaping the proceedings, only to surrender their cameras once they were themselves detained. Also surrendered were several automatic weapons, two fragmentary grenades, five 9-mm. pistols, a flare pistol, a knife, and a Daisy BB gun. Once SOUTHCOM treaty affairs representatives arrived, the video equipment minus the film footage was returned, and the men were escorted out of the Green area.

That the thirteen had been disarmed at gunpoint made the incident newsworthy. What lent it even greater import was the fact that one of the men was Noriega's brother-in-law. The humiliation he suffered simply by being detained ensured retaliation, and, a few days later, the Panama Defense Forces picked up four U.S. military policemen. This, in turn, led Cisneros to retaliate in kind, blocking the entrance to Fort Amador and picking up four PDF personnel. This forceful demonstration had the desired effect, and the MPs were released. As one JTF-Panama staff officer observed, Noriega could now have no doubt that the situation was going to be more difficult. "That was when life started to get a little bit more interesting," the officer added.[38]

Concerns raised by the PDF's "ambush" of the light armored vehicle did not delay the execution of Operation Alice two days later. The first phase of the Category IV Purple Storm kicked off around dawn on 10 August and consisted of a series of diversionary movements. On the Atlantic side, beginning at 0545, some of Colonel Hale's soldiers practiced an emergency withdrawal of ordnance from the Fort Espinar ammunition depot where, prior to Nimrod Dancer, U.S. vehicles engaged in the same procedure had been stopped by the Panama Defense Forces at gunpoint. Hale sent two trucks to do the job, and neither encountered any

---

[37] The following account of the events of 8 August is based on Msg, CDR, JTF-PM, to CINCSO, 090440Z Aug 89, sub: SITREP/COMJTF-PM/085; Intervs, author with Collier, 24 Jan 90, and Cisneros, 30 Jan 90; and Reynolds, *Just Cause*, pp. 15–16. Reynolds gives a 7 August date to the Sand Flea.

[38] Collier Interv, 24 Jan 90.

Marines in their light armored vehicles

resistance. But they did get the attention of the Panamanian military, which was, of course, the purpose of the maneuver.[39]

On the Pacific side, elements of the 5th Battalion, 87th Infantry, from Task Force Bayonet moved soon after daylight to secure the Ancon area, including Balboa High School, Quarry Heights, and Gorgas Army Hospital. Meanwhile, light armored vehicles from Task Force Semper Fi took up positions outside the PDF DNTT station near Fort Amador. At 0900, the second phase of Operation ALICE, the main effort, began when elements of the 1st Battalion, 508th Infantry, another Task Force Bayonet unit, conducted air assaults into three landing zones on Fort Amador. Soon thereafter, units from the NIMROD DANCER mechanized battalion moved to link up with the infantry, and the combined force then made its way down the causeway, securing key terrain on Naos Island and a landing beach on Perico Island. LCMs escorted by craft from Special Boat Unit 26 then brought in six Marine LAVs over the beachhead. Throughout, JTF-Panama's AFFOR component provided air cover and back-up air support for the ground troops and naval vessels. By 1150, the operation was over, with the U.S. units back at their bases. In the days preceding ALICE, there had been some feeling that it would be the "trigger" event, that it would provoke a strong reaction, but at no point did the Panama Defense Forces offer any opposition. A PDF guard at the causeway surrendered his weapon voluntarily, and two PDF vehicles that had been set in place to block the causeway were removed as the mechanized and infantry force approached.[40]

ALICE was considered a huge success. As one JTF-Panama staff officer boasted, the operation brought U.S. troops to Noriega's doorstep, resulting in a loss of face for

---

[39] Msg, CDR, JTF-PM, to CINCSO, 110543Z Aug 89, sub: SITREP/COMJTF-PM/087; Interv, author with Col David R. E. Hale, U.S. Army, 28 Sep 89, Fort Leavenworth, Kans.

[40] Msg, CDR, JTF-PM, to CINCSO, 110543Z Aug 89, sub: SITREP/COMJTF-PM/087; JCS Internal Staff Paper (and atchs.) to CJCS, 10 Aug 89, sub: Memorandum for Record—Exercise ALICE; Collier Interv, 24 Jan 90.

the dictator. The exercise also showed the regime that U.S. headquarters could put together a large force on short notice and shut down Fort Amador and the three islands off the causeway. Equally satisfying was the realization that operations security had not been compromised in any significant way. In accordance with what treaty affairs advisers had predicted, the Panama Defense Forces received just enough advance information to confuse them. They knew there was going to be an operation, but not where the main effort would be. Thus Noriega's propaganda specialists and the regime-controlled media showed up only for the Marines' portion of ALICE; they were not present to provide an anti-American slant to the sight of the large U.S. mechanized and infantry force advancing down the causeway.[41]

With its diversionary actions, Task Force Atlantic had played a supporting role in ALICE. A few weeks later, it had the opportunity to mount a full-fledged Category IV operation of its own. In his 30 May message to Crowe, Woerner had recommended reoccupying various military quarters and facilities that the United States had leased to the Panamanian government before the crisis. One of these buildings was Quarters 32 at Fort Espinar, ostensibly the residence of the PDF 8th Infantry Company commander. With the deterioration in U.S.-Panamanian relations, the Panama Defense Forces had stopped paying rent on the building, which SOUTHCOM treaty affairs personnel charged was not being used for its intended purpose anyway. The regime countered that the facility had been transferred to Panama in 1984, along with other portions of what was then called Fort Gulick. The United States rejected this position and, in March 1989, terminated the lease. As of late August, however, the PDF had not turned the building back to U.S. Forces. In a message to the Joint Staff on 31 August, Woerner notified the National Command Authority of his intention to reoccupy Quarters 32 on 2 September. The operation was code-named BEATRICE.[42]

BEATRICE was a Category IV operation because the Southern Command could not rule out the possibility that the Panama Defense Forces would fight to retain possession of Quarters 32, which was now being used as a billet for visiting VIPs.[43] The building was guarded 24 hours a day (one guard at night, two during daylight). Complicating matters, American family housing was located within twenty meters of the structure. In short, given the possibility of a hostile PDF reaction and the attendant risks to U.S. military dependents, JTF-Panama had to take exceptional care in planning the building's reoccupation. From the beginning, the undertaking was treated as a major tactical operation, with highly detailed preparations, sand table rehearsals, and continuous requests for legal advice. At one point, Cisneros and Hale meticulously drafted a statement that the latter would read to the PDF company commander at Espinar, notifying him of the impending takeover of

---

[41] Intervs, author with Francis, 14 Dec 89, and Pantier, 21 May 91.

[42] Msg, CINCSO to CJCS, 301426Z May 89, sub: Asserting Treaty Rights; JCS Internal Staff Paper (and atchs.) to CJCS, 1 Sep 89, sub: USCINCSO Category IV OPERATION BEATRICE. One of the attachments is Msg, CINCSO to Joint Staff, 311745Z Aug 89, sub: Notification of Category IV Activity, in which Woerner provided the background and concept of operations for BEATRICE.

[43] The account of Operation BEATRICE that follows is based on Msg, CINCSO to Joint Staff, 311745Z Aug 89. Intervs, author with Maj Harry Tunnell, U.S. Army, 13 May 98, Fort Leavenworth, Kans.; Maj Reginald Sikes, U.S. Army, 7 May 99, Fort Leavenworth, Kans.; Collier, 24 Jan 90; Hale, 28 Sep 89; and Maj Brian Clark, U.S. Army, 2 May 2000, Fort Leavenworth, Kans. Briefing, Col Hale to TRADOC Warfighter X Seminar, 28 Sep 89, Fort Leavenworth, Kans.

Quarters 32. The trick in writing the statement was to convey the inevitability of the action in forceful but not offensive terms, so as not to deny the officer a face-saving exit.

In case the PDF commander did not accept a graceful way out, Hale had the force he needed to accomplish the mission. According to the concept of operations Woerner forwarded to the Joint Chiefs and National Command Authority, a locksmith and an MP liaison team with dogs would go to Quarters 32 to take possession of the building. In support would be an infantry company(-), a Marine platoon with LAVs (secretly infiltrated into Espinar through the fort's back gate over the course of two nights), and a military police company. The infantry and light armored vehicles would be used to isolate the building and stop any PDF attempt to send reinforcements, while the military police working with a psychological operations team would provide security and information for noncombatants in the housing area. Snipers would take positions across from Quarters 32 with instructions to engage anyone pointing weapons at U.S. troops. The Panama Defense Forces, as required by law, would be apprised of the operation in advance and warned of the consequences of resisting.

Light fighters stationed at Espinar kept Quarters 32 under continuous surveillance. The night before BEATRICE, a Scout, after having observed the PDF guard on duty bringing in a woman companion, dutifully submitted a report on "that particular engagement." The next morning, only one guard was present when the U.S. team riding in HMMWVs approached to retake the quarters. The guard made a quick telephone call, then picked up a TV antenna, flipped the building's keys to the senior U.S. officer present, and walked off. A military police squad with an explosive-detecting dog proceeded to clear the house, after which BEATRICE was over. That the operation transpired without incident Hale attributed to the PDF's psychological state of mind. During NIMROD DANCER, the frenetic schedule of 7th Infantry Division exercises, especially at night, had worn down the 8th Infantry Company at Espinar to the point where, as Hale later contended concerning Quarters 32, "We were able to bluff them out of it."[44]

Operation BEATRICE, as initially presented by Woerner to the National Command Authority, had targeted two buildings for reoccupation, Quarters 32 at Espinar and Quarters 323 on Quarry Heights. The SOUTHCOM commander's concept of operations was briefed to Secretary of Defense Cheney, after which Woerner received approval for the Espinar target only. Concerns over PDF intentions and the sensitive location of Quarters 323 led to the deletion of the second target, at least for the time being.[45] This decision and others like it, such as the postponement of ALICE, underscored the point that U.S. officers in Panama could not take for granted NCA approval for Category III and IV proposals. As was necessary and appropriate, the Bush administration would consider all requests in the context of broader political and diplomatic issues. Given this broader perspective, policy makers in Washington, after discussing risks and ramifications, might arrive at conclusions at variance with SOUTHCOM and JTF-Panama projections.

---

[44] Briefing, Col Hale to TRADOC Warfighter X Seminar, 28 Sep 89.
[45] In all, Woerner had called for the reoccupation of four facilities. By the time he left Panama, all four had been reoccupied without incident.

In some cases when the National Command Authority or the Pentagon expressed doubts about a proposed operation, JTF-Panama would revise the plan so as to allay specific concerns and elicit the necessary approval. There were times, however, when Cisneros wondered if officials back in Washington were being too cautious in their assessments. The general, as his admirers and even some of his detractors acknowledged, had an almost intuitive ability to anticipate how Noriega and the Panama Defense Forces would react to a specific military initiative. On rare occasions when Cisneros feared a fainthearted response from Washington to what he considered a safe and prudent undertaking, he would obviate involvement of higher headquarters simply by designating his plan Category I or II. As either, he could execute it on his own authority, without having to pass it up the chain of command to a point where, he might suspect, the measure in question could appear more deserving of a Category III or IV classification.[46]

Into September, the prognosis that the Panamanian military would not forcefully resist most initiatives to assert U.S. treaty rights remained unchanged. On those few occasions when U.S. officials worried that a николN DANCER operation might actually provoke an armed reaction or some other undesirable PDF response, commanders and staff adjusted their mix of psychological operations, surprise, and overwhelming force to discourage any such outcome. Yet, to say that the Panama Defense Forces would not overreact was not to say that it would not react at all. At issue was what kind of response to expect. Although Woerner, Loeffke, Cisneros, and others proved adept at predicting how the PDF would handle most U.S. challenges, the problem was in determining how to respond to the response. For example, after the success of Operation ALICE, the Noriega regime placed signs on the Amador Causeway proclaiming that it had reverted to Panamanian control and that U.S. forces could no longer wear their uniforms there. To challenge both claims, Woerner had to ask the National Command Authority for permission (which he received) to conduct another major causeway operation, ANNE MARIE, in mid-September.[47]

In this continuous process of action and reaction, calculations predicting how the Panama Defense Forces would respond to any U.S. initiative invariably distinguished between the institution itself and the individuals within it. SOUTHCOM and JTF-Panama assurances of PDF passivity during most U.S. exercises and operations generally applied to the institution. What an individual might do under pressure or in the heat of the moment was another matter and cause for concern. Anxiety on this point had existed throughout the crisis and pertained not just to planned confrontations but also to daily encounters, routine and otherwise, between Panamanian and U.S. forces. Concern increased, however, as U.S. policy became more aggressive under National Security Directive-17, and as troops and police on both sides found themselves caught up in the more truculent rhetoric and posturing.

Maj. Alan Mansfield, the Pacific-side provost marshal at Fort Clayton, witnessed how the more contentious and combative mood affected his daily responsibilities and those of the military police under his command. Writing to a

---

[46] Cisneros Interv, 30 Jan 90.

[47] JCS Internal Staff Paper (and atchs.) to CJCS, 13 Sep 89, sub: USCINCSO Category IV Exercise—ANN MARIE. (In Woerner's message attached to the staff paper, the commander spelled the operation as the planners had named it, Anne Marie.)

friend, Mansfield reported with pleasure that the "new rules of engagement give the MPs a lot of leeway." "Things are completely different now—any time the PDF violate the treaty in the freedom of movement arena, we meet the violation with a pile of forces." He went on to describe four examples that illustrated his point, one of which involved a female MP, Capt. Anna Patilla, responding to an incident (unspecified in the letter) at the DNTT. When she arrived, PDF members at the scene with their commanding officer, a lieutenant, locked and loaded their AK47s. In reply, "She pulled her pistol and told LT Rodriguez that if they pointed their weapons she would shoot him." To be threatened by a woman with a gun was a singular humiliation for any male PDF officer.

Mansfield went on to relate how, during the heightened tension, the Panama Defense Forces had charged him with "acts against the security of Panama and attempted murder of members of the PDF." When he learned of the charges, he sought a meeting with Captain Cortizo, the PDF's 5th Infantry Company commander at Fort Amador. "I told him that I was tired of certain personalities in the PDF and I was going to order them shot the next time they pointed a gun at one of my people. I talked all this war talk and more, then I left the building and went about my business." Mansfield was posturing for effect, a technique he had perfected over the course of the two-year crisis, but he was also clearly enjoying himself. Nor did he appear to regret that the "PDF run every time we try to talk to them. We no longer have joint patrols or a joint MP Desk. According to CPT Cortizo, the PDF are afraid to work with us."[48]

If the military police were becoming more assertive in the conduct of their duties, so, too, were other JTF-Panama units as they went through their daily routines. Patrols were but one example. Designed to collect information and show the flag, they did not fall under NSD-17 unless there were special circumstances. Yet, from mid-July on, in keeping with the spirit of the tougher U.S. policy (and without violating the provisions of the canal treaties), they became "more active," in Hale's words. At Fort Espinar, for example, squad-size patrols went out three times a day, twice during daylight, once at night. Whereas, in the early phases of NIMROD DANCER, they had kept to the roads and other established routes, once policy had been ratcheted up, they expanded their movements into White areas and into the jungle behind PDF positions. This kind of aggressive patrolling kept Panamanian units off-balance, forcing them to guess and react even as they were getting used to the increased tempo of U.S. operations.[49]

Shortly before the end of his five-month tour in Panama, Colonel Hale summarized the results of "Operation RATCHET." In late May, he stated, when JTF-Panama had begun asserting U.S. treaty rights, the command had sought minimal goals without being more provocative than need be. A firefight was something to be avoided, and the rules of engagement almost ensured an American "bleeding first." Under the new phase recommended by Woerner and others at the end of May and authorized by President Bush in NSD-17, exercises and operations to assert treaty rights began to "push the limits of the treaty." U.S. forces were more aggressive and more provocative, even at the risk of an armed confrontation. Working against such an incident was the fact that the new phase had evolved through a process of

---

[48] Ltr, Alan and Patty [Mansfield] to Tony [Schilling], 9 Sep 89.
[49] Quote from Interv, author with Hale, 28 Sep 89. Interv, author with Sikes, 7 May 99.

gradual escalation, allowing the Panama Defense Forces to acclimate to one level of activity before U.S. forces moved to a more intense level. In Hale's opinion, if he had done in May what he was doing in August and September, there almost certainly would have been a firefight at the outset of NIMROD DANCER.[50]

Cisneros was certainly comfortable with the even more hard-nosed approach authorized by NSD-17; he had been one of the key figures responsible for crafting it. But Woerner was the one who had recommended it to Washington, and he still had misgivings about the direction in which events were heading. Some in Panama suspected that a showdown with Panamanian armed forces would come on or around 1 September, the day a new—and, from the U.S. perspective, illegitimate—government in Panama would take office, but that milestone passed without incident.[51] In fact, according to Col. Mike Snell, the relatively new commander of the 193d Infantry Brigade, confrontations with the Panama Defense Forces fell off precipitously during most of September. On 5 September, Woerner sent a message to Crowe reiterating the purpose of U.S. military activity in the crisis: to protect American lives and property, to demonstrate U.S. treaty rights, and to train to be able to execute, if necessary, existing contingency plans. Those points, he indicated, had been reaffirmed with subordinate commanders following the political events of 1 September. He also acknowledged that the U.S. military in Panama needed to demonstrate its resolve to Noriega's "new" handpicked regime. Then, having conveyed those points to the chairman, he went on to note emphatically, "I do not intend to execute operations solely for the purpose of 'picking a fight.'"[52] Woerner recognized that the United States might have to employ military force to end the crisis, an option he still believed should be used only as a last resort. But he was also unwilling to goad the Panamanian military into providing Washington with a pretext for using force.

That Woerner refused to engage in gratuitous provocations was rapidly becoming a moot point. When he conveyed that message to Crowe, the general had only three weeks left before retirement, and he was fully aware that there were officers above him and under him who were beginning to believe that a military solution was the only alternative to a prolongation of the uncertainty, distractions, and drain on U.S. resources caused by the ongoing crisis. During the past four months, JTF-Panama had executed Purple Storms, contingency readiness exercises, and Sand Fleas under NIMROD DANCER and NSD-17. The exercises boosted morale, provided valuable lessons and experience, generated information, and enabled commanders to adjust command and control mechanisms. Yet, the crisis seemed no closer to resolution than it had at its outset two years before. Asserting U.S. treaty rights may have kept the Panama Defense Forces off-balance, but officers within that

---

[50] Quotes from Hale Interv, 28 Sep 89. Briefing, Col Hale to TRADOC Warfighter X Seminar, 28 Sep 89.

[51] On 1 September 1989, Francesco Antonio Rodriquez Poveda, a "close crony of Noriega's," was sworn in as the new Panamanian president. In response, President Bush refused to recognize the new government or to have diplomatic relations with it. From the administration's perspective, Panama was "without any legitimate government." Lt. Gen. Edward M. Flanagan Jr., U.S. Army (Ret.), *Battle for Panama: Inside Operation Just Cause* (Washington, D.C.: Brassey's, 1993), pp. 1–19.

[52] Snell Interv, 16 Dec 89. Quotes from Msg, CINCSO to CJCS, 5 Sep 89, sub: USCINCSO's Intent for U.S. Military Activities in Panama.

organization did not appear ready to move against their commander. Nor did they seem to be overly intimidated by JTF-Panama's operations and exercises. In the Pentagon, General Kelly alluded to the lack of conclusive results when he used the phrase "SOUTHCOM Follies" to describe the military measures Woerner had employed since the Panamanian elections.[53]

Woerner also knew that President Bush, having witnessed the failure to end the crisis through diplomacy, economic sanctions, OAS involvement, and tougher military measures, was running out of options and that many of his key advisers were running out of patience. Admiral Crowe, himself looking at his last few weeks in uniform, had reluctantly reached the conclusion that the United States might have to execute BLUE SPOON. According to journalist Bob Woodward, in September the admiral told certain key officers on the Joint Staff, "I don't know when it's going to happen, I don't know what's going to precipitate it, but I am convinced that we are going to have to go in with military force into Panama to resolve the situation, and we need to be ready to do it."[54]

For over two years of crisis in Panama, Woerner and Crowe had managed to counter what they considered to be the rash proposals of several civilian presidential advisers, especially under President Reagan, as well as the periodic planning critiques of senior officers in the Pentagon and at Fort Bragg. Now both men were retiring. What position would General Colin Powell, Crowe's successor, take on Panama? And what about the Thurman factor? Like Woerner, General Max Thurman, soon to take over as SOUTHCOM's commander, was extremely intelligent, but unlike Woerner, he was not a specialist in Latin American affairs. He also had a reputation for blunt talk, not necessarily an attribute in a situation that was as politically sensitive as it was militarily complex. How did Thurman intend to handle the crisis he would walk into as Woerner's successor? Woerner could only speculate. What he knew for certain was that on 30 September, he himself would cease to be an active participant, whatever the outcome.

---

[53] Woodward, *The Commanders*, p. 100.

[54] Ibid., p. 116. In *Operation Just Cause*, pp. 64–65, Donnelly, Roth, and Baker also mention Crowe's pessimistic view, quoting the admiral as saying to Kelly and another staff officer, "I am absolutely 100 percent convinced that the only way the situation is going to get resolved in Panama is with military force. You guys better be ready. . . . I can't tell you when it is going to happen and I can't tell you what the trigger is going to be, but I'm convinced that's the only way it's going to be resolved." The three journalists also write that Brent Scowcroft, President Bush's national security adviser, had reached a conclusion similar to Crowe's.

9

From Black Tuesday to Blue Spoon
October–December 1989

The SOUTHCOM change of command ceremony took place on 30 September 1989. Among the dignitaries in attendance were Army Chief of Staff General Carl Vuono and the Vice Chairman of the Joint Chiefs of Staff, Air Force General Robert Herres. Admiral Crowe, who had welcomed Woerner to his new command two years before, was not present. He had been honored at his own retirement ceremony in Annapolis the previous day. Former National Security Adviser, General Colin Powell, would succeed him as chairman of the Joint Chiefs.

After the Southern Command flag was passed from Woerner to General Maxwell R. Thurman, the new commander praised his predecessor, highlighted the strategic significance of Latin America, commented on SOUTHCOM's missions in the theater, and emphasized the "important new challenge" of ridding the earth of "the scourge of drugs." The only reference to the U.S.-Panama crisis in the brief speech was when Thurman quoted from President Bush's 11 May message the passage that denounced the Noriega regime and committed the United States to the cause of Panamanian democracy. If those listening expected to acquire a sense of how the new commander would deal with the dictator, they were disappointed. The talk was largely ceremonial, more platitude than policy.[1] What was generally recognized, at least among the U.S. officers present, was that the outgoing and incoming commanders had decidedly different personalities and ways of operating.

General Max Thurman

In the days leading up to his retirement, Woerner received accolades from many who had served under his command or worked with him in some capacity during his tour at Quarry Heights. The praise was often peppered with implied criticism of the way the general had been relieved. Thus Woerner's political adviser, John J. Youle, who chose to retire along with his boss, stated that "General Woerner has been right in every analysis, every policy recommendation, regarding Panama over the past 2½ years," an observation clearly critical of President George H. W. Bush's decision to "make a change."[2]

---

[1] An account of the change of command ceremony and a transcript of General Thurman's remarks can be found in the *Tropic Times*, 2 Oct 89.

[2] Ibid., 29 Sep 89. The phrase "make a change," used by General Vuono to inform Woerner of the president's decision, is in Woodward, *The Commanders*, p. 96.

General Woerner talks at the change of command ceremony.

Such kind remarks and other expressions of loyalty were gratifying, as Woerner prepared to reenter private life after thirty-four years in the Army. In the meantime, however, he still had to oversee the daily operations of a unified command and, of critical importance to him, to do what he could to ensure a smooth transition in leadership. To that end, he directed his staff to prepare extensive read-ahead books of policy statements, analyses, documents, and briefings for the benefit of his successor, with whom he planned to meet personally to discuss the myriad issues affecting the U.S. military in Latin America.

For his part, General Thurman was trying to learn as much as he could about his new assignment. In July, when he received a telephone call from General Vuono informing him of Woerner's "unprogrammed retirement" and asking if he would take the reins at the Southern Command, the 58-year-old Thurman was planning his own retirement after thirty-six years in the Army. His had been a distinguished career that ranged from a deployment to Lebanon when the United States intervened there in 1958, to two tours in Vietnam, to helping rebuild a shattered and demoralized U.S. Army once that war ended. As part of this latter achievement, he had revitalized the Army's Recruiting Command, no small feat given the antimilitary feelings in much of the country at the time. Promoted to lieutenant general, he moved on to become the Army's deputy chief of staff for personnel in 1981. Two years later, he received his fourth star and an appointment as vice chief of staff of the Army, a position that often placed him in the "joint" arena, attending meetings of the Joint Chiefs in their conference room, the Tank, and dealing with other service chiefs and their subordinates. In 1989, when Vuono offered him the command in Panama, Thurman was less than a month away from stepping down as commander of the Training and Doctrine Command, the "brains" of the Army, located at Fort Monroe, Virginia. He had held the position for two years, during which time he had been diagnosed as having asthma. Concerned about Panama's allergens, he waited to consult with his doctors and have a physical examination before accepting the new assignment.

Unlike Woerner, Thurman had a solid constituency in the U.S. capital, not only among the Pentagon's senior officers, but on Capitol Hill as well. "I was well-known in the Washington community," he observed as a matter of fact. "That was where General Woerner was having most of his difficulties."[3] Also, unlike Woerner, he did not have an extensive knowledge of Latin America, an area he had visited only about a half-dozen times in the performance of his military duties. In the time available to him between Vuono's call and the change of command at Quarry Heights, he was not going to become an expert on the region, but he could devour as much pertinent information as possible. Given his habits, the amount would be considerable. Over the years, he had acquired a reputation as a workaholic. A bachelor, he kept his office lights burning late, worked weekends, seemed to sleep little, and often resumed work before dawn. He had a penchant for detail, insisted on accuracy, and expected his subordinates to be well informed. Once he had accepted the command in Panama, he immersed himself in preparing for the new assignment, using as his "base of operations" a house in Alexandria, Virginia, owned by his brother, John R. Thurman, himself a retired Army lieutenant general. He also acquired an office in the Pentagon and brought in an executive officer to assist him.

General Thurman

During several weeks of extensive study for the SOUTHCOM command, Thurman read voraciously, attended numerous meetings and briefings, took an intensive course in Spanish, and, in general, began to develop a feel for what he would encounter after the 30 September ceremony. In Washington, he visited the "deputy dogs" and the "top dogs" in various agencies and organizations connected with U.S. Latin American policies: the National Security Council, Drug Enforcement Administration, Central Intelligence Agency, Treasury Department, and White House. He called on his "buddies" in Congress and was introduced to members of the committees with which he would have to deal. "I also resolved that I would be friends with the State Department," he recalled later. "I spent an enormous amount of my time and energy getting to know the Assistant Secretary of State [for Inter-American Affairs] Bernard Aronson." Of the numerous meetings Thurman attended, some covered general issues, some focused on the drug war, and some dwelt on the crisis in Panama. At the Pentagon, he met with Crowe, who told him, "I want you to take a fresh look at everything."[4]

---

[3] Except where noted, this and other quotations regarding Thurman's preparation for the SOUTHCOM position are taken from Interv, Col Richard H. Mackey with General Maxwell R. Thurman, U.S. Army (Ret.), 1992, U.S. Army War College/U.S. Army Military History Institute (USAWC/USAMHI) Senior Officer Oral History Program, Project 1992–1.

[4] Woodward, *The Commanders*, p. 103. Thurman later paraphrased Crowe as directing him, "Operate as if it is a clean sweep, fore and aft; it's a complete, new deal." Interv, John Partin with

"Everything" included the Prayer Book, which took Thurman to Fort Bragg on 4 August for a day-long briefing. General James J. Lindsay, the commander in chief of the U.S. Special Operations Command, accompanied Thurman. At Bragg, Maj. Gen. Gary Luck, the commander of the Joint Special Operations Command (JSOC), was there to brief the special operations version of the Blue Spoon operation order, while Lt. Cols. Bob Pantier and William Bennett flew up from Panama to represent JTF-Panama and the Southern Command, respectively. Lt. Gen. Carl Stiner, the XVIII Airborne Corps commander, was not able to attend, so his deputy, Maj. Gen. William A. Roosma, and planner Lt. Col. Timothy McMahon spoke for the corps.

The briefing lasted eight hours and was broken into three parts: a general overview of the Prayer Book, the Blue Spoon operations assigned to Luck's joint special operations task force, and JTF-Panama's conventional portion of Blue Spoon. Possibly influenced by the Prayer Book's critics in the Pentagon, Thurman indicated that he was not comfortable with fundamental aspects of the existing plan; it was, he said, an "unworkable operation." The gradual buildup of U.S. troops from outside Panama, called for in the Post Time plan, violated the tenets of operations security and surprise and, in his view, "depended on everybody standing fast on the PDF side while the operation went down." The concept, he later recalled, reminded him of the piecemeal approach the United States had adopted in Vietnam, with disastrous results. In addition to these reservations, he did not like the idea of having the special and conventional Blue Spoon operations run by two different headquarters answering directly to the SOUTHCOM commander, a violation, in his mind, of the military principle of unity of command.

Thurman emphasized to all present that he had not yet been confirmed as the commander in chief, Southern Command; that he in no way intended to encroach on General Woerner's prerogatives; and that he had no authority to direct the assembled group to do anything. "You guys have to obey your current boss," he recalled saying, referring to Woerner. But, having observed propriety, he went on to add that, once he took command in Panama, he would direct the various headquarters working on the Prayer Book, and Blue Spoon in particular, to come up with a different concept. The gradual buildup would have to be jettisoned in favor of a rapid assault, employing surprise and overwhelming combat power. Furthermore, in the interest of unity of command, the joint special operations task force would have to be placed under the conventional joint task force from the XVIII Airborne Corps. Thurman asked Luck, "Do you have any problems with this?" Luck answered that he did not, even though the command and control arrangement proposed by Thurman technically violated a near-sacred principle within the special operations community that special operations units with their unorthodox methods and requirements should not be placed under a commander of conventional forces. Beginning with World War II, recent history was replete with the tragic results of conventional commanders, acting out of ignorance, misunderstanding, or indifference, misusing unconventional forces assigned to them. Yet Luck's reply to Thurman did not ignore either the principle or the history. The JSOC commander simply assumed (correctly, as events turned out) that, under the realignment, the joint special operations task force would answer to a joint task force commanded by

---

General Maxwell R. Thurman, U.S. Army, 12 Apr 90, Fort Benning, Ga.

Stiner, a general who had extensive special operations experience and who himself had commanded the Joint Special Operations Command. Stiner understood how to employ Special Operations Forces and recognized their strengths and limitations on the battlefield; under his control, the unconventional forces called for in BLUE SPOON ran no risk of being misused.[5]

Luck's assumption begged the question of when during the execution of BLUE SPOON the SOUTHCOM commander would call upon Stiner and the XVIII Airborne Corps to take charge of the operation. Woerner had deliberately left the answer vague, sticking to his plan to have a conventional joint task force from Fort Bragg deploy only after hostilities had begun and only if they had escalated to a level necessitating the corps' involvement. This meant that, initially, JTF-Panama would run conventional BLUE SPOON operations. If, at some point in the battle, Woerner determined that the XVIII Airborne Corps was needed, there would be a handoff of command and control responsibilities in the midst of the fighting. Thurman had studied this arrangement and foresaw a potentially awkward transition. So, well before taking over the Southern Command, he let Kelly, Vuono, and others know that he intended to put "one guy in charge" from the outset: in the event of a U.S. invasion of Panama, the XVIII Airborne Corps commander would be the Southern Command's principal "war fighter." Also militating for this streamlined arrangement was Thurman's opinion of the SOUTHCOM staff, which he regarded as a group of foreign area specialists, not warriors. "The staff in Panama isn't big enough, doesn't have enough people on it, is not smart enough, to do the warfighting game," he claimed. The XVIII Airborne Corps staff, on the other hand, was twice as large as SOUTHCOM's and specialized in planning contingency operations. For Thurman, common sense dictated that an XVIII Airborne Corps joint task force be responsible for executing BLUE SPOON from beginning to end, an arrangement he expected the Joint Chiefs to endorse soon after the 30 September change of command ceremony.[6]

Stiner personally received informal notification of this revised arrangement when, on 5 August, he attended the ceremony at Fort Monroe in which Thurman stepped down as the TRADOC commander. Once the official observances ended, Thurman left the reviewing stand and went over to his friend of sixteen years. Sticking his finger in Stiner's chest, he said in his crisp voice, "Carlos, you are my man for Panama. I hold you responsible for all contingency planning and any combat operations."[7]

---

[5] The account of the meeting at Fort Bragg is taken from Woodward, *The Commanders*, p. 104; Donnelly, Roth, and Baker, *Operation Just Cause*, p. 55; Cole, *Operation Just Cause*, p. 13. Quotes from Interv, Partin with Thurman, 12 Apr 90. Interv, author with Lt Col Robert Pantier, U.S. Army, 21 May 91, Fort Leavenworth, Kans.; Telephone Interv, author with Maj David Huntoon, 27 Jun 90; Conversation, author with Lt Col Timothy McMahon, 20 Dec 89, Fort Clayton, Panama. Concerning Thurman's guidance that the joint special operations task force should come under the operational control of the conventional joint task force, the argument would also be made that Stiner, besides ensuring that the unconventional forces would not be misused, could also ensure that the special operations forces would not interfere in conventional operations.

[6] Quotes from Thurman Interv, 12 Apr 90. Woodward, *The Commanders*, pp. 103–04.

[7] Woodward, *The Commanders*, p. 101. Donnelly, Roth, and Baker, *Operation Just Cause,* p. 55, give a fuller version of what Thurman said to Stiner. "Carlos, I've talked to the chief and I've talked to the chairman, and you are my man for everything that has to be done there. I'm putting you in charge of all forces and you've got it: planning, execution, the whole business. I have looked at my

General Stiner

Thurman's remarks on the PRAYER BOOK to Pentagon officials, to the planners assembled at Bragg, and to General Stiner rendered Woerner something of a lame duck—an idiom used by one of Stiner's subordinates—insofar as planning for U.S. military contingencies in Panama was concerned. Any doubts on that score seemed dispelled when, in response to guidance from the Joint Chiefs, the new director of operations at the Southern Command, Brig. Gen. William Hartzog, began reviewing the PRAYER BOOK in July with an eye to devising an "alternative" to the existing concept of operations. Woerner monitored the process, but, according to Hartzog, did not get actively involved in the review or offer any "earthshaking or decisive guidance." As for Thurman, Hartzog met with him in Washington, informed him of the project, and gave him a progress report. The alternative plan was code-named BANNER SAVIOR, and its contents satisfied in many respects the criticism Kelly, Stiner, Luck, and now Thurman had expressed about POST TIME and BLUE SPOON. The principle of surprise would be added to that of mass, conventional and special operations would be integrated, and the list of targets would be expanded. After Thurman received the BANNER SAVIOR briefing, he offered his thoughts on the evolving plan, again making clear that he had yet to be confirmed as the new SOUTHCOM commander. As events turned out, BANNER SAVIOR would be a "short-lived" project, to use Hartzog's words. But the initiative, while it lasted, facilitated Hartzog's interaction with the XVIII Airborne Corps where, as a result of Thurman's visit, Stiner had directed his two Panama planners, Colonel McMahon and Major Huntoon, to prepare a new BLUE SPOON operation order compatible with the incoming SOUTHCOM commander's statements of intent.[8]

In the final few weeks before assuming his new command, Thurman used what he called his "garden leave" to intensify even further his preparations for Panama. There were numerous meetings in August and September, including the one Woerner had anticipated. When the two generals met, Thurman alluded to the circumstances of Woerner's departure, saying, "I want you to know I had nothing

---

staff and I have told the chairman and I have told the chief that it cannot run a contingency operation. He said you can have it and I'm holding you responsible." Stiner recollects Thurman contacting him before the visit to Bragg and the change of command ceremony. According to Stiner, General Vuono telephoned him even before the announcement of Woerner's retirement and told him he needed to talk to Thurman. Thurman himself called Stiner about a week later, telling him, "You're my JTF; I'm going to hold you responsible and I will turn everything over to you. And I hold you responsible for doing the whole thing." Intervs, Robert K. Wright Jr., U.S. Army Center of Military History, with Lt Gen Carl W. Stiner, U.S. Army, 2, 7, 27 Mar 90 and 11 Jun 90, Fort Bragg, N.C.

[8] Interv, author with Brig Gen William Hartzog, U.S. Army, and Col. Tom Braaten, USMC, 29 Jun 90, Quarry Heights, Panama.

to do with this." To which Woerner replied, "If I thought you did, I wouldn't be here." Thurman took possession of the thick briefing books the SOUTHCOM staff had prepared, but on the whole, Woerner regarded the meeting itself as not being very "substantive." Rather than discussing the full range of hemispheric issues, he later related, the talks focused narrowly on the crisis in Panama.[9]

Late in September, Thurman briefed Admiral Crowe and the Joint Chiefs on his "views about everything down there," meaning in the Southern Command's area of responsibility. When he came to the crisis and the PRAYER BOOK, he stated forcefully that he could not support the current BLUE SPOON operation order and intended to change it. Crowe, according to Thurman, said, "Well, you go down and change the plan the way you want to. When you get done, bring it back up here." At no point did the admiral criticize the existing plan, which he had supported for over a year and which the Joint Chiefs themselves had approved.[10]

En route to Panama, Thurman changed into his battle dress uniform (BDU). "I wanted there to be no mistaking that a warrior had arrived," he said later. "Now a lot of people would laugh at that because they don't perceive me to be a warrior. They look at me as a manager. But the whole purpose was to say, 'This is a different climate now guys. You have a new guy on the block. Make sure that all the Panamanians reporting back to Noriega don't get the sense that there is some guy coming down in his aloha shirt. There was a guy coming down wearing his pistol and his fatigues.' The first order I gave after I assumed command was that fatigues would be the uniform of the day."[11]

The SOUTHCOM change of command took place on a Saturday morning at Fort Clayton. To enhance security, JTF-Panama simultaneously ran Operation RIO BRAVO as a diversion, sending a mechanized company into Fort Amador to relieve an MP quick reaction force.[12] Once the ceremony was over, Thurman went to his headquarters at Quarry Heights to settle in. The next day, Sunday, was to be his first "working day," as he sought to determine "what the lay of the land was" through a series of briefings that lasted until 1800. In the process, his staff and other subordinates received their initiation into what was widely known as the Thurman Effect.[13] Not that the new commander unleashed his modus operandi upon unsuspecting minions: his reputation for long hours, hard work, predawn briefings, blunt talk, probing questions, and relentless demands had preceded him. So, too, had the nicknames he had acquired along the way—Mad Max, the Maxatollah, the Emperor Maximilian. There were a few present who had previously served under him and could testify to his agile mind, acute intellect, and sharp tongue-lashings, as well as to the fact that he demanded and got results.

---

[9] The Thurman-Woerner exchange is quoted in Woodward, *The Commanders*, p. 98. Woerner's assessment of the meeting is in Interv, General Frederick F. Woerner Jr., U.S. Army (Ret.), U.S. Army Military History Institute, Carlisle Barracks, Pa.

[10] Thurman Interv, 12 Apr 90.

[11] Thurman Interv, 1992, USAWC/USAMHI, Project 1992–1.

[12] On Operation RIO BRAVO, see Msg, CINCSO to JCS, 011556Z Oct 89, sub: Situation Report 149.

[13] The so-called Thurman Effect is discussed in Donnelly, Roth, and Baker, *Operation Just Cause*, pp. 52, 67; Woodward, *The Commanders*, p. 94; Lt. Gen. Edward M. Flanagan Jr., U.S. Army (Ret.), *Battle for Panama: Inside Operation Just Cause* (Washington, D.C.: Brassey's, 1993), pp. 22–23. Several officers who had served under Thurman also offered comments—including those presented in the quotations—to the author on the general's way of conducting business.

The Army was Thurman's "wife," according to one metaphor, and several officers who had worked for him attested that he served her fully, faithfully, and zealously. For some, the marital comparison was proffered as a compliment; for others, especially those with families on accompanied tours, as a reproach. Those adhering to the latter view argued that Thurman, having no experience himself with family life, had no understanding of it and thus gave little thought to how essential it was to his subordinates. "I don't think he ever knew or cared that I had a wife and children," lamented one SOUTHCOM staff officer after spending over a hundred consecutive days working late at the headquarters. Given one night off to have dinner with his wife, this same officer had just raised a forkful of spaghetti to his mouth when the telephone rang. General Thurman wanted him back in the office, not to tackle some major issue but, in the officer's opinion, to address some "silly thing"; the plate of pasta went flying against the dining room wall. Another story had a staff officer waking up at 0330 in a cold sweat, to be assured by his spouse, "It's OK. The general hasn't called."

All that said, one should not conclude that Thurman's subordinates at Quarry Heights objected to hard work, long hours, and high standards of accountability. During periods of heightened tension in the two-year crisis with Noriega, working past midnight and, after a few hours sleep, returning to work before dawn had been routine for many SOUTHCOM and component officers. As for Thurman's rough handling of advisers or briefers who seemed poorly informed or poorly prepared, the argument could be made that, if you did not have a thorough working knowledge of the specific issues assigned to you, the general had every right to call that to your attention in whatever manner he chose. What most critics of the Thurman Effect questioned was not the work it entailed but whether a steady subjection to consecutive work days, long hours, unexpected phone calls, and brusque treatment, when combined with a seeming lack of concern about the personal needs of the staff, offered the best way to achieve positive results without adversely affecting headquarters morale. Not helping matters were the rumors circulating before Thurman's arrival that he considered the Southern Command a "Sleepy Hollow," a sinecure for Latin Americanists within the military as well as for officers who were not quite competent enough to serve in more prestigious and demanding organizations. Once ensconced at Quarry Heights, Thurman sometimes reinforced this impression by relying disproportionately on only a handful of his staff, notably General Hartzog and Marine Col. Tom Braaten, the two ranking officers in the Operations Directorate. Other staff officers he seemed to keep at arm's length, to a degree that implied a lack of respect or confidence. In one meeting, just a few days into his command, he reached down into the ranks to make a young Navy lieutenant in the Military Intelligence Directorate his principal adviser on Noriega, a clear indication that he found that officer's superiors wanting in some way. He also turned to outside experts to analyze his headquarters for the purpose of recommending organizational and operational changes. In light of these and similar actions, U.S. officers in Panama were soon experiencing and, in many cases, lamenting their own version of the Thurman Effect.

"BLACK TUESDAY": THE 3 OCTOBER COUP ATTEMPT

Characteristically, Thurman was still in his office Sunday night, 1 October 1989, when he received a telephone call from Hartzog. The headquarters, Hartzog declared, had received a report claiming that a Panamanian officer was planning to mount a coup d'état against Noriega the next morning. If the report proved true, Thurman, in just his second day as the SOUTHCOM commander, would be facing a pivotal moment in a crisis that had defied resolution for over two years.[14]

Following the call from Hartzog, Thurman convened a meeting in the Tunnel, where he learned that the wife of a Panamanian major had contacted a female friend of hers who worked as a secretary at the Southern Command. When the secretary could not locate her boss, she phoned her father, who knew Thurman's personal secretary. He relayed the information regarding an imminent coup to her, and she, in turn, got in touch with a lieutenant colonel in the SOUTHCOM Secretary, Joint Staff office, who immediately informed Hartzog and others. Thurman, in his own words, was "spooked" over the unorthodox chain—wives, friends, fathers, and stenographers—through which such portentous information had arrived at Quarry Heights. It was too haphazard, too chancy, almost lackadaisical, and just plain bizarre. Yet he could not ignore the report. He therefore asked the CIA chief of station and the CIA representative to the Southern Command to meet with the major's wife.

The woman turned out to be Adela Bonilla de Giroldi, wife of Maj. Moisés Giroldi Vega, the 38-year-old commander of the PDF 4th Infantry Company, charged with security at the Comandancia. The two CIA agents drove to the house of Thurman's secretary, where they met with the señora. She told them of the coup plot and her husband's request to meet with a U.S. decision maker, meaning a high-ranking officer from the Southern Command, perhaps the commander himself. Having conveyed this message, Sra. Giroldi went to pick up her husband, and the two agents returned to the Tunnel to discuss the meeting with Thurman. They then went back to the secretary's house to meet the major.

The ensuing conversation took fewer than thirty minutes, during which Major Giroldi, appearing "nervous" and "scared," refused to get out of his truck. Essentially, he told the two men that the coup was scheduled for the next morning and that, in addition to his own 4th Company, he had the support of two other PDF units, the 1st Public Order Company, or Dobermans, at the Comandancia and the cavalry squadron at Panama Viejo. Furthermore, the commander of Battalion 2000 at Fort Cimarrón had agreed not to get involved. The main threats to the coup, as Giroldi assessed them, were the 5th Infantry Company at Fort Amador, the 7th Infantry Company at Rio Hato, and the elite UESAT units. Since the move against Noriega would take place at the Comandancia, Giroldi wanted U.S. forces to block certain approach routes to stop any unit that might attempt to rescue the general. Two avenues the major mentioned specifically were the Bridge of the Americas that Rio Hato–based units would have to cross and the main road leading from Fort Amador to the Comandancia.[15] He

---

[14] The account of the 3 October coup in this section is based on reconstructions from a variety of sources. The fullest journalistic account of the events between 1 October and 3 October can be found in Kempe, *Divorcing the Dictator*, pp. 369–97. Kempe clearly had access to key U.S. officials together with some of the survivors of the coup attempt. Various chronologies and oral histories helped to flesh out Kempe's account and to support or refute the events he describes. Woodward, *The Commanders*, pp. 119–25, also offers an inside analysis, most of which is not contradicted by official accounts.

[15] In *Divorcing the Dictator*, Kempe calls attention to a dispute over what Giroldi asked for in the way of U.S. support. After the coup had failed, Sra. Giroldi claimed that she and her hus-

also asked that the families of the rebel leaders be granted safe haven on American bases if necessary. During the short conversation, Giroldi emphasized that the coup would be strongly nationalistic and that he intended to proceed with or without U.S. support. In one gesture to demonstrate the patriotic motives behind his undertaking, he refused to give his American interlocutors a telephone number at which he could be reached once the coup was under way.

The CIA representatives were convinced of Giroldi's sincerity. Thurman was not so sure. That Giroldi and Noriega were very close was no secret. The dictator was godfather to the Giroldis' son and had been best man when the couple renewed their wedding vows (as all PDF officers were directed to do at Noriega's behest). Giroldi rated such special attention from Noriega because of the key role he had played in putting down the coup attempt against the strongman in March 1988. Thereafter, Noriega had personally looked after the young officer's professional welfare, promoting him to major and ultimately making him head of the security unit at the Comandancia. Giroldi, one author has noted, was one of a handful of people Noriega trusted around him with a machine gun. Why, then, was the major considering action against his benefactor? Giroldi and his wife claimed that increasing signs of Noriega's instability—his drinking and belligerence, as well as other excesses and abuses—rendered the PDF commander unfit to lead. Noriega had become an embarrassment and a liability to Panama's national interest and honor, and drastic action was required to remove him from power.

The nature of that action also troubled Thurman, as it did the CIA agents. Giroldi did not intend to arrest or kill Noriega. Rather, he planned to seize the Comandancia once the general was inside, invite other units to defect, deny Noriega access to critical communications and staff, and, then, once the dictator realized the hopelessness of his isolated position, convince him to retire, together with several senior Panamanian officers. There would be no need to incarcerate Noriega, and no need to turn him over to the Americans, despite the criminal indictments against him in the United States. The whole matter, in short, was to be handled in a gentlemanly way, with Noriega stepping aside graciously once he accepted the fact that he had been deposed. The plan, while conforming to the Panamanian tradition of fairly bloodless coups, failed to impress the two CIA agents who estimated the chances of success at less than fifty-fifty.

Thurman was even less optimistic, regarding the plot as "preposterous." More than that, its near surrealistic elements reinforced his suspicion that Giroldi was either incompetent or, worse, a fraud. The whole scheme, Thurman had to consider, might be a setup, "a ruse" as he put it, designed specifically to lure a U.S. commander new to his post into committing American troops to a nonexistent revolt, a move that would make him a laughingstock and undermine his credibility. There was something else that caused Thurman to suspect a "sting operation." Unknown to all but a handful of SOUTHCOM officers, a command-wide, no-notice contingency readiness exercise was scheduled to begin at 0400 Monday. Under JTF-Panama, certain U.S. forces would be assembled at their bases, armed, and deployed around sunrise to all American housing areas in the former Canal

---

band had specifically requested that U.S. forces block all ("*todas*") of the main routes leading to the Comandancia and that the Southern Command provide air cover as well. The official U.S. version is that the Giroldis asked that only two routes—the Bridge of the Americas and the road out of Fort Amador—be blocked and that there was no mention of air cover.

Zone. As Thurman later recounted, "I said, 'That sorry bastard has found out and he is preempting to see what I am going to do about all that.' So he wants to find out who Thurman is."[16]

Around midnight, General Cisneros received a telephone call from Quarry Heights, telling him to cancel the no-notice exercise and report to the Tunnel. When he arrived, he learned of the CIA contacts with Giroldi. Thurman, Cisneros said later, was justifiably cautious. The USARSO commander himself was wary, yet tended to give credence to the plot and viewed it as an opportunity the Southern Command could exploit. Going ahead with the predawn deployments, he argued, would signal moral support for the coup without involving U.S. troops in anything more than a training event, the kind they had been conducting routinely over the past several months. Thurman demurred. He would not reinstate the readiness exercise. So Cisneros changed his tack, requesting that Thurman instead authorize him to move an infantry company into Fort Amador to secure vulnerable American housing areas if necessary. Amador, Cisneros explained, was a potential "terrorist target," an installation that the Panamanian military had indicated could come under attack should the United States take direct action against Noriega. Helping to alleviate any concern on Thurman's part that the insertion of the company might be playing into Noriega's hands, Cisneros proposed a low-profile movement, with the soldiers arriving dressed for physical training, their weapons and combat gear stashed out of sight in the bottom of their trucks. Around 0800, they could change clothes and be ready to secure the fort and to contain the Panama Defense Forces there, should Thurman direct them to do so. After Cisneros laid out the finer details of his proposed deception, Thurman gave his approval. He also told Cisneros to put JTF-Panama on a thirty-minute alert posture for a contingency readiness exercise, just in case one should prove necessary. He further determined that, if the coup did take place, the rebels' family members should be taken onto U.S. bases, as Giroldi had requested.

With these decisions out of the way, Thurman received a briefing on Giroldi from his military intelligence staff about an hour before dawn. Brig. Gen. Mike Schneider, the Southern Command's director of intelligence, was relatively new to his post, so he let Ken Pierce, a young Navy lieutenant who had been in Panama about a year and a half, take the lead. Thurman was impressed, to the point of making Pierce his personal "Panama analyst." As the Navy officer recalled, "My chain of command that morning effectively became me to General Thurman. . . . Actually, there were five levels in the chain of command between me and General Thurman that were brushed aside."[17] For the remainder of the crisis, Pierce would never be far from Thurman's elbow.

In the wee hours of Monday, 2 October, officials in Washington received their first notification of the impending upheaval in Panama. The CIA sent an urgent message for the National Command Authority, providing an account of the meetings between the two agents and the Giroldis. Meanwhile, John Maisto, the chargé d'affaires in the U.S. Embassy in Panama City, alerted the State Department. From Quarry Heights, Thurman called Lt. Gen. Tom Kelly, starting a chain of phone calls in Washington: Kelly to Colin Powell, Powell to Secretary of Defense Cheney, and

---

[16] Thurman Interv, 12 Apr 90.

[17] Interv, author with Lt Cdr Kenneth D. Pierce, USN, 21 May 98, Fort Leavenworth, Kans.

Cheney to President Bush's national security adviser, Brent Scowcroft. After talking to Cheney, Powell headed to the National Military Communications Center in the Pentagon, where a crisis action team was quickly set up to monitor developments. With little more information to go on than what was available to those meeting with Thurman in the Tunnel, the officers present in the communications center shared SOUTHCOM's skepticism. Giroldi's plan seemed shaky, his motives and reliability questionable. After receiving an intelligence update, Powell decided he would recommend blocking the Amador route, a fairly safe measure. He had qualms, however, about shutting down the Bridge of the Americas, an action that could only be interpreted as American involvement in the coup attempt and that would place U.S. troops dangerously close to the Comandancia.

Shortly after dawn, a company from the 1st Battalion, 508th Infantry (Airborne), entered Fort Amador and began jogging on the causeway. A bit later, Thurman issued a warning order to JTF-Panama to be prepared to block Fort Amador and the Bridge of the Americas but not to do so without a direct order from his headquarters. Nearly all U.S. forces would be on full alert without necessarily knowing why, and Cisneros was told to reduce the reaction times of specific units, should they be ordered into action. Soon after 0800, various aircraft including an AC–130 were put on one-hour alert status at Howard Air Force Base. Still later that morning, JTF-Panama's Marine Forces component placed a Fleet Anti-Terrorist Security Team platoon near the Bridge of the Americas. Located with the platoon were ten heavy road graders from USARSO's 536th Engineer Battalion that could be used to block traffic should the order come. In another precautionary move, JTF-Panama fire support elements were placed on call.

Meanwhile, in Washington, the president and senior national security advisers who had not yet heard about the planned coup received a briefing on the situation. An hour later, at 0900 EDT (Eastern Daylight Time—Washington time running one hour ahead of Panama time), President Bush convened a meeting in the Oval Office. After being advised to take a generally cautious approach, he reportedly responded, "Look, you've had me out there for the last couple of months begging these guys to start a coup. If someone's actually willing to do one, we have to help them."[18] He went on to state his intention to have U.S. forces block Fort Amador and the Bridge of the Americas if such actions proved necessary to protect American lives and installations. He also indicated that America's willingness to support a coup would be strengthened if the plotters included in their planned statement references to democracy and the need for international support. At 0930, Bush cut back the number of advisers in his office and conducted further discussions. The urgency of the talks diminished, however, when a message arrived that the coup had been postponed; the message did not give a new date. To several present, this only confirmed their suspicions that the whole enterprise was either bogus or "half-baked." There was no further need to take up the president's valuable time with something that had not occurred and, in the minds of some, would not.

While Bush moved on to other pressing business, senior U.S. officials in Washington and Panama, however skeptical they might be, had to be prepared just in case Giroldi did launch a coup attempt. Lawyers at the State Department and the Southern Command offered opinions on the legality of using U.S. troops to block

---

[18] Baker, *Politics of Diplomacy*, p. 185.

Fort Amador and the Bridge of the Americas. (Blocking Amador was allowed under the treaty, they concluded; blocking the bridge was more problematic.) Also at the State Department, Michael Kozak, a veteran of the crisis, talked with Maisto in Panama about the president's desire to have the coup plotters include a call for democratic elections and international support in whatever public pronouncement they planned to make justifying their action. Around midday, a State Department drafted message containing these sentiments made its way to Panama and into the hands of Sra. Giroldi to deliver to her husband.

At Quarry Heights, Thurman stayed in the Tunnel most of Monday, assessing incoming information and discussing various courses of action and appropriate rules of engagement. In a conversation with Powell, he indicated that he would justify whatever military action he took "in the name of protection of U.S. citizens," almost always a safe legal argument. When a note from Sra. Giroldi arrived, indicating that the coup had been postponed only until the next day, Tuesday, 3 October, it did little to allay Thurman's serious doubts about Major Giroldi's intentions. In fact, information Thurman received throughout the day only increased his skepticism. Postponement of the coup had allowed U.S. officials to take a closer look at the Panamanian major, with the CIA reporting that Giroldi had a history of being involved in entrapment operations. The most recent episode had been in June when he was purported to have circulated rumors of a coup in order to "ferret out" disloyal elements within the Panama Defense Forces. In support of this assessment, Lieutenant Pierce pointed out that in the past nineteen months, there had been twenty instances of rumored coup attempts, the products of wishful thinking, disinformation, or the Panama rumor mill. Giroldi, one SOUTHCOM intelligence officer advised, "is totally corrupt." By Monday afternoon, the command position being relayed to the Joint Chiefs of Staff was that Giroldi was probably on a mission to spread "bogus disinformation" (a superb example of a nonsensical redundancy).

That being said, the Southern Command still had to follow a prudent course and be ready to act just in case Giroldi turned out to be on the level. Having been informed of the legality and legal ramifications of certain specific actions, Thurman again talked with Cisneros to determine what posture JTF-Panama would assume on Tuesday. And again, Cisneros later recalled, "we got into it," by which he meant "a whole day of arguing." If a coup attempt did occur, both generals assumed, it would probably take place in the morning. Cisneros once more advocated putting a force into Fort Amador, this time a company from the mechanized battalion attached to JTF-Panama during Operation NIMROD DANCER. Thurman was cautious as before, expressing concern over the perceptions the move would generate about U.S. involvement in a coup. Finally, when he was told the Panamanian military would be notified in advance that the deployment was a routine training exercise, he decided to go with the plan, which, after being forwarded to the Pentagon, was approved by the Joint Chiefs. Thurman also told Cisneros to have JTF-Panama prepared Tuesday morning to conduct an on-order contingency readiness exercise, and he directed that various aircraft at Howard Air Force Base again be placed on full alert. Around 1800 Monday, the command's Center for Treaty Affairs informed the Panama Defense Forces of the mechanized company's training exercise at Amador the next morning. Some U.S. officers believed that Giroldi, if telling the truth, would learn of this information and interpret it as American support for his undertaking. Sometime before midnight, the Southern Command also informed Powell and the Joint Chiefs that, according to the latest information received from Sra. Giroldi, the coup would begin the next morning at 0800, Panama time.

Sometime before that hour on Tuesday, 3 October, U.S. marines again took up positions near the Bridge of the Americas. Cisneros had instructed them to look "menacing" but not to block the highway over the bridge unless specifically ordered to do so. Cisneros himself was following the mechanized company en route to Fort Amador. Shortly before 0800, reports reached him of disturbances within the Comandancia compound, whereupon he ordered the company to move faster to its destination. The coup, he surmised, was under way, although he could not be sure.

That was the problem. No ranking U.S. officers or officials could be certain as to what exactly was happening. Neither the Southern Command nor U.S. Army, South, had direct contact with Giroldi or any other officer involved in the plot. As initial reports of troop activity and gunfire at the PDF headquarters began arriving at Quarry Heights, Thurman tried to acquire a clearer picture of what was going on. He had several intelligence sources to draw on, CNN would be closely monitored, and there was always the vantage point the Southern Command enjoyed from its perch on Ancon Hill, from which staff officers could look down directly into the Comandancia compound. Yet, despite the flow of information he received at his command post in the Tunnel, Thurman was not able that morning to determine or, in some cases, even to approximate in a timely way what was transpiring. This uncertainty, taken in conjunction with the suspicions he and some of his staff harbored concerning the rebel officers' motives and intentions, created doubts in the first hour or so as to whether a coup was actually in progress. The shots being reported could have been staged, part of the ruse Thurman still suspected.

Given such doubts, Thurman's initial response was measured. Within an hour of the first reports of gunfire, he closed Howard, raised the Personnel Movement Limitations level from Alpha to Delta, ordered Department of Defense dependent schools secured, and launched several aircraft for reconnaissance. During that same period, though, when Cisneros sought permission to execute the preplanned contingency readiness exercise, Thurman refused. In light of the sketchy information available to him at the time, he thought it premature to be maneuvering large numbers of U.S. forces, even if the measures they contemplated were purely defensive.

In Washington, meanwhile, Robert Gates, the president's deputy national security adviser, met with Bush at 0940 to pass on what was then known about developments in Panama. Scowcroft, Baker, and White House Chief of Staff John Sununu soon joined the meeting, a portion of which turned into a "walking briefing" as Bush hurried from the Oval Office, through the West Wing, to the Rose Garden to greet the president of Mexico. According to an informed account, the hurried discussion with the president lacked depth. There simply was not sufficient time to weigh U.S. options. One key adviser, the secretary of defense, was not even present. He was escorting the Soviet defense minister to Gettysburg, Pennsylvania, for a tour of the battlefield. Powell informed Cheney of the situation by phone, after which the secretary returned to Washington. Thus, as events unfolded rapidly in Panama and as the appropriate U.S. agencies tried to monitor the fast-moving developments, key top-level administration officials were distracted by other activities, unable at first to give their undivided attention to the coup attempt, the fate of which would likely be determined in only a matter of hours. In the meantime, officers at the Southern Command awaited specific guidance from the White House or Pentagon.

By 1000 in Panama, reports reaching Quarry Heights confirmed that a coup was in progress, a conclusion supported by the arrival of the Giroldi family at Fort Clayton seeking refuge. Further information indicated that Giroldi's 4th Infantry Company controlled the Comandancia compound, and that Noriega, his bodyguards, and some of his staff were on the premises, their status unknown. Responding to the updated reports, Thurman decided that the time had come to authorize JTF-Panama to execute the preplanned contingency readiness exercise, although he expressly stated that Fort Amador and the Bridge of the Americas should not be blocked at that time. Cisneros received the order shortly before 1000 and passed it down to the various JTF-Panama units on alert. Within thirty minutes of being notified, most had reached and secured their designated positions at U.S. bases, facilities, and housing areas. In accordance with the law, Thurman's treaty affairs people notified the Panama Defense Forces of the exercise, of its legal grounding in the right of the United States to protect American interests in Panama and to defend the canal, and of the Southern Command's intention to stay out of whatever was the cause of that morning's turmoil.

In the midst of all this, word reached Quarry Heights that units from the PDF's 7th Infantry Company at Rio Hato were flying into Panama City, thus rendering irrelevant any roadblock U.S. marines might set up at the Bridge of the Americas. Once on the ground, the company's lead elements headed for the Comandancia to launch a counterattack against Giroldi. When their initial assault failed, the attackers tried talking with the rebel officers in an effort to buy time until more units loyal to Noriega could arrive. Thurman, aware of the troop movements, issued an order at 1101 for U.S. forces at Fort Amador to seal off the installation. Accordingly, M113s moved onto the causeway, thereby containing UESAT units on Flamenco Island, while other vehicles blocked the main gate, thus freezing the PDF's 5th Infantry Company in place. That company had gone on full alert at the outset of the coup attempt, but, confronted with armed American troops right outside its barracks, the commander, Captain Cortizo, issued instructions for his men to sit tight.

At this point, the mood in Washington was upbeat. Shortly before noon, the president was finally free to convene a forty-minute meeting with his advisers in the Oval Office, where he expressed his opinion that indigenous backing for the coup was essential to its success and that the Panamanian opposition needed to get involved in support of the rebel officers. While the White House meeting was in progress, those officers were finally releasing a public statement, announcing their intention to have Noriega and other senior officers retire for the good of the country, whose economic condition, they said, continued to deteriorate. The statement went on to emphasize that the junior officers involved in the coup were acting on their own (that is, without U.S. involvement) and that they supported elections sometime in the near future. To Thurman and other American decision makers, this pronouncement fell far short of expectations. It did nothing to illuminate

Noriega's current and future status, while the commitment to democracy sought by Washington seemed vague at best.

The situation by this time had reached a critical point, and U.S. officials in Panama and Washington had yet to determine what further courses of action to take. Forcing the issue were the Panamanian units loyal to Noriega that were preparing to move in force against Giroldi. Additional troops from the 7th Infantry Company continued to arrive at Tocumen airfield, while units from Battalion 2000, realizing that their noncommittal stance could lead to reprisals if Noriega triumphed, decided to join the countercoup. When these and other loyalist elements began their march on the Comandancia, they did so via one of the main avenues running through Panama City, thus avoiding the U.S. roadblock at Fort Amador and U.S. troops at the Bridge of the Americas. If the Southern Command sought to prevent these pro-Noriega troops from proceeding, JTF-Panama would have to move its own units into the heart of the capital, and quickly. The U.S. force required to block the city's principal thoroughfares would not be large, and such a move would probably compel the PDF loyalists to reconsider their commitment to the dictator. But the measure would also mean involving the United States directly in the coup attempt, and orders to that effect could only come from the president.

Another matter U.S. decision makers had to address was the fate of Noriega, the man who had been at the center of the two-year crisis since its inception. Giroldi had already asserted that he had no intention of harming the dictator. But would he be willing to turn him over to the United States? And if so, how would the transfer be arranged? If not, should U.S. troops enter the Comandancia to seize Noriega by force? In Panama, the Southern Command and the U.S. Embassy worked on a set of options to cover each possibility. Washington did the same, with communication between the Joint Chiefs and Thurman's control center being quite good but with the secure phone line between the embassy and the State Department experiencing problems. What was completely lacking was any communication between SOUTHCOM headquarters and the rebels. Thurman apparently made no attempt to contact Giroldi, who, as noted, had refused to provide the CIA agents a phone number at which he could be reached inside the Comandancia. Nor was the major able to telephone the general. As Thurman later testified, he had not made available to the plotters a number at which Giroldi could call him. "The operation seemed flaky," Thurman explained, "and I did not want him to have a number to coup management."

Late Tuesday morning, Giroldi finally decided to establish contact with the U.S. military, not with Thurman but with Cisneros. Around 1100, he sent two of his fellow conspirators to Fort Clayton. When Cisneros heard of their arrival, he contacted Quarry Heights to request instructions and received the green light to meet with the two officers. To those with Thurman in the Tunnel, however, the new SOUTHCOM commander was clearly unhappy. "Why the hell are they over at Fort Clayton?" he demanded of Schneider and Pierce. "How'd they get there and why are they there? Are they there to surrender? Are they going to give us Noriega? What's going on?" Receiving no answer, he asked the same questions of Hartzog and Braaten, with no better results. As Pierce later observed, the development at Fort Clayton was "completely unexpected"; it was a "surprise variable" that Thurman did not welcome. Yet he had no choice but to acquiesce in the meeting.[19]

---

[19] All quotes from Woodward, *The Commanders*, p. 121. Pierce Interv, 21 May 98.

Of the two conspirators ushered into the USARSO commander's office, Capt. Javier Licona, commander of the cavalry squadron that had sided with Giroldi, took the lead in the ensuing discussion. According to Cisneros, the first point Licona made upon entering the room was that the rebels had Noriega in their hands but were not going to turn him over to the United States in light of the indictments against him, which would mean extradition and a trial. Giroldi apparently still maintained that the dictator could be persuaded to retire with dignity. Cisneros replied that keeping Noriega at the Comandancia was a big mistake. The PDF commander, he believed, would not retire under any circumstances. If the rebels were not willing to turn Noriega over to U.S. authorities, they should at least remove him from his headquarters compound to some undisclosed location. Cisneros sensed that, despite Licona's words to the contrary, the captain personally favored giving up the dictator but that he could not agree to such arrangements without Giroldi's approval.

Licona also raised the issue of American support for the coup, declaring that the rebels only wanted U.S. troops to block Fort Amador—he obviously did not know that Thurman had already issued that order—and the Bridge of the Americas and to control areas for which the United States was responsible under the treaty. The rebels, for their part, would be responsible for the areas under their control. Licona deemed this arrangement essential lest there be an accidental confrontation between U.S. and rebel forces. To Cisneros, the captain's requests no longer reflected the reality in the streets. When he informed the two officers of the 7th Infantry Company's deployment by air to Panama City, he tried to convince them of the urgent need to make critical decisions. Licona, though, insisted only that U.S. troops block the Bridge of the Americas, so Cisneros called the Southern Command and received permission to order the symbolic but otherwise meaningless gesture.

After Cisneros reported the substance of his meeting with the rebel officers to Quarry Heights, Thurman's staff relayed the information to the embassy, the CIA, and the Joint Chiefs. At some point in this process, either through a misprint in a telegram or through a misunderstanding of what Licona had said, the report reaching Washington indicated that the rebels were prepared to turn Noriega over to American authorities. This arrived at a time when three courses of action designed to accomplish that goal were being hammered out by Thurman and Maisto. One option envisaged the rebels bringing Noriega to a U.S. base, perhaps on a helicopter provided by the Southern Command. Another had a small group of U.S. authorities entering the Comandancia, with rebel permission, to take custody of the dictator. The third had U.S. troops moving into the Comandancia to seize Noriega by force. Thurman forwarded the plan to Washington and discussed each measure with Powell. By noon, the Joint Chiefs had replied that he should be ready to move on either the first or second option if approved but not to consider using force for the time being.

Around 1345 EDT, the president held another meeting with his advisers in the Oval Office, and out of those discussions emanated further guidance on several critical points. Cisneros was to renew contact with the rebel officers and have them confirm that Giroldi really did have custody of Noriega. If that were the case, Bush directed that the rebels be asked to turn the dictator over to the United States and to renew their call for democratic elections. The assumption, based in part on the erroneous transmission of Licona's meeting with Cisneros, was that the rebels would accede to both requests. As a precautionary measure, however, the Southern Command was to proceed with making plans to take Noriega from the Comandancia by force.

Thurman was at last receiving some concrete guidance from Washington. But it was too late. Even while the Oval Office meeting was in progress, the main counterattack against the rebels was succeeding. By the time President Bush and his advisers had finished their deliberations, shortly after 1300, Panama time, the attempted coup was over. Panamanian radio and television proclaimed that Noriega was safe and remained in charge of the Panama Defense Forces. From Quarry Heights, observers could see rebel soldiers stacking arms and putting their hands above their heads. Bush learned of the outcome around 1430 EDT. Since May, he had been on record as urging the Panama Defense Forces to oust its commander. Now a group of officers had tried and failed. The repercussions would be extensive.

RAMIFICATIONS

The 3 October 1989 coup attempt signaled a major turning point in the U.S.-Panama crisis—Secretary of State Baker called it a "watershed"—with immediate ramifications for each country. In Panama, Noriega moved quickly to cement his authority over the Panama Defense Forces and punish the coup plotters.[20] Within twenty-four hours of the uprising, Giroldi and several officers and enlisted men who had actively supported him were dead, a lethal bullet, not confinement, being the retribution meted out, an unusual penalty in Panama for a military conspiracy. Giroldi apparently was singled out for especially brutal treatment. His niece told the press that his body had numerous bullet wounds and leg, rib, and skull fractures. Informants within the Panamanian military provided further details, revealing that several high-ranking officers who had displayed questionable loyalty during the coup attempt had been forced to take part in the executions. Other officers whose loyalty was in question, including three full colonels within Noriega's inner circle, found themselves out of favor, demoted or arrested. Among the PDF rank and file, several hundred were also incarcerated. Other coup plots were purportedly uncovered, and further executions were reported by Panamanian physicians who received the remains of the victims. In stark contrast, those officers who helped rescue their commander were rewarded, some with promotions. Captain Cortizo, for example, whose 5th Infantry Company at Fort Amador had stayed in the barracks rather than challenge U.S. troops, had been vocal after the coup in spreading the word of Noriega's triumph. His cheerleading won him quick elevation to the rank of major.

While the Panama Defense Forces was the principal object of Noriega's retribution and rewards, he also moved rapidly in the political arena to shore up his influence. Members of the opposition, even Guillermo Endara, were detained, a reminder as to who still wielded power in the country. On 11 October, district representatives answerable to Noriega enacted a series of "war laws" that suspended constitutional guarantees and concentrated more power in the dictator's hands. The general seemed not only to have survived the attempt to depose him but to have strengthened his position in its wake. The incident of 3 October had been a close

---

[20] This summary of the measures taken by Noriega after the coup attempt failed is based on Briefing script, SOUTHCOM, 13 October Attaché Briefing, n.d.; *Time*, 16 Oct 89; Kempe, *Divorcing the Dictator*, pp. 393–97. Quoted word from Baker, *Politics of Diplomacy,* p. 187.

call, but it appeared to be working to his long-term advantage.

Some observers at Quarry Heights and Fort Clayton were not so sure. The regime's excessive reprisals had spread fear and damaged morale throughout the Panama Defense Forces. Furthermore, the disruption caused by Noriega's extensive personnel and organizational changes was bound to have an adverse effect on the military's discipline and stability. True, there was little to prevent Noriega from asserting his authority and keeping his subordinates in line, except that in the days and weeks after the coup attempt, the erratic behavior, the rages, and the heavy drinking that had caused Giroldi to turn against him actually worsened.

Noriega waves his fist to supporters after the failed October 1989 coup.

Given these conditions, U.S. officials could not rule out another plot to oust the PDF commander, although Cisneros for one thought that unlikely. More probable, he and others believed, would be some incident between U.S. forces and a Panamanian military racked by uncertainty and suspicion and led by officers now fully conscious of the need to demonstrate their unswerving loyalty to Noriega. How such an incident might play out was anybody's guess.

While analyzing the post-coup configuration, intentions, and mood of the Panama Defense Forces and the implications for American policy, the Southern Command also tried to find out what exactly had happened at the Comandancia on 3 October. In the investigation that followed, intelligence not available or processed during the coup attempt, debriefings of surviving rebels like Licona, and contacts with informants still inside the Panamanian military helped flesh out the skeletal accounts Thurman had received while the event was in progress. As a more complete picture came into focus, U.S. authorities learned that Giroldi had informed his 4th Infantry Company of the planned revolt just minutes before Noriega arrived at the Comandancia Tuesday morning. Once the dictator and his entourage were inside the compound, they were apprehended but apparently not placed under arrest. Early on, either Noriega or someone with him acquired access to communications equipment, using it to call in loyal units and to move others like Battalion 2000 off the fence. At one point, Giroldi considered sending the PDF commander to Fort Clayton, but Noriega himself talked the major out of it, so Giroldi sent Licona and another officer instead. The rebel leader also contacted other military commanders throughout the country to determine whether or not they supported his uprising. Later, as units loyal to Noriega mounted their counterattack, the general taunted Giroldi, yelling at the major either to shoot him or to kill himself. Giroldi did neither. At that point, according to some sources,

Noriega took a pistol and shot an officer standing next to Giroldi in the head. The coup attempt collapsed soon thereafter.[21]

Thurman was still incredulous: how could Giroldi have expected success from a scheme that left Noriega walking and talking throughout the effort to oust him? At one session in the Tunnel, Cisneros tried to explain that the idea of a coup d'état by telephone poll was not that far-fetched in Panama. What Giroldi had obviously not anticipated was Noriega's brutal behavior during and after the uprising. Thurman listened but remained skeptical, clearly not persuaded by what Cisneros was saying.[22] In fact, during the three days from the first contact with Sra. Giroldi to the failure of the coup, the new SOUTHCOM commander had not readily solicited or easily accepted Cisneros' advice. Thurman had turned instead for information to a handful of officers on his own staff. To be sure, Thurman had brought Cisneros to Quarry Heights soon after the CIA's initial meeting with the Giroldis, but the subsequent conversation centered on the options open to JTF-Panama; it did not draw extensively on Cisneros' experience and expertise regarding the crisis and the Panama Defense Forces. Cisneros later described the experience: "We sat down and we started talking . . . we started *listening* to General Thurman."[23] What particularly troubled Cisneros was the failure to let him communicate directly with Giroldi, either before or during the coup. "I don't know why, for the life of me," he recounted, Thurman failed to ask such questions as "'Do you know Giroldi?' 'What do you think about him?' 'What should we tell him?' 'How can we influence him?' I mean no one knew how to exert influence more than I did here. That was an ability that I had. Nobody captured that. Nobody wanted to." Cisneros did not make these points arrogantly or egotistically; other officers who had observed his behavior in the crisis for over two years conceded his knack for knowing how to deal with Noriega and the Panamanian military. Indeed, on 3 October, Giroldi himself had reinforced that perception when he sent Licona and the other rebel officer not the short distance up Ancon Hill to Quarry Heights but several miles down the road to Fort Clayton, where, once they arrived, the two had asked specifically for Cisneros. In the weeks and months to come, when the general reexamined the coup attempt and the way he believed his expertise had been squandered, his emotions encompassed sadness, frustration, anger, and just a touch of resignation. An opportunity, he believed, one that, if permitted, he might have been better able to exploit, had been lost.

Lost, too, was any chance for a close working relationship between Thurman and Cisneros based on mutual trust and respect. Cisneros later described his relationship with Thurman as "very bad," attributing much of the friction to the fact that he, Cisneros, was Hispanic; that he enjoyed ready access to important Panamanians; and that, during the events surrounding the coup, his recommendations to employ JTF-Panama more decisively might have been misinterpreted by his superiors as a desire

---

[21] Briefing script, SOUTHCOM, 13 October Attaché Briefing, n.d.; *Time*, 16 Oct 89; Kempe, *Divorcing the Dictator*, pp. 381–93; Baker, *Politics of Diplomacy*, p. 186.

[22] An account of Cisneros' efforts to explain a coup by "telephone poll" is in Pierce Interv, 21 May 98.

[23] Cisneros discussed his relationship with Thurman in Interv, author with Maj Gen Marc Cisneros, U.S. Army, 30 Jan 90, Fort Clayton, Panama. In more informal but off-the-record conversations, other USARSO and SOUTHCOM officers confirmed the friction and speculated on the reasons for it.

on his part "to start a war." Other observers noted that Cisneros' status as a holdover from the Woerner days and, thus, in Thurman's mind, a part of the "Sleepy Hollow" gang may have contributed to the chilly relationship, as well. Some officers even went so far as to claim that the new SOUTHCOM commander suspected his Army component commander had "gone native" over the years, becoming so personally caught up in the crisis as to lose his objectivity and ability to devise imaginative approaches, a charge that struck Cisneros as gratuitous and deplorable. Whatever the causes, the strained relationship between the two generals was apparent to virtually everyone at SOUTHCOM and USARSO headquarters. In late December, it would come to a head during Operation JUST CAUSE. In the meantime, each man conducted his day-to-day business with the other formally and with formality.

For at least two weeks after 3 October, Thurman spent much of his time meeting and talking with officials in Washington. There, the Bush administration was under attack on several fronts for failing to take more decisive action during the coup attempt. Prominent Democrats in Congress such as Senators John Kerry of Massachusetts and Sam Nunn of Georgia and Congressman Les Aspin of Wisconsin led the charge, but a number of Republicans such as Senator Jesse Helms of North Carolina were firing their own salvos, as were some Panamanian opposition leaders. "Keystone Kops" was one unflattering reference used to characterize the response of the president and his advisers. More substantively, critics charged that Bush, having encouraged the Panama Defense Forces to move against their leader, had been too busy or too indecisive to order the action necessary to make sure the coup, once initiated, succeeded. This failure to follow through not only doomed the coup attempt, but also served to undermine U.S. credibility in the international arena. As former CIA director Richard Helms stated, "The oldest rule in the exercise of power is that if a nation tells the world it wants to get rid of a corrupt government, as did the U.S. in Panama, that nation had better have the means and the will to carry it through once the opportunity develops." The question of presidential will surfaced repeatedly, recalling for many the "wimp factor" references that had dogged Bush during his bid for the White House the previous year.

Not just the president's personality and resolve but his style of crisis management also came under critical scrutiny. As Henry Kissinger remarked, crisis situations rarely provided a leader with a clear picture or adequate information on which to act. Given this truism, Bush, some argued, had further complicated matters by having information from three different and often contradictory sources (the State Department, Pentagon, and CIA) funneled, or "stovepiped," directly to him, without benefit of interagency analysis. Besides that, he had failed to meet with his advisers for an in-depth discussion of the coup attempt until it was too late. More cautious commentators, to be sure, questioned the wisdom of additional American involvement in Giroldi's machinations. If U.S. troops, for example, had blocked all avenues leading to the Comandancia or had moved to seize Noriega by force, they would probably have found themselves in the untenable position of having to fight rebels and loyalists alike. Still, however comforting Bush might find these endorsements of the minor role played by the United States on 3 October, they could not dispel the perception that the president's limited course of action was not one he had mandated but rather one that had been dictated by the rapid movement of events spinning out of control. In short, the impression began to take hold after the failed coup that the administration's excursion into crisis management had suffered from distractions, poor communications, inadequate information, and, at the critical moments, indecision.[24]

In the face of this criticism, administration officials initially took the position that the president and his advisers had possessed little knowledge of the coup plot and that U.S. troops had not made any moves to support the rebels. These denials were quickly discredited, after which the administration went on the offensive against its critics, emphasizing the wisdom President Bush had shown in distancing the United States from a very questionable enterprise. The goals of the coup plotters were vague at best. Beyond forcing Noriega to retire, the conspirators seemed to have few if any specific ideas of what would happen in Panama, a position hardly worthy of U.S. support. Besides, who was this Giroldi, anyway? According to one Pentagon source, he was "a bastard, a sort of mini-Noriega." Secretary Baker, after denouncing the critics as "armchair generals," offered a loftier rebuttal when he declared, "You don't [risk American lives] on the basis of someone else's plans and in response to rapidly changing circumstances."[25] Refusing to act hastily under the pressure of fast-moving events was a sign of wisdom, not weakness or indecision.

Thurman, who would meet at the White House with the president and his advisers on 16 October and testify the next day before Congress, was delighted by Baker's statement and endorsed it in President Bush's presence. In his congressional testimony and in the numerous coup-related briefings he would give over the following weeks, his words began to resemble a mantra: the coup, he said repeatedly, was "ill-motivated, ill-conceived, ill-led, and fatally flawed."[26]

Yet, however vigorously the president's men defended their actions during the coup attempt, at heart many realized an opportunity had been missed. Baker would later reveal the "soul-searching" that beset Bush's inner circle, concluding that "It is an understatement to say that administration decision making was less than crisp. As a result, we revamped our entire crisis-management processes." In the president's words, "Amateur hour is over." No one in authority confided to Thurman what would happen should circumstances similar to 3 October arise in the future, but the SOUTHCOM commander returned from Washington convinced that, if only for political reasons, Bush could not allow the appearance of another debacle in Panama. As the general later recalled, "I said, 'Get your ducks in a row because he's not going through this again.' . . . I said to myself as I flew back down there. . . . 'Get your s——t straight because if this ever happens again or if an American is hurt, then there will be a takedown here. That will be the end of it.'"[27]

Cisneros, whom Thurman had been ordered to bring to Washington with him, returned with the same impression. Despite the different perspectives from which the two generals assessed the crisis, they had arrived at a similar conclusion: a major incident, be it another coup attempt or a U.S.-PDF confrontation, was almost

---

[24] On the Bush administration being under attack for its handling of the coup, see Baker, *Politics of Diplomacy*, pp. 186 (reference to "Keystone Kops")–87; Woodward, *The Commanders*, pp. 127–28. Helms quote from *Time*, 16 Oct 89, and see also 23 Oct 89, 30 Oct 89, 6 Nov 89.

[25] Baker, *Politics of Diplomacy*, pp. 186–87. On the administration's response to its critics, see also Kempe, *Divorcing the Dictator*, pp. 393–95; Woodward, *The Commanders*, p. 128; *Time*, 16 Oct 89, 23 Oct 89, 30 Oct 89, 6 Nov 89.

[26] On two occasions in early December 1989, the author heard Thurman's briefings covering the event of the coup attempt.

[27] First and second quotes from Baker, *Politics of Diplomacy*, p. 186. Third quote from Woodward, *The Commanders*, p. 128. Last quote from Thurman Interv, 12 Apr 90.

certain to result in a BLUE SPOON execution order. Cisneros still thought another coup unlikely in the near future. What Panamanian officer would want to suffer Giroldi's fate? Still, should there be another attempt, Washington seemed prepared to commit U.S. troops to the endeavor. This sort of automatic commitment seemed unwise to Cisneros, but what troubled him more was the very real prospect of an incident, provoked most likely by an errant member of the Panama Defense Forces, escalating out of control. Giving voice to this fear, he told U.S. troops arriving in Panama in mid-October during the scheduled rotations for security enhancement and NIMROD DANCER units that, unlike the forces that had preceded them, they were likely to get into a conflict.[28]

OPERATION ORDER 1–90 AND OPERATION PLAN 90–2

Thurman, in his testimony before Congress, claimed there had been no plan for SOUTHCOM forces to support the kind of revolt within the Panamanian military that had occurred on 3 October.[29] This position was technically correct, although some U.S. officers in Panama believed that any military measures required that Tuesday could have been implemented in the framework of a Purple Storm or contingency readiness exercise. But such actions would have been improvised to accommodate the circumstances of the coup attempt, and the consequences would have been unpredictable. For President Bush, this debate over what could have been only buttressed his determination that, in the future, U.S. forces in Panama be prepared to deal effectively with any unexpected turn of events. "I want some follow-through planning," he is reported to have told his National Security Council.[30]

Powell conveyed this sentiment to Thurman, realizing that the SOUTHCOM commander needed no prodding. Revising the PRAYER BOOK had been one of Thurman's priorities when he arrived in Panama. What the abortive coup did was provide the planners at Quarry Heights, Fort Bragg, and Fort Clayton additional factors to consider as they overhauled BLUE SPOON. Powell merely wanted to hear that the effort was making progress. Thurman, who had been in continuous contact with the chairman since the coup, assured him that it was.

In fact, there had been substantial progress on rewriting BLUE SPOON well before the coup attempt. Hartzog, as previously noted, had been working on BANNER SAVIOR from July through September, whereas Stiner, following the briefings that had been given to Thurman in early August at Fort Bragg, had directed Lt. Col. Tim McMahon and Maj. Dave Huntoon to write an XVIII Airborne Corps version of BLUE SPOON based on Thurman's comments and the corps' preferences for a swift and massive assault. Even before the change of command in Panama, the two planners had drafted a new document, JTF-South OPLAN 90–1. Woerner was aware of the undertaking but made no protest; 90–1 was, as Huntoon later observed, a corps, not

---

[28] Cisneros Interv, 30 Jan 90.

[29] Except where noted, this section on the revision of BLUE SPOON is based on the following sources: Donnelly, Roth, and Baker, *Operation Just Cause*, pp. 55–62, 70–89; Woodward, *The Commanders*, pp. 128–31, 134–35, 139–41; Cole, *Operation Just Cause*, pp. 17–24; Intervs, Mackey with Thurman, 1992, USAWC/USAMHI, Project 1992–1; Partin with Thurman, 12 Apr 90; author with Hartzog and Braaten, 29 Jun 90; and Lt Col David Huntoon, U.S. Army, 7 Apr 92, Fort Bragg, N.C. Telephone Interv, author with Huntoon, 27 Jun 90; Conversation, author with McMahon, 20 Dec 89.

[30] Woodward, *The Commanders*, p. 128.

a SOUTHCOM, plan. Hartzog and his subordinates, especially Lt. Col. Bill Bennett, kept in touch with the corps operations shop, thus ensuring that BANNER SAVIOR and 90–1 developed along parallel lines, with planners in each headquarters staying abreast of what their counterparts were doing.

After the coup attempt, Thurman met several times with commanders and planners from the SOUTHCOM operations directorate, the XVIII Airborne Corps, the Joint Special Operations Command, and JTF-Panama. At one session in Panama, he issued the formal guidance all anticipated and, to some degree, was already in effect. The XVIII Airborne Corps would be the principal planner for BLUE SPOON operations and the war-fighting headquarters should the full plan be executed. The Southern Command would provide the corps only general guidance, contained in a new version of the CINCSO BLUE SPOON operation order. For Hartzog, this meant stopping work on BANNER SAVIOR and transferring the concepts he had developed therein to the revised BLUE SPOON. The new plan was to cover a variety of contingencies from another coup attempt to an all-out U.S. invasion, and it was to consider what U.S. forces in Panama alone could accomplish in each of three scenarios determined by the amount of advance warning: no notification, little notification, or adequate notification. JTF-Panama would have to handle any sudden outbreak of violence. If forces outside Panama were needed—and the assumption was they would be—they would be brought in quickly and strike hard. The gradual buildup so critical to Woerner's strategy of putting pressure on the Panamanian military was thus jettisoned, to be replaced by a combination of mass and surprise, both principles of war being essential to the concept of operations for which the Joint Staff in Washington, together with the Joint Special Operations Command and the XVIII Airborne Corps, had lobbied in the past. Finally, Thurman, as anticipated, formally changed the command and control arrangements for BLUE SPOON. If the plan were fully executed, not only would the XVIII Airborne Corps serve from the outset as the joint task force in charge of conducting military operations but, as a measure to ensure unity of command, would have operational control over the BLUE SPOON joint special operations task force as well.

After listening to Thurman's guidance, Col. Tom Needham, the XVIII Airborne Corps director of operations, made the point that OPLAN 90–1 drafted by McMahon and Huntoon contained almost everything the SOUTHCOM commander wanted. Thurman and Hartzog agreed. What was lacking was only an explicit reference to another coup attempt that Thurman needed to satisfy Washington, but that was easily incorporated. More important were the revisions required in light of lessons drawn from the PDF's behavior on 3 October and from Noriega's actions in the aftermath. The ease with which the 7th Infantry Company had flown into Panama City, together with the belated move by Battalion 2000 to take part in the countercoup, had to be factored into the new BLUE SPOON. Furthermore, Noriega had relocated a number of units after the coup. The bulk of the elite UESAT, for example, was moved from Flamenco Island, where U.S. forces had kept it bottled up on 3 October, to Panama Viejo in the capital city. To these considerations, Thurman introduced a new piece of guidance of great significance: the Panama Defense Forces would still have to be "decapitated," but, in contrast to previous plans that envisaged only the removal of Noriega and the top military leadership, the destruction or radical reorientation of the entire institution was now to be a U.S. objective. For the planners, all these concerns meant expanding the scope of U.S. operations beyond select command, control, and communications nodes along the Panama City–Colón axis, adding new targets to the existing lists, and readjusting the forces assigned to what had to that point been peripheral objectives. At most targets, the aim was to "fix in-place" and "neutralize" all PDF units. Neutralization meant making them ineffective, through combat operations if necessary but through other less lethal means if the situation allowed.

Armed with Thurman's post-coup guidance, officers at the Southern Command, JTF-Panama, and the joint special operations task force reworked their respective BLUE SPOON operation orders and plans, producing working drafts by mid-October. When Thurman flew to Washington soon thereafter to meet with the president and to appear before Congress, he and Stiner were able to give Powell and Kelly a comprehensive planning update. Stiner extolled the conceptual changes incorporated in the revised plan but emphasized that full-scale execution of BLUE SPOON—the option he preferred—would depend on receiving adequate support from the Military Airlift Command. The request for airlift was not a mere formality. As the assembled officers knew, worldwide demands kept up to 80 percent of MAC's fleet operating at any given time. The Air Force, therefore, needed to know and acknowledge the magnitude of the BLUE SPOON airlift requirement, based as it was on employing more troops in a much shorter time than called for in previous versions of the plan. Complicating the issue, Thurman could not provide a specific date when the aircraft would be needed, only that they would have to be assembled within thirty-six hours of the command being notified.

Three days after Thurman returned from Washington, he held another major planning session in the Tunnel at which drafts of the principal plans were presented for review. The new CINCSO BLUE SPOON plan, designated OPORD 1–90, limited itself as promised to general guidance. The mission statement had the Southern Command conducting "joint offensive operations to neutralize the PDF and other combatants." U.S. forces, the statement continued, had to be prepared to rescue any American citizens detained by the Panama Defense Forces and "to conduct restoration of law and order operations." They also had to be ready "to conduct all missions simultaneously and to assist the emergent government of Panama in stabilization operations on the completion of combat operations." Included in the concept of operations was the "removal of Noriega from power and Panama, the removal of Noriega's cronies and accomplices from office, the creation of a PDF responsive to and supportive of an emergent democratic government of Panama, and a freely elected [government of Panama] which is allowed to govern."[31]

The CINCSO operation order recognized that execution of BLUE SPOON might come in response to a surprise "trigger event" or as the result of the "deliberate" reaction by Washington to some serious provocation. In the former case, JTF-Panama would undertake operations, with reinforcements from the United States joining the fight once they arrived in the country. In the latter case, in-country and deployed U.S.-based troops would conduct simultaneous operations under Joint Task Force-South (JTF-South), the designated XVIII Airborne Corps war-fighting headquarters for BLUE SPOON. "From a military perspective," 1–90 made clear, "deliberate execution of the OPORD is preferred; however, when the situation is viewed against

---

[31] CINCSO OPORD 1–90 (BLUE SPOON), 30 October 1989. The information in the text is taken from a copy of the operation order.

the backdrop of international, regional, and national politics the reactive execution of the OPORD is more likely."[32] The operation order went on to identify specific objectives, the task forces involved and their responsibilities, and the command and control arrangements applicable under each scenario. With the required appendixes attached, the new CINCSO BLUE SPOON ran only fifty-five pages, far shorter than previous versions that had envisaged the Southern Command as the war-fighting headquarters directing operations of a conventional joint task force and a special operations joint task force.

Reflecting SOUTHCOM's very general conceptual guidance (which, in turn, reflected what Hartzog, McMahon, and Huntoon had been working on in their respective planning shops well before October), the operational details of BLUE SPOON were set forth in the XVIII Airborne Corps' JTF-South OPLAN 90–2. The concept of operations presented therein covered five phases: predeployment and crisis action, in-place force operations, assault force operations, stabilizing force operations, and redeployment. In keeping with Thurman's directive, OPLAN 90–2 stated as its "principal objective" the neutralization of the Panama Defense Forces and the protection of American lives, sites, and facilities. The in-place U.S. forces would have primary responsibility for the "protection mission"; they would also join with deploying assault forces to "conduct rapid and aggressive force-oriented attacks to isolate, neutralize, and, if necessary, destroy the PDF." The capture of Noriega would be an integral part of these operations. Military action against the Panama Defense Forces, the plan stated, should be completed within three days; follow-on operations to stabilize Panama and restructure Panama's armed forces would take up to a month to complete.[33]

OPLAN 90–2 explicitly posited another coup attempt as the event that would precipitate execution of BLUE SPOON, but the planners knew that any number of incidents could have the same effect. Whatever the cause, once the National Command Authority had decided to execute the plan, elements from the XVIII Airborne Corps would deploy as JTF-South and direct the military operations assigned to the various task forces under its control. Most of the task forces involved Army units, but despite this fact, McMahon and Huntoon had deliberately omitted an Army Forces component headquarters from the chain of command. The corps would act as the ARFOR, while JTF-South would issue orders directly to the subordinate task forces (*Chart 6*).

Many of the objectives assigned to a given task force had not changed from previous versions of BLUE SPOON. Others had. One major revision involved shifting Ranger units slated to attack the Comandancia to an air assault on Panamanian military encampments at Rio Hato, now a "primary" target as a direct consequence of the 3 October experience. Replacing the Rangers at the PDF headquarters would be Task Force Gator, a force cobbled primarily from the NIMROD DANCER mechanized battalion and from elements of the 193d Infantry Brigade. As another consequence of the failed coup, certain units under Special Operations Command, South, found themselves assigned new targets, including the Pacora River bridge located along a main road north of the city over which any reinforcements from Battalion 2000 at Fort Cimarrón would have to travel to reach the Comandancia downtown.

---

[32] Ibid.

[33] Joint Task Force-South OPLAN 90–2, 3 November 1989. The information in the text is taken from a copy of the operation plan.

Chart 6—Blue Spoon on the Eve of Operation Just Cause
Operation Plan 90–2 Command and Control

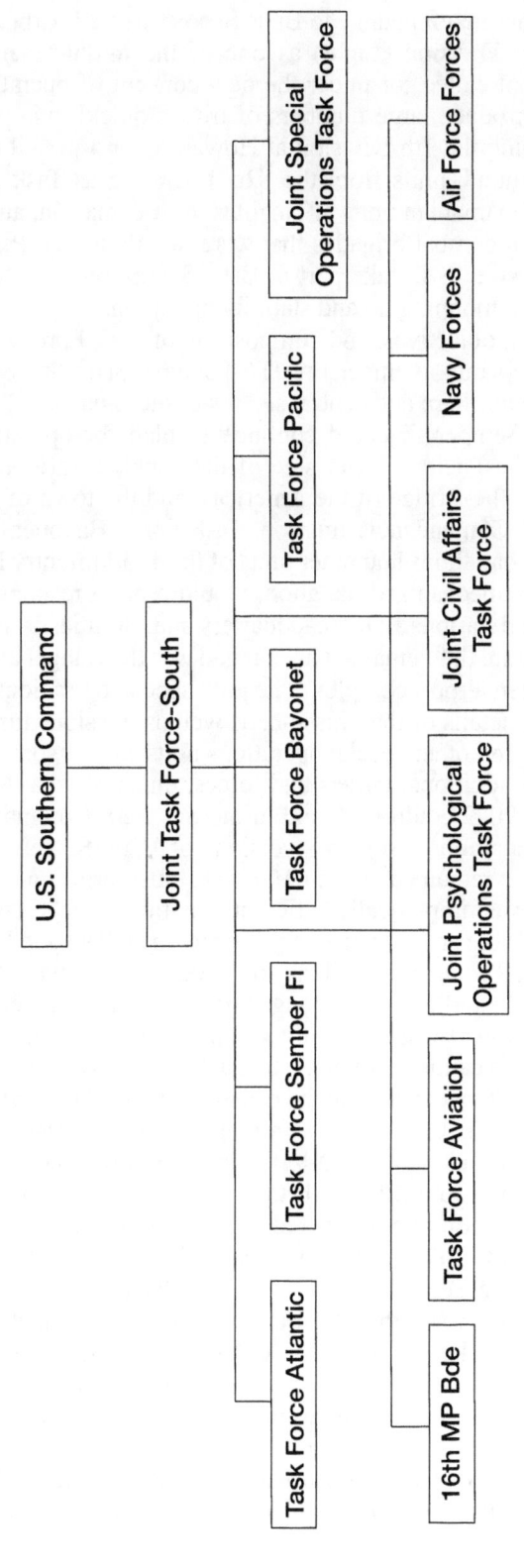

In yet another major change to BLUE SPOON, the 82d Airborne Division replaced the 7th Infantry Division (Light) as one of the initial assault forces. Given the rapid deployment called for under the new concept of operations, using the 82d's capability to introduce large numbers of troops quickly via parachute made more sense than landing the 7th Division at Howard over a period of hours, if not days. Once on the ground, units from the 82d, operating as Task Force Pacific, would move against Panamanian units at Tinajitas, Fort Cimarrón, and Panama Viejo. The two 7th Division combat brigades that were not already in Panama as part of Task Force Atlantic would still take part in BLUE SPOON, but as a follow-on force, to be used primarily in mopping up and stability operations.

The mission, objectives, and composition of Task Force Atlantic would remain pretty much the same as under the JTF-Panama BLUE SPOON, with the task force operating in the northern and central sectors of the canal area. Similarly, the marines of Task Force Semper Fi could continue to plan for operations restricted to the west bank on the Pacific Ocean side of the canal, an area that included Howard Air Force Base, the Bridge of the Americas, and the town of Arraiján. Besides the newly acquired Comandancia mission, Task Force Bayonet, composed mainly of the two combat battalions and other units of the 193d Infantry Brigade as well as the NIMROD DANCER mechanized battalion, would remain responsible for taking down Fort Amador and various PDF headquarters and facilities in Panama City. Another BLUE SPOON feature that remained unchanged was the Ranger assault that targeted the Torrijos-Tocumen airport complex. The joint special operations task force continued to fine-tune the details of that mission, as well as missions for Navy SEALs, Army Special Forces, and other special operations units and personnel.

Despite the additional targets and forces, much of what was contained in JTF-South OPLAN 90–2 could be found in the Southern Command, JTF-Panama, and joint special operations task force versions of BLUE SPOON written under General Woerner. H-hour remained set at 0100, and most targets and assignments did not change. What was dramatically different was the concept, "the idea," as Huntoon noted, "that we were going to hit everything in one fell swoop." That and the decision to neutralize the Panamanian military resulted in a plan with "many moving parts," as Powell observed after one briefing. For officers acquainted with the vagaries of the fog and friction of war once military operations were under way, the chairman's remark served as a cautionary note. Not that Stiner needed reminding. On the basis of his extensive military experience, he had already told Thurman, "It won't go exactly as planned."[34] But BLUE SPOON was a plan that, in contrast to Woerner's, now had the wholehearted backing of the XVIII Airborne Corps, the Joint Special Operations Command, and the Joint Staff. All that remained was for the Joint Chiefs to sign on, which they did after being briefed in the Tank in early November. The approved version of CINCSO OPORD 1–90 was dated 30 October 1989; the published version of Joint Task Force-South OPLAN 90–2, was dated 3 November.

There was one issue that the BLUE SPOON revisions and detailed briefings did not address at any length. Both the CINCSO operation order and the JTF-South operation plan regarded law and order and stability operations as integral parts of the U.S. military mission during an invasion, yet little effort had been made to link

---

[34] Huntoon's comments are in Huntoon Interv, 7 Apr 92. Powell's and Stiner's comments are in Donnelly, Roth, and Baker, *Operation Just Cause*, p. 79 and p. 89, respectively.

the new BLUE SPOON plan to BLIND LOGIC, the PRAYER BOOK operation order for civil-military operations and nation building in a post-invasion Panama.[35] In March, and again in May 1989, planners responsible for civil affairs in the SOUTHCOM Policy, Strategy, and Programs Directorate had reviewed and revised BLIND LOGIC. One of the plan's original assumptions in 1988 was that there would be a presidential call-up of reserve units necessary for post-conflict stability operations. At the time the plan was reexamined a year later, however, a presidential call-up no longer seemed likely. The planners thus began looking at the deployment of "pre-selected volunteers" in the reserves as an alternative. BLIND LOGIC also assumed that there would be a U.S. military government established in Panama if BLUE SPOON were executed. Without having received word to the contrary, the civil affairs planners at Quarry Heights kept that assumption intact. Finally, the revised operation order also took into account the probability—which would become a certainty after Thurman's arrival—that the XVIII Airborne Corps would be the war-fighting joint task force and, during BLUE SPOON, would control the support forces for civil-military operations. BLIND LOGIC therefore identified the conditions that would allow control of those units to be transferred, once the principal combat objectives had been achieved, from JTF-South to a civil-military operations task force responsible for stability operations and nation building.

Soon after Operation NIMROD DANCER got under way in May, a team from the XVIII Airborne Corps under Major Huntoon arrived in Panama, thus providing the civil affairs planners at Quarry Heights a chance to coordinate with a corps representative face-to-face on a variety of issues linking BLUE SPOON to BLIND LOGIC. One issue involved the corps' responsibility as JTF-South to ensure that the support troops for restoring Panama arrived in a timely fashion—meaning, during BLUE SPOON—and that, once combat subsided, the transfer of control over these people to a civil-military operations task force went smoothly. More important, the corps had to understand fully that BLUE SPOON itself envisaged certain stability operations that required more than lip service from officers preoccupied with planning combat operations. Coordinating talks on these and related issues between SOUTHCOM planners and Huntoon's team in Panama went well enough, but, according to one participant stationed at Quarry Heights, whatever progress was made suffered a setback when the XVIII Airborne Corps command and staff back at Fort Bragg failed to follow through by taking the civil-military aspects of BLUE SPOON seriously or by regarding the planning for them as a formal tasking.

The lack of coordination between BLUE SPOON and BLIND LOGIC persisted after the SOUTHCOM change of command at the end of September. When Thurman arrived in Panama, he did not even know about BLIND LOGIC, and during the turmoil of his first days and weeks in command, he offered his planners no guidance on postcombat reconstruction issues, nor did he direct the XVIII Airborne Corps to take BLIND LOGIC into account when making the changes he wanted in BLUE SPOON. At some point after the corps made the 7th Infantry Division (Light) a follow-on force under BLUE SPOON, a staff officer at Fort Ord, realizing that elements of the division were thus likely to pick up responsibility for stability operations, contacted Huntoon with an urgent request to discuss the transition from wartime to postwar

---

[35] The following account of BLIND LOGIC planning is taken mainly from Fishel, *The Fog of Peace*. See also Interv, author with Maj Harry Tomlin, U.S. Army, 22 Mar 91, Fort Leavenworth, Kans.

civil-military operations. Huntoon agreed and said the issue would be placed on the agenda for the planning session in Panama scheduled for mid-December. When that meeting convened, however, events had altered the agenda significantly.

Despite the failure to integrate BLUE SPOON and BLIND LOGIC with respect to civil-military operations, the planning process for U.S. combat operations in Panama would in retrospect be hailed as a highly successful endeavor. It would also be heralded as a validation of the Goldwater-Nichols Act and the measures contained in that law to promote joint military cooperation and operations. On this second point, the accolades, while well deserved, should have been tempered with some modest reservations. BLUE SPOON, although a joint undertaking, was dominated by the Army. Of the 26,000 troops called for in the plan, the overwhelming majority of them would be "green suiters." True, the marines in Panama would participate as their own task force. However, just one day after the Joint Chiefs approved the plan, the Marine Corps offered Stiner additional units for combat in Panama, only to have Stiner politely decline. The force he already had was large enough to execute BLUE SPOON, and the introduction of more marines from Camp Lejeune would only complicate matters. As for the Navy, although SOUTHCOM's small naval component was included in the plan, the efforts begun under Woerner to incorporate an aircraft carrier battle group had never gotten off the ground. In the final plan, carrier-based Navy fighters would provide air cover for the Army and special operations forces deploying from the United States, but this was a naval interdiction operation in support of BLUE SPOON, not the kind of direct participation envisaged in the original SOUTHCOM plans. All this leaves open for speculation the question of how smoothly joint planning would have proceeded had the Army and its sister services shared nearly equal roles in the proposed operation.

THE ROAD TO JUST CAUSE

If, in the aftermath of the 3 October coup attempt, most U.S. officials involved in the crisis accepted the inevitability of some trigger event that would lead to open hostilities, "We hadn't the foggiest notion" according to Hartzog, "of when this thing would occur." In the meantime, the Southern Command and JTF-Panama continued to monitor the situation and conduct day-to-day operations in an atmosphere that was highly charged and likely to become more so. Thurman, while continuing to weather the criticism generated by the abortive coup, was virtually putting his headquarters on a wartime footing. Through November, Purple Storms and Sand Fleas, some initiated as high-risk Category III and IV undertakings, intensified and were increasingly geared to rehearsing missions found in the newly approved version of BLUE SPOON. For the anticipated showdown with the Panama Defense Forces, Thurman wanted there to be more firepower already in place. Stiner concurred, and in mid-November, four M551 Sheridan armored reconnaissance vehicles (also regarded as light tanks) and six AH–64 Apache attack helicopters arrived in Panama under cover of darkness. (The Sheridans were concealed at the Empire Range, the Apaches in a hangar at Howard Air Force Base.) Entering the country openly in the days and weeks following the coup attempt were units and personnel replacing those security enhancement and NIMROD DANCER forces whose time had come to return to their home bases. Fresh to the crisis, these newly arrived troops quickly realized that, in the words of one officer, "This is a disaster waiting to happen."[36]

---

[36] Hartzog quote from Interv, author with Hartzog and Braaten, 29 Jun 90. Quotes on impending disaster from Interv, author with Brig Gen Keith Kellogg and Lt Col Gregory Gardner, 9 Apr 92, Fort

The officer making this prediction was Col. Keith Kellogg, the commander of 3d Brigade, 7th Infantry Division (Light), rotating in to take over from Colonel Hale as commander of Task Force Atlantic. The tense environment Kellogg encountered was to his liking. Perhaps unaware of the strict restraints the White House, the Southern Command, and JTF-Panama had placed on the troops during most of the crisis, he viewed Hale's tour of duty as having been driven by too many political considerations; these, he believed, had caused young U.S. soldiers to think too much about what was proper conduct in light of the restrictions placed on them and not enough about how to perform their duties aggressively and with confidence. Kellogg wanted to "make it much more black and white and take the onus away from [the soldiers] on having to make real hard decisions." Whereas Hale had adjusted to the political dimensions of the crisis, Kellogg desired a freer hand, and under Thurman, he anticipated having it. Thurman "wasn't going to take any crap from the Panamanians," Kellogg noted with approval; he "wasn't afraid to get into a nose-to-nose, hard-ass confrontation with them." That being the case, the colonel wanted his men to be "much more aggressive" in exercising American treaty rights "to the fullest." Panamanian armed forces should be kept busy reacting to U.S. initiatives, not vice versa. Looking back on this period in the crisis, Kellogg later declared, "I thought we turned up the heat quite a bit." Perhaps too high, in the view of some. On one occasion, troops under Kellogg responded to a drive-by shooting by blocking off a main Panamanian road. When Cisneros found out, he placed a call to Kellogg's headquarters and ordered the roadblock removed. This was not the first or last time Cisneros, himself an advocate of putting more pressure on the Panama Defense Forces provided it was done in a measured and calculated way, would consider it necessary to rein in his new Task Force Atlantic commander.[37]

Despite the concerns, expectations, intensified activities, and higher tensions precipitated by the coup attempt, the trigger event many U.S. officers anticipated did not occur in October or November. There was, however, one false alarm. Around the Thanksgiving holiday, the Southern Command received word from an informant that Colombian drug traffickers, acting in retaliation for some U.S. initiative in the drug war, were going to set off car bombs aimed at killing Americans, especially military personnel, in Panama.[38] Thurman realized that, if this actually happened, President Bush might hold Noriega accountable—given the dictator's reputed ties to the Colombian cartel—and authorize the execution of BLUE SPOON. So as not to be

---

Bragg, N.C. Donnelly, Roth, and Baker, *Operation Just Cause*, p. 86; Woodward, *The Commanders*, pp. 132, 141.

[37] The text including quotes is based on Interv, author with Kellogg and Gardner, 9 Apr 92. On the Pacific side of JTF-Panama's area of responsibility, newly arrived units, once acclimated to the political-military nature of the crisis, continued to exercise close to the same degree of restraint as their predecessors. For example, according to a platoon leader in the mechanized battalion that had rotated in, he had been in Panama for only a few weeks when, in the midst of a Sand Flea exercise, his vehicles rounded a corner in Panama City and unexpectedly encountered armed Panamanian military personnel. The Panamanians were equally surprised and reflexively raised their weapons in the direction of the U.S. troops. As the platoon leader recalled, had this happened his first week in Panama, he would have ordered his men to open fire. Having had time to adjust to the requirements of the crisis, however, he and his men just kept on moving. The potential incident went largely unnoticed. Telephone Interv, author with 1st Lt Douglas L. Rubin, 5–6, 11 Apr 90.

[38] The November bomb scare is covered in Woodward, *The Commanders*, pp. 142–44; Cole, *Operation Just Cause*, pp. 24–25; Donnelly, Roth, and Baker, *Operation Just Cause*, pp. 91–93.

caught flatfooted, the general ordered an increase in security at U.S. installations and facilities throughout the country. Soon, drivers trying to enter Fort Clayton or visit the commissary found their travel impeded by concertina wire, concrete barriers, and rigorous identification checks. The measures unleashed an avalanche of complaints, offset somewhat by acknowledgments that the steps were probably necessary, the inconveniences unavoidable.

As an additional precaution during the bomb scare, Thurman activated JTF-South, calling Stiner and his staff back to Panama in between two scheduled BLUE SPOON planning sessions. The corps personnel would now have an opportunity to rehearse their role as the joint task force called for in the plans. At best, the arrangement would be instructive as a practice run; in the worst case, those involved might actually find themselves at war. In making this move, Thurman acted on his own authority, informing General Powell in Washington only after the fact. The Joint Chiefs chairman was not happy. The Southern Command, he let Thurman know, did not control the XVIII Airborne Corps and could not order it to do anything without the express approval of higher authorities. Thurman countered that the urgency of the situation had required him to act as he did. The explanation did little to dispel the chairman's concerns over Thurman's disregard of proper procedure, but, accepting the fait accompli, Powell let the arrangement stand. As expected, the activation of JTF-South served a useful purpose. Stiner's people gained experience working with JTF-Panama personnel in the USARSO Emergency Operations Center, and this interaction revealed additional issues that would have to be addressed in the planning process.

One particular security measure enacted during the bomb scare, while restricted solely to Gorgas Army Hospital on Ancon Hill, resulted in U.S. soldiers engaging in an "eyeball to eyeball" confrontation with Noriega's Dignity Battalions.[39] According to the informant who had generated the scare, the hospital would be targeted for a car bombing. The building's vulnerability to such an attack was undeniable, given that several parking lots were located close to it. On the Saturday before Thanksgiving, 18 November, representatives from the U.S. Forces Joint Committee met with PDF members of the Joint Committee and Combined Board to discuss the need, in light of the bomb threats, to inspect vehicles coming to the hospital and to close off parking areas within seventy-five meters of the facility. The U.S. officials asked for the cooperation of the Panamanian armed forces in helping American troops implement these measures. Soon thereafter, a unit from the 1st Battalion, 508th Infantry (Airborne), commanded by Lt. Col. Billy Ray Fitzgerald at Fort Kobbe, arrived at Gorgas and began stringing concertina wire and emplacing other barriers to shut off the parking lots close to the hospital. Some of the restricted areas, however, also included parking places used by personnel at Panama's Ministry of Health nearby. As the area was being secured, therefore, some Panamanians complained to the U.S. soldiers that what they were doing was not fair. This, however, seemed to be the extent of any protest.

On Monday morning, 20 November, all that changed, as the regime's intention to use the U.S. security measures to score propaganda points became apparent. The maneuvering began when Major Cortizo arrived on the scene, removed some of the concertina wire strung across a parking lot entrance, and waved a number of people

---

[39] The account of the confrontation at Gorgas Army Hospital that follows is based on Woodward, *The Commanders*, pp. 142, 144; *Tropic Times*, 22 Nov 89. Quotes from Interv, author with Lt Col Billy Ray Fitzgerald, U.S. Army, 27 Jan 90.

Soldiers in an M113 armored personnel carrier guard an entrance to Gorgas Army Hospital.

in to park their cars, to the cheers of other Panamanians in the vicinity. An effort by Center for Treaty Affairs personnel dispatched from Quarry Heights to calm the situation failed, as what would become a Dignity Battalion rally began to take shape. As the crowd grew, several protesters began taunting the U.S. troops still present at the hospital, across the street from the demonstration. Some soldiers had voodoo powder thrown at them, while all were subjected to harangues and patriotic music over speakers brought in for the occasion. As the protest continued, Col. Mike Snell directed Fitzgerald to wait until the wee hours of the morning, then advance farther across the parking lot, putting additional barriers, including concrete culverts, into place. Any demonstration on Tuesday would thus have to be staged a greater distance from the hospital.

When the protesters, who did in fact return on Tuesday, saw the newly emplaced barriers, the demonstration quickly escalated into what Fitzgerald described as "a real mess." At one point, men from a Panamanian electric company owned by a Dignity Battalion leader arrived with cranes to remove the culverts. Under orders to prevent this, Fitzgerald called on the mechanized battalion to send him some M113 armored personnel carriers, which he used to block the cranes. By this time, several hundred demonstrators had gathered and had maneuvered right up to the curb of the hospital. As the taunts grew louder, Fitzgerald had the M113s rev their engines as a countermeasure. In a display of machismo, some of the "DigBats" raised their T-shirts to reveal pistols, and some began spitting on the Americans. Before the confrontation could get completely out of control, however, U.S. and Panamanian officials announced an agreement, whereby the regime recognized the increased danger U.S. forces faced because of the bomb threats and accepted responsibility for inspecting vehicles at two parking facilities near Gorgas. Both sides claimed victory in the confrontation, while each experienced a sense of relief that events had not spiraled out of control.

The November bomb scare came to a sudden end after a competent polygraph team arrived in Panama to test the informant and concluded that he had perpetrated a colossal hoax. Thurman then canceled or cut back on several of the security measures, although the concertina wire and concrete barriers on and near U.S. facilities remained in place. Going into December, tensions in Panama eased ever so slightly. To be sure, Stiner and what he called his "group of twenty" staff officers continued to visit the Southern Command for planning sessions, now scheduled at least once a month, but the group would arrive in civilian clothes, generally at night, to avoid attracting attention or causing an unwanted provocation. JTF-Panama units continued to conduct Sand Fleas, Purple Storms, and contingency readiness exercises, in effect rehearsing (still unknowingly in the case of the troops) portions of the new operation plan. Early in the month, though, Cisneros was told to reduce the intensity of the exercises in advance of a drug summit to be held in Panama. This was also a time when conventional wisdom held that "nothing ever happens in Panama during a holiday season." The same could almost be said of crisis-related activities in the United States. At Fort Bragg and elsewhere along the East Coast during the first half of December, the 82d Airborne Division and Special Operations Forces conducted a series of BLUE SPOON rehearsals for which precise mock-ups and line-outs of the actual targets in Panama had been constructed. There were two major rehearsals, the second of which was over by mid-month. The results would help to identify problems, streamline procedures, and update plans. In the meantime, as in Panama, almost everyone involved turned their thoughts to the holiday season, to parties, and to family and friends. At Quarry Heights, Fort Clayton, Fort Bragg, and the Pentagon, the safe bet was that the anticipated trigger event for BLUE SPOON would not occur before the new year.[40]

Then, on 15 December 1989, just as the holiday spirit was getting into full swing, Noriega gave an inflammatory speech before the National Assembly of Representatives, which dutifully passed a resolution declaring, "The Republic of Panama is declared to be in a state of war while [U.S.] aggression lasts." The same document also proclaimed Noriega "Maximum Leader for national liberation" and head of government. At the Southern Command and USARSO headquarters, viewers of the televised performance did not take it seriously. They dismissed it, correctly, as high theater designed to shore up the dictator's political position. But, as hindsight would suggest, the speech possibly encouraged the Panamanian military, many members of which were still under suspicion because of the abortive coup, to demonstrate their loyalty and their patriotism by taking a more combative approach toward U.S. service personnel. Whatever the motives at play, the next night, Saturday, 16 December, ended in a deadly confrontation.

Virtually every U.S. headquarters in Panama was holding a holiday party that evening. At Fort Amador, Cisneros hosted the USARSO festivities. Hartzog, for his part, had arranged a celebration for his staff and their families. Some of these soirées were formal affairs, requiring dress uniforms. There were lavish dinners, toasts, speeches, and entertainment. At Hartzog's quarters, the revelers had almost finished a song parody, "The Twelve Days of Thurman," when the brigadier general received

---

[40] Interv, author with Hartzog and Braaten, 29 Jun 90. Concerning expectations of when the trigger event would occur, the Thurman Papers in the U.S. Army Military History Institute at Carlisle Barracks, Pennsylvania, contain briefing slides that, presumably for gaming purposes, used a date in mid-January.

a telephone call. The Panama Defense Forces had shot an American officer, Hartzog was told, possibly killing him. At Amador, Cisneros was in the middle of remarks to the guests when he received word of the shooting. He quickly canceled the rest of the party and, with several of his staff, headed for Fort Clayton.

By 2200, much of what had happened was known. Four U.S. officers riding through Panama City had ended up at a roadblock in front of the Comandancia. Soon after their car was stopped, the situation with the Panamanian guards manning the checkpoint had become abusive. Concerned about his and his passengers' safety, the driver decided to run the roadblock, and the Panamanians opened fire, one bullet hitting U.S. Marine Lt. Robert Paz, who was sitting in the backseat. Before the driver could reach a hospital, Paz had bled to death.

What the American officers assembled at Quarry Heights and Fort Clayton did not know was whether the incident had broader ramifications. Was there, for example, another coup attempt under way into which the marines had had the misfortune to stumble? Was this a preemptive strike by the Panamanian military against United States forces? For several hours, the Southern Command and JTF-Panama gathered as much information as they could. Reconnaissance aircraft were launched to determine if there were any Panamanian troop movements. Meanwhile, JTF-Panama units went on heightened alert, with some moving to defensive positions on or around key U.S. installations as a result of a hastily called contingency readiness exercise. Analysts soon concluded that the shooting had been an isolated incident, not a preparatory or premeditated act. By midnight, the urgency and frenetic activity of the previous hours had subsided. Somewhat surprisingly, there was no visible sense of outrage over the killing of an American marine. As a group of officers in the operations center at Fort Clayton opined in matter-of-fact terms, running a roadblock anywhere, even in a friendly country, can bring one under fire.

The outrage came on Sunday when reports circulated that, minutes after the shooting, PDF personnel had detained a U.S. Navy lieutenant and his wife who had witnessed the incident. Before being released, the lieutenant had been brutally and repeatedly punched and kicked, even after he had fallen to the floor. His wife had been made to stand facing a wall with her hands raised above her head. At least one Panamanian officer made sexual threats and fondled her until she ultimately passed out. Among the U.S. officers privy to the news, the episode provoked the anger not in evidence the previous night. Even so, indignation did not automatically translate into action. The critical question was whether the Bush administration, despite its more belligerent rhetoric since the October coup attempt, was really prepared to use military force in Panama. Many officers at Quarry Heights and Fort Clayton thought not, believing that the State Department or the Southern Command's Center for Treaty Affairs would simply protest the PDF's behavior, then, as in so many cases in the past, let the matter drop. At a JTF-Panama meeting held around noon, Cisneros said that he could not predict what the president would do. What was important at the moment was to put the Panamanian armed forces off their guard, just in case Bush decided to take military action. Cisneros thus ordered units that had been put on heightened alert Saturday night to adopt a lower profile. He then went around the conference table, asking each of his commanders and staff officers if there were any problems, or "war stoppers," that would prevent them from executing their BLUE SPOON missions. Only a few minor issues surfaced. That finished, he voiced his two principal concerns should there be hostilities: poor communications and friendly fire incidents. The units slated for combat needed to do all they could to minimize the chances of either occurring.[41]

As this meeting was under way, President Bush was at a White House Christmas party. At 1400 EDT, he slipped away to his residence on the second floor to receive a briefing on the Panamanian situation. Joining him in his quarters were his key military and foreign policy advisers. Cheney and Powell had conferred earlier in the day and had agreed to recommend a full-scale invasion of Panama to the president. The Joint Chiefs of Staff had concurred. During the meeting with Bush, General Kelly delivered the BLUE SPOON briefing with some passion, and the president asked several hard and detailed questions. His approval was not a foregone conclusion. Yet the fact remained that the discipline and stability of the Panama Defense Forces seemed to be disintegrating, calling into question the safety of American citizens in Panama to a degree that had not existed previously. After about an hour and forty minutes, Bush summarized the situation: "This guy," meaning Noriega, "is not going to lay off. It will only get worse." He then looked at Powell and said, "Okay, let's go. We're going to go."[42]

After two and a half years, the crisis between the United States and Panama was going to be resolved through the use of military force. BLUE SPOON, which had started out nearly two years before as one phase of the ELABORATE MAZE operation order, was going to be executed. The world would know it as Operation JUST CAUSE.

---

[41] The account of the events from Saturday night to Sunday afternoon is based on notes the author took, 15–17 December 1989, while in Panama.

[42] Woodward, *The Commanders*, pp. 160–71.

10

Conclusions

The crisis in Panama began in June 1987 with demonstrations against the dictatorial regime of General Manuel Antonio Noriega Moreno, the commander of the Panama Defense Forces, who had been accused by a former subordinate of drug-trafficking, election fraud, and murder. Over the ensuing months, as the domestic turmoil intensified, the general's increasing resort to anti-American rhetoric and activities as a means of deflecting internal criticism precipitated a confrontation with the Reagan administration in Washington, D.C. That aspect of the crisis was exacerbated in February 1988, when two federal grand juries in Florida returned sealed indictments against the dictator. By the end of the month, tensions between the two governments had reached the point where the U.S. Southern Command, headquartered in the former Panama Canal Zone, began writing contingency plans for increasing the number of U.S. forces in the country, evacuating American citizens, and conducting defensive and offensive military operations to remove Noriega from power. As staff officers revised those plans over the course of nearly two years, U.S. troops based in Panama were significantly augmented on two occasions: the first occurring in March and April 1988 for the purpose of security enhancement and the second, in May 1989, for the purpose of asserting U.S. rights under the 1979 Panama Canal treaties (*Table*). As a result of these crisis-related measures, when President George H. W. Bush ordered the invasion of Panama in December 1989, the plans for executing the appropriate military operations had been finely tuned, and a large portion of the conventional force needed to perform the tactical missions was already on the scene and prepared to act. The result was an overwhelming success from a strictly military standpoint. Despite the fog and friction inherent in warfare, the stage for Operation JUST CAUSE had been so well set that the production was performed with comparatively few muffed lines.

The foregoing synopsis reflects a common but skewed approach to assessing U.S. military involvement in the Panama crisis from June 1987 to December 1989. After the Bush administration employed armed force to resolve the confrontation with Noriega, several writers—civilians and military, official historians, professional authors, and journalists—applied their talents to recounting the plans and the combat operations executed on 20 December and after. In the process, the military dimension of the contentious 2½ years preceding the invasion was treated as background material, covered in an introductory chapter or two, with emphasis on

Table—Buildup of U.S. Forces in Panama, 1988–1989

Stationed in Panama

U.S. Navy, South
U.S. Air Force, South
U.S. Marines, South
U.S. Army, South (USARSO)
    193d Infantry Brigade
    92d Military Police (MP) Battalion
    228th Aviation Battalion
Special Operations Command, South
    3d Battalion, 7th Special Forces Group (Airborne)
617th Special Operations Aviation Detachment

1988 Security Enhancement Augmentation

MP brigade
MP battalions
Task Force Hawk (7th Infantry Division [Light] aviation assets)
U.S. Marine company

1989 Nimrod Dancer Buildup

Brigade headquarters, 7th Infantry Division (Light)
Battalion, 7th Infantry Division (Light)
Mechanized battalion, 5th Infantry Division (Mechanized)
U.S. Marine light armored infantry company
Battalion in Jungle Operations Training Center

1989 Eloquent Banquet Insertions

AH–64 Apache helicopters
OH–58 Kiowa helicopters
M551 Sheridan armored reconnaissance vehicles

Total forces as of December 1989: 13,171

Of the total, Army forces: 9,254

Conclusions

those events and undertakings—U.S. contingency planning, the 1989 Panamanian elections and subsequent American troop buildup, and the 3 October failed coup—whose cumulative effect was to increase the likelihood of all-out hostilities. Almost without exception, there appeared in print no comprehensive account or in-depth analysis of the day-to-day military activities undertaken during the crisis by the U.S. Southern Command and, at the operational and tactical levels, Joint Task Force-Panama and its component task forces.[1] The omission, while understandable, had the effect of underscoring the insights taken from Operation JUST CAUSE while ignoring or downplaying other, equally important and valuable insights from the protracted pre-invasion period, some of which contradicted the positive lessons being gleaned from the invasion. For example, the analysts who praised JUST CAUSE as a model of interservice cooperation consonant with the Goldwater-Nichols Act of 1986 were generally unaware of the intense friction that, beginning with the security enhancement buildup in early 1988, had permeated dealings between the Army-dominated JTF-Panama headquarters and its Marine Forces component. Likewise, many observers applauding the incorporation and interaction of conventional and special operations forces in the invasion remained ignorant of the largely unsuccessful efforts within JTF-Panama throughout the crisis to arrange a workable command, control, and operational relationship between these two disparate types of forces.

As a corrective to the approach taken in most accounts, this study has attempted to assess the military dimension of the pre-invasion crisis on its own merits and not simply as a prelude to JUST CAUSE. The perspective is that of the officers who had to cope with the tense, unfolding drama on a daily basis while civilian and military decision makers in Washington and Panama sought to resolve the confrontation through peaceful means. To these people, the outcome was far from certain, and the use of force was by no means accepted as inevitable, at least until the last two months before the invasion. When examined in detail, the activities of the U.S. military relating to Panama during the period June 1987 to mid-December 1989 offer observations and insights that were relevant to, if not always appreciated by, civilian and military decision makers at the time, that are still relevant today, and that will remain so for the foreseeable future.

The Twilight Zone

From the outset, the crisis in Panama involved the U.S. military in circumstances that could not be formally categorized or easily defined. Since the United States

---

[1] Of the principal publications on the Panama crisis and Operation JUST CAUSE, Woodward's *The Commanders* provides a thorough and accurate account of the military dimensions of the crisis preceding the U.S. invasion, but from the perspective of the Reagan-Bush administrations, the Pentagon, the Southern Command, and Fort Bragg; the book makes only passing references to the activities of JTF-Panama and its components. Two official histories, Cole's *Operation Just Cause* and Fishel's *The Fog of Peace*, both address periodic milestones in the crisis from June 1987 to December 1989, but mainly in terms of contingency plans and the process in which they were drafted. The Marine Corps' official history does contain a detailed account of military activities from early 1988 to late 1989, but almost exclusively, as one would expect, from the perspective of Marine Forces-Panama. In the best commercial publication on the invasion to date, Donnelly, Roth, and Baker, *Operation Just Cause*, the first one hundred pages give a more detailed account than found elsewhere on the military aspects of the crisis up to President Bush's decision to use armed force. Some of this material, however, needs to be updated.

was not at war with the Noriega regime or the Panama Defense Forces, the situation could only be described technically as one of peace. In fact, the crisis occupied what USARSO's chief of staff, Col. Arnie Rossi, referred to as the Twilight Zone between peace and war, a status not supported by any corpus of legal statutes and only marginally covered at the time in U.S. military doctrine for low intensity conflict. Consequently, the Southern Command often found the peacetime laws and rules it applied in dealing with the crisis inadequate tools for accomplishing its objectives.

Operating in the Twilight Zone raised more than just legal and doctrinal problems. In peacetime, there was little need to worry unduly about the safety of the tens of thousands of U.S. military dependents and other American citizens living in Panama. In war, those citizens would presumably be evacuated. In the limbo between the two conditions, their situation was more precarious, as they remained in the country, generally going about their business without obstruction, but, at various times in the crisis, harassed in a variety of ways that included, on rare occasions, physical injury. What the Southern Command had to be concerned with was the sporadic but calculated intimidation of these Americans through acts that, however annoying or dangerous, fell short of the kind of direct threats to their lives and well-being that would have befallen them in wartime. Such expedients as Personnel Movement Limitations, town hall meetings, public affairs initiatives, and increased patrolling of U.S. housing areas helped to reduce the risks to Americans in Panama but did little to reduce the command's vulnerability to charges that it was not doing enough to protect its personnel. In the meantime, military planners pondered what would happen to the American community in the event of hostilities.

Dealing with a conflict in the Twilight Zone also affected the guidance the Southern Command received on what courses of action to follow. The dangers implicit in the deteriorating situation were enough to make Panama the object of discussion in Washington, but, without the clarity of a war and with seemingly more important issues in other parts of the world vying for the attention of both President Reagan and President Bush, the discussions were too often unfocused or, worse, they became bureaucratic turf battles that undermined attempts to devise an effective interagency strategy and policy. General Woerner, as the SOUTHCOM commander, was persistent in pushing for a multifaceted approach that would combine international, political, economic, and military pressure on Panama's regime and armed forces in such a way as to compel a "Panamanian solution" to the crisis, but his entreaties could never overcome the entrenched positions of the various U.S. agencies involved. In his view, the incremental, disconnected measures—especially the economic sanctions—enacted by the White House and Congress only served to prolong the crisis, not end it.

If a comprehensive strategy for dealing with the crisis was nonexistent and policy guidance often inadequate, Woerner did repeatedly receive one message that was very clear: U.S. forces in Panama were not to start a war. During most of the crisis, Quarry Heights and Washington were in complete agreement on this point, although not necessarily for the same reasons. Generals Woerner, Loeffke, Cisneros, and Stewart hoped to avoid hostilities because of the negative impact they would have on America's influence and image throughout most of Latin America. The White House, on the other hand, while not unmoved by this same sentiment, was more concerned in 1988 about the negative effect hostilities might have on the American presidential election that year and on U.S. military capabilities elsewhere in the world. Even after President Bush took office in 1989 and enunciated a tougher policy toward Noriega, the Southern Command, amid the directives it received to assert U.S. treaty rights in Panama and to put pressure on the Panamanian military, was also enjoined, once again, not to start a war.

The impact of this injunction was twofold. First, since most American military personnel stationed in Panama were unaware of such behind-the-scenes restrictions placed on Woerner, they blamed the general for not being more aggressive in taking a stand against the Noriega regime's campaign of harassment, much of which violated U.S. treaty rights in Panama. Yet for Woerner to have taken a stronger stand against these infringements would have risked precipitating the hostilities he was under instructions to avoid. Second, efforts to keep the crisis from spinning out of control meant restraining the activities of the U.S. military units that came into day-to-day contact with the Panama Defense Forces. The principal means of exercising this restraint was through restrictive rules of engagement that, based on peacetime requirements, were designed to limit the use of deadly force by U.S. troops to an extremely narrow range of conditions. Flag officers and legal authorities in the Southern Command, the Joint Chiefs of Staff, and JTF-Panama generally consulted one another before promulgating what they considered to be rules of engagement appropriate to the situation. Once the rules were issued, Woerner, Loeffke, and their respective staffs with few but noteworthy exceptions demanded rigorous adherence. Relying on intelligence sources and their own expertise concerning Panama, they knew that Noriega and the Panama Defense Forces, despite their harassment campaigns and their violations of U.S. treaty rights, also sought to avoid open hostilities. Thus, war, if it came, was likely to be the result of an accident—some incident in which one side or the other overreacted in a tense situation. The strict and restrictive rules of engagement issued by the Southern Command and JTF-Panama would at least diminish the chances of an inadvertent war precipitated by American forces.

At the tactical level, many troops—especially the marines and the NIMROD DANCER augmentation units—complained that the rules were too passive and reactive, placing U.S. forces at a disadvantage in any confrontation with armed Panamanians. Among the critics were those who believed the rules of engagement almost guaranteed that an American would take the first bullet in any standoff that went wrong. In other words, the rules seemed to abridge the individual's inherent right of self-defense in the face of hostile actions or hostile intent.

There were other complaints about the rules of engagement. Some commanders of the tactical units maintained that the rules were too complex, at times ambiguous, and continuously changing in their details. The constraints they incorporated also implied that trained U.S. military personnel could not be trusted to know when to use their weapons. Furthermore, soldiers or marines contemplating the use of deadly force for legitimate reasons might hesitate, wondering whether their actions might land them in serious trouble with higher headquarters. That hesitation, the argument went, could have fatal consequences. The controversy surrounding the rules of engagement was never resolved to everyone's satisfaction during the course of the crisis. Still, however one viewed the limitations placed on American military activities, the fact remains that, aside from two significant but contained firefights in 1988, there were few shooting incidents between U.S. and Panamanian forces, a strong indication that Woerner, Cisneros, Loeffke, and others did have an accurate understanding of their adversary. When a U.S. officer was shot and killed on 16 December 1989—the trigger event for the invasion of Panama—the circumstances had nothing to do with rules of engagement or related issues.

To many soldiers and marines in Panama—again, especially those who entered the crisis in augmentation units from outside the country—operating under such constraints violated the "warrior" ethos they had brought with them. Whether these troops referred to their environment as low intensity conflict, unorthodox operations, or the Twilight Zone, most considered what they confronted and what they were required to do as having little or no relation to the scenarios for which they had been trained and prepared. The warriors who entered Panama were oriented to a linear battlefield on which one conventional force would fire and maneuver against a conventional enemy force, a mirror-image of their own, without restrictions on the use of nonnuclear firepower and without civilians getting in the way. In the Panama crisis, a sizable portion of the canal area—and, potentially, the entire country—was the battlefield, and the enemy, meaning the Panama Defense Forces and Dignity Battalions, constituted an unavoidable presence in urban areas whose population included U.S. military personnel and their dependents living "on the economy" and thousands of Panamanians friendly to the United States. On a daily basis, the warriors routinely pulled guard duty, conducted training events, and, during Operation NIMROD DANCER, asserted U.S. treaty rights. Their orders in each of these endeavors were to use force only as a last resort.

Coming to grips with the ambiguity, complexity, dynamics, and unorthodox aspects of the crisis required adjustments that some soldiers and marines were able to make, while others were not. In one example of the first instance, a platoon leader in a mechanized company whose unit had arrived in Panama in late 1989 made the adjustment in a couple of weeks. Thus, when on an exercise with the platoon's three M113 armored personnel carriers, he rounded a corner and found himself facing a surprised group of armed Panamanian soldiers who promptly pointed their weapons at his men, the young officer just kept on going. But he stated afterward that, had this happened on his first day or week in Panama, he would have opened fire on the group. From the perspective of JTF-Panama, the headquarters that had operational control of these tactical forces, the fact that most of the U.S. combat units arriving in the country possessed little or no training in the unorthodox requirements and nuances of the Twilight Zone was a source of great concern.

JOINT OPERATIONS

All units under JTF-Panama experienced working with units and personnel from other services on a weekly if not daily basis. Soon after Woerner activated the joint task force, Loeffke, as its commanding general, let his component commanders and their staffs know that he wanted unit training events, exercises, and operations to be planned and conducted on a joint basis. The success of this program, which allowed each service to adjust to different standard operating procedures, force structure, equipment, tactics, and jargon employed by its sister services, was something in which the organization as a whole took a great deal of pride. JTF-Panama was less successful, however, in promoting joint working relationships in certain other areas. The three most serious problems centered on staffing the headquarters, relations with the Marine Forces component, and friction between special operations and conventional forces. Regarding the first, Colonel Cope, the JTF-Panama operations officer through most of the crisis, once remarked that the joint headquarters consisted of U.S. Army, South, personnel and "about ten other guys," meaning that Army officers filled most key positions, except in times of acute crisis.[2] On a daily basis, only the Navy sent staff officers to help JTF-Panama in its operations center.

As for the marines, high-ranking officers at both the Southern Command and JTF-Panama, to include Woerner and Loeffke, formed the impression early on that the Leathernecks were "trigger happy," inclined to use force at the slightest provocation, which was exactly what the unified command and joint task force were trying to avoid. Marine Forces-Panama, for its part, believed that both higher headquarters evinced an inadequate concern for the personal safety of the marines in the field. Some Marine officers even believed that Woerner, Loeffke, and their staffs were setting them up, unintentionally to be sure, for another Beirut, the horrendous memory of which was fewer than five years old when the first Marine company sent to Panama for security enhancement duties arrived in April 1988. The friction between the Marine Forces component and the headquarters to which it answered in Panama began on the nights of 11 and 12 April 1988 when, in sequence, a marine on the Arraiján Tank Farm was killed by friendly fire and, the next night, the marines engaged in a two-hour firefight. That friction persisted late into the crisis, to subside somewhat once Thurman took over for Woerner and Cisneros had replaced Loeffke. For the most part, though, the conflicting mind-sets of the marines in the field and the commanders and staffs at Quarry Heights and Fort Clayton could not be reconciled through joint training events and the high level of cooperation attained in other, less volatile areas.

The third case in point was the friction that developed early on between JTF-Panama and the Special Operations Command, South, over the question of who had operational control of special operations forces and how those elite forces would interact with conventional forces when engaged in crisis-related activities. For Loeffke and the SOCSOUTH commander, Colonel Fry, the incident near Howard Air Force Base on 20–21 April 1988 brought both issues to the fore, in the most fractious of ways. In Loeffke's opinion, the special operators needed to be under his operational control when conducting crisis-related missions; they also needed to coordinate those missions with conventional units in the area assigned to JTF-Panama. Fry's response was that SOCSOUTH was a subunified command that answered only to the SOUTHCOM commander and that the safety of the small teams he fielded relied on operations security, which meant that they could share very little information with their conventional counterparts. For over a year, Loeffke and Fry tried unsuccessfully to work out an acceptable command and control arrangement. When they both left Panama at the end of June 1989, the points of friction still existed. At the time, some observers blamed the impasse on the personalities of two hard-headed and determined individuals, only to find that the pair's successors would continue to fight the same turf battles. The persistence of this problem, together with the staffing issue and the friction with the marines,

---

[2] Interv, author with Col John A. Cope Jr., U.S. Army, 29 Mar 89, Fort Clayton, Panama.

was a source of concern but did not diminish the resounding success of JTF-Panama's overall record of promoting interservice cooperation, coordination, and interoperability.

At Quarry Heights, a quarter-century of joint experience within the unified command militated against the kind of problems JTF-Panama struggled with at the operational and tactical levels. Where the Southern Command encountered joint difficulties with respect to the Panama crisis was primarily in the conduct of contingency planning. The original CINCSO ELABORATE MAZE operation order of March 1988 called for three subordinate headquarters to be under the SOUTHCOM commander should hostilities occur in Panama: JTF-Panama, a joint special operations task force, and a U.S. Navy aircraft carrier battle group. The staff at Quarry Heights had some doubts about establishing JTF-Panama, but the pressures generated by planning needs and various developments in the crisis overrode most of those concerns. The joint special operations task force, which Woerner readily activated, coordinated with the Southern Command and JTF-Panama planners almost daily and proved cooperative throughout the planning process, even though some contentious issues did arise and although not all the special operators involved at Fort Bragg were enamored of Woerner's concept for what became the BLUE SPOON plan for U.S. combat operations in Panama.

The same commitment to a cooperative joint relationship, however, was not forthcoming from the Navy's Atlantic Command, which balked at putting a carrier battle group under the control of an Army general, no matter what Goldwater-Nichols intended or the Joint Chiefs of Staff directed. At one point, Woerner appealed directly to Admiral Crowe to intercede. The Joint Chiefs chairman sided with the general, but the Navy continued to be recalcitrant, and the issue was not resolved until after the 3 October 1989 coup attempt, at which time SOUTHCOM planners simply dropped the carrier group from the BLUE SPOON operation order. After Operation JUST CAUSE, when General Thurman and others would herald the joint composition of the invasion force as a vindication of Goldwater-Nichols, there were veterans of the crisis who were inclined to add a disclaimer or two.

PERSONALITIES

The bulk of U.S. military training and education emphasizes organizations, processes, doctrine, technology, and other impersonal factors. The subject of leadership to some degree addresses the issue of personality, but generally places greater weight on techniques and personnel management, overlooking the fact that, in any human endeavor, the interplay of different personalities is often critical to understanding the outcome. This was certainly the case in the Panama crisis. Three examples should suffice to make the case. To begin with, there was General Woerner, a commander with a vast knowledge of Latin America and extensive military experience in the area, including Panama. From the perspective of many officers serving with him, his expertise was put to excellent use during the crisis, a fact that Admiral Crowe in the Pentagon recognized as well. To his critics, though, Woerner's reputation as an "intellectual" signaled a possible tendency to overanalyze problems, while his expertise with respect to Latin America fueled groundless speculation that he had "gone native." Once what had been regarded as his attributes became a source of suspicion among policy makers in Washington and his peers in the Pentagon and elsewhere, his effectiveness in the crisis was reduced. That notwithstanding, at the time he was relieved, he could say that he had carried out his orders and, more important, had kept the crisis from escalating unnecessarily to the point that U.S. intervention would be required. His successor, General Max Thurman, only knew what he had absorbed about Latin America in the short time he had as SOUTHCOM's commander-designate. Thurman was critical of Woerner's strategy and plans and lacked Woerner's wariness of "outsiders," meaning primarily the XVIII Airborne Corps. How Thurman would have handled the crisis had he been the SOUTHCOM commander in 1987 and 1988 can only be imagined; the same is true of how Woerner would have acted during the 3 October coup attempt or during the execution of Operation JUST CAUSE. Conjecture, however, would probably yield in both cases scenarios very different from the events that actually transpired.

Brig. Gen., later Maj. Gen., Marc Cisneros, like Woerner, knew much about Panama and, after Woerner's departure, was the highest ranking officer in the country with any institutional memory for what had happened during the more than two years of crisis. Cisneros also had a knack for determining what Noriega and the Panama Defense Forces would do at critical moments, or how they would react to U.S. initiatives. Yet, if some thought Cisneros would become an indispensable adviser to General Thurman, they were greatly mistaken. Considered part of the "Woerner crowd," plus being a person of Hispanic heritage, Cisneros was kept at arm's length during his service as one of Thurman's component commanders. On those occasions when he was encouraged to express his best judgment, his views often conflicted with those of the four-star. Cisneros' largely unsuccessful efforts to explain the nuances of the 3 October coup attempt to Thurman, whom the USARSO commander believed to be letting ego get the better of common sense, illustrate the point.

Other examples of the importance of personalities in the Panama crisis abound. All contribute to the conclusion that, in examining any such ongoing conflict, the personal dimension must be given the weight it deserves along with the impersonal factors that are also at work and generally highly emphasized in postconflict analyses. The actors—in this study, mainly the military leaders involved—should not be treated as interchangeable parts whose participation and interaction have only a marginal effect on the course of events.

In addition to the aforementioned observations, there are many other "lessons" that the U.S. military derived or should have derived from its involvement in the Panama crisis from June 1987 to mid-December 1989. Many are highlighted in the main text of this study; readers will infer others; and still others will surface as classified documents are released and the crisis is examined by writers asking different questions of the material. In concluding this volume, the point to reiterate is that the role of the U.S. military in Panama during more than two years of crisis should not be viewed as simply setting the stage for Operation JUST CAUSE, an invasion that few officers saw as inevitable until mid-October 1989. The daily activities of the U.S. Southern Command and, under it, JTF-Panama during this 2½-year period must be examined and analyzed on their own merits and from the perspective of individuals looking toward the future, uncertain of its outcome. What one observes from this perspective is an example of crisis management in which the U.S. military played a dominant—sometimes predominant—role while receiving inadequate guidance, fighting for scarce resources, continuing to carry out theater-wide missions, enduring internal frictions, and at times operating under severe constraints generated by both military and political considerations. In a generic sense, U.S. military operations well before the Panama crisis were affected by these or similar issues, and that pattern holds true today. As a case study, the military's role in the political-military confrontation with Noriega stands on its own as informative and instructive. Together with studies of similar endeavors, it has much to say to officers who at some point in their careers will experience military operations in similar "Twilight Zones."

Bibliography

Primary Sources

Most of the documents, oral histories, and other primary sources cited in the footnotes to each chapter were collected at a variety of locations during the U.S.-Panamanian crisis or soon after its resolution in Operations Just Cause and Promote Liberty. In the case of the documents, the vast majority were taken from operational files, xeroxed, and returned to the files. Most of those files no longer exist, although some of the material contained in them is likely to be located in the archives or history offices of the Joint History Office in the Pentagon; U.S. Army, South, now at Fort Sam Houston, Texas; the U.S. Army Center of Military History in Washington, D.C.; the U.S. Army Forces Command at Fort McPherson, Georgia; the U.S. Army Military History Institute and the U.S. Army War College at Carlisle Barracks, Pennsylvania; the U.S. Army Special Operations Command at Fort Bragg, North Carolina; the U.S. Marine Corps History Division (formerly the U.S. Marine Corps History and Museums Division) at Quantico, Virginia; the U.S. Southern Command, now in Dade County, Florida; and the U.S. Special Operations Command at MacDill Air Force Base, Florida.

In the case of the oral history interviews cited in the footnotes, most were conducted by the author, but many came from other sources: the XVIII Airborne Corps at Fort Bragg, North Carolina; the U.S. Army Center for Army Lessons Learned at Fort Leavenworth, Kansas; the U.S. Army Center of Military History; the U.S. Army Military History Institute and U.S. Army Strategic Studies Institute at Carlisle Barracks; the U.S. Army Forces Command; the U.S. Marine Corps History Division; and the U.S. Special Operations Command.

With few exceptions, the author has placed the primary sources cited in this study into a discrete research collection. As of this writing, that collection is located at the Combined Arms Research Library (CARL) at Fort Leavenworth, Kansas. Existing plans call for keeping that collection intact, even though its location may shift after completion of the second, and final, volume in this study of the crisis.

Unpublished Material

Kraus, Theresa L. Working Chronology for Operation Just Cause. Washington, D.C.: U.S. Army Center of Military History, 1990.
Loeffke, Maj Gen Bernard, U.S. Army. Diary.

Marcella, Gabriel, and General Frederick F. Woerner Jr., U.S. Army (Ret.). *The Road to War: The U.S.-Panamanian Crisis, 1987–1989.* Draft article. 6 May 1991.

Neller, Maj Robert B., U.S. Marine Corps (USMC). *Marines in Panama: 1988–1990.* Paper, USMC Staff College, Quantico, Va., 1991.

Sikes, Reginald. *Operation NIMROD DANCER: A Personal View of Lessons Learned.* Paper, A645, U.S. Army Command and General Staff College, Fort Leavenworth, Kans., 15 Feb 98.

U.S. Southern Command. Joint After Action Report. Operation JUST CAUSE. 14 Feb 91.

Woodrow. Lt Col Paul J. *'Ni Un Paso Atras'-The Crisis in Panama, 1987–1989.* U.S. Army War College Personal Experience Monograph. Carlisle Barracks, Pa.: U.S. Army War College, 12 April 1992.

DOCUMENT COLLECTIONS

Thurman, Maxwell, Papers. U.S. Army Military History Institute, Carlisle Barracks, Pa.

USMC Command Chronologies for Panama. U.S. Marine Corps History Division, Quantico, Va.

Woerner, Frederick, Jr., Papers. U.S. Army Military History Institute, Carlisle Barracks, Pa.

BOOKS

Baker, James A., III, with Thomas M. DeFrank. *The Politics of Diplomacy: Revolution, War, and Peace, 1989–1992.* New York: G. P. Putnam's Sons, 1995.

Buckley, Kevin. *Panama: The Whole Story.* New York: Simon & Schuster, 1991.

Cole, Ronald H. *Operation Just Cause: The Planning and Execution of Joint Operations in Panama, February 1988–January 1990.* Washington, D.C.: Joint History Office, Office of the Chairman of the Joint Chiefs of Staff, 1995.

Conniff, Michael L. *Panama and the United States: The Forced Alliance.* Athens, Ga.: University of Georgia Press, 1992.

Dinges, John. *Our Man in Panama: How General Noriega Used the United States and Made Millions in Drugs and Arms.* New York: Random House, 1990.

_____. *Our Man in Panama: The Shrewd Rise and Brutal Fall of Manuel Noriega.* Rev. ed. New York: Times Books, 1991.

Donnelly, Thomas; Margaret Roth; and Caleb Baker. *Operation Just Cause: The Storming of Panama.* New York: Lexington Books, 1991.

Fishel, John T. *The Fog of Peace: Planning and Executing the Restoration of Panama.* Carlisle Barracks, Pa.: Strategic Studies Institute, 1992.

_____. "Planning For Post-Conflict Panama: What It Tells Us About Phase IV Operations." In *Turning Victory into Success: Military Operations After the Campaign*, edited by Brian M. De Toy. Fort Leavenworth, Kans.: Combat Studies Institute Press, 2005.

Flanagan, Lt. Gen. Edward M., Jr., U.S. Army (Ret.). *Battle for Panama: Inside Operation Just Cause.* Washington, D.C.: Brassey's, 1993.

Kempe, Frederick. *Divorcing the Dictator: America's Bungled Affair with Noriega.* New York: G. P. Putnam's Sons, 1990.

BIBLIOGRAPHY

Meditz, Sandra W., and Dennis M. Hanratty, eds. *Panama: A Country Study*. Washington, D.C.: Headquarters, Department of the Army, 1989.

Reynolds, Lt. Col. Nicholas E. *Just Cause: Marine Operations in Panama, 1988–1990*. Washington, D.C.: U.S. Marine Corps History and Museums Division, 1996.

Scranton, Margaret E. *The Noriega Years: U.S.-Panamanian Relations, 1981–1990*. Boulder, Colo.: Lynne Rienner Publishers, 1991.

Woodward, Bob. *The Commanders*. New York: Simon & Schuster, 1991.

NEWSPAPERS, BULLETINS, AND MAGAZINES

Air Force Times, *Army Times*, *New York Times*, *Southern Command News*, *Time*, *Tropic Times*, and *Washington Post*.

Department of State Bulletin. 89 (July 1989): 70–71.

Livingstone, Neil. "Just Cause Jailbreak." *Soldier of Fortune* (October 1990).

Abbreviations and Acronyms

AAR	After action report
AFB	Air Force base
AFFOR	Air Force Forces
AFOSI	Air Force Office of Special Investigations
AIDS	Acquired Immune Deficiency Syndrome
AO	Area of operations
APC	Armored personnel carrier
ARFOR	Army Forces
ARFORPM	Army Forces-Panama
BCE	Battlefield coordination element
BDU	Battle dress uniform
CARL	Combined Arms Research Library
CAT	Crisis action team
CCN	Spanish acronym for National Civic Crusade
CG	Commanding general
CGSC	U.S. Army Command and General Staff College
CIA	Central Intelligence Agency
CINCFOR	Commander in chief, U.S. Forces Command
CINCSO	Commander in chief, U.S. Southern Command
CJCS	Chairman, Joint Chiefs of Staff
CMO	Civil-military operations
CMOTF	Civil-military operations task force
CMR	Countermortar radar
CNN	Cable News Network
CO	Commanding officer
COMARFORPM	Commander, Army Forces-Panama
COMJSOTF	Commander, joint special operations task force
COMJTF-Panama	Commander, Joint Task Force-Panama
COMJTFPM	Commander, Joint Task Force-Panama
COMMARFORPM	Commander, Marine Forces-Panama
COMSOCSO	Commander, Special Operations Command, South
COMSOCSOUTH	Commander, Special Operations Command, South

COMUSNAVSO	Commander, U.S. Navy, South
CRE	Contingency readiness exercise
CSA	Chief of staff, Army
DA	Department of the Army
DCSINT	Deputy chief of staff for intelligence
DCSOPS	Deputy chief of staff for operations
DENI	National Investigation Department
DEROS	Date eligible to return from overseas
DF	Disposition form
DIA	Defense Intelligence Agency
DJS	Director, Joint Staff
DNTT	*Dirección nacional de transporte terrestre*
DoDDS	Department of Defense Dependent Schools
DRB	Division ready brigade
EDT	Eastern Daylight Time
FAST	Marine Fleet Anti-Terrorist Security Team
FBIS	Foreign Broadcast Information Service
FOM	Freedom of movement
FORSCOM	U.S. Forces Command
FRAGO	Fragmentary order
FSE	Fire support element
HMMWV	High mobility multipurpose wheeled vehicle
HQDA	Headquarters, Department of the Army
HUMINT	Intelligence collected and provided by human sources
IEEPA	International Emergency Economic Powers Act
INSCOM	U.S. Army Intelligence and Security Command
INTREP	Intelligence report
INTSUM	Intelligence summary
J–2	Joint intelligence directorate or officer
J–4	Joint logistics directorate or officer
JCIT	JUST CAUSE interview tapes
JCS	Joint Chiefs of Staff
JOPS	Joint Operation Planning System
JOTC	Jungle Operations Training Center
JSOTF	Joint special operations task force
JTF	Joint task force
LAI	Light amphibious infantry
LANTCOM	U.S. Atlantic Command
LAV	Light armored vehicle
LCM	Landing craft, mechanized

Abbreviations and Acronyms

LIC	Low intensity conflict
LOI	Letter of instruction
LNO	Liaison officer
MAC	Military Airlift Command
MARFOR	Marine Forces
MEB	Marine Expeditionary Brigade
MFR	Memorandum for the Record
MHI	U.S. Army Military History Institute
MI	Military intelligence
MILGRP	Military group
MP	Military police
NAVFOR	Navy Forces
NAVINVSERVRA	Naval Investigative Service Agency
NAVSO	U.S. Navy, South
NCC	National Civic Crusade
NSD	National security directive
OAS	Organization of American States
OPG	Operations Planning Group
OPLAN	Operation plan
OPORD	Operation order
PCC	Panama Canal Commission
PDF	Panama Defense Forces
PML	Personnel movement limitation
PRD	Democratic Revolutionary Party (Partido Revolucionario Democrático)
PSYOP	Psychological operations
QRF	Quick reaction force
ROC	Rules of confrontation
ROE	Rules of engagement
ROPP	Reduction of off-post personnel
RPG	Rocket-propelled grenade
S–3	Operations directorate or officer
SAM	Surface-to-air missile
SAW	Squad automatic weapon
SCJ–3	Southern Command's Operations Directorate
SCJ–5	Southern Command's Policy, Strategy, and Programs Directorate
SCN	Southern Command Network
SCTA	Southern Command's Center for Treaty Affairs
SEAL	Navy Sea-Air-Land
SF	Special Forces

SGS	Secretary of the General Staff
SJA	Staff judge advocate
SOCOM	U.S. Special Operations Command
SOCSOUTH	Special Operations Command, South
SOUTHCOM	U.S. Southern Command
STA	Surveillance and target acquisition
TACSAT	Tactical satellite
TAOR	Tactical area of responsibility
TDY	Temporary duty
TRANSCOM	Transportation Command
UESAT	Spanish acronym for the PDF's special operations unit
USAF	U.S. Air Force
USAMHI	U.S. Army Military History Institute
USARSO	U.S. Army, South
USAWC	U.S. Army War College
USCINCEUR	U.S. commander in chief, Europe
USCINCLANT	U.S. commander in chief, U.S. Atlantic Command
USG	U.S. government
USMC	U.S. Marine Corps
USSOUTHCOM	U.S. Southern Command

Index

✯ ✯ ✯

1st Battalion, 228th Aviation, 50, 70, 200, 204
1st Battalion, 5th Infantry Division (Mechanized), 175
1st Battalion, 9th Infantry, 178, 180
1st Battalion, 508th Infantry, 193d Infantry Brigade, 72n17, 73, 177, 220, 234, 252, 272
  Company B, 77
  Company C, 78, 79, 80
  Corozal exercise, 209
  and Las Minas incident, 140
1st Public Order Company, 249. *See also* Panama Defense Forces (PDF).
1st Special Operations Command, 45, 48
1st Special Operations Wing (Air Force), 46
2d Battalion, 8th Field Artillery, 174
2d Battalion, 9th Infantry, 174, 188, 207n39
3d Battalion, 4th Marines, Company I, 67, 68, 69, 72, 73, 74, 75, 76
3d Battalion, 7th Special Forces Group, 77, 96
3d Brigade, 7th Infantry Division (Light), 271
4th Infantry Company (PDF), 249, 255, 259
5th Battalion, 87th Infantry, 81n35, 214, 234
5th Infantry Company (PDF), 255
  housed at Fort Amador, 29, 47, 71, 210, 225, 226, 249, 258
  and LAV exercise, 211
5th Infantry Division (Mechanized), 174, 220
6th Marine Expeditionary Brigade, 67, 75
7th Infantry Company (PDF) ("Wild Boars"), 97, 116, 249, 255, 256, 264
7th Infantry Division (Light), 59, 155, 171, 179, 210, 268, 269. *See also* PURPLE STRIKE.
  in convoys, 204
  deployment of, 129, 173, 174, 188, 220, 236
  and ELABORATE MAZE, 50
  and ELDER STATESMAN, 93
  and JOTC battalion, 178
  and POST TIME, 93n55
  and Task Force Hawk, 127, 128
  "warrior" attitude of, 186
7th Special Forces Group, 45, 46, 47, 78
8th Infantry Company (PDF), 188, 189, 220, 235
9th Infantry ("Manchus"), 7th Infantry Division (Light), 174, 180
16th Military Police Brigade, 56, 59, 70, 128
XVIII Airborne Corps, 129–34, 220, 244, 264, 265, 266, 285
  and Hartzog, 246
  and Joint Task Force-Charlie, 155

XVIII Airborne Corps—*Continued*
  planners, 133, 196, 222, 263, 269
28th Public Affairs Detachment, 176
29th Military Intelligence Battalion, 189
75th Ranger Regiment, 46, 47
82d Airborne Division, 132, 147, 274
160th Special Operations Aviation Regiment, 46
193d Infantry Brigade, 79, 114, 181, 220, 223, 226, 239. *See also* LIGHTNING THRUST I; Operation NIMROD DANCER.
  and Arraiján Tank Farm, 70, 72, 77
  and convoys, 201
  and ELABORATE MAZE, 50
  and Task Force Bayonet, 179
324th Support Group, 114
361st Civil Affairs Brigade, 44n18
407th Military Intelligence Brigade, 22, 23
503d Military Police Battalion, 55
519th Military Police Battalion, 56, 59, 77
536th Engineer Battalion, 252
549th Military Police Company, 179
617th Special Operations Aviation Detachment, 77

A–10 Warthogs, 201, 204, 208
ABC News, 52, 57
Abrams, Elliott, 57, 58, 105, 136, 138, 146
  on Noriega, 14, 19, 64
  on sanctions, 40
AC–130 Spectre gunships, 47, 77, 85, 96, 130, 215, 252
  and Arraiján Tank Farm firefight, 70, 72n17, 75
  and BLUE SPOON, 95, 221
  and joint training, 111
  and NIMROD DANCER, 172, 177, 189
  used to track intruders, 79, 80, 82
AH–1 Cobras, 59, 77, 172, 201, 206
  and Arraiján Tank Farm firefight, 70, 71
  training of, 112
AH–6 Little Birds, 95
AH–64 Apache helicopters, 232, 270
Air Force Dog Flight, 51
Air Force Forces (AFFOR), 61, 201

Air Force security, 66, 85, 88, 172
Airbase Ground Defense Flight, 51, 52
Aircraft carrier battle group, 50, 155
AirLand Battle doctrine, 34, 35
Albrook Air Station, 30, 45, 50, 85, 187, 213, 223
  and BLUE SPOON, 94
  troops billeted at, 175
  vulnerability of, 96
Arias Calderón, Ricardo, 157, 168, 169
Arias Madrid, Arnulfo, 3, 6, 10, 11, 157
Arias Madrid, Harmodio, 3
Armored personnel carriers (APCs), 172, 175
Army Arrival/Departure Airfield Control Group, 51
Army counterintelligence detachment, 51
Army Forces (ARFOR), 61, 93, 266
Army Forces-Panama (ARFORPM), 93n55
Army Movement Control Team, 51
Army Recruiting Command, 242
Army Special Forces, 268
Army Times, 146
Army Training and Evaluation Program, 45
Aronson, Bernard, 136, 138, 223, 228n26, 243
Arraiján, Panama, 268
Arraiján Tank Farm, 52, 66, 75, 81n35, 111, 114
  debriefing after action, 71, 72
  defenses of, 67–68, 126
  firefights at, 65n5, 70–71, 81, 97, 98n65, 127, 212, 283
  guard duty at, 116–17
  Halloween incident at, 117, 125
  intruders, 69, 116, 185
  and rules of engagement, 119, 123
Aspin, Les, 261
Augustine, Maj. Dan, 48, 49, 60, 92, 93, 94, 155, 199

Baker, Howard, 98, 99
Baker, James D., 136, 137–38, 150, 153, 254
  on Noriega, 196

on October 1989 coup attempt, 258, 262
on Panamanian elections, 162
on Woerner's retirement, 224n13
Balboa, Panama City, 143
Balboa High School, 234
Barefield, Lt. Col. Robert, 77, 78, 79
Barletta, Nicolás Ardito, 11, 13
Battalion 2000. *See* Panama Defense Forces (PDF).
Bay of Panama, 47, 112
Beaumont, Louisiana, 175
Bellatrix, USNS, 175
Bennett, Lt. Col. William, 244, 264
Bergdorf, Lt. Col. Charles, 222
BLACK TOUCAN, 36
"Black Tuesday" (October 1989 coup), 248–58, 259, 279. *See also* Giroldi Vega, Maj. Moisés.
BLADE JEWEL, 182, 217–22, 223, 228
BLIND LOGIC, 44n18, 156, 269–70
BLUE SPOON, 89, 97, 129, 133, 180, 272, 274. *See also* 7th Infantry Division (Light); XVIII Airborne Corps; BLIND LOGIC; JTF-Panama.
and aircraft carrier battle group, 91, 155
airlift requirements, 265
changes and refinements to, 155, 160, 196, 221, 222, 268
civil-military operations under, 90, 92
conventional operations in, 221, 244, 245
Crowe on, 240
elements of, 221
and evacuation of U.S. citizens, 130
execution of, 225, 263, 265, 266
force list, 132
Kelly on, 137
OPORD 1–90, 265
phases of, 95
rehearsals, 274
SOUTHCOM commander role, 91, 92
and Special Operations Forces, 90, 244, 265

targets, 90, 208, 266
task forces, 95
Thurman on, 247
trigger event, 274
Bolt, Col. William J., 185, 204, 205, 215, 223
193d Infantry Brigade commander, 56, 85, 180, 201
commands Task Force Bayonet, 178
Bomb scare, 271n38, 272, 274
Bonney, Col. Charles E., 125n50
Braaten, Col. Thomas A., 199, 211, 248, 256
Bradley infantry fighting vehicle, 175
Bridge of the Americas, 175, 268
Arraiján Tank Farm firefight, 70, 81
and October 1989 coup attempt, 249, 250n15, 252, 253, 254, 255, 256, 257
Brite, S. Sgt. John C., 127n54
Brown, Richard, 228n26
Bush, George H. W., and his administration, 108, 134, 157, 167, 218, 236, 240
and additional troops sent to Panama, 171
and assertion of treaty rights, 238
assessment of crisis, 187
campaign of, 100, 106
and convoys' purpose, 199
and Muse affair, 160–61
on NIMROD DANCER, 220
on Noriega, 135, 137, 138, 151, 170, 183, 191, 281
and October 1989 coup attempt against Noriega, 252, 254, 255, 257, 261, 262
and Operation JUST CAUSE, 1, 277
and Organization of American States, 194, 232
on Panamanian elections, 152, 156, 158, 162, 166
pressures Noriega, 192, 194, 216, 227
and relocation of U.S. dependents, 217
and school bus detention, 146

297

Bush, George H. W., and his administration—*Continued*
and Woerner's retirement, 167, 224n13, 241

C–141 (aircraft), 130, 174
Cable News Network. *See* CNN (Cable News Network).
Cadillac-Gage V–300 armored reconnaissance vehicles, 211, 213
Camp Lejeune, North Carolina, 67, 173, 191, 270
Camp Rousseau, 175, 179, 183, 186
Carcel Modelo, 160, 161, 170, 184
Carleton, Col. Charles, 125n50
Carlucci, Frank, 40, 51, 55, 101n72
Carter, Jimmy, 7, 8, 156, 166, 167, 168
Carter-Torrijos Treaty. *See* Panama Canal Treaties (1979).
Casey, William, 20
Casino Gambit, 45, 48
Castillo, Col. Elías, 71, 74
Cavezza, Maj. Gen. Carmen, 186, 187
CBS News, 57
Center for Army Lessons Learned (Fort Leavenworth), 113
Center for Treaty Affairs. *See* U.S. Southern Command (SOUTHCOM).
Central American Chambers of Commerce, 138
Central Intelligence Agency (CIA), 14, 20, 141, 218, 243
  interagency campaign to oust Noriega, 98, 100, 105
  and Muse affair, 159, 160
  and October 1989 coup attempt, 249, 250, 251, 256, 260, 261
  and support of Noriega's opponents, 152, 158
Cerro Gordo, Panama, 47
Cheney, Richard, 136, 150, 177, 236, 276
  and October 1989 coup attempt, 251, 254
  on Woerner's relief, 224
Chiriquí Province, Panama, 10, 167

Chorrillos Military Academy, 10
Christian Democratic Party, 157
Cisneros, Brig. Gen. Marc, 24, 74, 115, 223, 224, 225, 231, 275, 282, 285
  on XVIII Airborne Corps, 131, 132
  and Arraiján Tank Farm firefight, 72
  assertion of treaty rights, 232, 233, 235, 239, 271, 274
  avoids provocative actions, 280
  carrier battle group command issue, 91
  and contingency readiness exercises, 226
  convoys, 199, 206
  and crisis action planning, 37
  and Elaborate Maze, 47
  on harassment, 30, 148
  and intrusions at Howard Air Force Base, 79, 80, 82
  and Navy, 76
  and Nimrod Dancer, 177
  on Noriega, 224
  and October 1989 coup attempt against Noriega, 251, 252, 253, 254, 255, 256, 257, 259, 260, 262
  and Operation Alice, 232
  and Prayer Book review, 133
  presidential election preparations, 161
  and psychological operations, 226, 227
  on reporting procedures, 87, 88
  and rules of engagement, 123–24, 125n50
  on school bus detention, 149n30
  and SOUTHCOM Operations Directorate, 89
  and Thurman, 260, 261
Claymore antipersonnel mines, 78, 80
CNN (Cable News Network), 23, 57, 88
Collier, Maj. Mark C., 199, 200, 230
Colón, Panama, 3, 38, 49, 58, 94, 265
  demonstrations in, 14
  and Krystal Ball, 91, 92

INDEX

Colón Province, Panama, 10
Comandancia, 46, 47, 160, 189, 215, 249, 266
    and BLUE SPOON, 90, 94, 266, 268
    and October 1989 coup attempt, 250, 252, 254, 255, 257, 259, 261
Combined Board. *See* Panama Canal Commission (PCC).
Command and General Staff College, Fort Leavenworth, 199
Communications, 203–05
Conley, Col. William J., 67, 68, 75, 76, 85, 88, 121, 219
    and Arraiján Tank Farm firefight, 70, 71, 72n17, 73
    on joint training, 111
Contingency planning, 35–40, 48, 49, 63, 279, 284
    XVIII Airborne Corps capability for, 245
    Hale and, 180
    and USARSO, 60
Contingency readiness exercises (CREs), 226
Convoys, 197, 213. *See also* Freedom of movement operations.
    air cover, 201, 207
    air-ground reaction force, 198
    armed escorts of, 199, 207
    communications, 205, 206
    definition of, 142–43
    reassertion of treaty rights, 196–207
    rehearsals, 204–05
Cope, Col. John A. "Jay," Jr., 55, 60, 85, 155, 181, 212, 223, 283
    and Arraiján Tank Farm firefight, 70, 71
    on BLADE JEWEL, 219
    concern about "warrior" appearance, 186
    contingency planning role, 48, 49
    and convoys, 199, 205
    on dissemination of information, 88
    and ELABORATE MAZE, 61, 92, 93
    and Fort Espinar, 189
    joint training and, 110–11, 113n23
    "lessons learned" file of, 113
    and military police, 56, 59
    Panamanian election preparations, 163
    reporting accuracy issues, 87
    rules of engagement issues, 124–25, 126
    on training in low intensity conflicts, 112–13
Corozal, Panama, 160
Cortizo, Capt. Moisés, 71, 72, 97, 189, 238, 255, 258, 272
Crowe, Admiral William, 18, 20, 58, 154, 227, 228, 235, 239, 241
    and XVIII Airborne Corps, 132, 133
    and Arraiján Tank Farm firefight report, 72
    and BLUE SPOON, 240
    and Bush candidacy, 101n72
    freedom of movement operations, 197–98, 200, 207
    and harassment issues, 142, 148
    human rights and presidential election, 151
    integration of conventional and special forces, 84n40
    and Noriega's removal, 46, 57, 191, 222
    and personnel relocations, 220
    phased force buildup preferred by, 61
    on plans for carrier battle group, 91, 284
    on sanctions, 40, 41, 42
    and Thurman, 243, 247
    and troop deployments, 171n23
    and Woerner, 50, 126, 137, 139, 165, 170, 224
Cuba, 13, 22, 33, 65–66, 155, 172, 222
Curundu airfield, 85, 90

D'Amato, Alfonse, 98n65
David, Panama, 47, 90, 91
Davis, Arthur, 14, 19, 156, 162, 166, 169, 196
    on increasing pressure on Noriega, 150, 153
    recalled, 170, 192

Dearborn, Capt. Mike, 48, 94
Deliberate Planning Process, 36
Delvalle, Eric Arturo, 13, 21, 28, 30, 42, 57, 103
  dismissal of, 31, 40, 74
  on sanctions, 41
  and state of emergency, 18, 19
Democratic Revolutionary Party *See* Partido Revolucionario Democrático (PRD).
Department of Defense Dependent Schools (DoDDS), 160, 165, 169, 254
DEVIL I (exercise), 208
Diablo Heights, Panama City, 143
Díaz Herrera, Col. Roberto, 14, 15, 18
Dignity Battalions, 58, 65, 168, 184, 215, 272, 273, 282
DNTT (*dirección nacional de transporte terreste*), 145, 234, 238
Dobermans. *See* Panama Defense Forces (PDF).
Dornan, Robert, 146
Doyle, Col. James J., Jr., 163, 173, 178, 180, 185, 211
Duque, Carlos, 157

ELABORATE MAZE, 38, 40, 51, 58, 92, 276, 284. *See also* ELDER STATESMAN; PRAYER BOOK.
  and BLUE SPOON, 90
  consolidation of, 89
  evacuation plans, 89, 94
  Kelly reviews, 43
  and Marine expeditionary brigade, 67
  OPORD 1–88, 49
  phases of, 39, 44, 46, 48, 59, 60, 89
  SOCSOUTH participates in planning, 45
  and Task Forces, 47
  troop list, 50, 55
ELDER STATESMAN, 89, 92, 93, 94. *See also* POST TIME.
Endara, Guillermo, 157, 168, 169, 258

Farfan antenna site, 66, 67, 76
Findlay, Capt. Mike, 221
Fissures. *See* Woerner, General Frederick F., Jr.
Fitzgerald, Lt. Col. Billy Ray, 272, 273
Flamenco Island, 47, 231, 264
Florida National Guard, 51
FM 100–20 (low intensity conflict field manual), 34
Ford, Guillermo "Billy," 157, 168, 169
Fort Amador, Panama, 21, 75, 85, 96, 141, 238, 274. *See also* 5th Infantry Company (PDF); Operations.
  American housing at, 29, 218, 220
  asserting treaty rights at, 232, 233
  and BLUE SPOON, 90, 94, 95
  causeway, 228, 237
  and helicopter accident, 215
  joint exercise at, 210, 211, 212, 213
  MP quick reaction force at, 209
  and October 1989 coup attempt, 251, 252, 253, 255, 257
  Purple Storm exercise at, 231
  shooting near, 227
Fort Bragg, North Carolina, 51, 55, 96, 128n57, 139, 244
  1st Special Operations Command at, 45, 48
  and XVIII Airborne Corps, 130
  and BLUE SPOON, 92
  and gradual buildup, 137
  joint special operations task force, 222
  Noriega trained at, 10
  planning at, 95, 131, 133, 196, 222, 246
  and PRAYER BOOK, 94
Fort Cimarrón, Panama, 47, 90, 249, 266, 268
Fort Clayton, Panama, 85, 109, 163, 175, 181, 215, 218
  Cisneros takes command at, 223–25
  and convoys, 201, 204, 205, 206
  and JTF-Panama, 70, 75, 127
  NIMROD DANCER, 182
  operations center at, 1

relocation center at, 219
reports from, 87
review of security enhancement forces, 129
U.S. Army, South, at, 25
Fort Davis, Panama, 188, 189, 201, 204, 205, 206n56
Fort Espinar, Panama, 29, 47, 204, 232, 233, 238
   7th Infantry company billeted at, 188, 207n39, 210
   American housing at, 29
   and BLUE SPOON, 94, 95
   "invasion" of, 188–89, 192, 209
   Quarters 32, 235, 236
Fort Gulick, Panama, 235
Fort Kobbe, Panama, 85
   and 1st Battalion, 508th Infantry, 140, 272
   and Arraiján Tank Farm firefight, 70, 77, 78n32, 79, 80
Fort Leavenworth, Kansas, 113, 199
Fort Lewis, Washington, 176
Fort McPherson, Georgia, 172, 173
Fort Monroe, Virginia, 242, 245
Fort Ord, California, 173, 179, 180
Fort Polk, Louisiana, 174, 175, 185
Fort Rucker, Alabama, 214
Fort Sherman, Panama, 174, 179, 186, 189, 201, 220
Francis, Lt. Col. Brett, 181–82
Freedom of movement operations, 197, 203–04, 205–06, 217, 222, 227. *See also* Convoys.
Fry, Col. Chuck, 45, 82, 84n40, 95, 111, 223
   and intruders, 77, 79, 80, 124
   and Loeffke, 84, 283

Gaillard Highway, 187
Galeta Island, 76
Gates, Robert, 254
General strike, 195
Giroldi, Adela Bonilla de, 249, 251, 253, 260
Giroldi Vega, Maj. Moisés, 249–51, 252–54, 255–57, 258, 259–60, 261–62

Gneckow, Rear Adm. Jerry G., 75, 125n50, 210
Goldwater-Nichols Department of Defense Reorganization Act of 1986, 91, 270, 279, 284
Gorgas Army Hospital, 68, 145, 176, 234, 272
Graves, Capt. William, 79, 80

Hale, Col. David R. E., 184, 185, 191, 210, 238, 239. *See also* Rules of confrontation.
   and BLUE SPOON, 220
   and convoys, 201, 204
   and Fort Espinar "invasion," 188
   and Operation ALICE, 233
   and Operation BEATRICE, 235, 236
   and rules of engagement, 202, 203
   and Task Force Atlantic, 179, 180–81, 271
   "warrior" impression of troops, 186, 187
Hartzog, Brig. Gen. William, 246, 266, 270, 274–75
   and Operation BANNER SAVIOR, 263, 264
   relationship with Thurman, 248, 256
Harvest Bare shelters, 183
Harvest Eagle shelters, 183, 219
Hay–Bunau-Varilla Treaty, 3, 7
Hayden, Col. T., 125n50
Helms, Jesse, 261
Helms, Richard, 261
Herrera Hassán, Col. Eduardo, 57
Herres, General Robert, 229, 241
Herrick, Maj. Chuck, 48, 94
Hersh, Seymour M., 13, 14
Higginbotham, Col. Norman D., 182, 183
High mobility multipurpose wheeled vehicles (HMMWVs), 55, 200, 201, 236
Howard Air Force Base, 80, 81, 82, 160, 206, 228, 270, 283
   and Arraiján Tank Farm firefight, 70
   and BLUE SPOON, 95, 268
   election observers arrive at, 166, 167

Howard Air Force Base—*Continued*
   and helicopter accident, 214
   hostile surveillance of, 66
   housing at, 175, 183
   and Nimrod Dancer, 174n31
   Observation Post 2, 78, 80
   and October 1989 coup attempt, 252, 253, 254
   Proud Warrior, 208
   security at, 66, 76, 85, 177
   security enhancement troops arrive at, 51, 56
   vulnerability of, 76, 88, 96
Huff, Lt. Col. William, III, 215
Hull-Alfaro Treaty, 3
Human rights issues, 151–52
Huntoon, Maj. David, 132, 221
   and Blue Spoon, 222, 246, 263–64, 266, 268, 269
   and Prayer Book, 131–32, 196
Hurlburt Air Force Base, Florida, 45, 48

Inter-American Defense Board, 223
Inter-American Defense College, 223
Inter-American Highway, 67, 69, 71, 173
Interagency Policy Review Group, 99
International Emergency Economic Powers Act of 1977 (IEEPA), 63, 143

Joint Chiefs of Staff (JCS), 20, 99, 126, 216, 270, 272, 276. *See also* Task Force Gator.
   and XVIII Airborne Corps, 132
   and Arraiján Tank Farm firefight, 72, 88
   authorized contingency planning, 31, 34, 36, 37, 49
   and Bradley fighting vehicle, 175
   and convoys, 196, 200, 202
   on Elaborate Maze, 38, 43, 44, 59
   on evacuation of noncombatants, 44, 89
   and exercises, 128
   marine rifle company deployed by, 67
   on Marriott Hotel incident, 57, 67
   and October 1989 coup attempt, 253, 254, 256, 257
   and Operation Nimrod Dancer, 171, 176
   and NSD–17, 232
   and Prayer Book, 97, 246
   Publication 2, 9
   publications of, 111
   and redeployments, 128
   and rules of engagement, 119, 120, 124, 125, 201, 202
   and school bus detention, 146
   and security enhancement buildup, 51, 52
   and Thurman, 242, 247
   and Woerner, 58–59, 87, 88, 89, 100, 107, 207
Joint Operations Planning System, 36, 37, 173
Joint Readiness Training Center, 112, 185
Joint Special Operations Command (JSOC), 48, 129, 155, 244, 245, 264, 268
Joint special operations task force (JSOTF), 39, 46, 49, 129, 137, 222, 268
   and XVIII Airborne Corps, 133–34
   and Blue Spoon, 90, 91, 92, 94
   operation order for, 44, 45
Joint Staff, 43, 88, 93, 104, 240
   and Blue Spoon, 265
   and convoys, 196, 197
   and Nimrod Dancer, 173
   Operation Alice, 232
   and security enhancement deployments, 128, 170
Joint Task Force-Charlie, 155
Joint Task Force-Panama. *See* JTF-Panama.
Joint Task Force (JTF)-South, 265, 266, 268
Joint training, 109–13, 181, 185, 209, 226. *See also* Purple Storms.
JTF-Panama, 79, 87, 217, 226, 237, 270, 279. *See also* Blind Logic; Prayer Book.

INDEX

and XVIII Airborne Corps, 132
activated, 36, 48, 60n50, 61, 282
additional troop requests, 89 165, 170, 171
and Arraiján Tank Farm firefight, 72
and BLUE SPOON, 90, 91, 94, 95, 129–30, 221, 226, 244, 265, 268
and combat support units, 114
commanded by USARSO commanding general, 61
communications, 61, 111–12
conventional and special forces relations, 81, 82, 84
and convoys, 199, 203, 204, 207
and death of Marine Lt. Robert Paz, 275
deception plans, 208
and ELABORATE MAZE, 39, 47, 49, 60
ELDER STATESMAN development, 92, 93
and evacuation plan for U.S. civilians, 94
Fort Clayton operations center for, 70, 117
fragmentary order, 163, 180, 206
and harassment of American citizens, 147
intelligence summary, 97, 203
and intrusions at U.S. facilities, 126
joint operations and training, 109–13, 181, 210
JSOTF missions supported by, 90
logistical issues, 183
marines and, 74, 76, 90–91, 212, 283
and NIMROD DANCER, 175, 178, 182, 239
Noriega regime pressured by, 230
NSD-17, 239
and October 1989 coup attempt, 250, 251, 252, 253, 255, 260
Operation ALICE, 232–33
OPLAN 2–89, 205
OPLAN 90–1, 263
OPORD 1–88, 85
and Panamanian elections, 156, 161–64

POST TIME, 226
Purple Storms, 239
and quick reaction force, 209
reporting procedures and issues, 87–88, 88n45, 180
responsibilities of, 84, 85, 109
and rules of engagement, 120, 122, 123
Sand Fleas, 239
security enhancement deployments, 119
and SOUTHCOM, 109–10
and Task Force Atlantic, 187
and Thurman, 264
and Woerner, 104, 206n36
Jungle Operations Training Center (JOTC), 47, 117, 165, 177, 180
Justines, Col. Marco, 38

Keith, Maj. Eddie, 68
Kellogg, Col. Keith, 271
Kelly, Lt. Gen. Thomas, 43, 104, 131, 228, 240, 245
and XVIII Airborne Corps, 132, 133
on BLUE SPOON, 137, 276
on information distribution, 88
and October 1989 coup attempt, 251
and Operation BANNER SAVIOR, 246
Kerry, John, 261
KINDLE LIBERTY, 21
Kissinger, Henry, 261
KLONDIKE KEY, 89, 90, 92, 94, 96, 156, 220
Kozak, Michael, 54, 103, 127, 150, 151, 153
and October 1989 coup attempt, 253
talks with Noriega, 63, 98, 100, 106, 114
KRYSTAL BALL, 44n18, 89, 90, 91–92, 96, 156

La Chorrera, Panama, 97
Landing craft, mechanized (LCM)–8s, 208
Las Minas, Panama, 140
Law 20. *See* Panama Defense Forces (PDF).

Lesnowicz, Maj. Ed, 221
Licona, Capt. Javier, 257, 259
Light amphibious infantry (LAI) elements, 165, 178, 201
Light armored vehicle (LAV)–25, 173, 234
Light fighters. *See* 7th Infantry Division (Light).
LIGHTNING THRUST I, 209
Lindsay, General James J., 45, 48, 51, 244
Loeffke, Maj. Gen. Bernard, 46, 53, 98, 146, 177, 199, 223, 226
   and 7th Infantry (Light), 171
   XVIII Airborne Corps action opposed by, 130, 131
   and Amador exercise, 211n48
   and Arraiján Tank Farm, 71, 72, 73, 74, 77, 111, 125n50
   on BLACK TOUCAN, 36
   on BLADE JEWEL, 219
   and BLUE SPOON, 221
   on collateral activities, 209
   and combat service units, 114
   command and control issues and, 75, 76, 82, 180
   on communications issues, 111–12, 203, 204, 205n32
   and convoy operations, 198, 205, 206, 207
   on Cubans in Panama, 66
   on dissemination of information, 88
   on evacuation of civilians, 30, 51, 94
   Hale meets with, 185n54
   on harassment, 143, 147, 148
   on helicopter accident, 214, 215, 216
   joint training and, 110, 111, 113, 181
   and JTF-Panama, 61, 75, 84, 110
   and Las Minas incident, 140
   and light infantry battalion, 171n23
   on marines, 85, 210, 212–13, 283
   military action opposed by, 50
   morale issues and, 142
   use of MPs, 56–57
   on Noriega, 55
   and Ostrander affair, 141n14
   on Panamanian elections, 163, 164
   and PDF, 25, 172, 237
   phased buildup preferred by, 61
   planning staff augmented, 49
   on rules of engagement, 117, 119–20, 123, 124, 125, 126, 281
   and school bus detention, 146, 149n30
   on security enhancement forces, 59, 89, 128
   on special operations forces, 80n34, 82, 84
   on State Department, 54–55
   and Task Force Atlantic, 179
   on "warrior" image of troops, 187
Low intensity conflict (LIC), 34, 35, 112, 113
Luck, Lt. Gen. Gary, 96, 244, 246

M113 armored personnel carrier, 175, 187, 225, 255, 273, 282
M551 Sheridan armored reconnaissance vehicle, 270
MacDill Air Force Base, Florida, 45, 177
Macías, Col. Leonidas, 53
Mack, Connie, 167, 168
Madden Dam, 74, 213
Maisto, John, 251, 253, 257
Mansfield, Maj. Alan, 25, 145, 215, 237–38
Marcella, Gabriel, 43n16
Marine Fleet Anti-Terrorist Security Team (FAST), 51, 52, 66–67, 76, 200–201, 252
Marine Forces (MARFOR), 61, 75, 76, 77, 85, 233, 283. *See also* Task Forces; U.S. Marine Corps.
   Amador exercise, 210, 211
   amphibious landing staged, 191
   area of responsibility, 114, 115
   and light armored vehicles (LAVs), 173;
   and October 1989 coup attempt against Noriega, 252
   Panamanian election preparations, 163

and rules of engagement, 115,
121–22, 124, 125, 185
and special operations units, 84
Marriott Hotel, Panama City, 57, 59, 89
Marsh, John O., Jr., 141
Martyrs' Day, 25
McCain, John, 166–67, 218
McCutchon, Lt. Col. John, 38, 89, 129, 132
McMahon, Lt. Col. Timothy L., 131, 244, 246, 263, 264, 266
Meade, Brig. Gen. David, 228n26
Mechanized infantry, 164, 185, 187, 188, 220, 253, 273
Menser, Lt. Col. Michael, 199, 200, 205, 230
Military Airlift Command (MAC), 51, 172, 173, 265
Military Area of Coordination, 23
Military intelligence, 22, 97, 115, 123
Military police, 51, 55–56, 77, 114, 185, 238
    and convoys, 200, 204
    at Fort Amador, 208
    at Fort Espinar, 189
    and NIMROD DANCER, 179
    on redeployments, 128
    responsibilities of, 66
    and school bus detention, 145
Military Police Command, 55
Military Times Media Group, 146
Morgan, Col. Paul, 66n6, 71, 115
Murtha, John, 166
Muse, Kurt, 158, 159, 161
Muse affair, 158–61

Naos Island, 231, 234
Narco-trafficking, 105
National Assembly of Representatives, Panama, 274
National Civic Crusade (NCC), 15, 28, 54, 64, 97, 106
    demonstrations by, 18, 19, 53
    and PDF, 108, 109
National Command Authority, 37, 87, 216, 237, 266
    and evacuation of civilians, 89, 94

freedom of movement operations, 197, 198
and NIMROD DANCER, 171
and October 1989 coup attempt, 251
Operation ALICE, 232
Operation BEATRICE, 235, 236
National Investigation Department (DENI), 144, 160
National Liberal Republican Movement, 157
National Military Communications Center, 252
National Security Council, 14, 128, 218, 228n26, 243, 263
National Security Directive-17. *See* NSD–17.
National Training Center, 112, 128
Navy Forces (NAVFOR), 61, 111, 155, 210
NBC News, 57
Needham, Col. Thomas H., 131
Nevgloski, 1st Sgt. Alexander, 73
New York Times, 13, 138, 141, 142
Nicaragua, 9, 12, 15, 20, 22, 33, 60, 66n5
Nieves, Petty Officer Michael, 146
Noriega Hurtado, Luis Carlos, 9
Noriega Moreno, General Manuel Antonio, 2, 9–14, 38, 45, 77, 104, 123, 136
    allegations against, 13
    Arias coup led by, 10
    on Arraiján Tank Farm firefight, 73, 97
    Cuban arms deal, 65
    demonstrations directed by, 24, 135
    and ELABORATE MAZE, 45
    on electoral interference by United States, 158
    foreign advisers, 66n5
    harassment of Americans by, 39, 50, 65
    indictment against, 28, 36, 135, 277
    Kozak negotiates with, 63, 98, 100, 103, 114, 127
    and Las Minas incident, 140

Noriega Moreno, General Manuel Antonio—*Continued*
  March 1988 coup attempt against, 54, 64, 65, 93, 106
  Marriott raid, 59
  as "Maximum Leader," 274
  October 1989 coup attempt against, 248–58
  organized opposition to, 14–15
  Panama Defense Forces chief, 11, 14, 277
  propaganda campaign of, 42, 52n32, 64, 65, 235
  and psychological operations, 10, 72
  psychological profile of, 107
  reaction to redeployments, 129
  response to demonstrations, 19
  response to sanctions, 42
  and Spadafora, 12
  special operational element created by, 97
  and Torrijos, 10
  U.S. information source, 14, 20
  U.S. military options against, 45–46, 48–49, 57, 58, 61–62, 96–97, 150–51, 222, 264–65, 266
  U.S. pressure on, 99, 218
NSD–17, 232, 237, 238
Nunn, Sam, 261

OA–37 Dragonflys, 201, 204
October 1989 coup. *See* "Black Tuesday" (October 1989 coup).
OH–58 Kiowas, 59, 70, 201, 204, 213
Okinawa, USS, 47
Operation NIMROD DANCER, 174, 176, 186, 209, 263, 269, 270
  asserting U.S. treaty rights, 282
  conventional forces in, 172
  demands on JTF-Panama, 182
  deployments, 172, 174n31, 175, 184
  and helicopter accident, 215
  impacts BLUE SPOON, 220
  impacts POST TIME, 220, 221
  and joint training, 178
  and logistics, 182, 183
  morale of forces, 187–88
  and October 1989 coup attempt, 253
  and Operation ALICE, 234
  operations of, 189, 236, 239
  and Panama Triad, 192
  and PDF, 192
  PRAYER BOOK, 223
  results of, 217, 222
  rules of engagement, 281
Operations. *See also* Operations Planning Group (OPG).
  ALICE, 232, 233, 234, 235, 237
  ANNE MARIE, 237
  BANNER SAVIOR, 246, 263
  BEATRICE, 235, 236
  GOLDEN PHEASANT, 60
  JUST CAUSE, 1, 69, 261, 276, 277, 279, 284
  RATCHET, 231, 238
  RIO BRAVO, 247
Operations Planning Group (OPG), 199, 200, 201, 230
OPLAN (Operation Plan) 2–89, 205
OPLAN 90–1, 263, 264
OPLAN 90–2, 266, 268
OPLAN 6000–86, 35, 36, 38
OPORD (Operation Order) 1–88. *See* ELABORATE MAZE.
OPORD 1–90. *See* BLUE SPOON.
OPORD 2–88. *See* ELABORATE MAZE.
OPORD 5–88. *See* BLUE SPOON.
OPORD 6–88. *See* KRYSTAL BALL.
Organization of American States (OAS), 170, 188–89, 194, 196, 229, 240
  delegation in Panama, 200, 205, 231
  mediation efforts of, 192
  meets on crisis, 228
  Noriega condemned by, 184
  Woerner on, 195, 196n9
Ostrander, Dr. Marcos, 141, 160

Pacora River bridge, 47, 266
Paitilla airfield, 47, 90
Pan-American Highway. *See* Inter-American Highway.

INDEX

Panama, 2–3, 6–9, 54, 92, 231. *See also* Panama presidential elections.
  and KINDLE LIBERTY, 21
  opposition to Noriega, 14–15, 64, 97, 108, 184, 194–95, 196
  sanctions against, 20, 40–43
  SOUTHCOM relations with, 21–32
  U.S. intelligence gathering in, 13
Panama Air Force, 172
Panama Canal, 2–3, 33, 42, 47
Panama Canal Causeway, 231
Panama Canal Commission (PCC), 7, 9, 99, 100, 163, 230
  Combined Board, 8, 21, 28, 142, 188, 206, 272
  and sanctions, 41, 42
Panama Canal Treaties (1979), 7, 135, 155, 206, 277
Panama Canal Zone, 6, 7, 9, 10, 15, 22, 277
Panama City, Panama, 15, 50, 51, 91, 94, 95, 175
  and Arraiján Tank Farm firefight, 71
  and death of Marine Lt. Robert Paz, 275
  decline of harassment in, 184
  and ELABORATE MAZE, 49
  evacuation plans, 94
  and KRYSTAL BALL, 92
  and October 1989 coup attempt, 255, 264
  PDF headquarters in, 1, 38, 46
  targets in and around, 130
  U.S. housing leased in, 143
  violence in, 183
Panama crisis action team, 57
Panama Defense Forces (PDF), 18, 30n31, 93n55, 97, 123, 141, 280. *See also* Dignity Battalions.
  Battalion 2000, 19, 249, 259, 264, 266
  and BLUE SPOON, 95, 130
  and convoys, 36, 142, 143, 202, 205, 206n35
  Doberman unit, 14, 15, 249
  ELABORATE MAZE and, 39, 45
  and elections, 167
  foreign advisers and weapons, 58, 66, 97, 117
  harassment of Americans, 24, 29, 30, 39, 50, 65, 104, 136, 139, 140–41, 144
  increased U.S. military pressure on, 226–28, 237
  interference with U.S. freedom of movement, 142, 143, 154
  jungle operations school, 97
  at Las Minas, 140
  Law 20 establishes, 11
  left-wing groups controlled by, 35
  Marriott Hotel incident, 57, 64
  and Muse affair, 159
  and NIMROD DANCER, 209
  and Noriega, 11, 31, 37, 184, 191, 239–40, 277
  and October 1989 coup attempt against Noriega, 253, 258, 259, 260
  and opposition, 64, 108, 109
  and Dr. Ostrander, 141
  psychological operations, 126, 141, 144, 227
  purged, 53
  radio stations closed by, 28
  school bus detained by, 145
  training, 126, 172
  tránsitos, 139
  UESAT, 47, 264
  use of deadly force, 202
  violates treaties, 136
  Woerner on, 42, 105, 154
Panama Directorate of Engineering and Housing, 209
Panama Ministry of Government and Justice, 72
Panama Ministry of Health, 272
Panama Ministry of Housing, 143
Panama National Assembly, 31
Panama presidential elections, 129, 153, 165–70, 222, 279
  Bush policies geared to, 137, 157
  candidates, 157–58
  and human rights, 151–52
  SOUTHCOM preparations for, 155, 156, 161–65

307

Panama Relocation Center, 182
Panama Review Group, 41
Panama Triad, 192, 196, 229
Panama Viejo, Panama, 47, 90, 249, 264, 268
Panamanian Student Federation, 10
Pangram, 219
Pantier, Lt. Col. Robert, 57, 93, 129, 132, 133, 177, 221, 244
Partido Laborista Agrario, 11
Partido Revolucionario Democrático (PRD), 9, 11
Patilla, Capt. Anna, 238
Paz, Lt. Robert, 1n1, 275
Paz y Salvo ("Peace and Safety") certificates, 143–44, 145
Perico Island, 231, 234
Perry, Lt. Col. Robert, 160
Personnel Movement Limitation, 23, 24, 165, 169, 186, 254, 280
Pierce, Lt. Ken, 251, 553, 456
Policy Coordination Committee, 228
Post Time, 93, 94, 130, 165, 244
   7th Infantry Division (Light), 173
   and XVIII Airborne Corps, 132
   additional units for, 221
   fragmentary order, 163
   operation plan of, 93n55
   revisions to, 129, 155
Powell, General Colin, 50, 55, 101n72, 240, 241, 263, 265, 268, 276
   and October 1989 coup attempt against Noriega, 251–52, 253–55, 257
Prayer Book, 89–97, 181, 196, 220–21, 223
   and XVIII Airborne Corps, 131
   and Blind Logic, 269
   and Nimrod Dancer, 178
   reviews and updates of, 133, 246, 155
   Thurman on, 244, 247
Presidential Selected Reserve Call-up, 92
Price, William, 228n26
Program Development Group, 160
Proud Warrior, 208
Psychological operations, 50, 226, 227

Puentes, Capt. Carlos, 48, 93
Purple Storms, 181, 226, 231, 233, 239, 263, 270
Purple Strike, 209

Quarry Heights, 15, 25, 57, 85, 109–10, 127, 129, 229, 232, 234
Quezada, Maj. Fernando, 53
Quick reaction force (QRF), 56, 197, 200, 201, 208, 225

Reagan, Ronald W., and his administration, 8, 33, 56, 58, 136, 277, 280
   approach to crisis in Panama, 24, 29, 53, 55, 104, 105
   Delvalle administration recognized by, 31, 40
   and Marriott Hotel incident, 61
   military force in Panama opposed by, 62, 63, 97, 106–07, 137
   on Noriega, 13, 14, 19, 28, 58, 100
   on Panamanian presidential elections, 134
   Panamanians demonstrate against, 135
   on redeployments, 127
   sanctions implemented by, 20, 40, 42, 50, 103, 143
   security enhancement forces approved by, 148
Reduction of Off-Post Personnel program, 217
Rio Hato, 47, 49, 66, 90, 91, 249, 255, 266
Ritter, Jorge, 194
Roberts, Col. Thomas W., 121, 124, 126, 127
Rodman Ammunition Supply Point, 88, 114, 126, 127, 173
   guard duty at, 116–17
   intruders at, 77, 97, 116, 185
   and rules of engagement, 119, 123
Rodman Naval Station, 68, 70, 72n17, 85, 96, 211
   guards at, 66, 67
   security police at, 75, 76
   vulnerability of, 96
Roosevelt, Theodore, 3

INDEX

Roosma, Maj. Gen. William A., 244
Rossi, Col. Arnold T., 60, 61, 92, 117, 132, 180, 220
   on accuracy of reports, 87
   and Arraiján Tank Farm firefight, 70, 71, 72, 75, 79
   on BLADE JEWEL, 219
   on command and control issues, 76
   on communications, 112
   and evacuation plans, 49, 94
   and Fort Espinar action, 189
   and harassment of U.S. civilians, 142n16
   on intruders, 115
   and low intensity conflict, 34n1
   and Martyrs' Day demonstrations, 25
   and Operation ALICE, 232
   on Panamanian presidential election preparations, 161, 163
   on rules of engagement, 121, 122
   on Sand Fleas, 226
   on security responsibilities, 85, 114
   on special operations forces, 84
   tour extended, 223
   and troop deployments, 178
   on the "Twilight Zone," 35, 280
   use of MPs, 55
Ruffer, Lt. Col. James, 160
Rules of confrontation, 203, 209
Rules of engagement (ROE), 36–37, 49, 115, 116–17, 118–27, 209, 238, 281
   and Amador exercise, 210, 211, 213
   and deadly force, 201, 281
   and NIMROD DANCER, 186
   peacetime, 52, 118, 197, 202

Sanctions. *See* Panama.
Sand Fleas (exercises), 226, 231, 233, 239, 270, 271n37, 274
Sandinistas, 12, 60
School bus detention, 145–46
Schneider, Brig. Gen. Mike, 251, 256
SCN (Southern Command Network), 23, 107, 161
Sconyers, Col. Ronald T., 161

Scott Air Force Base, Illinois, 172
Scowcroft, Brent, 139, 150, 240n54, 251, 254
Sea-Air-Land (SEAL) forces, 46–47, 268
Security enhancement forces, 50–57, 114, 125, 148, 210
   additional troops for, 58, 59, 63, 112, 128, 170
   and JTF-Panama, 60, 97
   missions of, 76, 77, 88, 122
   redeployments, 127, 129
   rules of engagement and, 118, 119, 120
Shultz, George P., 13, 53, 55, 137
   on Noriega, 57, 58, 100
Sierra Miñon, Panama, 114
Sneddon, Maj. Bruce, 48, 49
Snell, Col. Michael J., 223, 239, 273
Solis Palma, Manuel, 31, 41, 103, 108, 143
Somoza Debayle, Anastasio, 12
SOUTHCOM. *See* U.S. Southern Command (SOUTHCOM).
Southern Command Network. *See* SCN (Southern Command Network).
Southern Command News, 23, 24, 29
Spadafora, Dr. Hugo, 12, 13, 14, 19
Spanish-American War, 3
Special Boat Unit 26, 47, 79, 234
Special Forces, 81, 82, 114
Special Operations Command, South (SOCSOUTH), 47, 78, 124, 266. *See also* U.S. Special Operations Command (SOCOM).
   and BLUE SPOON, 95, 96
   and JTF-Panama, 45, 81, 82, 84, 283
Special Operations Forces, 15, 45, 46, 124, 245, 270
   and BLUE SPOON, 90, 95, 273, 274
   relationship with conventional forces, 81, 82, 84
Special Security Antiterrorist Unit (UESAT), 116, 249
Stewart, Brig. Gen. John F., Jr., 108–09, 115, 223, 280
Stiner, Lt. Gen. Carl W., 220, 221, 244, 245n5,n7, 263, 265, 270, 273

Stiner, Lt. Gen. Carl W.—*Continued*
   and XVIII Airborne Corps, 122, 134
   and BANNER SAVIOR, 246
   and bomb scare, 272
   experience of, 245, 268
Strategic Air Command (SAC), 51, 172
Strategic Military Council (Panama), 53
Stringham, Col. Joseph S., 45, 46, 47, 48, 53n35, 60n50, 95
Sununu, John, 254

Tactical satellite communications (TACSAT), 205
Tarter, Capt. Daniel, 213, 214
Task Force Atlantic, 178, 180–81, 201, 210, 268, 271
   activated, 179, 220
   and convoys, 204, 213
   and Fort Espinar, 189
   and JTF-Panama, 187
   morale of, 188
   Operation ALICE, 235
Task Forces
   Bayonet, 178, 179, 180, 234, 268
   Gator, 266
   Gray, 77, 78, 79, 82
   Hawk, 112, 127, 128, 176, 179, 189
   Pacific, 268
   Semper Fi, 178, 233, 234, 268
Thatcher Highway. *See* Inter-American Highway.
Thiry, Col. Gar E., 25, 30, 161
Thurman, General Maxwell R., 224, 240, 241–48, 264, 270, 273, 283, 284
   and BLIND LOGIC, 269
   on BLUE SPOON, 246, 268
   and bomb scare, 272, 274
   and Cisneros, 260, 261
   and Kellogg, 271
   and October 1989 coup attempt against Noriega, 249, 250, 251, 253, 254, 255, 256, 257, 258, 259
   on PRAYER BOOK, 263
Tigris River, 178
Tinajitas, Panama, 47, 90, 96, 268

Tornow, Brig. Gen. Robin, 201
Torrijos Herrera, Brig. Gen. Omar, 6, 10, 11, 14
   and canal treaties, 7, 8
   and Nicaragua, 9, 12
   and Spadafora, 12
Torrijos-Tocumen airport complex, 47, 90, 146, 158
   and BLUE SPOON, 95, 96, 130, 268
   and October 1989 coup attempt against Noriega, 256
TOTAL WARRIOR exercises, 42, 51, 52
Tower, John, 135–36, 138
Transisthmian highway, 201, 204
Transportation Command (TRANSCOM), 172
Travis Air Force Base, California, 174
Tropic Times, 29, 107, 149, 161, 162, 165

UH–1 Hueys, 70
UH–60 Black Hawks, 59, 70, 176, 208
U.S. Army Assistance Agency for Latin America, 15
U.S. Army Empire Range, 112
U.S. Army National Guard, 42, 175
U.S. Army, South (USARSO), 1n1, 29, 30n31, 61, 67
   XVIII Airborne Corps used by, 131, 132, 133
   and 193d Infantry Brigade, 23, 55
   BLADE JEWEL impacts, 218–19
   Cisneros commands, 230
   civil disturbance responses, 30
   core of JTF-Panama, 36, 60
   ELABORATE MAZE planning by, 92
   Emergency Operations Center, 272
   Fort Clayton headquarters for, 25
   and intelligence, 22, 23
   and logistical issues, 183
   marines reinforced by units from, 77
   and NIMROD DANCER, 175–76, 183
   on Noriega speech, 274
   and October 1989 coup attempt against Noriega, 254
   OPORDs developed by, 35
   and Ostrander incident, 141

planning cell in, 93
Plans Division of, 155
and PRAYER BOOK, 92
Provost Marshal Office, 145
as reaction force, 24
staff judge advocate general, 212
Stringham on, 60n50
study group, 49
taxed by demands on, 48, 131
and TOTAL WARRIOR exercises, 42
travel restrictions of, 187
on use of MPs, 56
U.S. Army Training and Doctrine Command (TRADOC), 199, 224, 242
U.S. Atlantic Command (LANTCOM), 51, 76, 91, 97, 155, 172
U.S. Caribbean Command. *See* U.S. Southern Command (SOUTHCOM).
U.S. Congress, 20
U.S. Department of the Army, 30, 49
U.S. Department of Defense, 105, 107, 172, 213–14
U.S. Drug Enforcement Administration, 13, 14, 105, 243
U.S. Embassy, Panama City, 23, 52n32, 92, 99, 108, 256, 257
  command post exercises and, 163
  demonstrations at, 19
  guards at, 162
U.S. Forces Command (FORSCOM), 128, 172, 173
U.S. Forces Joint Committee, 272
U.S. House of Representatives Foreign Affairs Committee, 137–38
U.S. Marine Corps, 35, 50, 59, 63, 210, 211, 270, 281. *See also* Marine Forces (MARFOR).
  aviation assets of, 67
  Loeffke on, 212–13
  morale of, 188
  Operation ALICE, 235
  security enhancement rifle company, 127
  security forces, 66
  warrior ethos of, 282
U.S. Navy, South (NAVSO), 67, 76

U.S. Pacific Command, 171
U.S. Senate, 13, 19, 100
U.S. Southern Command (SOUTHCOM), 15, 82, 105, 217, 270, 279, 280
  and XVIII Airborne Corps, 133
  additional troops for, 154, 164, 170
  Arraiján Tank Farm firefight, 72
  and assertion of treaty rights, 227
  and BLUE SPOON, 94, 95, 244, 265
  CAPSTONE reserve unit, 44n18
  and carrier battle group, 155, 270
  Center for Treaty Affairs, 24, 71, 109, 139, 147, 160, 161, 230, 253, 273
  change of command, 247, 269
  Civil Affairs Branch, 92
  components of, 15, 60
  contingency planning by, 30, 31, 34, 63, 277
  convoy procedures of, 196, 200, 202, 206n36, 207
  crisis action teams, 22
  and debriefings, 120
  deception plans used by, 208
  deployment adjustments, 52
  and evacuation of civilians, 94
  and freedom of movement exercises, 197, 198, 203
  Guidance Message 1, 87
  on harassment of Americans, 140, 141, 143, 144, 147
  intelligence sections of, 22
  and intrusions, 126
  isolation campaign against Noriega, 196
  and joint special operations task force, 44
  and JTF-Panama, 44, 61, 88
  and KLONDIKE KEY, 96
  and Kozak negotiations, 98
  marines on, 74, 283
  Military Intelligence Directorate, 248
  and NIMROD DANCER, 177
  and October 1989 coup attempt, 250n15, 252, 253, 254, 255, 256, 257, 258, 259

311

U.S. Southern Command (SOUTHCOM)
—*Continued*
and Operation Alice, 232–33
Operation Beatrice, 235
Operations Directorate, 30, 74, 89, 96, 199, 248
and OPLAN 6000–86, 35
and Panamanian presidential elections, 136, 156, 161–64, 165, 166
and PDF, 20, 21–32, 237
Policy, Strategy, and Programs Directorate, 44, 92, 96, 99, 106, 269
and Post Time, 93, 94, 96
and Prayer Book, 129, 155, 156
Public Affairs Office, 23, 52, 73, 141, 165
redeployment schedule, 129
relocation of American civilians, 141
reporting procedures, 87–88, 180
restrictions on, 271
and rules of engagement, 118, 119, 122, 123, 124, 281
and shooting incidents, 117
videotaping, 231
Woerner on, 18n13
U.S. Special Operations Command (SOCOM), 45, 48, 244. *See also* Special Operations Command, South (SOCSOUTH).
U.S. State Department, 14, 58, 59, 98, 99, 105, 228n26
and Elaborate Maze, 49
military action in Panama desired by, 43, 218
and Muse affair, 160
negotiations with Noriega, 54, 135
and October 1989 coup attempt, 251, 252, 253, 256, 261
and Panamanian presidential elections, 162
on redeployments, 128
and sanctions, 19, 20, 40–41
on SOUTHCOM, 141
special group to monitor crisis, 171

Thurman and, 243
travel advisory to Panama issued by, 171
on Woerner's Panama scenario, 108
U.S. Treasury Department, 63, 243
U.S. Treaty Implementation Plan, 107
USARSO. *See* U.S. Army, South (USARSO).
Ustick, Rear Adm. Richard C., 57, 125n50, 142, 144, 148, 154

Valore, Capt. Joseph P., 67, 75, 76
at Arraiján Tank Farm, 68, 70–71, 72, 73, 77
Villahermosa, Cpl. Ricardo M., 68, 72
Voice of Liberty, The, 159
Volant Solo (aircraft), 96
Vuono, General Carl, 241, 242, 243, 245, 246n7
Loeffke reports to, 29, 51, 52, 59, 61, 74, 75, 89, 114, 209
on Woerner's relief, 223, 224

Walker, William, 54, 63
Washington Post, 142, 191
Weinberger, Caspar, 20
Westward Ho, 233
Woerner, General Frederick F., Jr., 24, 38, 101n72, 217, 223, 231, 285
on XVIII Airborne Corps, 131, 132, 133, 134
193d Infantry Brigade commander, 15
and Abrams, 136n3
Amador exercise, 212
and Arraiján Tank Farm firefight, 72
on augmentation force, 52
on Blade Jewel, 220
Blue Spoon, 90, 91, 92, 96, 133, 230, 268, 284
and Bush administration, 136, 137–39
Central American Chambers of Commerce speech, 138
and collateral operations, 207, 227, 228
comprehensive program desired by, 151, 153–54

on convoys, 154–55, 199, 200, 206, 207, 228
covert psychological operations of, 108
and crisis action planning team, 43
and Crowe, 40, 41–42, 50, 224
ELABORATE MAZE, 47, 48, 89
on ELDER STATESMAN, 89
fissures campaign, 97–101, 106, 192, 195, 196, 217
force increase recommended by, 50, 51, 89, 98, 154, 155, 165
interagency approach desired, 151, 156, 280
on intruders, 77
and JTF-Panama, 282
and KLONDIKE KEY, 89, 94
and Las Minas incident, 140
LAV exercise, 211
low intensity conflict, 34n1
and Marriott Hotel incident, 57
and Noriega, 21, 29, 31, 53n35, 74, 222
OPLAN 90–1, 263
on OPLAN 6000–86, 36, 37
OPORD 2–89 approved by, 205
and Organization of American States, 194
on Panamanian elections, 151, 152, 157, 158, 164, 166, 167, 171, 174
on Panamanian opposition, 152, 195
on PDF, 21, 31, 42, 99, 141, 172, 196, 197, 237, 282
phased plan desired by, 37, 61, 129, 137
and PMLs, 23
and POST TIME, 133
on redeployments, 127
reoccupation of U.S. facilities, 235, 236, 238
and reports, 87, 88
retirement of, 241, 246n7
and rules of engagement, 119, 120, 123, 124, 125, 126
on sanctions against Panama, 20, 41, 43n16
and school bus detention, 146, 149n30
and security enhancement forces, 55, 59, 125, 128, 170
on Special Operations Forces, 82
and Stringham, 45, 50
and Thurman, 244, 246–47
and triad concept, 196, 229
and use of MPs, 56
Wong, Col. Guillermo, 215
Woodward, Bob, 240

Youle, John J., 241

www.ingramcontent.com/pod-product-compliance
Lightning Source LLC
Chambersburg PA
CBHW082144230426
43672CB00015B/2845